Dancing with Śiva

शिवेन सह नर्तनम्
सनातनधर्मप्रश्नोत्तरम्

Books by Sivaya Subramuniyaswami

RISHI COLLECTION

Dancing with Śiva
Living with Śiva
Merging with Śiva
Gems of Wisdom
Raja Yoga

HINDU COLLECTION

Satguru Speaks on Hindu Family Life
Satguru Speaks on Hindu Renaissance
Satguru Speaks on Lord Ganesha
Satguru Speaks on Hindu Prosperity
Satguru Speaks on Teenage Sexuality
Satguru Speaks on Becoming a Hindu
Satguru Speaks on Praying to the Gods
Satguru Speaks on Home Worship

OTHER PUBLICATIONS

Holy Orders of Sannyasa
Holy Tirukural in English
Holy Natchintanai Songbook
Hinduism Today international newspaper

Dancing with Śiva

Hinduism's Contemporary Catechism

शिवेन सह नर्तनम्
सनातनधर्मप्रश्नोत्तरम्

Satguru Sivaya
Subramuniyaswami

Published by
Himalayan Academy
India • USA

Fourth Edition

Dancing with Śiva: Hinduism's Contemporary Catechism was first published by Himalayan Academy in 1979. Second edition 1987. Third edition 1991. Designed, typeset and illustrated by the *swāmīs* of the Śaiva Siddhānta Yoga Order and published by Himalayan Academy, 1819 Second Street, Concord, California 94519 USA.

Published by
Himalayan Academy
India • USA

PRINTED IN USA

Library of Congress Catalog Card Number 93-77806
ISBN 0-945497-48-2. ISBN 0-945497-47-4 (paper)

ெ

Dedication

Grantha Nivedana

ग्रन्थनिवेदन

GANESHA, THE LORD OF CATEGORIES, WHO REMOVED ALL BARRIERS TO THE MANIFESTATION OF THIS CONTEMPORARY HINDU CATECHISM, to Him we offer reverent obeisance. This holy text is dedicated to my *satguru,* Sage Yogaswāmī of Sri Lanka, perfect *siddha yogi* and illumined master who knew the Unknowable and held Truth in the palm of his hand. As monarch of the Nandinātha Sampradāya's Kailāsa Paramparā, this obedient disciple of Chellappaswāmī infused in me all that you will find herein. He commanded all to seek within, to know the Self and to see God Śiva everywhere and in everyone. Among his great sayings: "Know thy Self by thyself. Śiva is doing it all. All is Śiva. Be still."

Well over 2,000 years ago our great *paramaguru,* Ṛishi Tirumular, aptly conveyed the spirit of *Dancing with Śiva:*

> *The thirty-six elements dance. Sadāśiva dances. Consciousness dances. Śiva-Śakti dances. The animate and inanimate dance. All these and the* Vedas *dance when the Supreme dances His dance of bliss. The seven worlds as His golden abode, the five* chakras *as His pedestal, the central* kuṇḍalinī śakti *as His divine stage, thus in rapture He dances, He who is Transcendent Light. He dances with the celestials. He dances in the golden hall. He dances with the three Gods. He dances with the assembly of silent sages. He dances in song. He dances in ultimate energy. He dances in souls—He who is the Lord of Dances.* Tat Astu.

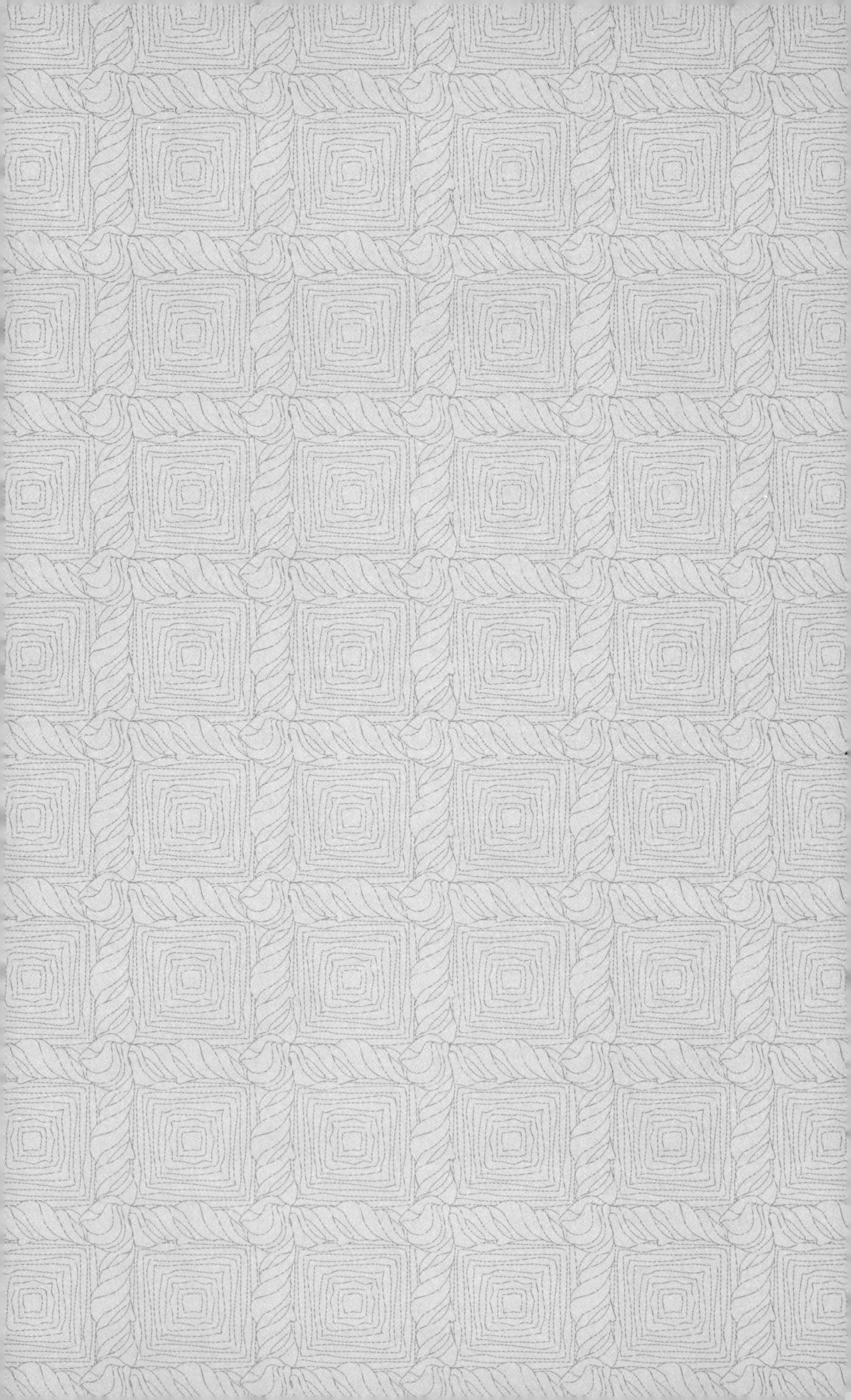

Contents

Anukramaṇī

अनुक्रमणी

Dedication—*Nivedaṇa* i
Introduction—*Bhūmikā* xvii
The Beliefs of Hinduism, world map, etc. xx
About This Edition of *Dancing with Śiva* . . . xxvi
Ways to Study and Teach *Dancing with Śiva* . xxix
Sanskṛit Pronunciation—*Ucchāraṇa Vyākhyā*. . xxxv

UPANISHAD ONE
ETERNAL TRUTHS—*Sanātana Dharma*

Maṇḍala 1: Self Realization—*Paramātma Darśana*

ŚLOKA . . . . PAGE
1 Who Am I? Where Did I Come From? 5
2 Where Am I Going? What Is My Path? 7
3 What Is Meant by "Dancing with Śiva"? 9
4 How Can We Learn to Dance with Śiva? 11
5 What is the Ultimate Goal of Earthly Life? 13
Scriptures Speak on Self Realization 14

Maṇḍala 2: Hinduism
6 What Are Hinduism's Principal Sects? 19
7 What Is the Deeply Mystical Śaiva Sect? 21
8 What Is the Magic and Power of Śāktism? 23
9 What Is the Devotional Vaishṇava Sect? 25
10 What Is the Universalistic Smārta Sect? 27
Scriptures Speak on Religion 28

Maṇḍala 3: Śaivite Hinduism—*Śaiva Dharma*
11 What Is the Nature of Śaivite Theology? 33
12 How Do Śaivites Regard Other Faiths? 35

ŚLOKA .... PAGE

13 How Does Śaivism Stay Contemporary? 37
14 What Is the Nature of Life for Śaivites? 39
15 What Is the Symbolism of Śiva's Dance? 41
Scriptures Speak on Śaivism 42

UPANISHAD TWO
GOD AND THE GODS—*Deva-Devatā*

Maṇḍala 4: Our Supreme God—*Śiva*
16 What Is the Nature of Our God Śiva? 49
17 What Is God Śiva's Unmanifest Reality? 51
18 What Is God Śiva's Pure Consciousness? 53
19 What Is the Nature of the Primal Soul? 55
20 What Are God Śiva's Traditional Forms? 57
Scriptures Speak on Śiva 58

Maṇḍala 5: Lords of Dharma—*Gaṇeśa Kārttikeya*
21 Do Other Gods Exist Apart from Śiva? 63
22 What Is the Nature of Lord Gaṇeśa? 65
23 What Is Lord Gaṇeśa's Special Duty? 67
24 What Is the Nature of Lord Kārttikeya? 69
25 What Does Lord Kārttikeya's Vel Signify? 71
Scriptures Speak on Lords of Dharma 72

UPANISHAD THREE
OUR IMMORTAL SOUL—*Amṛitātma*

Maṇḍala 6: The Nature of the Soul—*Ātmasvarūpa*
26 What Is Our Individual Soul Nature? 79
27 How Is Our Soul Different from Śiva? 81
28 How Is Our Soul Identical with Śiva? 83
29 Why Are We Not Omniscient Like Śiva? 85
30 How Do Hindus Understand Moksha? 87
Scriptures Speak on the Soul 88

ŚLOKA .... PAGE

Maṇḍala 7: Karma and Rebirth—*Saṁsāra*

31 How Do Hindus Understand Karma? 93
32 Is There Good Karma and Bad Karma? 95
33 What Is the Process of Reincarnation? 97
34 How Should We View Death and Dying? 99
35 How Does One Best Prepare for Death? 101
Scriptures Speak on Saṁsāra 102

Maṇḍala 8: The Way to Liberation—*San Mārga*

36 What Are the Four Stages on the Path? 107
37 What Is the Nature of the Charyā Pāda? 109
38 What Is the Nature of the Kriyā Pāda? 111
39 What Is the Nature of the Yoga Pāda? 113
40 What Is the Nature of the Jñāna Pāda? 115
Scriptures Speak on Liberation 116

UPANISHAD FOUR
THE WORLD—*Śivamaya*

Maṇḍala 9: The Three Worlds—*Triloka*

41 Where Did This Universe Come from? 123
42 What Is the Nature of the Physical Plane? 125
43 What Is the Nature of the Subtle Plane? 127
44 What Is the Nature of the Causal Plane? 129
45 Does the Universe Ever End? Is It Real? 131
Scriptures Speak on Three Worlds 132

Maṇḍala 10: The Goodness of All—*Sarvabhadra*

46 Are Souls and World Essentially Good? 137
47 Why Do Some Souls Act in Evil Ways? 139
48 What Is the Source of Good and Evil? 141
49 How Can a Benevolent God Permit Evil? 143
50 Should One Avoid Worldly Involvement? 145
Scriptures Speak on Goodness 146

ŚLOKA .... PAGE

Maṇḍala 11: Sin and Suffering—*Pāpa Duḥkha*
51 Why Is There Suffering in the World? 151
52 What Is Sin? How Can We Atone for It? 153
53 Does Hell Really Exist? Is There a Satan? 155
54 What Is the Consequence of Sinful Acts? 157
55 Does God Ever Punish Wrongdoers? 159
Scriptures Speak on Sin and Suffering 160

UPANISHAD FIVE
RIGHT LIVING—*Dharma*

Maṇḍala 12: Four Dharmas—*Chaturdharma*
56 What Is Dharma? What Are Its Forms? 167
57 What Is Signified by Universal Dharma? 169
58 What Is the Nature of Social Dharma? 171
59 What Is the Nature of Human Dharma? 173
60 What Is the Nature of Personal Dharma? 175
Scriptures Speak on Four Dharmas 176

Maṇḍala 13: Good Conduct—*Sadāchāra*
61 What Is the Meaning of Good Conduct? 181
62 What Are Good Conduct's Four Keys? 183
63 From Whom Is Good Conduct Learned? 185
64 What Are the Ten Classical Restraints? 187
65 What Are the Ten Classical Observances? 189
Scriptures Speak on Good Conduct 190

Maṇḍala 14: Noninjury—*Ahiṁsā*
66 What Is the Great Virtue Called Ahiṁsā? 195
67 What Is the Inner Source of Noninjury? 197
68 What Is the Inner Source of Violence? 199
69 Is Vegetarianism Integral to Noninjury? 201
70 How Can Peace on Earth Be Achieved? 203
Scriptures Speak on Noninjury 204

ŚLOKA .... PAGE

UPANISHAD SIX
FAMILY LIFE—*Gṛihastha Dharma*

Maṇḍala 15: Husband and Wife—*Dampati*

71 What Is the Central Purpose of Marriage? 211
72 What Are the Duties of the Husband? 213
73 What Are Special Duties of the Wife? 215
74 What Is the Hindu View of Sexuality? 217
75 What Is the Relation of Sex to Marriage? 219
Scriptures Speak on Husband and Wife 220

Maṇḍala 16: Marriage—*Vivāha*

76 What Is the Basis for a Happy Marriage? 225
77 Must We Marry Within Our Religion? 227
78 How Are Hindu Marriages Arranged? 229
79 What Is the Hindu Family Structure? 231
80 How Are Marital Problems Reconciled? 233
Scriptures Speak on Marriage 234

Maṇḍala 17: Children—*Apatya*

81 What Is the Fulfillment of a Marriage? 239
82 What Are the Main Duties of Parents? 241
83 How Strictly Must Children Be Guided? 243
84 Should All Youths Be Urged to Marry? 245
85 How Is Family Harmony Maintained? 247
Scriptures Speak on Children 248

UPANISHAD SEVEN
SACRED CULTURE—*Maṅgala Kriyā*

Maṇḍala 18: Ways of Wisdom—*Bodhi Tantra*

86 How Do We Overcome Life's Obstacles? 255
87 What Are the Hindu's Daily Yoga Practices? 257
88 How Are Āyurveda and Jyotisha Used? 259
89 How Do Hindus Regard Art and Culture? 261

ŚLOKA .... PAGE

90 What Is the Hindu Outlook on Giving? 263
Scriptures Speak on Ways of Wisdom 264

Maṇḍala 19: Sacraments—*Saṁskāra*

91 What Are Hinduism's Rites of Passage? 269
92 What Are the Sacraments of Childhood? 271
93 What Are the Sacraments of Adulthood? 273
94 What Are the Child-bearing Sacraments? 275
95 Are There Rites for the Wisdom Years? 277
Scriptures Speak on Sacraments 278

Maṇḍala 20: Festivals—*Utsava*

96 What Are the Festival Days of Śaivism? 283
97 What Are the Primary Festivals to Śiva? 285
98 What Are the Major Gaṇeśa Festivals? 287
99 What Are the Main Kārttikeya Festivals? 289
100 What Are Other Important Festivals? 291
Scriptures Speak on Festivals 292

UPANISHAD EIGHT
SACRED WORSHIP—*Upāsanā*

Maṇḍala 21: Śiva Temples—*Śivālaya*

101 What Is the Nature of the Śiva Temple? 299
102 How Are Temples Founded and Built? 301
103 When Should One Attend the Temple? 303
104 How Does One Attend a Śiva Temple? 305
105 What Occurs Within the Śiva Temple? 307
Scriptures Speak on Śiva Temples 308

Maṇḍala 22: Temple Rites—*Pūjā*

106 What Is the Inner Importance of Pūjā? 313
107 What Is the Special Rite Called Ārchanā? 315
108 What Is the Nature of Image Worship? 317
109 Who Are the Priests of Śiva Temples? 319

ŚLOKA .... PAGE

110 What Does the Pujārī Do during Pūjā? 321
Scriptures Speak on Temples Rites 322

Maṇḍala 23: Love of God—*Bhakti*

111 Is Temple Worship Only for Beginners? 327
112 How Do Devotees Prepare for Worship? 329
113 How Do Our Prayers Reach the Gods? 331
114 Do Śaivites Worship Only in Temples? 333
115 What Is the Home Shrine's Significance? 335
Scriptures Speak on Love of God 336

UPANISHAD NINE
HOLY MEN AND WOMEN—*Mahātma*

Maṇḍala 24: Monastic Life—*Vairāgya*

116 What Is the Hindu Monastic Tradition? 343
117 What Are the Goals of Renunciate Life? 345
118 What Is the Sannyāsin's Kuṇḍalinī Path? 347
119 What Is the Sannyāsin's Initiation Rite? 349
120 What Are the Holy Orders of Sannyāsa 351
Scriptures Speak on Monastic Life 352

Maṇḍala 25: Knowers of God—*Jñānī*

121 Who Are Hinduism's Spiritual Leaders? 357
122 What Is a Saint, a Sage and a Satguru? 359
123 Are There Other Terms for Holy Ones? 361
124 What Is the Nature of Guru Protocol? 363
125 What Is the Satguru's Special Function? 365
Scriptures Speak on Knowers of God 366

UPANISHAD TEN
SACRED SCRIPTURE—*Śāstra*

Maṇḍala 26: Revealed Scripture—*Śruti*

126 What Are Hindu Revealed Scriptures? 373
127 What Is the Nature of the Veda Texts? 375

ŚLOKA .... PAGE

128 How Are the Vedas Significant Today?.......... 377
129 What Is the Nature of the Holy Āgamas? 379
130 How Are the Āgamas Significant Today?........ 381
Scriptures Speak on Śruti 382

Maṇḍala 27: Secondary Scripture—*Smṛiti*

131 Do Smṛiti and Sacred Literature Differ? 387
132 What Texts Amplify Vedas and Āgamas?........ 389
133 Does Hinduism Have Epics and Myths? 391
134 Are there Other Types of Sacred Texts? 393
135 What Is the Source of This Catechism? 395
Scriptures Speak on Śmṛiti 396

Maṇḍala 28: Affirmations of Faith—*Mantra*

136 What Is the Holy Namaḥ Śivāya Mantra? 401
137 How Is Namaḥ Śivāya Properly Chanted?....... 403
138 Is Initiation Necessary to Perform Japa? 405
139 What Is Śaivism's Affirmation of Faith? 407
140 How Is the Affirmation of Faith Used? 409
Scriptures Speak on Affirmation............... 410

UPANISHAD ELEVEN
MONISTIC THEISM—*Advaita Īśvaravāda*

Maṇḍala 29: Monism and Dualism–*Advaita Dvaita*

141 What Are the Many Hindu Philosophies?....... 417
142 How Do Monism and Dualism Differ? 419
143 Are Monism and Dualism Reconcilable? 421
144 What Is the View of Monistic Theism? 423
145 Is Monistic Theism Found in the Vedas?........ 425
Scriptures Speak on One and Two 426

Maṇḍala 30: Views of Reality—*Siddhānta*

146 What Are Śaiva Siddhānta's Two Schools? 431
147 What Are the Two Views on Creation? 433

ŚLOKA .... PAGE

148 What Are the Views on God and Soul? 435
149 What Are the Differing Views on Evil? 437
150 What Are the Views on Mahāpralaya? 439
Scriptures Speak on Siddhānta 440

UPANISHAD TWELVE
PASSING ON THE POWER—*Sampradāya*

Maṇḍala 31: Himalayan Lineage—*Kailāsa Paramparā*
151 What Is Hinduism's Nātha Sampradāya? 447
152 What Is the Lofty Kailāsa Paramparā? 449
153 Who Were the Early Kailāsa Preceptors? 451
154 Who Were Kadaitswāmī and Chellappan? 453
155 Who Are the Most Recent Kailāsa Gurus? 455
Scriptures Speak on Paramparā 456

RESOURCES—*Upagrantha*
1. A Śaivite Creed—*Śaiva Śraddhādhāraṇā* 461
2. Six Schools of Śaivism—*Shaṭśaiva Sampradāya* 491
3. Truth Is One, Paths Are Many
Ekam Sat, Anekāḥ Panthāḥ 523
4. Hindu Timeline—*Bhārata Kālachakra* 605
5. A Children's Primer—*Bālaka Pustaka* 649

Conclusion—*Nirvāhaṇa* 673
Lexicon—*Śabda Kośa* 675
Charts: Hindu Cosmology, Tattvas, Chakras 865
Index—*Sūchī* 871
Scriptural Quote Index—*Śāstra Uddharaṇasūchī* ... 937
Scriptural Bibliography—*Śāstra Vidyānusevana* 945
Supplementary reading—*Granthavidyā* 951
Colophon—*Anytaśabda* 959

Author's Introduction

Granthakāra Bhūmikā

ग्रन्थकारभूमिका

IT IS NO ACCIDENT THAT YOU HAVE FOUND THIS BOOK AND THE TREASURES IT CONTAINS. IT'S ALL PART OF THE DIVINE DANCE OF DESTINY. THE treasure you hold in the palm of your hand is divine knowledge, knowledge about you and God, knowledge about how to live a spiritual life, knowledge about what Hindus teach and believe. All of this and more awaits you in the chapters that follow. Follow it, and one day you will hold Truth in the palm of your hand—just as simply.

While other religions are precisely defined by explicit and often unyielding beliefs, Hinduism condones no such constraints. For the Hindu, intuition is far more important than intellect; experience supercedes dogma; and personal realization is held infinitely more precious than outer expressions or affiliations of faith. Philosopher S. Rādhākṛishṇan said it well: "The mechanical faith which depends on authority and wishes to enjoy the consolations of religion without the labor of being religious is quite different from the religious faith which has its roots in experience."

Hindu religious philosophy is based on experience, on personal discovery and testing of things. It does not say, "Believe as others do or suffer." Rather, it says, "Know thy Self, inquire and be free." There are no heretics in Hinduism, for God is everywhere and in all things. In such an open laboratory, Hindu spirituality has grown over the millennia so diverse and rich that it defies definition. Even knowledgeable Hindus, after a lifetime of study, will hesitate to say that Hinduism is one thing and not another. Indeed, the very idea of a Hindu catechism is, for many, unthinkable, a perilous and impertinent pursuit. Until now, no one has attempted such a complete overview, making this a rare, and perhaps remarkable, book. One might even say an inevitable one. If, therefore, in undertaking the impossible we have overlooked any lineage, neglected any tradition or vital issue, please call to mind that it is human to err and only God is perfect and find room in your heart to overlook any oversight.

A simple warning is due. This collection of customs and beliefs is not a detached, scholastic analysis of Hinduism, but a view from the inside, a view of the religion as Hindus themselves would wish their tradition honored and explained to others. Nor is this yet another dogma added to the mountains of doctrines and decrees which have crushed the human spirit throughout history. Every instinct in Hinduism rebels against the doctrine which is oppressive or narrow-minded. Every instinct in Hinduism rejoices in tolerance and in acknowledgement of the many paths, even those that seem to contradict its own. When you believe that God is everywhere, in all there is wherever it is, it becomes impossible to hate or injure or seek to aggressively convert others. That is the spirit of this book. It is a transcript of the life lived by hundreds of millions of people, one out of six of the human family. Like Hinduism itself, this contemporary catechism is an ongoing revelation—a dance more than a doctrine.

Dancing with Śiva! What an extraordinary expression of our closeness to God, our creative interplay with God. The Cosmic Dance describes the Hindu view of existence, from the first thunder of the drum in His right hand announcing the Beginning, to the final all-consuming flames in His left hand pronouncing the End, which but heralds a new Beginning. Thus, dancing with Śiva is everything we do, everything we think and say and feel, from our seeming birth to our so-called death. It is man and God forever engaged in sacred movement.

The ancient sages chose the dance to depict God for good

reason. Esoterically, movement is the most primal act of existence. Without this simple thing, there would be no universe, no us, no experience, nothing. Light is movement. Thought is movement. Atoms are movement. Life is movement. And, the Hindu holds, God is movement. Also, dance is the only creative act in which there is perfect oneness of the creator and his creation. Unlike a painting, a poem, an invention or any other artistic impulse, when the dance is over there is no product, no thing to save and enjoy. As with life, we may perceive the dance, never possess it. One cannot separate the dancer from dancing, just as one cannot separate God from the world or from ourselves. Of special meaning is the place where Śiva dances: in the *chitsabhā,* the hall of consciousness. In other words, it happens within each of us.

The vast complexity of Śiva's Cosmic Dance is traditionally represented in 108 poses. Over twenty centuries ago, Ṛishi Tirumular of the Nandinātha Sampradāya's Kailāsa Paramparā praised God Śiva's never-ending dance with loving eloquence: "In all worlds He is, the Holy Lord. In darkness He is, light He is. In sun He is, in moon He is. Everywhere He is. The Lord is in all creation. None knows His coming and going. He is distant. He is near. Multiple He is. One He is. Water, earth, sky, fire and wind, the spark within the body—all these He is. He is the walking *jīva* here below. Deathless He is."

It is imperative at this time in our history—when the world, our Earth, is on the brink of an inner and outer space age—that we continue to value and learn from ancient Hindu wisdom. Long, long ago, great sages of India unfolded these eternal truths from within themselves and recorded them as written scripture to be sung out through the voices of their representatives today. So great was their insight. Truly, this eternal wisdom lives now and will live on into the next generation, the next and the next. Hear the famed prayer offered by *ṛishis* of yore: "Lead me from unreality to reality. Lead me from darkness to light. Lead me from death to immortality."

The Beliefs of Hinduism

Hinduism, more than any other religion, has encompassed the full spectrum of philosophic positions, and to this day venerates living exponents of each. Thus it is that one teacher will praise devotion as the ultimate path, while another, spurning devotion, says liberation comes only upon the shattering of this universe's illusory appearance. How then to understand Hinduism? From the Himalayan vaults, ten thousand streams of thought descend, their cool waters giving life to all below. These flow together, their convergences becoming broad tributaries. From these, two mighty rivers are born which have through history watered and made green the growth of Indian spirituality—one is Vedānta and the other Siddhānta. This contemporary catechism is the confluence of these two potent traditions into a single torrent, the inundation of the Sanātana Dharma in full, fierce flood and force.

What Do Most Hindus Believe?

There are nine beliefs, or *śraddhā,* which though not exhaustive, offer a simple summary of Hindu spirituality.

1. Hindus believe in the divinity of the *Vedas,* the world's most ancient scripture, and venerate the *Āgamas* as equally revealed. These primordial hymns are God's word and the bedrock of Sanātana Dharma, the eternal religion which has neither beginning nor end.
2. Hindus believe in a one, all-pervasive Supreme Being who is both immanent and transcendent, both Creator and Unmanifest Reality.
3. Hindus believe that the universe undergoes endless cycles of creation, preservation and dissolution.
4. Hindus believe in *karma,* the law of cause and effect by which each individual creates his own destiny by his thoughts, words and deeds.
5. Hindus believe that the soul reincarnates, evolving

through many births until all *karmas* have been resolved, and *moksha*, spiritual knowledge and liberation from the cycle of rebirth, is attained. Not a single soul will be eternally deprived of this destiny.

6. Hindus believe that divine beings exist in unseen worlds and that temple worship, rituals, sacraments as well as personal devotionals create a communion with these *devas* and Gods.
7. Hindus believe that a spiritually awakened master, or *satguru*, is essential to know the Transcendent Absolute, as are personal discipline, good conduct, purification, pilgrimage, self-inquiry and meditation.
8. Hindus believe that all life is sacred, to be loved and revered, and therefore practice *ahiṁsā*, "noninjury."
9. Hindus believe that no particular religion teaches the only way to salvation above all others, but that all genuine religious paths are facets of God's Pure Love and Light, deserving tolerance and understanding.

World Religions at a Glance, and Hindu Population Map
We list here how the number of Hindus compares with other religions and provide a map indicating where Hindus reside in the world. Main statistical sources: *World Christian Encyclopedia* and the Worldwatch Institute.

1993 World Population: 5.2 billion

Hindus:	1 billion	Taoists:	50 million
Muslims:	1 billion	Other Faiths:	50 million
Catholics:	1.5 billion	Shintoists:	30 million
Protestants:	600 million	Jews:	12 million
Nonbelievers:	600 million	Sikhs:	9 million
Confucian:	400 million	Jains:	6 million
Buddhists:	350 million	Zoroastrians:	125,000
Tribals:	100 million	**Total:**	**5.2 Billion**

Where Hindus Live

Algeria..........500	Czech Republic and Slovakia...100	Columbia........50	Guinea...........50
Barbados.......100	Chad.............20	Cuba...........100	Hungary.........50
Brazil.............50	Chile.............20	Equador........500	Iceland............6
Brunei..........500	China............50	Finland.........100	Ireland...........20
Cameroon.......50	Congo.........100	Gabon..........100	Israel...........100
C. African Rep..20		Ghana..........500	Italy.............200

While India is home to 93% of the world's 816 million Hindus, nearly 60 million are scattered widely across the globe. This map shows larger communities, with smaller ones listed below.

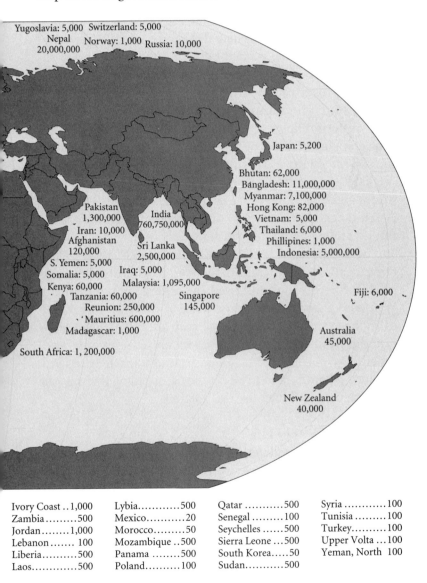

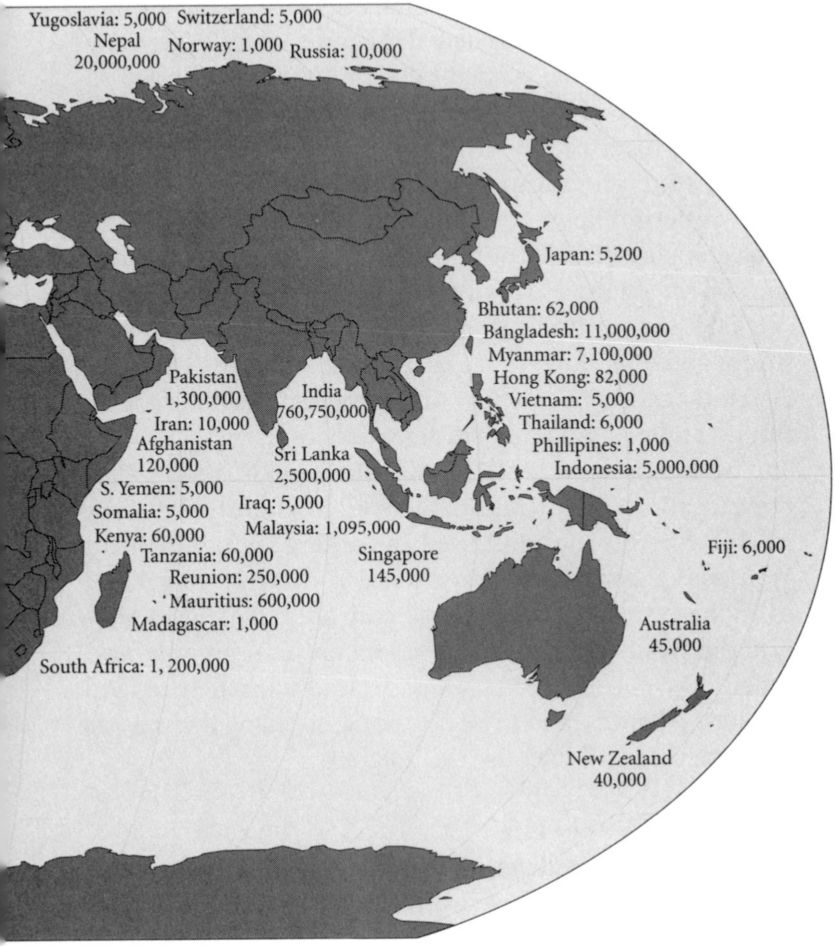

Ivory Coast .. 1,000	Lybia........... 500	Qatar 500	Syria 100
Zambia......... 500	Mexico.......... 20	Senegal 100	Tunisia 100
Jordan........ 1,000	Morocco......... 50	Seychelles 500	Turkey.......... 100
Lebanon....... 100	Mozambique .. 500	Sierra Leone ... 500	Upper Volta ... 100
Liberia.......... 500	Panama 500	South Korea..... 50	Yeman, North 100
Laos............ 500	Poland......... 100	Sudan.......... 500	

Hinduism Is an Eastern Religion

To place Hinduism in the context of world thought, it is first important to note that it is a religion of the East. This is a vital fact, for there is a vast difference between the way seekers in the East and the West have traditionally viewed the ultimate questions: "Who am I? Where did I come from? Where am I going?" The East has tended to be unitive, idealistic and introspective. The West has tended to be dualistic, materialistic and extroverted. Looking at it simply, the major Eastern religions are Hinduism, Jainism, Buddhism and Sikhism. The Western religions are Judaism, Christianity and Islam. This comparison does not include the Oriental faiths: Confucianism, Shinto and Taoism.

The Eastern mind tends to see God everywhere, in all things and, therefore, to see everything as sacred. The Western mind considers it heresy to believe that God pervades all things, and makes a strong difference between what is sacred and what is profane. While the Eastern mind holds to *karma,* reincarnation and liberation, the Westerner postulates a single life for the soul, followed by reward or punishment. Whereas personal inner experience is the crux of religion from the Eastern view, belief and faith are valued most highly in the West. While Eastern religions are accommodating of other views, believing that all paths lead ultimately to God, Western religions tend to be dogmatic, stressing theirs as the one true God and the one true religion.

The Hindu View of Life

The soul, in its intelligence, searches for its Self, slowly ascending the path that leads to enlightenment and liberation. It is an arduous, delightful journey through the cycles of birth, death and rebirth culminating in Self Realization, the direct and personal spiritual experience of God, of the Self, of Truth. This alone among all things in the cosmos can bring freedom from the bondages of ignorance and desire. This is the highest realization. There is none greater. Hindus believe that all women and men are on this path and that all will ultimately reach its summit. It is a glorious and encouraging concept—that every single soul will reach Truth, *moksha*, none left to suffer forever for human frailties and faults.

Hinduism is our planet's original and oldest living religion, with no single founder. For as long as man has lived and roamed across Earth's land and water masses, breathed its air and worshiped in awe its fire, the Sanātana Dharma has been a guide of righteous life for evolving souls. Shortly into the twenty-first century, Hindu adherents will number over a billion. All of them are Hindus, yes, but they represent a broad range of beliefs, *sādhanas* and mystic goals.

While Hindus believe many diverse and exotic things, there are several bedrock concepts on which virtually all concur. All Hindus worship one Supreme Reality, though they call it by many names, and teach that all souls will ultimately realize the truth of the *Vedas* and *Āgamas.* Hindus believe that there is no eternal hell, no damnation. They concur that there is no intrinsic evil. All is good. All is God. In contrast, Western faiths postulate a living evil force, embodied in Satan that directly opposes the will of God.

Hindus believe that the universe was created out of God and is permeated by Him—a Supreme Being who both is form and pervades form, who creates, sustains and destroys the universe only to recreate it again in unending cycles. Hindus accept all genuine spiritual paths—from pure monism, which concludes that "God alone exists," to theistic dualism, which asks, "When shall I know His Grace?" Each soul is free to find his own way, whether by devotion, austerity, meditation, *yoga* or selfless service (*sevā*). Hinduism's three pillars are temple worship, scripture and the *guru*-disciple tradition. Hinduism strongly declares the validity of the three worlds of existence and the myriad Gods and *devas* residing within them. Festivals, pilgrimage, chanting of holy hymns and home worship are dynamic practices. Love, nonviolence, good conduct and the law of *dharma* define the Hindu path. Hinduism explains that the soul reincarnates until all *karmas* are resolved and God Realization is attained.

Hindus wear the sectarian marks, called *tilaka,* on their foreheads as sacred symbols, distinctive insignia of their heritage. Hinduism is a mystical religion, leading devotees to personally experience its eternal truths within themselves, finally reaching the pinnacle of consciousness where man and God are forever one. They prefer cremation of the body upon death, rather than burial, believing that the soul lives on and will inhabit a new body on earth.

While Hinduism has many sacred scriptures, all sects ascribe the highest authority to the *Vedas* and *Āgamas,* though their *Āgamas* differ somewhat. Hinduism's nearly one billion adherents have tens of thousands of sacred temples and shrines, mostly in India, but now located in every community of the global village where Hindus have settled. Its spiritual core is its holy men and women—millions of *sādhus, yogīs, swāmīs, vairāgīs,* saints and *satgurus* who have dedicated their lives to full-time service, devotion and God Realization, and to proclaiming the eternal truths of the Sanātana Dharma.

About this Edition of *Dancing with Śiva*

In this fourth edition of *Dancing with Śiva: Hinduism's Contemporary Catechism, Sanātana Dharma Praśnottaram,* the questions and answers have been brought into the ancient form of terse *ślokas,* also known as *sūtras,* followed by longer explanations called *bhāshya.* In the *Purāṇas* we find a description of this style: "Those who know, say that a *sūtra* is brief, with no uncertainty, rich in substance, general, without useless words, and irrefutable." A mystical meaning is spoken in the *Mṛigendra Āgama*: "In it, as in a seed, grows the tree which is the subject of the treatise as a whole, such is the original *sūtra* which scintillates, adorned with words such as *atha*."

In olden days in India, before paper was invented, *ślokas* were written on palm leaves (*olai*) in the South, scribed into the tough surface, or written on specially-prepared birch bark *(bhūrja pattra)* in the North. The unbound pages were small, about two inches high and six or eight inches wide. Verses written on them were usually uniform in length, two, three or four lines. To carry forward the refined finesse of those Vedic times, the *ślokas* and *bhāshyas* of this modern catechism have been composed to precise lengths—each *śloka* exactly four lines long and each *bhāshya* exactly twenty-one lines, not a millimeter more or less.

The book has more than tripled in size since the 309-page 1990 edition. First, I instructed a few of my *sannyāsins* to redo the artwork. You will see that they have combined traditional images with computerized technology to produce a unique art form that is the best of the East and the best of the West. More sacred symbols were added, and over 150 reproductions of Rājput paintings were selected from sources all over the world, chosen for their aptness to the many subjects covered.

Then I brought in hundreds of verses from Hindu scripture, mostly from the *Vedas*. There is a scriptural quote for each *bhāshya*, and at the end of every chapter, or *maṇḍala*, there are two full pages of scripture elaborating the subject under discussion. We are hopeful that this anthology of hymns will inspire readers to dive deeper into the beauties of the *Vedas* and *Āgamas* on their own.

We then expanded by several hundred the number of Sanskṛit terms in the book, and incorporated the diacritical marks into the special Minion family of fonts. We typeset the main lexicon entries in Devanāgarī, with the able editing assistance of several Sanskṛit scholars. In the lexicon, we worked ardently to more fully amplify the essential concepts so briefly presented in the terse *ślokas* and *bhāshyas*. Thus, over the months, what began as a simple glossary of terms steadily grew. The result is really an encyclopedic dictionary. Many terms can be defined in various ways, according to one's philosophical perspective. By understanding the terms as defined in this lexicon, one can better understand their meaning in the body of the text.

Next, we assembled a timeline, a detailed chronology of ancient Bhārat and modern India, a record of Hindu events placed in the context of world historic landmarks. I believe this chronology is the only one of its kind and encourage teachers to teach it and students to study it to understand the way Hindu history flows alongside the other great human civilizations.

Last but not least, in the final weeks of production, we added a new section called "Truth Is One, Paths Are Many," drawn from the international newspaper, *Hinduism Today.* This 60-page resource offers a brief summary of the beliefs and paths of attainment of the world's major religions, faiths and philosophies and several point-counterpoints, including a comparison of Eastern and Western thought. For the past ten years it has been widely used as an educational tool in universities and various interfaith gatherings, and I felt it should definitely be part of this book. The timeline, lexicon and Truth Is One are each complete studies unto themselves.

One of the limitations we encountered was how to speak of the genderless God without implying that the Divine is either man or woman. Working through the constraints of the English language, we just didn't know what to do with the words *he, she, him, her, hers* and *his* in reference to God and the Gods. To speak of God in the neuter form, *It,* seemed a worse solution, for that indicates a cold and indifferent Deity. Another possibility was to speak of God as *She* and *He* alternately. But this would require also using *God* and *Goddess* alternately, since *God* itself is a masculine term. English seems to offer no reasonable way around the use of masculine pronouns, so, reluctantly, we have referred to God and Gods in mostly masculine terms. One consolation is that this problem also exists in the original Sanskṛit, so we emerged from the dilemma by accepting the precedent set by the *Vedas* and *Āgamas* to describe the Supreme Lord.

In producing this modern catechism, or *praśnottaram* (literally, "questions and answers"), we kept in mind the need to provide resources so that Hindu institutions and communities around the globe could have, at their fingertips, authentic teachings from which they could locally develop classes and courses and various kinds of study. We encourage scholars, *paṇḍitas, swāmīs* and elders everywhere to work with us in translating *Dancing with Śiva* into many of the world's more than 3,000 languages.

Ways to Study *Dancing with Śiva*

It is our belief that a full study of this catechism will provide a basic understanding of the Hindu religion as it is lived today. We have taught its earlier editions for over forty years in many countries, and we know that it is competent to change the lives of people, to bring them closer to their inner Divinity, to strengthen husband and wife relationships, cement family unity and establish strong, unbreakable connections with God and the Gods. The key is study, by which we do not mean mere recitation, but living the life described in our venerable traditions. There are seven ways this book can be routinely studied, whether individually or in groups, small or large.

1. The twelve parts, called *upanishads,* in this catechism, one for each month of the year, may be used as lecture notes or personal study for the month. Each of the twelve is a completely different subject. An *upanishad* is a collection of one, two or three *maṇḍalas.*

2. The thirty-one chapters, called *maṇḍalas,* each contain-

ing five *ślokas,* may be studied one each day for a month and then repeated time and time again.

3. There are 155 *ślokas.* An ideal way to study the catechism by yourself is to take one *śloka* and its accompanying *bhāshya* each day. Study it, meditate on it. Apply it to your own life. Then move on to the next. This will give a daily study of over five months.

4. Another way to study the book is the "subject study," choosing concepts which interest you and following their threads throughout the book. For example, using the index, one could take the word *soul* and explore its various references—the soul's creation, its evolution, old souls and young souls. This can be even more interesting if you explore the lexicon references as well. Tracing the meaning of terms in this way through the index and lexicon is a wonderful tool for lectures, classes, teaching of children and your own personal enjoyment.

5. The fifth way is to read and meditate on the profound Vedic verses, which are found, more than any other scripture, in this *praśnottaram.* They are as alive today as the day they were spoken thousands of years ago. Is it really what they say that stirs the higher consciousness, or is it what they do to the inner currents of the body as they stimulate spirituality?

6. Another way is to simply read the book, cover to cover.

7. A final way, since this book has been magically impressed into the *ākāśa,* is to hold it in your hands and absorb its knowledge or put it under your pillow at night.

How to Teach *Dancing with Śiva*

For those who are serious about conducting regular lectures or classes on *Dancing with Śiva, Hinduism's Contemporary Catechism,* we have created the following simple guide. This system has several objectives: 1) it gives you a systematic way of presenting the material, without repeating yourself; 2) it relieves you from having to decide what you are going to talk about when lecture or class time comes around and 3) it creates a powerful harmony of minds around the globe among all who are teaching and learning the subject matter at the same time.

The cardinal principle is that there is one *maṇḍala* (containing five *ślokas* and *bhāshyas*, and two pages of scriptural verses) for each day of the month. So, for example, if you are giving a lecture on the 12th day of the month, your subject matter should be one or more of the five *ślokas* of *maṇḍala* 12, "The Four Dharmas." These five *ślokas* and their *bhāshyas* create a complete concept and are more than ample for a well-rounded lecture or seminar.

January 12: Maṇḍala 12 (five *ślokas* and *bhāshyas)*
January 13: Maṇḍala 13 (five *ślokas* and *bhāshyas)*
January 14: Maṇḍala 14 (five *ślokas* and *bhāshyas)*
January 15: Maṇḍala 14 (five *ślokas* and *bhāshyas)*
etc.

In addition, the art and sacred symbols can be used when explaining concepts to children, adding a visual dimension to their young understanding. The entire book can be used as a coloring book as it is, or by making enlarged copies of the black and white photos on a photocopy machine. Children enjoy animation, and more adventuresome parents may wish to turn portions into an educational video series for their community or nation. Children love toys and games, and interesting charades and memorization games can be developed by inventive parents and teachers. After all, it is in giving our tradition to the children that we assure its perpetuation into the future.

Only days before this catechism was sent off to the printer, the night before Mahāśivarātri, we saw the final results in color of the March, 1993, edition of *Hinduism Today,* in which we had reprinted the very popular primer for children covering Hinduism from A to Z in an illustrated and fun way. For older youth, there appeared a more mature summary, a traditional explanation of the five main precepts and practices. We were inspired to incorporate both of these in this book for parents to teach their children. The 1992 Bali Conference of the World Hindu Federation of Nepal decreed that such a simple presentation of the minimal duties for parents to pass on Sanātana Dharma to their children be outlined and spread worldwide. With that in mind, we added to *Dancing with Śiva* a new resource section called "A Children's Primer," which includes Hinduism A to Z, the Five Precepts and Five Practices, and an illustrated summary of the essential Hindu *saṁskāras,* or rites of passage.

Awake! Arise!

As you proceed through *Dancing with Śiva, Hinduism's Contemporary Catechism, Sanātana Dharma Praśnottaram,* you will come to see that it contains a new presentation of very ancient knowledge. You will soon realize that, somewhere within you, you already know these truths. You will find yourself traveling back in your memory, perhaps for several lives, and remembering that you have studied them before in the same way that you are studying them now.

This textbook gives an organized approach as to what to say to the youth and the adults of our religion. It also gives truth-seekers who have discovered the mystical realities a coherent and complete philosophical context through which they can understand and continue to pursue the often unbidden experiences they encounter. It validates their inner realizations and gives them the confidence to persevere.

A new breed of souls is even now coming up in the world. They are fearless because they are strong. They do not fear death, ill-health or lack of knowledge. Their only qualification is that they love and worship God and the Gods. They have no magic formula. They are selling nothing. They need nothing. They are who they are. You may be one of them.

So, proceed with confidence. Success is assured. You cannot fail if *bhakti* is integrated with *jñāna,* Siddhānta with Vedānta, *Āgamas* with *Vedas,* and Hindu Dharma with everyday life. Yea, this is the secure path, the safe path, leading to knowledge, experience and recognition, then realization, of your true, divine, eternal Self. Awake, arise and stop not until the goal is reached! It is no accident that you have found this book and the treasures it contains.

Love and blessings to you from this and inner worlds,

Satguru Sivaya Subramuniyaswami
Jagadāchārya of the Nandinātha
Sampradāya's Kailāsa Paramparā,
Guru Mahāsannidhānam,
Kauai Aadheenam, Hawaii,
Mahāśivarātri, February 18, 1993, Hindu year 5094

> O *Infinite Effulgence, praise be to thee. Hail! . . .*
> *Thou who is water, fire, wind, ether too! Hail thou who creates all souls but is Himself uncreated. Hail thou the culmination of all souls, hail!. . . To the one who embodies within Himself the Vedic hymns and Vedic sacrifice, truth and untruth, light and darkness, joy and sorrow, the divided and undivided, the attachment and release, the beginning and ultimate end— to Him our songs of praise we sing.*
>
> SAINT MANIKKAVASAGAR

Sanskṛit Pronunciation

VOWELS
Vowels marked like ā are sounded twice as long as short vowels. The dipthongs, e, ai, o and au, are always long.

अ a as in about
आ ा ā ...tar, father
इ ि i ...fill, lily
ई ी ī ...machine
उ ु u ...full, bush
ऊ ू ū ...allude
ऋ ृ ṛi ...merrily
ॠ ॄ ṛī ...marine
ऌ lṛi ...revelry
ए े e ...prey
ऐ ै ai ...aisle
ओ ो o ...go, stone
औ ौ au ...*Haus*

GUTTURAL CONSONANTS
Sounded in the throat.

क् k ...kite, seek
ख् kh ...inkhorn
ग् g ...good
घ् gh ...loghouse
ङ् ṅ ...sing

PALATAL CONSONANTS
Sounded at the roof of the mouth.

च् ch ...church
छ् çh ...churchill
ज् j ...jump
झ् jh ...he*dg*ehog
ञ् ñ ...hinge

CEREBRAL CONSONANTS
Pronounced with the tongue turned up and back against the roof of the mouth (retroflex).

ट् ṭ ...true
ठ् ṭh ...nuthook
ड् ḍ ...drum
ढ् ḍh ...redhaired
ण् ṇ ...none

DENTAL CONSONANTS
Sounded with the tip of the tongue at the back of the upper front teeth.

त् t ...tub
थ् th ...anthill
द् d ...dot
ध् dh ...adhere
न् n ...not

LABIAL CONSONANTS
Sounded at the lips.

प् p ...pot
फ् ph ...uphill
ब् b ...bear
भ् bh ...abhor
म् m ...map

SEMIVOWELS

य् y ...yet (palatal)
र् r ...road (cereb.)
ल् l ...lull (dental)
व् v ...voice (labial), but more like *w* after consonants.
ह् h ...hear (gutteral)

SIBILANTS

श् ś ...sure (palatal)
ष् sh ...shut (cerebral)
स् s ...saint (dental)

ANUSVĀRA
The dot over Devanāgarī letters represents the nasal of the type of the letter it precedes; e.g.: अंग = *aṅga.* It is transliterated as ṁ or as the actual nasal (ṅ, ñ, n, ṇ, m). At the end of words it is म् *(m).*

VISĀRGA (:) ḥ
Pronounced like *huh* (with a short, stopping sound), or *hih,* after i, ī and e.

ASPIRATES
The *h* following a consonant indicates aspiration, the addition of air. Thus, *th* should not be confused with the *th* in the word *then.*

SPECIAL CHARACTERS
ज्ञ् jñ ...a nasalized sound, like *gya* or *jya.*
क्ष् = क्+ ष् ksh

CONVENTIONS
1. In this text, generally, the root forms of Sanskṛit words are used, without case endings.
2. च्छ is transliterated as cçh, and चच as cch.
3. Most Tamil words are written without diacritical marks.
4. Geographical terms, e.g., *Himalaya,* are marked with diacriticals only as main lexicon entries.

Sanātana Dharma Upanishad

सनातनधर्म उपनिषद्

Eternal Truths

Paramātma Darśana Maṇḍala

परमात्मदर्शनमण्डल

Self Realization

Praṇava, Aum, is the root *mantra* and primal sound from which all creation issues forth. It is associated with Lord Gaṇeśa. Its three syllables stand at the beginning and end of every sacred verse, every human act. Aum.

Who Am I? Where Did I Come From?

ŚLOKA 1

Ṛishis proclaim that we are not our body, mind or emotions. We are divine souls on a wondrous journey. We came from God, live in God and are evolving into oneness with God. We are, in truth, the Truth we seek. Aum.

BHĀSHYA

We are immortal souls living and growing in the great school of earthly experience in which we have lived many lives. Vedic *ṛishis* have given us courage by uttering the simple truth, "God is the Life of our life." A great sage carried it further by saying, there is one thing God cannot do: God cannot separate Himself from us. This is because God is our life. God is the life in the birds. God is the life in the fish. God is the life in the animals. Becoming aware of this Life energy in all that lives is becoming aware of God's loving presence within us. We are the undying consciousness and energy flowing through all things. Deep inside we are perfect this very moment, and we have only to discover and live up to this perfection to be whole. Our energy and God's energy are the same, ever coming out of the void. We are all beautiful children of God. Each day we should try to see the life energy in trees, birds, animals and people. When we do, we are seeing God Śiva in action. The *Vedas* affirm, "He who knows God as the Life of life, the Eye of the eye, the Ear of the ear, the Mind of the mind—he indeed comprehends fully the Cause of all causes." Aum Namaḥ Śivāya.

Where Am I Going? What Is My Path?

ŚLOKA 2

We are all growing toward God, and experience is the path. Through experience we mature out of fear into fearlessness, out of anger into love, out of conflict into peace, out of darkness into light and union in God. Aum.

BHĀSHYA

We have taken birth in a physical body to grow and evolve into our divine potential. We are inwardly already one with God. Our religion contains the knowledge of how to realize this oneness and not create unwanted experiences along the way. The peerless path is following the way of our spiritual forefathers, discovering the mystical meaning of the scriptures. The peerless path is commitment, study, discipline, practice and the maturing of *yoga* into wisdom. In the beginning stages, we suffer until we learn. Learning leads us to service; and selfless service is the beginning of spiritual striving. Service leads us to understanding. Understanding leads us to meditate deeply and without distractions. Finally, meditation leads us to surrender in God. This is the straight and certain path, the San Mārga, leading to Self Realization—the inmost purpose of life—and subsequently to *moksha,* freedom from rebirth. The *Vedas* wisely affirm, "By austerity, goodness is obtained. From goodness, understanding is reached. From understanding, the Self is obtained, and he who obtains the Self is freed from the cycle of birth and death." Aum Namaḥ Śivāya.

What Is Meant by "Dancing with Śiva"?

ŚLOKA 3

All motion begins in God and ends in God. The whole universe is engaged in a whirling flow of change and activity. This is Śiva's dance. We are all dancing with Śiva, and He with us. Ultimately, we are Śiva dancing. Aum.

BHĀSHYA

The world is seen as it truly is—sacred—when we behold Śiva's cosmic dance. Everything in the universe, all that we see, hear and imagine, is movement. Galaxies soar in movement; atoms swirl in movement. All movement is Śiva's dance. When we fight this movement and think it should be other than it is, we are reluctantly dancing with Śiva. We are stubbornly resisting, holding ourselves apart, criticizing the natural processes and movements around us. It is by understanding the eternal truths that we bring all areas of our mind into the knowledge of how to accept what is and not wish it to be otherwise. Once this happens, we begin to consciously dance with Śiva, to move with the sacred flow that surrounds us, to accept praise and blame, joy and sorrow, prosperity and adversity in equanimity, the fruit of understanding. We are then gracefully, in unrestrained surrender, dancing with Śiva. The *Vedas* state, "The cosmic soul is truly the whole universe, the immortal source of all creation, all action, all meditation. Whoever discovers Him, hidden deep within, cuts through the bonds of ignorance even during his life on earth." Aum Namaḥ Śivāya.

How Can We Learn to Dance with Śiva?

ŚLOKA 4

Dance is movement, and the most exquisite dance is the most disciplined dance. Hindu spiritual disciplines lead to oneness with God through self-reflection, surrender, personal transformation and the many *yogas.* Aum.

BHĀSHYA

To progress on the path, we study the *Vedas,* other scriptures and our *guru's* teachings and make every effort to apply these philosophical truths to daily experience. We strive to understand the mind in its fourfold nature: *chitta,* consciousness; *manas,* instinctive mind; *buddhi,* intellectual mind; and *ahaṁkāra,* ego or I-maker. We perform *japa,* meditation and *yoga* each day. Such spiritual discipline is known as *sādhana.* It is the mystical, mental, physical and devotional exercise that enables us to dance with Śiva by bringing inner advancement, changes in perception and improvements in character. *Sādhana* allows us to live in the refined and cultured soul nature, rather than in the outer, instinctive or intellectual spheres. For consistent progress, *sādhana* should be performed regularly, without fail, at the same time each day, preferably in the early hours before dawn. The most important *sādhanas* are the challenges and practices given by one's *guru.* The *Vedas* caution, "The Self cannot be attained by the weak, nor by the careless, nor through aimless disciplines. But if one who knows strives by right means, his soul enters the abode of God." Aum Namaḥ Śivāya.

What Is the Ultimate Goal of Earthly Life?

ŚLOKA 5

The ultimate goal of life on earth is to realize the Self, the rare attainment of *nirvikalpa samādhi*. Each soul discovers its Śivaness, Absolute Reality, Paraśiva—the timeless, formless, spaceless Self God. Aum Namaḥ Śivāya.

BHĀSHYA

The realization of the Self, Paraśiva, is the destiny of each soul, attainable through renunciation, sustained meditation and frying the seeds of *karmas* yet to germinate. It is the gateway to *moksha*, liberation from rebirth. The Self lies beyond the thinking mind, beyond the feeling nature, beyond action or any movement of even the highest state of consciousness. The Self God is more solid than a neutron star, more elusive than empty space, more intimate than thought and feeling. It is ultimate reality itself, the innermost Truth all seekers seek. It is well worth striving for. It is well worth struggling to bring the mind under the dominion of the will. After the Self is realized, the mind is seen for the unreality that it truly is. Because Self Realization must be experienced in a physical body, the soul cycles back again and again into flesh to dance with Śiva, live with Śiva and ultimately merge with Śiva in undifferentiated oneness. Yea, *jīva* is actually Śiva. The *Vedas* explain, "As water poured into water, milk poured into milk, *ghee* into *ghee* become one without differentiation, even so the individual soul and the Supreme Self become one." Aum Namaḥ Śivāya.

Scriptures Speak on Self Realization

Lead me from unreality to reality. Lead me from darkness to light. Lead me from death to immortality. ***Yajur Veda***

He is the Supreme Brahman, the Self of all, the chief foundation of this world, subtler than the subtle, eternal. That thou art; thou art That. ***Atharva Veda***

One should meditate on the *ātman,* which consists of spirit, whose embodiment is life, whose form is light, whose essence is space, which changes its form at will, swift as thought. ***Yajur Veda***

Subtlest of the subtle, greatest of the great, the *ātman* is hidden in the cave of the heart of all beings. He who, free from all urges, beholds Him overcomes sorrow, seeing by grace of the Creator, the Lord and His glory. ***Yajur Veda***

Perishable is matter. Immortal, imperishable the Lord, who, the One, controls the perishable and also the soul. Meditating on Him, uniting with Him, becoming more and more like Him, one is freed at the last from the world's illusion. ***Yajur Veda***

I am the Supreme Brahman! I am the Lord of the universe! Such is the settled conviction of the *muktas.* All other experiences lead to bondage. When the Self is clearly realized not to be the body, the realizer gains peace and becomes free from all desires. ***Devīkālottara Āgama***

Realize the Self always to be neither above nor below, nor on either side, not without nor within, but to be eternal and shining beyond the sublime world. ***Sarvajñānottara Āgama***

That which is neither conscious nor unconscious, which is invisible, impalpable, indefinable, unthinkable, unnameable, whose very essence consists of the experience of its own self, which absorbs all diversity, is tranquil and benign, without a second, which is what they call the fourth state—that is the *ātman*. This it is which should be known. *Atharva Veda*

On the emergence of spontaneous supreme knowledge occurs that state of movement in the vast unlimited expanse of consciousness which is Śiva's state, the supreme state of Reality. *Śiva Sūtras*

When the Creator dances, the worlds He created dance. To the measure that He dances in our knowledge, our thoughts, too, dance. When He in heart endearing dances, the several elements, too, dance. Witness in rapture surpassing the dance of Him who is a glowing flame. *Tirumantiram*

O God of mercy, who performs the dance of illimitable happiness in the hall of inconceivable intelligence! The *Ṛig* and the other *Vedas* are thundering forth in words, announcing to us that all are thy slaves, all things belong to thee, all actions are thine, that thou pervades everywhere, that this is thy nature. Such is the teaching of those who, though they never speak, yet broke silence for our sake. *Tayumanavar*

Just as light shines, dispelling darkness, so also the Supreme Self shines, dispelling ignorance. Just as a lamp spontaneously goes out if not fed with oil, so also the ego becomes extinct if one meditates unceasingly and becomes merged in the Self. There is no higher gain than the Self. *Sarvajñānottara Āgama*

The Supreme Lord is not two. To me belongs the glory of meditating that I, His devoted servant, am He. As one imagines, so one becomes. Therefore, practice the meditation of "I am He." Then all your actions will become His action. *Natchintanai*

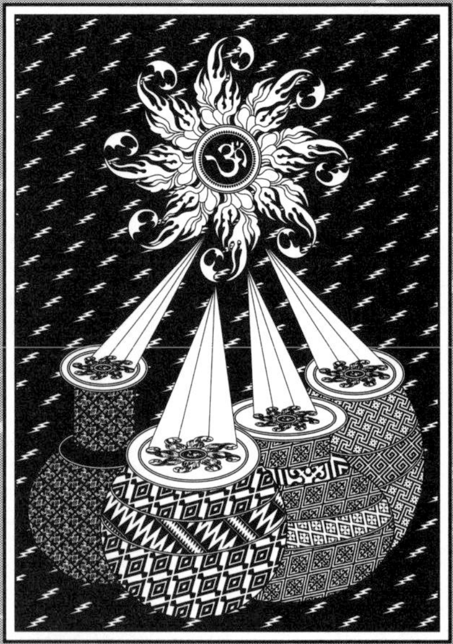

Hindu Maṇḍala

हिन्दुमण्डल

Hinduism

Vaṭa, the banyan tree, *Ficus indicus*, symbolizes Hinduism, which branches out in all directions, draws from many roots, spreads shade far and wide, yet stems from one great trunk. Śiva as Silent Sage sits beneath it. Aum.

What Are Hinduism's Principal Sects?

ŚLOKA 6

The Sanātana Dharma, or "eternal faith," known today as Hinduism, is a family of religions that accept the authority of the *Vedas.* Its four principal denominations are Śaivism, Śāktism, Vaishṇavism and Smārtism. Aum.

BHĀSHYA

The world's billion Hindus, one-sixth of the human family, are organized in four main denominations, each distinguished by its Supreme Deity. For Vaishṇavites, Lord Vishṇu is God. For Śaivites, God is Śiva. For Śāktas, Goddess Śakti is supreme. For Smārtas, liberal Hindus, the choice of Deity is left to the devotee. Each has a multitude of *guru* lineages, religious leaders, priesthoods, sacred literature, monastic communities, schools, pilgrimage centers and tens of thousands of temples. They possess a wealth of art and architecture, philosophy and scholarship. These four sects hold such divergent beliefs that each is a complete and independent religion. Yet, they share a vast heritage of culture and belief—*karma, dharma,* reincarnation, all-pervasive Divinity, temple worship, sacraments, manifold Deities, the *guru-śishya* tradition and the *Vedas* as scriptural authority. While India is home to most Hindus, large communities flourish worldwide. The *Vedas* elaborate, "He is Brahmā. He is Śiva. He is Indra. He is the immutable, the supreme, the self-luminous. He is Vishṇu. He is life. He is time. He is the fire, and He is the moon." Aum Namaḥ Śivāya.

What Is the Deeply Mystical Śaiva Sect?

ŚLOKA 7

Śaivism is the world's oldest religion. Worshiping God Śiva, the compassionate One, it stresses potent disciplines, high philosophy, the *guru's* centrality and *bhakti-rāja-siddha yoga* leading to oneness with Śiva within. Aum.

BHĀSHYA

Śaivism is ancient, truly ageless, for it has no beginning. It is the precursor of the many-faceted religion now termed Hinduism. Scholars trace the roots of Śiva worship back more than 8,000 years to the advanced Indus Valley civilization. But sacred writings tell us there never was a time when Śaivism did not exist. Modern history records six main schools: Śaiva Siddhānta, Pāśupatism, Kashmīr Śaivism, Vīra Śaivism, Siddha Siddhānta and Śiva Advaita. Śaivism's grandeur and beauty are found in a practical culture, an enlightened view of man's place in the universe and a profound system of temple mysticism and *siddha yoga*. It provides knowledge of man's evolution from God and back to God, of the soul's unfoldment and awakening guided by enlightened sages. Like all the sects, its majority are devout families, headed by hundreds of orders of *swāmīs* and *sādhus* who follow the fiery, world-renouncing path to *moksha*. The *Vedas* state, "By knowing Śiva, the Auspicious One who is hidden in all things, exceedingly fine, like film arising from clarified butter, the One embracer of the universe—by realizing God, one is released from all fetters." Aum Namaḥ Śivāya.

What Is the Magic and Power of Śāktism?

ŚLOKA 8

Śāktism reveres the Supreme as the Divine Mother, Śakti or Devī, in Her many forms, both gentle and fierce. Śāktas use *mantra, tantra, yantra, yoga* and *pūjā* to invoke cosmic forces and awaken the *kuṇḍalinī* power. Aum.

BHĀSHYA

While worship of the Divine Mother extends beyond the pale of history, Śākta Hinduism arose as an organized sect in India around the fifth century. Today it has four expressions—devotional, folk-shamanic, *yogic* and universalist—all invoking the fierce power of Kālī or Durgā, or the benign grace of Pārvatī or Ambikā. Śākta devotionalists use *pūjā* rites, especially to the *Śrī Chakra yantra,* to establish intimacy with the Goddess. Shamanic Śāktism employs magic, trance mediumship, firewalking and animal sacrifice for healing, fertility, prophecy and power. Śākta *yogīs* seek to awaken the sleeping Goddess Kuṇḍalinī and unite her with Śiva in the *sahasrāra chakra.* Śākta universalists follow the reformed Vedāntic tradition exemplified by Śrī Rāmakṛishṇa. "Left-hand" *tantric* rites transcend traditional ethical codes. Śāktism is chiefly *advaitic,* defining the soul's destiny as complete identity with the Unmanifest, Śiva. Central scriptures are the *Vedas, Śākta Āgamas* and *Purāṇas.* The *Devī Gītā* extols, "We bow down to the universal soul of all. Above and below and in all four directions, Mother of the universe, we bow." Aum Chaṇḍikāyai Namaḥ.

What Is the Devotional Vaishṇava Sect?

ŚLOKA 9

Vaishṇavism is an ancient Hindu sect centering on the worship of Lord Vishṇu and His incarnations, especially Kṛishṇa and Rāma. Largely dualistic, profoundly devotional, it is rich in saints, temples and scriptures. Aum.

BHĀSHYA

The worship of Vishṇu, meaning "pervader," dates back to Vedic times. The Pañcharātra and Bhāgavata sects were popular prior to 300 BCE. Today's five Vaishṇava schools emerged in the middle ages, founded by Rāmānuja, Mādhva, Nimbārka, Vallabha and Chaitanya. Vaishṇavism stresses *prapatti,* single-pointed surrender to Vishṇu, or His ten or more incarnations, called *avatāras.* *Japa* is a key devotional *sādhana,* as is ecstatic chanting and dancing, called *kīrtana.* Temple worship and festivals are elaborately observed. Philosophically, Vaishṇavism ranges from Mādhva's pure dualism to Rāmānuja's qualified nondualism to Vallabha's nearly monistic vision. God and soul are everlastingly distinct. The soul's destiny, through God's grace, is to eternally worship and enjoy Him. While generally nonascetic, advocating *bhakti* as the highest path, Vaishṇavism has a strong monastic community. Central scriptures are the *Vedas, Vaishṇava Āgamas, Itihāsas* and *Purāṇas.* The *Bhagavad Gītā* states, "On those who meditate on Me and worship with undivided heart, I confer attainment of what they have not, and preserve what they have." Aum Namo Nārāyaṇāya.

What Is the Universalistic Smārta Sect?

ŚLOKA 10

Smārtism is an ancient *brāhminical* tradition reformed by Śaṅkara in the ninth century. Worshiping six forms of God, this liberal Hindu path is monistic, nonsectarian, meditative and philosophical. Aum Namaḥ Śivāya.

BHĀSHYA

Smārta means a follower of classical *smṛiti,* particularly the *Dharma Śāstras, Purāṇas* and *Itihāsas.* Smārtas revere the *Vedas* and honor the *Āgamas.* Today this faith is synonymous with the teachings of Ādi Śaṅkara, the monk-philosopher, known as *shaṇmata sthāpanāchārya,* "founder of the six-sect system." He campaigned India-wide to consolidate the Hindu faiths of his time under the banner of Advaita Vedānta. To unify the worship, he popularized the ancient Smārta five-Deity altar—Gaṇapati, Sūrya, Vishṇu, Śiva and Śakti—and added Kumāra. From these, devotees may choose their "preferred Deity," or *Ishṭa Devatā.* Each God is but a reflection of the one Saguṇa Brahman. Śaṅkara organized hundreds of monasteries into a ten-order, *daśanāmī* system, which now has five pontifical centers. He wrote profuse commentaries on the *Upanishads, Brahma Sūtras* and *Bhagavad Gītā.* Śaṅkara proclaimed, "It is the one Reality which appears to our ignorance as a manifold universe of names and forms and changes. Like the gold of which many ornaments are made, it remains in itself unchanged. Such is Brahman, and That art Thou." Aum Namaḥ Śivāya.

Scriptures Speak on Religion

They call Him Indra, Mitra, Varuṇa, Agni or the heavenly sunbird Garutmat. The seers call in many ways that which is One; they speak of Agni, Yama, Mātariśvan. *Ṛig Veda*

Him who is without beginning and without end, in the midst of confusion, the Creator of all, of manifold form, the One embracer of the universe—by knowing God, one is released from all fetters. *Yajur Veda*

Who by His grandeur has emerged sole sovereign of every living thing that breathes and slumbers, He who is Lord of man and four-legged creatures—what God shall we adore with our oblation? *Ṛig Veda*

The Primordial Vastness is the sky. The Primordial Vastness is the sphere of space. The Primordial Vastness is the mother, the father, the son. The Primordial Vastness is all the Gods, the five sorts of men, all that was born and shall be born. *Ṛig Veda*

May I attain to Vishṇu's glorious mansion where the faithful rejoice, where, close beside the Strider, within His highest footstep springs the well of purest honey. *Ṛig Veda*

I am the ruling Queen, the amasser of treasures, full of wisdom, first of those worthy of worship. In various places, divine powers have set Me. I enter many homes and take numerous forms. *Ṛig Veda*

Whatever exists and wherever it exists is permeated by the same divine power and force. *Yajur Veda*

Recognition of the world as the manifestation of Śakti is worship of Śakti. Pure knowledge, unrelated to objects, is absolute. *Devīkālottara Āgama*

When milk is poured into milk, oil into oil, water into water, they blend in absolute oneness. So also the illumined seer, the knower of the *ātman,* becomes one with the *ātman.* *Crest-Jewel of Discrimination*

Let us worship Him, the pure-formed One, the cloud which, emitting a rain of unthinkable joy, satiates the hearts and eyes of its followers, as if millions of rain clouds had poured down, the stay of the Great Silence, called by many names, described by many religions, the embodiment of ineffable degrees of spiritual happiness. *Tayumanavar*

Oh God of mercy who performs the dance of illimitable happiness in the hall of inconceivable Intelligence! Oh thou Preceptor who art named Nīlakaṇṭha! Oh thou Preceptor of wisdom who art of the form of Vishṇu! Oh thou Preceptor who art of the form of the four-headed Brahmā, the author of *Vedas!* O thou who discharges the duties of a Preceptor in all religions! Oh thou who as Preceptor enlightens in love those followers who have implored thee not to abandon them. *Tayumanavar*

Give reverence to your tradition's God, who the whole world and all that lives pervades. *Natchintanai*

He is the Ancient One. He created the beings of earth and heaven in days of yore in order divine. The six faiths seek the feet but of the One Primal, Peerless God. And in them all, He pervades in measure appropriate. *Tirumantiram*

Śaiva Dharma Maṇḍala

शैवधर्ममण्डल

Śaivite Hinduism

Tripuṇḍra is a Śaivite's great mark, three stripes of white *vibhūti* on the brow. This holy ash signifies purity and the burning away of *āṇava, karma* and *māyā.* The *bindu,* or dot, at the third eye quickens spiritual insight. Aum.

What Is the Nature of Śaivite Theology?

ŚLOKA 11

Śaivism proclaims: God Śiva is Love, both immanent and transcendent, both the creator and the creation. This world is the arena of our evolution, which leads by stages to *moksha,* liberation from birth and death. Aum.

BHĀSHYA

Śaivism is a unique religion in which God is both manifest and unmanifest, dual and nondual, within us and outside of us. It is not strictly pantheistic, polytheistic or monotheistic. Its predominant theology is known as monistic theism, panentheism, or Advaita Īsvaravāda. Monism, the opposite of dualism, is the doctrine that reality is a one whole or existence without independent parts. Theism is belief in God and the Gods, both immanent and transcendent. Śaivism is monistic in its belief in a one reality and in the *advaitic,* or nondual, identity of man with that reality. Śaivism is theistic in its belief in the Gods, and in God Śiva as a loving, personal Lord, immanent in the world. Śaivism expresses the oneness of Pati-*paśu-pāśa,* God-soul-world, encompassing the nondual and the dual, faithfully carrying forth both Vedānta and Siddhānta, the pristine Sanātana Dharma of the *Vedas* and *Śaiva Āgamas.* The *Tirumantiram* states, "Śuddha Śaivas meditate on these as their religious path: Oneself, Absolute Reality and the Primal Soul; the categories three: God, soul and bonds; immaculate liberation and all that fetters the soul." Aum Namaḥ Śivāya.

How Do Śaivites Regard Other Faiths?

ŚLOKA 12

Religious beliefs are manifold and different. Śaivites, understanding the strength of this diversity, wholeheartedly respect and encourage all who believe in God. They honor the fact that Truth is one, paths are many. Aum.

BHĀSHYA

Since the inner intent of all religions is to bind man back to God, Śaivite Hindus seek not to interfere with anyone's faith or practice. We believe that there is no exclusive path, no one way for all. Śaivites profoundly know that God Śiva is the same Supreme Being in whom peoples of all faiths find solace, peace and liberation. Nonetheless, we realize that all religions are not the same. Each has its unique beliefs, practices, goals and paths of attainment, and the doctrines of one often conflict with those of another. Even this should never be cause for religious tension or intolerance. Śaivites respect all religious traditions and the people within them. They know that good citizens and stable societies are created from groups of religious people. Śaivite leaders support and participate in ecumenical gatherings with all religions. Still, Śaivites defend their faith, proceed contentedly with their practices and avoid the enchantment of other ways, be they ancient or modern. The *Vedas* explain, "Let us have concord with our own people, and concord with people who are strangers to us. Aśvins, create between us and the strangers a unity of hearts." Aum Namaḥ Śivāya.

How Does Śaivism Stay Contemporary?

ŚLOKA 13

Inner truths never change, but outer forms of practice and observance do evolve. Śaivism seeks to preserve its mystical teachings while adapting to the cultural, social and technological changes of each recurrent age. Aum.

BHĀSHYA

Śaivism is an orthodox religion, conservative in its ways and yet pliant and understanding. It is simultaneously the most demanding spiritual path and the most forgiving. Śaivites have persisted through many ages through successfully adapting work, service and skills according to the times while internalizing worship and holding firmly to the eternal values. The outer form of service or occupation does not change the spiritual search. Be he a skilled farmer, factory worker, village merchant, computer programmer or corporate executive, the Śaivite is served well by his religion. Śaivism has all of the facilities for the education of humankind back to the Source. Each futuristic age does not reflect a difference in the Śaivite's relationship with his family, *kula guru,* teacher, *satguru,* Gods or God in his daily religious life. The Śaiva Dharma: it is now as it always was. The *Vedas* implore: "O self-luminous Divine, remove the veil of ignorance from before me, that I may behold your light. Reveal to me the spirit of the scriptures. May the truth of the scriptures be ever present to me. May I seek day and night to realize what I learn from the sages." Aum Namaḥ Śivāya.

What Is the Nature of Life for Śaivites?

ŚLOKA 14

To the Śaivite Hindu, all of life is sacred. All of life is religion. Thus, Śaivite art is sacred art, Śaivite music is devotional music, and the Śaivite's business is not only his livelihood, it is his service to man and God. Aum.

BHĀSHYA

Each Śaivite is unique in his or her quest, yet all seek the same things in life: to be happy and secure, loved and appreciated, creative and useful. Śaivism has an established culture which fulfills these essential human wants and helps us understand the world and our place in it. To all devotees it gives guidance in the qualities of character so necessary in spiritual life: patience, compassion, broad-mindedness, humility, industriousness and devotion. Śaivism centers around the home and the temple. Monastic life is its core and its power. Family life is strong and precious. Śaivism possesses a wealth of art and architecture, traditions of music, art, drama and dance, and a treasury of philosophy and scholarship. Śaivite temples provide worship services daily. Scriptures give ethical guidelines. *Satgurus* offer advanced spiritual initiation. These three—temples, scriptures and *satgurus*—are our pillars of faith. The *Vedas* implore, "O learned people, may we with our ears listen to what is beneficial, may we see with our eyes what is beneficial. May we, engaged in your praises, enjoy with firm limbs and sound bodies, a full term of life dedicated to God." Aum Namaḥ Śivāya.

What Is the Symbolism of Śiva's Dance?

ŚLOKA 15

The symbolism of Śiva Naṭarāja is religion, art and science merged as one. In God's endless dance of creation, preservation, destruction and paired graces is hidden a deep understanding of our universe. Aum Namaḥ Śivāya.

BHĀSHYA

Naṭarāja, the King of Dance, has four arms. The upper right hand holds the drum from which creation issues forth. The lower right hand is raised in blessing, betokening preservation. The upper left hand holds a flame, which is destruction, the dissolution of form. The right leg, representing obscuring grace, stands upon Apasmārapurusha, a soul temporarily earth-bound by its own sloth, confusion and forgetfulness. The uplifted left leg is revealing grace, which releases the mature soul from bondage. The lower left hand gestures toward that holy foot in assurance that Śiva's grace is the refuge for everyone, the way to liberation. The circle of fire represents the cosmos and especially consciousness. The all-devouring form looming above is Mahākāla, "Great Time." The cobra around Naṭarāja's waist is *kuṇḍalinī śakti,* the soul-impelling cosmic power resident within all. Naṭarāja's dance is not just a symbol. It is taking place within each of us, at the atomic level, this very moment. The *Āgamas* proclaim, "The birth of the world, its maintenance, its destruction, the soul's obscuration and liberation are the five acts of His dance." Aum Namaḥ Śivāya.

Scriptures Speak on Śaivism

To the strong Rudra bring we these, our songs of praise, to Him the Lord of heroes, He with braided hair, that it be well with our cattle and our men, that in this village all be healthy and well fed. ***Ṛig Veda***

Instill in us a wholesome, happy mind, with goodwill and understanding. Then shall we ever delight in your friendship like cows who gladly rejoice in meadows green. This is my joyful message. ***Ṛig Veda***

He is the never-created creator of all: He knows all. He is pure consciousness, the creator of time, all-powerful, all-knowing. He is the Lord of the soul and of nature and of the three conditions of nature. From Him comes the transmigration of life and liberation, bondage in time and freedom in eternity. ***Yajur Veda***

All this universe is in the glory of God, of Śiva, the God of love. The heads and faces of men are His own, and He is in the hearts of all. ***Yajur Veda***

God is, in truth, the whole universe: what was, what is and what beyond shall ever be. He is the God of life immortal and of all life that lives by food. His hands and feet are everywhere. He has heads and mouths everywhere. He sees all, He hears all. He is in all, and He Is. ***Yajur Veda***

He is the God of forms infinite, in whose glory all things are, smaller than the smallest atom, and yet the creator of all, ever living in the mystery of His creation. In the vision of this God of love there is everlasting peace. ***Yajur Veda***

Devoid of beginning, duration and ending, by nature immaculate, powerful, omniscient, supremely perfect—thus is Śiva spoken of in Śaivite tradition. *Ajita Āgama*

Unequalled, free from pain, subtle, all-pervading, unending, unchanging, incapable of decay, sovereign—such is the essence of Śiva, Lord of the summit of all paths. *Svāyambhuva Āgama*

The path of Śiva is the proven path. It led them to Hara.
It is the royal path that renowned souls have walked. By this path divine, the devout pervade the universe. That path do seek, enter and persevere. *Tirumantiram*

They are not for outward form and attire,
nor for pomp and ceremony. Uprooting all bond and desire, abiding in the immaculate Lord, they bring to dire destruction the soul's egoity and its troublesome attachments. They, indeed, are pure Śaivas. *Tirumantiram*

If you could see the arch of his brow, the budding
smile on lips red as the kovai fruit, cool, matted hair, the milk-white ash on coral skin and the sweet golden foot raised up in dance, then even human birth on this wide earth would become a thing worth having. *Tirumurai*

Hara, Hara! Śiva, Śiva, who in Thy lover's heart
dost dwell, who art the essence of the *Vedas*! O wealth! O jewel! O beauteous king, our ruler whom the poets praise, who art commingled with the eyes that see and dost like the sunlight everything pervade! *Natchintanai*

With body as temple, with mind ever subject to Him, with truthfulness as purity, with the light of the mind as his Liṅga, with love as melted butter and milk together with the holy water, let us offer sacrifice to the Lord. *Tirumurai*

Deva-Devatā Upanishad

देवदेवता उपनिषद्

God and Gods

Śiva Maṇḍala

शिवमण्डल

Our Supreme God

Naṭarāja is Śiva as "King of Dance." Carved in stone or caste in bronze, His *ānanda tāṇḍava,* the fierce ballet of bliss, dances the cosmos into and out of existence within the fiery arch of flames denoting consciousness. Aum.

What Is the Nature of Our God Śiva?

ŚLOKA 16

God Śiva is all and in all, one without a second, the Supreme Being and only Absolute Reality. He is Pati, our Lord, immanent and transcendent. To create, preserve, destroy, conceal and reveal are His five powers. Aum.

BHĀSHYA

God Śiva is a one being, yet we understand Him in three perfections: Absolute Reality, Pure Consciousness and Primal Soul. As Absolute Reality, Śiva is unmanifest, unchanging and transcendent, the Self God, timeless, formless and spaceless. As Pure Consciousness, Śiva is the manifest primal substance, pure love and light flowing through all form, existing everywhere in time and space as infinite intelligence and power. As Primal Soul, Śiva is the five-fold manifestation: Brahmā, the creator; Vishṇu, the preserver; Rudra, the destroyer; Maheśvara, the veiling Lord, and Sadāśiva, the revealer. He is our personal Lord, source of all three worlds. Our divine father-mother protects, nurtures and guides us, veiling Truth as we evolve, revealing it when we are mature enough to receive God's bountiful grace. God Śiva is all and in all, great beyond our conception, a sacred mystery that can be known in direct communion. Yea, when Śiva is known, all is known. The *Vedas* state: "That part of Him which is characterized by *tamas* is called Rudra. That part of Him which belongs to *rajas* is Brahmā. That part of Him which belongs to *sattva* is Vishṇu." Aum Namaḥ Śivāya.

ಶಿವ ಶಿವ

What Is God Śiva's Unmanifest Reality?

ŚLOKA 17

Paraśiva is God Śiva's Unmanifest Reality or Absolute Being, distinguished from His other two perfections, which are manifest and of the nature of form. Paraśiva is the fullness of everything, the absence of nothing. Aum.

BHĀSHYA

Paraśiva, the Self God, must be realized to be known, does not exist, yet seems to exist; yet existence itself and all states of mind, being and experiential patterns could not exist but for this ultimate reality of God. Such is the great mystery that *yogīs, ṛishis,* saints and sages have realized through the ages. To discover Paraśiva, the *yogī* penetrates deep into contemplation. As thoughts arise in his mind, mental concepts of the world or of the God he seeks, he silently repeats, "*Neti, neti*—it is not this; it is not that." His quieted consciousness expands into Satchidānanda. He is everywhere, permeating all form in this blissful state. He remembers his goal, which lies beyond bliss, and holds firmly to "*Neti, neti*—this is not that for which I seek." Through *prāṇāyāma,* through *mantra,* through *tantra,* wielding an indomitable will, the last forces of form, time and space subside, as the *yogī,* deep in *nirvikalpa samādhi,* merges into Paraśiva. The *Vedas* explain, "Self-resplendent, formless, unoriginated and pure, that all-pervading being is both within and without. He transcends even the transcendent, unmanifest, causal state of the universe." Aum Namaḥ Śivāya.

What Is God Śiva's Pure Consciousness?

ŚLOKA 18

Parāśakti is pure consciousness, the substratum or primal substance flowing through all form. It is Śiva's inscrutable presence, the ultimate ground and being of all that exists, without which nothing could endure. Aum.

BHĀSHYA

Parāśakti, "Supreme Energy," is called by many names: silence, love, being, power and all-knowingness. It is Satchidānanda—existence-consciousness-bliss—that pristine force of being which is undifferentiated, totally aware of itself, without an object of its awareness. It radiates as divine light, energy and knowing. Out of Paraśiva ever comes Parāśakti, the first manifestation of mind, superconsciousness or infinite knowing. God Śiva knows in infinite, all-abiding, loving superconsciousness. Śiva knows from deep within all of His creations to their surface. His Being is within every animate and inanimate form. Should God Śiva remove His all-pervasive Parāśakti from any one or all of the three worlds, they would crumble, disintegrate and fade away. Śiva's Śakti is the sustaining power and presence throughout the universe. This unbounded force has neither beginning nor end. Verily, it is the Divine Mind of Lord Śiva. The *Vedas* say, "He is God, hidden in all beings, their inmost soul who is in all. He watches the works of creation, lives in all things, watches all things. He is pure consciousness, beyond the three conditions of nature." Aum Namaḥ Śivāya.

What Is the Nature of the Primal Soul?

ŚLOKA 19

Parameśvara is the uncreated, ever-existent Primal Soul, Śiva-Śakti, creator and supreme ruler of Mahādevas and beings of all three worlds. Abiding in His creation, our personal Lord rules from within, not from above. Aum.

BHĀSHYA

Parameśvara, "Supreme Lord," Mother of the universe, is the eternal, sovereign one, worshiped by all the Gods and sentient beings. So loved is Śiva-Śakti that all have an intimate relationship. So vast is His vastness, so overpowering is He that men cringe to transgress His will. So talked of is He that His name is on the lips of everyone—for He is the primal sound. Being the first and perfect form, God Śiva in this third perfection of His being—the Primal Soul, the manifest and personal Lord—naturally creates souls in His image and likeness. To love God is to know God. To know God is to feel His love for you. Such a compassionate God—a being, whose resplendent body may be seen in mystic vision—cares for the minutiae such as we and a universe such as ours. Many are the mystics who have seen the brilliant milk-white form of Śiva's glowing body with its red-locked hair, graceful arms and legs, large hands, perfect face, loving eyes and musing smile. The *Āgamas* say, "Parameśvara is the cause of the five manifest aspects: emanation, *sṛishṭi;* preservation, *sthiti;* dissolution, *saṁhāra;* concealment, *tirobhāva;* and revelation, *anugraha.*" Aum Namaḥ Śivāya.

What Are God Śiva's Traditional Forms?

ŚLOKA 20

Our adoration of the one great God Śiva is directed toward diverse images and icons. Primary among them are Śivaliṅga, Naṭarāja, Ardhanārīśvara, Dakshiṇāmūrti, Hari-Hara, Bhairava and the *triśūla.* Aum Namaḥ Śivāya.

BHĀSHYA

Every form is a form of Śiva. Tradition has given us several of special sacredness. The Śivaliṅga was the first image of Divinity. After it all other icons evolved from mystic visions. We contemplate God Śiva as Paraśiva when we worship the Śivaliṅga. Its simple elliptical shape speaks silently of God's unspeakable Absolute Being. We exalt Śiva as Parāśakti or Satchidānanda, God's living omnipresence, when we worship any form of His never-separate Śakti, especially Ardhanārīśvara, whose right half is masculine and left half is feminine, and in whom all opposites are reconciled. We adore Him as Parameśvara, the Primal Soul, when we worship Naṭarāja, the Divine Dancer who animates the universe. Thus we worship Śiva's three perfections in three forms, yet knowing that He is a one Being, fully present in each of them. He is also Dakshiṇāmūrti, the silent teacher; Hari-Hara—half-Śiva, half-Vishṇu—and Bhairava, the fierce wielder of *triśūla,* the trident of love, wisdom and action. The *Tirumantiram* declares, "Everywhere is the Holy Form. Everywhere is Śiva-Śakti. Everywhere is Chidambaram; Everywhere is Divine Dance." Aum Namaḥ Śivāya.

Scriptures Speak on Śiva

There the eye goes not, nor words, nor mind. We know not. We cannot understand how He can be explained. He is above the known, and He is above the unknown. Thus have we heard from the ancient sages who explained this truth to us. *Sāma Veda*

This *ātman* is the Lord of all beings, the King of all beings. Just as the spokes are fixed in the hub and the rim of a chariot wheel, in the same way all these beings, all the Gods, all the worlds, all life breaths, all these selves, are fixed in the *ātman*. *Yajur Veda*

Fire is His head, the sun and moon His eyes, space His ears, the *Vedas* His speech, the wind His breath, the universe His heart. From His feet the earth has originated. Verily, He is the inner Self of all beings. *Atharva Veda*

He, the Self, is not this, not this. He is ungraspable, for He is not grasped. He is indestructible, for He cannot be destroyed, He is unattached, for He does not cling to anything. He is unbound, He does not suffer, nor is He injured. *Yajur Veda*

To Rudra, Lord of sacrifice, of hymns and balmy medicines, we pray for joy and health and strength. He shines in splendor like the sun, refulgent as bright gold is He, the good, the best among the Gods. *Ṛig Veda*

Now, that golden Person who is seen within the sun has a golden beard and golden hair. He is exceedingly brilliant all, even to the fingernail tips. His eyes are even as a Kapyasa lotus flower. His name is high. He is raised high above all evils. Verily, he who knows this rises high above all evils. *Sāma Veda*

The bodily form of the Almighty, being constituted of powers, is not comparable to ours. Most conspicuous is the absence of *āṇava.* His bodily form, having a head, etc., is composed of five *mantras,* corresponding each to the five activities—Īśa, Tat Purusha, Aghora, Vāma and Aja. ***Mṛigendra Āgama***

As movement within wind, as sugar within sugarcane, as *ghee* within milk, as juice within fruit, as fragrance within flower, thus does the Lord pervade all. ***Tirumantiram***

Himself creates. Himself preserves. Himself destroys. Himself obscures. Himself, all these He does and then grants *mukti*—Himself the all-pervading Lord. ***Tirumantiram***

An earring of bright, new gold glows on one ear; a coiled conch shell sways on the other. On one side He chants the melodies of the ritual *Veda;* on the other He gently smiles. Matted hair adorned with sweet *konrai* blossoms on one half of His head, and a woman's curls on the other, He comes. The one is the nature of His form, the other, of Hers; and both are the very essence of His beauty. ***Tirumurai***

Bearing Gaṅgā on spreading, matted locks, the forehead eye sparkling, the breath spirating as tempestuous wind, the immaculate form shining radiant as the clear sky, the holy feet stretching to the ends of earth, the blemishless heart serving as pedestal, the *Vedas* chanting aloud of themselves, the right hand that grants refuge and the left hand that grants favors both appropriately gesturing, the *nāda* sound of drum filling the air all around—thus Śiva dances. ***Tayumanavar***

Love of Śiva's feet eradicates bad *karma.* Love of Śiva's feet grants you clarity of mind. Love of Śiva's feet imbues the heart with gladness. Love of Śiva's feet is consciousness itself. ***Natchintanai***

Gaṇeśa-Kārttikeya Maṇḍala

गणेशकार्त्तिकेयमण्डल

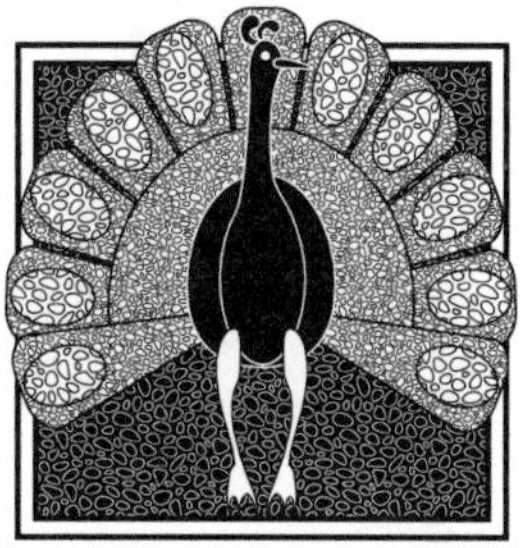

Lords of Dharma

Mayūra, "peacock," is Lord Murugan's mount, swift and beautiful like Kārttikeya Himself. The proud display of the dancing peacock symbolizes religion in full, unfolded glory. His shrill cry warns of approaching harm. Aum.

Do Other Gods Exist Apart from Śiva?

ŚLOKA 21

Supreme God Śiva has created all the Gods and given them distinct existence and powers, and yet He pervades them wholly. They are separate but inseparable. At the deepest level, nothing exists apart from Him. Aum.

BHĀSHYA

God Śiva is the Supreme Being, the Lord of lords. He alone prevails everywhere. Not an atom moves except by His will. Gaṇeśa, Kārttikeya, Indra, Agni and all the 330 million Gods of Hinduism are beings just as we are, created by Lord Śiva and destined to enjoy union with Him. The Gods are souls of high evolution. They are very old and mature souls, mighty beings who live in the Śivaloka. Though neither male nor female, they may be popularly depicted as Gods and Goddesses. The *devas* are benevolent beings of light abiding in the higher Antarloka. They help guide evolution from their world between births. The *asuras* are demonic beings of darkness, immature souls who temporarily inhabit Naraka, the lower Antarloka. *Devas* and *asuras* are usually subject to rebirth. We worship Śiva and the Gods. We neither worship the *devas* nor invoke the *asuras.* Kārttikeya, Gaṇeśa and all the Gods, *devas* and *asuras* worship Śiva. The *Vedas* explain, "From Him, also, are born the Gods, in manifold ways, the celestials, men, cattle, birds, the in-breath and the out-breath, rice and barley, austerity, faith, truth, chastity and the law." Aum Namaḥ Śivāya.

What Is the Nature of Lord Gaṇeśa?

ŚLOKA 22

Lord Gaṇeśa is the elephant-faced Patron of Art and Science, the Lord of Obstacles and Guardian of Dharma. His will prevails as the force of righteousness, the embodiment of Śiva's *karmic* law in all three worlds. Aum.

BHĀSHYA

Lord Śiva, the Almighty Power, created heaven and earth and the God Lord Gaṇeśa to oversee the intricate *karmas* and *dharmas* within the heavens and all the earths. Lord Gaṇeśa was created as a governor and interplanetary, intergalactic Lord. His knowledge is infinite, His judgment is just. It is none other than Lord Gaṇeśa and His mighty band of *gaṇas* who gently help souls out of the Naraka abyss and adjust them into higher consciousness after due penance has been paid, guiding them on the right path toward *dharmic* destiny. He is intricate of mind, loving pomp, delighting in all things sweet and enjoying adulation. Lord Śiva proclaimed that this son be worshiped first, even before Himself. Verily, He is the Lord of Karma. All Mahādevas, minor Gods, *devas* and sentient beings must worship Gaṇeśa before any responsible act could hope to be successful. Those who do not are subject to their own barriers. Yea, worship of Him sets the pattern of one's destiny. The *Tirumantiram* says, "Five-armed is He, elephant-faced with tusks protruding, crescent-shaped, son of Śiva, wisdom's flower, in heart enshrined, His feet I praise." Aum Namaḥ Śivāya.

What Is Lord Gaṇeśa's Special Duty?

ŚLOKA 23

As Lord of Obstacles, Gaṇeśa wields the noose and the goad, icons of His benevolent power of preventing or permitting events to happen in our life. Thus, we invoke His grace and wisdom before any worship or task. Aum.

BHĀSHYA

Lord Gaṇeśa, the God of time and memory, strategically seated on the *mūlādhāra chakra,* poised between the higher and lower *chakras,* stabilizes all sentient beings. He holds the architect's plans of the divine masterpiece of universal past and future. Only good comes from Lord Gaṇeśa, who by taking the form of an elephant distinguishes Himself from other Gods. The *charyā pāda* begins with His worship. He staves off misfortune for those who perform penance in His name. He guides our *karma* from within us through the timing of events. Before any important undertaking, we supplicate Him to clear obstacles from the path, if it be His will. This Lord of Obstacles prevents us from hurting ourselves through living under an incomplete concept or making a request unneeded or beginning an endeavor not well thought out. Before we petition Him, He expects us to use all of our faculties to arrive at the decision He would have made. The *Āgamas* declare, "These Lords who, it is said, on the pure path, attend to the various duties deriving from a higher realm of *māyā* are at the prow of the effects of the higher realm of *māyā.*" Aum Namaḥ Śivāya.

What Is the Nature of Lord Kārttikeya?

ŚLOKA 24

Lord Kārttikeya, Murugan, first *guru* and Pleiadean master of *kuṇḍalinī yoga*, was born of God Śiva's mind. His dynamic power awakens spiritual cognition to propel souls onward in their evolution to Śiva's feet. Aum.

BHĀSHYA

Lord Kārttikeya flies through the mind's vast substance from planet to planet. He could well be called the Emancipator, ever available to the call of those in distress. Lord Kārttikeya, God of will, direct cognition and the purest, child-like divine love, propels us onward on the righteous way through religion, His Father's law. Majestically seated on the *maṇipūra chakra*, this scarlet-hued God blesses mankind and strengthens our will when we lift to the inner sky through *sādhana* and *yoga*. The *yoga pāda* begins with the worship of Him. The *yogī*, locked in meditation, venerates Kārttikeya, Skanda, as his mind becomes as calm as Śaravaṇa, the lake of Divine Essence. The *kuṇḍalinī* force within everyone is held and controlled by this powerful God, first among renunciates, dear to all *sannyāsins*. Revered as Murugan in the South, He is commander in chief of the great devonic army, a fine, dynamic soldier of the within, a fearless defender of righteousness. He is Divinity emulated in form. The *Vedas* say, "To such a one who has his stains wiped away, the venerable Sanatkumāra shows the further shore of darkness. Him they call Skanda." Aum Namaḥ Śivāya.

What Does Lord Kārttikeya's Vel Signify?

ŚLOKA 25

The lancelike *vel* wielded by Lord Kārttikeya, or Skanda, embodies discrimination and spiritual insight. Its blade is wide, long and keen, just as our knowledge must be broad, deep and penetrating. Aum Namaḥ Śivāya.

BHĀSHYA

The *śakti* power of the *vel,* the eminent, intricate power of righteousness over wrongdoing, conquers confusion within the realms below. The holy *vel,* that when thrown always hits its mark and of itself returns to Kārttikeya's mighty hand, rewards us when righteousness prevails and becomes the *kuṇḍalinī* serpent's unleashed power thwarting our every effort with punishing remorse when we transgress *dharma's* law. Thus, the holy *vel* is our release from ignorance into knowledge, our release from vanity into modesty, our release from sinfulness into purity through *tapas.* When we perform penance and beseech His blessing, this merciful God hurls His *vel* into the astral plane, piercing discordant sounds, colors and shapes, removing the mind's darkness. He is the King of kings, the power in their scepters. Standing behind the temporal majesty, He advises and authorizes. His *vel* empowering the ruler, justice prevails, wisdom enriches the minds of citizens, rain is abundant, crops flourish and plenty fills the larders. The *Tirumurai* says, "In the gloom of fear, His six-fold face gleams. In perils unbounded, His *vel* betokens, 'Fear not.'" Aum Namaḥ Śivāya.

Scriptures Speak on Lords of Dharma

As the God evoked faith from the mighty *asuras*, so may my prayer for the generous worshiper be accepted! *Ṛig Veda*

He who is source and origin of the Gods, the Lord of all, Rudra, the Mighty Sage who produced in ancient days the Golden Germ—may He endow us with purity of mind! *Yajur Veda*

Great are the Gods who were born from Nonbeing. Yet men aver this Nonbeing to be the single limb of the Support, the great Beyond. *Atharva Veda*

In whose one limb all the Gods, three and thirty in number, are affixed—tell me of that Support—who may He be? *Atharva Veda*

"Agni, Vāyu, Āditya who is the time (Prajāpati), *prāṇa*, food, Brahmā, Rudra, Vishṇu. From among these, some, meditating, adore one, others another. Please tell us: who among them is adored most, who is He?" Then he said to them: "These, indeed, are the foremost appeared forms of the highest, immortal, incorporeal Brahman." *Yajur Veda*

In Him exists neither action nor organ of action; no one is found His equal or superior to Him. His supreme power is revealed in manifold forms; inherent to His nature is the working of His strength and wisdom. *Yajur Veda*

I'll not sell you, not for a thousand or ten thousand pieces! O Indra, you are more to me than a father. I count a brother naught compared to you. You and a mother, O Bountiful, vie with each other in generous giving and in bestowal of joy. *Ṛig Veda*

In the heart of those who recount His name, He reveals His gracious feet. Thus He appears to those who chant the hallowed name *Murugan.* He stands immanent in all. *Tirumurai*

The moon, sun and fire are in unison radiating their resplendent effulgence. Radiating the luminous sparks is Murugan, who lights up the world by His peerless light. *Kathirgama Purāṇa*

Let us know that Supreme Being and meditate upon
Him, the Supreme General of the great *deva* army. May
He enlighten us and lead us to be one with Him,
Lord Skanda. *Shaṇmukha Gāyatrī*

If you worship the elephant-faced Vināyaka, your life will expand bountifully. If you worship the white-tusked Vināyaka, your desires and doubts will flee. Therefore, worship Him with love-offerings of jack, hoppers, plantain and mango fruits and thus mitigate the burden of deeds. *Saint Auvaiyar*

He has one tusk and four arms. Two of His hands hold a noose and a hook, while the other hands show the gestures of removing fear and granting boons. A mouse is seen on His flag. Red, obese, He has ears like winnowing baskets. He is dressed in red, with limbs painted with red sandalpaste. *Gaṇapati Upanishad*

Murugan, Kumāran, Guhan—to utter and melt and have divine experience—when shall Thou grant this, O *guru* supreme, worshiped by the *devas* devout and mortals alike, O abode of virtues eight! *Kandar Anubhuti*

The God with the elephantine visage I shall never forget—
Śaṅkara's son, with massive belly and the *thodu* in His ear,
the Lord who gave His grace to Indra, of whom *mantra*
is His very form. *Natchintanai*

Amṛitātma Upanishad

अमृतात्म उपनिषद्

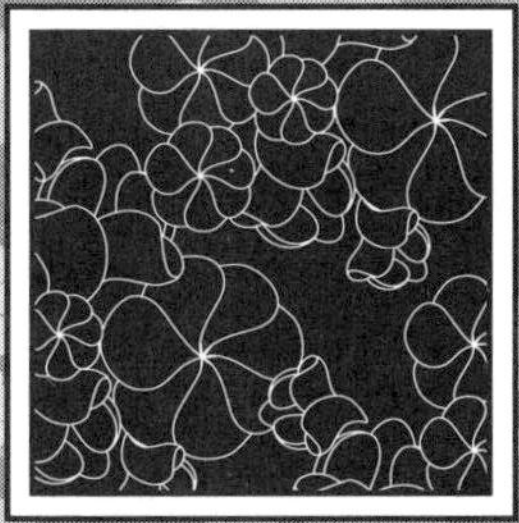

Our Immortal Soul

Ātmasvarūpa Maṇḍala

आत्मस्वरूपमण्डल

The Nature of the Soul

Nandi is Lord Śiva's mount, or *vāhana.* This huge white bull with a black tail, whose name means "joyful," disciplined animality kneeling at Śiva's feet, is the ideal devotee, the pure joy and strength of Śaiva Dharma. Aum.

What Is Our Individual Soul Nature?

ŚLOKA 26

Our individual soul is the immortal and spiritual body of light that animates life and reincarnates again and again until all necessary *karmas* are created and resolved and its essential unity with God is fully realized. Aum.

BHĀSHYA

Our soul is God Śiva's emanational creation, the source of all our higher functions, including knowledge, will and love. Our soul is neither male nor female. It is that which never dies, even when its four outer sheaths—physical, *prāṇic*, instinctive and mental—change form and perish as they naturally do. The physical body is the *annamaya kośa*. The *prāṇic* sheath of vitality is the *prāṇamaya kośa*. The instinctive-intellectual sheath is the *manomaya kośa*. The mental, or cognitive, sheath is the *vijñānamaya kośa*. The inmost soul body is the blissful, ever-giving-wisdom *ānandamaya kośa*. Parāśakti is the soul's superconscious mind—God Śiva's mind. Paraśiva is the soul's inmost core. We are not the physical body, mind or emotions. We are the immortal soul, *ātman*. The sum of our true existence is *ānandamaya kośa* and its essence, Parāśakti and Paraśiva. The *Vedas* expostulate, "The soul is born and unfolds in a body, with dreams and desires and the food of life. And then it is reborn in new bodies, in accordance with its former works. The quality of the soul determines its future body; earthly or airy, heavy or light." Aum Namaḥ Śivāya.

How Is Our Soul Different from Śiva?

ŚLOKA 27

Our soul body was created in the image and likeness of the Primal Soul, God Śiva, but it differs from the Primal Soul in that it is immature. While Śiva is unevolutionary perfection, we are in the process of evolving. Aum.

BHĀSHYA

To understand the mysteries of the soul, we distinguish between the soul body and its essence. As a soul body, we are individual and unique, different from all others, a self-effulgent being of light which evolves and matures through an evolutionary process. This soul body is of the nature of God Śiva, but is different from Śiva in that it is less resplendent than the Primal Soul and still evolving, while God is unevolutionary perfection. We may liken the soul body to an acorn, which contains the mighty oak tree but is a small seed yet to develop. The soul body matures through experience, evolving through many lives into the splendor of God Śiva, ultimately realizing Śiva totally in *nirvikalpa samādhi*. Even after Self Realization is attained, the soul body continues to evolve in this and other worlds until it merges with the Primal Soul, as a drop of water merges with its source, the ocean. Yea, this is the destiny of all souls without exception. The *Vedas* say, "As oil in sesame seeds, as butter in cream, as water in river beds, as fire in friction sticks, so is the *ātman* grasped in one's own self when one searches for Him with truthfulness and austerity." Aum Namaḥ Śivāya.

How Is Our Soul Identical with Śiva?

ŚLOKA 28

The essence of our soul, which was never created, is immanent love and transcendent reality and is identical and eternally one with God Śiva. At the core of our being, we already are That—perfect at this very moment. Aum.

BHĀSHYA

At the core of the subtle soul body is Parāśakti, or Satchidānanda, immanent love; and at the core of that is Paraśiva, transcendent reality. At this depth of our being there exists no separate identity or difference—all are One. Thus, deep within our soul we are identical with God now and forever. These two divine perfections are not aspects of the evolving soul, but the nucleus of the soul which does not change or evolve. From an absolute perspective, our soul is already in nondual union with God, but to be realized to be known. We are That. We do not become That. Deep within this physical body, with its turbulent emotions and getting-educated mind, is pure perfection identical to Śiva's own perfections of Parāśakti and Paraśiva. In this sacred mystery we find the paradoxes of oneness and twoness, of being and becoming, of created and uncreated existence subtly delineated. Yea, in the depth of our being, we are as He is. The *Vedas* explain, "The one controller, the inner Self of all things, who makes His one form manifold, to the wise who perceive Him as abiding in the soul, to them is eternal bliss—to no others." Aum Namaḥ Śivāya.

Why Are We Not Omniscient Like Śiva?

ŚLOKA 29

The three bonds of *āṇava, karma* and *māyā* veil our sight. This is Śiva's purposeful limiting of awareness which allows us to evolve. In the superconscious depths of our soul, we share God Śiva's all-knowingness. Aum.

BHĀSHYA

Just as children are kept from knowing all about adult life until they have matured into understanding, so too is the soul's knowledge limited. We learn what we need to know, and we understand what we have experienced. Only this narrowing of our awareness, coupled with a sense of individualized ego, allows us to look upon the world and our part in it from a practical, human point of view. *Pāśa* is the soul's triple bondage: *māyā, karma* and *āṇava.* Without the world of *māyā,* the soul could not evolve through experience. *Karma* is the law of cause and effect, action and reaction governing *māyā. Āṇava* is the individuating veil of duality, source of ignorance and finitude. *Māyā* is the classroom, *karma* the teacher, and *āṇava* the student's ignorance. The three bonds, or *malas,* are given by Lord Śiva to help and protect us as we unfold. Yet, God Śiva's all-knowingness may be experienced for brief periods by the meditator who turns within to his own essence. The *Tirumantiram* explains, "When the soul attains Self-knowledge, then it becomes one with Śiva. The *malas* perish, birth's cycle ends and the lustrous light of wisdom dawns." Aum Namaḥ Śivāya.

How Do Hindus Understand Moksha?

ŚLOKA 30

The destiny of all souls is *moksha,* liberation from rebirth on the physical plane. Our soul then continues evolving in the Antarloka and Śivaloka, and finally merges with Śiva like water returning to the sea. Aum Namaḥ Śivāya.

BHĀSHYA

Moksha comes when earthly *karma* has been resolved, *dharma* well performed and God fully realized. Each soul must have performed well through many lives the *varṇa dharmas,* or four castes, and lived through life's varied experiences, in order to not be pulled back to physical birth by a deed left undone. All souls are destined to achieve *moksha,* but not necessarily in this life. Hindus know this and do not delude themselves that this life is the last. While seeking and attaining profound realizations, they know there is much to be done in fulfilling life's other goals, *purushārthas—dharma,* righteousness; *artha,* wealth; and *kāma,* pleasure. Old souls renounce worldly ambitions and take up *sannyāsa* in quest of Paraśiva, even at a young age. Toward life's end, all Hindus strive for Self Realization, the gateway to liberation. After *moksha,* subtle *karmas* are made in inner realms and swiftly resolved, like writing on water. At the end of each soul's evolution comes *viśvagrāsa,* total absorption in Śiva. The *Vedas* say, "If here one is able to realize Him before the death of the body, he will be liberated from the bondage of the world." Aum Namaḥ Śivāya.

Scriptures Speak on the Soul

The *ātman* pervades all like butter hidden in milk. He is the source of Self-knowledge and ascetic fervor. This is the Brahman teaching, the highest goal! This is the Brahman teaching, the highest goal! ***Yajur Veda***

The inspired Self is not born nor does He die; He springs from nothing and becomes nothing. Unborn, permanent, unchanging, primordial, He is not destroyed when the body is destroyed. ***Yajur Veda***

Now, the teaching concerning the *ātman:* the *ātman* is below, it is above, it is behind, it is before, it is in the South, it is in the North. The *ātman* indeed is all that is. He who sees, reflects and knows this—he has joy in the *ātman.* ***Sāma Veda***

Verily, he is pure, steadfast and unswerving, stainless, unagitated, desireless, fixed like a spectator and self-abiding. As an enjoyer of righteousness, he covers himself with a veil made of qualities; [yet] he remains fixed—yea, he remains fixed! ***Yajur Veda***

He who with the truth of the *ātman,* unified, perceives the truth of Brahman as with a lamp, who knows God, the unborn, the stable, free from all forms of being, is released from all fetters. ***Yajur Veda***

A part of Infinite Consciousness becomes our own finite consciousness, with powers of discrimination and definition and with false conceptions. He is, in truth, Prajāpati and Viśva, the Source of Creation and the Universal in us all. This Spirit is consciousness and gives consciousness to the body. He is the driver of the chariot. ***Yajur Veda***

He who dwells in the light, yet is other than the light, whom the light does not know, whose body is the light, who controls the light from within—He is the *ātman* within you. ***Yajur Veda***

Pure consciousness, taking form as knowledge and action, is present in the soul everywhere and always, for the soul is universal in its unfettered state. ***Mṛigendra Āgama***

The three impurities are *āṇava, māyā* and the one caused by actions. ***Suprabheda Āgama***

When the state is attained where one becomes Śiva, the *malas*—the bonds diverse, mental states and experiences that arose for the individualized soul—will all fade like the beams of the moon in the presence of the rising sun. ***Tirumantiram***

When *jīva* attains the state of neutrality to deeds good and evil, then does divine grace in *guru* form descend, remove attributes all and implant *jñāna* that is unto a heavenly cool shade. The *jīva* is without egoity, and the impurities three are finished. He is Śiva who all this does. ***Tirumantiram***

In the primal play of the Lord were *jīvas* created. Enveloped in mighty *malas* were they. Discarding them, they realized themselves and besought the feet of their hoary Lord. Thus they became Śiva, with birth no more to be. ***Tirumantiram***

A goldsmith fashions several ornaments out of gold. So God, the great goldsmith, makes many ornaments—different souls—out of the one Universal Spirit. ***Natchintanai***

The *ātman* is eternal. This is the conclusion at which great souls have arrived from their experience. ***Natchintanai***

Saṁsāra Maṇḍala

संसारमण्डल

Karma and Rebirth

Gaṇeśa is the Lord of Obstacles and Ruler of Dharma. Seated upon His throne, He guides our *karmas* through creating and removing obstacles from our path. We seek His permission and blessings in every undertaking. Aum.

How Do Hindus Understand Karma?

ŚLOKA 31

Karma literally means "deed or act" and more broadly names the universal principle of cause and effect, action and reaction which governs all life. *Karma* is a natural law of the mind, just as gravity is a law of matter. Aum.

BHĀSHYA

Karma is not fate, for man acts with free will creating his own destiny. The *Vedas* tell us, if we sow goodness, we will reap goodness; if we sow evil, we will reap evil. *Karma* refers to the totality of our actions and their concomitant reactions in this and previous lives, all of which determines our future. It is the interplay between our experience and how we respond to it that makes *karma* devastating or helpfully invigorating. The conquest of *karma* lies in intelligent action and dispassionate reaction. Not all *karmas* rebound immediately. Some accumulate and return unexpectedly in this or other births. The several kinds of *karma* are: personal, family, community, national, global and universal. Ancient *ṛishis* perceived personal *karma's* three-fold edict. The first is *sañchita,* the sum total of past *karmas* yet to be resolved. The second is *prārabdha,* that portion of *sañchita* to be experienced in this life. *kriyamāna,* the third type, is *karma* we are currently creating. The *Vedas* propound, "Here they say that a person consists of desires. And as is his desire, so is his will. As is his will, so is his deed. Whatever deed he does, that he will reap." Aum Namaḥ Śivāya.

Is There Good Karma and Bad Karma?

ŚLOKA 32

In the highest sense, there is no good or bad *karma.* All experience offers opportunities for spiritual growth. Selfless acts yield positive, uplifting conditions. Selfish acts yield conditions of negativity and confusion. Aum.

BHĀSHYA

Karma itself is neither good nor bad but a neutral principle that governs energy and motion of thought, word and deed. All experience helps us grow. Good, loving actions bring to us lovingness through others. Mean, selfish acts bring back to us pain and suffering. Kindness produces sweet fruits, called *puṇya.* Unkindness yields spoiled fruits, called *pāpa.* As we mature, life after life, we go through much pain and joy. Actions that are in tune with *dharma* help us along the path, while *adharmic* actions impede our progress. The divine law is: whatever *karma* we are experiencing in our life is just what we need at the moment, and nothing can happen but that we have the strength to meet it. Even harsh *karma,* when faced in wisdom, can be the greatest catalyst for spiritual unfoldment. Performing daily *sādhana,* keeping good company, pilgrimaging to holy places, seeing to others' needs—these evoke the higher energies, direct the mind to useful thoughts and avoid the creation of troublesome new *karmas.* The *Vedas* explain, "According as one acts, so does he become. One becomes virtuous by virtuous action, bad by bad action." Aum Namaḥ Śivāya.

What Is the Process of Reincarnation?

ŚLOKA 33

Reincarnation, *punarjanma,* is the natural process of birth, death and rebirth. At death we drop off the physical body and continue evolving in the inner worlds in our subtle bodies, until we again enter into birth. Aum.

BHĀSHYA

Through the ages, reincarnation has been the great consoling element within Hinduism, eliminating the fear of death, explaining why one person is born a genius and another an idiot. We are not the body in which we live but the immortal soul which inhabits many bodies in its evolutionary journey through *saṁsāra.* After death, we continue to exist in unseen worlds, enjoying or suffering the harvest of earthly deeds until it comes time for yet another physical birth. Because certain *karmas* can be resolved only in the physical world, we must enter another physical body to continue our evolution. After soaring into the causal plane, we enter a new womb. Subsequently the old *manomaya kośa* is slowly sloughed off and a new one created. The actions set in motion in previous lives form the tendencies and conditions of the next. Reincarnation ceases when *karma* is resolved, God is realized and *moksha* attained. The *Vedas* say, "After death, the soul goes to the next world bearing in mind the subtle impressions of its deeds, and after reaping their harvest returns again to this world of action. Thus, he who has desires continues subject to rebirth." Aum Namaḥ Śivāya.

How Should We View Death and Dying?

ŚLOKA 34

Our soul never dies; only the physical body dies. We neither fear death nor look forward to it, but revere it as a most exalted experience. Life, death and the afterlife are all part of our path to perfect oneness with God. Aum.

BHĀSHYA

For Hindus, death is nobly referred to as *mahāprasthāna,* "the great journey." When the lessons of this life have been learned and *karmas* reach a point of intensity, the soul leaves the physical body, which then returns its elements to the earth. The awareness, will, memory and intelligence which we think of as ourselves continue to exist in the soul body. Death is a most natural experience, not to be feared. It is a quick transition from the physical world to the astral plane, like walking through a door, leaving one room and entering another. Knowing this, we approach death as a *sādhana,* as a spiritual opportunity, bringing a level of detachment which is difficult to achieve in the tumult of life and an urgency to strive more than ever in our search for the Divine Self. To be near a realized soul at the time he or she gives up the body yields blessings surpassing those of a thousand and eight visits to holy persons at other times. The *Vedas* explain, "As a caterpillar coming to the end of a blade of grass draws itself together in taking the next step, so does the soul in the process of transition strike down this body and dispel its ignorance." Aum Namaḥ Śivāya.

How Does One Best Prepare for Death?

ŚLOKA 35

Blessed with the knowledge of impending transition, we settle affairs and take refuge in *japa,* worship, scripture and *yoga*—seeking the highest realizations as we consciously, joyously release the world. Aum Namaḥ Śivāya.

BHĀSHYA

Before dying, Hindus diligently fulfill obligations, make amends and resolve differences by forgiving themselves and others, lest unresolved *karmas* bear fruit in future births. That done, we turn to God through meditation, surrender and scriptural study. As a conscious death is our ideal, we avoid drugs, artificial life-extension and suicide. Suicide only postpones and intensifies the *karma* one seeks escape from, requiring several lives to return to the evolutionary point that existed at the moment of suicide. In cases of terminal illness, under strict community regulation, tradition does allow *prāyopaveśa,* self-willed religious death by fasting. When nearing transition, if hospitalized, we return home to be among loved ones. In the final hours of life, we seek the Self God within and focus on our *mantra* as kindred keep prayerful vigil. At death, we leave the body through the crown *chakra,* entering the clear white light and beyond in quest of *videhamukti.* The *Vedas* affirm, "When a person comes to weakness, be it through old age or disease, he frees himself from these limbs just as a mango, a fig or a berry releases itself from its stalk." Aum Namaḥ Śivāya.

Scriptures Speak on Saṁsāra

Desireless, wise, immortal, self-existent, full of bliss, lacking in nothing, is the one who knows the wise, unaging, youthful *ātman*. He fears not death! ***Atharva Veda***

He, however, who has not understanding, who is unmindful and ever impure, reaches not the goal, but goes on to reincarnation. He, however, who has understanding, who is mindful and ever pure, reaches the goal from which he is born no more. ***Yajur Veda***

Go, my breath, to the immortal Breath. Then may this body end in ashes! Remember, O my mind, the deeds of the past, remember the deeds, remember the deeds! ***Yajur Veda***

O Māghavan, verily, this body is mortal. It has been appropriated by death. But it is the standing ground of that deathless, bodiless Self *(ātman)*. Verily, he who is incorporate has been appropriated by pleasure and pain. Verily, there is no freedom from pleasure and pain for one while he is incorporate. Verily, while one is bodiless, pleasure and pain do not touch him. ***Sāma Veda***

Through the ripening of the fruits of his actions he does not attain any rest, like a worm caught within a whirlpool. The desire for liberation arises in human beings at the end of many births, through the ripening of their past virtuous conduct. ***Yajur Veda***

He lives as long as he lives. Then when he dies, they carry him to the fire. His fire, in truth, becomes the fire; fuel, the fuel; smoke, the smoke; flame, the flame; coals, the coals; sparks, the sparks. In this fire the Gods offer a person. From this oblation the man arises, having the color of light. ***Yajur Veda***

Thus acting from the principle of *māyā* itself down to the lowest level, *karma*, even when it manifests as good, is an obstacle still, because it is not toward liberation that it leads. *Karma* does not dissolve without its various fruits being tasted and consumed. *Mṛigendra Āgama*

A twice-born, gone to the end of the *Veda*, knowing that life is impermanent, may abandon the body there by fasting to death according to prescription. After worshiping the Gods and honoring the *munis*, the *siddhā* may go to heaven, the eternal realm of Brahmā. *Mahābhārata*

Even as the snake sloughs off its skin, even as the bird leaves its shell, even as in its waking state the *jīva* forgets happenings of the dream state—thus does *jīva* from one body to another migrate until, with grace of Hara, it reaches where it is destined to be, and there experiences the two *karmas*, good and evil. *Tirumantiram*

I pray Thee for undying love. I pray Thee for the birthless state; but were I to be born again, for the grace of never forgetting Thee. Still more do I pray to be at Thy feet singing joyfully while Thou dancest. *Tirumurai*

All suffering recoils on the wrongdoer himself. Therefore, those who desire not to suffer refrain from causing others pain. If a man inflicts sorrow on another in the morning, sorrow will come to him unbidden in the afternoon. *Tirukural*

The Life of my life, whose nature 'tis to hold the fire in His hand, essence of Truth of purest gold, who neither comes nor goes, the Mighty One who doth all souls pervade—in this great world, for those who thus meditate on Him, all future births will end. *Natchintanai*

San Mārga Maṇḍala

सन्मार्गमण्डल

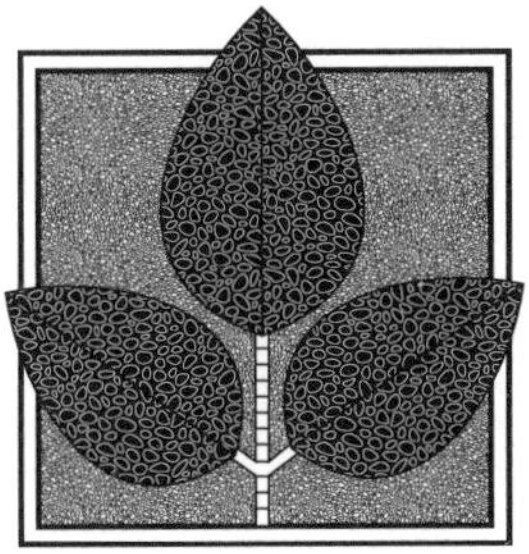

The Way to Liberation

Bilva is the *bael* tree. Its fruit, flowers and leaves are all sacred to Śiva, liberation's summit. Planting *Aegle marmelos* trees around home or temple is sanctifying, as is worshiping a Liṅga with *bilva* leaves and water. Aum.

What Are the Four Stages on the Path?

ŚLOKA 36

The path of enlightenment is divided naturally into four stages: *charyā,* virtue and selfless service; *kriyā,* worshipful *sādhanas; yoga,* meditation under a *guru's* guidance; and *jñāna,* the wisdom state of the realized soul. Aum.

BHĀSHYA

Charyā, kriyā, yoga and *jñāna* are the sequence of the soul's evolutionary process, much like the natural development of a butterfly from egg to larvae, from larvae to pupa, from pupa to caterpillar, and then the final metamorphosis from caterpillar to butterfly. These are four *pādas,* or stages, through which each human soul must pass, through many births, in order to attain its final goal. Before entering this path, the soul is immersed in the lower nature, bound in fear and lust, hurtful rage, jealousy, confusion, selfishness, consciencelessness and malice. Then it awakens into *charyā,* unselfish religious service, or *karma yoga.* Once matured in *charyā,* it enters *kriyā,* devotion or *bhakti yoga,* and finally blossoms into *kuṇḍalinī yoga. Jñāna* is the state of enlightened wisdom reached toward the path's end as a result of Self Realization. The four *pādas* are not alternative ways, but progressive, cumulative phases of a one path, San Mārga. The *Tirumantiram* affirms, "Being the Life of life is splendrous *jñāna* worship. Beholding the Light of life is great *yoga* worship. Giving life by invocation is external worship. Expressing adoration is *charyā.*" Aum Namaḥ Śivāya.

What Is the Nature of the Charyā Pāda?

ŚLOKA 37

Charyā is the performance of altruistic religious service and living according to traditional ethical conduct and culture, by which the outer nature is purified. It is the stage of overcoming basic instinctive patterns. Aum.

BHĀSHYA

Charyā, literally "conduct," is the first stage of religiousness and the foundation for the next three stages. It is also called the *dāsa mārga,* meaning "path of servitude," for here the soul relates to God as servant to master. The disciplines of *charyā* include humble service, attending the temple, performing one's duty to community and family, honoring holy men, respecting elders, atoning for misdeeds and fulfilling the ten classical restraints called *yamas.* Within a strong society, one performs *charyā* whether he wants to or not. Young or rebellious souls often resist and resent, whereas mature souls fulfill these obligations most naturally. Right behavior and self-sacrificing service are never outgrown. The keynote of *charyā,* or *karma yoga,* is *sevā,* religious service given without the least thought of reward, which has the magical effect of softening the ego and bringing forth the soul's innate devotion. The *Tirumantiram* explains, "The simple temple duties, lighting the lamps, picking flowers, lovingly polishing the floors, sweeping, singing the Lord's praise, ringing the bell and fetching ceremonial water—these constitute the *dāsa mārga.*" Aum Namaḥ Śivāya.

What Is the Nature of the Kriyā Pāda?

ŚLOKA 38

Kriyā is joyous and regular worship, both internal and external, in the home and temple. It includes *pūjā, japa,* penance, fasting and scriptural learning, by which our understanding and love of God and Gods deepen. Aum.

BHĀSHYA

Hinduism demands deep devotion through *bhakti yoga* in the *kriyā pāda,* softening the intellect and unfolding love. In *kriyā,* the second stage of religiousness, our *sādhana,* which was mostly external in *charyā,* is now also internal. *Kriyā,* literally "action or rite," is a stirring of the soul in awareness of the Divine, overcoming the obstinacy of the instinctive-intellectual mind. We now look upon the Deity image not just as carved stone, but as the living presence of the God. We perform ritual and *pūjā* not because we have to but because we want to. We are drawn to the temple to satisfy our longing. We sing joyfully. We absorb and intuit the wisdom of the *Vedas* and *Āgamas.* We perform pilgrimage and fulfill the sacraments. We practice diligently the ten classical observances called *niyamas.* Our relationship with God in *kriyā* is as a son to his parents and thus this stage is called the *satputra mārga.* The *Tirumantiram* instructs, "*Pūjā,* reading the scriptures, singing hymns, performing *japa* and unsullied austerity, truthfulness, restraint of envy, and offering of food—these and other self-purifying acts constitute the flawless *satputra mārga.*" Aum Namaḥ Śivāya.

What Is the Nature of the Yoga Pāda?

ŚLOKA 39

Yoga is internalized worship which leads to union with God. It is the regular practice of meditation, detachment and austerities under the guidance of a *satguru* through whose grace we attain the realization of Paraśiva. Aum.

BHĀSHYA

Yoga, "union," is the process of uniting with God within oneself, a stage arrived at through perfecting *charyā* and *kriyā.* As God is now like a friend to us, *yoga* is known as the *sakhā mārga.* This system of inner discovery begins with *āsana*—sitting quietly in *yogic* posture—and *prāṇāyāma,* breath control. *Pratyāhāra,* sense withdrawal, brings awareness into *dhāraṇā,* concentration, then into *dhyāna,* meditation. Over the years, under ideal conditions, the *kuṇḍalinī* fire of consciousness ascends to the higher *chakras,* burning the dross of ignorance and past *karmas. Dhyāna* finally leads to enstasy—first to *savikalpa samādhi,* "the contemplative experience of Satchidānanda, and ultimately to *nirvikalpa samādhi,* Paraśiva. Truly a living *satguru* is needed as a steady guide to traverse this path. When *yoga* is practiced by one perfected in *kriyā,* the Gods receive the *yogī* into their midst through his awakened, fiery *kuṇḍalinī.* The *Vedas* enjoin the *yogī,* "With earnest effort hold the senses in check. Controlling the breath, regulate the vital activities. As a charioteer holds back his restive horses, so does a persevering aspirant restrain his mind." Aum Namaḥ Śivāya.

What Is the Nature of the Jñāna Pāda?

ŚLOKA 40

Jñāna is divine wisdom emanating from an enlightened being, a soul in its maturity, immersed in Śivaness, the blessed realization of God, while living out earthly *karma.* *Jñāna* is the fruition of *yoga tapas.* Aum Namaḥ Śivāya.

BHĀSHYA

The instinctive mind in the young soul is firm and well-knit together. The intellectual mind in the adolescent soul is complicated, and he sees the physical world as his only reality. The subsuperconscious mind in the mystically inclined soul well perfected in *kriyā* longs for realization of Śiva's two perfections, Satchidānanda and Paraśiva. Through *yoga* he bursts into the superconscious mind, experiencing bliss, all-knowingness and perfect silence. It is when the *yogī's* intellect is shattered that he soars into Paraśiva and comes out a *jñānī.* Each time he enters that unspeakable *nirvikalpa samādhi,* he returns to consciousness more and more the knower. He is the liberated one, the *jīvanmukta,* the epitome of *kaivalya*—perfect freedom—far-seeing, filled with light, filled with love. One does not become a *jñānī* simply by reading and understanding philosophy. The state of *jñāna* lies in the realm of intuition, beyond the intellect. The *Vedas* say, "Having realized the Self, the *ṛishis,* perfected souls, satisfied with their knowledge, passion-free, tranquil—those wise beings, having attained the omnipresent on all sides—enter into the All itself." Aum Namaḥ Śivāya.

Scriptures Speak on Liberation

Like the household fire, devotees seek the glory of the Lord even from afar and enshrine it in their inner chamber for enlightenment. The glory of our Lord is full of splendor, all-illuminative and worthy to be honored in every heart. *Ṛig Veda*

For the great-souled, the surest way to liberation is the conviction that "I am Brahman." The two terms, what leads to bondage and what leads to liberation, are the sense of mineness and the absence of the sense of mineness. *Yajur Veda*

When the nets of dispositions (good and bad) are dissolved without any residue, when the accumulated deeds virtuous and vicious are completely destroyed to the very roots, the past and the future alike, owing to the removal of all impediments, bring about the direct and immediate perception (of Brahman) as of the *āmalaka* fruit on the palm of the hand, then (the knower of Brahman) becomes one liberated while in life. *Yajur Veda*

He remains aloof, but not aloof, in the body, but not in the body; his inmost Self becomes the All-Pervading. Having purified his heart and accomplished his perfect thinking, the *yogin* sees: I am the All, the Highest Bliss. *Yajur Veda*

When the *yogin* unites his breath with Aum or is united with the All in manifold ways, it is called *yoga*. This oneness of breath, mind and senses, the renunciation of all existence—this is termed *yoga*. *Yajur Veda*

When cease the five (sense) knowledges, together with the mind, and the intellect stirs not—that, they say, is the highest course. *Yajur Veda*

It should be known that effort for *yogic* realization by *yogīs* must proceed in eight steps: *yama, niyama, āsana, prāṇāyāma, pratyāhāra, dhāraṇā, dhyāna* and *samādhi.* ***Suprabheda Āgama***

He alone is learned, he alone is fortunate and successful, whose mind is no longer unstable as air, but is held firm. That is the way to liberation, that is the highest virtue, that is wisdom, that is strength and that is the merit of those who seek. ***Devīkālottara Āgama***

Never does a man attain *moksha* by his own skill; by no means other than the grace of Śiva, the dispeller of evil, is such an attainment possible. ***Paushkara Āgama***

To see him, to adore him, to meditate on him, to touch him, to sing of him, to bear his holy feet on humbled head—they that render devotion to *guru* in diverse ways thus—they indeed walk the San Mārga that to liberation leads. ***Tirumantiram***

Self-control will place a man among the Gods, but the lack of it will lead him into deepest darkness. ***Tirukural***

The One Entity—blissful, entire and all-pervading—alone exists, and nothing else; he who constantly realizes this knowledge is freed from death and the sorrow of the world-wheel. ***Śiva Saṁhitā***

Listen while I tell you the path to liberation: truth, patience, calmness and discipline of self, discrimination between the eternal and the passing, devotion to the humble servants of the Lord, rising in the early morning and bathing before daybreak, repeating in the way prescribed the flawless Letters Five, worshiping the *guru's* feet, applying holy ash, eating but when hungry, with the whole heart giving praise. ***Natchintanai***

Śivamaya Upanishad

शिवमय उपनिषद्

The World

Triloka Maṇḍala

त्रिलोकमण्डल

The Three Worlds

Padma is the lotus flower, *Nelumbo nucifera,* perfection of beauty, associated with Deities and the *chakras,* especially the 1,000-petaled *sahasrāra.* Rooted in the mud, its blossom is a promise of purity and unfoldment. Aum.

Where Did This Universe Come from?

ŚLOKA 41

Supreme God Śiva created the world and all things in it. He creates and sustains from moment to moment every atom of the seen physical and unseen spiritual universe. Everything is within Him. He is within everything. Aum.

BHĀSHYA

God Śiva created us. He created the earth and all things upon it, animate and inanimate. He created time and gravity, the vast spaces and the uncounted stars. He created night and day, joy and sorrow, love and hate, birth and death. He created the gross and the subtle, this world and the other worlds. There are three worlds of existence: the physical, subtle and causal, termed Bhūloka, Antarloka and Śivaloka. The Creator of all, Śiva Himself is uncreated. As supreme Mahādeva, Śiva wills into manifestation all souls and all form, issuing them from Himself like light from a fire or waves from an ocean. *Ṛishis* describe this perpetual process as the unfoldment of thirty-six *tattvas,* stages of manifestation, from the Śiva *tattva*—Parāśakti and *nāda*—to the five elements. Creation is not the making of a separate thing, but an emanation of Himself. Lord Śiva creates, constantly sustains the form of His creations and absorbs them back into Himself. The *Vedas* elucidate, "As a spider spins and withdraws its web, as herbs grow on the earth, as hair grows on the head and body of a person, so also from the Imperishable arises this universe." Aum Namaḥ Śivāya.

What Is the Nature of the Physical Plane?

ŚLOKA 42

The physical plane, or Bhūloka, is the world of gross or material substance in which phenomena are perceived by the five senses. It is the most limited of worlds, the least permanent and the most subject to change. Aum.

BHĀSHYA

The material world is where we have our experiences, manufacture *karma* and fulfill the desires and duties of life in a physical body. It is in the Bhūloka that consciousness is limited, that awareness of the other two worlds is not always remembered. It is the external plane, made of gross matter, which is really just energy. The world is remarkable in its unending variety and enthralling novelty. Mystics call it the unfoldment of *prakṛiti,* primal nature, and liken it to a bubble on the ocean's surface. It arises, lives and bursts to return to the source. This physical world, though necessary to our evolution, is the embodiment of impermanence, of constant change. Thus, we take care not to become overly attached to it. It is mystically subjective, not objective. It is dense but not solid. It is sentient, even sacred. It is rocks and rainbows, liquid, gas and conflagration, all held in a setting of space. The *Vedas* affirm, "The knower, the author of time, the possessor of qualities and all knowledge, it is He who envelopes the universe. Controlled by Him, this work of creation unfolds itself—that which is regarded as earth, water, fire, air and ether." Aum Namaḥ Śivāya.

राजपूजाधनंधान्यं॥नित्यंकल्याणमेववा॥पुत्रदारार्थमा
द्ररूपंविनिर्दिशेत्॥ ॥

What Is the Nature of the Subtle Plane?

ŚLOKA 43

The subtle plane, or Antarloka, is the mental-emotional sphere that we function in through thought and feeling and reside in fully during sleep and after death. It is the astral world that exists within the physical plane. Aum.

BHĀSHYA

The astral plane is for the most part exactly duplicated in the physical plane, though it is of a more intense rate of vibration. Beings in the higher Antarloka are trained in technology, the arts and increments of culture to take up bodies in the Bhūloka, to improve and enhance conditions within it. It is in this more advanced realm that new inventions are invented, new species created, ideas unfolded, futures envisioned, environments balanced, scientists trained and artists taught finesse. We function constantly, though perhaps not consciously, in this subtle plane by our every thought and emotion. Here, during sleep and after death, we meet others who are sleeping or who have died. We attend inner-plane schools, there to advance our knowledge. The Antarloka spans the spectrum of consciousness from the hellish Naraka regions beginning at the *pātāla chakra* within the feet, to the heavenly realm of divine love in the *viśuddha chakra* within the throat. The *Vedas* recount, "Now, there are, of a truth, three worlds: the world of men, the world of the fathers, and the world of the Gods. The world of the Gods is verily the best of worlds." Aum Namaḥ Śivāya.

What Is the Nature of the Causal Plane?

ŚLOKA 44

The causal plane, or Śivaloka, pulsates at the core of being, deep within the subtle plane. It is the superconscious world where the Gods and highly evolved souls live and can be accessed through *yoga* and temple worship. Aum.

BHĀSHYA

The causal plane is the world of light and blessedness, the highest of heavenly regions, extolled in the scriptures of all faiths. It is the foundation of existence, the source of visions, the point of conception, the apex of creation. The causal plane is the abode of Lord Śiva and His entourage of Mahādevas and other highly evolved souls who exist in their own self-effulgent form—radiant bodies of centillions of quantum light particles. Even for embodied souls, this refined realm is not distant, but exists within man. It is ever-present, ever-available as the clear white light that illumines the mind, accessed within the throat and cranial *chakras*—*viśuddha, ājñā* and *sahasrāra*—in the sublime practices of *yoga* and temple worship. It is in the causal plane that the mature soul, unshrouded of the physical body's strong instinctive pulls and astral body's harsh intellectual stranglehold, resides fully conscious in its self-effulgent form. The Śivaloka is the natural refuge of all souls. The *Vedas* intone, "Where men move at will, in the threefold sphere, in the third heaven of heavens, where are realms full of light, in that radiant world make me immortal." Aum Namaḥ Śivāya.

Does the Universe Ever End? Is It Real?

ŚLOKA 45

The universe ends at *mahāpralaya*, when time, form and space dissolve in God Śiva, only to be created again in the next cosmic cycle. We call it relatively real to distinguish it from the unchanging Reality. Aum Namaḥ Śivāya.

BHĀSHYA

This universe, and indeed all of existence, is *māyā*, Śiva's mirific energy. While God is absolutely real, His emanated world is relatively real. Being relatively real does not mean the universe is illusory or nonexistent, but that it is impermanent and subject to change. It is an error to say that the universe is mere illusion, for it is entirely real when experienced in ordinary consciousness, and its existence is required to lead us to God. The universe is born, evolves and dissolves in cycles much as the seasons come and go through the year. These cycles are inconceivably immense, ending in *mahāpralaya* when the universe undergoes dissolution. All three worlds, including time and space, dissolve in God Śiva. This is His ultimate grace—the evolution of all souls is perfect and complete as they lose individuality and return to Him. Then God Śiva exists alone in His three perfections until He again issues forth creation. The *Vedas* state, "Truly, God is One; there can be no second. He alone governs these worlds with His powers. He stands facing beings. He, the herdsman, after bringing forth all worlds, reabsorbs them at the end of time." Aum Namaḥ Śivāya.

Scriptures Speak on Three Worlds

As threads come out of the spider, as little sparks come out of the fire, so all the senses, all the worlds, all the Gods, yea, all beings, issue forth from the Self. *Yajur Veda*

In heaven there is no fear at all. Thou, O Death, art not there. Nor in that place does the thought of growing old make one tremble. There, free from hunger and from thirst, and far from the reach of sorrow, all rejoice and are glad. *Yajur Veda*

This universe is a tree eternally existing, its root aloft, its branches spread below. The pure root of the tree is Brahman, the immortal, in whom the three worlds have their being, whom none can transcend, who is verily the Self. *Yajur Veda*

The spirit of man has two dwellings: this world and the world beyond. There is also a third dwelling place: the land of sleep and dreams. Resting in this borderland, the spirit of man can behold his dwelling in this world and in the other world afar; and wandering in this borderland, he beholds behind him the sorrows of this world, and in front of him he sees the joys of the beyond. *Yajur Veda*

May God—who, in the mystery of His vision and power, transforms His white radiance into His many-colored creation, from whom all things come and into whom they all return—grant us the grace of pure vision. *Yajur Veda*

When a man knows God, he is free: his sorrows have an end, and birth and death are no more. When in inner union he is beyond the world of the body, then the third world, the world of the Spirit, is found, where the power of the All is, and man has all—for he is one with the One. *Yajur Veda*

Without beginning art thou, beyond time, beyond space; thou art He from whom sprang the three worlds. ***Yajur Veda***

These worlds, tiered one above the other from the lowest to the highest, make up the universe of transmigration. Knowers of Reality describe it as the place of effective experience. ***Mṛigendra Āgama***

All these visibles and invisibles, movables and immovables, are pervaded by Me. All the worlds existing in the *tattvas* from Śakti to *pṛithivī* [earth] exist in me. Whatever is heard or seen, internally or externally, is pervaded by Me. ***Sarvajñānottara Āgama***

The gross body with presence prominent, the subtle body that invisible takes shape and the causal body that by inference is—all these bodies disappear when merging in the Lord's feet. ***Tirumantiram***

The universe, animate and inanimate, is His body. The universe, animate and inanimate, is His play. The universe, animate and inanimate, is He. The whole universe, animate and inanimate, is a wonder. ***Natchintanai***

O! Transcendent One extending through both earth and heaven! Ever bright with glory! The King of Śivaloka! The Lord Śiva presiding at *Tiruperunturai!* I have no sustenance other than You. ***Tirumurai***

The Supreme dwells within the lotus of the heart. Those who reach His splendid feet dwell endearingly within unearthly realms. ***Tirukural***

There is no baser folly than the infatuation that looks upon the transient as if it were everlasting. ***Tirukural***

Sarvabhadra Maṇḍala

सर्वभद्रमण्डल

The Goodness of All

Swastika is the symbol of auspiciousness and good fortune—literally, "It is well." The right-angled arms of this ancient sun-sign denote the indirect way that Divinity is apprehended: by intuition and not by intellect. Aum.

Are Souls and World Essentially Good?

ŚLOKA 46

The intrinsic and real nature of all beings is their soul, which is goodness. The world, too, is God's flawless creation. All is in perfect balance. There are changes, and they may appear evil, but there is no intrinsic evil. Aum.

BHĀSHYA

The soul radiates love, is a child of God going through its evolutionary process of growing up into the image and likeness of the Lord. Goodness and mercy, compassion and caring are the intrinsic, inherent or indwelling nature of the soul. Wisdom and pure knowledge, happiness and joy are the intrinsic nature of the soul. Can we believe the soul is anything but goodness itself, purity and all the refined qualities found within superconsciousness? When God is everywhere, how can there be a place for evil? The soul is constantly one with God in its ever-present Satchidānanda state at every point in its evolution. How, then, arises the concept of evil and suffering? *Āṇava, karma* and *māyā,* the play toys of the soul, are the source of this seeming suffering. Like a child, we play with the toys of *āṇava* in the playground of *māyā,* fall and are bruised by *karma,* then run to our loving Lord for solace and release into spiritual maturity. The *Vedas* pointedly state, "As the sun, the eye of the whole world, is not sullied by the external faults of the eyes, so the one inner soul of all things is not sullied by the sorrow in the world, being external to it." Aum Namaḥ Śivāya.

Why Do Some Souls Act in Evil Ways?

ŚLOKA 47

People act in evil ways who have lost touch with their soul nature and live totally in the outer, instinctive mind. What the ignorant see as evil, the enlightened see as the actions of low-minded and immature individuals. Aum.

BHĀSHYA

Evil is often looked upon as a force against God. But the Hindu knows that all forces are God's forces, even the waywardness of *adharma.* This is sometimes difficult to understand when we see the pains and problems caused by men against men. Looking deeper, we see that what is called evil has its own mysterious purpose in life. Yes, bad things do happen. Still, the wise never blame God, for they know these to be the return of man's self-created *karmas,* difficult but necessary experiences for his spiritual evolution. Whenever we are injured or hurt, we understand that our suffering is but the fulfillment of a *karma* we once initiated, for which our injurer is but the instrument who, when his *karma* cycles around, will be the injured. Those who perform seemingly evil deeds are not yet in touch with the ever-present God consciousness of their immortal soul. The *Vedas* rightly admonish, "Borne along and defiled by the stream of qualities, unsteady, wavering, bewildered, full of desire, distracted, one goes on into the state of self-conceit. In thinking, 'This is I' and 'That is mine' one binds himself with himself, as does a bird with a snare." Aum Namaḥ Śivāya.

What Is the Source of Good and Evil?

ŚLOKA 48

Instead of seeing good and evil in the world, we understand the nature of the embodied soul in three interrelated parts: instinctive or physical-emotional; intellectual or mental; and superconscious or spiritual. Aum.

BHĀSHYA

Evil has no source, unless the source of evil's seeming be ignorance itself. Still, it is good to fear unrighteousness. The ignorant complain, justify, fear and criticize "sinful deeds," setting themselves apart as lofty puritans. When the outer, or lower, instinctive nature dominates, one is prone to anger, fear, greed, jealousy, hatred and backbiting. When the intellect is prominent, arrogance and analytical thinking preside. When the superconscious soul comes forth the refined qualities are born—compassion, insight, modesty and the others. The animal instincts of the young soul are strong. The intellect, yet to be developed, is nonexistent to control these strong instinctive impulses. When the intellect is developed, the instinctive nature subsides. When the soul unfolds and overshadows the well-developed intellect, this mental harness is loosened and removed. When we encounter wickedness in others, let us be compassionate, for truly there is no intrinsic evil. The *Vedas* say, "Mind is indeed the source of bondage and also the source of liberation. To be bound to things of this world: this is bondage. To be free from them: this is liberation." Aum Namaḥ Śivāya.

How Can a Benevolent God Permit Evil?

ŚLOKA 49

Ultimately, there is no good or bad. God did not create evil as a force distinct from good. He granted to souls the loving edicts of *dharma* and experiential choices from very subtle to most crude, thus to learn and evolve. Aum.

BHĀSHYA

From the pinnacle of consciousness, one sees the harmony of life. Similarly, from a mountaintop, we see the natural role of a raging ocean and the steep cliffs below—they are beautiful. From the bottom of the mountain, the ocean can appear ominous and the cliffs treacherous. When through meditation, we view the universe from the inside out, we see that there is not one thing out of place or wrong. This releases the human concepts of right and wrong, good and bad. Our benevolent Lord created everything in perfect balance. Good or evil, kindness or hurtfulness return to us as the result, the fruit, of our own actions of the past. The four *dharmas* are God's wisdom lighting our path. That which is known as evil arises from the instinctive-intellectual nature, which the Lord created as dimensions of experience to strengthen our soul and further its spiritual evolution. Let us be compassionate, for truly there is no intrinsic evil. The *Vedas* admonish, "Being overcome by the fruits of his action, he enters a good or an evil womb, so that his course is downward or upward, and he wanders around, overcome by the pairs of opposites." Aum Namaḥ Śivāya.

Should One Avoid Worldly Involvement?

ŚLOKA 50

The world is the bountiful creation of a benevolent God, who means for us to live positively in it, facing *karma* and fulfilling *dharma.* We must not despise or fear the world. Life is meant to be lived joyously. Aum Namaḥ Śivāya.

BHĀSHYA

The world is the place where our destiny is shaped, our desires fulfilled and our soul matured. In the world, we grow from ignorance into wisdom, from darkness into light and from a consciousness of death to immortality. The whole world is an *āśrama* in which all are doing *sādhana.* We must love the world, which is God's creation. Those who despise, hate and fear the world do not understand the intrinsic goodness of all. The world is a glorious place, not to be feared. It is a gracious gift from Śiva Himself, a playground for His children in which to interrelate young souls with the old—the young experiencing their *karma* while the old hold firmly to their *dharma.* The young grow; the old know. Not fearing the world does not give us permission to become immersed in worldliness. To the contrary, it means remaining affectionately detached, like a drop of water on a lotus leaf, being in the world but not of it, walking in the rain without getting wet. The *Vedas* warn, "Behold the universe in the glory of God: and all that lives and moves on earth. Leaving the transient, find joy in the Eternal. Set not your heart on another's possession." Aum Namaḥ Śivāya.

Scriptures Speak on Goodness

As one not knowing that a golden treasure lies buried beneath his feet may walk over it again and again yet never find it—so all beings live every moment in the city of Brahman yet never find Him, because of the veil of illusion by which He is concealed. *Sāma Veda*

He who knows the fine-drawn thread of which the creatures that we see are spun, who knows the thread of that same thread—he also knows Brahman, the Ultimate. *Atharva Veda*

Sin of the mind, depart far away! Why do you utter improper suggestions? Depart from this place! I do not want you! Go to the trees and the forests! My mind will remain here along with our homes and our cattle. *Atharva Veda*

O Lord, lead us along the right path to prosperity. O God, You know all our deeds. Take from us our deceitful sin. To you, then, we shall offer our prayers. *Yajur Veda*

As water descending on mountain crags wastes its energies among the gullies, so he who views things as separate wastes his energies in their pursuit. But as pure water poured into pure becomes the self-same, wholly pure—so, too, becomes the self of the silent sage, of the one, O Gautama, who has understanding. *Yajur Veda*

When he knows the *ātman*—the Self, the inner life, who enjoys like a bee the sweetness of the flowers of the senses, the Lord of what was and of what will be—then he goes beyond fear. This, in truth, is That. *Yajur Veda*

He who is pure of mind, intellect and ego, the senses
and their perceptions is pure, in fact, and finds everything pure
as well. *Sarvajñānottara Āgama*

Turn away from confusion, ignorance, delusion, dream, sleep or wakefulness, for the Supreme is different from the gross body, from the subtle *prāṇa*, from thought or intellect or ego. Meditate on consciousness and become one with it. *Devīkālottara Āgama*

How is it they received God Śiva's grace, you ask?
In the battle of life, their bewildered thoughts wandered. They trained their course and, freed of darkness, sought the Lord and adored His precious, holy feet. *Tirumantiram*

Joy and sorrow—both are *māyā*. The *ātman*, never from love divided, is the very form of knowledge. Therefore, these two will not touch you. Can a mirage wash away the earth? *Natchintanai*

O man! Be a little patient and see! You will understand who you are. Do not grieve over that which does not merit grief. Joy and sorrow are of the world. You are a conscious being. Nothing can affect you. Arise! Be awake! Open the door of heaven with the key of Śivadhyāna and look! Everything will be revealed. *Natchintanai*

O, ye, my men! Try to get into the habit of meditating and praying to Śiva, the Supreme. All your old sins will disappear as the filmy dew evaporates as soon as the sun rises. *Tirumurai*

Without virtue and penitence, devoid of love and learning, as a leather puppet I went around and fell. He showed me the love and the path and the way to reach the world wherefrom there is no return. *Tirumurai*

Pāpa-Duḥkha Maṇḍala

पापदुःखमण्डल

Sin and Suffering

Mahākāla, "Great Time," presides above creation's golden arch. Devouring instants and eons, with a ferocious face, He is Time beyond time, reminder of this world's transitoriness, that sin and suffering will pass. Aum.

Why Is There Suffering in the World?

ŚLOKA 51

The nature of the world is duality. It contains each thing and its opposite: joy and sorrow, goodness and evil, love and hate. Through experience of these, we learn and evolve, finally seeking Truth beyond all opposites. Aum.

BHĀSHYA

There is a divine purpose even in the existence of suffering in the world. Suffering cannot be totally avoided. It is a natural part of human life and the impetus for much spiritual growth for the soul. Knowing this, the wise accept suffering from any source, be it hurricanes, earthquakes, floods, famine, wars, disease or inexplicable tragedies. Just as the intense fire of the furnace purifies gold, so does suffering purify the soul to resplendence. So also does suffering offer us the important realization that true happiness and freedom cannot be found in the world, for earthly joy is inextricably bound to sorrow, and worldly freedom to bondage. Having learned this, devotees seek a *satguru* who teaches them to understand suffering, and brings them into the intentional hardships of *sādhana* and *tapas* leading to liberation from the cycles of experience in the realm of duality. The *Āgamas* explain, "That which appears as cold or as hot, fresh or spoiled, good fortune and bad, love and hate, effort and laziness, the exalted and the depraved, the rich and the poor, the well-founded and the ill-founded, all this is God Himself; none other than Him can we know." Aum Namaḥ Śivāya.

What Is Sin? How Can We Atone for It?

ŚLOKA 52

Sin is the intentional transgression of divine law. There is no inherent or "original" sin. Neither is there mortal sin by which the soul is forever lost. Through *sādhana,* worship and austerities, sins can be atoned for. Aum.

BHĀSHYA

What men term sin, the wise call ignorance. Man's true nature is not sullied by sin. Sin is related only to the lower, instinctive-intellectual nature as a transgression of *dharma.* Still, sin is real and to be avoided, for our wrongful actions return to us as sorrow through the law of *karma.* Sin is terminable, and its effects may be compensated for by penance, or *prāyaśchitta,* and good deeds which settle the *karmic* debt. The young soul, less in tune with his soul nature, is inclined toward sin; the old soul seldom transgresses divine law. Sins are the crippling distortions of intellect bound in emotion. When we sin, we take the energy and distort it to our instinctive favor. When we are unjust and mean, hateful and holding resentments year after year and no one but ourselves knows of our intrigue and corruption, we suffer. As the soul evolves, it eventually feels the great burden of faults and misdeeds and wishes to atone. Penance is performed, and the soul seeks absolution from society and beseeches God's exonerating grace. The *Vedas* say, "Loose me from my sin as from a bond that binds me. May my life swell the stream of your river of Right." Aum Namaḥ Śivāya.

Does Hell Really Exist? Is There a Satan?

ŚLOKA 53

There is no eternal hell, nor is there a Satan. However, there are hellish states of mind and woeful births for those who think and act wrongfully—temporary tormenting conditions that lift the fiery forces within. Aum.

BHĀSHYA

Hell, termed Naraka, is the lower astral realm of the seven *chakras* below the *mūlādhāra*. It is a place of fire and heat, anguish and dismay, of confusion, despair and depression. Here anger, jealousy, argument, mental conflict and tormenting moods plague the mind. Access to hell is brought about by our own thoughts, words, deeds and emotions—suppressed, antagonistic feelings that court demons and their aggressive forces. Hell is not eternal. Nor is there a Satan who tempts man and opposes God's power, though there are devilish beings called *asuras*, immature souls caught in the abyss of deception and hurtfulness. We do not have to die to suffer the Naraka regions, for hellish states of mind are also experienced in the physical world. If we do die in a hellish state of consciousness—burdened by unresolved hatred, remorse, resentment, fear and distorted patterns of thought—we arrive in Naraka fully equipped to join others in this temporary astral purgatory. The *Vedas* say, "Sunless and demonic, verily, are those worlds, and enveloped in blinding darkness, to which all those people who are enemies of their own souls go after death." Aum Namaḥ Śivāya.

What Is the Consequence of Sinful Acts?

ŚLOKA 54

When we do not think, speak and act virtuously, we create negative *karmas* and bring suffering upon ourselves and others. We suffer when we act instinctively and intellectually without superconscious guidance. Aum.

BHĀSHYA

We are happy, serene and stable when we follow good conduct, when we listen to our conscience, the knowing voice of the soul. The superconscious mind, the mind of our soul, knows and inspires good conduct, out of which comes a refined, sustainable culture. Wrongdoing and vice lead us away from God, deep into the darkness of doubt, despair and self-condemnation. This brings the *asuras* around us. We are out of harmony with ourselves and our family and must seek companionship elsewhere, amongst those who are also crude, unmindful, greedy and lacking in self-control. In this bad company, burdensome new *karma* is created, as good conduct cannot be followed. This *pāpa* accumulates, blinding us to the religious life we once lived. Penance and throwing ourselves upon the mercy of God and the Gods are the only release for the unvirtuous, those who conduct themselves poorly. Fortunately, our Gods are compassionate and love their devotees. The ancient *Vedas* elucidate, "The mind is said to be twofold: the pure and also the impure; impure by union with desire—pure when from desire completely free!" Aum Namaḥ Śivāya.

Does God Ever Punish Wrongdoers?

ŚLOKA 55

God is perfect goodness, love and truth. He is not wrathful or vengeful. He does not condemn or punish wrongdoers. Jealousy, vengefulness and vanity are qualities of man's instinctive nature, not of God. Aum Namaḥ Śivāya.

BHĀSHYA

There is no reason to ever fear God, whose right-hand gesture, *abhaya mudrā,* indicates "fear not," and whose left hand invites approach. God is with us always, even when we are unaware of that holy presence. He is His creation. It is an extension of Himself; and God is never apart from it nor limited by it. When we act wrongly, we create negative *karma* for ourselves and must then live through experiences of suffering to fulfill the law of *karma.* Such *karmas* may be painful, but they were generated from our own thoughts and deeds. God never punishes us, even if we do not believe in Him. It is by means of worship of and meditation on God that our self-created sufferings are softened and assuaged. God is the God of all—of the believers within all religions, and of the nonbelievers, too. God does not destroy the wicked and redeem the righteous; but grants the precious gift of liberation to all souls. The *Āgamas* state, "When the soul gradually reduces and then stops altogether its participation in darkness and inauspicious powers, the Friend of the World, God, reveals to the soul the limitless character of its knowledge and activity." Aum Namaḥ Śivāya.

Scriptures Speak on Sin and Suffering

When, to a man who knows, all beings have become one with his own Self, when furthermore he perceives this oneness, how then can sorrow or delusion touch him? ***Yajur Veda***

I glorify Him who is of wonderful radiance like the sun, who is the giver of happiness, lovely, benevolent, and the One whom all welcome like a guest. He bestows vigor upon the worshipers; may He, the fire divine, remove our sorrow and give us heroic strength and all sustaining riches. ***Ṛig Veda***

I go for refuge to God who is One in the silence of eternity, pure radiance of beauty and perfection, in whom we find our peace. He is the bridge supreme which leads to immortality, and the spirit of fire which burns the dross of lower life. ***Yajur Veda***

When a seer sees the creator of golden hue, the Lord, the Person, the source of Brahmā, then being a knower, shaking off good and evil and free from stain, he attains supreme equality with the Lord. ***Atharva Veda***

Only by a tranquil mind does one destroy all action, good or bad. Once the self is pacified, one abides in the Self and attains everlasting bliss. If the mind becomes as firmly established in Brahman as it is usually attached to the sense objects, who, then, will not be released from bondage? ***Yajur Veda***

Words cannot describe the joy of the soul whose impurities are cleansed in deep contemplation—who is one with his *ātman,* his own Spirit. Only those who feel this joy know what it is. ***Yajur Veda***

Even though he causes pain to his patient by applying certain remedies, the physician is not taken to be the cause of the suffering, because in the final analysis he has produced the good that was sought after. ***Mṛigendra Āgama***

Disputes, worldly associations and quarrels should be avoided. Not even spiritual disputations should be indulged in, whether good or bad. Jealousy, slander, pomp, passion, envy, love, anger, fear and misery should all disappear gradually and entirely. ***Devākālottara Āgama***

And even if thou wert the greatest of sinners, with the help of the vessel of wisdom thou shalt cross the sea of evil. Even as a burning fire burns all fuel into ashes, the fire of eternal wisdom burns into ashes all works. ***Bhagavad Gītā***

The virtuous wife, devotee true and *jñāni* great—those who have done exceeding harm to shock these, their life and wealth will in a year disappear. ***Tirumantiram***

A physician takes various roots, mixes them together into one medicine and with it cures the disease. Likewise, the great All-Knowing Physician, by giving to the soul its body, faculties, the world and all its experiences, cures its disease and establishes it in the bliss of liberation. ***Natchintanai***

O, my Lord, the five senses have taken possession of my body and driven me away from your holy feet. I am confused and troubled at heart, like the curd which is being churned. Bestow enlightenment upon me. ***Tirumurai***

As the intense fire of the furnace refines gold to brilliancy, so does the burning suffering of austerity purify the soul to resplendence. ***Tirukural***

Dharma Upanishad

धर्म उपनिषद्

Right Living

HINDUISM TODAY
HINDUISM

Chaturdharma Maṇḍala

चतुर्धर्ममण्डल

Four Dharmas

Aṅkuśa, the goad held in Lord Ganeśa's right hand, is used to remove obstacles from *dharma's* path. It is the force by which all wrongful things are repelled from us, the sharp prod which spurs the dullards onward. Aum.

What Is Dharma? What Are Its Forms?

ŚLOKA 56

Dharma is the law of being, the orderly fulfillment of an inherent nature and destiny. *Dharma* is of four main divisions, which are God's law at work on four levels of our existence: universal, human, social and personal. Aum.

BHĀSHYA

When God created the universe, He endowed it with order, with the laws to govern creation. *Dharma* is God's divine law prevailing on every level of existence, from the sustaining cosmic order to religious and moral laws which bind us in harmony with that order. We are maintained by *dharma,* held in our most perfect relationship within a complex universe. Every form of life, every group of men, has its *dharma,* the law of its being. When we follow *dharma,* we are in conformity with the Truth that inheres and instructs the universe, and we naturally abide in closeness to God. *Adharma* is opposition to divine law. *Dharma* prevails in the laws of nature and is expressed in our culture and heritage. It is piety and ethical practice, duty and obligation. It is the path which leads us to liberation. Universal *dharma* is known as *ṛita.* Social *dharma* is *varṇa dharma.* Human *dharma* is known as *āśrama dharma.* Our personal *dharma* is *svadharma.* Hinduism, the purest expression of these four timeless *dharmas,* is called Sanātana Dharma. The *Vedas* proclaim, "There is nothing higher than *dharma.* Verily, that which is *dharma* is Truth." Aum Namaḥ Śivāya.

What Is Signified by Universal Dharma?

ŚLOKA 57

Universal law, known in the *Vedas* as *ṛita,* is cosmic order, God's rule at work throughout the physical province. It is the infinite intelligence or consciousness in nature, the sustaining cosmic design and organizing force. Aum.

BHĀSHYA

Ṛita is the underlying divine principle and universal law regulating nature, from the voyage of stars in vast galactic orbits to the flux of infinitesimal subatomic energies. *Ṛita* is the Tao. It is destiny and the road to destiny. When we are in tune with universal *dharma,* and realize that man is an integral part of nature and not above it or dominating it, then we are in tune with God. All Hindus feel they are guests on the planet with responsibilities to nature, which when fulfilled balance its responsibilities to them. The physical body was gathered from nature and returns to it. Nature is exquisitely complex and orderly. The coconut always yields a coconut tree, a lotus a lotus, a rose a rose, not another species. How constant nature is, and yet how diverse, for in mass producing its creations, no two ever look exactly alike. Yes, the Hindu knows himself to be a part of nature and seeks to bring his life into harmony with the universal path, the sustaining cosmic force. The *Vedas* proclaim, "Earth is upheld by Truth. Heaven is upheld by the sun. The solar regions are supported by eternal laws, *ṛita.* The elixir of divine love is supreme in heaven." Aum Namaḥ Śivāya.

What Is the Nature of Social Dharma?

ŚLOKA 58

Social law, or *varṇa dharma,* consists of the occupation, duties and responsibilities we must fulfill as a member of our nation, community and family. An important aspect of this *dharma* is religious and moral law. Aum.

BHĀSHYA

Every human society defines a complex stratification of community interaction. Scholarly, pious souls of exceptional learning are the wise *brāhmins.* Lawmakers and law-enforcers are the guardian *kshatriyas.* Bankers and businessmen are merchant *vaiśyas.* Laborers, workers and artisans are *śūdras.* In addition to these four classes, or *varṇas,* are hundreds of castes, or *jātis.* In Hindu societies, class and caste, which dictates one's occupation and community, is largely hereditary. However, these birth-imposed categories can be transcended by the ambitious who enter new careers through education, skill and persistence. Social *dharma* is fulfilled in adherence to the laws of our nation, to our community responsibilities and to our obligations among family and friends. A comprehensive system of duties, morals and religious observances make up God's law at work in our daily life. Rightly followed, *varṇa dharma* enhances individual and family progress and ensures the continuity of culture. The *Vedas* say, "When a man is born, whoever he may be, there is born simultaneously a debt to the Gods, to the sages, to the ancestors and to men." Aum Namaḥ Śivāya.

What Is the Nature of Human Dharma?

ŚLOKA 59

Human law, or *āśrama dharma,* is the natural expression and maturing of the body, mind and emotions through four progressive stages of earthly life: student, householder, elder advisor and religious solitaire. Aum.

BHĀSHYA

The four *āśramas* are "stages of striving," in pursuit of the *purushārthas:* righteousness, wealth, pleasure and liberation. Our first 24 years of life are a time of intense learning. Around age 12, we enter formally the *brahmacharya āśrama* and undertake the study and skills that will serve us in later life. From 24 to 48, in the *gṛihastha āśrama,* we work together as husband and wife to raise the family, increasing wealth and knowledge through our profession, serving the community and sustaining the members of the other three *āśramas.* In the *vānaprastha āśrama,* from 48 to 72, slowly retiring from public life, we share our experience by advising and guiding younger generations. After age 72, as the physical forces wane, we turn fully to scripture, worship and *yoga.* This is the *sannyāsa āśrama,* which differs from the formal life of ochre-robed monks. Thus, our human *dharma* is a natural awakening, expression, maturing and withdrawal from worldly involvement. The *Vedas* say, "Pursuit of the duties of the stage of life to which each one belongs—that, verily, is the rule! Others are like branches of a stem. With this, one tends upwards; otherwise, downwards." Aum Namaḥ Śivāya.

What Is the Nature of Personal Dharma?

ŚLOKA 60

Personal law, or *svadharma,* is our own perfect individual pattern in life. It is the sum of our accumulated seed *karmas* as they relate to the collective effect on us of *ṛita, āśrama* and *varṇa dharma.* Aum Namaḥ Śivāya.

BHĀSHYA

Each human being has an individual, personal *dharma.* This *dharma* is determined by two things: the *karmas,* both good and bad, from past lives; and the three *dharmas* of this life—universal, human and social. *Svadharma,* "one's own law," is molded by our background and experiences, tendencies and desires—indicated by astrology—all of which determine our personality, profession and associations. The key to discovering and understanding personal *dharma* is the worship of Lord Gaṇeśa, the God of memory, time and wisdom, who knows our past lives and can clarify our most perfect pattern, our right path in life. When we follow this unique pattern—guided by *guru,* wise elders and the knowing voice of our soul—we are content and at peace with ourselves and the world. *Dharma* is to the individual what its normal development is to a seed—the orderly fulfillment of an inherent nature and destiny. A Vedic prayer implores, "That splendor that resides in an elephant, in a king, among men, or within the waters, with which the Gods in the beginning came to Godhood, with that same splendor make me splendid, O Lord." Aum Namaḥ Śivāya.

Scriptures Speak on Four Dharmas

We all have various thoughts and plans, and diverse are the callings of men. The carpenter seeks out that which is cracked; the physician, the ailing; the priest, the *soma* press. *Ṛig Veda*

The daughter of heaven has revealed Herself in the eastern region, all clothed in light. Faithfully She follows the path of *ṛita dharma*; well understanding, She measures out the regions. *Ṛig Veda*

The hands are alike but in their work they differ. So also, two cows, offspring of a single mother, may yet give differing yields of milk. Even twins are not the same in strength, or kinsmen in bounty. *Ṛig Veda*

A man should think on wealth and strive to win it by adoration on the path of Order, counsel himself with his own mental insight, and grasp still nobler vigor with his spirit. *Ṛig Veda*

Who, weary of Brahman studentship, having fully learnt the *Vedas*, is discharged by the teacher he had ever obeyed, such a one is called the *āśramin*. Choosing a wife of equally high birth, he should deposit the sacred fires, and bring to those Deities the Brahman sacrifice day and night until, dividing among the children his property, abstaining from conjugal pleasures, he gives himself to the forest life, wandering in a pure region. Living on water and on air, and on such fruit as proper, fire within body, he abides on earth without obligations, without tears. *Atharva Veda*

A hundred uninitiated are equal to one *brahmachārī*. A hundred *brahmachārīs* are equal to one *gṛihastha*. A hundred *gṛihasthas* are equal to one *vānaprastha*. A hundred *vānaprasthas* are equal to one *sannyāsin*. *Atharva Veda*

In how many parts was He transformed when they cut the Purusha in pieces? What did His mouth become? What His arms, what His thighs, what His feet? His mouth then became the *brāhmaṇa,* from the arms the *rājanya* was made, the *vaiśya* from the thighs, from the feet the *śūdra* came forth. *Ṛig Veda*

The works of *brāhmins, kshatriyas, vaiśyas* and *śūdras* are different, in harmony with the three powers of their born nature. The works of a *brāhmin* are peace, self-harmony, austerity and purity, loving forgiveness and righteousness, vision, wisdom and faith. These are the works of a *kshatriya:* a heroic mind, inner fire, constancy, resourcefulness, courage in battle, generosity and noble leadership. Trade, agriculture and the rearing of cattle is the work of a *vaiśya.* And the work of the *śūdra* is service. They all attain perfection when they find joy in their work. *Bhagavad Gītā*

A man attains perfection when his work is worship of God, from whom all things come and who is in all. Greater is thine own work, even if this be humble, than the work of another, even if this be great. When a man does the work God gives him, no sin can touch this man. *Bhagavad Gītā*

A *sattvic* he is, his thoughts centered on Paratattva,
his vision clear through conflicting faiths, abhorrent of recurring cycles of births, straight in *dharma's* path he easy walks. He, sure, is disciple good and true. *Tirumantiram*

He who understands his duty to society truly lives. All others shall be counted among the dead. *Tirukural*

By the laws of *dharma* that govern body and mind, you
must fear sin and act righteously. Wise men, by thinking and behaving in this way, become worthy to gain bliss both here and hereafter. *Natchintanai*

Sadāchāra Maṇḍala

सदाचारमण्डल

Good Conduct

Añjali, the gesture of two hands brought together near the heart, means to "honor or celebrate." It is our Hindu greeting, two joined as one, the bringing together of matter and spirit, the self meeting the Self in all. Aum.

What Is the Meaning of Good Conduct?

ŚLOKA 61

Good conduct is right thought, right speech and right action. It is virtuous deeds in harmony with divine law, reflecting the soul's innate purity. As a staff is used to climb a mountain, so must virtue be used in life. Aum.

BHĀSHYA

Good conduct, *sadāchāra,* determines our behavior in day-to-day life. We should be uplifting to our fellow man, not critical or injurious. We should be loving and kind, not hateful or mean. We should express the soul's beautiful qualities of self-control, modesty and honesty. We should be a good example to others and a joy to be around, not a person to be avoided. Good conduct is the sum of spiritual living and comes through keeping good company. When heart and mind are freed of baseness, when desires have been tempered and excesses avoided, *dharma* is known and followed, and good conduct naturally arises. The Hindu fosters humility and shuns arrogance, seeks to assist, never to hinder, finds good in others and forgets their faults. There is no other way to be called a true devotee, but to conduct ourself properly within ourself and among our fellow men. The *Vedas* say, "Let there be no neglect of Truth. Let there be no neglect of *dharma.* Let there be no neglect of welfare. Let there be no neglect of prosperity. Let there be no neglect of study and teaching. Let there be no neglect of the duties to the Gods and the ancestors." Aum Namaḥ Śivāya.

What Are Good Conduct's Four Keys?

ŚLOKA 62

Purity, devotion, humility and charity are the four keys to good conduct. Of these, purity is the cardinal virtue. We cultivate purity by thinking, speaking and doing only that which is conceived in compassion for all. Aum.

BHĀSHYA

Purity is the pristine and natural state of the soul. We cultivate purity by refraining from anger and retaliation, by maintaining a clean and healthy body, and by guarding our virginity until marriage. We cultivate purity by seeking good company and by living a disciplined life. Devotion is love of God, Gods and *guru,* and dedication to family and friends. We cultivate devotion through being loyal and trustworthy. We cultivate devotion through worship and selfless service. Humility is mildness, modesty, reverence and unpretentiousness. We cultivate humility by taking the experiences of life in understanding and not in reaction, and by seeing God everywhere. We cultivate humility through showing patience with circumstances and forbearance with people. Charity is selfless concern and caring for our fellow man. It is generous giving without thought of reward, always sharing and never hoarding. We cultivate charity through giving to the hungry, the sick, the homeless, the elderly and the unfortunate. The *Vedas* explain, "As to a mountain that's enflamed, deer and birds do not resort—so, with knowers of God, sins find no shelter." Aum Namaḥ Śivāya.

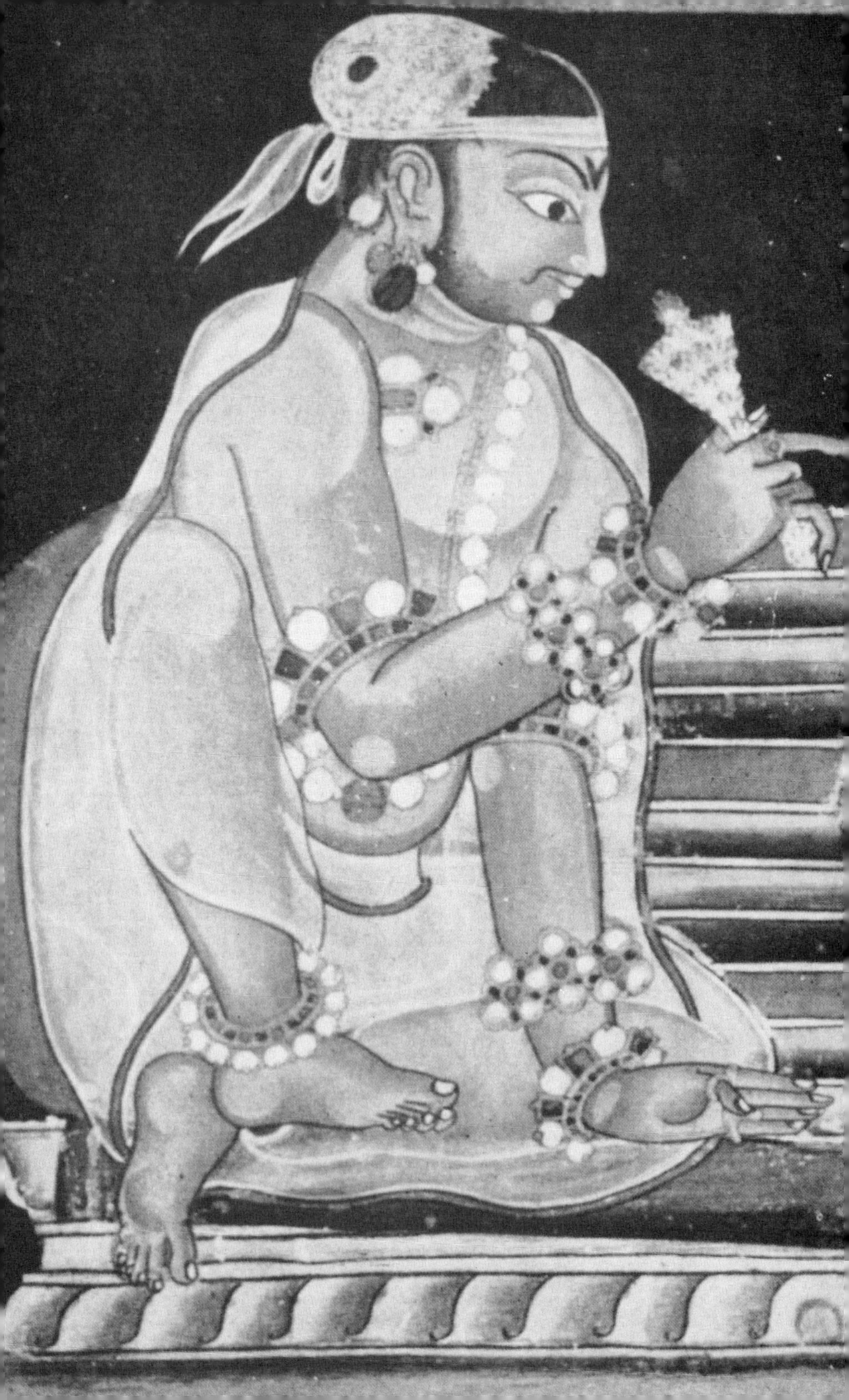

From Whom Is Good Conduct Learned?

ŚLOKA 63

The first teacher in matters of good conduct is our conscience. To know what is right and what is wrong we can also turn to God, to our *satguru* and *swāmīs,* to scripture and to our elders, family and trusted friends. Aum.

BHĀSHYA

Divine laws cannot be avoided. They do not rule us from above but are wrought into our very nature. Even death cannot efface the *karma* created by evil deeds. Good conduct alone can resolve woeful *karmas.* Therefore, it is essential that we learn and adhere to good conduct. Good people are the best teachers of good conduct, and should be sought out and heeded when we need help or advice. Talk with them, the wise ones, and in good judgment be guided accordingly. Ethical scriptures should be read and studied regularly and their wisdom followed. The loud voice of our soul, ever heard within our conscience, is a worthy guide. When we grasp the subtle mechanism of *karma,* we wisely follow the good path. Good conduct, or *sadāchāra,* for the Hindu is summarized in five obligatory duties, called *pañcha nitya karmas:* virtuous living, *dharma*; worship, *upāsanā;* holy days, *utsava*; pilgrimage, *tīrthayātrā;* and sacraments, *saṁskāras.* The *Vedas* offer this guidance, "If you have doubt concerning conduct, follow the example of high souls who are competent to judge, devout, not led by others, not harsh, but lovers of virtue." Aum Namaḥ Śivāya.

What Are the Ten Classical Restraints?

ŚLOKA 64

Hinduism's ethical restraints are contained in ten simple precepts called *yamas.* They define the codes of conduct by which we harness our instinctive forces and cultivate the innate, pristine qualities of our soul. Aum.

BHĀSHYA

The *yamas* and *niyamas* are scriptural injunctions for all aspects of thought and behavior. They are advice and simple guidelines, not commandments. The ten *yamas,* defining the ideals of *charyā,* are: 1) *ahiṁsā,* "noninjury," do not harm others by thought, word or deed; 2) *satya,* "truthfulness," refrain from lying and betraying promises; 3) *asteya,* "nonstealing," neither steal nor covet nor enter into debt; 4) *brahmacharya,* "divine conduct," control lust by remaining celibate when single, leading to faithfulness in marriage; 5) *kshamā,* "patience," restrain intolerance with people and impatience with circumstances; 6) *dhṛiti,* "steadfastness," overcome nonperseverance, fear, indecision and changeableness; 7) *dayā,* "compassion," conquer callous, cruel and insensitive feelings toward all beings; 8) *ārjava,* "honesty," renounce deception and wrongdoing; 9) *mitāhāra,* "moderate appetite," neither eat too much, nor consume meat, fish, fowl or eggs; 10) *śaucha,* "purity," avoid impurity in body, mind and speech. The *Vedas* proclaim, "To them belongs yon stainless Brahma world in whom there is no crookedness and falsehood, nor trickery." Aum Namaḥ Śivāya.

What Are the Ten Classical Observances?

ŚLOKA 65

Hinduism's religious tenets are contained in ten terse precepts called *niyamas*. They summarize the essential practices that we observe and the soulful virtues and qualities we strive daily to perfect. Aum Namaḥ Śivāya.

BHĀSHYA

Good conduct is a combination of avoiding unethical behavior and performing virtuous, spiritualizing acts. The accumulated wisdom of thousands of years of Hindu culture has evolved ten *niyamas*, or religious observances. These precepts defining the ideals of *kriyā* are: 1) *hrī*, "remorse," be modest and show shame for misdeeds; 2) *santosha*, "contentment," seek joy and serenity in life; 3) *dāna*, "giving," tithe and give creatively without thought of reward; 4) *āstikya*, "faith," believe firmly in God, Gods, *guru* and the path to enlightenment; 5) *Īśvarapūjāna*, "worship," cultivate devotion through daily *pūjā* and meditation; 6) *siddhānta śravaṇa*, "scriptural listening," study the teachings and listen to the wise of one's lineage; 7) *mati*, "cognition," develop a spiritual will and intellect with a *guru's* guidance; 8) *vrata*, "sacred vows," fulfill religious vows, rules and observances faithfully; 9) *japa*, "recitation," chant holy *mantras* daily; 10) *tapas*, "austerity," perform *sādhana*, penance, *tapas* and sacrifice. The *Vedas* state, "They indeed possess that Brahma world who possess austerity and chastity, and in whom the truth is established." Aum Namaḥ Śivāya.

Scriptures Speak on Good Conduct

You are in truth the visible Brahman. I will proclaim you as the visible Brahman. I will speak the right. I will speak the truth. May this protect me. May it protect my teacher! May this protect me. May it protect my teacher! Aum, peace, peace, peace! ***Yajur Veda***

The one who has not turned away from wickedness, who has no peace, who is not concentrated, whose mind is restless—he cannot realize the *ātman*, who is known by wisdom. ***Yajur Veda***

The ten abstinences are nonviolence, truth, nonstealing, chastity, kindness, rectitude, forgiveness, endurance, temperance in food and purity. ***Yajur Veda***

May He protect us both. May He be pleased with us both. May we work together with vigor; may our study make us illumined. May there be no dislike between us. Aum, peace, peace. ***Yajur Veda***

The subtle Self is known by thought in which the senses in five different forms have centered. The whole of men's thought is pervaded by the senses. When thought is purified, the Self shines forth. ***Atharva Veda***

They say of a man who speaks the truth, "He speaks the *dharma*," or of a man who speaks the *dharma*, "he speaks the truth." Verily, both these are the same thing. ***Yajur Veda***

Rescue the mind from qualities, make it pure and fix it in the heart. That consciousness which manifests clearly thereafter must alone be aimed at and striven for. ***Devīkālottara Āgama***

Let the aspirant for liberation behave in an unselfish and kind way and give aid to all, let him undergo penance, and let him study this *Āgama*. ***Devīkālottara Āgama***

One who has recoiled from sensual pleasures and devoted himself to undefiled, pure wisdom is sure to achieve everlasting *moksha*, even if he does not consciously seek it. ***Devīkālottara Āgama***

I walk with those who go after God. I live with those who sing His praise. The Lord blesses those who seek Him. With those who unite in Him, I unite in their feet. ***Tirumantiram***

Tapas, *japa*, serenity, belief in God, charity, vows in Śaiva way and Siddhānta learning, sacrificial offerings, Śiva *pūjā* and speech pure—with these ten the one in *niyama* perfects his way. ***Tirumantiram***

More precious than life itself is rectitude. Those who practice rectitude possess everything that is worthwhile. Humility, truthfulness, avoidance of killing and stealing, refraining from slandering others, absence of covetousness and so forth—these are the characteristics of a life of rectitude. ***Natchintanai***

Keep the mind free of impurity. That alone is the practice of virtue. All else is nothing but empty display. ***Tirukural***

Virtue yields heaven's honor and earth's wealth. What is there then that is more fruitful for a man? Be unremitting in the doing of good deeds. Do them with all your might and by every possible means. ***Tirukural***

Purity of mind and purity of conduct—these two depend upon the purity of a man's companions. ***Tirukural***

Ahiṁsā Maṇḍala

अहिंसामण्डल

Noninjury

Go, the cow, is a symbol of the earth, the nourisher, the ever-giving, undemanding provider. To the Hindu, all animals are sacred, and we acknowledge this reverence of life in our special affection for the gentle cow. Aum.

What Is the Great Virtue Called Ahiṁsā?

ŚLOKA 66

Ahiṁsā, or noninjury, is the first and foremost ethical principle of every Hindu. It is gentleness and nonviolence, whether physical, mental or emotional. It is abstaining from causing hurt or harm to all beings. Aum.

BHĀSHYA

To the Hindu the ground is sacred. The rivers are sacred. The sky is sacred. The sun is sacred. His wife is a Goddess. Her husband is a God. Their children are *devas.* Their home is a shrine. Life is a pilgrimage to liberation from rebirth, and no violence can be carried to the higher reaches of that ascent. While nonviolence speaks only to the most extreme forms of wrongdoing, *ahiṁsā,* which includes not killing, goes much deeper to prohibit the subtle abuse and the simple hurt. Ṛishi Patañjali described *ahiṁsā* as the great vow and foremost spiritual discipline which Truth-seekers must follow strictly and without fail. This extends to harm of all kinds caused by one's thoughts, words and deeds—including injury to the natural environment. Even the intent to injure, even violence committed in a dream, is a violation of *ahiṁsā.* Vedic *ṛishis* who revealed *dharma* proclaimed *ahiṁsā* as the way to achieve harmony with our environment, peace between peoples and compassion within ourselves. The Vedic edict is: "*Ahiṁsā* is not causing pain to any living being at any time through the actions of one's mind, speech or body." Aum Namaḥ Śivāya.

What Is the Inner Source of Noninjury?

ŚLOKA 67

Two beliefs form the philosophical basis of noninjury. The first is the law of *karma,* by which harm caused to others unfailingly returns to oneself. The second is that the Divine shines forth in all peoples and things. Aum.

BHĀSHYA

The Hindu is thoroughly convinced that violence he commits will return to him by a cosmic process that is unerring. He knows that, by *karma's* law, what we have done to others will be done to us, if not in this life then in another. He knows that he may one day be in the same position of anyone he is inclined to harm or persecute, perhaps incarnating in the society he most opposed in order to equalize his hates and fears into a greater understanding. The belief in the existence of God everywhere, as an all-pervasive, self-effulgent energy and consciousness, creates the attitude of sublime tolerance and acceptance toward others. Even *tolerance* is insufficient to describe the compassion and reverence the Hindu holds for the intrinsic sacredness within all things. Therefore, the actions of all Hindus living in the higher nature are rendered benign, or *ahiṁsā.* One would not hurt that which he reveres. The *Vedas* pronounce, "He who, dwelling in all things, yet is other than all things, whom all things do not know, whose body all things are, who controls all things from within—He is your soul, the Inner Controller, the Immortal." Aum Namaḥ Śivāya.

What Is the Inner Source of Violence?

ŚLOKA 68

Violence is a reflection of lower, instinctive consciousness—fear, anger, greed, jealousy and hate—based in the mentality of separateness and unconnectedness, of good and bad, winners and losers, mine and yours. Aum.

BHĀSHYA

Every belief creates certain attitudes. Attitudes govern our actions. Our actions can thus be traced to our inmost beliefs about ourself and the world around us. If those beliefs are erroneous, our actions will not be in tune with the universal *dharma.* For instance, the beliefs in the duality of self and other, of eternal heaven and hell, victors and vanquished, white forces and dark forces, create the attitudes that we must be on our guard, and are justified in giving injury, physically, mentally and emotionally to those whom we judge as bad, pagan, alien or unworthy. Such thinking leads to rationalizing so-called righteous wars and conflicts. As long as our beliefs are dualistic, we will continue to generate antagonism, and that will erupt here and there in violence. Those living in the lower, instinctive nature are society's antagonists. They are self-assertive, territorial, competitive, jealous, angry, fearful and rarely penitent of their hurtfulness. Many take sport in killing for the sake of killing, thieving for the sake of theft. The *Vedas* indicate, "This soul, verily, is overcome by nature's qualities. Now, because of being overcome, he goes on to confusedness." Aum Namaḥ Śivāya.

Is Vegetarianism Integral to Noninjury?

ŚLOKA 69

Hindus teach vegetarianism as a way to live with a minimum of hurt to other beings, for to consume meat, fish, fowl or eggs is to participate indirectly in acts of cruelty and violence against the animal kingdom. Aum.

BHĀSHYA

The abhorrence of injury and killing of any kind leads quite naturally to a vegetarian diet, *śākāhāra.* The meat-eater's desire for meat drives another to kill and provide that meat. The act of the butcher begins with the desire of the consumer. Meat-eating contributes to a mentality of violence, for with the chemically complex meat ingested, one absorbs the slaughtered creature's fear, pain and terror. These qualities are nourished within the meat-eater, perpetuating the cycle of cruelty and confusion. When the individual's consciousness lifts and expands, he will abhor violence and not be able to even digest the meat, fish, fowl and eggs he was formerly consuming. India's greatest saints have confirmed that one cannot eat meat and live a peaceful, harmonious life. Man's appetite for meat inflicts devastating harm on the earth itself, stripping its precious forests to make way for pastures. The *Tirukural* candidly states, "How can he practice true compassion who eats the flesh of an animal to fatten his own flesh? Greater than a thousand *ghee* offerings consumed in sacrificial fires is not to sacrifice and consume any living creature." Aum Namaḥ Śivāya.

How Can Peace on Earth Be Achieved?

ŚLOKA 70

Peace is a reflection of spiritual consciousness. It begins within each person, and extends to the home, neighborhood, nation and beyond. It comes when the higher nature takes charge of the lower nature. Aum Namaḥ Śivāya.

BHĀSHYA

Until we have peace in our own heart, we can't hope for peace in the world. Peace is the natural state of the mind. It is there, inside, to be discovered in meditation, maintained through self-control, and then radiated out to others. The best way to promote peace is to teach families to be peaceful within their own homes by settling all conflicts quickly. At a national and international level, we will enjoy more peace as we become more tolerant. Religious leaders can help by teaching their congregations how to live in a world of differences without feeling threatened, without forcing their ways or will on others. World bodies can make laws which deplore and work to prevent crimes of violence. It is only when the higher-nature people are in charge that peace will truly come. There is no other way, because the problems of conflict reside within the low-minded group who only know retaliation as a way of life. The *Vedas* beseech, "Peace be to the earth and to airy spaces! Peace be to heaven, peace to the waters, peace to the plants and peace to the trees! May all the Gods grant to me peace! By this invocation of peace may peace be diffused!" Aum Namaḥ Śivāya.

Scriptures Speak on Noninjury

Nonviolence is all the offerings. Renunciation is the priestly honorarium. The final purification is death. Thus all the Divinities are established in this body. *Yajur Veda*

If we have injured space, the earth or heaven, or if we have offended mother or father, from that may Agni, fire of the house, absolve us and guide us safely to the world of goodness. *Atharva Veda*

You must not use your God-given body for killing God's creatures, whether they are human, animal or whatever. *Yajur Veda*

To the heavens be peace, to the sky and the earth; to the waters be peace, to plants and all trees; to the Gods be peace, to Brahman be peace, to all men be peace, again and again—peace also to me! *Yajur Veda*

Protect both our species, two-legged and four-legged. Both food and water for their needs supply. May they with us increase in stature and strength. Save us from hurt all our days, O Powers! *Ṛig Veda*

O earthen vessel, strengthen me. May all beings regard me with friendly eyes! May I look upon all creatures with friendly eyes! With a friend's eye may we regard each other! *Yajur Veda*

No pain should be caused to any created being or thing. *Devīkālottara Āgama*

When mindstuff is firmly based in waves of *ahiṁsā*, all living beings cease their enmity in the presence of such a person. *Yoga Sūtras*

Hiṁsā is to act against the spirit divine of the *Vedas.* It is to act against the dictates of *dharma. Ahiṁsā* is the understanding of the fundamental truth that the *ātman* is imperishable, immutable and all-pervading. ***Sūta Saṁhitā***

He who sees that the Lord of all is ever the same in all that is—immortal in the field of mortality—he sees the truth. And when a man sees that the God in himself is the same God in all that is, he hurts not himself by hurting others. Then he goes, indeed, to the highest path. ***Bhagavad Gītā***

The purchaser of flesh performs *hiṁsā* (violence) by his wealth; he who eats flesh does so by enjoying its taste; the killer does *hiṁsā* by actually tying and killing the animal. Thus, there are three forms of killing: he who brings flesh or sends for it, he who cuts off the limbs of an animal, and he who purchases, sells or cooks flesh and eats it—all of these are to be considered meat-eaters. ***Mahābhārata***

Nonviolence, truth, freedom from anger, renunciation, serenity, aversion to fault-finding, sympathy for all beings, peace from greedy cravings, gentleness, modesty, steadiness, energy, forgiveness, fortitude, purity, a good will, freedom from pride—these belong to a man who is born for heaven. ***Bhagavad Gītā***

Meat can never be obtained without injury to living creatures, and injury to sentient beings is detrimental to the attainment of heavenly bliss; let him therefore shun meat. ***Manu Dharma Śāstras***

Worthless are those who injure others vengefully, while those who stoically endure are like stored gold. Let him who wishes to be free from affliction's pain avoid inflicting harm on others. ***Tirukural***

Gṛihastha Upanishad

गृहस्थ उपनिषद्

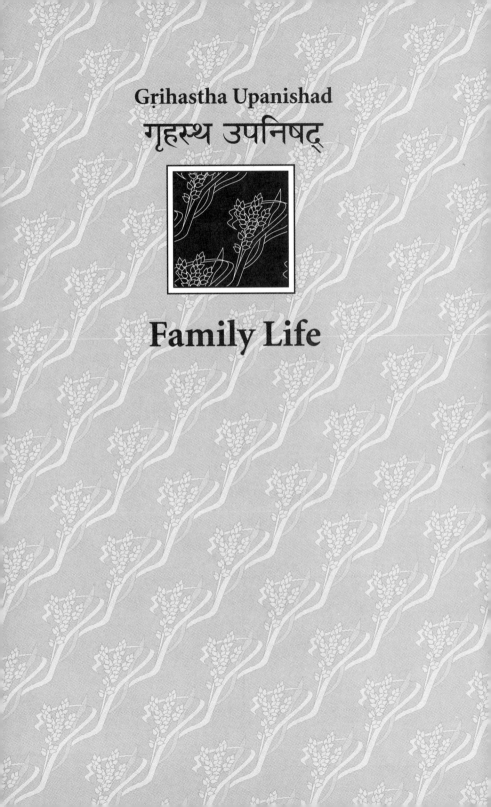

Family Life

Dampati Maṇḍala

दंपतिमण्डल

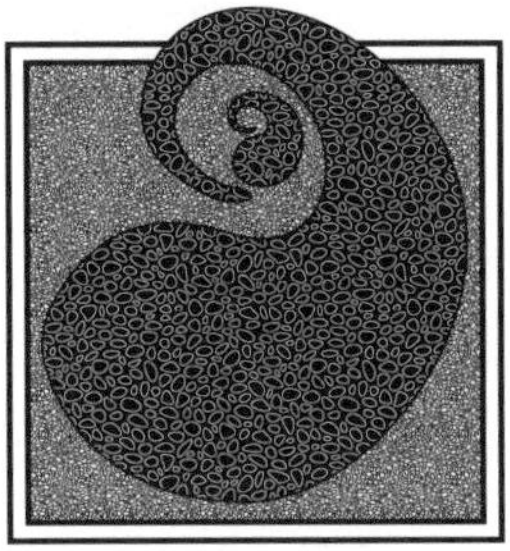

Husband and Wife

Mankolam, the pleasing paisley design, is modeled after a mango and associated with Lord Gaṇeśa. Mangos are the sweetest of fruits, symbolizing auspiciousness and the happy fulfillment of legitimate worldly desires. Aum.

What Is the Central Purpose of Marriage?

ŚLOKA 71

The two purposes of marriage are: the mutual support, both spiritual and material, of man and wife; and bringing children into the world. Marriage is a religious sacrament, a human contract and a civil institution. Aum.

BHĀSHYA

Through marriage, a man and a woman each fulfill their *dharma,* becoming physically, emotionally and spiritually complete. He needs her tenderness, companionship and encouragement, while she needs his strength, love and understanding. Their union results in the birth of children and the perpetuation of the human race. Marriage is a three-fold state: it is a sacrament, a contract and an institution. As a sacrament, it is a spiritual union in which man and woman utter certain vows one to another and thus bind themselves together for life and for their souls' mutual benefit. As a contract, it is a personal agreement to live together as husband and wife, he to provide shelter, protection, sustenance, and she to care for the home and bear and nurture their children. As an institution, marriage is the lawful custom in society, bringing stability to the family and the social order. Marriage is a *jīvayajña,* a sacrifice of each small self to the greater good of the family and society. The *Vedas* exclaim, "I am he, you are she, I am song, you are verse, I am heaven, you are earth. We two shall here together dwell, becoming parents of children." Aum Namaḥ Śivāya.

What Are the Duties of the Husband?

ŚLOKA 72

It is the husband's duty, his *purusha dharma,* to protect and provide for his wife and children. He, as head of the family, *grihesvara,* is responsible for its spiritual, economic, physical, mental and emotional security. Aum.

BHĀSHYA

By their physical, mental and emotional differences, the man is suited to work in the world and the woman to bear and raise their children in the home. The husband is, first, an equal participant in the procreation and upbringing of the future generation. Second, he is the generator of economic resources necessary for society and the immediate family. The husband must be caring, understanding, masculine, loving, affectionate, and an unselfish provider, to the best of his ability and through honest means. He is well equipped physically and mentally for the stress and demands placed upon him. When he performs his *dharma* well, the family is materially and emotionally secure. Still, he is not restricted from participation in household chores, remembering that the home is the wife's domain and she is its mistress. The *Vedas* implore, "Through this oblation, which invokes prosperity, may this bridegroom flourish anew; may he, with his manly energies, flourish the wife they have brought to him. May he excel in strength, excel in royalty! May this couple be inexhaustible in wealth that bestows luster a thousand fold!" Aum Namaḥ Śivāya.

What Are Special Duties of the Wife?

ŚLOKA 73

It is the wife's duty, her *strī dharma,* to bear, nurse and raise the children. She is the able homemaker, standing beside her husband as the mother and educator of their children and the home's silent leader, *gṛihiṇī.* Aum.

BHĀSHYA

The biological differences between man and woman are part of their human *dharma.* The two together constitute a whole. They are equal partners in joy and sorrow, companions and helpmates, yet their functions differ. The Hindu home and family is the fortress of the Sanātana Dharma, which the wife and mother is duty-bound to maintain and thus to perpetuate the faith and create fine citizens. As long as the husband is capable of supporting the family, a woman should not leave the home to work in the world, though she may earn through home industry. The spiritual and emotional loss suffered by the children and the bad *karma* accrued from having a wife and mother work outside the home is never offset by the financial gain. The woman's more intuitive and emotional qualities of femininity, gentleness, modesty, kindness and compassion are needed for the children's proper care and development. The *Vedas* encourage, "May happiness await you with your children! Watch over this house as mistress of the home. Unite yourself wholly with your husband. Thus authority in speech till old age will be yours." Aum Namaḥ Śivāya.

What Is the Hindu View of Sexuality?

ŚLOKA 74

The purpose of sexual union is to express and foster love's beautiful intimacy and to draw husband and wife together for procreation. While offering community guidance, Hinduism does not legislate sexual matters. Aum.

BHĀSHYA

Sexual intercourse is a natural reproductive function, a part of the instinctive nature, and its pleasures draw man and woman together that a child may be conceived. It also serves through its intimacy to express and nurture love. It is love which endows sexual intercourse with its higher qualities, transforming it from an animal function to a human fulfillment. Intensely personal matters of sex as they affect the family or individual are not legislated, but left to the judgment of those involved, subject to community laws and customs. Hinduism neither condones nor condemns birth control, sterilization, masturbation, homosexuality, petting, polygamy or pornography. It does not exclude or draw harsh conclusions against any part of human nature, though scripture prohibits adultery and forbids abortion except to save a mother's life. Advice in such matters should be sought from parents, elders and spiritual leaders. The only rigid rule is wisdom, guided by tradition and virtue. The *Vedas* beseech, "May all the divine powers together with the waters join our two hearts in one! May the Messenger, the Creator and holy Obedience unite us." Aum Namaḥ Śivāya.

What Is the Relation of Sex to Marriage?

ŚLOKA 75

Wisdom demands that the intimacies of sexual intercourse be confined to marriage. Marriages that are free of prior relationships are the truest and strongest, seldom ending in separation or divorce. Aum Namaḥ Śivāya.

BHĀSHYA

When a virgin man and woman marry and share physical intimacy with each other, their union is very strong and their marriage stable. This is because their psychic nerve currents, or *nāḍīs,* grow together and they form a one body and a one mind. Conversely, if the man or woman have had intercourse before the marriage, the emotional-psychic closeness of the marriage will suffer, and this in proportion to the extent of promiscuity. For a marriage to succeed, sexual intercourse must be preserved for husband and wife. Each should grow to understand the other's needs and take care to neither deny intercourse to the married partner nor make excessive demands. A healthy, unrepressed attitude should be kept regarding sexual matters. Boys and girls must be taught to value and protect their chastity as a sacred treasure, and to save the special gift of intimacy for their spouse. They should be taught the importance of loyalty in marriage and to avoid even the thought of adultery. The *Vedas* intone, "Sweet be the glances we exchange, our faces showing true concord. Enshrine me in your heart and let one spirit dwell with us." Aum Namaḥ Śivāya.

Scriptures Speak on Man and Wife

O Divines, may the husband and wife who with one accord offer the elixer of dedication with pure heart and propitiate you with the milk of sweet devotional prayers, constantly associated—may they acquire appropriate food, may they be able to offer sacrifice, and may they never fail in strength and vigor. *Ṛig Veda*

May Prajāpati grant to us an issue, Aryaman keep us till death in holy marriage! Free from ill omens, enter the home of your husband. Bring blessing to both humans and cattle. *Ṛig Veda*

May the Provident One lead you, holding your hand! May the two Aśvins transport you on their chariot! Enter your house as that household's mistress. May authority in speech ever be yours! *Ṛig Veda*

O man and woman, having acquired knowledge from the learned, proclaim amongst the wise the fact of your intention of entering the married life. Attain to fame, observing the noble virtue of non-violence, and uplift your soul. Shun crookedness. Converse together happily. Living in a peaceful home, spoil not your life. Spoil not your progeny. In this world, pass your life happily, on this wide earth full of enjoyment! *Yajur Veda*

Love, children, happiness and wealth will come to answer your hopes. Devoted to your husband's needs, be girded for immortality! *Atharva Veda*

Not evil-eyed nor harmful to your husband, kind to dumb beasts, radiant, gentle-hearted, pleasing, beloved by the Gods, bring forth heroes. To menfolk and beasts alike bring blessing. *Ṛig Veda*

Divine Architect of the universe, well pleased, may you give us procreant vigor, whence a brave son—skilled in action, lover of divine powers and resolute like grinding stones—be born. *Ṛig Veda*

Unite, O Lord, this couple like a pair of lovebirds. May they surrounded by children be, living both long and happily. *Atharva Veda*

May the Lord of the clouds protect our stores, piled high in our homes! May the Lord of the clouds give us vitality in our homes, granting goods and riches! *Atharva Veda*

Let there be faithfulness to each other until death. This, in short, should be known as the highest duty of husband and wife. So let husband and wife ever strive, doing all their duties, that they may not, separated from each other, wander apart. *Manu Dharma Śāstras*

You are firm and I see you. Be firm with me, O flourishing one! Bṛihaspati has given you to me, so live with me a hundred years bearing children by me, your husband. *Pāraskara Gṛihya Sūtras*

A worthy wife is the blessing of a home, and good children are its precious adornment. *Tirukural*

There is no greater dignity than that of the man who declares, "I will never cease in laboring to advance my family." *Tirukural*

Whatever the work may be, a man should train himself to carry it out with perseverance, devotion and joy. By disciplining himself in this way he will acquire steadiness of mind, that is to say, the mind will become one-pointed. *Natchintanai*

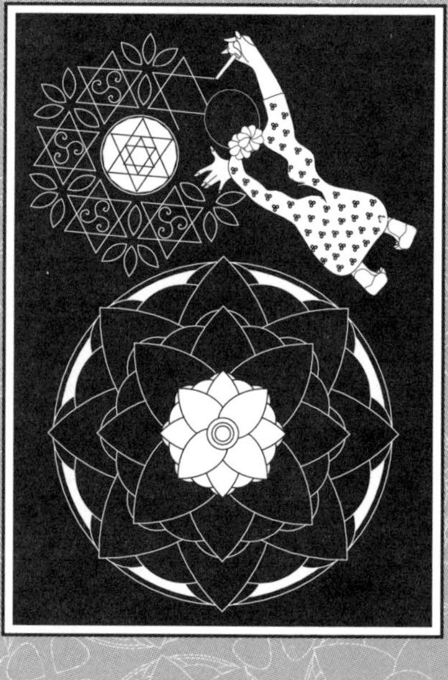

Vivāha Maṇḍala

विवाहमण्डल

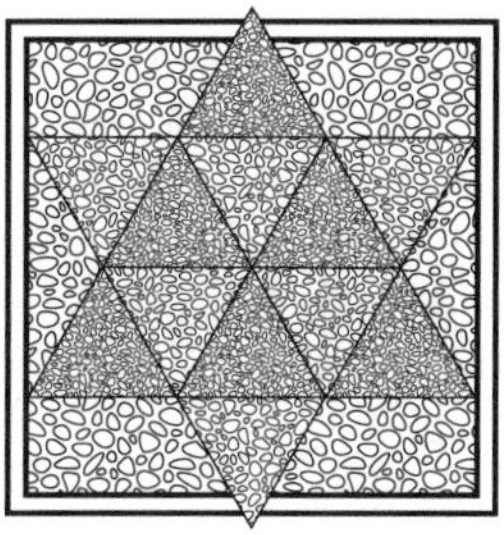

Marriage

Shaṭkoṇa, "six-pointed star," is two interlocking triangles; the upper stands for Śiva, *purusha* and fire, the lower for Śakti, *prakṛiti* and water. Their union gives birth to Sanatkumāra, whose sacred number is six. Aum.

What Is the Basis for a Happy Marriage?

ŚLOKA 76

A happy marriage is based first and foremost on a mature love, not a romantic ideal of love. It requires selflessness and constant attention. A successful marriage is one which both partners work at making successful. Aum.

BHĀSHYA

While not all marriages must be arranged, there is wisdom in arranged marriages, which have always been an important part of Hindu culture. Their success lies the families' judgment to base the union on pragmatic matters which will outlast the sweetest infatuation and endure through the years. The ideal age for women is from 18 to 25, men from 21 to 30. Stability is enhanced if the boy has completed his education, established earnings through a profession and is at least five years older than the girl. Mature love includes accepting obligations, duties and even difficulties. The couple should be prepared to work with their marriage, not expecting it to take care of itself. It is good for bride and groom to write out a covenant by hand, each pledging to fulfill certain duties and promises. They should approach the marriage as holy, advancing both partners spiritually. It is important to marry a spouse who is dependable, chaste and serious about raising children in the Hindu way, and then worship and pray together. The *Vedas* say, "Devoted to sacrifice, gathering wealth, they serve the Immortal and honor the Gods, united in mutual love." Aum Namaḥ Śivāya.

Must We Marry Within Our Religion?

ŚLOKA 77

Tradition requires that the wife adopt the religion and lifestyle of her husband. Thus, Hindu women wanting to continue their family culture and religion will, in wisdom, marry a spouse of the same sect and lineage. Aum.

BHĀSHYA

The mutual spiritual unfoldment of man and wife is a central purpose of marriage. When we marry outside our religion, we create disharmony and conflict for ourselves and our children. Such a marriage draws us away from religious involvement instead of deeper into its fulfillment. For marriage to serve its spiritual purpose to the highest, husband and wife should hold the same beliefs and share the same religious practices. Their harmony of minds will be reflected in the children. A man's choice of spouse is a simple decision, because his wife is bound to follow him. For a woman, it is a far more important decision, because her choice determines the future of her religious and social life. While his lifestyle will not change, her's will. Should a Hindu marry a non-Hindu, traditional wisdom dictates that the wife conform to her husband's heritage, and that the children be raised in his faith, with no conflicting beliefs or customs. The husband may be invited to convert to her faith before marriage. The *Vedas* pray, "United your resolve, united your hearts, may your spirits be one, that you may long together dwell in unity and concord!" Aum Namaḥ Śivāya.

How Are Hindu Marriages Arranged?

ŚLOKA 78

Marriage is a union not only of boy and girl, but of their families, too. Not leaving such crucial matters to chance, all family members participate in finding the most suitable spouse for the eligible son or daughter. Aum.

BHĀSHYA

In seeking a bride for a son, or a groom for a daughter, the goal is to find a mate compatible in age, physique, education, social status, religion, character and personality. Elders may first seek a partner among families they know and esteem for the kinship bonds the marriage would bring. Astrology is always consulted for compatibility. Of course, mutual attraction and full consent of the couple are crucial. Once a potential spouse is selected, informal inquiries are made by a relative or friend. If the response is encouraging, the father of the girl meets the father of the boy and presents a proposal. Next, the families gather at the girl's home to get acquainted and to allow the couple to meet and discuss their expectations. If all agree to the match, the boy's mother adorns the girl with a gold necklace, or gifts are exchanged between families, signifying a firm betrothal. Rejoicing begins with the engagement ceremony and culminates on the wedding day. The *Vedas* say, "Straight be the paths and thornless on which our friends will travel to present our suit! May Aryaman and Bhaga lead us together! May heaven grant us a stable marriage!" Aum Namaḥ Śivāya.

What Is the Hindu Family Structure?

ŚLOKA 79

The main Hindu social unit is the joint family, usually consisting of several generations living together under the guidance of the father and mother. Each joint family is part of a greater body called the extended family. Aum.

BHĀSHYA

A joint family lives under one roof. It includes a father and mother, their sons, grandsons and great-grandsons and all their spouses, as well as all daughters, granddaughters and great-granddaughters until they are married. The head of the family is the father, assisted by his wife, or in his absence the eldest son, encouraged by his mother, and in his absence, the next eldest brother. The family head delegates responsibilities to members according to their abilities. The mother oversees household activities, nurturance, hospitality and gift-giving. Religious observances are the eldest son's responsibility. The joint family is founded on selfless sharing, community ownership and the fact that each member's voice and opinion is important. The extended family includes one or more joint families, community elders, married daughters and their kindred, close friends and business associates. It is headed by the family *guru*, priests and *paṇḍitas*. The *Vedas* offer blessings: "Dwell in this home; never be parted! Enjoy the full duration of your days, with sons and grandsons playing to the end, rejoicing in your home to your heart's content." Aum Namaḥ Śivāya.

How Are Marital Problems Reconciled?

ŚLOKA 80

When problems arise in marriage, Hindus study the scriptures and seek advice of family, elders and spiritual leaders. A good marriage requires that the husband be masculine and the wife feminine. Aum Namaḥ Śivāya.

BHĀSHYA

Success in marriage depends on learning to discuss problems with each other freely and constructively. Criticizing one another, even mentally, must be strictly avoided, for that erodes a marriage most quickly. Under no circumstance should a husband hit or abuse his wife, nor should a wife dominate or torment her husband. It is important to not be jealous or overly protective, but to have trust in one another and live up to that trust. Problems should be resolved daily before sleep. If inharmony persists, advice of elders should be sought. A reading and reaffirmation of original marriage covenants and an astrological assessment may provide a common point of reference and a foundation for mutual sacrifice and understanding. The husband who does not take the lead is not fulfilling his duty. The wife who takes an aggressive lead in the marriage makes her husband weak. She must be shy to make him bold. Couples keep a healthy attitude toward sex, never offering it as reward or withholding it as punishment. The *Vedas* say, "Bẹ courteous, planning and working in harness together. Approach, conversing pleasantly, like-minded, united." Aum Namaḥ Śivāya.

Scriptures Speak on Marriage

Of one mind and one purpose I make you, following one leader. Be like the Gods, ever deathless! Never stop loving. *Atharva Veda*

Have your eating and drinking in common. I bind you together. Assemble for worship of the Lord, like spokes around a hub. *Atharva Veda*

Thus steadfast and firm as a horse, we shall offer our praises, Omniscient Lord, forever. Replete with food and with riches, being close to you always, may we never suffer reverses! *Atharva Veda*

May Mitra, Varuṇa and Aryaman grant us freedom and space enough for us and for our children! May we find pleasant pathways, good to travel! Preserve us evermore, O Gods, with blessings! *Ṛig Veda*

Let this man be again bedewed with this presented sacrifice, and comfort with the sap of life the bride whom they have brought to him. *Atharva Veda*

Act like a queen to your husband's father; to your husband's mother likewise, and his sister. To all your husband's brothers be queen. *Ṛig Veda*

The Lord brings us riches, food in daily abundance, renown and hero sons to gladden our hearts. So, like a father to his sons, be to us easy of entreaty. Stay with us, O Lord, for our joy. *Ṛig Veda*

When family life possesses love and virtue, that is both its essence and fruition. *Tirukural*

May our minds move in accord. May our thinking be in harmony—common the purpose and common the desire. May our prayers and worship be alike, and may our devotional offerings be one and the same. *Ṛig Veda*

May this our Lord of cloudy sky, bedewed with liquid drops preserve unequalled riches in our homes. Lord of the cloudy sky, bestow vigor and strength on our abodes. Let wealth and treasure come to us. *Atharva Veda*

The gift of a daughter, after decking her with costly garments and honoring her by presents of jewels, to a man learned in the *Veda* and of good conduct whom the father himself invites, is called the Brāhma rite. *Manu Dharma Śāstras*

Endowed with the qualities of beauty and goodness, possessing wealth and fame, obtaining as many enjoyments as they desire and being most righteous, they will live a hundred years. *Manu Dharma Śāstras*

Women must be honored and adorned by their fathers, brothers, husbands and brothers-in-law, who desire their own welfare. Where women are honored, there the Gods are pleased. But where they are not honored, no sacred rite yields rewards. *Manu Dharma Śāstras*

I hold your heart in serving fellowship, your mind follows my mind. In my word you rejoice with all your heart. You are joined to me by the Lord of all creatures. *Pāraskara Gṛihya Sūtras*

The foremost duty of the householder is to duly serve these five: ancestors, God, guests, kindred and himself. *Tirukural*

Apatya Maṇḍala

अपत्यमण्डल

Children

Mūshika is Lord Gaṇeśa's mount, the mouse, traditionally associated with abundance in family life. Under cover of darkness, seldom visible yet always at work, Mūshika is like God's unseen grace in our lives. Aum.

What Is the Fulfillment of a Marriage?

ŚLOKA 81

Children are the greatest source of happiness in marriage. Householder life is made rich and complete when sons and daughters are born, at which time the marriage becomes a family and a new generation begins. Aum.

BHĀSHYA

The total fulfillment of the *gṛihastha dharma* is children. Marriage remains incomplete until the first child is born or adopted. The birth of the first child cements the family together. At the birth itself, the community of guardian *devas* of the husband, wife and child are eminently present. Their collective vibration showers blessings upon the home, making of it a full place, a warm place. It is the duty of the husband and wife to become father and mother. This process begins prior to conception with prayer, meditation and a conscious desire to bring a high soul into human birth and continues with providing the best possible conditions for its upbringing. Raising several children rewards the parents and their offspring as well. Large families are more cohesive, more stable, and are encouraged within the limits of the family's ability to care for them. Parents, along with all members of the extended family, are responsible to nurture the future generation through childhood into puberty and adulthood. The *Vedas* exclaim, "Blessed with sons and daughters, may they enjoy their full extent of life, decked with ornaments of gold." Aum Namaḥ Śivāya.

What Are the Main Duties of Parents?

ŚLOKA 82

The fundamental duty of parents is to provide food, shelter and clothing and to keep their children safe and healthy. The secondary duty is to bestow education, including instruction in morality and religious life. Aum.

BHĀSHYA

Assuring the health and well-being of their offspring is the most essential duty of parents to their children, never to be neglected. Beyond this, parents should provide a good example to their children, being certain that they are taught the Hindu religious heritage and culture along with good values, ethics, strength of character and discipline. Sons and daughters should worship regularly at *pūjā* with the parents, and the Hindu sacraments should all be provided. Education in all matters is the duty of the parents, including teaching them frankly about sex, its sacredness and the necessity to remain chaste until marriage. Children must learn to respect and observe civil law and to honor and obey their elders. Parents must love their children dearly, and teach them to love. The best way to teach is by example: by their own life, parents teach their children how to live. The *Vedas* declare, "Of one heart and mind I make you, devoid of hate. Love one another as a cow loves the calf she has borne. Let the son be courteous to his father, of one mind with his mother. Let the wife speak words that are gentle and sweet to her husband." Aum Namaḥ Śivāya.

How Strictly Must Children Be Guided?

ŚLOKA 83

Parents should be most diligent in guiding their children toward virtue, protecting them from all bad company and influences, being strict yet never harsh or mean, allowing them prudent freedom in which to grow. Aum.

BHĀSHYA

Children are constantly learning, and that learning must be guided carefully by the parents. The young's education, recreation and companions must be supervised. They should be taught the scriptures of their lineage. Their religious education is almost always in the hands of the parents. They should be disciplined to study hard, and challenged to excel and fulfill their natural talents. They should be praised and rewarded for their accomplishments. Children need and seek guidance, and only the parents can truly provide it. In general, it is the mother who provides love and encouragement, while the father corrects and disciplines. A child's faults if not corrected will be carried into adult life. Still, care should be taken to not be overly restrictive either. Children should never be struck, beaten, abused or ruled through a sense of fear. Children, be they young or old, have a *karma* and a *dharma* of their own. Their parents have a debt to pay them; and they have a debt to return later in life. The *Vedas* plead, "O friend of men, protect my children. O adorable one, protect my cattle. O sword of flame, protect my nourishment." Aum Namaḥ Śivāya.

Should All Youths Be Urged to Marry?

ŚLOKA 84

All but the rare few inclined to monastic life should be encouraged to marry and schooled in the skills they will need to fulfill *dharma.* Young boys destined to be monastics should be raised as their *satguru's* progeny. Aum.

BHĀSHYA

Traditionally, boys with monastic tendencies are encouraged and provided special training under their *satguru's* direction. It is considered a great blessing for the family to have a son become a monastic and later a *swāmī.* Generally, children should be taught to follow and prepare themselves for the householder path. Most boys will choose married life, and should be schooled in professional, technical skills. Girls are taught the refinements of household culture. Both girls and boys should be trained in the sacred Vedic arts and sciences, including the sixty-four crafts and social skills, called *kalās.* Boys benefit greatly when taught the profession of their father from a very young age. The mother is the role model for her daughters, whom she raises as the mothers of future families. Sons and daughters who are gay may not benefit from marriage, and should be taught to remain loyal in relationships and be prepared to cope with community challenges. The *Vedas* pray, "May you, O love divine, flow for the acquisition of food of wisdom and for the prosperity of the enlightened person who praises you; may you grant him excellent progeny." Aum Namaḥ Śivāya.

How Is Family Harmony Maintained?

ŚLOKA 85

In the Hindu family, mutual respect, love and understanding are the bedrock of harmony. By not fighting, arguing or criticizing, members cultivate a spiritual environment in which all may progress. Aum Namaḥ Śivāya.

BHĀSHYA

For a harmonious joint family, it is vital to make the home strong, the center of activity and creativity, kept beautiful and clean, a sanctuary for each member. While striving to increase wealth, the wise families live within their means, content with what they have. Activities are planned to bring the family close through shared experiences. A gentle but firm hierarchy of respect for elders is maintained throughout the family. In general, the younger, in humility, defers to the elder, allowing him or her the last word. The elder is equally obliged to not misuse authority. Older children are responsible for the safety and care of their younger brothers and sisters. Disputes among children are settled by their mother, but not kept a secret from the father. Actual discipline in the case of misconduct is carried out by the father. When disputes arise in the extended family, responsibility for restoring harmony falls first to the men. However, any concerned member can take the lead if necessary. The *Vedas* say of *gṛihastha* life, "I will utter a prayer for such concord among family members as binds together the Gods, among whom is no hatred." Aum Namaḥ Śivāya.

Scriptures Speak on Children

O Lord of the home, best finder of riches for our children are you. Grant to us splendor and strength, O Master of our home. *Yajur Veda*

I am inclined to adore you, the two sages, the ministrants at the places of work and worship of men, from whom all the prosperity is derived. May you raise our offspring to a higher stature and help us to acquire precious treasures preserved amongst nature's bounties, when the worship is being conducted. *Ṛig Veda*

I know not how to stretch the threads or weave or discern the pattern of those who weave in the contest. Whose son will be the one to speak so well as to surpass, advancing from below, his father? *Ṛig Veda*

Keen of mind and keen of sight, free from sickness, free from sin, rich in children, may we see you rise as a friend, O Sun, till a long life's end! *Ṛig Veda*

Never may brother hate brother or sister hurt sister. United in heart and in purpose, commune sweetly together. *Atharva Veda*

To you, O Lord, the Priest, beloved of all men, we bring our praise with reverence. Keep watch over our children and ourselves, we pray. Guard both our lives and our cattle. *Atharva Veda*

Let there be no neglect of the duties to the Gods and the fathers. Be one to whom the mother is a God. Be one to whom the father is a God. Be one to whom the teacher is a God. Be one to whom the guest is a God. *Yajur Veda*

If he should desire, "Let me be born here again," in whatever family he directs his attention, either the family of a *brāhmin* or the family of a king, into that he will be born. *Sāma Veda*

By honoring his mother he gains this world, by honoring his father the middle sphere; but by obedience to his teacher, the world of Brahman. All duties have been fulfilled by him who honors those three. *Manu Dharma Śāstras*

Among those who strive for liberation, the foremost are they who live the blessed state of family life as it should be lived. *Tirukural*

"Sweet are the sounds of the flute and the lute," say those who have not heard the prattle of their own children. *Tirukural*

The father's duty to his son is to make him worthy of precedence in the assembly of the wise. The son's duty to his father is to make the world ask, "By what great austerities did he merit such a son?" *Tirukural*

Of all a man's blessings we know of none greater than the begetting of children endowed with wisdom. What pleasure it is to human beings everywhere when their children possess knowledge surpassing their own! *Tirukural*

Study well. Be obedient. Hear and follow the advice of your father, mother, brothers and sisters, and your aunt and uncle. You alone always set a good example in obedience. *Natchintanai*

Do not neglect your duty, my son. Be not troubled by sorrow or care. Do not stray from the path of *dharma*, my son. Awake and know yourself! *Natchintanai*

Maṅgala Kriyā Upanishad

मङ्गलक्रिया उपनिषद्

Sacred Culture

Bodhi Tantra Maṇḍala

बोधितन्त्रमण्डल

Ways of Wisdom

Konrai, Golden Shower, blossoms are the flowering symbol of Śiva's honeyed grace in our life. Associated with His shrines and temples throughout India, the *Cassia fistula* is lauded in numberless *Tirumurai* hymns. Aum.

How Do We Overcome Life's Obstacles?

ŚLOKA 86

Just as a small leaf can obscure the sun when held before our eyes, so can the past cloud the present and hide our divinity. With Vedic methods, or *tantras,* we remove impediments to reveal the ever-present inner light. Aum.

BHĀSHYA

An ancient *Upanishad* defines twenty obstacles, *upasarga,* to spiritual progress: hunger, thirst, laziness, passion, lust, fear, shame, anxiety, excitement, adversity, sorrow, despair, anger, arrogance, delusion, greed, stinginess, ambitiousness, death and birth. Another obstacle is the intellect which, unguided by intuition, merely juggles memory and reason as a way of life. The experience of these impediments creates reactions that combine with the sum of all past impressions, *saṁskāras,* both positive and negative. Residing in the subconscious mind, these are the source of subliminal traits or tendencies, called *vāsanās,* which shape our attitudes and motivations. The troublesome *vāsanās* clouding the mind must be reconciled and released. There are beneficial *tantras* by which absolution can be attained for unhindered living, including *āyurveda, jyotisha,* daily *sādhana,* temple worship, selfless giving, the creative arts and the several *yogas.* The *Vedas* explain, "Even as a mirror covered with dust shines brightly when cleaned, so the embodied soul, seeing the truth of *ātman,* realizes oneness, attains the goal of life and becomes free from sorrow." Aum Namaḥ Śivāya.

What Are the Hindu's Daily Yoga Practices?

ŚLOKA 87

Devout Hindus perform daily vigil, called *saṇdhyā upāsanā,* usually before dawn. This sacred period of *pūjā, japa,* chanting, singing, *haṭha yoga,* meditation and scriptural study is the foundation of personal life. Aum.

BHĀSHYA

Each day hundreds of millions of Hindus awaken for the last fifth of the night, bathe, don fresh clothing, apply sectarian marks, called *tilaka,* and sit in a clean, quiet place for religious disciplines. Facing east or north, the devotional *pūjā* rites of *bhakti yoga* are performed. *Haṭha yoga,* hymn singing, *japa* and chanting are often included. Then follows scriptural study and meditation, listening to the sound current and contemplating the moonlike inner light during *brāhma muhūrta,* the auspicious hour-and-a-half period before dawn. The duly initiated practice advanced *yogas,* such as those revealed in *Merging with Śiva*—but only as directed by their *guru,* knowing that unless firmly harnessed, the *kuṇḍalinī* can manifest uncontrollable desires. Through the day, *karma yoga,* selfless religious service, is performed at every opportunity. Besides these *yogas* of doing, Hindus practice the central *yoga* of being—living a joyful, positive, harmonious life. The *Vedas* declare, "The mind, indeed, is this fleeting world. Therefore, it should be purified with great effort. One becomes like that which is in one's mind—this is the everlasting secret." Aum Namaḥ Śivāya.

How Are Āyurveda and Jyotisha Used?

ŚLOKA 88

Āyurveda is the Hindu science of life, a complete, holistic medical system. *Jyotisha,* or Vedic astrology, is the knowledge of right timing and future potentialities. Both are vital tools for happy, productive living. Aum.

BHĀSHYA

Āyurveda, rooted in the *Atharva Upaveda,* deals with both the prevention and cure of disease. Its eight medical arts, with their *mantras, tantras* and *yogas,* are based on spiritual well-being and encompass every human need, physical, mental and emotional. *Āyurveda* teaches that the true healing powers reside in the mind at the quantum level. Wellness depends on the correct balance of three bodily humors, called *doshas,* maintained by a nutritious vegetarian diet, *dharmic* living and natural healing remedies. The kindred science of Vedic astrology, revealed in the *Jyotisha Vedāṅga,* likewise is vital to every Hindu's life. It propounds a dynamic cosmos of which we are an integral part, and charts the complex influence on us of important stars and planets, according to our birth chart. Knowing that the stars enliven positive and negative *karmas* we have brought into this life, in wisdom we choose an auspicious time, *śubha muhūrta,* for every important event. An orthodox Hindu family is not complete without its *jyotisha śāstrī* or *āyurveda vaidya.* The *Vedas* beseech, "Peaceful for us be the planets and the moon, peaceful the sun and *rāhu.*" Aum Namaḥ Śivāya.

How Do Hindus Regard Art and Culture?

ŚLOKA 89

Hindus of every sect cherish art and culture as sacred. Music, art, drama and the dance are expressions of spiritual experience established in *śāstras* by God-inspired *ṛishis* as an integral flowering of temple worship. Aum.

BHĀSHYA

Art and culture, from the Hindu perspective, are the sublime fruits of a profound civilization. Every Hindu strives to perfect an art or craft to manifest creative benefits for family and community. The home is a spiritual extension of the temple. Graced with the sounds of Indian sacred music, it is adorned with religious pictures, symbols and icons. The shrine is the most lavish room. Children are raised to appreciate Hindu art, music and culture, carefully trained in the sixty-four *kalās* and protected from alien influences. Human relationships are kept harmonious and uplifting through the attitudes, customs and refinements of Asian protocol, as revealed in *Living with Śiva.* Hindu attire is elegantly modest. Sectarian marks, called *tilaka,* are worn on the brow as emblems of sectarian identity. *Mantra* and prayer sanctify even simple daily acts—awakening, bathing, greetings, meals, meetings, outings, daily tasks and sleep. Annual festivals and pilgrimage offer a complete departure from worldly concerns. The *Vedas* proclaim, "Let the drum sound forth and let the lute resound, let the strings vibrate the exalted prayer to God." Aum Namaḥ Śivāya.

What Is the Hindu Outlook on Giving?

ŚLOKA 90

Generous, selfless giving is among *dharma's* central fulfillments. Hospitality, charity and support of God's work on earth arises from the belief that the underlying purpose of life is spiritual, not material. Aum Namaḥ Śivāya.

BHĀSHYA

Nowhere is giving better unfolded than in the ancient *Tirukural,* which says, "Of all duties, benevolence is unequaled in this world, and even in celestial realms. It is to meet the needs of the deserving that the worthy labor arduously to acquire wealth." Even the poorest Hindu practices charity according to his means. In this unselfish tradition, guests are treated as God. Friends, acquaintances, even strangers, are humbled by the overwhelming hospitality received. We share with the less fortunate. We care for the aged. We honor *swāmīs* with gifts of food, money and clothes. We encourage the spirit of helping and giving, called *dāna,* within the family, between families and their monastic and priestly communities. Many devout Hindus take the *daśama bhāga vrata,* a vow to pay ten percent of their income each month to an institution of their choice to perpetuate Sanātana Dharma. This centuries-old tithing practice is called *daśamāṁśa.* The *Vedas* wisely warn, "The powerful man should give to one in straits; let him consider the road that lies ahead! Riches revolve just like a chariot's wheels, coming to one man now, then to another." Aum Namaḥ Śivāya.

Scriptures Speak on Wisdom's Ways

May the Goddess of culture, associated with the models of other cultures, may the Goddess of wisdom in company with men, ordinary and intellectual, may the fire divine, and may the Goddess of divine speech with masters of language come to bless us and enshrine our hearts. *Ṛig Veda*

In vain the foolish man accumulates food. I tell you, truly, it will be his downfall! He gathers to himself neither friend nor comrade. Alone he eats; alone he sits in sin. The ploughshare cleaving the soil helps satisfy hunger. The traveler, using his legs, achieves his goal. The priest who speaks surpasses the one who is silent. The friend who gives is better than the miser. *Ṛig Veda*

Śilpani, works of art of man, are an imitation of divine forms. By employing their rhythms, a metrical reconstitution is effected of the limited human personality. *Ṛig Veda*

There are five great sacrifices, namely, the great ritual services: the sacrifice to all beings, sacrifice to men, sacrifice to the ancestors, sacrifice to the Gods, sacrifice to Brahman. *Yajur Veda*

Find a quiet retreat for the practice of *yoga*, sheltered from the wind, level and clean, free from rubbish, smoldering fires and ugliness, and where the sound of waters and the beauty of the place help thought and contemplation. *Yajur Veda*

Lightness, healthiness, steadiness, clearness of complexion, pleasantness of voice, sweetness of odor, and slight excretions—these, they say, are the first results of the progress of *yoga.* *Yajur Veda*

Vāsanā is divided into two, the pure and the impure. If thou art led by the pure *vāsanās*, thou shalt thereby soon reach by degrees My Seat. But should the old, impure *vāsanās* land thee in danger, they should be overcome through efforts. ***Yajur Veda***

Works of sacrifice, gift and self-harmony should not be abandoned, but should indeed be performed, for these are works of purification. But even these works, Arjuna, should be done in the freedom of a pure offering, and without expectation of a reward. This is My final word. ***Bhagavad Gītā***

Easy for all to offer in worship a green leaf to the Lord. Easy for all to give a mouthful to the cow. Easy for all to give a handful when sitting down to eat. Easy for all to speak pleasant words to others. ***Tirumantiram***

So let my star be the sun or the moon, Mars or Mercury or Jupiter; let it be Venus, or Saturn or the two snakes!
All the planets and stars are good stars for us, all bring good luck to Śiva's devotees! ***Tirumurai***

Plough with truth. Plant the seed of desire for knowledge. Weed out falsehood. Irrigate the mind with the water of patience. Supervise your work by introspection and self-analysis. Build the fence of *yama* and *niyama*, or right conduct and right rules. You will soon attain Śivānanda, or eternal bliss of Śiva. ***Tirumurai***

Moderately, moderately eat for your sustenance.
Take pains at all times to assimilate knowledge. In your youth, learn the arts and the sciences. To the mean and the miserly be not attached. Foster, foster the friendship of well-nurtured people. Live in happiness, saying you are lacking in nothing. Look after, look after your brothers and kinfolk. Inwardly and outwardly let your life be the same. ***Natchintanai***

Saṁskāra Maṇḍala

संस्कारमण्डल

Sacraments

Homakuṇḍa, the fire altar, is the symbol of ancient Vedic rites. It is through the fire element, denoting divine consciousness, that we make offerings to the Gods. Hindu sacraments are solemnized before the *homa* fire. Aum.

What Are Hinduism's Rites of Passage?

ŚLOKA 91

Hindus celebrate life's crucial junctures by holy sacraments, or rites of passage, called *saṁskāras,* which impress the subconscious mind, inspire family and community sharing and invoke the Gods' blessings. Aum.

BHĀSHYA

For the Hindu, life is a sacred journey in which each milestone, marking major biological and emotional stages, is consecrated through sacred ceremony. Family and friends draw near, lending support, advice and encouragement. Through Vedic rites and *mantras,* family members or priests invoke the Gods for blessings and protection during important turning points, praying for the individual's spiritual and social development. There are many sacraments, from the rite of conception to the funeral ceremony. Each one, properly observed, empowers spiritual life and preserves Hindu culture, as the soul consciously accepts each succeeding discovery and duty in the order of God's creation. The essential *saṁskāras* are the rites of conception, the three-month blessing, hair-parting, birth, name-giving, head-shaving, first feeding, ear-piercing, first learning, puberty, marriage, elders' vows and last rites. The holy *Vedas* proclaim, "From Him come hymns, songs and sacrificial formulas, initiations, sacrifices, rites and all offerings. From Him come the year, the sacrificer and the worlds in which the moon shines forth, and the sun." Aum Namaḥ Śivāya.

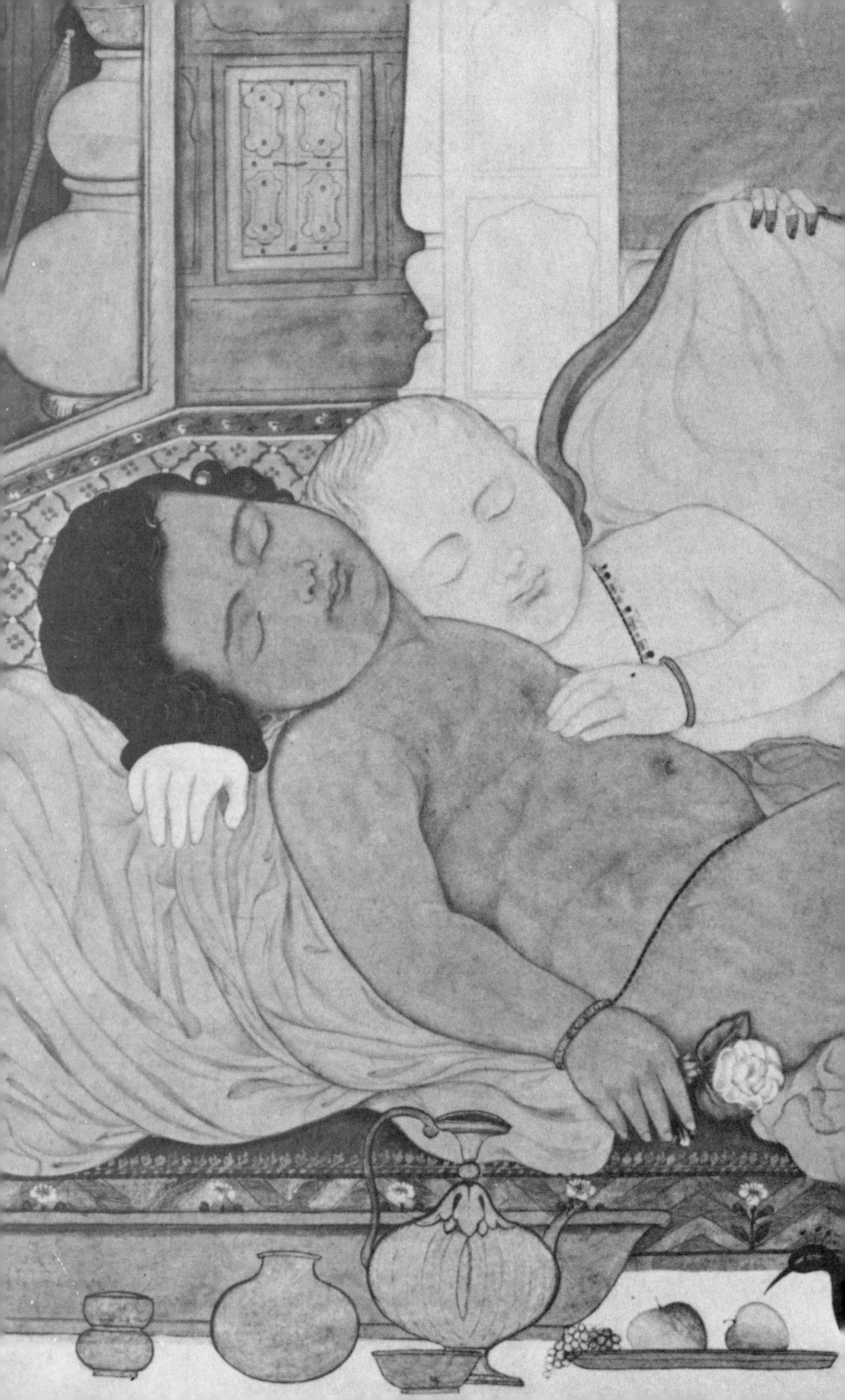

What Are the Sacraments of Childhood?

ŚLOKA 92

The essential religious sacraments of childhood are the *nāmakaraṇa,* name-giving; *chūḍākaraṇa,* head-shaving; *annaprāśana,* first solid food; *karṇavedha,* ear-piercing; and *vidyārambha,* commencement of formal study. Aum.

BHĀSHYA

Saṁskāras impress upon a child its holiness and innate possibilities for spiritual advancement. The *nāmakaraṇa* occurs in the temple or home, eleven to forty-one days after birth. The baby's name, astrologically chosen, is whispered in the right ear by the father, marking the formal entry into Hinduism. The head-shaving, *chūḍākaraṇa,* is performed at the temple between the thirty-first day and the fourth year. The *annaprāśana* celebrates the child's first solid food, when sweet rice is fed to the baby by the father or the family *guru.* Ear-piercing, *karṇavedha,* held for both girls and boys during the first, third or fifth year, endows the spirit of health and wealth. Girls are adorned with gold earrings, bangles and anklets; boys with two earrings and other gold jewelry. The *vidyārambha* begins formal education, when children write their first letter in a tray of rice. The *upanayana* begins, and the *samāvartana* ends, a youth's religious study. The *Vedas* beseech, "I bend to our cause at this solemn moment, O Gods, your divine and holy attention. May a thousand streams gush forth from this offering, like milk from a bountiful, pasture-fed cow." Aum Namaḥ Śivāya.

What Are the Sacraments of Adulthood?

ŚLOKA 93

The most important sacrament of adulthood is the *vivāha saṁskāra,* or marriage rite, preceded by a pledge of betrothal. A boy's or girl's coming of age is also consecrated through special ceremony in the home. Aum.

BHĀSHYA

As puberty dawns, the *ṛitu kāla* home-ceremony acknowledges a girl's first menses, and the *keśānta kāla* celebrates a boy's first beard-shaving. New clothing and jewelry fit for royalty are presented to and worn by the youth, who is joyously welcomed into the young adult community. Girls receive their first *sārī,* boys their first razor. Chastity is vowed until marriage. The next sacrament is the betrothal ceremony, called *niśchitārtha* or *vāgdāna,* in which a man and woman are declared formally engaged by their parents with the exchange of jewelry and other gifts. Based on this commitment, they and their families begin planning a shared future. In the marriage sacrament, or *vivāha,* seven steps before God and Gods and tying the wedding pendant consecrate the union of husband and wife. This sacrament is performed before the *homa* fire in a wedding hall or temple and is occasioned by elaborate celebration. The *Gṛihya Sūtras* pronounce, "One step for strength, two steps for vitality, three steps for prosperity, four steps for happiness, five steps for cattle, six steps for seasons, seven steps for friendship. To me be devoted." Aum Namaḥ Śivāya.

What Are the Child-Bearing Sacraments?

ŚLOKA 94

The essential child-bearing *saṁskāras* are the *garbhādhāna,* rite of conception; the *punsavana,* third-month blessing; the *sīmantonnaya,* hair-parting ceremony; and the *jātakarma,* welcoming the new-born child. Aum.

BHĀSHYA

Conception, pregnancy's crucial stages and birth itself are all sanctified through sacred ceremonies performed privately by the husband. In the rite of conception, *garbhādhāna,* physical union is consecrated through prayer, *mantra* and invocation with the conscious purpose of bringing a high soul into physical birth. At the first stirring of life in the womb, in the rite called *punsavana,* special prayers are intoned for the protection and safe development of child and mother. Between the fourth and seventh months, in the *sīmantonnaya,* or hair-parting sacrament, the husband lovingly combs his wife's hair, whispers sweet words praising her beauty and offers gifts of jewelry to express his affection and support. Through the *jātakarma saṁskāra,* the father welcomes the newborn child into the world, feeding it a taste of honey and clarified butter and praying for its long life, intelligence and well-being. The *Vedas* proclaim, "That in which the prayers, the songs and formulas are fixed firm like spokes in the hub of a cartwheel, in which are interwoven the hearts of all beings—may that spirit be graciously disposed toward me!" Aum Namaḥ Śivāya.

Are There Rites for the Wisdom Years?

ŚLOKA 95

Entrance into the elder advisor stage at age 48, the marriage renewal at age 60, and the dawn of renunciation at 72 may be signified by ceremony. Funeral rites, *antyeshṭi,* solemnize the transition called death. Aum Namaḥ Śivāya.

BHĀSHYA

Hindu society values and protects its senior members, honoring their experience and heeding their wise advice. Age 48 marks the entrance into the *vānaprastha āśrama,* celebrated in some communities by special ceremony. At age 60, husband and wife reaffirm marriage vows in a sacred ablution ceremony called *shashṭyābda pūrti.* Age 72 marks the advent of withdrawal from society, the *sannyāsa āśrama,* sometimes ritually acknowledged but never confused with *sannyāsa dīkshā.* The *antyeshṭi,* or funeral ceremony, is a home sacrament performed by the family, assisted by a priest. Rites include guiding the individual's transition into the higher planes, preparing the body, cremation, bone-gathering, dispersal of ashes, home purification and commemorative ceremonies, *śrāddha,* one week, one month and one year from the day of death, and sometimes longer, according to local custom. Through the *antyeshṭi,* the soul is released to the holy feet of Śiva. The *Vedas* counsel, "Attain your prime; then welcome old age, striving by turns in the contest of life. May the Ordainer, maker of good things, be pleased to grant you length of days." Aum Namaḥ Śivāya.

Scriptures Speak on Sacraments

Life universal shall guard and surround you. May Pūshan protect and precede you on the way! May Savitṛi, the God, to that place lead you where go and dwell the doers of good deeds! *Ṛig Veda*

As days follow days in orderly succession, as seasons faithfully succeed one another, so shape the lives of these, O Supporter, that the younger may not forsake his elder. *Ṛig Veda*

I take thy hand in mine for happy fortune that thou may reach old age with me, thy husband. "This woman, strewing grains, prays thus, 'May I bring bliss to my relations. May my husband live long. *Svāhā!*' " *Ṛig Veda & Śāṅkhāyana Gṛihya Sūtras*

After completing the life of a student, let a man become a householder. After completing the life of a householder, let him become a forest dweller, let him renounce all things. Or he may renounce all things directly from the student state or from the householder's state, as well as from that of the forest dweller. *Yajur Veda*

Having reached the last order of life, one should sit in a solitary place in a relaxed posture, with pure heart, with head, neck and body straight, controlling all the sense organs, having bowed with devotion to the master. *Atharva Veda*

That the father and mother give birth to him from mutual desire, so that he is born from the womb, let this be known as his physical birth. But that birth which is given, according to the ordinance, through the Sāvitrī, by the preceptor who has mastered the *Vedas*, that is the true birth, the unaging and immortal. *Manu Dharma Śāstras*

With holy rites prescribed by the *Veda* must the ceremony on conception and other sacraments be performed for twice-born men, which sanctify the body and purify in this life and after death. *Manu Dharma Śāstras*

Let the father perform or cause to be performed the *nāmadheya*, the rite of naming the child, on the tenth or twelfth day after birth, or on a lucky lunar day, in a lucky *muhūrta* under an auspicious constellation. *Manu Dharma Śāstras*

The names of women should be easy to pronounce, not imply anything dreadful, possess a plain meaning, be pleasing and auspicious, end in long vowels and contain a word of benediction. *Manu Dharma Śāstras*

Having studied the *Vedas* in accordance with the rule, having begat sons according to the sacred law and having offered sacrifices according to his ability, he may direct his mind to final liberation. *Manu Dharma Śāstras*

The boy grows to youth and youth as surely to old age decays. But time's changes teach them not that nothing abides. He pervades this earth and the space beyond. I long for His feet and desire there to remain. *Tirumantiram*

When the son is one year old, the *chūḍākaraṇa*, the tonsure of his head, should be performed, or before the lapse of the third year. When he is sixteen years old, the *keśānta,* the shaving of his beard, is to be done, or according as it is considered auspicious by all. *Pāraskara Gṛihya Sūtras*

Knowingly or even unknowingly, intentionally or even unintentionally, a mortal, having gone to death in the Gaṅgā, obtains heaven and *moksha.* *Padma Purāṇa*

Utsava Maṇḍala

उत्सवमण्डल

Festivals

Ghaṇṭa is the bell used in ritual *pūjā*, which engages all senses, including hearing. Its ringing summons the Gods, stimulates the inner ear and reminds us that, like sound, the world may be perceived but not possessed. Aum.

What Are the Festival Days of Śaivism?

ŚLOKA 96

Festivals are special times of communion with God and Gods, of family and community sharing and *sādhana.* Śaivites observe numerous festivals in the temple and the home, and special holy days each week and month. Aum.

BHĀSHYA

Monday is the Hindu holy day in the North of India, and Friday in the South, set aside each week for attending the temple, cleaning and decorating the home shrine, devout prayer, *japa* and scriptural study. These are not days of rest, for we carry on our usual work. Among the major Deity festivals are Mahāśivarātri, Vaikāsi Viśākham, Gaṇeśa Chaturthī, Skanda Shashṭhī, Kṛittikā Dīpa, Vināyaka Vratam, Ārdrā Darśana and Tai Pusam. Temples also hold a ten-day annual festival called Brahmotsava, often on the Uttarāphalgunī *nakshatra* in March-April, as well as honor the anniversary day of their founding. Festivals are auspicious and sacred days of family and community togetherness, and of *sādhana,* fasting, meditation, worship and retreat from worldly concerns. Śaivites offer special prayers to Śiva, Gaṇeśa and Kārttikeya on propitious days each month according to the Hindu sacred calendar. The *Vedas* proclaim, "Behold now a man who unwinds and sets the thread, a man who unwinds it right up to the vault of heaven. Here are the pegs; they are fastened to the place of worship. The *Sāma Veda* hymns are used for weaving shuttles." Aum Namaḥ Śivāya.

What Are the Primary Festivals to Śiva?

ŚLOKA 97

Mahāśivarātri, Śiva's great night, venerates Paraśiva. Kṛittikā Dīpa celebrates the infinite light of Parāśakti. Ārdrā Darśana invokes the blessings of Parameśvara—Lord Śiva Naṭarāja in His blissful Cosmic Dance. Aum.

BHĀSHYA

Mahāśivarātri is the night before the new-moon day in February-March. We observe it both as a discipline and a festivity, keeping a strict fast and all-night vigil, meditating, intoning Śiva's 1,008 names, singing His praise, chanting Śrī Rudram, bathing the Śivaliṅga and being near the *vairāgīs* as they strive to realize Paraśiva. On Kṛittikā Dīpa, the Kṛittikā *nakshatra* in November-December, we honor—with oil lamps everywhere, village bonfires and special temple *ārati*—God Śiva as an infinite pillar of light. This is an important festival in Murugan temples. On Ārdrā Darśana, during the Ārdrā *nakshatra* of December-January, Lord Naṭarāja receives elaborate *abhisheka* and is beseeched for *yogic* union, prosperity and matrimonial success. He is again lavishly invoked on the Uttarāphalgunī *nakshatra* in June-July and on four other days each year. Special monthly days for Śiva worship are the two 13th *tithis*, called *pradosha*. The *Vedas* proclaim, "The Lord, God, all-pervading and omnipresent, dwells in the heart of all beings. Full of grace, He ultimately gives liberation to all creatures by turning their faces toward Himself." Aum Namaḥ Śivāya.

What Are the Major Gaṇeśa Festivals?

ŚLOKA 98

Gaṇeśa Chaturthī is a joyous celebration of Gaṇeśa's birthday. Vināyaka Vratam is twenty-one days of fasting and daily temple worship. Pañcha Gaṇapati is a five-day family festival of harmony and gift-giving. Aum.

BHĀSHYA

On Gaṇeśa Chaturthī, in August-September, elaborate temple *pūjās* are held. Worship is also given in the home shrine to a clay image of Gaṇeśa that we make or obtain. At the end of the day, or after ten days, we join others in a grand parade, called *visarjana,* to a river, temple tank, lake or seashore, where we immerse the image, symbolizing Gaṇeśa's release into universal consciousness. During the twenty-one days of Vināyaka Vratam, in November-December, devotees vow to attend daily Gaṇeśa *pūjā,* fasting on water and taking a full meal after sunset. Pañcha Gaṇapati, December 21 to 25, is a modern five-day festival of gift-giving, dear to children. Families invoke His five *śaktis,* one on each day—creating harmony in the home, concord among relatives, neighbors and friends, good business and public relations, cultural upliftment and heartfelt charity. Gaṇeśa's monthly holy day is Chaturthī, the fourth *tithi* after the new moon. The *Vedas* implore, "O Lord of Categories, thou art the Lord, the seer of seers, unrivaled in wealth, king of elders, lord of the principle of principles. Hear us and take thy place, bringing with thee all enjoyments." Aum Namaḥ Śivāya.

What Are the Main Kārttikeya Festivals?

ŚLOKA 99

Vaikāsi Viśākham celebrates the anniversary of Lord Kārttikeya's creation. Skanda Shashṭhī is a six-day festival honoring His conquest of light over darkness. Tai Pusam is a time of *sādhana* and public penance. Aum.

BHĀSHYA

On Vaikāsi Viśākham day, Lord Kārttikeya's birthstar, Viśākhā *nakshatra*, in May-June, elaborate *abhisheka* is conducted in all His temples. It is a time of gift-giving to *paṇḍitas* and great souls, weddings, feedings for the poor, caring for trees, spiritual initiation, *dīkshā*, and conclaves of holy men. Skanda Shashṭhī is celebrated on the six days after the new moon in October-November with festive processions and *pūjās* invoking His protection and grace. It honors Kārttikeya's receiving the *vel*, His lance of spiritual illumination, *jñāna śakti*, and culminates in a dramatic victory celebration of spiritual light over *asuric* darkness. Tai Pusam occurs on Pushya *nakshatra* in January-February. During this festival we fast and perform public penance, called *kavadi*, seeking Kārttikeya's blessings to dispel our selfishness, pride and vanity. His special monthly days are Kṛittikā *nakshatra* and Shashṭhi, the sixth *tithi* after the new moon. The *Vedas* say, "Like the cry of watchful birds swimming in water, like the loud claps of thundering rain clouds, like the joyful streams gushing from the mountain, so have our hymns sounded forth to the Lord." Aum Namaḥ Śivāya.

What Are Other Important Festivals?

ŚLOKA 100

Besides the temple festivals, there is a multitude of home, community and national celebrations, notably Dīpāvalī, Hindu New Year, Tai Pongal, *guru pūjā* days, *kumbha melas,* Jayantī and Guru Pūrṇimā. Aum Namaḥ Śivāya.

BHĀSHYA

Dīpāvalī, the "festival of lights" in October-November, is a most popular festival, esteemed as a day of Hindu solidarity, when all sects gather in love and trust. It begins the financial year and is celebrated by opening new accounts, giving greeting cards, clothing and other gifts and by lighting rows of oil lamps. Family bonds are strengthened and forgivenesses sought. The several Hindu New Years are important observations. Tai Pongal, in January-February, is a harvest thanksgiving and invocation for prosperity. God Sūrya, the Sun, is honored, and daughters are presented with gifts. We venerate saints and sages by conducting *guru pūjā* on the anniversary of their passing, or *mahāsamādhi.* We celebrate our *satguru's* birthday, or Jayantī, with special *pūjā* to his *śrī pādukā,* "sandals," or holy feet. We honor him again on Guru Pūrṇimā, the full moon of July. *Kumbha melas,* humanity's largest gatherings, are held at four pilgrimage centers in India every three years. The *Vedas* proclaim, "Thus have we now approached the All-Knower, the one who is the best procurer of good things. Endow us, O Majesty, with strength and glory." Aum Namaḥ Śivāya.

Scriptures Speak on Festivals

Supported by whose protection heaven and earth, shining brightly and inspired in their spirit, manifest this glory, with whose effulgence does the risen sun shine forth? To whom else, besides that giver of happiness, can we offer all our devotion? ***Ṛig Veda***

Let us now invoke for our aid the Lord of Speech, the Designer of all things that are, the inspirer of wisdom! May He, the ever-kindly, be well disposed to our summons, and may He, whose work is goodness, grant us His blessing! ***Ṛig Veda***

The gift of wealth and victory in deeds, sweetest of garlands, honor and fame, too, love and esteem are His bounties— so even *devas* adore the elephant-faced One, in devotion sweet with cooped hands. ***Tirumurai***

Wherever I hear the sound of drums, the music of hymns, the *Vedas* chanted, there my heart remembers God our Master, the Lord who dwells in Itaimarutu. ***Tirumurai***

The Lord of Citticcaram shrine in Naraiyur, who has the river in His hair, the poison stain on His throat and the *Veda* on His tongue, goes resplendent in ceremonial dress as His devotees and perfected sages sing and dance His widespread fame, and the sound of festival drums beaten on the streets, where the temple car is pulled, spreads on every side. ***Tirumurai***

Pumpavai, O beautiful girl! Would you go without having seen, on the streets of great Mayilai, always busy with festive crowds, the festival of Uttarāphalgunī with its great sound of celebration, at which beautiful women sing and distribute alms, at the Lord's Kapaliccaram shrine, center of many festivals? ***Tirumurai***

You took for your shrine the good temple at Itaimarutu where, for the blessing of the world, scholars praise you with the *Vedic* chant, and great seers and Gods gather to bathe on the day of the Pusam festival in the month of Tai. ***Tirumurai***

Folk from far and near, good men and rogues and those who pray every day for an end to disease—our Lord of Arur is kinsman to all those who cry, "O my jewel, golden one, dear husband! My son!" Such is the splendor of Ārdrā day in Arur town! ***Tirumurai***

As the blare of the moon-white conch, the *parai* drum's beat and the jingle of the cymbals of dancing devotees spread everywhere, peacocks, thinking that the rains have come, dance in delight. Such is the splendor of Ārdrā day in Arur town! ***Tirumurai***

Hail! Śaṅkara, Dispenser of Bliss! Hail! The oldest in Śivaloka! Hail! Our youngest youth appearing to extricate us from affliction! Hail! Matchless One! Hail! The Lord of *devas*! Hail! ***Tirumurai***

By drinking the water after washing the holy feet of the *guru* and sprinkling the remains on the head, man attains the fruit of bathing in all the sacred waters of all sacred rivers and of all pilgrimages. ***Guru Gītā***

I'll wreathe Him in garland. I'll hug Him to heart. I'll sing Him His name and dance with gifts of flowers. Singing and dancing, seek the Lord. This alone I know. ***Tirumantiram***

Why think and suffer further for the insubstantial body, that is transient as a dew drop on a blade of grass? While on this earth, extol with love the holy feet of Him who has six faces. ***Natchintanai***

Upāsanā Upanishad

उपासना उपनिषद्

Sacred Worship

Śivālaya Maṇḍala

शिवालयमण्डल

Śiva Temples

Gopuras are the towering stone gateways through which pilgrims enter the South-Indian temple. Richly ornamented with myriad sculptures of the divine pantheon, their tiers symbolize the several planes of existence. Aum.

What Is the Nature of the Śiva Temple?

ŚLOKA 101

The Śiva temple is the abode of God Śiva and Gods and the precinct in which the three worlds consciously commune. It is specially sanctified, possessing a ray of spiritual energy connecting it to the celestial worlds. Aum.

BHĀSHYA

The three pillars of Śaivism are the temples, the scriptures and the *satgurus.* These we revere, for they sustain and preserve the ancient wisdom. Śiva temples, whether they be small village sanctuaries or towering citadels, are esteemed as God's home and consecrated abode. In the Śiva temple we draw close to God Śiva and find a refuge from the world. His grace, permeating everywhere, is most easily known within the precincts of the Śiva temple. It is in the purified milieu of the temple that the three worlds commune most perfectly, that devotees can establish harmony with inner-plane spiritual beings. When the spiritual energy, *śakti,* invoked by the *pūjā* permeates the sanctum sanctorum and floods out to the world, Śaivites know they are in a most holy place where God and the Gods commune with them. Within most Śiva temples are private rooms, sanctums, for Lord Gaṇeśa and Lord Kārttikeya, and shrines for the many Gods and saints. The *Vedas* explain, "Even as the radiance of the sun enlightens all regions, above, below, and slantwise, so that only God, glorious and worthy of worship, rules over all His creation." Aum Namaḥ Śivāya.

How Are Temples Founded and Built?

ŚLOKA 102

Śiva temples are founded by God Himself, often designated in a vision or dream of a devout Śaivite, then erected by temple craftsmen usually following Āgamic law. In such a holy place, holiness itself can reside. Aum.

BHĀSHYA

Because of its holiness, a Śiva temple is most often and properly established by God Śiva through His devotees and not founded by men. Once the site is known, hereditary temple architects, known as *sthapatis,* are commissioned to design and construct the temple. By tradition, every stone is set in place according to the sacred architecture found in the Āgamic scriptures. When properly consecrated, the temple becomes a place upon the earth in which the three worlds can communicate for the upliftment of mankind and the fulfillment of Śiva's *dharmic* law. Śiva has deliberately established many temples to communicate His love to His children throughout the world, who live in every country of the world and long for their Lord's ever-present love. They build temples in His name and install His image, chant His praises and thus invoke His presence. Lord Śiva accepts all these temples as His own and sends a divine ray to vivify and vitalize them. Śiva's *Vedas* annunciate, "Brahman is the priest, Brahman the sacrifice; by Brahman the posts are erected. From Brahman the officiating priest was born; in Brahman is concealed the oblation." Aum Namaḥ Śivāya.

When Should One Attend the Temple?

ŚLOKA 103

We attend the temple to commune with God Śiva, Kārttikeya or Gaṇeśa at least once each week and additionally on auspicious days of the month, yearly festival days and on the holiest day of the year, Mahāśivarātri. Aum.

BHĀSHYA

Śaivites consider it most important to live near a Śiva temple, and we build one wherever we find ourselves in the world. This is a most meritorious act, earning blessings in this life and the next. Religious life centers around the temple. It is here in God's home that we nurture our relationship with the Divine. Not wanting to stay away too long, we visit the temple weekly, though women never go during their monthly period. We strive to attend each major festival, when the *śakti* of the Deity is most powerful, and pilgrimage to a far-off temple annually. Devout Śiva *bhaktas* attend daily *pūjā* in the temple. All Śaivites visit the temple on Śiva's most sacred day of the year, Mahāśivarātri. Śaivite temples are the most ancient of all. Being the homes of the Gods and God, they are approached with great reverence and humility. Draw near the temple as you would approach a king, a governor, a president of a great realm, anticipating with a little trepidation your audience with him. The *Vedas* say, "May the Lord find pleasure in our song of praise! Priest among men, may he offer due homage to the heavenly beings! Great, O Lord, is your renown." Aum Namaḥ Śivāya.

How Does One Attend a Śiva Temple?

ŚLOKA 104

Approaching with deep reverence, we begin our worship with Gaṇeśa, circumambulate the temple and proceed to the main sanctum for *pūjā.* After receiving the sacraments, we sit quietly before taking our leave. Aum.

BHĀSHYA

With offerings in hand, leaving our shoes outside, we enter through the *gopura,* or temple tower, wash hands, feet and mouth, and seek blessings at Lord Gaṇeśa's shrine. Next we follow the outer *prakara,* or hallway, clockwise around the *mahāmaṇḍapa,* central chambers. Inside we leave our worldly thoughts at the *balipīṭha,* or offering place, then prostrate before the *dhvajastambha,* temple flagpole, and worship Nandi, the sacred bull. Next we circumambulate the central sanctum, *garbhagṛiha,* usually three times, returning to its entrance for worship. During *pūjā,* we stand with hands folded or in *añjali mudrā,* though according to temple custom, it may be proper to sit quietly or sing devotional hymns. After the *āratī,* or waving of the camphor light before the Deity, we prostrate (*ashṭāṅga praṇāma* for men, and *pañchāṅga praṇāma* for women) and rise to receive the *prasāda,* accepting them in the right hand. We walk around the *garbhagṛiha* one final time before taking our leave. The *Vedas* affirm, "If a man first takes firm hold on faith and then offers his sacrifice, then in that man's sacrifice both Gods and men place confidence." Aum Namaḥ Śivāya.

What Occurs Within the Śiva Temple?

ŚLOKA 105

Activities within a Śiva temple vary from the daily round of *pūjās* to the elaborate celebrations on annual festival days. Even amid large crowds, our worship is personal and individual, not congregational. Aum Namaḥ Śivāya.

BHĀSHYA

Besides the daily round of *pūjās,* many other events take place within the temple: pilgrims offering vows, priests chanting the *Vedas,* processions, elephants giving blessings, garlands being woven, weddings or philosophical discourses in pillared halls, devotional singing, feedings for the impoverished, dance and cultural performances, ritual bath in the stone tank, meditation, religious instruction, and many festival-related events. Generally, there are seven times when *pūjās* are held: at five, six and nine in the morning, at noon, and at six, eight and ten in the evening. The outer worship is approaching God properly, presenting ourselves acceptably. It is to offer our love, our adoration and then to speak out our prayer, our petition. The inner worship is to enjoy God's presence and not rush away, to stay, to sit, to meditate awhile and bask in the *śakti,* endeavoring to realize the Self within. The *Vedas* say, "'Come, come!' these radiant offerings invite the worshiper, conveying him thither on the rays of the sun, addressing him pleasantly with words of praise, 'This world of Brahman is yours in its purity, gained by your own good works.'" Aum Namaḥ Śivāya.

Scriptures Speak on Śiva Temples

You who are worthy of men's prayers, our leader, our God, rich in heroes—may we install you glowing and glistening! Shine forth at night and at morn! Your favor has kindled our hearths! By your favor we shall be great! ***Ṛig Veda***

Of lords the Lord Supreme, of kings the King, of Gods the God, Him let us worship—transcendent, Lord of all worlds and wholly worthy of worship. ***Yajur Veda***

A man comes to Thee in fearful wonder and says: "Thou art God who never was born. Let thy face, Rudra, shine upon me, and let thy love be my eternal protection." ***Yajur Veda***

For the purpose of protection of all, a Liṅga is variously caused to be built in villages by Gods, by seers and by ordinary men. ***Kāraṇa Āgama***

Cutting all the stones to be cut, carving all the stones to be carved, boring all the stones to be bored, such are the three aspects of the *śilpi's* art. The architect and the *sūtragrāhin* build the temples and craft the images, but it is with the *takshaka* that the architect effects the opening of the eyes of these images, and similar rites. ***Suprabheda Āgama***

Having worshiped Nandi in the Southeast—two-eyed, two-armed, black in color, having the formidable three-pointed trident of Śiva, with a crest and twisted locks of hair—in the Southwest, he should especially worship Mahākāla, black in color, two-eyed, two-armed, with white garment, two-legged, having an awesome form, equipped with a noose and a tusk, and endowed with all ornaments. ***Kāraṇa Āgama***

He should repeat the Śiva *mantra* according to his ability, and (there should be) circumambulation, obeisance and surrender of the self. ***Kāraṇa Āgama***

I bow before that Sadāśivaliṅga which is worshiped by the multitude of Gods with genuine thoughts, full of faith and devotion, and whose splendor is like that of a million suns. ***Liṅgāshṭakam***

The Pati is the blessed Śivaliṅga. The *paśu* is the mighty bull standing in front. The *pāśa* is the altar. Thus, in the temple, the Lord stands for those who, searching, see. ***Tirumantiram***

When in Śiva's temple, worship ceases, harm befalls the ruler, scanty are the rains, theft and robbery abound in the land. Thus did my holy Nandinātha declare. ***Tirumantiram***

Of what use is the body that never walked around the temple of Śiva, offering Him flowers in the worship rite? Of what use is this body? ***Tirumurai***

The unholy town where no temple stands, the town where men do not wear the holy ash, the town which does not resound with sacred song, the town which is not resplendent with many shrines, the town where the white conch is not reverently blown, the town where festive canopies and white flags are not seen, the town where devotees do not gather flowers for the worship rite, that town is no town. It is a mere wilderness. ***Tirumurai***

He approached and entered the temple where the Lord who has the golden mountain for His bow dwells in delight. He circumambulated it, prostrated himself at the sacred courtyard, entered the presence of the three-eyed God, the bull-rider crowned with matted, red hair. ***Periyapurāṇam***

Pūjā Maṇḍala

पूजामण्डल

Temple Rites

Kalaśa, a husked coconut circled by five mango leaves on a pot, is used in *pūjā* to represent any God, especially Lord Gaṇeśa. Breaking a coconut before His shrine is the ego's shattering to reveal the sweet fruit inside. Aum.

What Is the Inner Importance of Pūjā?

ŚLOKA 106

The traditional rite of worship, called *pūjā,* is a sanctified act of the highest importance for the Hindu. It is the invoking of God Śiva and the Gods and the heartfelt expression of our love, devotion and surrender. Aum.

BHĀSHYA

Pūjā is a ceremony in which the ringing of bells, passing of flames, presenting of offerings and chanting invoke the *devas* and Mahādevas, who then come to bless and help us. *Pūjā* is our holy communion, full of wonder and tender affections. It is that part of our day which we share most closely and consciously with our beloved Deity; and thus it is for Śaivites the axis of religious life. Our worship through *pūjā,* outlined in the *Śaiva Āgamas,* may be an expression of festive celebration of important events in life, of adoration and thanksgiving, penance and confession, prayerful supplication and requests, or contemplation at the deepest levels of superconsciousness. *Pūjā* may be conducted on highly auspicious days in a most elaborate, orthodox and strict manner by the temple *pujārīs,* or it may be offered in the simplest form each morning and evening in the home shrine by any devotee. The *Vedas* proclaim, "Sacrifice resembles a loom with threads extended this way and that, composed of innumerable rituals. Behold now the fathers weaving the fabric; seated on the outstretched loom. 'Lengthwise! Crosswise!' they cry." Aum Namaḥ Śivāya.

What Is the Special Rite Called Archana?

ŚLOKA 107

Archana is an abbreviated form of temple *pūjā* in which the name, birth star and spiritual lineage of a devotee are intoned to the God by the priest to invoke special, individual, family or group blessings and assistance. Aum.

BHĀSHYA

If we wish to receive the Deity's blessing for something special that is happening in our life, we may request an *archana*. This is arranged and paid for within the temple itself. We give a basket or tray to the priest, or *pujārī*, upon which have been placed certain articles to be offered to the Deity: usually a flower garland, bananas and a coconut (carefully washed and not even breathed upon), holy ash, incense, camphor, rosewater and a contribution for the *pujārī*. The *pujārī* asks for our name, which we tell him aloud, and our *nakshatra*, or birth star. Then he asks for our *gotra*—the name of the *ṛishi* with which our family is associated. He then intones these, our credentials, before the Deity along with a Sanskṛit verse. A brief *pūjā*, in which the 108 names of the God are chanted, is then performed specifically on our behalf and special blessings received. At the end, the *pujārī* will return most of the offerings as *prasāda*. The *Vedas* implore, "By your favors granted enable us, O Lord, once again to leap over the pitfalls that face us. Be a high tower, powerful and broad, for both us and our children. To our people bring well-being and peace." Aum Namaḥ Śivāya.

What is the Nature of Image Worship?

ŚLOKA 108

We worship God Śiva and the Gods who by their infinite powers spiritually hover over and indwell the image, or *mūrti,* which we revere as their temporary body. We commune with them through the ritual act of *pūjā.* Aum.

BHĀSHYA

The stone or metal Deity images are not mere symbols of the Gods; they are the form through which their love, power and blessings flood forth into this world. We may liken this mystery to our ability to communicate with others through the telephone. We do not talk to the telephone; rather we use a telephone as a means of communication with another person who is perhaps thousands of miles away. Without the telephone, we could not converse across such distances; and without the sanctified *mūrti* in the temple or shrine we cannot easily commune with the Deity. His vibration and presence can be felt in the image, and He can use the image as a temporary physical-plane body or channel. As we progress in our worship, we begin to adore the image as the Deity's physical body, for we know that He is actually present and conscious in it during *pūjā,* aware of our thoughts and feelings and even sensing the *pujārī's* gentle touch on the metal or stone. The *Vedas* exclaim, "Come down to us, Rudra, who art in the high mountains. Come and let the light of thy face, free from fear and evil, shine upon us. Come to us with thy love." Aum Namaḥ Śivāya.

Who Are the Priests of Śiva Temples?

ŚLOKA 109

Ādiśaiva priests are the hereditary *pujārīs,* who care for the temple and conduct its varied rites and rituals as humble servants of God. They are trained in the complex arts of worship, generally from a young age. Aum.

BHĀSHYA

Every temple has its own staff of priests. Some temples appoint only one, while others have a large extended family of priests to take care of the many shrines and elaborate festivals. Most are well trained from early childhood in the intricate liturgy. Śiva temple *pujārīs* are usually *brāhmins* from the Ādiśaiva lineage, though in certain temples they are not. These men of God must be fully knowledgeable of the metaphysical and ontological tenets of the religion and learn hundreds of *mantras* and chants required in the ritual worship. When fully trained, they are duly ordained as Śivāchāryas to perform *parārtha pūjā* in a consecrated Śiva temple. Generally, *pujārīs* do not attend to the personal problems of devotees. They are God's servants, tending His temple home and its related duties, never standing between the devotee and God. Officiating priests are almost always married men, while their assistants may be *brahmachārīs* or widowers. The *Āgamas* explain, "Only a well-qualified priest may perform both *ātmārtha pūjā,* worship for one's self, and *parārtha pūjā,* worship for others. Such an Ādiśaiva is a Śaiva *brāhmin* and a teacher." Aum Namaḥ Śivāya.

What Does the Pujārī Do During Pūjā?

ŚLOKA 110

During the *pūjā,* through *mantras, mudrās* and mystical ritual, the priest invokes the Deity. All observances are precisely detailed in the *Āgamas;* every act, every intoned syllable is rich in esoteric meaning. Aum Namaḥ Śivāya.

BHĀSHYA

The *pujārī* performs strict ablutions and disciplines to prepare himself for his sacred duty. Before the *pūjā,* he ritually purifies the atmosphere. As the *pūjā* begins, he meditates on Lord Gaṇeśa, praying that all obstacles may be removed. He then beseeches the God to indwell the image, to accept the prayers of the votaries, and to shower blessings and love on all. Calling the name of the Deity and chanting *mantras* and hymns from the *Vedas* and *Āgamas,* the *pujārī* makes offerings of unbroken rice, burning camphor, incense, holy ash, water, red turmeric powder, flowers and food. Sometimes offerings of milk, rosewater, sandalwood paste and yogurt are poured over the *mūrti* as an oblation, called *abhisheka.* Bells are loudly rung, conch shells sounded, and musicians may play the temple drums and woodwinds. The *pujārī* treats the Deity with utmost care, attending to Him as the King of kings. When the *pūjā* has ended, the *pujārī* passes the now sanctified offerings to those present. The *Vedas* state, "Daily the sacrifice is spread. Daily the sacrifice is completed. Daily it unites the worshiper to heaven. Daily by sacrifice to heaven he ascends." Aum Namaḥ Śivāya.

Scriptures Speak on Temple Rites

The devout performers of solemn ceremonies, aspiring for chariots, as if, are led to the doors of the chamber of the Lord. Ladles, placed to the East, are plying the fire with melted butter at the fire sacrifice, as the mother cow licks her calf. *Ṛig Veda*

As hungry children here below sit round about their mother, even so all beings expectantly sit round the *agnihotra.* *Sāma Veda*

May the forefathers of ancient days protect me in this my prayer, in this my act, in this my priestly duty, in this my performance, in this my thought, in this my purpose and desire, in this my calling on the Gods! All Hail! *Atharva Veda*

A Liṅga sprung up by itself and an image in the shape of a God are said to be intended for worship for the purpose of others. The merit to the worshiper of worship for all others is the same as the merit of worship for oneself. *Kāraṇa Āgama*

Offerings of perfumed substances, flowers, incense, lamps and fresh fruits—these are the five elements of the traditional *pūjā* which culminates with the offering of the lamps. *Kāmika Āgama*

The worship rites from the very beginning, worship of the Liṅga and its support, must be done by an Ādiśaiva in the manner described in the *Āgamas.* *Kāraṇa Āgama*

As fire in a basin flames by means of air, thus Lord Śiva is born, is made manifest before the eyes of the devotee, by *mantra,* in the Liṅga. *Kāraṇa Āgama*

The twice-born *gurukal* should twice place the triple sectarian marks of ash mixed with water. Having scattered all sins by this twofold protection of his body, the Gurukkal should now be competent to perform all the sacrificial rites. *Kāraṇa Āgama*

In the beginning of worship, at the conclusion of the rite, in the offering of water, in the anointing of the image, in the bathing of the image, in the offering of light, in the sprinkling of the image with sandal, in the bathing of the image with consecrated liquids, in the offering of incense, in the act of worship, and in all other things to be done, the Śivāchārya should strike the great bell. *Kāraṇa Āgama*

He should bathe the Liṅga, repeating the Vyoma-Vyāpi Mantra, and with sesame oil, and with curd, milk and *ghee*, with coconut water, with honey, repeating the Pañchabrahman, he should carefully rub the Liṅga with fine rice-flour paste, repeating the Hṛidayā Mantra. *Kāraṇa Āgama*

First there is the invocation; second, the establishing of the God; third, water for washing the feet should be offered; fourth, water for sipping; fifth, the placing of *ārghya,* water; sixth, sprinkling water as ablution; seventh, garment and sandal; eighth, worship with flowers; ninth, incense and light should be offered; tenth, offering of food; eleventh, oblation should be performed; twelfth, the holy fire, an oblation of clarified butter; thirteenth, an oblation; fourteenth, song and music; fifteenth, dancing; and sixteenth, the act of leaving. *Kāraṇa Āgama*

Seers can reach Him because He is visible; worshipers, too, can see Him. But if they possess love for Him, Hara, who is the first cause of the ancient universe, will manifest Himself to their mind as light. *Tirumurai*

Bhakti Maṇḍala

भक्तिमण्डल

Love of God

Kuttuvilaku, the standing oil lamp, symbolizes the dispelling of ignorance and awakening of the divine light within us. Its soft glow illumines the temple or shrine room, keeping the atmosphere pure and serene. Aum.

Is Temple Worship Only for Beginners?

ŚLOKA 111

Temple worship is for all men and women at every level of spiritual development. Its meaning and experience deepen as we unfold spiritually through the stages of service, devotion, *yoga* and enlightened wisdom. Aum.

BHĀSHYA

We never outgrow temple worship. It simply becomes more profound and meaningful as we progress through four spiritual levels. In the *charyā pāda,* the stage of selfless service, we attend the temple because we have to, because it is expected of us. In the *kriyā pāda,* the stage of worshipful *sādhanas,* we attend because we want to; our love of God is the motivation. In the *yoga pāda,* we worship God internally, in the sanctum of the heart; yet even the *yogī* immersed in the superconscious depths of mind has not outgrown the temple. It is there—God's home on the earth plane—when the *yogī* returns to normal consciousness. So perfect is the temple worship of those who have traversed the *jñāna pāda* that they themselves become worship's object—living, moving temples. Yea, temple worship is never outgrown. The *Vedas* give praise, "Homage to Him who presides over all things, that which was and that which shall be; to whom alone belongs the heaven, to that all-powerful Brahman be homage! From Fullness He pours forth the full; the full spreads, merging with the full. We eagerly would know from whence He thus replenishes Himself." Aum Namaḥ Śivāya.

How Do Devotees Prepare for Worship?

ŚLOKA 112

We visit a Śiva temple after bathing, dressing in clean clothes and preparing an offering, which can be as simple as a few flowers or fruits. We bring the mind to the holy feet of the Deity even as preparations begin. Aum.

BHĀSHYA

Visiting the home of God Śiva or of a God, the temple, is not without its trepidation, protocol and proper conduct, preceded by preparation that we administrate ourselves. Our worship is only as meaningful and effective as we make it. Before we attend or conduct a *pūjā*, we should carefully bathe the body, rinse the mouth and dress in fresh clothing—*sārīs* for women and *dhotīs* or *veshtis* and shawls for men where this is the custom. Throughout these preparations we may sing hymns or chant *mantras* or God's holy names silently or aloud, taking care to keep the mind free from worldly matters. We then gather offerings for the Deity. If mealtime is near, we eat only after *pūjā* has been concluded. Although the outer details of our worship are important, it is our inner feelings and thoughts, our love and devotion, which are the truest offering we can make. The *Vedas* testify, "The Gods, led by the spirit, honor faith in their worship. Faith is composed of the heart's intention. Light comes through faith. Through faith men come to prayer, faith in the morning, faith at noon and at the setting of the sun. O faith, give us faith!" Aum Namaḥ Śivāya.

How Do Our Prayers Reach the Gods?

ŚLOKA 113

Through temple worship, the three worlds become open to one another, and the beings within them are able to communicate. By means of the mystical arts of *pūjā*, the worlds act in concert, and prayers are received. Aum.

BHĀSHYA

The three worlds are connected when *pūjā* is performed and worship is begun. There are certain rites that can be performed to enable individuals to communicate directly with beings in the inner worlds. Prayers are given and received in many ways. Among the most intimate, personal forms of communication is the written prayer to the *devas* or to God. Burned in Agni's sacred fire, it disintegrates in the physical world and quickly re-forms in the astral world. When a prayer is burned in a temple wherein this practice is consecrated, its astral image is received and read by the *devas*, and properly dispatched and answered, within the confines of our *karmic* pattern. Prayers may also be conveyed by slowly, mentally enunciating the words, visualizing them rising up the spine, through the top of the head, reaching beyond to the feet of God. The *devas* will not intervene unless asked. This is the inner law. The *Vedas* avow, "He shines forth at dawn like the sunlight, deploying the sacrifice in the manner of priests unfolding their prayerful thoughts. Agni, the God who knows well all the generations, visits the Gods as a messenger, most efficacious." Aum Namaḥ Śivāya.

Do Śaivites Worship Only in Temples?

ŚLOKA 114

One can worship God anywhere and be in contact with the inner worlds—in the temple, in the home shrine and in the *yogī's* contemplation. However, in the holy Śiva temple the three worlds most perfectly commune. Aum.

BHĀSHYA

In the shrine room gather messengers of the Mahādeva being worshiped to hear the prayers of the devotee and carry them to their Master. The Gods can be worshiped anywhere when the proper *saṅkalpa,* preparation, has been performed. God's presence is everywhere, through everything, in everything, for Śiva is the creator of all things, the manifestor of time, form and the space between forms. Śiva is worshiped in the mind, in the heart, through the throat, in the head of the *yogī* locked in *yoga.* So great is the power of worship, communion and communication with the centillion *devas,* that when a little bell is rung, a flame appears in the lamp, the vermilion spot is placed, the flower appears and is offered, God Śiva and the Gods are invoked. Contemplating the aftermath of *pūjā* or *abhisheka,* we feel the *sānnidhya* or divine presence of Parāśakti, tender motherly love, permeating to the outer walls around the temple. The *Vedas* proclaim, "Assemble all, with prayer to the Lord of Heaven, He is the One, the all-pervading, the guest of men. He, the ancient of days, abides in the present. Him, the One, the many follow on their path." Aum Namaḥ Śivāya.

What Is the Home Shrine's Significance?

ŚLOKA 115

Every Śaivite maintains a home shrine. It is the most beautiful room in the house, an extension of the temple, the abode for Deities and *devas,* and a holy refuge for daily worship and meditation. Aum Namaḥ Śivāya.

BHĀSHYA

Every Śaivite home centers around the home shrine, a special room set aside and maintained to create a temple-like atmosphere in which we conduct *pūjā,* read scripture, perform *sādhana,* meditate, sing *bhajana* and do *japa.* Here the presence of the Gods is always felt, and we remember them especially morning and evening and before meals, which we offer to them before we partake. Worship traditionally begins before dawn, with the simple act of dedication for the coming day. After a bath, morning *pūjā* is performed which includes the repetition of the Gāyatrī or other *mantras* and is followed by *sādhanas* given by one's *guru.* The form of home worship, *ātmārtha pūjā,* is simple: the Deities are invoked and offerings are made. After the final *āratī,* or offering of the light, we supplicate them to bestow their grace on us, our family and all devotees. Evening devotionals include a simple *āratī, bhajana,* meditation and reading of scripture, which carries one to lofty celestial realms during sleep. The *Āgamas* affirm, "Worship of one's chosen Liṅga by anyone in their own home for divine protection is called *ātmārtha pūjā.*" Aum Namaḥ Śivāya.

Scriptures Speak on Love of God

Yes, may the man who within his home pleases you all his days with songs and with offerings receive a rich reward, be loaded with your gifts! To him be happiness! This is our prayer. *Ṛig Veda*

Aum. O terrestrial sphere! O sphere of space! O celestial sphere! Let us contemplate the splendor of the Solar Spirit, the Divine Creator. May He guide our minds. *Ṛig Veda, Gāyatrī Mantra*

For you is my offering, to you I will pray, to you who are worthy of homage and worship. You, O God, are a spring in the desert for the man who is thirsty for you, O Everliving. *Ṛig Veda*

All that God does shall win our praise. We magnify His name with hymns, seeking boons from the Mighty. *Ṛig Veda*

The rites of oblation, O lovers of truth, which the sages divined from the sacred verses, were variously expounded in the threefold *Veda*. Perform them with constant care. This is your path to the world of holy action. *Atharva Veda*

Whatever the merit in any sacrifice, austerity, offering, pilgrimage or place, the merit of worship of the Śivaliṅga equals that merit multiplied by hundreds of thousands. *Kāraṇa Āgama*

In the forenoon with a white garment, in midday with a red garment, with a yellow garment in the evening, and with any of them in the night, the worshiper, drawing the God near with the Sadyojāta Mantra, should cause Him to be firmly established by means of the Vāma Mantra and the Aghora Mantra. *Kāraṇa Āgama*

First there should be purification of one's self; secondly, purification of the site; thirdly, there should be the cleansing of the worship materials, fourthly, purification of the Liṅga; fifthly, purification of the *mantras* should be done. Thus there is the five-fold purification. *Kāraṇa Āgama*

Even the incompetent, indeed, should worship, ending with the offering of sacrificial food, ending with light. He who daily does this shall obtain progress toward the Auspicious. *Kāraṇa Āgama*

There is no difference between devotion and perfect knowledge. A person who is engrossed in devotion enjoys perpetual happiness. And perfect knowledge never descends in a vicious person averse to devotion. *Śiva Purāṇa*

They labor hard and gather flowers and carry water pure. They adore the Lord in unfailing piety and at His shining Feet lay flowers and stand and pray, and unto the rain-laden clouds forever prosperous shall they be. *Tirumantiram*

It is devotion to God, Śiva *bhakti,* alone that makes a man blessed. Everything else is useless. Therefore, without break, practice Śivadhyāna. Do not be afraid of anything. Victory will be yours! *Natchintanai*

He folded his hands in adoration and praised the Lord's feet. His deep love melted in a stream, the flood from his eyes gushed out and spread over his body. *Periyapurāṇam*

What has learning profited a man, if it has not lead him to worship the good feet of Him who is pure knowledge itself? They alone dispel the mind's distress who take refuge at the feet of the Incomparable One. *Tirukural*

Mahātma Upanishad

महात्म उपनिषद्

Holy Men and Women

Vairāgya Maṇḍala

वैराग्यमण्डल

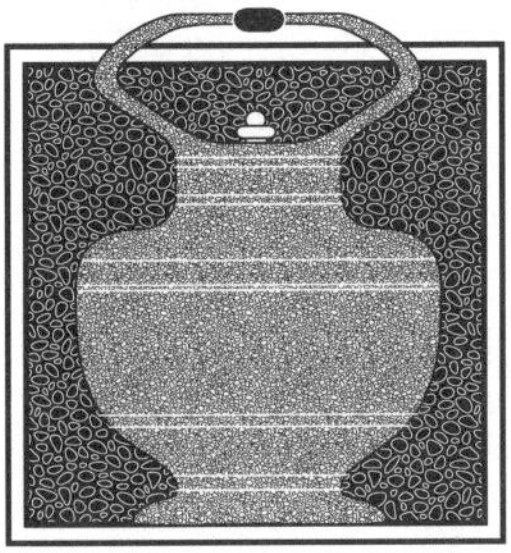

Monastic Life

Kamaṇḍalu, the water vessel, is carried by the Hindu monastic. It symbolizes his simple, self-contained life, his freedom from worldly needs, his constant *sādhana* and *tapas*, and his oath to seek God everywhere. Aum.

What Is the Hindu Monastic Tradition?

ŚLOKA 116

In the Hindu tradition there have always existed among men a few for whom the world held no attraction and *karmas* were on the wane. Some are solitary mendicants. Others reside with their brothers in monasteries. Aum.

BHĀSHYA

Certain men are by nature inclined toward realization of the Self, and disinclined toward desires of family, wealth and property. Some among them are *sādhus* dressed in white. They are anchorites living in the seclusion of distant caves and remote forests or wandering as homeless mendicants, itinerant pilgrims to the holy sanctuaries of Hinduism. Others dwell as cenobites assembled with fellow monastics, often in the *āśrama, aadheenam* or *maṭha* of their *satguru.* These monks, both anchorite and cenobite, may live with no formal vows or take certain simple vows. When initiated into the order of *sannyāsa,* they don the saffron robes and bind themselves to a universal body of Hindu renunciates whose existence has never ceased. Scriptural doctrine states that the two paths, householder and renunciate, are distinct in their *dharmas* and attainments, affirming that true renunciation may not be achieved by those in the world even by virtue of a genuine attitude of detachment. The holy *Vedas* declare, "The man who has found Him becomes a silent monk. Desiring Him alone as their world, ascetics leave their homes and wander about." Aum Namaḥ Śivāya.

What Are the Goals of Renunciate Life?

ŚLOKA 117

The two fundamental objectives of *sannyāsa* are to promote the spiritual progress of the individual, bringing him into God Realization, and to protect and perpetuate the religion through his illumined leadership. Aum.

BHĀSHYA

Renunciation and asceticism have been an integral component of Vedic culture from the earliest days, the most highly esteemed path of the Hindu Dharma. Monastic life has both an individual and a universal objective. At the individual level, it is a life of selflessness in which the monastic has made the supreme sacrifice of renouncing all personal ambition, all involvement in worldly matters, that he might direct his consciousness and energies fully toward God Śiva. Guided by the *satguru* along the *sādhana mārga*, the initiated *sannyāsin* unfolds through the years into deeper and deeper realizations. Ultimately, if he persists, he comes into direct knowing of Paraśiva, Transcendent Reality. At the universal level, Hindu monasticism fosters the religion by preserving the truths of the Sanātana Dharma. Competent *swāmīs* are the teachers, the theologians, the exemplars of their faith, the torchbearers lighting the way for all. The ancient *Vedas* elucidate, "The ascetic who wears discolored robes, whose head is shaved, who does not possess anything, who is pure and free from hatred, who lives on alms, he becomes absorbed in Brahman." Aum Namaḥ Śivāya.

What Is the Sannyāsin's Kuṇḍalinī Path?

ŚLOKA 118

The *sannyāsin* balances within himself both the male and female energies. Complete unto himself, he is whole and independent. Having attained an equilibrium of *iḍā* and *piṅgalā*, he becomes a knower of the known. Aum.

BHĀSHYA

There arises within the *sannyāsin* a pure energy, neither masculine nor feminine. This is the *sushumṇā* current coming into power through which he gains control of the *kuṇḍalinī* force and eventually, after years of careful guidance, attains *nirvikalpa samādhi.* Eventually, in one life or another, all will turn to the renunciate path. However, it would be equally improper for a renunciate-minded soul to enter family life as for a householder to seek to be a *sannyāsin.* A word of warning. Be cautious of those who promise great *kuṇḍalinī* awakenings and spiritual rewards from severe practices without preparation, initiation and renunciation. Those entering the serious life of *sannyāsa* must be prepared to follow the traditional path of unrewarded *sādhana* through the years, apart from dear family and friends. Such is the way to reach the truth of *yoga.* It takes many, many years for the soul to thus ripen and mature. The *Tirumantiram* affirms, "Many are the births and deaths forgotten by souls shrouded in ignorance, enveloped in *mala's* darkness. At the moment Great Śiva's grace is gained, the renunciate attains the splendorous light." Aum Namaḥ Śivāya.

What Is the Sannyāsin's Initiation Rite?

ŚLOKA 119

Young, unmarried men of the Hindu religion may qualify for renunciation, called *sannyāsa dīkshā,* which may be conferred by any legitimate *sannyāsin.* But the most spiritually potent initiation comes from a *satguru.* Aum.

BHĀSHYA

Traditionally, *sannyāsa dīkshā* is restricted to unmarried men, though some modern orders have accepted qualified women. As a rule in most orders, if a candidate enters monastic training before age twenty-five and meets other qualifications, he may, generally after a minimum of twelve years of preparation and training, take the *sannyāsin's* lifetime vows, called holy orders of *sannyāsa.* Only a *sannyāsin* can bring another into the ancient order of *sannyāsa.* However, since the purpose is God Realization, most candidates seek initiation from a spiritually advanced knower of God who can bring them into Paraśiva. *Sannyāsa dīkshā* is given in simple or most formal ways. The formal rites include the shaving of the head, conveyance of certain esoteric teachings, abjuration of the worldly life and *dharma,* administration of monastic vows, conducting of the novitiate's funeral rites and the giving of the *kavi* vestments. The *Vedas* proclaim, "The Self within the body, pure and resplendent, is attained through the cultivation of truth, austerity, right knowledge and chastity. When their impurities dwindle, the ascetics behold Him." Aum Namaḥ Śivāya.

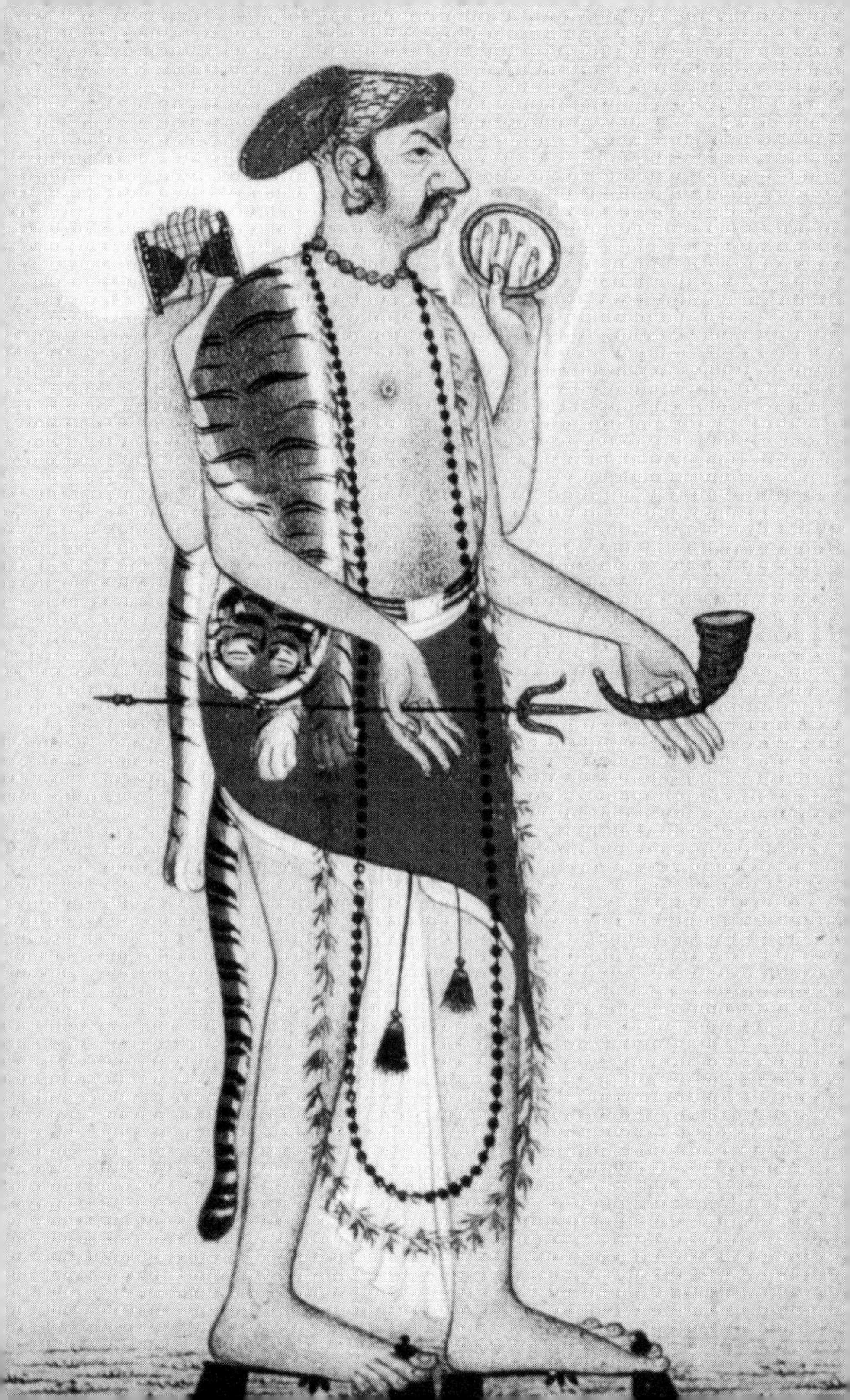

What Are the Holy Orders of Sannyāsa?

ŚLOKA 120

The holy orders of *sannyāsa* are lifetime vows of poverty, obedience and chastity, never to be relinquished or rescinded. The *sannyāsins* are the religious leaders, the bedrock of the Sanātana Dharma. Aum Namaḥ Śivāya.

BHĀSHYA

The *sannyāsin's* first sacred vow is renunciation, the surrendering of the limited identity of the ego that the soul may soar to the depths of impersonal Being. It is a repudiation of worldly *dharma* and involvement, and thus includes poverty and simplicity. The *sannyāsin* owns nothing, not even the robes he is given to wear. The second vow is obedience—a pledge to follow the traditional ways of the *sannyāsa dharma* and the specific directions of his *satguru.* It embraces obedience to his own conscience, to scripture, to God and the Gods and to his illustrious *guru paramparā.* The third vow is purity—a pledge to remain pure in thought, word and deed, to be continent throughout life, to protect the mind from all lower instincts: deceit, hatred, fear, jealousy, anger, pride, lust, covetousness and so forth. It includes the observance of *ahiṁsā,* noninjuriousness, and adherence to a vegetarian diet. Some orders also give vows of humility and confidentiality. The *Vedas* elucidate, "Henceforth being pure, clean, void, tranquil, breathless, selfless, endless, undecaying, steadfast, eternal, unborn, independent, he abides in his own greatness." Aum Namaḥ Śivāya.

Scriptures Speak on Monastic Life

Girded by the wind, they have donned ocher mud for a garment. So soon as the Gods have entered within them, they follow the wings of the wind, these silent ascetics. ***Ṛig Veda***

Let him approach with humility a *guru* who is learned in the scriptures and established in Brahman. To such a seeker, whose mind is tranquil and senses controlled, and who has approached him in the proper manner, let the learned *guru* impart the science of Brahman, through which the true, Imperishable Being is realized. ***Atharva Veda***

Within him is fire, within him is drink, within him both earth and heaven. He is the sun which views the whole world, he is indeed light itself—the long-haired ascetic. ***Ṛig Veda***

Having transcended the desire for sons, the desire for wealth, the desire for worlds, they go about as mendicants. For the desire for sons is the desire for wealth, and the desire for wealth is the desire for worlds. All these are nothing but desires. He, the *ātman,* is not this, not this. ***Yajur Veda***

Having realized with mind and heart, having become wise, you will no longer move on the path of death. Therefore, they call renunciation the ardor surpassing all others. ***Yajur Veda***

What people call salvation is really continence. For through continence man is freed from ignorance. And what is known as the vow of silence, that too is really continence. For a man through continence realizes the Self and lives in quiet contemplation. ***Yajur Veda***

Know, Arjuna, that what men call renunciation is the authentic *yoga*, for without renouncing all desire no man becomes a *yogin*. The silent sage climbing toward *yoga* uses work as a means. Quiescence and serenity are the proper course for one who has attained. ***Bhagavad Gītā***

In the one who has conquered his self and is peaceful, the Supreme Self, in heat or cold, joy or pain, honor or disgrace, abides in serenity. He who is full of wisdom and understanding, calm and controlled, to whom a clod, a stone and gold are the same, is in truth a *yogin*. ***Bhagavad Gītā***

A myriad times are they born and die. In a million follies they forget this; and in the darkness of *mala* are enveloped. When at last the hidden Grace of Śiva bursts forth and chases the night away, then is the moment for the soul to renounce. When it does, a radiant light it becomes. ***Tirumantiram***

Hail, O *sannyāsin*, you who knows no guile! Establish in your heart and worship there that Taintless One—Pañchākshara's inmost core, whom neither Vishṇu nor Brahmā had power to comprehend. You who regards all others as yourself—who in this world can be compared with you? The powerful *karma* your past deeds have wrought will vanish without trace. Daily, on the thought "Is not this *jīva* Śiva?" you must meditate. ***Natchintanai***

On those who wholeheartedly surrender their possessions, souls and bodies, Naṭarāja, the Gracious Giver, will at once bestow His golden lotus feet. That is the truth! ***Natchintanai***

The scriptures exalt above every other good the greatness of virtuous renunciates. Those who renounce totally reach the highest peak; the rest remain enamored in delusion's net. ***Tirukural***

Jñāni Maṇḍala

ज्ञानिमण्डल

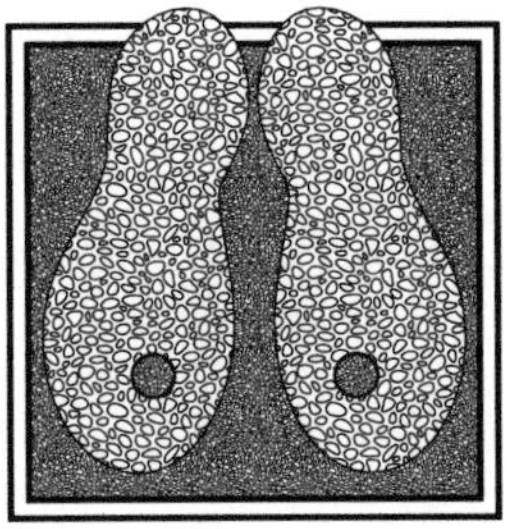

Knowers of God

Śrī pādukā, the sacred sandals worn by saints, sages and *satgurus,* symbolize the preceptor's holy feet, which are the source of his grace. Prostrating before him, we humbly touch his feet for release from worldliness. Aum.

Who Are Hinduism's Spiritual Leaders?

ŚLOKA 121

The saints, sages and *satgurus* who commune with God and Gods through devotion and meditation are Hinduism's holy men and women. We revere them and strive to follow their example and words of wisdom. Aum.

BHĀSHYA

There are and have always been many holy men and women within the Sanātana Dharma. They are considered holy because of their loving surrender to God and the Gods, their dedication to our faith, their accomplishments and profound realizations. Their knowing is more important than their learning, their purity more essential than their position. It is very difficult to be so disciplined and devoted, and so we honor and love those who have attained God's grace, and worship the divine within them, not their personality or humanness. Because of Hinduism's great diversity and decentralized organization, holy ones are not universally canonized, for there is no single ecclesiastical hierarchy to do this. Still, saints, sages and *satgurus* are sanctified by followers within their own *sampradāya.* Each within his or her own sphere of devotees is the authority on religious matters, listened to and obeyed as such. The *Vedas* declare, "Not understanding, and yet desirous to do so, I ask the wise who know, myself not knowing: 'Who may He be, the One in the form of the Unborn, who props in their place the six universal regions?' " Aum Namaḥ Śivāya.

What Is a Saint, a Sage and a Satguru?

ŚLOKA 122

Saints, devoid of ego, reflect the peace, humility and purity of a devout life. Sages, though perfectly liberated, may outwardly appear detached and ordinary. *Satgurus,* also fully enlightened, guide others on the path. Aum.

BHĀSHYA

The saints, or *sants,* of Hinduism are honored as exemplars of our faith. Often living the householder *dharma,* they teach us how to act and how to serve the Gods. The purity of the saint's heart is evident in his or her words and deportment. There are others in our religion who are inwardly pure and awakened, but who do not outwardly display their attainment. These are known as sages and often live as secluded *munis* or wander as homeless mendicants, remaining aloof from the world. *Satgurus* are the masterful guides and mystical awakeners who bring us into the fullness of spiritual life. They are initiated *swāmīs* of recognized spiritual lineages. Sages and *satgurus* are the most honored among holy men, beings of the highest attainment. Both are unmarried renunciates. Sages are generally *nirvāṇīs,* reposing within their realization; *satgurus* are *upadeśīs,* actively guiding others to Truth. The *Vedas* offer this praise, "We celebrate with dedicated acts the greatness of the illustrious supermen amidst enlightened persons, who are pure, most wise, thought-inspirers, and who enjoy both kinds of our oblations—physical and spiritual." Aum Namaḥ Śivāya.

Are There Other Terms for Holy Ones?

ŚLOKA 123

Many terms name Hindu masters, teachers and aspirants including: *jīvanmukta, ṛishi, muni, siddha, mahātma, guru, swāmī, sannyāsin, tapasvin, yogī, sādhu, sādhaka, paṇḍita, āchārya, śāstrī, pujārī, śishya* and *brahmachārī.* Aum.

BHĀSHYA

A *jīvanmukta* is a liberated soul. *Ṛishi* refers to a venerated sage or seer. A *muni* is an ecstatic mystic, especially one living in seclusion or vowed to silence. *Siddha* refers to a perfected being or one who has attained magical powers. *Mahātmā* denotes a great soul or renowned *guru.* The term *guru* usually describes a spiritual master, but can connote a teacher of any subject. A *sannyāsin,* or *swāmī,* is a formally ordained renunciate monk. A *tapasvin* is an ascetic seeking purification through rigorous disciplines. The *yogī* is dedicated to intense meditation for inner attainment. *Sādhu* is a general term for a holy man or wandering mendicant. A *sādhaka* is a serious seeker of the Self, and is often a monk. The *āchārya,* like the *paṇḍita,* is a respected teacher and advisor. *Śāstrī* refers to an expert in scripture. A *pujārī* is a temple priest. A *śishya* is a formal disciple. A *brahmachārī* is a celibate student, often under simple vows. Some titles have feminine equivalents, such as *sādhvī, yoginī* and *brahmachāriṇī.* The *Vedas* explain, "The *brahmachārī* moves, strengthening both the worlds. In him the *devas* meet in concord; he upholds earth and heaven." Aum Namaḥ Śivāya.

What Is the Nature of Guru Protocol?

ŚLOKA 124

Guru protocol, as outlined in the *Kulārṇava Tantra* and *Guru Gītā,* defines the traditional ways of relating to one's spiritual preceptor to draw forth his wisdom and blessings and fully understand his inner nature. Aum.

BHĀSHYA

Guru protocol can be understood in three parts: devotional acts, codes of harmony and prohibitions. Devotional acts include serving the *guru,* prostrating daily and offering a gift in love, chanting his name and meditating on his inner form as the embodiment of the Divine, partaking of *ucçhishṭa*—waters from his holy sandals, and his food leavings—emulating his awakened qualities, seeking initiation and striving for Self Realization as he directs. Codes of harmony include seeking his blessings, obeying his directions, keeping no secrets and honoring his lofty presence. Prohibitions include never contradicting or arguing with the *guru,* never criticizing him, nor listening to criticism by others, not imitating his dress or deportment, not standing or sitting above him, nor walking or driving ahead of him; not assuming authority in his presence, nor uttering words of falsehood or contempt, and not initiating conversation or asking questions unless invited. The *Kulārṇava Tantra* explains, "Be always in service of the *guru,* ever in his presence, giving up desire and anger, humble and devoted, lauding in spirit, upright in doing his work." Aum Namaḥ Śivāya.

What Is the Satguru's Unique Function?

ŚLOKA 125

To transcend the mind and reach the ultimate goal, seekers need the guidance of a *satguru,* an enlightened master who has followed the path to its natural end and can lead them to the Divine within themselves. Aum Namaḥ Śivāya.

BHĀSHYA

The *satguru* is the devotee's spiritual guide and preceptor, friend and companion on the path. Having become religion's consummation, the *satguru* can see where others are and know what their next step should be. Nothing is more precious than the first soul-quickening, life-changing *śaktipāta* from a *guru.* Nothing is more central to spiritual awakening than the progressive *dīkshās,* or initiations, he bestows. A *satguru* is needed because the mind is so cunning and the ego is a self-perpetuating mechanism. It is he who inspires, assists, guides and impels the *śishya* toward the Self of himself. The *satguru,* perfected in his relationship with Śiva, administrates the *sādhana* and *tapas* that slowly incinerate the seeds of *sañchita karmas.* It is his task to preside over the annihilation of the *śishya's* ego and subconscious dross, all the while guiding the awakened *kuṇḍalinī* force so that safe, steady progress can be made from stage to stage. The *Āgamas* affirm, "Individuals who become, by the grace of Śiva, eager to extricate themselves from worldly fetters, obtain initiation from a competent preceptor into the path that leads to Śivasāyujya." Aum Namaḥ Śivāya.

Scriptures Speak on Knowers of God

He should be known as one liberated while alive.
He is blessed and is of fulfilled duties. After giving up the state of being liberated while alive, when the time arrives for his quitting the body, he enters on the state of disembodied liberation, even as the air attains the state of nonmovement. *Yajur Veda*

Purified, empty, peaceful, breathless, selfless, infinite, indestructible, stable, eternal, unborn, free, he is established in his own glory. Having seen the Self who is established in His own glory, he looks upon the wheel of life as a wheel that rolls on. *Yajur Veda*

He should fulfill, according to the rules ordained, for twelve years the observance of *brahmacharya*, such as the service of the *guru.* *Atharva Veda*

The Self resides within the lotus of the heart. Knowing this, consecrated to the Self, the sage enters daily that holy sanctuary. Absorbed in the Self, the sage is freed from identity with the body and lives in blissful consciousness. *Sāma Veda*

Let him approach him properly with mind and senses tranquil and peaceful. Then will this master disclose the essence of the knowledge of Brahman whereby may be known the imperishable Real, the Person. *Atharva Veda*

Without regard for themselves, without urges and efforts, absorbed in contemplation and established in the higher Self, they endeavor to remove evil deeds and surrender their bodies by renunciation. Such is a *paramahaṁsa,* such indeed is a *paramahaṁsa!* *Yajur Veda*

Earnest seekers who worship enlightened ones at sight—with perfume, flowers, water, fruits, incense, clothing and food, or by word, deed and thought—are absolved then and there. ***Devīkālottara Āgama***

The *guru* who has attained Self Realization can alone help the aspirant in acquiring it. ***Śiva Sūtras***

Those who themselves have seen the Truth can be thy teachers of wisdom. Ask from them, bow unto them, be thou unto them a servant. ***Bhagavad Gītā***

One should worship his *guru* by daily performing full prostrations to him. By worship, one attains steadiness and ultimately realizes one's own true nature. ***Guru Gītā***

At the root of *dhyāna* is the form of the *guru.* At the root of *pūjā* are the feet of the *guru.* At the root of *mantra* is the word of the *guru,* and at the root of all liberation is the grace of the *guru.* ***Kulārṇava Tantra***

Where there is a holy man of divine worth who pursues the Lord, that all space embraces; there enemies are none. Rains in abundance fall. Full is the people's contentment. No evil befalls that land. ***Tirumantiram***

The heart of the holy trembles not in fear. All passions stilled, it enjoys calm unruffled. Neither is there death nor pain, nor night nor day, nor fruits of *karma* to experience. That, truly, is the state of those who have renounced desire. ***Tirumantiram***

He who has realized by himself his soul's Self will be worshiped by all other souls. ***Tirukural***

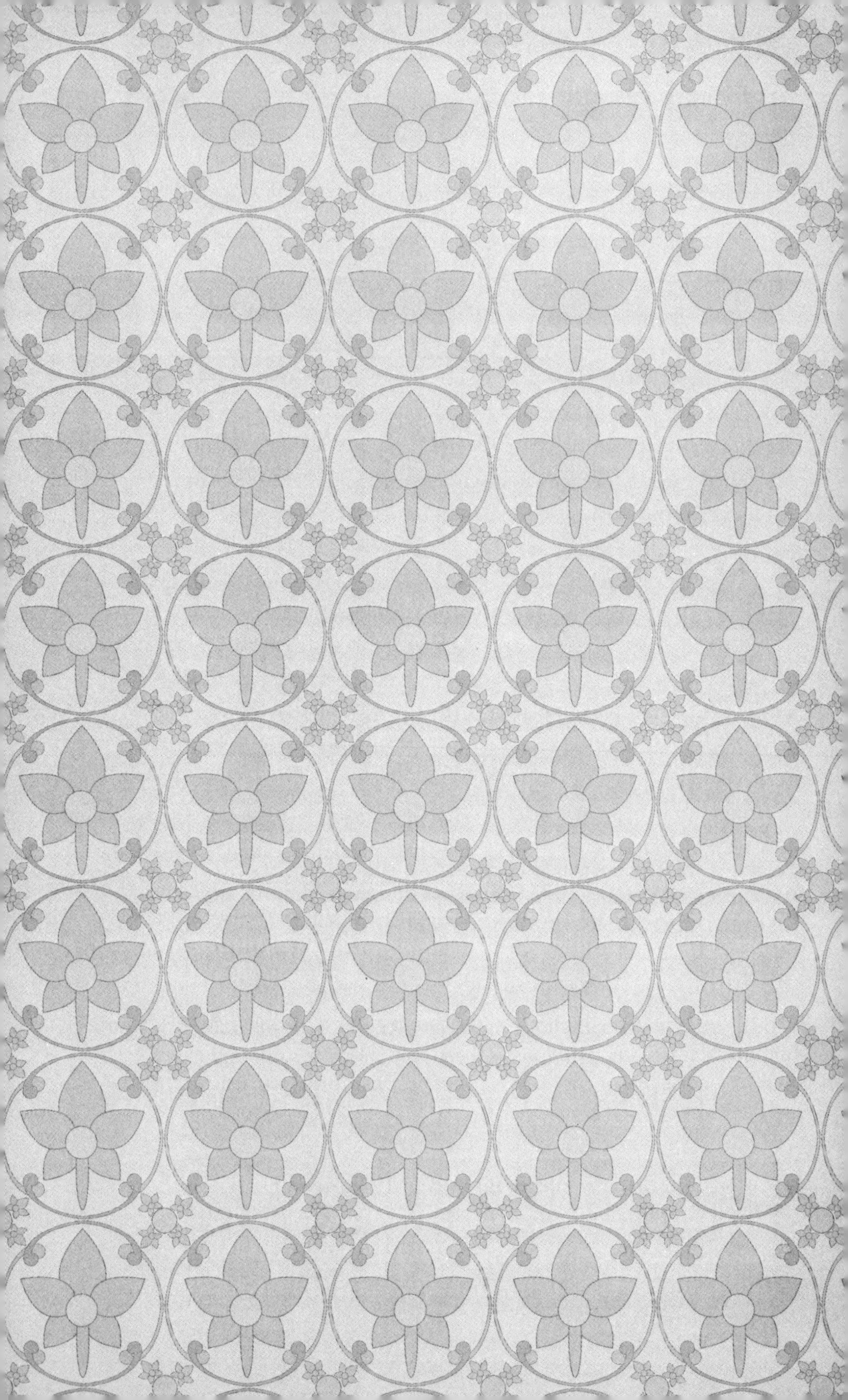

Śāstra Upanishad

शास्त्र उपनिषद्

Sacred Scripture

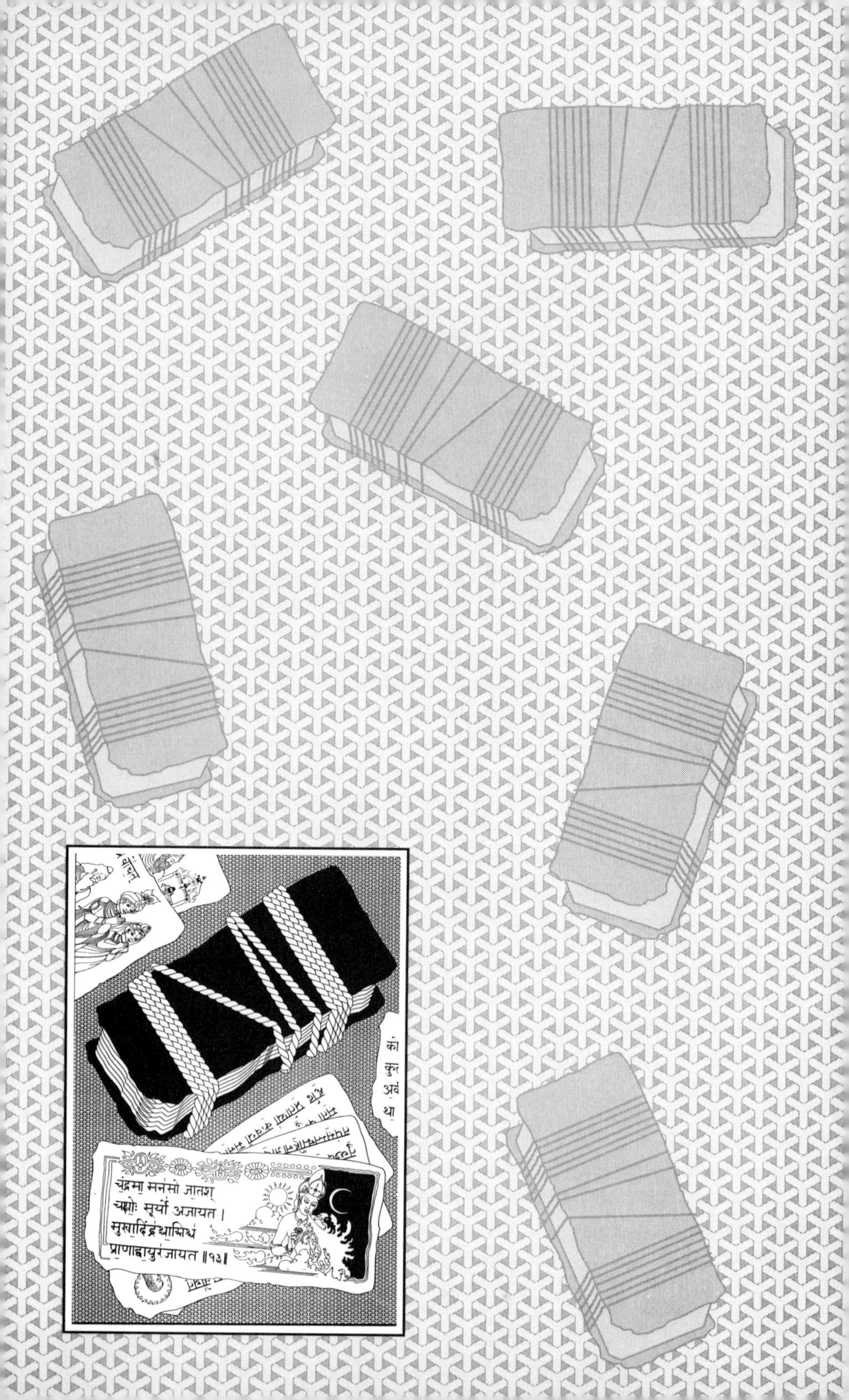
चंद्रमा मनसो जातश्
चक्षोः सूर्यो अजायत ।
मुखादिंद्रश्चाग्निश्च
प्राणाद्वायुरजायत ॥१३॥

Śruti Maṇḍala

श्रुतिमण्डल

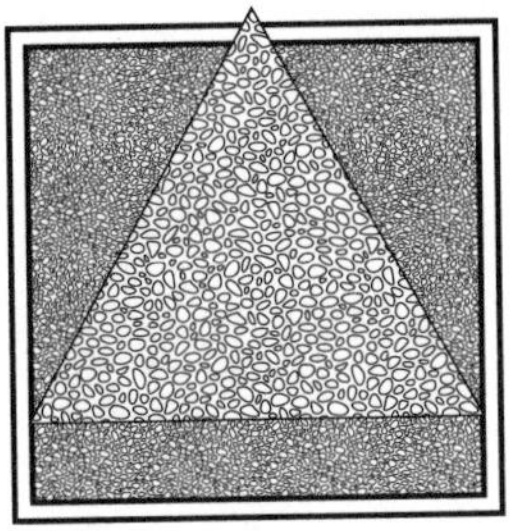

Revealed Scripture

Trikoṇa, the triangle, is a symbol of God Śiva which, like the Śivaliṅga, denotes His Absolute Being. It represents the element fire and portrays the process of spiritual ascent and liberation spoken of in scripture. Aum.

What Are Hindu Revealed Scriptures?

ŚLOKA 126

The *Vedas* and *Āgamas*, revealed by God, are Hinduism's sovereign scriptures, called *śruti*, "that which is heard." Their timeless truths are expressed in the most extraordinarily profound mystical poetry known to man. Aum.

BHĀSHYA

Veda, from *vid*, "to know," means "supreme wisdom or science." Similarly, *Āgama*, which names the sacred sectarian revelations, means "descent of knowledge." The *Vedas* and *Āgamas* are eternal truths transmitted by God through great clairaudient and clairvoyant *ṛishis*. They are Hinduism's primary and most authoritative scriptures, expounding life's sacredness and man's purpose on the planet. These psalms of wisdom were disclosed over many centuries, memorized and orally conveyed from generation to generation within priestly families, then finally written down in Sanskṛit in the last few millennia. The subtly symbolic language of *śruti*, the cherished word of God, is lyrical and lofty. In imparting religious practice, rules and doctrine, the *Vedas* are general and the *Āgamas* specific. The *Vedas* extol and invoke a multiplicity of Gods through elaborate fire rituals called *yajña*. The *Āgamas* center around a single Deity and His worship with water, flowers and lights in sanctified temples and shrines. The *Tirumantiram* lauds, "Two are the scriptures that Lord Śiva revealed—the primal *Vedas* and the perfect *Āgamas*." Aum Namaḥ Śivāya.

What Is the Nature of the Veda Texts?

ŚLOKA 127

The holy *Vedas,* man's oldest scripture, dating back 6,000 to 8,000 years, are a collection of four books: the *Ṛig, Sāma, Yajur* and *Atharva.* Each has four sections: hymns, rites, interpretation and philosophical instruction. Aum.

BHĀSHYA

The oldest and core portions of the *Vedas* are the four *Saṁhitās,* "hymn collections." They consist of invocations to the One Divine and the divinities of nature, such as the Sun, the Rain, the Wind, the Fire and the Dawn—as well as prayers for matrimony, progeny, prosperity, concord, domestic rites, formulas for magic, and more. They are composed in beautiful metrical verses, generally of three or four lines. The heart of the entire *Veda* is the 10,552-verse *Ṛig Saṁhitā.* The *Sāma* and *Yajur Saṁhitās,* each with about 2,000 verses, are mainly liturgical selections from the *Ṛig;* whereas most of the *Atharva Saṁhitā's* nearly 6,000 verses of prayers, charms and rites are unique. The *Sāma* is arranged for melodious chanting, the *Yajur* for cadenced intonation. Besides its *Saṁhitā,* each *Veda* includes one or two *Brāhmaṇas,* ceremonial handbooks, and *Āraṇyakas,* ritual interpretations, plus many inestimable *Upanishads,* metaphysical dialogs. In all there are over 100,000 Vedic verses, and some prose, in dozens of texts. The *Tirumantiram* confirms, "There is no *dharma* other than what the *Vedas* say. *Dharma's* central core the *Vedas* proclaim." Aum Namaḥ Śivāya.

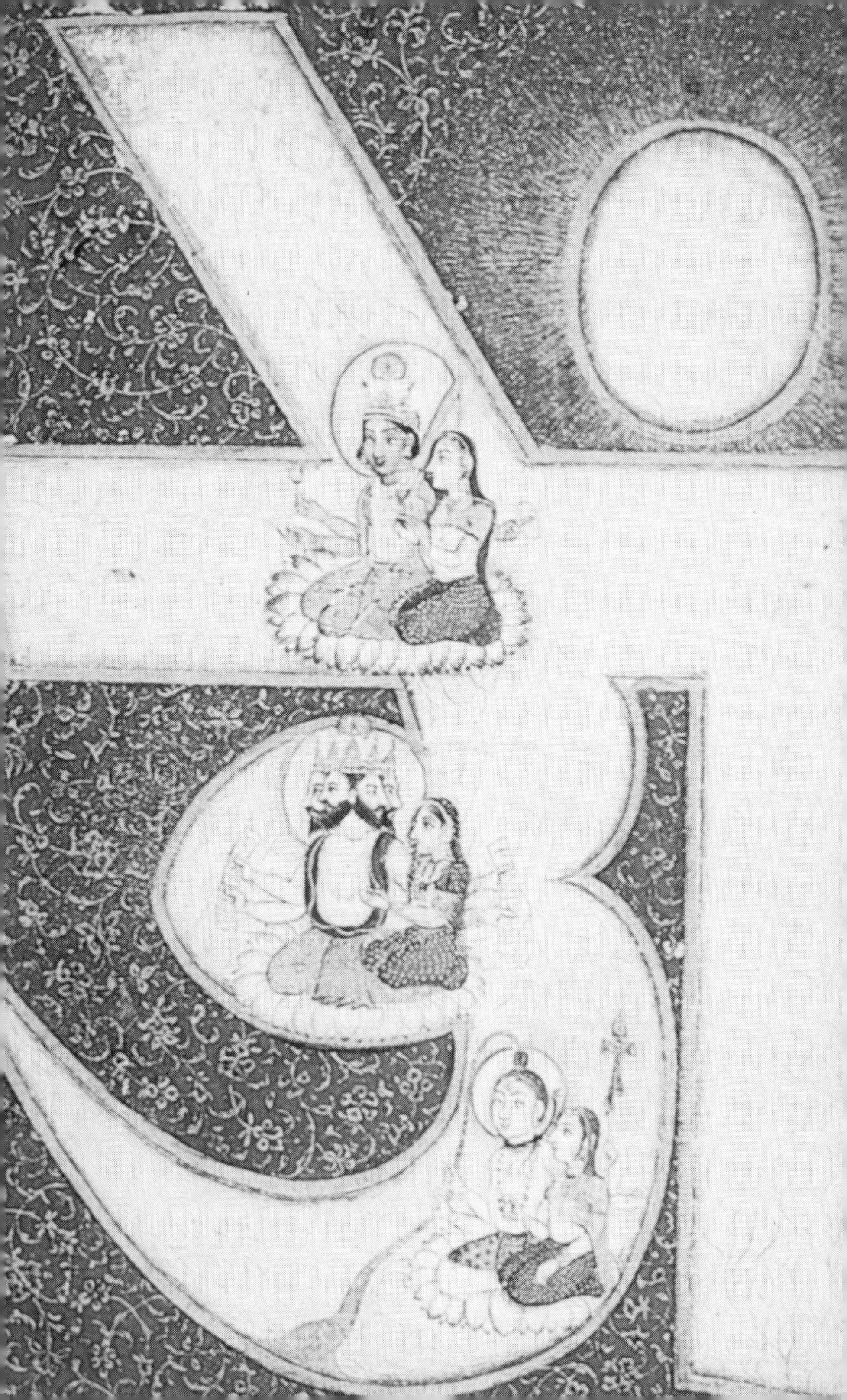

How Are the Vedas Significant Today?

ŚLOKA 128

The *Vedas,* the ultimate scriptural authority, permeate Hinduism's thought, ritual and meditation. They open a rare window into ancient Bhārata society, proclaiming life's sacredness and the way to oneness with God. Aum.

BHĀSHYA

Like the Taoist *Tao te Ching,* the Buddhist *Dhammapada,* the Sikh *Ādi Granth,* the Jewish *Torah,* the Christian *Bible* and the Muslim *Koran*—the *Veda* is the Hindu holy book. For untold centuries unto today, it has remained the sustaining force and authoritative doctrine, guiding followers in ways of worship, duty and enlightenment—*upāsanā, dharma* and *jñāna.* The *Vedas* are the meditative and philosophical focus for millions of monks and a billion seekers. Their stanzas are chanted from memory by priests and laymen daily as liturgy in temple worship and domestic ritual. All Hindus wholeheartedly accept the *Vedas,* yet each draws selectively, interprets freely and amplifies abundantly. Over time, this tolerant allegiance has woven the varied tapestry of Bhārata Dharma. Today the *Vedas* are published in Sanskṛit, English, French, German and other languages. But it is the metaphysical and popular *Upanishads* which have been most amply and ably translated. The *Vedas* say, "Just as the spokes are affixed to the hub of a wheel, so are all things established in life, the *Ṛig* and *Yajur* and *Sāma Veda,* sacrifice, the nobility and also the priesthood." Aum Namaḥ Śivāya.

What Is the Nature of the Holy Āgamas?

ŚLOKA 129

The *Āgamas,* Sanātana Dharma's second authority, are revelations on sacred living, worship, *yoga* and philosophy. Śaivism, Śāktism and Vaishṇavism each exalts its own array of *Āgamas,* many over 2,000 years old. Aum.

BHĀSHYA

In the vast Āgamic literature, tradition counts 92 main *Śaiva Āgamas*—10 Śiva, 18 Rudra and 64 Bhairava—77 *Śākta Āgamas* and 108 *Vaishṇava Pañcharātra Āgamas.* Most *Āgamas* are of four parts, called *pādas,* and possess thousands of metered Sanskṛit verses, usually of two lines. The *charyā pāda* details daily religious observance, right conduct, the *guru-śishya* relationship, community life, house design and town planning. The *kriyā pāda,* commonly the longest, extols worship and temples in meticulous detail—from site selection, architectural design and iconography, to rules for priests and the intricacies of daily *pūjā,* annual festivals and home-shrine devotionals. The *yoga pāda* discloses the interior way of meditation, of *rāja yoga, mantra* and *tantra* which stimulates the awakening of the slumbering serpent, *kuṇḍalinī.* The *jñāna pāda* narrates the nature of God, soul and world, and the means for liberation. The *Tirumantiram* declares, "*Veda* and *Āgama* are Iraivan's scriptures. Both are truth: one is general, the other specific. While some say these words of God reach two different conclusions, the wise see no difference." Aum Namaḥ Śivāya.

ॐ अथ हृत्पद्मनाहतचक्रे ॥ हृ दयस्थाने रक्तवर्णो न
मोगुणमकारकदेवो देव ना उमाशक्तिः ॥ द्विवाय
गर्भऋषिः ॥ वेदीवाहनं प्राणवायुः ॥ ज्योतिः ॥ क
लोकावरणं देहस्थधमा वस्था ॥ पुष्पेनीवाक मा
मवेदं ॥ ब्रह्मस्थन्याभिः ॥ ॥ शिवलिंगधामाभूमि
का ॥ सायुज्यता ॥ मोक्षदा दशकला ॥ १२ श्वेतमोजा
११ ॥ कामवासादिपं ३ योने ॥ वाहिमोजा ११

रुद्राणी ॥ १ ॥ नेजसा २
तापनी ३ सख
दा ४ चेतना
५ मी वा ६
धेनि ७ उमा
८ मो री ९
मा नं दा १०
ज्वाला ११ मम
लिनी १२ देव
ना श्वेत पाजमेय
हृसमहत्ते १... ये ॥ १९ य
ले १४ ॥ षडेहृत्वनाहत चक्रे सेतव मौहृत
हिरिस्थिते ॥ यस्मत्तस्मव णेनापित्रेवामक्ष नपू
नकान ॥ श्वराहनं महाचक्रे सर्वधान्निम मनि
ने मनसाभाव येडीमानमहापा प

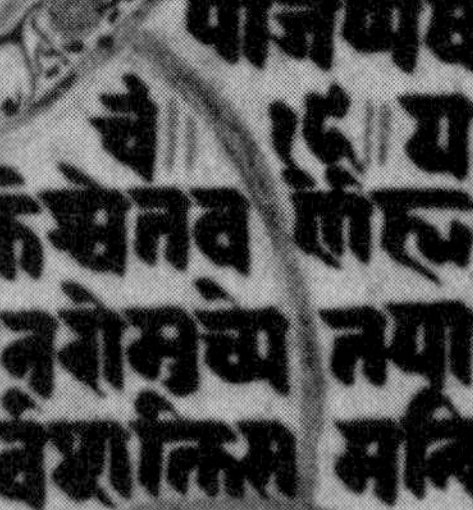

मूलमाके ॥ नस्माश्चकामिदरे
येध्येयेमग ननमाविन ॥ ॥ ॥ ॥

मूजामा नासिकेपोनामोहृभावेनष
जयेत ॥ श्वत्रमेधादिसमर्पयेत ॥ ॥ ८ ॥ ॥

How Are the Āgamas Significant Today?

ŚLOKA 130

While the *Vedas,* with myriad Deities, bind all Hindus together, the *Āgamas,* with a single supreme God, unify each sect in a oneness of thought, instilling in adherents the joyful arts of divine adoration. Aum Namaḥ Śivāya.

BHĀSHYA

God is love, and to love God is the pure path prescribed in the *Āgamas.* Veritably, these texts are God's own voice admonishing the *saṁsārī,* reincarnation's wanderer, to give up love of the transient and adore instead the Immortal. How to love the Divine, when and where, with what *mantras* and visualizations and at what auspicious times, all this is preserved in the *Āgamas.* The specific doctrines and practices of day-to-day Hinduism are nowhere more fully expounded than in these revelation hymns, delineating everything from daily work routines to astrology and cosmology. So overwhelming is Āgamic influence in the lives of most Hindus, particularly in temple liturgy and culture, that it is impossible to ponder modern Sanātana Dharma without these discourses. While many *Āgamas* have been published, most remain inaccessible, protected by families and guilds who are stewards of an intimate hereditary knowledge. The *Tirumantiram* says, "Nine are the *Āgamas* of yore, in time expanded into twenty-eight, they then took divisions three, into one truth of Vedānta-Siddhānta to accord. That is Śuddha Śaiva, rare and precious." Aum Namaḥ Śivāya.

Scriptures Speak on Śruti

The efforts of man are stated to be of two kinds, those that transcend scriptures and those that are according to scriptures. Those that transcend scriptures tend to harm, while those that are according to scriptures tend to Reality. ***Yajur Veda***

As when a fire is lit with damp fuel, different clouds of smoke come forth, in the same way from this great Being are breathed forth the *Ṛig Veda, Yajur Veda, Sāma Veda, Atharva Veda.* ***Yajur Veda***

There, where there is no darkness, nor night, nor day, nor being, nor nonbeing, there is the Auspicious One, alone, absolute and eternal. There is the glorious splendor of that Light from whom in the beginning sprang ancient wisdom. ***Yajur Veda***

Taking as a bow the great weapon of the *Upanishad*, one should put upon it an arrow sharpened by meditation. Stretching it with a thought directed to the essence of That, penetrate that Imperishable as the mark, my friend. ***Atharva Veda***

By the power of inner harmony and by the grace of God, Śvetāśvatara had the vision of Brahman. He then spoke to his nearest hermit-students about the supreme purification, about Brahman, whom the seers adore. ***Yajur Veda***

Aum. One should meditate on this syllable as the Udgītha chant, for every chant starts with *Aum.* Of this the explanation is as follows. The essence of all beings is the earth; the essence of the earth is water; the essence of water is plants; the essence of plants is man; the essence of man is speech; the essence of speech is the *Ṛig Veda*; the essence of the *Ṛig Veda* is the *Sāma Veda*, and the essence of the *Sāma Veda* is the Udgītha chant. ***Sāma Veda***

The Śaivism of Siddhānta is the Śaivism of the *Āgamas*, the first of which is the *Kāmika*. ***Kāraṇa Āgama***

In the beauteous *Veda*, aptly named the *Ṛig*, as the moving mood behind He stood. In the trembling chant of the Vedic priests He stood, Himself the eye of vision central. ***Tirumantiram***

All the world may well attain the bliss I have—who hold firmly to the heavenly secret the books impart, who chant the hymns that thrill the flesh and swell the heart. Strive, always strive, then it will come. ***Tirumantiram***

Behold the father of the elephant-faced Gaṇapati who dons the *konrai* garland and has matted locks, the author of the ageless *Vedas*, the Auspicious One. He is ours by virtue of spiritual efforts *(tapas)*. He abides in the hallowed temple of Rāmeśvaram. ***Tirumurai***

May the sun and moon be my protection! May all beings everywhere be my protection! May *mantras* and *tantras* be my protection! May the four *Vedas*, the *Śaiva Āgamas* and the whole world be my protection! ***Natchintanai***

A thousand scriptures speak of His attributes and signs, His shrines, His paths, His greatness—O, witless people, that your hearts have not been won! ***Tirumurai***

As heaven resounded with Hara's name, with the chants of the *Veda* and *Āgama*, and the hymns of the learned *brāhmins*, the Highest God in Notittanmalai showed me the path, the Lord who gives all blessings gave me a splendid elephant to ride. ***Tirumurai***

Smṛiti Maṇḍala

स्मृतिमण्डल

Secondary Scripture

Seval is the noble red rooster who heralds each dawn, calling all to awake and arise. He is a symbol of the imminence of spiritual unfoldment and wisdom. As a fighting cock, he crows from Lord Skanda's battle flag. Aum.

Do Smṛiti and Sacred Literature Differ?

ŚLOKA 131

Hindu sacred literature is a treasury of hymns, legend, mythology, philosophy, science and ethics. From among this vast body of writings, each lineage recognizes a select portion as its secondary scripture, called *smṛiti.* Aum.

BHĀSHYA

While the *Vedas* and *Agamas* are shared as part of every Hindu's primary scripture, *śruti,* each sect and lineage defines its own unique set of *smṛiti.* The sacred literature, *puṇya śāstra,* from which *smṛiti* is drawn consists of writings, both ancient and modern, in many languages. Especially central are the ancient Sanskṛitic texts, such as the *Itihāsas, Purāṇas* and *Dharma Śāstras,* which are widely termed the classical *smṛiti.* In reality, while many revere these as *smṛiti,* others regard them only as sacred literature. *Smṛiti* means "that which is remembered" and is known as "the tradition," for it derives from human insight and experience and preserves the course of culture. While *śruti* comes from God and is eternal and universal, the ever-growing *smṛiti* canon is written by man. Hinduism's sacred literature is the touchstone of theater and dance, music, song and pageantry, *yoga* and *sādhana,* metaphysics and ethics, exquisite art and hallowed sciences. The *Vedas* inquire, "In whom are set firm the firstborn seers, the hymns, the songs and the sacrificial formulas, in whom is established the single seer—tell me of that support—who may He be?" Aum Namaḥ Śivāya.

What Texts Amplify Vedas and Āgamas?

ŚLOKA 132

Many texts support the *Vedas* and *Āgamas. Vedāṅgas* detail conduct, astrology, language and etymology. *Upavedas* unfold politics, health, warfare and music. *Upāgamas* and *Paddhatis* elaborate the Āgamic wisdom. Aum.

BHĀSHYA

Much of Hinduism's practical knowledge is safeguarded in venerable texts which amplify *śruti.* The *Vedāṅgas* and *Upavedas* are collections of texts that augment and apply the *Vedas* as a comprehensive system of sacred living. *Jyotisha Vedāṅga* delineates auspicious timing for holy rites. *Kalpa Vedāṅga* defines public rituals in the *Śrauta* and *Śulba Sūtras,* domestic rites in the *Gṛihya Sūtras* and religious law in the *Dharma Śāstras.* Four other *Vedāṅgas* ensure the purity of *mantra* recitation, through knowledge of phonetics, grammar, poetry and the way of words. The *Upavedas* expound profound sciences: *Arthaveda* unfolds statecraft; *Āyurveda* sets forth medicine and health; *Dhanurveda* discusses military science; *Gāndharvaveda* illumines music and the arts; and *Sthāpatyaveda* explains architecture. In addition, the *Kāma Sūtras* detail erotic pleasures. The *Āgamas,* too, have ancillary texts, such as the *Upāgamas* and *Paddhatis,* which elaborate the ancient wisdom. The *Jñāneśvarī* says, "The *Vedas* in their perfection are as the beautiful image of the God, of which the flawless words are the resplendent body. The *smṛitis* are the limbs thereof." Aum Namaḥ Śivāya.

Does Hinduism Have Epics and Myths?

ŚLOKA 133

The *Mahābhārata* and *Rāmāyaṇa* are Hinduism's most renowned epic histories, called *Itihāsa.* The *Purāṇas* are popular folk narratives, teaching faith, belief and ethics in mythology, allegory, legend and symbolism. Aum.

BHĀSHYA

Hinduism's poetic stories of *ṛishis,* Gods, heroes and demons are sung by gifted *paṇḍitas* and traveling bards, narrated to children and portrayed in dramas and festivals. The *Mahābhārata,* the world's longest epic poem, is the legend of two ancient dynasties whose great battle of Kurukshetra is the scene of the *Bhagavad Gītā,* the eloquent spiritual dialog between Arjuna and Kṛishṇa. The *Rāmāyaṇa* relates the life of Rāma, a heroic king revered as the ideal man. The *Purāṇas,* like the *Mahābhārata,* are encyclopedic in scope, containing teachings on *sādhana,* philosophy, *dharma,* ritual, language and the arts, architecture, agriculture, magic charms and more. Of eighteen principal *Purāṇas,* six honor God as Śiva, six as Vishṇu and six as Brahmā. The witty *Pañchatantra,* eminent among the "story" literature, or *kathā,* portrays wisdom through animal fables and parables. The *Bhagavad Gītā* proclaims, "He who reads this sacred dialog of ours, by him I consider Myself worshiped through the sacrifice of knowledge. And the man who listens to it with faith and without scoffing, liberated, he shall attain to the happy realm of the righteous." Aum Namaḥ Śivāya.

Are There Other Types of Sacred Texts?

ŚLOKA 134

India's lofty philosophical texts expound diverse views in exacting dialectics. *Yoga* treatises unveil the mysterious path to ultimate *samādhis.* Intimate devotional hymns disclose the raptures of consummate Divine love. Aum.

BHĀSHYA

In addition to the epics, legends and supplements to the *Vedas* and *Āgamas,* there is a wealth of Hindu metaphysical, *yogic* and devotional writings. Considered foundational are the early texts defining the six philosophical *darśanas:* the *sūtras* by Kapila, Patañjali, Jaimini, Bādarāyaṇa, Kaṇāda and Gautama. Hailed as leading occult works on *yoga, āsanas, nāḍīs, chakras, kuṇḍalinī* and *samādhi* are the *Yoga Sūtras, Tirumantiram, Yoga Vāsishṭha, Śiva Sūtras, Siddha Siddhānta Paddhati, Jñāneśvarī, Haṭha Yoga Pradīpikā* and *Gheraṇḍa Saṁhitā.* Widely extolled among the *bhakti* literature are the *Bhagavad Gītā, Nārada Sūtras, Tiruvasagam,* the *Vachanas* of the Śivaśaraṇās and the hymns of mystic poets like Sūrdās, Tukaram, Rāmprasad, Mīrābāī, Andal, Vallabha, Tulasīdāsa, Tayumanavar, Lallā, Tagore, Auvaiyar and the saintly Nayanars and Alvars. The *Bhagavad Gītā* explains, "As a blazing fire reduces the wood to ashes, O Arjuna, so does the fire of knowledge reduce all activity to ashes. There is nothing on earth which possesses such power to cleanse as wisdom. The perfect *yogin* finds this knowledge in himself by himself in due time." Aum Namaḥ Śivāya.

What Is the Source of This Catechism?

ŚLOKA 135

The philosophical basis of this catechism is the monistic Śaiva Siddhānta of the Kailāsa Paramparā as expressed in the *Vedas, Śaiva Āgamas, Tirukural, Tirumurai, Tirumantiram* and contemporary scripture. Aum Namaḥ Śivāya.

BHĀSHYA

This catechism, *praśnottaram,* is the creation of the living lineage of seers known as the Kailāsa Paramparā, of the South Indian Śaivite school called Śuddha Śaiva Siddhānta, Advaita Siddhānta or monistic Śaiva Siddhānta. It reflects the teachings of the *Vedas* and *Śaiva Āgamas,* the profound Tamil scriptures *Tirumurai* and *Tirukural* and the revelations of contemporary Kailāsa *gurus.* The *Tirumurai* is a twelve-book collection of hymns of numerous Śaivite saints. Most important among these is the *Tirumantiram,* a *siddha yoga* treatise by Ṛishi Tirumular, recording the Śaiva tenets in 3,047 verses. It is prized as the confluence of Siddhānta and Vedānta. The *Tirukural,* containing 1,330 couplets by the weaver saint Tiruvalluvar, is among the world's greatest ethical scriptures, sworn on in South Indian courts of law. *Natchintanai* are the sacred hymns of Sri Lanka's Sage Yogaswāmī. Tayumanavar says, "I meditate on the great light of the Siddhānta, the thought of all thoughts, the life of all life, which, existing in all objects without distinction, causes a spring of inestimably pure and happy nectar to flow for the good of its followers." Aum Namaḥ Śivāya.

Scriptures Speak on Smṛiti

Just as the luminous day is born from light, so may the radiant singers shine far and wide! Truly, the poet's wisdom enhances the glory of the Ordinance decreed by God, the Powerful, the Ancient. ***Atharva Veda***

The Word, verily, is greater than name. The Word, in fact, makes known the *Ṛig Veda*, the *Yajur Veda*, the *Sāma Veda*, the *Atharva Veda* as the fourth, and the ancient lore as the fifth: the *Veda* of *Vedas*, the ritual for ancestors, calculus, the augural sciences, the knowledge of the signs of the times, ethics, political science, sacred knowledge, theology, knowledge of the spirits, military science, astrology, the science of snakes and of celestial beings. The Word also makes known heaven, earth, wind, space, the waters, fire, the Gods, men, animals, birds, grass and trees, all animals down to worms, insects and ants. It also makes known what is right and wrong, truth and untruth, good and evil, what is pleasing and what is unpleasing. Verily, if there were no Word, there would be knowledge neither of right and wrong, nor of truth and untruth, nor of the pleasing and unpleasing. The Word makes all this known. Meditate on the Word. ***Sāma Veda***

The man who rejects the words of the scriptures and follows the impulse of desire attains neither his perfection, nor joy, nor the Path Supreme. Let the scriptures be, therefore, thy authority as to what is right and what is not right. ***Bhagavad Gītā***

Just as gold is freed from its dross only by fire, and acquires its shining appearance from heat, so the mind of a living being, cleansed from the filth of his actions and his desires through his love for Me, is transformed into My transcendent likeness. The mind is purified through the hearing and uttering of sacred hymns in My praise. ***Bhāgavata Purāṇa***

If daily to his home the friends who love him come, and coming, bring delight to eyes that kindle bright, a man has found the whole of life within his soul. ***Pañchatantra***

He who worships the Liṅga, knowing it to be the first cause, the source of consciousness, the substance of the universe, is nearer to Me than any other being. ***Śiva Purāṇa***

With the help of the gardeners called Mind and Love,
plucking the flower called Steady Contemplation, offering the water of the flood of the Self's own bliss, worship the Lord with the sacred formula of silence! ***Lallā***

Who will finish this suffering of mine? Who will take my burden on himself? Thy name will carry me over the sea of this world. Thou dost run to help the distressed. Now run to me, Nārāyaṇa, to me, poor and wretched as I am. Consider neither my merit nor my faults. Tukārām implores thy mercy. ***Tukārām***

The pot is a God. The winnowing fan is a God.
The stone in the street is a God. The comb is a God. The bowstring is also a God. The bushel is a God and the spouted cup is a God. Gods, Gods, there are so many, there's no place left for a foot. There is only one God. He is our Lord of the meeting rivers. ***Vachanas of Basavaṇṇa***

They will find enduring joy who praise the auspicious
God who knows the four *Vedas* and the six sacred sciences,
who is Himself the sacred Word recited by scholars of the scripture. ***Tirumurai***

The eighteen *Purāṇas* are the rich ornaments, and the theories propounded in them are the gems for which the rhythmic style provides the settings. ***Jñāneśvarī***

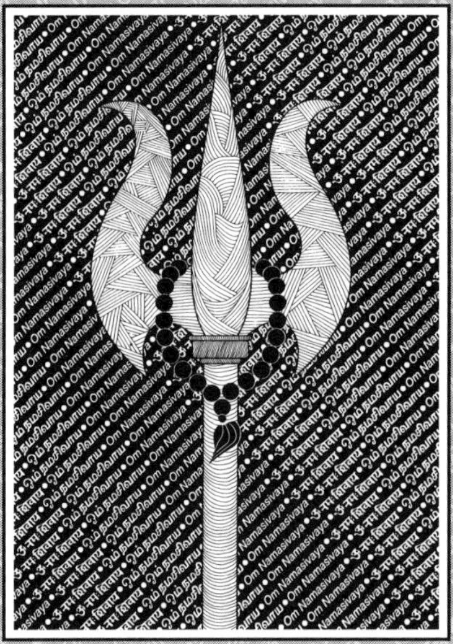
Om Namasivaya

Mantra Maṇḍala

मन्त्रमण्डल

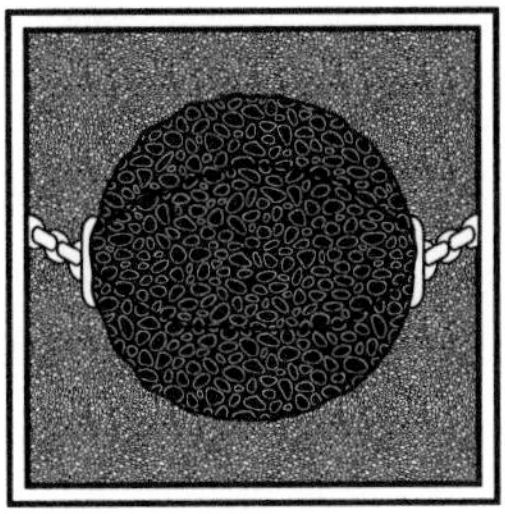

Mantra And Affirmation

Rudrāksha seeds, *Eleocarpus ganitrus,* are prized as the compassionate tears Lord Śiva shed for mankind's suffering. Śaivites wear *mālās* of them always as a symbol of God's love, chanting on each bead, "Aum Namaḥ Śivāya."

What Is the Holy Namaḥ Śivāya Mantra?

ŚLOKA 136

Namaḥ Śivāya is among the foremost Vedic *mantras.* It means "adoration to Śiva," and is called the Pañchākshara, or "five-letters." Within its celestial tones and hues resides all of the intuitive knowledge of Śaivism. Aum.

BHĀSHYA

Namaḥ Śivāya is the most holy name of God Śiva, recorded at the very center of the *Vedas* and elaborated in the *Śaiva Āgamas. Na* is the Lord's concealing grace, *Ma* is the world, *Śi* stands for Śiva, *Vā* is His revealing grace, *Ya* is the soul. The five elements, too, are embodied in this ancient formula for invocation. *Na* is earth, *Ma* is water, *Śi* is fire, *Vā* is air, and *Ya* is ether, or *ākāśa.* Many are its meanings. Namaḥ Śivāya has such power, the mere intonation of these syllables reaps its own reward in salvaging the soul from bondages of the treacherous instinctive mind and the steel bands of a perfected externalized intellect. Namaḥ Śivāya quells the instinct, cuts through the steel bands and turns this intellect within and on itself, to face itself and see its ignorance. Sages declare that *mantra* is life, that *mantra* is action, that *mantra* is love and that the repetition of *mantra, japa,* bursts forth wisdom from within. The holy *Natchintanai* proclaims, "Namaḥ Śivāya is in truth both *Āgama* and *Veda.* Namaḥ Śivāya represents all *mantras* and *tantras.* Namaḥ Śivāya is our souls, our bodies and possessions. Namaḥ Śivāya has become our sure protection." Aum Namaḥ Śivāya.

How Is Namaḥ Śivāya Properly Chanted?

ŚLOKA 137

The Pañchākshara Mantra, Namaḥ Śivāya, is repeated verbally or mentally, often while counting a *mālā* of *rudrāksha* beads, drawing the mind in upon itself to cognize Lord Śiva's infinite, all-pervasive presence. Aum.

BHĀSHYA

Japa yoga is the first *yoga* to be performed toward the goal of *jñāna.* In the temple perform *japa.* Under your favorite tree perform *japa.* Seated in a remote cave perform *japa.* Aum Namaḥ Śivāya can be performed on *rudrāksha* beads over and over when the sun is setting, when the sun is rising or high noon lights the day. "Aum Namaḥ Śivāya," the Śaivite chants. Aum Namaḥ Śivāya feeds his soul, brightens his intellect and quells his instinctive mind. Take the holy tears of Śiva, the auburn *rudrāksha* beads, into your hands. Push a bead over the middle finger with your thumb and hold as the intonation marks its passage. The duly initiated audibly repeats "Namaḥ Śivāya," and when *japa* is performed silently, mentally chants "Śivāya Namaḥ." There are many ways to chant this *mantra,* but perform it as you were initiated. Unauthorized experimentation is forbidden. Those prone to angry rage should never do *japa.* The *Tirumantiram* announces, "His feet are the letter *Na.* His navel is the letter *Ma.* His shoulders are the letter *Śi.* His mouth, the letter *Vā.* His radiant cranial center aloft is *Ya.* Thus is the five-lettered form of Śiva." Aum Namaḥ Śivāya.

Is Initiation Necessary to Perform Japa?

ŚLOKA 138

The most precious of all Śaivite *mantras,* Namaḥ Śivāya is freely sung and chanted by one and all. *Mantra dīkshā* bestows the permission and power for *japa yoga.* Without this initiation, its repetition bears lesser fruit. Aum.

BHĀSHYA

The Pañchākshara Mantra is the word of God, the name and total essence of Śiva. But to chant Namaḥ Śivāya and to be empowered to chant Namaḥ Śivāya is likened to the difference between writing a check without money in the bank and writing a check with money in the bank. Namaḥ Śivāya is the gateway to *yoga.* Initiation from an orthodox *guru* is given after preparation, training and attaining a certain level of purity and dedication. The *guru* bestows the authority to chant Namaḥ Śivāya. After initiation, the devotee is obligated to intone it regularly as instructed. This forges the *śishya's* permanent bond with the *guru* and his spiritual lineage, *sampradāya,* and fires the process of inner unfoldment. From the lips of my Satgurunātha I learned Namaḥ Śivāya, and it has been the central core of my life, strength and fulfillment of destiny. The secret of Namaḥ Śivāya is to hear it from the right lips at the right time. Then, and only then, is it the most powerful *mantra* for you. The *Śiva Saṁhitā* affirms, "Only the knowledge imparted by a *guru,* through his lips, is powerful and useful; otherwise it becomes fruitless, weak and very painful." Aum Namaḥ Śivāya.

What Is Śaivism's Affirmation of Faith?

ŚLOKA 139

The proclamation "God Śiva is Immanent Love and Transcendent Reality" is a potent affirmation of faith. Said in any of Earth's 3,000 languages, it summarizes the beliefs and doctrines of the Śaivite Hindu religion. Aum.

BHĀSHYA

An affirmation of faith is a terse, concise statement summarizing a complex philosophical tradition. "God Śiva is Immanent Love and Transcendent Reality," is what we have when we take the milk from the sacred cow of Śaivism, separate out the cream, churn that cream to rich butter and boil that butter into a precious few drops of *ghee*. "God Śiva is Immanent Love and Transcendent Reality" is the sweet *ghee* of the Śaivite Hindu religion. In the Sanskṛit language it is *Premaiva Śivamaya, Satyam eva Paraśivaḥ*. In the sweet Tamil language it is even more succinct and beautiful: *Anbe Śivamayam, Satyame Paraśivam*. In French it is *Dieu Śiva est Amour omniprésent et Réalité transcendante.* We strengthen our mind with positive affirmations that record the impressions of the distilled and ultimate truths of our religion so that these memories fortify us in times of distress, worldliness or anxiety. The *Tirumantiram* proclaims, "Transcending all, yet immanent in each He stands. For those bound in the world here below, He is the great treasure. Himself the Parapara Supreme, for all worlds He gave the way that His greatness extends." Aum Namaḥ Śivāya.

How Is the Affirmation of Faith Used?

ŚLOKA 140

Intoning the affirmation of faith, we positively assert that God is both manifest and unmanifest, both permeating the world and transcending it, both personal Divine Love and impersonal Reality. Aum Namaḥ Śivāya.

BHĀSHYA

On the lips of Śaivites throughout the world resounds the proclamation "God Śiva is Immanent Love and Transcendent Reality." It is a statement of fact, a summation of truth, even more potent when intoned in one's native language. "God Śiva is Immanent Love and Transcendent Reality," we repeat prior to sleep. "God Śiva is Immanent Love and Transcendent Reality," we say upon awakening as we recall the transcendent knowledge gained from the *ṛishis* during sleep. These sacred words we say as we bathe to prepare to face the day, God Śiva's day, reminding ourselves that His immanent love protects us, guides us, lifting our mind into the arena of useful thoughts and keeping us from harm's way. Devotees write this affirmation 1,008 times as a *sahasra lekhana sādhana*. It may be spoken 108 times daily in any language before initiation into Namaḥ Śivāya. Yea, the recitation of this affirmation draws devotees into Śiva-consciousness. The *Tirumantiram* says, "The ignorant prate that love and Śiva are two. They do not know that love alone is Śiva. When men know that love and Śiva are the same, love as Śiva they ever remain." Aum Namaḥ Śivāya.

Scriptures Speak on Affirmation

Namastārāya namaḥ śambhave cha mayobhave cha, namaḥ śaṅkarāya cha mayaskarāya cha, namaḥ śivāya cha śivatarāya cha.

* * *

Homage to the source of health, and to the source of delight. Homage to the maker of health and to the maker of delight. Homage to the Auspicious and to the more Auspicious. ***Yajur Veda***

From all knowledge, *yoga* practice and meditation, all that relates to the *Aum* sound is to be meditated on as the only blissful (Śiva). Indeed, the *Aum* sound is Śiva. ***Atharva Veda***

By means of the hymns one attains this world, by the sacrificial formulas the space in-between, by holy chant the world revealed by the sages. With the syllable *Aum* as his sole support, the wise man attains that which is peaceful, unaging, deathless, fearless—the Supreme. ***Atharva Veda***

Mantra yields early success due to practice done in previous life. Self-fulfilling, too, is the *mantra* which is received according to the line of tradition, with due *dīkshā,* obtained in the right way. Innumerable are the *mantras*; they but distract the mind. Only that *mantra* which is received through the grace of the *guru* gives all fulfillment. ***Kulārṇava Tantra***

Japa is the happy giver of enjoyment, salvation, self-fulfilling wish. Therefore, practice the *yoga* of *japa* and *dhyāna.* All blemishes due to transgressions of rule, from the *jīva* up to the Brahman, done knowingly or unknowingly, are wiped away by *japa.* ***Kulārṇava Tantra***

The bank of a river, the cave, the summit of a hill, the place of holy bath, the confluence of rivers, the holy forest, the vacant garden, the root of the *bilva* tree, the slope of the hill, the temple, the coast of the sea, one's own house—these are the places lauded for the *sādhana* of *mantra japa.* ***Kulārṇava Tantra***

Have faith in God. Believe in Him with all your heart. Think that in the world He is for you the sweetest of all sweet things. Think that there is nothing other than God. Sitting or standing, walking or lying down, think of Him. ***Natchintanai***

Through the Letters Five can God's holy feet be seen. Through the Letters Five, the whole world you can rule. Through the Letters Five, mind's action can be stilled. The Letters Five have come and entered my heart. ***Natchintanai***

Let not the effect of past deeds rise in quick succession and overpower you. Chant the Pañchākshara—the *mantra* of the five letters. ***Guru Vāchagam***

Thinking of Him, great love welling up in their heart, if they finger the *rudrāksha* beads, it will bring them the glory of the Gods. Chant our naked Lord's name. Say, "Namaḥ Śivāya!" ***Tirumurai***

The mystic expression "Namaḥ Śivāya" is the sacred name of Lord Śiva, is the sum and substance of the four *Vedas* and conveys in the sacred path souls which are full of devotion and do utter it with a melting heart and tears trickling from their eyes. ***Tirumurai***

The Lord of Appati is both inside and outside, form and no form. He is both the flood and the bank. He is the broad-rayed sun. Himself the highest mystery, He is in all hidden thoughts. He is thought and meaning, and embraces all who embrace Him. ***Tirumurai***

Advaita Īśvaravāda Upanishad

अद्वैत ईश्वरवाद उपनिषद्

Monistic Theism

Advaita-Dvaita Maṇḍala

अद्वैतद्वैतमण्डल

Monism and Dualism

Chandra is the moon, ruler of the watery realms and of emotion, testing place of migrating souls. *Sūrya* is the sun, ruler of intellect, source of truth. One is *piṅgalā* and lights the day; the other is *iḍā* and lights the night. Aum.

What Are the Many Hindu Philosophies?

ŚLOKA 141

From time immemorial, India's sages and philosophers have pondered the nature of reality. Out of their speculations have blossomed hundreds of schools of thought, all evolving from the rich soil of village Hinduism. Aum.

BHĀSHYA

At one end of Hinduism's complex spectrum is monism, *advaita,* which perceives a unity of God, soul and world, as in Śaṅkara's acosmic pantheism and Kashmīr Śaiva monism. At the other end is dualism, *dvaita*—exemplified by Mādhva and the early Pāśupatas—which teaches two or more separate realities. In between are views describing reality as one and yet not one, *dvaita-advaita,* such as Rāmānuja's Vaishṇava Vedānta and Śrīkaṇṭha's Śaiva Viśishṭādvaita. Hindu philosophy consists of many schools of Vedic and Āgamic thought, including the six classical *darśanas*—Nyāya, Vaiśeshika, Sāṅkhya, Yoga, Mīmāṁsā and Vedānta. Each theology expresses the quest for God and is influenced by the myth, mystery and cultural syncretism of contemporary, tribal, shamanic Hinduism alive in every village in every age. India also produced views, called *nāstika,* that reject the *Vedas* and are thus not part of Hinduism, such as Jainism, Sikhism, Buddhism and Chārvāka materialistic atheism. The *Vedas* state, "Theologians ask: What is the cause? Is it Brahmā? Whence are we born? Whereby do we live? And on what are we established?" Aum Namaḥ Śivāya.

How Do Monism and Dualism Differ?

ŚLOKA 142

To most monists God is immanent, temporal, becoming. He is creation itself, material cause, but not efficient cause. To most dualists, God is transcendent, eternal, Creator—efficient cause but not material cause. Aum.

BHĀSHYA

To explain creation, philosophers speak of three kinds of causes: efficient, instrumental and material. These are likened to a potter's molding a pot from clay. The potter, who makes the process happen, is the *efficient cause.* The wheel he uses to spin and mold the pot is the *instrumental cause,* thought of as God's power, or *śakti.* The clay is the *material cause.* Theistic dualists believe in God as Lord and Creator, but He remains ever separate from man and the world and is not the material cause. Among the notable dualists have been Kapila, Mādhva, Meykandar, Chaitanya, Aristotle, Augustine, Kant and virtually all Jewish, Christian and Muslim theologians. The most prevalent monism is pantheism, "all is God," and its views do not permit of a God who is Lord and Creator. He is immanent, temporal—material cause but not efficient cause. History's pantheists include Śaṅkara, Vivekānanda, Aurobindo, Plotinus, the Stoics, Spinoza and Aśvaghosha. The *Vedas* proclaim, "As a thousand sparks from a fire well blazing spring forth, each one like the rest, so from the Imperishable all kinds of beings come forth, my dear, and to Him return." Aum Namaḥ Śivāya.

Are Monism and Dualism Reconcilable?

ŚLOKA 143

Monists, from their mountaintop perspective, perceive a one reality in all things. Dualists, from the foothills, see God, souls and world as eternally separate. Monistic theism is the perfect reconciliation of these two views. Aum.

BHĀSHYA

Visualize a mountain and the path leading to its icy summit. As the climber traverses the lower ranges, he sees the meadows, the passes, the giant boulders. This we can liken to dualism, the natural, theistic state where God and man are different. Reaching the summit, the climber sees that the many parts are actually a one mountain. This realization is likened to pure monism. Unfortunately, many monists, reaching the summit, teach a denial of the foothills they themselves climbed on the way to their monistic platform. However, by going a little higher, lifting the *kuṇḍalinī* into the space above the mountain's peak, the entire Truth is known. The bottom and the top are viewed as a one whole, just as theism and monism are accepted by the awakened soul. Monistic theism, Advaita Īśvaravāda, reconciles the dichotomy of being and becoming, the apparent contradiction of God's eternality and temporal activity, the confusion of good and evil, the impasse of one and two. The *Vedas* affirm, "He who knows this becomes a knower of the One and of duality, he who has attained to the oneness of the One, to the self-same nature." Aum Namaḥ Śivāya.

What Is the View of Monistic Theism?

ŚLOKA 144

Monistic theism is the synthesis of monism and dualism. It says God is transcendent and immanent, eternal and temporal, Being and becoming, Creator and created, Absolute and relative, efficient and material cause. Aum.

BHĀSHYA

Both strict monism and dualism are fatally flawed, for neither alone encompasses the whole of truth. In other words, it is not a choice between the *God-is-man-and-world* view of pantheistic monism and the *God-is-separate-from-man-and-world* view of theistic dualism. It is both. *Panentheism,* which describes "all in God, and God in all," and monistic theism are Western terms for Advaita Īśvaravāda. It is the view that embraces the oneness of God and soul, monism, and the reality of the Personal God, theism. As panentheists, we believe in an eternal oneness of God and man at the level of Satchidānanda and Paraśiva. But a difference is acknowledged during the evolution of the soul body. Ultimately, even this difference merges in identity. Thus, there is perfectly beginningless oneness and a temporary difference which resolves itself in perfect identity. In the acceptance of this identity, monistic theists differ from most *viśishṭādvaitins.* The *Vedas* declare, "He moves and He moves not; He is far, yet is near. He is within all that is, yet is also outside. The man who sees all beings in the Self and the Self in all beings is free from all fear." Aum Namaḥ Śivāya.

Is Monistic Theism Found in the Vedas?

ŚLOKA 145

Again and again in the *Vedas* and from *satgurus* we hear "Aham Brahmāsmi," "I am God," and that God is both immanent and transcendent. Taken together, these are clear statements of monistic theism. Aum Namaḥ Śivāya.

BHĀSHYA

Monistic theism is the philosophy of the *Vedas.* Scholars have long noted that the Hindu scriptures are alternately monistic, describing the oneness of the individual soul and God, and theistic, describing the reality of the Personal God. One cannot read the *Vedas, Śaiva Āgamas* and hymns of the saints without being overwhelmed with theism as well as monism. Monistic theism is the essential teaching of Hinduism, of Śaivism. It is the conclusion of Tirumular, Vasugupta, Gorakshanātha, Bhāskara, Śrīkaṇṭha, Basavaṇṇa, Vallabha, Rāmakṛishṇa, Yogaswāmī, Nityānanda, Rādhākṛishṇan and thousands of others. It encompasses both Siddhānta and Vedānta. It says, God is and is in all things. It propounds the hopeful, glorious, exultant concept that every soul will finally merge with Śiva in undifferentiated oneness, none left to suffer forever because of human transgression. The *Vedas* wisely proclaim, "Higher and other than the world-tree, time and forms is He from whom this expanse proceeds—the bringer of *dharma,* the remover of evil, the lord of prosperity. Know Him as in one's own Self, as the immortal abode of all." Aum Namaḥ Śivāya.

Scriptures Speak on One and Two

There is on earth no diversity. He gets death after death who perceives here seeming diversity. As a unity only is It to be looked upon—this indemonstrable, enduring Being, spotless, beyond space, the unborn Soul, great, enduring. *Yajur Veda*

Contemplating Him who has neither beginning, middle, nor end—the One, the all-pervading, who is wisdom and bliss, the formless, the wonderful, whose consort is Umā, the highest Lord, the ruler, having three eyes and a blue throat, the peaceful—the silent sage reaches the source of Being, the universal witness, on the other shore of darkness. *Atharva Veda*

Where there is duality, there one sees another, one smells another, one tastes another, one speaks to another, one hears another, one knows another. But where everything has become one's own Self, with what should one see whom, with what should one smell whom, with what should one taste whom, with what should one speak to whom, with what should one hear whom, with what should one think of whom, with what should one touch whom, with what should one know whom? How can He be known by whom all this is made known? *Yajur Veda*

When the Great Being is seen as both the higher and the lower, then the knot of the heart is rent asunder, all doubts are dispelled and *karma* is destroyed. *Atharva Veda*

Than whom there is naught else higher, than whom there is naught smaller, naught greater, the One stands like a tree established in heaven. By Him, the Person, is this whole universe filled. *Yajur Veda*

Even as water becomes one with water, fire with fire, and air with air, so the mind becomes one with the Infinite Mind and thus attains final freedom. ***Yajur Veda***

One who is established in the contemplation of nondual unity will abide in the Self of everyone and realize the immanent, all-pervading One. There is no doubt of this. ***Sarvajñānottara Āgama***

O Six-Faced God! What is the use of putting it in so many words? Multiplicity of form exists only in the self, and the forms are externalized by the confused mind. They are objectively created simultaneously with thoughts of them. ***Sarvajñānottara Āgama***

The luminous Being of the perfect I-consciousness, inherent in the multitude of words, whose essence consists in the knowledge of the highest nondualism, is the secret of *mantra*. ***Śiva Sūtras***

I sought Him in terms of I and you. But He who knows not I from you taught me the truth that I indeed is you. And now I talk not of I and you. ***Tirumantiram***

Oh thou who pervades all space, both now and hereafter, as the Soul of souls! The *Vedas, Āgamas, Purāṇas, Itihāsas* and all other sciences inculcate fully the tenet of nonduality. It is the inexplicable duality that leads to the knowledge of nonduality. This is consonant with reason, experience, tradition, and is admitted by the dualists and nondualists. ***Tayumanavar***

When the *Vedas* and *Āgamas* all proclaim that the whole world is filled with God and that there is nothing else, how can we say that the world exists and the body exists? Is there anything more worthy of reproach than to attribute an independent reality to them? ***Natchintanai***

Siddhānta Maṇḍala

सिद्धान्तमण्डल

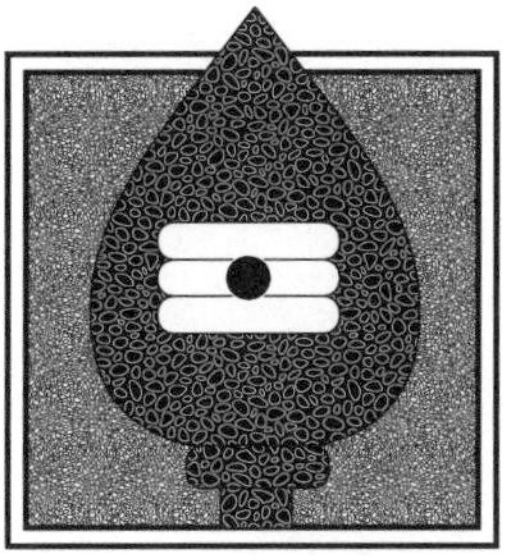

Views of Reality

Vel, the holy lance, is Lord Murugan's protective power, our safeguard in adversity. Its tip is wide, long and sharp, signifying incisive discrimination and spiritual knowledge, which must be broad, deep and penetrating. Aum.

What Are Śaiva Siddhānta's Two Schools?

ŚLOKA 146

There are two Śaiva Siddhānta schools: pluralistic theism, in the lines of Aghoraśiva and Meykandar, and Tirumular's monistic theism. While differing slightly, they share a religious heritage of belief, culture and practice. Aum.

BHĀSHYA

Here we compare the monistic Siddhānta of Ṛishi Tirumular that this catechism embodies and the pluralistic realism expounded by Meykandar and his disciples. They share far more in common than they hold in difference. In South India, their points of agreement are summarized as *guru,* preceptor; Liṅga, holy image of Śiva; *saṅga,* fellowship of devotees; and *valipadu,* ritual worship. Both agree that God Śiva is the efficient cause of creation, and also that His *Śakti* is the instrumental cause. Their differences arise around the question of material cause, the nature of the original substance, whether it is one with or apart from God. They also differ on the identity of the soul and God, evil and final dissolution. While monistic theists, Advaita Īśvaravādins, view the 2,200-year-old *Tirumantiram* as Siddhānta's authority, pluralists, Anekavādins, rely mainly on the 800-year-old *Aghoraśiva Paddhatis* and *Meykandar Śāstras.* The *Tirumantiram* inquires: "Who can know the greatness of our Lord? Who can measure His length and breadth? He is the mighty nameless Flame of whose unknown beginnings I venture to speak." Aum Namaḥ Śivāya.

What Are the Two Views on Creation?

ŚLOKA 147

Monistic theists believe that Śiva creates the cosmos as an emanation of Himself. He is His creation. Pluralistic theists hold that Śiva molds eternally existing matter to fashion the cosmos and is thus not His creation. Aum.

BHĀSHYA

Pluralistic Siddhāntins hold that God, souls and world—Pati, *paśu* and *pāśa*—are three eternally coexistent realities. By creation, this school understands that Śiva fashions existing matter, *māyā*, into various forms. In other words, God, like a potter, is the efficient cause of the cosmos. But He is not the material cause, the "clay" from which the cosmos is formed. Pluralists hold that any reason for the creation of *pāśa—āṇava, karma* and *māyā*—whether it be a divine desire, a demonstration of glory or merely a playful sport, makes the Creator less than perfect. Therefore, *pāśa* could never have been created. Monistic Siddhāntins totally reject the potter analogy. They teach that God is simultaneously the efficient, instrumental and material cause. Śiva is constantly emanating creation from Himself. His act of manifestation may be likened to heat issuing from a fire, a mountain from the earth or waves from the ocean. The heat is the fire, the mountain is the earth, the waves are not different from the ocean. The *Vedas* proclaim, "In That all this unites; from That all issues forth. He, omnipresent, is the warp and woof of all created things." Aum Namaḥ Śivāya.

What Are the Views on God and Soul?

ŚLOKA 148

For the monistic theist, the soul is an emanation of God Śiva and will merge back in Him as a river to the sea. For pluralists, God pervades but did not create the soul; thus, God and soul remain separate realities forever. Aum.

BHĀSHYA

Pluralistic Siddhāntins teach that Śiva pervades the soul, yet the soul is uncreated and exists eternally. It is amorphous, but has the qualities of willing, thinking and acting. It does not wholly merge in Him at the end of its evolution. Rather, it reaches His realm and enjoys the bliss of divine communion eternally. Like salt dissolved in water, soul and God are not two; neither are they perfectly one. For monistic Siddhāntins the soul emerges from God like a rain cloud drawn from the sea. Like a river, the soul passes through many births. The soul consists of an uncreated divine essence and a beautiful, effulgent, human-like form created by Śiva. While this form—called the *ānandamaya kośa* or soul body—is maturing, it is distinct from God. Even during this evolution, its essence, Satchidānanda and Paraśiva, is not different from Śiva. Finally, like a river flowing into the sea, the soul returns to its source. Soul and God are perfectly one. The *Vedas* say, "Just as the flowing rivers disappear in the ocean, casting off name and shape, even so the knower, freed from name and shape, attains to the Primal Soul, higher than the high." Aum Namaḥ Śivāya.

What Are the Differing Views on Evil?

ŚLOKA 149

For monistic theists, the world of *māyā* is Śiva's perfect creation, containing each thing and its opposite. For pluralistic theists, the world is tarnished with evil; thus *māyā* could not be the creation of a perfect God. Aum.

BHĀSHYA

Pluralistic Siddhāntins hold that the world of *māyā* is intrinsically evil and imperfect, for it is clearly full of sorrow, injustice, disease and death. The soul, too, is beginninglessly tainted with *āṇava,* or limitation. Pluralists contend that if God had created *māyā*—the material of the world—or the soul, surely He would have made them flawless, and there would be no evil, for imperfection cannot arise out of Perfection. Therefore, they conclude that *āṇava, karma* and *māyā* have always existed and the soul has been immersed in darkness and bondage without beginning. Monistic Siddhāntins hold that when viewed from higher consciousness, this world is seen as it truly is—perfect. There is no intrinsic evil. God Śiva has created the principle of opposites, which are the means for the soul's maturation—beauty and deformity, light and darkness, love and hate, joy and sorrow. All is God Śiva Himself, in Him and of Him. A perfect cosmos has issued forth from a perfect Creator. The *Tirumantiram* says, "All manifestations of nature are His grace. All animate and inanimate are His pure grace. As darkness, as light, the Lord's grace pervades." Aum Namaḥ Śivāya.

What Are the Views on Mahāpralaya?

ŚLOKA 150

Monistic theists hold that at *mahāpralaya,* cosmic dissolution, all creation is withdrawn into Śiva, and He alone exists. Pluralistic theists hold that world and souls persist in seed form and will later reemerge. Aum Namaḥ Śivāya.

BHĀSHYA

Pluralistic Siddhāntins contend that after *mahāpralaya*—the withdrawal of time, form and space into Śiva—souls and world are so close to Śiva that, for all practical purposes, He alone exists. Actually, they say, both world and souls continue to exist, not as things, but as "potentialities." As if in a deep sleep, souls, now in a bodiless state, rest. Individual *karmas* lie dormant to germinate later when creation again issues forth and nonliberated souls are re-embodied to continue their spiritual journey. Monistic Siddhāntins believe that souls persist through the lesser *pralayas* of the cosmic cycle, but hold that only Śiva exists following *mahāpralaya.* There is no "other," no separate souls, no separate world. The universe and all souls are absorbed in Śiva. *Pāśa—āṇava, karma* and *māyā*—is annihilated. In the intensity of pre-dissolution, when time itself is accelerated, all souls attain complete maturation, losing separateness through fulfilled merger with Śiva. Yea, *jīva* becomes Śiva. The *Vedas* boldly decree, "By His divine power He holds dominion over all the worlds. At the periods of creation and dissolution of the universe, He alone exists." Aum Namaḥ Śivāya.

Scriptures Speak on Siddhānta

Meditate on the Lord as the object of meditation, for by the Lord the whole world is set to activity. Brahmā, Vishṇu, Rudra and Indra have been brought forth by Him; similarly, all faculties along with creatures. His divine majesty has become the Cause, the Universe, the Blissful, as the ether standing unshaken in the mid-air. ***Atharva Veda***

Whoever has found and has awakened to the Self that has entered into this perilous inaccessible place, the body, he is the maker of the universe, for he is the maker of all. His is the world. Indeed, he is the world itself. ***Yajur Veda***

All the sacred books, all holy sacrifice and ritual and prayers, all the words of the *Vedas*, and the whole past and present and future, come from the Spirit. With *māyā*, His power of wonder, He made all things, and by *māyā* the human soul is bound. Know, therefore, that nature is *māyā*, but that God is the ruler of *māyā*, and that all beings in our universe are parts of His infinite splendor. ***Yajur Veda***

For the sake of experiencing the true and the false, the great Self has a dual nature. Yea, the great Self has a dual nature. Yea, the great Self has a dual nature! ***Yajur Veda***

The seer sees not death, nor sickness, nor any distress. The seer sees only the All, obtains the All entirely. ***Yajur Veda***

Inconceivable is this supreme *ātman*, immeasurable, unborn, inscrutable, unthinkable, He whose Self is infinite space. He alone remains awake when the universe is dissolved, and out of this space He awakens the world consisting of thought. ***Yajur Veda***

That intelligence which incites the functions into the paths of virtue or vice am I. All this universe, moveable and immoveable, is from Me. All things are preserved by Me. All are absorbed into Me at the time of *pralaya*. Because there exists nothing but Spirit, and I am that Spirit, there exists nothing else. ***Śiva Saṁhitā***

The Primal One, the indivisible great, Himself
into several divided. As form, formless and form-formless,
and as *guru* and as Śakti's Lord. In forms numerous He immanent
in *jīvas* became. ***Tirumantiram***

You and He are not two separate; you and He are but
one united; thus do you stand, freed of all sectarian shackles; adore
the Feet of Paraparai and with Śiva become One—that the way
Siddhānta fulfills. ***Tirumantiram***

It is the Primal One without past or future. Its form is free from age and sickness. It manifests as father and mother. It blossoms as the Self-Existent. It cannot be described as one or two. No artist can portray It. It is that which lies 'twixt good and evil. It ever abides in the hearts of the wise. It permits no distinction between Vedānta and Siddhānta. It is That which dances at the zenith beyond the realm of sound. ***Natchintanai***

Always my action is your action. I am not other than you, because the essence of myself which I call "I" does not exist apart from you. Herein lies the natural harmony between Vedānta and Siddhānta. ***Tayumanavar***

As wide earth, as fire and water, as sacrificer and wind that blows, as eternal moon and sun, as ether, as the eight-formed God, as cosmic good and evil, woman and man, all other forms and His own form, and all these as Himself, as yesterday and today and tomorrow, the God of the long, red hair stands, O Wonder! ***Tirumurai***

Sampradāya Upanishad

संप्रदाय उपनिषद्

Passing on the Power

Kailāsa Paramparā Maṇḍala

कैलासपरंपरामण्डल

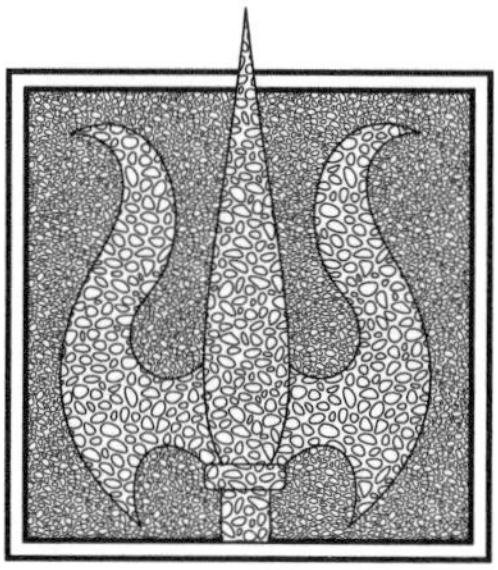

Himalayan Lineage

Triśūla, Śiva's trident carried by Himalayan *yogīs,* is the royal scepter of the Śaiva Dharma. Its triple prongs betoken desire, action and wisdom; *iḍā, piṅgalā* and *sushumṇā;* and the *guṇas—sattva, rajas* and *tamas.* Aum.

What Is Hinduism's Nātha Sampradāya?

ŚLOKA 151

The Nātha Sampradāya, "the masters' way," is the mystical fountainhead of Śaivism. The divine message of the eternal truths and how to succeed on the path to enlightenment are locked within the Nātha tradition. Aum.

BHĀSHYA

Nātha means "lord or adept," and *sampradāya* refers to a living theological tradition. The roots of this venerable heritage stretch back beyond recorded history, when awakened Nātha mystics worshiped the Lord of lords, Śiva, and in *yogic* contemplation experienced their identity in Him. The Nātha Sampradāya has revealed the search for the innermost divine Self, balanced by temple worship, fueled by *kuṇḍalinī yoga,* charted by monistic theism, illumined by a potent *guru-śishya* system, guided by soul-stirring scriptures and awakened by *sādhana* and *tapas.* Thus has it given mankind the mechanics for moving forward in evolution. Today two main Nātha streams are well known: the Nandinātha Sampradāya, made famous by Maharishi Nandinātha (ca 250 BCE), and the Ādinātha Sampradāya, carried forth by Siddha Yogī Gorakshanātha (ca 900). Yea, there is infinitely more to know of the mysterious Nāthas. The *Tirumantiram* states, "My peerless *satguru,* Nandinātha, of Śaivam honored high, showed us a holy path for soul's redemption. It is Śiva's divine path, San Mārga, for all the world to tread and forever be free." Aum Namaḥ Śivāya.

What Is the Lofty Kailāsa Paramparā?

ŚLOKA 152

The Kailāsa Paramparā is a millennia-old *guru* lineage of the Nandinātha Sampradāya. In this century it was embodied by Sage Yogaswāmī, who ordained me in Sri Lanka in 1949 to carry on the venerable tradition. Aum.

BHĀSHYA

The authenticity of Hindu teachings is perpetuated by lineages, *paramparā,* passed from *gurus* to their successors through ordination. The Kailāsa Paramparā extends back to, and far beyond, Maharishi Nandinātha and his eight disciples—Sanatkumāra, Sanakar, Sanadanar, Sananthanar, Śivayogamuni, Patañjali, Vyāgrapāda and Tirumular. This succession of *siddha yoga* adepts flourishes today in many streams, most notably in the Śaiva Siddhānta of South India. Our branch of this *paramparā* is the line of Ṛishi Tirumular (ca 200 BCE), of which the first known *satguru* in recent history was the Ṛishi from the Himalayas (ca 1770–1840). From him the power was passed to Siddha Kadaitswāmī of Bangalore (ca 1810–1875), then to Satguru Chellappāswāmī (1840–1915), then to Sage Yogaswāmī (1872–1964) of Sri Lanka, and finally to myself, Sivaya Subramuniyaswami (1927–). The *Tirumantiram* states, "Thus expounding, I bore His word down Kailāsa's unchanging path—the word of Him, the eternal, the truth effulgent, the limitless great, Nandinātha, the joyous one, He of the blissful dance that all impurity dispels." Aum Namaḥ Śivāya.

Who Were the Early Kailāsa Preceptors?

ŚLOKA 153

Among its ancient *gurus*, the Kailāsa Paramparā honors the illustrious Ṛishi Tirumular and his generations of successors. In recent history we especially revere the silent *siddha* called "Ṛishi from the Himalayas." Aum.

BHĀSHYA

Having achieved perfect enlightenment and the eight *siddhis* at the feet of Maharishi Nandinātha in the Himalayas, Ṛishi Tirumular was sent by his *satguru* to revive Śaiva Siddhānta in the South of India. Finally, he reached Tiruvavaduthurai, where, in the Tamil language, he recorded the truths of the *Śaiva Āgamas* and the precious *Vedas* in the *Tirumantiram*, a book of over 3,000 esoteric verses. Through the centuries, the Kailāsa mantle was passed from one *siddha yogī* to the next. Among these luminaries was the nameless Ṛishi from the Himalayas, who in the 1700s entered a teashop in a village near Bangalore, sat down and entered into deep *samādhi.* He did not move for seven years, nor did he speak. Streams of devotees came for his *darśana.* Their unspoken prayers and questions were mysteriously answered in dreams or in written, paper messages that manifested in the air and floated down. Then one day Ṛishi left the village, later to pass his power to Kadaitswāmī. The *Tirumantiram* expounds, "With Nandi's grace I sought the primal cause. With Nandi's grace I Sadāśiva became. With Nandi's grace truth divine I attained." Aum Namaḥ Śivāya.

Who Were Kadaitswāmī and Chellappan?

ŚLOKA 154

Kadaitswāmī was a dynamic *satguru* who revived Śaivism in Catholic-dominated Jaffna, Sri Lanka, in the 1800s. Chellappaswāmī was an ardent sage, ablaze with God consciousness, immersed in divine soliloquy. Aum.

BHĀSHYA

Kadaitswāmī was a powerful *siddha,* standing two meters tall, whose fiery marketplace talks converted thousands back to Śaivism. It is said he was a high court judge who refused to confer the death penalty and renounced his career at middle age to become a *sannyāsin.* Directed by his *satguru* to be a worker of miracles, he performed *siddhis* that are talked about to this day—turning iron to gold, drinking molten wax, disappearing and appearing elsewhere. Chellappaswāmī, initiated at age nineteen, lived alone in the *teradi* at Nallur temple. Absorbed in the inner Self, recognizing no duality, he uttered *advaitic* axioms in constant refrain: "There is no intrinsic evil. It was all finished long ago. All that is, is Truth. We know not!" The *Natchintanai* says, "Laughing, Chellappan roams in Nallur's precincts. Appearing like a man possessed, he scorns all outward show. Dark is his body; his only garment, rags. Now all my sins have gone, for he has burnt them up! Always repeating something softly to himself, he will impart the blessing of true life to anyone who ventures to come near him. And he has made a temple of my mind." Aum Namaḥ Śivāya.

Who Are the Most Recent Kailāsa Gurus?

ŚLOKA 155

Sage Yogaswāmī, source of *Natchintanai,* protector of *dharma,* was *satguru* of Sri Lanka for half a century. He ordained me with a slap on the back, commanding, "Go round the world and roar like a lion!" Aum Namaḥ Śivāya.

BHĀSHYA

Amid a festival crowd outside Nallur temple, a disheveled *sādhu* shook the bars from within the chariot shed, shouting, "Hey! Who are you?" and in that moment Yogaswāmī was transfixed. "There is not one wrong thing!" "It is as it is! Who knows?" Sage Chellappan said, and suddenly the world vanished. After Chellappan's *mahāsamādhi* in 1915, Yogaswāmī undertook five years of intense *sādhana.* Later, people of all walks of life, all nations, came for his *darśana.* He urged one and all to "Know thy Self by thyself." It was in his thatched, dung-floor hermitage in 1949 that we first met. I had just weeks before realized *Paraśiva* with his inner help while meditating in the caves of Jalani. "You are in me," he said. "I am in you," I responded. Later he ordained me "Subramuniyaswami" with a tremendous slap on the back, and with this *dīkshā* sent me as a *sannyāsin* to America, saying, "You will build temples. You will feed thousands." I was 22 at the time, and he was 77. In fulfillment of his orders have I, Sivaya Subramuniyaswami, composed these 155 *ślokas* and *bhāshyas,* telling an infinitesimal fraction of all that he infused in me. Aum Namaḥ Śivāya.

Scriptures Speak on Paramparā

There is no one greater in the three worlds than the *guru.* It is he who grants divine knowledge and should be worshiped with supreme devotion. ***Atharva Veda***

Abiding in the midst of ignorance, but thinking themselves wise and learned, fools aimlessly go hither and thither, like blind led by the blind. ***Atharva Veda***

Truth is the Supreme, the Supreme is Truth. Through Truth men never fall from the heavenly world, because Truth belongs to the saints. Therefore, they rejoice in Truth. ***Yajur Veda***

The supreme mystery in the *Veda's* end, which has been declared in former times, should not be given to one not tranquil, nor again to one who is not a son or a pupil. To one who has the highest devotion for God, and for his spiritual teacher even as for God, to him these matters which have been declared become manifest if he be a great soul—yea, become manifest if he be a great soul! ***Yajur Veda***

Disciples get, by devotion to the *guru,* the knowledge which the *guru* possesses. In the three worlds this fact is clearly enunciated by divine sages, the ancestors and learned men. ***Guru Gītā***

It is laid down by the Lord that there can be no *moksha,* liberation, without *dīkshā,* initiation; and initiation cannot be there without a teacher. Hence, it comes down the line of teachers, *paramparā.* ***Kulārṇava Tantra***

Though himself unattached, the *guru*, after testing him for some time, on command of the Lord, shall deliver the Truth to his disciple in order to vest him with authority. Of him who is so invested with authority, there is verily union with the Supreme Śiva. At the termination of the bodily life, his is the eternal liberation—this is declared by the Lord. Therefore, one should seek with all effort to have a *guru* of the unbroken tradition, born of Supreme Śiva himself. ***Kulārṇava Tantra***

Without a teacher, all philosophy, traditional knowledge and *mantras* are fruitless. Him alone the Gods laud who is the *guru*, keeping active what is handed down by tradition. ***Kulārṇava Tantra***

I adore the lotus feet of the teachers who have shown to us the source of the eternal ocean of bliss, born of the Self within, who have given us the remedy for the *hala-hala* poison of *saṁsāra*. ***Guru Gītā***

Night and day in Nallur's precincts, Chellappan danced in bliss. Even holy *yogīs* merged in silence do not know him. He keeps repeating, "All is truth," with radiant countenance. Night and day in Nallur's precincts, Chellappan danced in bliss. ***Natchintanai***

Seek the Nāthas who Nandinātha's grace received. First the *ṛishis* four, Śivayoga the holy next, then Patañjali, who in Sabhā's holy precincts worshiped. Vyāghra and I complete the number eight. ***Tirumantiram***

Nandinātha accepted the offering of my body, wealth and life. He then touched me, and his glance dispelled my distressful *karma*. He placed his feet on my head and imparted higher consciousness. Thus, he severed my burdensome cycle of birth. ***Tirumantiram***

Upagrantha

उपग्रन्थ

Resources

Śaiva Śraddhādhāraṇā

शैवश्रद्धाधारणा

A Śaivite Creed

Śivaliṅga is the ancient mark or symbol of God. This elliptical stone is a formless form betokening Paraśiva, That which can never be described or portrayed. The *pīṭha*, pedestal, represents Śiva's manifest Parāśakti. Aum.

A Śaivite Creed

EVERY RELIGION HAS A CREED OF ONE FORM OR ANOTHER, AN AUTHORITATIVE FORMULATION OF ITS BELIEFS. HISTORICALLY, CREEDS HAVE developed whenever religions migrate from their homelands. Until then, the beliefs are fully contained in the culture and taught to children as a natural part of growing up. But when followers settle in other countries where alien faiths predominate, the importance of a simple statement of faith arises. A creed is the distillation of volumes of knowledge into a series of easy-to-remember beliefs, or *śraddhā.* A creed is meant to summarize the specific teachings or articles of faith, to imbed and thus protect and transmit the beliefs. Creeds give strength to individuals seeking to understand life and religion. Creeds also allow members of one faith to express, in elementary and consistent terms, their traditions to members of another.

Though the vast array of doctrines within the Sanātana Dharma has not always been articulated in summary form, from ancient times unto today we have the well-known creedal *mahāvākya,* "great sayings," of the Vedic *Upanishads.* Now, in this technological age in which village integrity is being replaced by worldwide mobility, the importance of a creed becomes apparent if religious identity is to be preserved. We need two kinds of strength—that which is found in diversity and individual freedom to inquire and that which derives from a union of minds in upholding the universal principles of our faith. The twelve beliefs on the following pages embody the centuries-old central convictions of Śaivism, especially as postulated in the Advaita Iśvaravāda philosophy of Śaiva Siddhānta. Yea, this *Śaiva Dharma Śraddhādhāraṇā* is a total summation of *Dancing with Śiva, Hinduism's Contemporary Catechism.* Aum Namaḥ Śivaya.

Belief Number One

REGARDING GOD'S UNMANIFEST REALITY

Śiva's followers all believe that Lord Śiva is God, whose Absolute Being, Paraśiva, transcends time, form and space. The *yogī* silently exclaims, "It is not this. It is not that." Yea, such an inscrutable God is God Śiva. Aum.

Belief Number Two

REGARDING GOD'S MANIFEST NATURE OF ALL-PERVADING LOVE

Śiva's followers all believe that Lord Śiva is God, whose immanent nature of love, Parāśakti, is the substratum, primal substance or pure consciousness flowing through all form as energy, existence, knowledge and bliss. Aum.

Belief Number Three

REGARDING GOD AS PERSONAL LORD AND CREATOR OF ALL

Śiva's followers all believe that Lord Śiva is God, whose immanent nature is the Primal Soul, Supreme Mahādeva, Parameśvara, author of *Vedas* and *Āgamas*, the creator, preserver and destroyer of all that exists. Aum.

Belief Number Four

REGARDING THE ELEPHANT-FACED DEITY

Śiva's followers all believe in the Mahādeva Lord Gaṇeśa, son of Śiva-Śakti, to whom they must first supplicate before beginning any worship or task. His rule is compassionate. His law is just. Justice is His mind. Aum.

Belief Number Five

REGARDING THE DEITY KĀRTTIKEYA

Śiva's followers all believe in the Mahādeva Kārttikeya, son of Śiva-Śakti, whose *vel* of grace dissolves the bondages of ignorance. The *yogī*, locked in lotus, venerates Murugan. Thus restrained, his mind becomes calm. Aum.

Belief Number Six

REGARDING THE SOUL'S CREATION AND ITS IDENTITY WITH GOD

Śiva's followers all believe that each soul is created by Lord Śiva and is identical to Him, and that this identity will be fully realized by all souls when the bondage of *āṇava, karma* and *māyā* is removed by His grace. Aum.

Belief Number Seven

REGARDING THE GROSS, SUBTLE AND CAUSAL PLANES OF EXISTENCE

Śiva's followers all believe in three worlds of existence: the Bhūloka, where souls take on physical bodies; the Antarloka, where souls take on astral bodies; and the Śivaloka, where souls exist in their self-effulgent form. Aum.

Belief Number Eight

REGARDING KARMA, SAṀSĀRA AND LIBERATION FROM REBIRTH

Śiva's followers all believe in the law of *karma*—that one must reap the effects of all actions he has caused—and that each soul continues to reincarnate until all *karmas* are resolved and *moksha,* liberation, is attained. Aum.

Belief Number Nine

REGARDING THE FOUR MĀRGAS, OR STAGES OF INNER PROGRESS

Śiva's followers all believe that the performance of *charyā,* virtuous living, *kriyā,* temple worship, and *yoga,* leading to Paraśiva through the grace of the living *satguru,* is absolutely necessary to bring forth *jñāna,* wisdom. Aum.

Belief Number Ten

REGARDING THE GOODNESS OF ALL

Śiva's followers all believe there is no intrinsic evil. Evil has no source, unless the source of evil's seeming be ignorance itself. They are truly compassionate, knowing that ultimately there is no good or bad. All is Śiva's will. Aum.

Belief Number Eleven

REGARDING THE ESOTERIC PURPOSE OF TEMPLE WORSHIP

Śiva's followers all believe that religion is the harmonious working together of the three worlds and that this harmony can be created through temple worship, wherein the beings of all three worlds can communicate. Aum.

சி
வா
ய
ந
ம

Belief Number Twelve

REGARDING THE FIVE LETTERS

Śiva's followers all believe in the Pañchākshara Mantra, the five sacred syllables "Namaḥ Śivāya," as Śaivism's foremost and essential mantra. The secret of Namaḥ Śivāya is to hear it from the right lips at the right time. Aum.

Shaṭśaiva Sampradāya

षट्शैवसंप्रदाय

Six Schools of Śaivism

Nāga, the cobra, is a symbol of *kuṇḍalinī* power, cosmic energy coiled and slumbering within man. It inspires seekers to overcome misdeeds and suffering by lifting the serpent power up the spine into God Realization. Aum.

Six Schools of Śaivism

IN THE SEARCH FOR PEACE, ENLIGHTENMENT AND LIBERATION, NO PATH IS MORE TOLERANT, MORE MYSTICAL, MORE WIDESPREAD OR MORE ancient than Śaivite Hinduism. Through history Śaivism has developed a vast array of lineages and traditions, each with unique philosophic-cultural-linguistic characteristics, as it dominated India prior to 1100 from the Himalayas to Sri Lanka, from the Bay of Bengal to the Arabian Sea. Here we seek to present the essential features of six major traditions identifiable within the ongoing Śaiva context: Śaiva Siddhānta, Pāśupata Śaivism, Kashmīr Śaivism, Vīra Śaivism, Siddha Siddhānta and Śiva Advaita.

It should be understood that this formal and somewhat intellectual division, however useful, is by no means a comprehensive description of Śaivism, nor is it the only possible list. In practice, Śaivism is far more rich and varied than these divisions imply. Take for instance the Śaivism practiced by thirteen million people in Nepal or three million in Indonesia and fifty-five million Hinduized Javanese who worship Śiva as Batara. Ponder the millions upon millions of Smārtas and other universalists who have taken Gaṇeśa, Murugan or Śiva as their chosen Deity, or the legions of Ayyappan followers who worship devoutly in Lord Murugan's great South Indian sanctuaries. Consider the fact that only a handful of Kashmir's millions of Śiva worshipers would formally associate themselves with the school called Kashmīr Śaivism. Similarly, in the Indian state of Tamil Nadu, where there are over fifty million worshipers of Śiva, only a well-informed minority would knowingly subscribe to Śaiva Siddhānta.

Our discussion of these six schools and their related traditions is based upon historical information. There are wide gaps in the record, but we do know that at each point in which the veil of history lifts, the worship of Śiva is there. In the 8,000-year-old Indus Valley we find the famous seal of Śiva as Lord Paśupati. The seal shows Śiva seated in a *yogic* pose. In the *Rāmāyaṇa*, dated astronomically at 2000 BCE, Lord Rāma worshiped Śiva, as did his rival Rāvaṇa. In the *Mahābhārata*, dated at around 1300 BCE we find again the worship of Śiva. Buddha in 624 BCE was born into a Śaivite family, and records of his time talk of the Śaiva ascetics who wandered the hills looking much as they do today.

The *Śaiva Āgamas* form the foundation and circumference of all the schools of Śaivism. The system of philosophy set forth in the *Āgamas* is common to a remarkable degree among all these schools of thought. These *Āgamas* are theistic, that is, they all identify Śiva as the Supreme Lord, immanent and transcendent, capable of accepting worship as the personal Lord and of being realized through *yoga*. This above all else is the connecting strand through all the schools.

Philosophically, the Āgamic tradition includes the following principle doctrines: 1) the five powers of Śiva: creation, preservation, destruction, revealing and concealing grace; 2) The three categories, Pati, *paśu* and *pāśa*—God, souls and bonds; 3) the three bonds: *āṇava, karma* and *māyā;* 4) the three-fold power of Śiva—*icçhā, kriyā* and *jñāna śakti;* 5) the thirty-six *tattvas,* or categories of existence, from the five elements to God; 6) the need for the *satguru* and initiation; 7) the power of *mantra;* 8) the four *pādas: charyā, kriyā, yoga* and *jñāna.*

As we explore the individual schools and lineages within Śaivism, keep in mind that all adhere to these doctrines. Our discussion necessarily focuses on the differences between one school and another, but this is not meant to obscure the overwhelming similarity of belief and practice among them.

Monism, dualism and philosophies in-between are all conveyed in the *Śaiva Āgamas.* The various schools based on

Āgamas similarly vary in philosophic stance. Kashmīr Śaivite tradition says that Śiva revealed different philosophies for people of different understanding, so that each could advance on the spiritual path toward the recognition of the innate oneness of man and God.

Few worshipers of Śiva are now or were in the past familiar with the *Āgamas*. Reading and writing were the domain of a few specially trained scribes, and today the *Āgamas* remain mostly on the *olai* leaves upon which they have been transmitted for generations.

Āgamic philosophy and practices are conveyed to the common man through other channels, one of which is the *Śaiva Purāṇas*. These oral collections of stories about the Gods are interspersed with Āgamic philosophy. For example, the *Śiva Purāṇa* proclaims: "Śiva is the great *ātman* because He is the *ātman* of all, He is forever endowed with the great qualities. The devotee shall realize the identity of Śiva with himself: 'I am Śiva alone.' "

A second channel is the Śaivite temple itself, for the construction of the temples and the performance of the rituals are all set forth in the *Āgamas*—in fact it is one of their main subjects. The priests follow manuals called *paddhati*, which are summaries of the instructions for worship contained in the *Śaiva Āgamas*, specifically the *shoḍaśa upachāras*, or sixteen acts of *pūjā* worship, such as offering of food, incense and water. A third channel is the songs and *bhajanas* of the *sants*, which in their simplicity carry powerful philosophic import. A fourth is the on-going oral teachings of *gurus*, *swāmīs*, *paṇḍitas*, *śāstrīs*, priests and elders.

Such matters of agreement belie the fact that Śaivism is not a single, hierarchical system. Rather, it is a thousand traditions, great and small. Some are orthodox and pious, while others are iconoclastic and even—like the Kāpālikas and the Aghorīs—fiercely ascetic, eccentric or orgiastic. For some, Śiva is the powerful, terrible, awesome destroyer, but for most He is love itself, compassionate and gentle. For nearly all of the millions of Śiva's devotees, Śaivism is not, therefore, a school or philosophy; it is life itself. To them Śaivism means love of Śiva, and they simply follow the venerable traditions of their family and community. These men and women worship in the temples and mark life's passages by holy sacraments. They go on pilgrimages, perform daily prayers, meditations and *yogic* disciplines. They sing holy hymns, share Purāṇic folk narratives and recite scriptural verses. Still, it is useful for us all to understand the formal streams of thought which nurture and sustain our faith. Now, in our brief description of these six schools, we begin with today's most prominent form of Śaivism, Śaiva Siddhānta.

Śaiva Siddhānta

Śaiva Siddhānta is the oldest, most vigorous and extensively practiced Śaivite Hindu school today, encompassing millions of devotees, thousands of active temples and dozens of living monastic and ascetic traditions. Despite its popularity, Siddhānta's glorious past as an all-India denomination is relatively unknown and it is identified today primarily with its South Indian, Tamil form. The term *Śaiva Siddhānta* means "the final or established conclusions of Śaivism." It is the formalized theology of the divine revelations contained in the twenty-eight *Śaiva Āgamas.* The first known *guru* of the Śuddha, "pure," Śaiva Siddhānta tradition was Maharishi Nandinātha of Kashmir (ca 250 BCE), recorded in Pāṇini's book of grammar as the teacher of *ṛishis* Patañjali, Vyāghrapāda and Vasishṭha. The only surviving written work of Maharishi Nandinātha are twenty-six Sanskṛit verses, called the *Nandikeśvara Kāśikā,* in which he carried forward the ancient teachings. Because of his monistic approach, Nandinātha is often considered by scholars as an exponent of the Advaita school.

The next prominent *guru* on record is Ṛishi Tirumular,

a *siddha* in the line of Nandinātha who came from the Valley of Kashmir to South India to propound the sacred teachings of the twenty-eight *Śaiva Āgamas.* In his profound work the *Tirumantiram,* "Holy Incantation," Tirumular for the first time put the vast writings of the *Āgamas* and the Śuddha Siddhānta philosophy into the sweet Tamil language. Ṛishi Tirumular, like his *satguru,* Maharishi Nandinātha, propounds a monistic theism in which Śiva is both material and efficient cause, immanent and transcendent. Śiva creates souls and world through emanation from Himself, ultimately reabsorbing them in His oceanic Being, as water flows into water, fire into fire, ether into ether.

The *Tirumantiram* unfolds the way of Siddhānta as a progressive, four-fold path of *charyā,* virtuous and moral living; *kriyā,* temple worship; and *yoga*—internalized worship and union with Paraśiva through the grace of the living *satguru*—which leads to the state of *jñāna* and liberation. After liberation, the soul body continues to evolve until it fully merges with God—*jīva* becomes Śiva.

Tirumular's Śuddha Śaiva Siddhānta shares common distant roots with Mahāsiddhayogi Gorakshanātha's Siddha Siddhānta in that both are Nātha teaching lineages. Tirumular's lineage is known as the Nandinātha Sampradāya, Gorakshanātha's is called the Ādinātha Sampradāya.

Śaiva Siddhānta flowered in South India as a forceful *bhakti* movement infused with insights on *siddha yoga.* During the seventh to ninth centuries, saints Sambandar, Appar and Sundarar pilgrimaged from temple to temple, singing soulfully of Śiva's greatness. They were instrumental in successfully defending Śaivism against the threats of Buddhism and Jainism. Soon thereafter, a king's Prime Minister, Manikkavasagar, renounced a world of wealth and fame to seek and serve God. His heart-melting verses, called *Tiruvacagam,* are full of visionary experience, divine love and urgent striving for Truth. The songs of these four saints are part of the compendium known as *Tirumurai,* which along with the *Vedas* and *Śaiva Āgamas* form the scriptural basis of Śaiva Siddhānta in Tamil Nadu.

Besides the saints, philosophers and ascetics, there were innumerable *siddhas,* "accomplished ones," God-intoxicated men who roamed their way through the centuries as saints, *gurus,* inspired devotees or even despised outcastes. Śaiva Siddhānta makes a special claim on them, but their presence and revelation cut across all schools, philosophies and lineages to keep the true spirit of Śiva present on earth. These *siddhas* provided the central source of power to spur the religion from age to age. The well-known names include Sage Agastya, Bhoga Ṛishi, Tirumular and Gorakshanātha. They are revered by the Siddha Siddhāntins, Kashmīr Śaivites and even by the Nepalese branches of Buddhism.

In Central India, Śaiva Siddhānta of the Sanskṛit tradition was first institutionalized by Guhāvāsī Siddha (ca 675). The third successor in his line, Rudraśambhu, also known as Āmardaka Tīrthanātha, founded the Āmardaka monastic order (ca 775) in Andhra Pradesh. From this time, three monastic orders arose that were instrumental in Śaiva Siddhānta's diffusion throughout India. Along with the Āmardaka order (which identified with one of Śaivism's holiest cities, Ujjain) were the Mattamayūra Order, in the capital of the Chālukya dynasty, near the Punjab, and the Madhumateya order of Central India. Each of these developed numerous sub-orders, as the Siddhānta monastics, full of missionary spirit, used the influence of their royal patrons to propagate the teachings in neighboring kingdoms, particularly in South India. From Mattamayūra, they established monasteries in Maharashtra, Karnataka, Andhra and Kerala (ca 800).

Of the many *gurus* and *āchāryas* that followed, spreading Siddhānta through the whole of India, two *siddhas,* Sadyojyoti and Bṛihaspati of Central India (ca 850), are credited with the systematization of the theology in Sanskṛit.

Sadyojyoti, initiated by the Kashmir *guru* Ugrajyoti, propounded the Siddhānta philosophical views as found in the *Raurava Āgama.* He was succeeded by Rāmakaṇṭha I, Śrīkaṇṭha, Nārāyaṇakaṇṭha and Rāmakaṇṭha II, each of whom wrote numerous treatises on Śaiva Siddhānta.

Later, King Bhoja Paramāra of Gujarat (ca 1018) condensed the massive body of Siddhānta scriptural texts that preceded him into a one concise metaphysical treatise called *Tattva Prakāśa,* considered a foremost Sanskṛit scripture on Śaiva Siddhānta.

Affirming the monistic view of Śaiva Siddhānta was Śrīkumāra (ca 1056), stating in his commentary, *Tatparyadīpikā,* on Bhoja Paramāra's works, that Pati, *paśu* and *pāśa* are ultimately one, and that revelation declares that Śiva is one. He is the essence of everything. Śrīkumāra maintained that Śiva is both the efficient and the material cause of the universe.

Śaiva Siddhānta was readily accepted wherever it spread in India and continued to blossom until the Islamic invasions, which virtually annihilated all traces of Siddhānta from North and Central India, limiting its open practice to the southern areas of the subcontinent.

It was in the twelfth century that Aghoraśiva took up the task of amalgamating the Sanskṛit Siddhānta tradition of the North with the Southern, Tamil Siddhānta. As the head of a branch monastery of the Āmardaka Order in Chidambaram, Aghoraśiva gave a unique slant to Śaiva Siddhānta theology, paving the way for a new pluralistic school. In strongly refuting any monist interpretations of Siddhānta, Aghoraśiva brought a dramatic change in the understanding of the Godhead by classifying the first five principles, or *tattvas* (Nāda, Bindu, Sadāśiva, Īśvara and Śuddhavidyā), into the category of *pāśa* (bonds), stating they were effects of a cause and inherently unconscious substances. This was clearly a departure from the traditional teaching in which these five were part of the divine nature of God. Aghoraśiva thus inaugurated a new Siddhānta, divergent from the original monistic Śaiva Siddhānta of the Himalayas.

Despite Aghoraśiva's pluralistic viewpoint of Siddhānta, he was successful in preserving the invaluable Sanskṛitic rituals of the ancient Āgamic tradition through his writings. To this day, Aghoraśiva's Siddhānta philosophy is followed by almost all of the hereditary Śivāchārya temple priests, and his *Paddhati* texts on the *Āgamas* have become the standard *pūjā* manuals. His *Kriyākramadyotikā* is a vast work covering nearly all aspects of Śaiva Siddhānta ritual, including *dīkshā, saṁskāras, ātmārtha pūjā* and installation of Deities.

In the thirteenth century, another important development occurred in Śaiva Siddhānta when Meykandar wrote the twelve-verse *Śivajñānabodham.* This and subsequent works by other writers laid the foundation of the Meykandar Sampradāya, which propounds a pluralistic realism wherein God, souls and world are coexistent and without beginning. Śiva is efficient but not material cause. They view the soul's merging in Śiva as salt in water, an eternal oneness that is also twoness. This school's literature has so dominated scholarship that Śaiva Siddhānta is often erroneously identified as exclusively pluralistic. In truth, there are two interpretations, one monistic and another dualistic, of which the former is the original philosophical premise found in pre-Meykandar scriptures, including the *Upanishads.*

Śaiva Siddhānta is rich in its temple traditions, religious festivals, sacred arts, spiritual culture, priestly clans, monastic orders and *guru*-disciple lineages. All these still thrive. Today Śaiva Siddhānta is most prominent among sixty million Tamil Śaivites who live mostly in South India and Sri Lanka. Here and elsewhere in the world, prominent Siddhānta societies, temples and monasteries abound.

Pāśupata Śaivism

The Pāśupatas (from *Paśupati,* a name of Śiva meaning "Lord of souls") are the oldest known sect of Śaivite ascetic monks. They wandered, pounding the dust with iron tridents and stout staffs, their oily hair snarled in unkempt coils or tied in a knot, faces wrinkled with intense devotion, piercing eyes seeing more Śiva than world, loins wrapped in deer skin or bark. The Pāśupatas were *bhaktas* and benign sorcerers of Śiva, estranged from the priest-dominated Vedic society. Religious turbulence in India intensified as the dual waves of Śaivite Āgamic theism and Buddhism washed over the Gangetic plain.

The ways of the Pāśupatas were chronicled by several sometimes hostile contemporary commentators of that distant period, leaving us with a mixed impression of their life and philosophy. They originally allowed anyone to follow their path, which was not caste-discriminative. As the popularity of the Pāśupata lineage rose, high numbers of *brāhmins* defected to it to worship Śiva in unhindered abandon. Eventually it was preferred for a Pāśupata to come from the *brāhmin* caste. The relationship between these Pāśupata monks and the ash-smeared sādhus of Buddha's time, or the makers of the Indus Valley seal depicting Śiva as Pāśupata, is not known. They are perhaps the same, perhaps different.

The Pāśupata *sādhus* evoked sheer religious awe. Theirs was a brave, ego-stripping path meant to infuse the seeker with Lord Śiva's *kāruṇya,* "compassionate grace." Their austerity was leavened with *pūjā* rites to Śiva, with a profound awareness of the cosmos as Śiva's constant becoming and with an almost frolicsome spirit of love toward Him. *Sādhana* began with a strict code of ethics, called *yamas* and *niyamas,* stressing *brahmacharya,* "continence," *ahiṁsā,* "noninjury," and *tapas,* "asceticism." As detailed in their scriptures, their discipline was practiced in stages. First they assumed vows and practiced special disciplines among themselves which included Śiva-intoxicated laughing, singing and dancing.

Next they disappeared into mainstream society, living incognito. Here they performed outrageous acts to purposely invite public censure, such as babbling, making snorting sounds, walking as if crippled, talking nonsense, and wild gesturing. This *sādhana* was a means of self-purification, of rooting out egoism, of getting over the need to be accepted by the public, by friends or by neighbors, and to fully establish in the subconscious the knowledge that like and dislike, good and bad and all these human ways of thinking and feeling are equal if one's love of Lord Śiva is sufficiently strong. This was designed to break their links with human society and with their own humanness that came with them when they were born.

Returning to overt *sādhana,* they performed austerities, then abandoned all action to perform *kuṇḍalinī yoga* and so achieve perpetual nearness with God Śiva. When union matured, they acquired supernatural powers such as omniscience. The Pāśupatas believed that when a person is firm in virtue and able to accept with equanimity all abuse and insult, he is well established in the path of asceticism. Śrī Kauṇḍinya wrote in his sixth-century commentary, *Pañchārtha Bhāshya,* on the *Pāśupata Sūtra* that the Pāśupata *yogī* "should appear as though mad, like a pauper, his body covered with filth, letting his beard, nails and hair grow long, without any bodily care. Hereby he cuts himself off from the estates (*varṇa*) and stages of life (*āśramas*), and the power of dispassion is produced."

Pāśupatism is primarily an ascetic's path that rejects dialectical logic and prizes *sādhana* as a means to actuate Lord Śiva's *kāruṇya.* Seekers embrace strict *yama-niyama* vows, their *sādhanas* graduating from "action" to "nonaction." Worshipful action includes *pūjā,* penance, Namaḥ Śivāya *japa,* wearing sacred ash and showing abandoned love of God Śiva.

The sect was said to have been founded by Lord Śiva Himself, who imparted the doctrines to certain *maharishis.* Around 200 CE, Pāśupata's most historically prominent *satguru,* Lakulīśa, appeared in what is today India's state of Gujarat. According to the *Karavaṇa Māhātmya,* he was born to a *brāhmin* family, but died in his seventh month, after displaying remarkable spiritual powers. His mother cast his body into a river (a traditional form of infant burial), and a group of tortoises carried it to a powerful Śiva shrine. There the boy returned to life and was raised as an ascetic. By another account, Lakulīśa ("lord of the staff") was an anchorite who died and was revived by Lord Śiva, who entered his body to preach the Pāśupata Dharma to the world. The site of his appearance is a town known today as *Kayavarohana* ("to incarnate in another's body"). The miracle is still festively celebrated. Two stone inscriptions in the village honor the names of this *satguru's* four main *śishyas:* Kuśika, Gārgya, Maitreya and Kaurusha.

Satguru Lakulīśa was a dynamic Pāśupata reformist. In his *sūtras,* outlining the bold codes of conduct and *yoga* precepts, he restricted admittance to the three higher castes (*vaiśya, kshatriya* and *brāhmin*) in an attempt to link this school with Vedic orthodoxy. A popular householder path arose out of this exclusively ascetic order. Today numerous Pāśupata centers of worship are scattered across India, where Satguru Lakulīśa as Śiva is often enshrined, his image on the face of a Śivaliṅga, seated in lotus posture, virilely naked, holding a *daṇḍa* in his left hand and a citron fruit in his right. Their most revered temple, Somanātha, is in Gujarat a powerful, active temple which has endured several cycles of destruction and rebuilding.

A seventh-century Chinese traveler, Hiuen Tsiang, wrote that 10,000 Pāśupatas then occupied Varanasi. The Pāśupata tradition spread to Nepal in the eighth century, where the now famous Pāśupatināth Temple became a prime pilgrimage center and remains so to this day. At its medieval zenith, Pāśupatism blanketed Western, Northwestern and Southeastern India, where it received royal patronage. In the fifteenth century, it retreated to its strongholds of Gujarat, Nepal and the Himalayan hills.

Traditionally, the deepest Pāśupata teachings have been kept secret, reserved for initiates who were tried, tested and found most worthy. Central scriptures are the *Pāśupata Sūtras* (ascribed to the venerable Lakulīśa), Kauṇḍinya's commentary on them, *Pañchārtha Bhāshya* (ca 500) and the *Mṛigendra Āgama.*

The Pāśupata philosophy prior to Lakulīśa was dualistic. Little is known of it, as no writings remain. But scholars have discerned from references to Pāśupata by other ancient writers that it regarded Śiva as only the efficient cause of the universe, not the material. It posited five primarycategories—cause, effect, union, ritual and liberation. The later category was somewhat unusual, as the Pāśupatas believed the soul never merged in Śiva and that liberation was simply a state with no further pain. They taught that God can create changes in the world and in the destinies of men according to His own pleasure. God does not necessarily depend upon the person or his *karma* (actions).

Lakulīśa's Pāśupata system retained the idea of five categories, but regarded the goal of the soul as attainment of divine perfection. Further, he put God as the material cause of the universe, effectively moving the philosophy from dualism to dual-nondual. The soul, *paśu,* is prevented from closeness to Śiva by *pāśa,* "fetters." The soul retains its individuality in its liberated state, termed *sāyujya,* defined as closeness to but not complete union with God. Lord Śiva has no power over liberated souls.

The Kāpālika, "skull-bearers," sect developed out of the Pāśupatas and were likewise—but perhaps justifiably—vilified by their opponents. At worst, they are portrayed as drunken and licentious, engaged in human sacrifice and practicing the blackest of magic. Other portrayals are more benign. For example, in the early Sanskṛit drama *Mālatī-Mādhava,* a Kāpālika says with great insight, "Being exclusively devoted to alms alone, penance alone and rites alone—all this is easy to obtain. Being intent upon the Self alone, however, is a state difficult to obtain." Even today, followers of this sect are found begging food which they accept in a skull, preferably that of a *brāhmin.* Some scholars see a connection between the Kāpālikas and the later Gorakshanātha *yogīs.*

In the seventh century, another sect developed out of the Pāśupata tradition, the Kālāmukhas, "black-faced," who established a well-organized social structure with many temples and monasteries in what is now Karnataka and elsewhere. Like the earlier Pāśupatas, they suffered vilification at the hands of hostile commentators. Nothing is left of their scriptures, hence details of their philosophy and life is obscure. However, the esteem in which they were once held is reflected in an 1162 inscription on one of their temples stating, in part, that it was "a place devoted to the observances of Śaiva saints leading perpetually the life of celibate religious students, a place for the quiet study of four *Vedas,*... the *Yoga Śāstras* and the other kinds of learning, a place where food is always given to the poor, the helpless,...the musicians and bards whose duty it is to awaken their masters with music and songs,...and to the mendicants and all beggars,...a place where many helpless sick people are harbored and treated, a place of assurance of safety for all living creatures." The Vīra Śaiva school is thought by scholars to have developed out of and eventually replaced the Kālāmukhas, apparently taking over their temples and *āśramas.*

Today's reclusive Pāśupata monks live in Northern India and Nepal and influence followers worldwide.

Vīra Śaivism

Vīra Śaivism is one of the most dynamic of modern-day Śaivite schools. It was made popular by the remarkable South Indian *brāhmin* Śrī Basavaṇṇa (1105–1167). Adherents trace the roots of their faith back to the *ṛishis* of ancient times. Vīra, "heroic," Śaivites are also known as Liṅgāyats, "bearers of the Liṅga." All members are to constantly wear a Liṅga encased in a pendant around the neck. Of this practice, Thavathiru Śāntaliṅga Rāmasamy of Coimbatore recently said, "I can say that Vīra Śaiva worship is the best form of worship because Śivaliṅga is worn on our body and it unites the soul with the Omnipresence. We are always in touch with Lord Śiva, without even a few seconds break." Followers are also called *Liṅgavāntas* and *Śivaśaraṇās.*

Like the sixteenth-century Protestant revolt against Catholic authority, the Liṅgāyat movement championed the cause of the down-trodden, rebelling against a powerful *brāhminical* system which promoted social inequality through a caste system that branded a whole class of people (*harijans*) as polluted. Going against the way of the times, the Liṅgāyats rejected, Vedic authority, caste hierarchy, the system of four *āśramas,* a multiplicity of Gods, ritualistic (and self-aggrandizing) priestcraft, animal sacrifice, *karmic* bondage, the existence of inner worlds, duality of God and soul, temple worship and the traditions of ritual purity-pollution.

Vīra Śaiva tradition states that Basavaṇṇa was a reflective and defiant youth who rejected much of the Śaivism practiced in his day, tore off his sacred thread, *yājñopavīta,* at age 16 and fled to Sangama, Karnataka. He received shelter and encouragement from Īśānya Guru, a Śaivite *brāhmin* of the prevailing Kālāmukha sect, and studied under him at his monastery-temple complex for twelve years. There he developed a profound devotion to Śiva as Lord Kudalasaṅgama, "Lord of the meeting rivers." At age 28, Basavaṇṇa arrived at the insight that the brotherhood of man rests on the doctrine of a personalized, individual Godhood in the form of *Ishṭaliṅga* ("chosen, or personal Liṅga"). This spiritual realization gave rise to the central Vīra Śaiva belief that the human body is to be revered as a moving temple of the Lord, to be kept in a perpetual state of purity and sublimity.

Near the completion of his studies at Sangama, Basavaṇṇa had a vivid dream in which the Lord Kudalasangama touched his body gently, saying, "Basavaṇṇa, my son, the time has come at last for your departure from this place. There is Bijjala in Mangalavede. Carry on your work of building a just society from there." Having received these inner orders, he journeyed to Mangalavede and sought service in the court of Bijjala. He rose to become chief officer of the royal treasury, minister to this *mahārāja* in his troubled Śaivite country at odds with Buddhism and Jainism. This position led to the swift spreading of Basavaṇṇa's revolutionary message of a new, visionary religious society.

Basavaṇṇa wedded two wives, taking on the householder *dharma,* strengthening his teaching that all followers—not only renunciates—can live a holy life. He gave discourses each evening, denouncing caste hierarchy, magical practices, astrology, temple building and more, urging growing crowds of listeners to think rationally and worship Śiva as the God within themselves. Here Basavaṇṇa lived and preached for twenty years, developing a large Śaivite religious movement. The function of gathering for discourse became known as Śivānubhava Maṇḍapa, "hall of Śiva experience."

At age 48 he moved with King Bijjala to Kalyana, where, joined by Allama Prabhu, his fame continued to grow for the next fourteen years. Devotees of every walk of life flocked from all over India to join with him. Through the years, opposition to his egalitarian community grew strong among more conventional citizens. Tensions came to a head in 1167 when a *brāhmin* and *śūdra,* both Liṅgāyats, married. Outraged citizens appealed to King Bijjala, who took ruthless action and executed them both. The unstable political situation further disintegrated, and the King was shortly thereafter murdered by political opponents or possibly by Liṅgāyat radicals. Riots erupted and the Liṅgāyats were scattered far and wide. Basavaṇṇa, feeling his mission in the capital had come to an end, left for Sangama, and shortly thereafter died, at the age of 62. Leaders and followers transferred the institutional resources created in the urban Kalayana to the rural villages of Karnataka.

In spite of persecution, successful spiritual leadership left a legacy of sainthood, including many women saints. If Basavaṇṇa was the faith's intellectual and social architect, Allama Prabhu was its austerely mystical powerhouse. The doctrines of these two founders are contained in their *Vachanas,* or prose lyrics. Vīra Śaiva spiritual authority derives from the life and writings of these two knowers of Śiva and of numerous other Śivaśaraṇās, "those surrended to God." Roughly 450 writers of these scriptures have been identified. The *Vachanas,* "what is said," scorn the *Vedas,* mock ritual, and reject the legends of Gods and Goddesses. The authors of these verses saw formal religions as the "establishment," static institutions that promise man security and predictability, whereas they knew that religion must be dynamic, spontaneous, freed of bargains extracted in exchange for salvation. These scriptures reject "doing good" so one may go to heaven. Allama wrote, "Feed the poor, tell the truth, make water places for the thirsty and build tanks for a town. You may go to heaven after death, but you'll be nowhere near the truth of our Lord. And the man who knows our Lord, he gets no results." The *Vachanas* are incandescent poetry, full of humor, ridicule and the white heat of Truth-seeking, bristling with monotheism, commanding devotees to enter the awesome realm of personal spirituality.

These poems, written in the Kannada language, are central in the religious life of Liṅgāyats. Here are some samples.

Gaṇāchāra wrote, "They say I have been born, but I have no birth, Lord! They say I have died, but I have no death, O Lord!" Basavaṇṇa exclaimed, "Lord, the *brāhmin* priest does not act as he speaks. How is that? He goes one way, while the official code goes the other!" Allama Prabhu said, "Then, when there was neither beginning nor nonbeginning, when there was no conceit or arrogance, when there was neither peace nor peacelessness, when there was neither nothingness nor nonnothingness, when everything remained uncreated and raw, you, Guheśvara, were alone, all by yourself, present yet absent."

Ironically, in the centuries following these days of reform, Vīra Śaivism gradually reabsorbed much of what Basavaṇṇa had rejected. Thus emerged temple worship, certain traditions of ritual purity, giving gifts to *gurus,* and the stratification of society, headed up by two large hierarchical orders of *jaṅgamas*—resulting in the institutionalization of the crucial *guru*-disciple relationship, which by Vīra Śaiva precept should be very personal. Efforts were made to derive Vīra Śaiva theology from traditional Hindu scriptures such as *Āgamas* and *Sūtras*—a need rejected by the early *śaraṇās.* To this day, by rejecting the *Vedas,* Liṅgāyats continue to put themselves outside the fold of mainstream Hinduism, but in their acceptance of certain *Śaiva Āgamas,* align themselves with the other Śaiva sects. Vīra Śaivites generally regard their faith as a distinct and independent religion.

The original ideals, however, remain embedded in Liṅgāyat scripture, which is of three types: 1) the *Vachanas,* 2) historical narratives and biographies in verse and 3) specialized works on doctrine and theology. Among the most central texts are Basavaṇṇa's *Vachanas,* Allama Prabhu's *Mantra Gopya,* Chennabasavaṇṇa's *Kāraṇa Hasuge,* and the collected work called *Śūnya Sampādane.*

The monistic-theistic doctrine of Vīra Śaivism is called Śakti Viśishṭādvaita—a version of qualified nondualism which accepts both difference and nondifference between soul and God, like rays are to the sun. In brief, Śiva and the cosmic force, or existence, are one ("Śiva are you; you shall return to Śiva"). Yet, Śiva is beyond His creation, which is real, not illusory. God is both efficient and material cause. The soul in its liberated state attains undifferentiated union with Śiva. The Vīra Śaiva saint Reṇukāchārya said, "Like water placed in water, fire in fire, the soul that becomes mingled in the Supreme Brahman is not seen as distinct."

True union and identity of Śiva (Liṅga) and soul (*āṅga*) is life's goal, described as *śūnya,* or nothingness, which is not an empty void. One merges with Śiva by *shaṭsthala,* a progressive six-stage path of devotion and surrender: *bhakti* (devotion), *maheśa* (selfless service), *prasāda* (earnestly seeking Śiva's grace), *prāṇaliṅga* (experience of all as Śiva), *śaraṇā* (egoless refuge in Śiva), and *aikya* (oneness with Śiva). Each phase brings the seeker closer, until soul and God are fused in a final state of perpetual Śiva consciousness, as rivers merging in the ocean.

Vīra Śaivism's means of attainment depends on the *pañchāchāra* (five codes of conduct) and *ashṭāvaraṇa* (eight shields) to protect the body as the abode of the Lord. The five codes are *Liṅgāchāra* (daily worship of the Śivaliṅga), *sadāchāra* (attention to vocation and duty), Śivāchāra (acknowledging Śiva as the one God and equality among members), *bhṛityāchāra* (humility towards all creatures) and *gaṇāchāra* (defense of the community and its tenets).

The eight shields are *guru, Liṅga, jaṅgama* (wandering monk), *pādukā* (water from bathing the Liṅga or *guru's* feet), *prasāda* (sacred offering), *vibhūti* (holy ash), *rudrāksha* (holy beads) and *mantra* (Namaḥ Śivāya). One enters the Vīra Śaiva religion through formal initiation called Liṅga Dīkshā, a rite for both boys and girls which replaces the sacred thread ceremony and enjoins the devotee to worship the personal Śivaliṅga daily. Liṅgāyats place great emphasis on *this* life, on equality of all members (regardless of caste, education, sex, etc.), on intense social involvement and service to the community. Their faith stresses free will, affirms a purposeful world and avows a pure monotheism.

Today Vīra Śaivism is a vibrant faith, particularly strong in its religious homeland of Karnataka, South-Central India. Roughly forty million people live here, of which perhaps 25% are members of the Vīra Śaiva religion. There is hardly a village in the state without a *jaṅgama* and a *maṭha* (monastery). On the occasion of birth in a Liṅgāyat family, the child is entered into the faith that same day by a visiting *jaṅgama*, who bestows a small Śivaliṅga encased in a pendant tied to a thread. This same Liṅga is to be worn throughout life.

Kashmīr Śaivism

Kashmīr Śaivism, with its potent stress on man's recognition of an already existing oneness with Śiva, is the most single-mindedly monistic of the six schools. It arose in the ninth century in Northern India, then a tapestry of small feudal kingdoms. Mahārājas patronized the various religions. Buddhism was still strong. *Tantric* Śāktism flourished toward the Northeast. Śaivism had experienced a renaissance since the sixth century, and the most widespread Hindu God was Śiva.

According to the traditions of Kashmīr Śaivism, Lord Śiva originally set forth sixty-four systems, or philosophies, some monistic, some dualistic and some monistic theistic. Eventually these were lost, and Śiva commanded Sage Durvāsas to revive the knowledge. Sage Durvāsas' "mind-born sons" were assigned to teach the philosophies: Tryambaka (the monistic), Āmardaka (the dualistic) and Śrīnātha (monistic theistic). Thus, Tryambaka at an unknown time laid a new foundation for Kashmīr Śaiva philosophy.

Then, it is said, Lord Śiva Himself felt the need to resolve conflicting interpretations of the *Āgamas* and counter the encroachment of dualism on the ancient monistic doctrines.

In the early 800s, Śrī Vasugupta was living on Mahādeva Mountain near Srinagar. Tradition states that one night Lord Śiva appeared to him in a dream and told him of the whereabouts of a great scripture carved in rock. Upon awakening, Vasugupta rushed to the spot and found seventy-seven terse *sūtras* etched in stone, which he named the *Śiva Sūtras.* Vasugupta expounded the *Sūtras* to his followers, and gradually the philosophy spread. On this scriptural foundation arose the school known as Kashmīr Śaivism, Northern Śaivism, Pratyabhijñā Darśana ("recognition school"), or Trika-śāsana ("Trika system"). Trika, "three," refers to the school's three-fold treatment of the Divine: Śiva, Śakti and soul, as well as to three sets of scriptures and a number of other triads.

Kashmīr Śaivite literature is in three broad divisions: *Āgama Śāstra, Spanda Śāstra* and *Pratyabhijñā Śāstra. Āgama Śāstra* includes works of divine origin: specifically the *Śaiva Āgama* literature, but also including Vasugupta's *Śiva Sūtras.* The *Spanda Śāstra,* or *Spanda Kārikās* (of which only two *sūtras* are left), are both attributed to Vasugupta's disciple Kallaṭa (ca 850–900). These elaborate the principles of the *Śiva Sūtras.* The *Pratyabhijñā Śāstra's* principle components are the *Śiva Dṛishṭi* by Vasugupta's disciple, Somānanda, and the *Pratyabhijñā Sūtras* by Somānanda's pupil, Utpaladeva (ca 900-950). Abhinavagupta (ca 950-1000) wrote some forty works, including *Tantrāloka,* "Light on Tantra," a comprehensive text on Āgamic Śaiva philosophy and ritual. It was Abhinavagupta whose brilliant and encyclopedic works established Kashmīr Śaivism as an important philosophical school.

Kashmīr Śaivism provides an extremely rich and detailed understanding of the human psyche, and a clear and distinct path of *kuṇḍalinī-siddha yoga* to the goal of Self Realization. In its history the tradition produced numerous *siddhas,* adepts of remarkable insight and power. It is said that Abhinavagupta, after completing his last work on the Pratyabhijñā system, entered the Bhairava cave near Mangam with 1,200 disciples, and he and they were never seen again.

Kashmīr Śaivism is intensely monistic. It does not deny the existence of a personal God or of the Gods. But much more emphasis is put upon the personal meditation and reflection of the devotee and his guidance by a *guru*. Creation of the soul and world is explained as God Śiva's *ābhāsa,* "shining forth" of Himself in His dynamic aspect of Śakti, the first impulse, called *spanda.* As the Self of all, Śiva is immanent and transcendent, and performs through his Śakti the five actions of creation, preservation, destruction, revealing and concealing. The Kashmīr Śaivite is not so much concerned with worshiping a personal God as he is with attaining the transcendental state of Śiva consciousness.

An esoteric and contemplative path, Kashmīr Śaivism embraces both knowledge and devotion. *Sādhana* leads to the assimilation of the object (world) in the subject (I) until the Self (Śiva) stands revealed as one with the universe. The goal—liberation—is sustained recognition (*pratyabhijñā*) of one's true Self as nothing but Śiva. There is no merger of soul in God, as they are eternally nondifferent.

There are three *upāyas,* stages of attainment of God consciousness. These are not sequential, but do depend upon the evolution of the devotee. The first stage is *āṇavopāya,* which corresponds to the usual system of worship, *yogic* effort and purification through breath control. The second stage is *śāktopāya,* maintaining a constant awareness of Śiva through discrimination in one's thoughts. The third stage is *śāmbhavopāya* in which one attains instantly to God consciousness simply upon being told by the *guru* that the essential Self is Śiva. There is a forth stage, *anupāya,* "no means," which is the mature soul's recognition that there is nothing to be done, reached for or accomplished except to reside in one's own being, which is already of the nature of Śiva. Realization relies upon the *satguru,* whose grace is the blossoming of all *sādhana.*

Despite many renowned *gurus,* geographic isolation in the Kashmir Valley and latter Muslim domination kept the following relatively small. Scholars have recently brought the scriptures to light again, republishing surviving texts. The original *paramparā* was represented in recent times by Swāmī Lakshman Joo. Today various organizations promulgate the esoteric teachings to some extent worldwide. While the number of Kashmīr Śaivite formal followers is uncertain, the school remains an important influence in India. Many Kashmīr Śaivites have fled the presently war-torn Valley of Kashmir to settle in Jammu, New Delhi and elsewhere in North India. This diaspora of devout Śaivites may serve to spread the teachings into new areas.

Śiva Advaita

Śiva Advaita is the philosophy of Śrīkaṇṭha as expounded in his *Brahma Sūtra Bhāshya,* a Śaivite commentary on the *Brahma Sūtras* (ca 500-200 BCE). The *Brahma Sūtras* are 550 terse verses by Bādarāyaṇa summarizing the *Upanishads.* The *Brahma Sūtras,* the *Bhagavad Gītā* and the *Upanishads* are the three central scriptures of the various interpretations of Vedānta philosophy. Śaṅkara, Rāmānuja and Mādhva wrote commentaries on these books deriving three quite different philosophies—nondualism, qualified nondualism and dualism, respectively—from the same texts. Each claimed his to be the true interpretation of the *Vedas* and vigorously refuted all other interpretations. Śaṅkara was a monist and accorded worship of the personal God a lesser status. Rāmānuja and Mādhva, on the other hand, developed theistic philosophies in which devotion to Vishṇu was the highest path. There was as yet no school of Vedānta elevating devotion to Śiva to similar heights. Śrīkaṇṭha sought to fill this gap. The resulting philosophy is termed *Śiva Viśishṭādvaita* and is not unlike Rāmānuja's qualified nondualism. In the process of his commentary, Śrīkaṇṭha put Śaiva philosophy into Vedāntic terminology.

Śrīkaṇṭha lived in the eleventh century. Of his personal life virtually nothing is historically known, so the man remains a mystery. Nor did he catalyze a social movement that would vie with Vīra Śaivism or Śaiva Siddhānta. But from his writings it is clear that Śrīkaṇṭha was a masterful expositor and a devout lover of God Śiva. His influence was largely due to Appaya Dīkshita, who wrote a compelling commentary on Śrīkaṇṭha's work in the sixteenth century as part of a successful multi-pronged attempt to defend Śaivism against the inroads of Vaishṇava proselytization in South India.

According to Śrīkaṇṭha, Śiva created the world for no purpose except out of play or sport. Śiva is the efficient cause of creation. As His Śakti, He is also the material cause. Śiva assumes the form of the universe, transforms Himself into it, not directly but through His Śakti. Yet, He is transcendent, greater than and unaffected and unlimited by His creation. Śiva has a spiritual body and lives in a heaven more luminous than millions of suns, which liberated souls eventually can attain. Śrīkaṇṭha in his *Brahma Sūtra Bhāshya* said, "At the time of creation, preceded by the first vibrations of His energies—solely through an impulse of will, independently of any material cause, and out of His own substance—He creates, that is, manifests, the totality of conscious and unconscious things."

Purification, devotion and meditation upon Śiva as the Self—the *ākāśa* within the heart—define the path. Meditation is directed to the Self, Śiva, the One Existence that evolved into all form. Release comes only after certain preliminary attainments, including tranquility, faith and nonattachment. Bonds which fetter the soul can be shattered in the torrent of continuous contemplation on and identification with the Supreme, Śiva. Liberation depends on grace, not deeds.

Upon death, the liberated soul goes to Śiva along the

path of the Gods, without return to earthly existence. The individual soul continues to exist in the spiritual plane, enjoying the bliss of knowing all as Śiva, enjoying all experiences and powers, except that of creation of the universe. Ultimately, the soul does not become perfectly one with Brahman (or Śiva), but shares with Brahman all excellent qualities. Man is responsible, free to act as he wills to, for Śiva only fulfills needs according to the soul's *karma.* Śrīkaṇṭha wrote in *Brahma Sūtra Bhāshya,* "Śiva associates Himself with the triple energies [knowledge, will and action], enters into the total agglomerate of effects, and emerges as the universe, comprising the triad of Deities [Vishṇu, Brahmā and Rudra]. Who can comprehend the greatness of Śiva, the All-Powerful and the All-Knowing?"

Appaya Dīkshita (1554–1626) is a most unusual person in Hindu history. His commentaries on various schools of philosophy were so insightful that they are revered by those schools, even though he did not adhere to their philosophies. An ardent devotee of Lord Śiva, he compiled manuals on *pūjā* worship which are used to the present day by Śaivite priests. Additionally, he was an excellent devotional poet. Philosophically he adhered throughout his life to the *advaita* school of Ādi Śaṅkara. In his battles to reestablish the worship of Śiva against the Vaishṇavism of the day, his life came under threat numerous times. Śaivism was suffering setbacks in South India in the sixteenth century due largely to the patronage of Vaishṇavism by Rāmarāja, king of Vijayanagara, whose territory encompassed an area as large as modern Tamil Nadu. When Rāmarāja was killed at the fall of Vijayanagara in 1565, his successors ruling from other cities continued the patronage of Vaishṇavism. Appaya succeeded at this crucial juncture in gaining the patronage of King Chinna Bomman of Vellore, who ruled from 1559 to 1579. Bomman had once been subject to the king of Vijayanagara, but after the city fell, he declared his own independence.

Appaya Dīkshita set out to compose commentaries on the various philosophies of his day, including that of Śrīkaṇṭha. Appaya's commentaries on the writings of the dualist Mādhva are revered to this day by Mādhva's adherents. Through his 104 books, Appaya created more harmonious relations with the other systems of thought, promoted Śaivism from several philosophical approaches at once and contributed to the basic devotional worship of Śiva. The patronage of King Chinna Bomma assured the wide spread of Appaya's ideas through specially convened conferences of up to 500 scholars and extensive travel for both Appaya and the trained scholars who served as Śaiva missionaries. Appaya wrote in one text, "Since the summer heat of the evil-minded critics of Lord Śiva and His worship are awaiting in order to burn out and destroy the sprouts of Śiva *bhakti* or devotion that arise in the minds of the devotees, for which the seed is their accumulated merit in their previous births, this work, *Śivakārṇāmṛita,* with its verses made, as it were, of nectar, is written to help rejuvenate those sprouts."

Appaya Dīkshita concluded that the philosophies of Śrīkaṇṭha and those of other dualists or modified dualists were necessary steps to recognizing the truth of monism, *advaita.* He argued that Śrīkaṇṭha's emphasis on Saguṇa Brahman (God with qualities) rather than Nirguṇa Brahman (God without qualities) was meant to create, for the moment, faith and devotion in fellow Śaivites, for such devotion is a necessary prerequisite to the discipline needed to know the Transcendent Absolute, Paraśiva, Nirguṇa Brahman. Appaya Dīkshita said in *Śivarkamaṇi Dīpikā,* "Although *advaita* was the religion accepted and impressed by the great teachers of old like Śrī Śaṅkara [and the various scriptures], still an inclination for *advaita* is produced only by the grace of Lord Śiva and by that alone."

Śiva Advaita apparently has no community of followers or formal membership today, but may be understood as a highly insightful reconciliation of Vedānta and Siddhānta. Its importance is in its promotion by Appaya Dīkshita to revive Śaivism in the sixteenth century.

Siddha Siddhānta

Siddha Siddhānta, or Gorakshanātha Śaivism, is generally considered to have come in the lineage of the earlier ascetic orders of India. Gorakshanātha was a disciple of Matsyendranātha, patron saint of Nepal, revered by certain esoteric Buddhist schools as well as by Hindus. Gorakshanātha lived most likely in the tenth century and wrote in Hindi. Historians connect the Gorakshanātha lineage with that of the Pāśupatas and their later successors, as well as to the *siddha yoga* and Āgamic traditions. Gorakshanātha adherents themselves say that Matsyendranātha learned the secret Śaiva truths directly from Śiva, as Ādinātha, and he in turn passed them on to Gorakshanātha. The school systematized and developed the practice of *haṭha yoga* to a remarkable degree, indeed nearly all of what is today taught about *haṭha yoga* comes from this school.

Gorakshanātha, the preeminent *guru* and author of *Siddha Siddhānta Paddhati* ("tracks on the doctrines of the adepts"), was a man of awesome spiritual power and discerning practicality. As a renunciate, his early life is unknown, though he is thought to have been a native of Punjab. He mastered the highly occult Nātha *yoga* sciences after studying for twelve years under his famed *guru,* Matsyendranātha. Roaming North India from Assam to Kashmir, he worshiped Śiva in temples, realizing Him in the deepest of *samādhis* and awakening many of the powers of a Śaiva adept.

By creating twelve orders with monastery-temple complexes across the face of North India, Gorakshanātha popularized his school and effectively insulated pockets of Śaivism from Muslim dominance. Matsyendranātha had already established it in Nepal, where to this day he is deified as the country's patron saint. Scholars believe that Gorakshanātha's *yoga* represents a development out of the earlier Pāśupata and related ascetic orders, as there are many similarities of practice and philosophy.

To outer society, Gorakshanātha's *siddha yogīs* were mesmerizing, memorable men of renunciation—dressed in saffron robes, with flowing, jet-black hair, foreheads white with holy ash, large circular earrings, *rudrāksha* beads and a unique horn whistle on a hair-cord worn around the neck, signifying the primal vibration, Aum. Muslims called the Gorakshanāthis "Kanphaṭi," meaning "split-eared ones," referring to the rite of slitting the ear cartilage to insert sometimes monstrous earrings. Some Muslims even joined the Kanphaṭis, and heads of a few Gorakshanātha monasteries are known by the Muslim title *pir,* "holy father." This unusual ecumenical connection was of enormous benefit at a time of general religious persecution.

These Nāthas perceived the inner and outer universes as Śiva's cosmic body (Mahāsākāra Piṇḍa), as the continuous blossoming forth of Himself as Śakti (power) into an infinity of souls, worlds and forces. Earth and life, human frailties and human Divinity are Śiva manifest. As such, these men expressed spiritual exaltation in mankind and joyous devotion through temple worship and pilgrimage. But their daily focus was on internal worship and *kuṇḍalinī yoga.* Inside themselves they sought realization of Parāsamvid, the supreme transcendent state of Śiva.

Gorakshanātha, in *Viveka Mārtāṇḍa,* gives his view of *samādhi:* "*Samādhi* is the name of that state of phenomenal consciousness, in which there is the perfect realization of the absolute unity of the individual soul and the Universal Soul, and in which there is the perfect dissolution of all the mental processes. Just as a perfect union of salt and water is achieved through the process of *yoga,* so when the mind or the phenomenal consciousness is absolutely unified or identified with the soul through the process of the deepest concentration, this is called the state of *samādhi.* When the individuality of the individual soul is absolutely merged in the self-luminous transcendent unity of the Absolute Spirit (Śiva), and the phenomenal consciousness also is wholly dissolved in the Eternal, Infinite, Transcendent Consciousness, then perfect *samarasattva* (the essential unity of all existences) is realized, and this is called *samādhi.*"

Having achieved *samarasattva* (or *samarasa*), the *yogī* remains continually aware of the transcendent unity of God, even while being aware of the ordinary material world. This is the supreme achievement of the system.

The school is noted for its concept of *kāya siddhi,* extreme physical longevity, and even the claim of immortality for some. Indeed, Gorakshanātha himself and many of his followers are considered to be alive today, carrying on their work from hidden places. The precise methods of this are not delineated in their texts, but are taught directly by the *guru.*

Among the central scriptures are *Haṭha Yoga Pradīpikā* by Svātmarāma, *Gheraṇḍa Saṁhitā, Śiva Saṁhitā,* and *Jñānāmṛita,* which are among forty or so works attributed to Gorakshanātha or his followers. Most deal with *haṭha yoga.*

The Siddha Siddhānta theology embraces both transcendent Śiva (being) and immanent Śiva (becoming). Śiva is efficient and material cause. Creation and final return of soul and cosmos to Śiva are described as "bubbles arising and returning to water." Siddha Siddhānta accepts the *advaitic* experience of the advanced *yogī* while not denying the mixed experiences of oneness and twoness in ordinary realms of consciousness.

Through the centuries, a large householder community has also arisen which emulates the renunciate ideals. Today there are perhaps 750,000 adherents of Siddha Siddhānta Śaivism, who are often understood as Śāktas or *advaita tantrics.* In truth, they range from street magicians and snake charmers, to established citizens, to advanced *sādhus.* The school fans out through India, but is most prominent in North India and Nepal. Devotees are called *yogīs,* and stress is placed on world renunciation—even for householders. Over time and still today, the deeper theology has often been eclipsed by a dominant focus on *kuṇḍalinī-haṭha yoga.* Values and attitudes often hold followers apart from society. This sect is also most commonly known as Nātha, the Goraksha Pantha and Siddha Yogī Sampradāya. Other names include Ādinātha Sampradāya, Nāthamaṭha and Siddhamārga. The word *gorakh* or *goraksha* means "cowherd." (The name *Gorkhā* means an inhabitant of Nepal and is the same as *Gurkhā,* the famous martial tribe of that country.)

Today this Nātha tradition is represented by the Gorakshanātha *sādhus* and numerous other venerable orders of Himalayan monks who uphold the spirit of world renunciation in quest of the Self. Millions of modern-day seekers draw from their teachings, treasuring especially the sixteenth-century text by Svātmarāma, *Haṭha Yoga Pradīpikā,* "light on *haṭha yoga.*" From these strong, ancient roots, *yoga* schools have arisen in major cities in nearly every country of the world. They are aggressive. They are dynamic. They produce results, physically, mentally and emotionally. They usually do not include Hindu religion but for a minimal presentation of *pūjā, guru, karma, dharma* and the existence of an all-pervasive force, called energy. Because of this loosely-knit philosophical premise and the pragmatic results gained from the practices of *haṭha yoga, prāṇāyāma* and meditation, a large following of seekers from all religious backgrounds ever expands. Today these schools encompass *āyurveda,* astrology and various forms of holistic health practice. Advanced meditation is taught to the most sincere. Thus the ancient wisdom of Siddha Siddhānta survives in the modern age to improve the quality of life for mankind and aid truth seekers everywhere to attain their goal.

Six Schools of Saivism, Conclusion

Today, in one form or another, each of these six schools of Śaivism continue unhindered. Their leaders and *gurus* have reincarnated and are picking up the threads of the ancient past and bringing them forward to the twenty-first century. Seekers who worship Śiva are carefully choosing between one or another of them. *Gurus,* initiated, uninitiated or self-appointed by the spiritual forces within them, find themselves declaring God Śiva as Supreme Lord and aligning themselves with one or another of the Śaiva lineages. Non-Hindus have been attracted to the profound Śaiva philosophy, serving as unheralded missionaries. Many have fully converted to Saivism as the religion of their soul. In this modern age, toward the end of the twentieth century, Śaivism has gained a new strength and power. The schools of Śaivism relate and interrelate in love, kindness, compassion and understanding, share their strengths and fortify each other's weaknesses.

Our most eminent God Śiva knew His creations were not all the same. In different moods He created different kinds of souls at different times. Similarly, in His supreme wisdom, He created these six approaches to His grace upon one common Vedic-Āgamic foundation—one for *yogic* ascetics, one for heroic nonconformists, one for *kuṇḍalinī* mystics, one for the philosophically astute, one for immortal renunciates and one for devotional nondualists. None were forgotten. Yea, even today, Lord Śiva is ordaining leaders within the boundaries of these six philosophical streams to preach His message in sacred eloquence.

Ekam Sat Anekāḥ Panthāḥ

एकम् सत् अनेकाः पन्थाः

Truth Is One, Paths Are Many

Here in a lotus flower are assembled the world's major religions, each holding its uniquely profound perception of the many-petaled cosmos, symbolized by the lotus. In the center the Praṇava Aum denotes Truth Itself.

Truth Is One, Paths Are Many

IF RELIGION HAS EVER CONFUSED AND CONFOUNDED YOU, TAKE HEART! THIS NEXT RESOURCE SECTION WAS WRITTEN JUST FOR YOU. It is our humble attempt to gather from hundreds of sources a simple, in-a-nutshell summary of the world's major spiritual paths. The strength of this undertaking, brevity, is also its flaw. Complex and subtle distinctions, not to mention important exceptions, are consciously set aside for the sake of simplicity. There are hundreds of books addressing deeper matters, but none that we know of which have attempted a straightforward comparative summary. There is a need for no-nonsense reviews of religion, and this may hopefully begin to meet that need.

By juxtaposing a few of their major beliefs, we hope to highlight how other major world religions and important modern secular movements are similar to and differ from Hinduism. A leisurely hour with this section under a favorite tree will endow you with a good grasp of the essential truths of every major religion practiced today on the planet. It may also dispel the myth that all religions are one, that they all seek to lead adherents by the same means to the same Ultimate Reality. They don't, as a conscientious review will show. As you read through the 171 beliefs in this study, put a check by the ones you believe. Why, you might find that you are a Buddhist-Christian-Existentialist or a Taoist-new age-materialist. Place yourself in the cosmology of the beliefs of the world. Many have found this self-inquiry satisfying, others awesomely revealing.

> Pilgrim, pilgrimage and road—it was but myself toward my Self, and your arrival was but myself at my own door.
>
> SUFI MYSTIC, JAIAL AL-DIN RUMI (1207–73)

Hinduism

Hinduism

FOUNDED: Hinduism, the world's oldest religion, has no beginning—it predates recorded history.
FOUNDER: Hinduism has no human founder.
MAJOR SCRIPTURES: The *Vedas, Āgamas* and more.
ADHERENTS: Nearly one billion, mostly in India, Sri Lanka, Bangladesh, Bhutan, Nepal, Malaysia, Indonesia, Indian Ocean, Africa, Europe and North and South America.
SECTS: There are four main denominations: Śaivism, Śāktism, Vaishṇavism and Smārtism.

SYNOPSIS

Hinduism is a vast and profound religion. It worships one Supreme Reality (called by many names) and teaches that all souls ultimately realize Truth. There is no eternal hell, no damnation. It accepts all genuine spiritual paths—from pure monism ("God alone exists") to theistic dualism ("When shall I know His Grace?"). Each soul is free to find his own way, whether by devotion, austerity, meditation *(yoga)* or selfless service. Stress is placed on temple worship, scripture and the *guru-disciple* tradition. Festivals, pilgrimage, chanting of holy hymns and home worship are dynamic practices. Love, nonviolence, good conduct and the law of *dharma* define the Hindu path. Hinduism explains that the soul reincarnates until all *karmas* are resolved and God Realization is attained. The magnificent holy temples, the peaceful piety of the Hindu home, the subtle metaphysics and the science of *yoga* all play their part. Hinduism is a mystical religion, leading the devotee to personally experience the Truth within, finally reaching the pinnacle of consciousness where man and God are one.

GOALS OF THE FOUR MAJOR HINDU SECTS

ŚAIVISM: The primary goal of Śaivism is realizing one's identity with God Śiva, in perfect union and nondifferentiation. This is termed *nirvikalpa samādhi,* Self Realization, and may be attained in this life, granting *moksha,* permanent liberation from the cycles of birth and death. A secondary goal is *savikalpa samādhi,* the realization of Satchidānanda, a unitive experience within superconsciousness in which perfect Truth, knowledge and bliss are known. The soul's final destiny is *viśvagrāsa,* total merger in God Śiva.

ŚĀKTISM: The primary goal of Śāktism is *moksha,* defined as complete identification with God Śiva. A secondary goal for the Śāktas is to perform good works selflessly so that one may go, on death, to the heaven worlds and thereafter enjoy a good birth on earth, for heaven, too, is a transitory state. For Śāktas, God is both the formless Absolute (Śiva) and the manifest Divine (Śakti), worshiped as Pārvatī, Durgā, Kālī, Amman, Rājarājeśvarī, etc. Emphasis is given to the feminine manifest by which the masculine Unmanifest is ultimately reached.

VAISHṆAVISM: The primary goal of Vaishṇavites is *videha mukti,* liberation—attainable only after death—when the small self realizes union with God Vishṇu's body as a part of Him, yet maintains its pure individual personality. Lord Vishṇu—all-pervasive consciousness—is the soul of the universe, distinct from the world and from the *jīvas,* "embodied souls," which constitute His body. His transcendent Being is a celestial form residing in the city of Vaikuṇṭha, the home of all eternal values and perfection, where the soul joins Him upon *mukti,* liberation. A secondary goal—the experience of God's Grace—can be reached while yet embodied through taking refuge in Vishṇu's unbounded love. By loving and serving Vishṇu and meditating upon Him and His incarnations, our spiritual hunger grows and we experience His Grace flooding our whole being.

SMĀRTISM: The ultimate goal of Smārtas is *moksha,* to realize oneself as Brahman—the Absolute and only Reality—and become free from *saṁsāra,* the cycles of birth and death. For this, one must conquer the state of *avidyā,* or ignorance, which causes the world to appear as real. All illusion has vanished for the realized being, Jīvanmukta, even as he lives out life in the physical body. At death, his inner and outer bodies are extinguished. Brahman alone exists.

PATHS OF ATTAINMENT

ŚAIVISM: The path for Śaivites is divided into four progressive stages of belief and practice called *charyā, kriyā, yoga* and *jñāna.* The soul evolves through *karma* and reincarnation from the instinctive-intellectual sphere into virtuous and moral living, then into temple worship and devotion, followed by internalized worship or *yoga* and its meditative disciplines. Union with God Śiva comes through the grace of the *satguru* and culminates in the soul's maturity in the state of *jñāna,* or wisdom. Śaivism values both *bhakti* and *yoga,* devotional and contemplative *sādhanas.*

ŚĀKTISM: The spiritual practices in Śāktism are similar to those in Śaivism, though there is more emphasis in Śāktism on God's Power as opposed to Being, on *mantras* and *yantras,* and on embracing apparent opposites: male-female, absolute-relative, pleasure-pain, cause-effect, mind-body. Certain sects within Śāktism undertake "left-hand" *tantric* rites, consciously using the world of form to transmute and eventually transcend that world. The "left-hand" approach is somewhat occult in nature; it is considered a path for the few, not the many. The "right-hand" path is more conservative in nature.

VAISHṆAVISM: Most Vaishṇavites believe that religion is the performance of *bhakti sādhanas,* and that man can communicate with and receive the grace of Lord Vishṇu who manifests through the temple Deity, or idol. The path of *karma yoga* and *jñāna yoga* leads to *bhakti yoga.* Among the highest practices of all Vaishṇavites is chanting the holy names of the Avatāras, Vishṇu's incarnations, such as Rāma and Kṛishṇa. Through total self-surrender, called *prapatti,* to Lord Vishṇu, liberation from *saṁsāra* is attained.

SMĀRTISM: Most Smārta-Liberal Hindus believe that *moksha* is achieved through *jñāna yoga* alone—defined as an intellectual and meditative but *non-kuṇḍalinī-yoga* path. *Jñāna yoga's* progressive stages are scriptural study *(śravaṇa),* reflection *(manana)* and sustained meditation *(dhyāna).* Guided by a realized *guru* and avowed to the unreality of the world, the initiate meditates on himself as Brahman to break through the illusion of *māyā.* Devotees may also choose from three other non-successive paths to cultivate devotion, accrue good *karma* and purify the mind. These are *bhakti yoga, karma yoga* and *rāja yoga,* which certain Smārtas teach can also bring enlightenment.

HINDU BELIEFS

1. I believe in a one, all-pervasive Supreme Being who is both immanent and transcendent, both Creator and Unmanifest Reality.
2. I believe that the universe undergoes endless cycles of creation, preservation and dissolution.
3. I believe that all souls are evolving toward union with God and will ultimately find *moksha*: spiritual knowledge and liberation from the cycle of rebirth. Not a single soul will be eternally deprived of this destiny.
4. I believe in *karma*, the law of cause and effect by which each individual creates his own destiny by his thoughts, words and deeds.
5. I believe that the soul reincarnates, evolving through many births until all *karmas* have been resolved.
6. I believe that divine beings exist in unseen worlds and that temple worship, rituals, sacraments as well as personal devotionals create a communion with these *devas* and Gods.
7. I believe that a spiritually awakened master or *satguru* is essential to know the transcendent Absolute, as are personal discipline, good conduct, purification, self-inquiry and meditation.
8. I believe that all life is sacred, to be loved and revered, and therefore practice *ahiṁsā*, or nonviolence.
9. I believe that no particular religion teaches the only way to salvation above all others, but that all genuine religious paths are facets of God's pure love and light, deserving tolerance and understanding.

Buddhism

Buddhism

FOUNDED: Buddhism began about 2,500 years ago in India.
FOUNDER: Gautama Siddhartha, or the Buddha, "Enlightened One."
MAJOR SCRIPTURES: The *Tripitaka, Anguttara-Nikaya, Dhammapada, Sutta-Nipatta, Samyutta-Nikaya* and many others.
ADHERENTS: Over 300 million throughout China, Japan, Sri Lanka, Thailand, Burma, Indochina, Korea and Tibet.
SECTS: Buddhism today is divided into three main sects—Theravada, Tibetan and Mahāyāna. Zen Buddhism, well-known in the West, is a Japanese Mahāyāna school.

SYNOPSIS

The goal of life is *nirvāṇa* (salvation). Toward that end, the Buddha's essential teachings are contained in the Four Noble Truths:

1. The noble truth of suffering: life is pain. Being born is pain, growing old is pain, sickness is pain, death is pain. Union with what we dislike is pain, separation from what we like is pain, not obtaining what we desire is pain. This is the essential nature of life.
2. The noble truth of the cause of pain: it is the force of desire that leads to rebirth and further suffering, accompanied by delight and passion.
3. The noble truth of the cessation of pain: the complete cessation of desires, the forsaking, relinquishing and detaching of ourselves from desire and craving will automatically end the round of pleasure-pain, the wheel of birth and rebirth.
4. The noble truth of the path that leads to the cessation of pain: this is the Noble Eightfold Path, namely, right belief, right thought, right speech, right action, right livelihood, right effort, right mindfulness and right meditation.

GOALS OF BUDDHISM

The primary goal of the Buddhists is *nirvāṇa,* defined as the end of change, and literally meaning "to blow out" as one blows out a candle. The Theravada and Tibetan traditions describe the indescribable as "peace and tranquility," while the Mahāyāna tradition (which includes Zen) views it as "neither existence nor nonexistence," "emptiness and the unchanging essence of the Buddha," and "ultimate Reality." It is synonymous with release from the bonds of desire, ego, suffering and rebirth. Buddha never defined the term, except to say, "There is an unborn, an unoriginated, an unmade, an uncompounded," and it lies beyond the experiences of the senses. *Nirvāṇa* is not a state of annihilation, but of peace and reality. As with Jainism, Buddhism has no creator God and thus no union with Him.

PATH OF ATTAINMENT

Buddhism takes its followers through progressive stages, termed *dhyāna, samapatti* and *samādhi. Dhyāna* is meditation, which leads to moral and intellectual purification, and to detachment which leads to pure consciousness. The *samapattis,* or further *dhyānas,* lead through a progressive nullification of psychic, mental and emotional activity to a state which is perfect solitude, neither perception nor nonperception. This leads further to *samādhi,* the attainment of supernatural consciousness and, finally, entrance into the unspeakable *nirvāṇa.* Many Buddhists understand the ultimate destiny and goal to be a heaven of bliss where one can enjoy eternity with the Bodhisattvas.

BUDDHIST BELIEFS

1. I believe that the Supreme is completely transcendent and can be described as Sūnya, a void or state of nonbeing.
2. I believe in the Four Noble Truths: 1. that suffering exists; 2. that desire is the cause of suffering; 3. that suffering may be ended by the annihilation of desire; 4. that to end desire one must follow the Eight-Fold Path.
3. I believe in the Eight-Fold Path of right belief, right aims, right speech, right actions, right occupation, right endeavor, right mindfulness and right meditation.
4. I believe that life's aim is to end suffering through the annihilation of individual existence and absorption into *nirvāṇa,* the Real.
5. I believe in the "Middle Path," living moderately, avoiding extremes of luxury and asceticism.
6. I believe in the greatness of self-giving love and compassion toward all creatures that live, for these contain merit exceeding the giving of offerings to the Gods.
7. I believe in the sanctity of the Buddha and in the sacred scriptures of Buddhism: the *Tripitaka* (Three Baskets of Wisdom) and-or the *Mahāyāna Sūtras.*
8. I believe that man's true nature is divine and eternal, yet his individuality is subject to the change that affects all forms and is therefore transient, dissolving at liberation into *nirvāṇa.*
9. I believe in *dharma* (the Way), *karma* (cause and effect), reincarnation, the *saṅga* (brotherhood of seekers) and the passage on earth as an opportunity to end the cycle of birth and death.

Jainism

Jainism

FOUNDED: Jainism began about 2,500 years ago in India.
FOUNDER: Nataputta Vardhamana, known as Mahāvīra, "great hero."
MAJOR SCRIPTURES: The *Jain Āgamas* and *Siddhāntas.*
ADHERENTS: About six million, almost exclusively in Central and South India, especially in Bombay.
SECTS: There are two sects. The Digambara ("sky-clad") sect holds that a saint should own nothing, not even clothes, thus their practice of wearing only a loincloth. They believe that salvation in this birth is not possible for women. The Svetambara ("white-robed") sect disagrees with these points.

SYNOPSIS

Jainism strives for the realization of the highest perfection of man, which in its original purity is free from all pain and the bondage of birth and death. The term *Jain* is derived from the Sanskṛit *jina,* "conqueror," and implies conquest over this bondage imposed by the phenomenal world. Jainism does not consider it necessary to recognize a God or any being higher than the perfect man. Souls are beginningless and endless, eternally individual. It classes souls into three broad categories: those that are not yet evolved; those in the process of evolution and those that are liberated, free from rebirth. Jainism has strong monastic-ascetic leanings, even for householders. Its supreme ideal is *ahiṁsā,* equal kindness and reverence for all life. The *Jain Āgamas* teach great reverence for all forms of life, strict codes of vegetarianism, asceticism, nonviolence even in self-defense, and opposition to war. Jainism is, above all, a religion of love and compassion.

THE GOALS OF JAINISM

The primary goal of the Jains is becoming a Paramātman, a perfected soul. This is accomplished when all layers of *karma*, which is viewed as a substance, are removed, leading the soul to rise to the ceiling of the universe, from darkness to light, where, beyond the Gods and all currents of transmigration, the soul abides forever in the solitary bliss of *moksha*. *Moksha* is defined in Jainism as liberation, self-unity and integration, pure aloneness and endless calm, freedom from action and desire, freedom from *karma* and rebirth. *Moksha* is attainable in this world or at the time of death. When it is reached, man has fulfilled his destiny as the man-God. For the Jains there is no creator God and, therefore, no communion with Him. The nature of the soul is pure consciousness, power, bliss and omniscience.

PATH OF ATTAINMENT

The soul passes through various stages of spiritual development, called *guṇasthānas*, progressive manifestations of the innate faculties of knowledge and power accompanied by decreasing sinfulness and increasing purity. Souls attain better births according to the amount of personal *karma* they are able to eliminate during life. Between births, souls dwell in one of the seven hells, the sixteen heavens or fourteen celestial regions. Liberated souls abide at the top of the universe. All Jains take five vows, but it is the monk who practices celibacy and poverty. Jainism places great stress on *ahiṁsā*, asceticism, *yoga* and monasticism as the means of attainment. Temple *pūjās* are performed to the twenty-four Tīrthankaras or spiritual preceptors, literally "ford-crossers," those who take others across the ocean of *saṁsāra*.

JAIN BELIEFS

1. I believe in the spiritual lineage of the 24 Tīrthankaras ("ford-finders") of whom the ascetic sage Mahāvīra was the last—that they should be revered and worshiped above all else.
2. I believe in the sacredness of all life, that one must cease injury to sentient creatures, large and small, and that even unintentional killing creates *karma.*
3. I believe that God is neither Creator, Father nor Friend. Such human conceptions are limited. All that may be said of Him is: He is.
4. I believe that each man's soul is eternal and individual and that each must conquer himself by his own efforts and subordinate the worldly to the heavenly in order to attain *moksha,* or release.
5. I believe the conquest of oneself can only be achieved in ascetic discipline and strict religious observance, and that nonascetics and women will have their salvation in another life.
6. I believe that the principle governing the successions of life is *karma,* that our actions, both good and bad, bind us and that *karma* may only be consumed by purification, penance and austerity.
7. I believe in the *Jain Āgamas* and *Siddhāntas* as the sacred scriptures that guide man's moral and spiritual life.
8. I believe in the Three Jewels: right knowledge, right faith and right conduct.
9. I believe the ultimate goal of *moksha* is eternal release from *saṁsāra,* the "wheel of birth and death," and the concomitant attainment of Supreme Knowledge.

Sikhism

Sikhism

FOUNDED: Sikhism began about 500 years ago in Northern India, now the country of Pakistan.
FOUNDER: Guru Nānak.
MAJOR SCRIPTURE: The *Ādi Granth,* revered as the present *guru* of the faith.
ADHERENTS: Estimated at nine million, mostly in India's state of Punjab.
SECTS: Besides the *Khalsa,* there are the Ram Raiyas in Uttara Pradesh and two groups that have living *gurus*—Mandharis and Nirankaris.

SYNOPSIS

The Muslims began their invasions of India some 1,200 years ago. As a result of Islam's struggle with Hindu religion and culture, leaders sought a reconciliation between the two faiths, a middle path that embraced both. Sikhism (from *sikka,* meaning "disciple") united Hindu *bhakti* and Sufi mysticism most successfully. Sikhism began as a peaceful religion and patiently bore much persecution from the Muslims, but with the tenth *guru,* Gobind Singh, self-preservation forced a strong militarism aimed at protecting the faith and way of life against severe opposition. Sikhism stresses the importance of devotion, intense faith in the *guru,* the repetition of God's name *(nām)* as a means of salvation, opposition to the worship of idols, the brotherhood of all men and rejection of caste differences (though certain caste attitudes persist today). There have been no *gurus* in the main Sikh tradition since Guru Gobind Singh, whose last instructions to followers were to honor and cherish the teachings of the ten *gurus* as embodied in the scripture, *Ādi Granth.*

THE GOALS OF SIKHISM

The goal of Sikhism lies in *moksha* which is release and union with God, described as that of a lover with the beloved and resulting in self-transcendence, egolessness and enduring bliss, or *ānanda.* The Sikh is immersed in God, assimilated, identified with Him. It is the fulfillment of individuality in which man, freed of all limitations, becomes co-extensive and co-operant and co-present with God. In Sikhism, *moksha* means release into God's love. Man is not God, but is fulfilled in unitary, mystical consciousness with Him. God is the Personal Lord and Creator.

PATH OF ATTAINMENT

To lead man to the goal of *moksha,* Sikhism follows a path of *japa* and hymns. Through chanting of the Holy Names, Sat Nām, the soul is cleansed of its impurity, the ego is conquered and the wandering mind is stilled. This leads to a superconscious stillness. From here one enters into the divine light and thus attains the state of divine bliss. Once this highest goal is attained, the devotee must devote his awareness to the good of others. The highest goal can be realized only by God's grace, and this is obtained exclusively by following the *satguru* (or nowadays a *sant* or saint, since there are no living *gurus)* and by repeating the holy names of the Lord guided by the *Ādi Granth,* the scripture and sole repository of spiritual authority. For Sikhs there is no Deity worship, no symbol of Divinity.

SIKH BELIEFS

1. I believe in God as the sovereign One, the omnipotent, immortal and personal Creator, a being beyond time, who is called Sat Nām, for His name is Truth.
2. I believe that man grows spiritually by living truthfully, serving selflessly and by repetition of the Holy Name and Guru Nānak's Prayer, *Japaji.*
3. I believe that salvation lies in understanding the divine Truth and that man's surest path lies in faith, love, purity and devotion.
4. I believe in the scriptural and ethical authority of the *Ādi Granth* as God's revelation.
5. I believe that to know God the *guru* is essential as the guide who, himself absorbed in love of the Real, is able to awaken the soul to its true, divine nature.
6. I believe in the line of ten Sikh *gurus:* Guru Nānak, Guru Angad, Guru Amardas, Guru Rām Dās, Guru Arjan, Guru Har Govind, Guru Har Rai, Guru Har Kṛishṇan and Guru Tegh Bahadur—all these are my teachers.
7. I believe that the world is *māyā,* a vain and transitory illusion; only God is true as all else passes away.
8. I believe in adopting the last name "Singh," meaning "lion" and signifying courage, and in the five symbols: 1) white dress (purity), 2) sword (bravery), 3) iron bracelet (morality), 4) uncut hair and beard (renunciation), and 5) comb (cleanliness).
9. I believe in the natural path and stand opposed to fasting, vegetarianism, pilgrimage, caste, idolatry, celibacy and asceticism.

Taoism

Taoism

FOUNDED: Taoism began about 2,500 years ago in China.
FOUNDER: Lao-tzu, whom Confucius described as a dragon riding the wind and clouds.
MAJOR SCRIPTURE: The *Tao-te-Ching,* or "Book of Reason and Virtue," is among the shortest of all scriptures, containing only 5,000 words. Also central are the sacred writings of Chuang-tsu.
ADHERENTS: Estimated at 50 million, mostly in China and and other parts of Asia.
SECTS: Taoism is a potently mystical tradition, so interpretations have been diverse and its sects are many.

SYNOPSIS

The Tao, or Way, has never been put down in words; rather it is left for the seeker to discover within. Lao-tzu himself wrote, "The Tao that can be named is not the eternal Tao." Taoism is concerned with man's spiritual level of being, and in the *Tao-te-Ching* the awakened man is compared to bamboo: upright, simple and useful outside—and hollow inside. Effulgent emptiness is the spirit of Tao, but no words will capture its spontaneity, its eternal newness. Adherents of the faith are taught to see the Tao everywhere, in all beings and in all things. Taoist shrines are the homes of divine beings who guide the religion, bless and protect worshipers. A uniquely Taoist concept is *wu-wei,* nonaction. This does not mean no action, but rather not exceeding spontaneous action that accords with needs as they naturally arise; not indulging in calculated action and not acting so as to exceed the very minimum required for effective results. If we keep still and listen to the inner promptings of the Tao, we shall act effortlessly, efficiently, hardly giving the matter a thought. We will be ourselves, as we are.

THE GOALS OF TAOISM

The primary goal of Taoism may be described as the mystical intuition of the Tao, which is the Way, the Primal Meaning, the Undivided Unity, the Ultimate Reality. Both immanent and transcendent, the Tao is the natural way of all beings, it is the nameless beginning of heaven and earth, and it is the mother of all things. All things depend upon the Tao, all things return to it. Yet it lies hidden, transmitting its power and perfection to all things. He who has realized the Tao has uncovered the layers of consciousness so that he arrives at pure consciousness and sees the inner truth of everything. Only one who is free of desire can apprehend the Tao, thereafter leading a life of "actionless activity." There is no Personal God in Taoism, and thus no union with Him. There are three worlds and beings within them, and worship is part of the path.

PATH OF ATTAINMENT

One who follows the Tao follows the natural order of things, not seeking to improve upon nature or to legislate virtue to others. The Taoist observes *wu-wei,* or nondoing, like water which without effort seeks and finds its proper level. This path includes purifying oneself through stilling the appetites and the emotions, accomplished in part through meditation, breath control and other forms of inner discipline, generally under a master. The foremost practice is goodness or naturalness, and detachment from the Ten Thousand Things of the world.

TAOIST BELIEFS

1. I believe that the Eternal may be understood as the Tao, or "Way," which embraces the moral and physical order of the universe, the path of virtue which Heaven itself follows, and the Absolute—yet so great is it that "the Tao that can be described is not the Eternal Tao."
2. I believe in the unique greatness of the sage Lao-tsu and in his disciple Chuang-tsu.
3. I believe in the scriptural insights and final authority of the *Tao-te-Ching* and in the sacredness of Chuang-tsu's writings.
4. I believe that man aligns himself with the Eternal when he observes humility, simplicity, gentle yielding, serenity and effortless action.
5. I believe that the goal and the path of life are essentially the same, and that the Tao can be known only to exalted beings who realize it themselves—reflections of the Beyond are of no avail.
6. I believe the omniscient and impersonal Supreme is implacable, beyond concern for human woe, but that there exist lesser Divinities—from the high Gods who endure for eons, to the nature spirits and demons.
7. I believe that all actions create their opposing forces, and the wise will seek inaction in action.
8. I believe that man is one of the Ten Thousand Things of manifestation, is finite and will pass; only the Tao endures forever.
9. I believe in the oneness of all creation, in the spirituality of the material realms and in the brotherhood of all men.

Confucianism

Confucianism

FOUNDED: Confucianism began about 2,500 years ago in China.
FOUNDER: Supreme Sage K'ung-fu-tsu (Confucius) and Second Sage Meng-tzu (Mencius).
MAJOR SCRIPTURES: The *Analects, Doctrine of the Mean, Great Learning* and *Mencius.*
ADHERENTS: Estimated at 350 million, mostly in China, Japan, Burma and Thailand.
SECTS: There are no formal sects within Confucianism. Followers are free to profess other religions yet still be Confucianists.

SYNOPSIS

Confucianism is, and has been for over 25 centuries, the dominant philosophical system in China and the guiding light in almost every aspect of Chinese life. Confucius and his followers traveled throughout the many feudal states of the Chinese empire, persuading rulers to adopt his social reforms. They did not offer a point-by-point program, but stressed instead the "Way," or "One Thread," Jen (also translated as "humanity or love"), that runs through all Confucius' teachings. They urged individuals to strive for perfect virtue, righteousness (called Yi) and improvement of character. They taught the importance of harmony in the family, order in the state and peace in the empire, which they saw as inherently interdependent. Teachings emphasize a code of conduct, self-cultivation and propriety—and thus the attainment of social and national order. Stress is more on human duty and the ideal of the "superior man" than on a divine or supramundane Reality. Still, Confucius fasted, worshiped the ancestors, attended sacrifices and sought to live in harmony with Heaven. Confucianism is now enjoying a renaissance in China.

THE GOALS OF CONFUCIANISM

The primary goal of Confucianism is to create a true nobility through proper education and the inculcation of all the virtues. It is described as the return to the way of one's ancestors, and the classics are studied to discover the ancient way of virtue. Spiritual nobility is attainable by all men; it is a moral achievement. Confucius accepted the Tao, but placed emphasis on this return to an idealized age and the cultivation of the superior man, on the pragmatic rather than the mystical. The superior man's greatest virtue is benevolent love. The other great virtues are duty, wisdom, truth and propriety. Salvation is seen as realizing and living one's natural goodness, which is endowed by heaven through education. The superior man always knows the right and follows his knowledge.

PATH OF ATTAINMENT

Besides virtue, the five relationships offer the follower of Confucianism the means for progressing. These five relationships are to his ruler, his father, his wife, his elder brother and his friend. Ancestors are revered in Confucianism, and it is assumed that their spirit survives death. With respect to a Deity, Confucius was himself an agnostic, preferring to place emphasis on the ethical life here rather than to speak of a spiritual life beyond earthly existence, guiding men's minds not to the future, but to the present and the past.

CONFUCIAN BELIEFS

1. I believe in the presence of the Supreme Ruler in all things, and in Heaven as the Ethical Principle whose law is order, impersonal and yet interested in mankind.
2. I believe that the purpose of life is to pursue an orderly and reverent existence in accord with *Li*, propriety or virtue, so as to become the Superior Man.
3. I believe in the Golden Rule: "Never do to others what you would not like them to do to you."
4. I believe that Confucius, China's First Sage, is the Master of Life whose teachings embody the most profound understanding of earth and Heaven, and that Mencius is China's Second Sage.
5. I believe in the writings of Confucius as scriptural truth and in the Four Sacred Books: The *Analects, Doctrine of the Mean, Great Learning,* and *Mencius.*
6. I believe that each man has five relationships, entailing five duties to his fellow man: to his ruler, to his father, to his wife, to his elder brother and to his friend—the foremost being his familial duties.
7. I believe that human nature is inherently good, and evil is an unnatural condition arising from inharmony.
8. I believe that man is master of his own life and fate, free to conduct himself as he will, and that he should cultivate qualities of benevolence, righteousness, propriety, wisdom and sincerity.
9. I believe that the family is the most essential institution among men, and that religion should support the family and the state.

Shintoism

Shintoism

FOUNDED: Shintoism began around 2,500–3,000 years ago.
FOUNDER: Each of the thirteen ancient sects has its own founder.
MAJOR SCRIPTURES: *Kokiji* (Record of Ancient Things), *Nikongi* (Chronicles of Japan), a later work, *Yengishiki* (Institutes of the period of Yengi), and the *Collection of 10,000 Leaves* are the primary works, but they are not regarded as revealed scripture.
ADHERENTS: Estimated at 30 million, mostly in Japan. Most are also Buddhists.

SYNOPSIS

There are two main divisions. One is the thirteen ancient sects, all very similar. The second is known as State Shinto, and is a later synthesis finding its highest expression in the worship of the Emperor and loyalty to the State and family. Shinto (from the Chinese characters *Shin* and *Tao,* signifying the "Way of the Spirits") is called Kami-no-michi in its native Japan. Kami are the many Gods or nature spirits. Shinto shrines are many, over 100,000 in Japan. In the shrines no images are worshiped, rather it is considered that the Kami themselves are there. Fresh foods, water, incense, etc., are offered daily upon the altar. There is an inward belief in the sacredness of the whole of the universe, that man can be in tune with this sacredness. Stress is placed on truthfulness and purification through which man may remove the "dust" which conceals his inherently divine nature and thus receive the guidance and blessings of Kami. The Shintoist's ardent love of the motherland has found unique expression in the loyalty and devotion of the Japanese people to their state institutions.

THE GOALS OF SHINTOISM

The primary goal of Shintoism is to achieve immortality among the ancestral beings, the Kami. Kami is understood by the Shintoist as a supernatural, holy power living in or connected to the world of the spirit. All living things possess a Kami nature. Man's nature is the highest, for he possesses the most Kami. Salvation is living in the spirit world with these divine beings, the Kami.

PATH OF ATTAINMENT

Salvation is achieved in Shinto through observance of all tabus and the avoidance of persons and objects which might cause impurity or pollution. Prayers are made and offerings brought to the temples of the Gods and Goddesses, of which there are said to be 800 myriad in the universe. Man has no Supreme God to obey, but needs only know how to adjust to Kami in its various manifestations. A person's Kami nature survives death, and a man naturally desires to be worthy of being remembered with approbation by his descendants. Therefore, fulfillment of duty is a most important aspect of Shinto.

SHINTO BELIEFS

1. I believe in the "Way of the Gods," Kami-no-michi, which asserts nature's sacredness and uniquely reveals the supernatural.
2. I believe there is not a single Supreme Being, but myriad Gods, superior beings, among all the wonders of the universe which is not inanimate but filled everywhere with sentient life.
3. I believe in the scriptural authority of the great books known as the *Record of Ancient Things, Chronicles of Japan, Institutes of the Period of Yengi* and *Collection of 10,000 Leaves.*
4. I believe in the sanctity of cleanliness and purity—of body and spirit—and that impurity is a religious transgression.
5. I believe that the State is a divine institution whose laws should not be transgressed and to which individuals must sacrifice their own needs.
6. I believe in moral and spiritual uprightness as the cornerstone of religious ethics and in the supreme value of loyalty.
7. I believe that the supernatural reveals itself through all that is natural and beautiful, and value these above philosophical or theological doctrine.
8. I believe that whatever is, is Divine Spirit, that the world is a one brotherhood, that all men are capable of deep affinity with the Divine and that there exists no evil in the world whatsoever.
9. I believe in the practical use of ceremony and ritual, and in the worship of the Deities that animate nature, including the Sun Goddess, Star God and Storm God.

Zoroastrianism

Zoroastrianism

FOUNDED: Zoroastrianism began 2,600 years ago in ancient Iran.

FOUNDER: Spenta Zarathustra.

MAJOR SCRIPTURE: Portions of the *Zend Avesta* (Persian).

ADHERENTS: 125,000, mostly near Bombay, where they are called Parsis.

SECTS: The present-day sects are two, having split over a question of calendar.

SYNOPSIS

Two principles form the basis of Zoroastrian ethics: the maintenance of life and the struggle against evil. In order to maintain life, one must till the soil, raise cattle, marry and have children. Asceticism and celibacy are condemned; purity and avoidance of defilement (from death, demons, etc.) are valued. In order to combat evil, one must at all times oppose the forces of evil and people who side with them. Zoroastrianism stresses monotheism, while recognizing the universal sway of two opposite forces. The powers of good are led by Ahura Mazda (the Wise Lord) and the forces of evil by Angra Mainyu or Ahriman (the Evil Spirit). Each side has an array of warriors; bands of angels and archangels on one side and hosts of demons and archfiends on the other. Good will eventually triumph on Judgment Day, when a Messiah and Savior named Sayoshant will appear to punish the wicked and establish the righteous in a paradise on Earth. A central feature of the faith is the sacred fire that is constantly kept burning in every home, fueled by fragrant sandalwood. Fire is considered the only worshipful symbol, the great purifier and sustainer, of the nature of the sun itself.

THE GOALS OF ZOROASTRIANISM

The goal of Zoroastrianism is to be rewarded with a place in heaven where the soul will be with God, called Ahura Mazda, sharing His blessed existence forever.

PATH OF ATTAINMENT

Man's life, according to Zoroastrianism, is a moral struggle, not a search for knowledge or enlightenment. He is put on the earth to affirm and approve the world, not to deny it, not to escape from it. Salvation is found in obedience to the will of Ahura Mazda as revealed and taught by His prophet, Zoroaster. Man has but one life. He also has the freedom to choose between good and evil, the latter being embodied in Angra Mainyu who rebelled against God. At death, each is judged and consigned to his deserved abode.

Zoroastrians hold truth as the greatest virtue, followed by good thoughts, words and deeds. They value the ethical life most highly. Though there is a resurrection of the dead, a judgment and a kingdom of heaven on earth, followed by punishment of the wicked, all sins are eventually burned away and all of mankind exists forever with Ahura Mazda. Hell, for the Zoroastrian, is not eternal.

ZOROASTRIAN BELIEFS

1. I believe there are two Great Beings in the universe. One, Ahura Mazda, created man and all that is good, beautiful and true, while the other, Angra Mainyu, vivifies all that is evil, ugly and destructive.
2. I believe that man has free will to align himself with good or evil, and when all mankind is in harmony with the God Ahura Mazda, Angra Mainyu will be conquered.
3. I believe the soul is immortal and upon death crosses over Hell by a narrow bridge—the good crossing safely to Heaven and the evil falling into Hell.
4. I believe that a savior named Sayoshant will appear at the end of time, born of a virgin, reviving the dead, rewarding the good and punishing the evil, and thereafter Ahura Mazda will reign.
5. I believe that Zoroaster, also known as Zarathustra, is the foremost Prophet of God.
6. I believe in the scriptural authority of the *Zend Avesta.*
7. I believe that purity is the first virtue, truth the second and charity the third—and that man must discipline himself by good thoughts, words and deeds.
8. I believe that marriage excels continence, action excels contemplation and forgiveness excels revenge.
9. I believe in God as Seven Persons: Eternal Light; Right and Justice; Goodness and Love; Strength of Spirit; Piety and Faith; Health and Perfection; and Immortality—and that He may best be worshiped through the representation of fire.

Judaism

Judaism

FOUNDED: Judaism began about 3,700 years ago in Egypt-Canaan, now Israel.
FOUNDERS: Abraham, who started the lineage, and Moses, who emancipated the enslaved Jewish tribes from Egypt.
MAJOR SCRIPTURE: The *Torah* (the first five books of the *Old Testament*, and the *Talmud*).
ADHERENTS: About 12 million worldwide, over half in the United States.
SECTS: Jews are divided into Orthodox, Conservative and Reform sects, with other regional and ethnic divisions.

SYNOPSIS

The religion of the Jews is inseparable from their history as a people. Much of the *Torah* traces the ancestry of Abraham through Isaac, Jacob, Joseph and finally to Moses, the foremost of God's prophets in Hebrew history. It was Moses who gave Judaism the Ten Commandments and established the religious laws and traditions.

By far the most profound characteristic of Judaism is its strict monotheism. The Jews hold an unshakable belief in one God and one God only, whom they call Yahweh, from whom all creation flows. The Jewish people consider themselves a chosen people, apart from all the other peoples of the earth, by virtue of their covenant with Yahweh.

Much stress is placed on the hallowing of daily existence, worship in the synagogue, prayer and reading of the scriptures. Few religions can boast of such a close-knit family tradition as Judaism, making the home a great strength to the religion and a constant refuge to the faithful. Each day, morning and evening, every devout Jew affirms his faith by repeating Moses' prayer: "Hear, O Israel, the Lord our God, the Lord is One."

THE GOALS OF JUDAISM

The goal of Judaism lies in the strict obedience to the *Torah,* Jewish scripture, which can alleviate the plight of the individual and of society. Obeying God's law brings rewards in the future life when the Messiah will come to overthrow evil and reward the righteous in God's kingdom on the earth, the Day of the Lord. The soul thereafter will enjoy God's presence and love.

PATH OF ATTAINMENT

Man has two impulses: good and evil. He can either follow God's law or rebel and be influenced by Satan, who caused God's creation to go astray. It is the highest morality, possible through obedience to the *Torah,* which pleases God. One must follow justice, charity, ethics and honesty, being true to the one true God, Yahweh.

JUDAIC BELIEFS

1. I believe in the One God and Creator who is incorporeal and transcendent, beyond the limitation of form, yet who cares for the world and its creatures, rewarding the good and punishing the evil.
2. I believe in the Prophets, of which Moses was God's foremost, and in the Commandments revealed to him by God on Mount Sinai as man's highest law.
3. I believe in the *Torah* as God's word and scripture, composed of the five *Old Testament* books and the *Talmud.* They are God's only immutable law.
4. I believe that upon death the soul goes to Heaven (or to Hell first if it has been sinful), that one day the Messiah will appear on earth and there will be a Day of Judgment, and the dead shall physically arise to Life Everlasting.
5. I believe that the universe is not eternal, but was created by and will be destroyed by God.
6. I believe that no priest should intervene in the relationship of man and God, nor should God be represented in any form, nor should any being be worshiped other than the One God, Yahweh.
7. I believe in man's spiritualization through adherence to the law, justice, charity and honesty.
8. I believe that God has established a unique spiritual covenant with the Hebrew people to uphold for mankind the highest standards of monotheism and piety.
9. I believe in the duty of the family to make the home a House of God through devotions and ritual, prayers, sacred festivals and observation of the Holy Day.

Christianity

Christianity

FOUNDED: Christianity began about 2,000 years ago in what is now Israel.
FOUNDER: Jesus of Nazareth.
MAJOR SCRIPTURE: The *Bible, Old* and *New Testaments.*
ADHERENTS: Estimated at 1.5 billion.
SECTS: Christianity is divided into three main sects: Roman Catholic, Eastern Orthodox and Protestant. Among Protestants there are over 20,000 denominations.

SYNOPSIS

The majority of Christians adhere to the Apostles' Creed: "I believe in God, the Father Almighty, Maker of Heaven and Earth, and Jesus Christ, His only Son, our Lord, Who was conceived by the Holy Ghost, born of the Virgin Mary, suffered under Pontius Pilate, was crucified, dead and buried. He descended into Hell. The third day He rose again from the dead. He ascended unto Heaven and sitteth on the right hand of God, the Father Almighty. From thence He shall come to judge the quick and the dead. I believe in the Holy Ghost,...the communion of saints, the forgiveness of sins, the resurrection of the body and the life everlasting." Most Christian faith revolves around the basic principles of this creed, but with important exceptions to its various beliefs. Christianity has an unswerving conviction that it is the only true religion, the only path to salvation. This engenders a missionary zeal, an urgency to evangelize around the world.

Stress is placed on acceptance of Jesus as God and Savior, on good conduct, compassion, service to mankind, faith and preparation for the Final Judgment. Only good Christians will be saved and accepted into heaven. Today over half of all Christians are black. Membership is diminishing in developed nations but increasing in undeveloped nations.

THE GOALS OF CHRISTIANITY

The goal of Christianity is eternal life with God in heaven, a perfect existence in which God's glory and bliss are shared. It is also a personal life, enjoyed differently by souls according to the amount of grace achieved in life.

PATH OF ATTAINMENT

Man's plight is caused by disobedience to God's will. Man needs redemption from the forces which would enslave and destroy him—fear, selfishness, hopelessness, desire and the supernatural forces of the Devil, sin and death against which he is powerless. His salvation comes only through faith in Jesus Christ, that is, in acceptance of Jesus' resurrection from the dead as proof of God's power over the forces of sin and death. The good Christian lives a life of virtue and obedience to God out of gratitude to God for sacrificing Jesus for the sins of all who come to accept Jesus Christ as personal Savior and Lord. Jesus is to return again to judge the world and bring God's rule to the earth. Through following the law of God as found in the *Holy Bible* and through God's grace, man attains salvation. Those who do not achieve this blessedness are, after death, consigned to a hell of eternal suffering and damnation.

CHRISTIAN BELIEFS

1. I believe in God the Father, Creator of the universe, reigning forever distinct over man, His beloved creation.
2. I believe man is born a sinner, and that he may know salvation only through the Savior, Jesus Christ, God's only begotten Son.
3. I believe that Jesus Christ was born of Mary, a virgin.
4. I believe that Jesus Christ was crucified on the cross, then resurrected from the dead and now sits at the right hand of the Father as the final judge of the dead, and that He will return again as prophesied.
5. I believe that the soul is embodied for a single lifetime, but is immortal and accountable to God for all thoughts and actions.
6. I believe in the historical truth of the *Holy Bible,* that it is sacred scripture of the highest authority and the only word of God.
7. I believe that upon death and according to its earthly deeds and its acceptance of the Christian faith, the soul enters Heaven, Purgatory or Hell. There it awaits the Last Judgment when the dead shall rise again, the redeemed to enjoy life everlasting and the unsaved to suffer eternally.
8. I believe in the intrinsic goodness of mankind and the affirmative nature of life, and in the priceless value of love, charity and faith.
9. I believe in the Holy Trinity of God who reveals Himself as Father, Son and Holy Ghost, and in the existence of Satan, the personification of evil, deception and darkness.

Islam

Islam

FOUNDED: Islam began about 1,400 years ago in present-day Saudi Arabia.
FOUNDER: Prophet Mohammed.
MAJOR SCRIPTURES: The *Koran.*
ADHERENTS: Over one billion, mostly in the Middle East, Indonesia, Pakistan, Bangladesh, Africa, China and Eastern Europe.
SECTS: There are two main divisions within Islam. The Sunnis are followers of the political successors of Mohammed. The Shiites are followers of Mohammed's family successors, all martyred at an early age.

SYNOPSIS

Islam means "submission," surrender to the will of God, called Allah. Those who submit are called Muslims. Islam is based upon five "pillars," or principle acts of faith to which every Muslim in the world adheres. These are: 1) Faith in Allah: "There is no God but Allah, and Mohammed is His Prophet." 2) Praying five times daily: kneeling in the direction of Mecca, the holy city. 3) Giving of alms: a share of each Muslim's income is given to support the mosque and the poor. 4) Fasting: throughout Ramadan, the ninth month of the Muslim calendar, the faithful fast from sunrise to sunset. 5) Pilgrimage: the binding force of the peoples who have embraced Islam. At least once in life every believer must go to Mecca, the holy city. They go dressed in simple, seamless white garments.

Islam teaches absolute monotheism and Mohammed's primacy as God's last Prophet on earth. Stress is on the brotherhood of believers, nondifference of religious and secular life, obedience to God's Law, abstinence from alcohol, good conduct and the limitation of all except Allah. Today Islam is the world's fastest-growing religion.

THE GOALS OF ISLAM

The primary goal of Islam is to enjoy eternal life, both physical and spiritual, in heaven with Allah. Heaven is a paradise in which all the joys and pleasures abound, in which one lives amid beautiful gardens and fountains, enjoying the choicest foods served by sweet maidens. Man is the noblest creation of God, ranking above the angels. It is the sacred duty of Muslims to convert others to the Islamic faith. Islam has an ardent conviction that it is the only true religion, the only path to salvation. From this belief arises an extraordinary zeal, to share the faith and to convert others. The ideal human society is an Islamic theocracy.

PATH OF ATTAINMENT

Total submission to Allah is the single path to salvation, and even that is no guarantee, for Allah may desire even a faithful soul to experience misery. The good Muslim surrenders all pride, the chief among sins, and follows explicitly the will of Allah as revealed in the *Koran* by His last and greatest prophet, Mohammed. This and this alone brings a full and meaningful life and avoids the terrors of Hell which befall sinners and infidels. He believes in the Five Doctrines and observes the Five Pillars. The virtues of truthfulness, temperance and humility before God are foremost for Islam, and the practices of fasting, pilgrimage, prayer and charity to the Muslim community are most necessary to please Allah. The five doctrines are: 1) There is only one true God, Allah. 2) There are angels, chief of whom is Gabriel. 3) There are four inspired books: the *Torah* of Moses, the *Zabur* (Psalms) of David, the *Injil* (Evangel) of Jesus, and the *Koran,* Allah's final message, which supercedes all other scriptures. 4) There have been numerous prophets of Allah, including Mohammed, the Last Prophet. 5) There will be a final day of judgment and resurrection. A sixth but optional doctrine is belief in *kismit,* "fate or destiny."

ISLAMIC BELIEFS

1. I believe that Allah is the Supreme Creator and Sustainer, all-knowing and transcendent and yet the arbiter of good and evil, the final judge of men.
2. I believe in the Five Pillars of Faith: 1) praying five times daily, 2) charity through alms-giving, 3) fasting during the ninth month, 4) pilgrimage to Holy Mecca, Saudi Arabia, and 5) profession of faith by acknowledging, "There is no God but Allah, and Mohammed is His Prophet."
3. I believe in the *Koran* as the Word of God and sacred scripture mediated through the Angel Gabriel to Mohammed.
4. I believe in the direct communion of each man with God, that all are equal in the eyes of God and therefore priests or other intercessors are unneeded.
5. I believe in the pure transcendence of God, great beyond imagining—no form or idol can be worshiped in His Name.
6. I believe that the soul of man is immortal, embodied once on earth, then entering Heaven or Hell upon death according to its conduct and faith on earth.
7. I believe in the Last Judgment and that man should stand in humble awe and fear of God's wrathful and vengeful power.
8. I believe that truthfulness should be observed in all circumstances, even though it may bring injury or pain.
9. I believe that salvation is only obtained through God's grace and not through man's efforts, yet man should do good and avoid all sins, especially drunkenness, usury and gambling.

Faiths

Faiths

In his search of the Divine, man has created innumerable smaller "faiths." These spiritual paths are often charismatic or mystical in source or nature and have a powerful spiritual presence and purpose despite being numerically small. A few examples are explored here in nine beliefs. Following this, we explore some larger movements, which are not necessarily spiritual in nature, but are important currents of thought and belief which shape modern politics and society.

SPIRITUALISM: Spiritualism holds that there is another, perhaps deeper, reality on "the other side" which can be contacted by mediums or psychics who have sufficient sensitivity. It is one of the oldest forms of communion.

SHAMANISM: This broad term includes the thousands of tribal faiths which have existed on every continent since long before recorded history. Beliefs include a deep sense of the sacredness of life and of the earth, communion with spirit guides and in the ability of man to live in harmony with and influence nature.

THEOSOPHY: Founded in the late 1800s by Madame Blavatsky, Theosophy emphasizes mystical experience, esoteric doctrine and monism. They seek universal brotherhood, and explore the unexplained laws of nature, and the powers latent in man.

UNIVERSALISM: Many faiths are based on universalist principles, often as a conscious effort to avoid certain doctrines which are seen as narrow or sectarian. Universalism arises in all religions, whether Christian (Unitarianism), Islam (Baha'i), Jain (Rajneeshism) or Hindu (dozens of all-religions movements, such as those of Sāī Bāba, Kṛishṇamūrti and Mahārshi Mahesh Yogī).

OTHER FAITHS

Among thousands of other faiths are: indigenous people's tribal religions, humanitarianism, neo-Indian religion, shamanism, Anthroposophy, Swedenborgianism, Gnosticism, Neoplatonism, Scientology, Eckankar, channeling, witchcraft, Paganism, occultism, Subud, mysticism, Freemasonry, Satan worship, mysticism, Huna, Sufism, Baha'i, Rosicrucianism, Christian Science and Religious Science.

A SAMPLING OF BELIEFS OF FAITHS

1. I believe in the fundamental unity and common source of all religions (Baha'i and Universalism).
2. I believe man's natural spirituality is best expressed in loving and practical aid to his fellow man, rather than metaphysical inquiry (Humanitarianism).
3. I believe in the unity of religions, the efficacy of devotion, *sādhana* and service and in Satya Sāī Bāba as the living Incarnation of God (Saiism).
4. I believe that spiritual progress comes through analysis of current and past life experiences which resolve past *karma* most directly (Scientology).
5. I believe that there is no God beyond the Divine within man and no truth beyond existential freedom, that all religions imprison man, causing repression, fear and poverty (Rajneeshism).
6. I believe man's sense of the sacred can be fulfilled naturally, without formal worship, houses of God, ceremony, creeds or theology (various faiths).
7. I believe religion consists of unitive and direct mystical experience which should be the objective of every religious aspirant (mysticism).
8. I believe that the cultivation of occult powers including ESP, astral travel, past life readings, etc., is the highest pursuit of that which is spiritual (occultism).

9. I believe in the intimate relationship of man, Spirit and the earth—which is a living, sacred being—and in the brotherhood of all creatures (indigenous tribalism).

DRUG CULTURE

"Drug culture" refers to the philosophy and way of life developed in Western societies during the 1960s. Its adherents follow a lifestyle based on the use of various natural and man-made drugs such as marijuana, hashish, peyote, mescaline, cocaine, LSD and chemical designer drugs.

DRUG CULTURE BELIEFS

1. I believe that one can achieve the ultimate goal of enlightenment, as understood by any religion, through the use of drugs.
2. I believe that the psychedelic drug experience, properly handled, fulfills the role of a spiritual teacher or *guru.*
3. I believe that drugs give mystical experiences of various types identical to and therefore equally as valid as those achieved through *yoga,* penance, grace, etc.
4. I believe that the knowledge gained on drugs is more valid than the traditional knowledge given by society or religion because it is direct, personal experience of a higher order.
5. I believe that people who take drugs are more "aware" or "enlightened" than those who do not.
6. I believe that one can solve his personal psychological problems or "hangups" by taking drugs.
7. I believe in living simply, close to nature and in harmony with others and that sexual relationships need not be restricted by the traditional morals imposed by society.
8. I believe that the ideal life is to completely drop out of society, becoming self-sufficient and associating with

others of a like mind, and that those who do not drop out of society but continue to involve themselves in mundane materialism are living in a lower consciousness.

9. I believe that the meaning of life is found in intense self-revelatory experiences, which can be attained through drugs that open the doors of perception to higher consciousness.

NEW AGE

The term *new age* was coined in the 1970s to denote an awakening of the mass consciousness to deeper realities and the need for individual attunement with universal, higher consciousness and creative transformation. In practice, new-age thinking embraces myriad enlightenment teachings (mostly of Eastern origin)—from crystallography to Zen, parapsychology to holistic medicine.

NEW AGE BELIEFS

1. I believe in the one Eternal Source or Ultimate Reality, called by many names, which flows through all forms of nature and can be known through spiritual realization and experience.
2. I believe in unseen worlds and beings who may interact with our world, and that some are benevolent and help guide and protect us, while others are malevolent, and that channeling, or mediumship, is a means of contacting such souls.
3. I believe that the world is a dynamic, conscious entity; that mankind is but one part of the cosmic ecology and that, as stewards, we must treat the world responsibly, with love, respect and reverence.
4. I believe that consciousness is present in and conveyed through some structures more than others. Thus, for example, crystals are powerful sources or channels of

knowledge and spiritual strength.

5. I believe in meditation, trance, rebirthing, self-healing, channeling, past-life regression, crystals, sexual *tantras,* drugs and more as effective tools in the quest for wholeness and oneness with the sacred, and that one should continue to explore alternatives and not feel restricted to the disciplines of any one system of thought.
6. I believe the world has entered the New Age, the age of Aquarius, awakening to the consciousness of love, selflessness, compassion and creativity, from the old age of hatred, war, ignorance and greed. Those who perceive this vision should share it with others to uplift society.
7. I believe that traditional religions are outmoded and that we are moving toward a universal brotherhood; yet, the Eastern religions and so-called primitive faiths are rich reservoirs of truth and spiritual practice.
8. I believe in nonconformity and noncommitment: that each person is responsible to his-her own conscience only and not to the dictates of society which often unduly hamper freedom of expression, and that even spiritual *gurus* are to be approached with circumspection.
9. I believe that many of society's traditional economic and social structures are outmoded and should be abandoned for ones which reflect new-age consciousness, and that dropping out of society is a valid new-age alternative.

ECOLOGY MOVEMENT

In the 1980s there arose an earth-ethics movement complete with philosophy, an immense following and compelling missionary zeal. It deemed the present global environmental imbalance so severe as to threaten future generations' quality of life, perhaps even leading to the extinction of the human race. There is a wide philosophical range among adherents: 1) man-centered conservationists seek to preserve natural resources for human enjoyment, 2) environmentalists work to preserve ecosystems and species and 3) "deep ecologists" call for spiritualization of human life in consonance with a sacred nature. In the 1990s this movement brought together organizational, tribal, religious and political leaders from hundreds of nations to focus on global concerns at immense international conferences. Adherents believe the world community must act speedily to preserve nature and protect humanity from disaster.

BELIEFS OF THE ECOLOGY MOVEMENT

1. I believe that all nature is sacred and One and that each life form has intrinsic value in a cosmos where elements, plants, animals and humans are intimately interconnected, essential to and dependent on the whole.
2. I believe that every human being has the right to a healthy, pristine, undiminished environment, and that we are morally obliged to work toward assuring this right for future generations.
3. I believe that all living beings have an inalienable right to exist, and that through our ignorance, assisted by modern science, we have wrongly disrupted the balance of life and brought about the unforgivable extinction of vast numbers of plant and animal species.
4. I believe that the sacredness of life demands the practice of nonviolence, that differences must be resolved by consultation rather than conflict. Nations must work toward complete disarmament and termination of all weapons production and trade.
5. I believe we must change our system of values away from materialism and consumerism, transform our hearts and minds, make simple and concrete changes in our way of life and renew our deepest religious impulses as we create a global society.

6. I believe it is imperative that mankind rediscover the value of frugality, avoid waste, implement sustainable systems of nonpolluting farming, manufacturing and energy production to ensure the ability of future generations to meet their needs. Simplicity of life fosters both inner freedom and outer sustainability.
7. I believe that biological, cultural and religious diversity are essential to the purpose of life, and that all species of life and all human traditions, especially indigenous faiths, must be preserved through peaceful co-existence, protection of habitats through wilderness preservation and sustainable life practices.
8. I believe that the present ecological crisis is, at its heart, a spiritual crisis for the human race and affirm the importance of respecting all spiritual traditions, promoting those that foster concern and responsibility for the environment and vigorously challenging those that do not.
9. I believe that overpopulation poses one of the greatest threats to the natural environment and to the quality of human life, and that to establish a sustainable earth community we must promote the extended family and make greater efforts to educate women and children.

FUNDAMENTALISM

Fundamentalism describes any religious or philosophical group marked by extreme dogmatism and intolerance. There are fundamentalist denominations within virtually every religion and faith—including Christianity, Judaism, Islam, Buddhism, Sikhism and Hinduism—all believing in a literal interpretation of their scripture as *the* exclusive truth, the one and only way which all souls must follow to attain salvation. Historically, fundamentalism, especially when coupled with evangelical zeal, has led to aggression and violence against nonbelievers.

FUNDAMENTALISM BELIEFS

1. I believe that there is only one acceptable perception of truth, and it is stated in our scriptures; and all who do not accept this doctrine are following false paths and are destined to eternal damnation.
2. I believe that the gospel was spoken at one point in time by our messiah, the one and only true representative of God, and is not subject to or in need of adaptation through time or circumstance.
3. I believe that the members of our faith have been divinely commissioned by God and are duty-bound to spread His holy word throughout the world.
4. I believe that government should reflect and embody the beliefs of my faith, and that even nonbelievers should abide by our religious law as the law of the land.
5. I believe that there is in this world a battle between the believers, representing the forces of light, and the non-believers, representing the forces of darkness, and that ultimately good will conquer evil.
6. I believe that, if necessary, force and violence should be used to bring nonbelievers and dissidents to accept the truth of our religious doctrine, and that the use of such force is justifiable in the name of God.
7. I believe that free inquiry and the questioning of our religious doctrine is the first step to heresy and should be guarded against, and that modern liberties are forms of self-indulgence and sin.
8. I believe that our codes of morality are God's absolute commandments and are not subject to change, revision or reinterpretation.
9. I believe that education for children should consist of strict and exclusive learning of our teachings and careful censorship of other forms of thought and belief.

Atheistic Philosophies

Atheistic Philosophies

In this section we will examine the beliefs of four philosophies or world views that exclude God: materialism, Communism, existentialism, and secular humanism. Of course, there are many smaller ism's that could be listed here, but these are among the most prevalent. Their ideas and teachings have great influence throughout the world, especially through Western universities and the Western news media.

MATERIALISM

Materialism is "the opinion that nothing exists except matter and its movements and modifications." In practice it is "devotion to material needs or desires to the neglect of spiritual matters; a way of life, opinion or tendency based entirely upon material interests" *(Oxford English Dictionary).* There is a vast range of philosophies based on materialism, often embracing the philosophy of Western science, including determinism, or predetermination, the view that events occur by natural law and the results can be only one way.

MATERIALIST BELIEFS

1. I believe that all religious endeavor is a waste of time and energy, that there is no God, and all so-called paranormal or psychic phenomenon is quackery and superstition.
2. I believe that there is no such thing as the soul; death of the body is death of the mind, and there is no reincarnation or afterlife.
3. I believe that the material universe, governed by natural laws and chance, is the ultimate and only reality and that all apparently nonmaterial substances, such as mind, are explicable as modifications of matter.
4. I believe that science is the means of understanding all the secrets of the universe, for all phenomenon is the result of material processes which are governed by pre-

dictable, natural laws.

5. I believe that free will is an illusion; that each event, being a fortuitous combination of particles and forces, can only happen in one way and is thus predetermined (deterministic materialism).
6. I believe that there is no objective "higher purpose" in life, no absolute basis for ethics or morality and no retribution for sin or reward for virtue. Seeking pleasure and avoiding pain are the only two goals rational men will pursue—what pleases me is good, what pains me is bad (hedonistic materialism).
7. I believe that all novel qualities of existence can be derived from changing material conditions—that men's mental and spiritual life, their ideas and aims, reflect their material conditions of existence (dialectical materialism).
8. I believe that though not all things consist of matter or its modifications, whatever exists can be satisfactorily explained in natural terms (modified or naturalistic materialism).
9. I believe that man, the highest and most complex of the evolutionary process prevailing throughout the universe, may continue to evolve into an even more perfect being or higher species (utopian materialism).

COMMUNISM

Communism emerged around the turn of the 20th century in present-day Russia as "a hypothetical stage of socialism, as formulated by Marx, Engels, Lenin and others, to be characterized by a classless and stateless society and the equal distribution of economic goods and to be achieved by revolutionary and dictatorial, rather than gradualistic, means" *(Webster's New World Dictionary)*. Communism is proudly atheistic and seeks to liberate mankind from superstition and "spiritual bondage."

COMMUNIST BELIEFS

1. I believe there is no God, that this physical world is the only reality, physical beings are the only real beings, and reason is man's highest faculty.
2. I believe religion is "the opiate of the people," a bourgeoisie tool of oppression that should be eliminated and its resources redirected to improving world conditions to lift mankind from its misery.
3. I believe mysticism and religion are primitive and fraught with error, prejudice and superstition, and that modern science, based on materialism and empirical evidence, is the only respectable avenue to useful knowledge.
4. I believe that each person has but a single life in which to attain all he deems worthwhile and express his finer qualities in service to the greater social good.
5. I believe that as in the case of nature, history evolves in a continuous line from lower to higher forms, from tribalism, feudalism and capitalism to its final maturity in socialism, and that the collapse of capitalism and the establishment of socialism will usher in a utopian age of peace and plenty, when state control will no longer be needed.
6. I believe that all men are created equal and are inherently good, and that distinctive attitudes, personalities and experiences are determined solely by one's environment; therefore, to uplift mankind, improve the environment.
7. I believe that the views expressed by our great Marxist revolutionaries represent the one and only correct world outlook, and that it is imperative to overthrow the capitalist regimes, through violent revolution if necessary, to usher in a new order.
8. I believe that the world's wealth should be shared equally, and that unequal distribution caused by class distinctions, is the root of all social evils, driving men to greed,

selfishness and exploitation. Economic necessity is the basic moving force in society.

9. I believe there is no knowable providential order, that death is permanent, that God does not exist and that the highest life is one of intense consciousness.

EXISTENTIALISM

Existentialism arose in Europe in the mid-19th century. It teaches that God does not exist, or cannot be known, and affirms individuality and freedom. Stress is on transcendence of the mundane world through exaltation of will, the meaninglessness of existence and the absence of a substratum upon which to base truths or values. Man simply exists, free to create his own meaning in life.

EXISTENTIALIST BELIEFS

1. I believe that there is no knowable providential order in nature or in the larger realm of existence or cosmos.
2. I believe that the being of man is ultimately meaningless, which is to say that man knows not why he exists and cannot rise to the knowledge of his destiny.
3. I believe that each man is an individual and should break his dependence on society and rely solely upon his own individual life, spirit, personality and thought.
4. I believe that immortality is not a characteristic of man. Death is only realistically seen as an ultimate end and radical fact which cannot be overcome. Man should not tolerate even an anguished hope of personal survival.
5. I believe that harmony and security in human relationships are impossible to achieve, and the only satisfactory attitude toward others is based upon explicit recognition of this fact.
6. I believe that "Evil is not an illusion. It is not the effect of passions which might be cured, or a fear which might be

overcome. It is not an ignorance which might be enlightened. Evil cannot be redeemed" (Sartre).

7. I believe that God does not exist.
8. I believe that the highest and best life is lived in the intensity of being fully conscious of the life experience. This experience necessarily contains problems, struggle, suffering and conflict. This is man's unalterable reality within which his free creative action and choice gives birth to the fullness of consciousness which would otherwise be deadened by security and contentment.
9. I believe that the soul of man is not whole without such unpleasant things as death, anxiety, guilt, fear and trembling, and despair. It would be the final error of reason to deny that these emotions exist, or to strive to manipulate them out of existence. Therefore, it can be said that nothing can be accomplished by denying that man is essentially a troubled being, except to make more trouble.

SECULAR HUMANISM

Humanism is "a modern, nontheistic, rationalist movement that holds that man is capable of self-fulfillment, ethical conduct, etc., without recourse to supernaturalism" *(Webster's New World Dictionary).* By the term *secular* this stream distinguishes itself from theistic (Christian) humanism. Secular humanism evolved out of 18th-century rejection of revealed Christianity and the emergence of modern science and free thought. Modern secular humanists condemn and refute all assertions of divine or paranormal phenomenon.

SECULAR HUMANIST BELIEFS

1. I believe in nontheism, as there is no rational proof for the existence of God, and do not delude myself with thoughts of a supreme being.
2. I believe that traditional religions and faiths preach false

doctrines, are oppressive and lead their followers toward ignorance, bigotry and dogmatism, and that it is my duty to be actively skeptical of and challenge the illusions of orthodox religions and all attempts to explain the world in supernatural terms.

3. I believe in the preservation and enhancement of the human species as my ultimate concern, and in the global human family, which must preserve the earth for future generations through developing a secular, planetary morality and system of law.
4. I believe that living a good, moral life is the best means for individual and collective happiness and that morality has a rational, secular basis.
5. I believe in expanding human rights and intellectual and moral freedom, and in secular democracy, with strict separation of church and state, as the means of eliminating discrimination and attaining equality and justice for all.
6. I believe in the development of the creative human potential through education in the arts and sciences and in the paramount importance of free inquiry in an open, pluralistic, universalist society.
7. I believe in the application and development of reason and modern science as the highest means to understanding the universe, solving human problems and enabling each individual to realize his greatest potential.
8. I believe in striving for fulfillment and happiness in this life and reject all notions of reincarnation and afterlife as false and baseless, seeking my fullest capacity as a human being here and now, serving others and creating a better, more just world.
9. I believe in Darwin's theory of evolution as scientific fact, and in naturalism, holding that the known world is all that exists, and that it has no supernatural or spiritual creation, control or significance.

Religious Comparisons

Comparing Eastern Views and Western Views

In the following analysis, using one of several common religious categorizations, we compare the Eastern religions with the Western ones on many points of belief. The Eastern religions are Hinduism, Jainism, Buddhism and Sikhism. The Western religions are Judaism, Zoroastrianism, Christianity and Islam. We can see immediately that there is a vast difference between Eastern and Western religions, with the Eastern goals being unitive and introspective and the Western goals being dualistic, extroverted. The Eastern mind tends to see God everywhere, in all things, and to see everything as sacred. The Western mind considers it heresy to believe that God pervades all things, and makes a strong difference between what is sacred and what is profane. In general we notice the Eastern holding to *karma*, reincarnation and liberation, the Western postulating a single life for the soul, followed by reward or punishment.

Keep in mind that this is not a comprehensive comparison, as it does not take into account the East Asia religions—Taoism, Confucianism and Shinto.

To discover your own belief patterns, take a pencil and put a check mark next to the view—Eastern or Western—which is closest to your own belief on each of the subjects.

We might note here that the Eastern religions described here all originated in India, and that Jainism, Buddhism and Sikhism were offshoots of Hinduism. Among the Western faiths, Judaism, Christianity and Islam all share a common root in Abraham, and in recent times the term *Abrahamic* has been coined to denote these three world religions. Naturally there are important exceptions to the views expressed (for example, Buddhism does not believe in a Personal God). Nevertheless these broad generalities are useful, as they give a scholarly window into the East and the West.

DIFFERENCES

On Creation

EASTERN VIEW: The universe exists in endless cycles of creation, preservation and destruction. There is no absolute end to the world, neither is there a duality of God and world, but a unity.

WESTERN VIEW: The world was created by God and at some point in the future will be forever destroyed by Him. He is distinct from it, and rules it from above. Stresses a dualistic nature of the world.

On the True God

EASTERN VIEW: There is but one true and absolute God. All religions speak of Him. All souls are destined to receive God's grace through a process that takes them through diverse experiences on many paths according to their understanding, temperament and maturity of soul. God is pure Love and Consciousness.

WESTERN VIEW: There is but one true God and one true religion. Those who accept it will enjoy God's grace; all others, unless they repent and come to my God, will suffer eternally in hell. God is loving as well as wrathful.

On Proof of God's Existence

EASTERN VIEW: Proof of God's existence and love lies in direct communion, and indirectly through enlightened *gurus*, the God-Realized men of all ages, and the revealed scriptures they bring forth in every age.

WESTERN VIEW: Proof of God's love and promise for man is in the person of His Prophet and in His unchanging and unique revealed scripture.

On Personal Experience of God

EASTERN VIEW: Personal, inner and often mystical experience of God is the crux of religion. Man can and ultimately must know God during earthly life. Individually oriented and introspective.

WESTERN VIEW: It is presumptuous for man to seek personal knowledge of God. The linchpin of religion is not experience but belief and faith, coupled with a virtuous life. Socially oriented and extroverted.

On the Path to God, and Divine Judgment

EASTERN VIEW: Man is free to choose his form of worship, for all paths lead ultimately to God. Sin is only of the mind, not of the soul, which is pure. There is no Judgment Day for God does not judge or punish. He lovingly guides all souls back to Himself.

WESTERN VIEW: Only one path leads to God, others are false and futile. Everyone must convert to the one true religion. Failing that, the soul, laden with sin, will be damned on Judgment Day.

On Man's Plight

EASTERN VIEW: Man's plight is but his soul's immaturity. He is ever on a progressive path which leads from ignorance to knowledge, from death to immortality.

WESTERN VIEW: Man's plight is due to disobedience to God's will, to nonbelief and nonacceptance of His law.

On Hell

EASTERN VIEW: God is Love and is inextricably one with the soul, guiding it through *karmas* into the fulfillment of *dharma* and finally to *moksha,* liberation. Hell is a lower astral realm, not a physical place; nor is it eternal. Hell exists as a period of *karmic* intensity or suffering, a state of mind in life or between lives.

WESTERN VIEW: On Judgment Day the physical body of every

soul that ever lived is brought to life, and God consigns pure souls to heaven and sinners to hell, a physical place where the body burns without being consumed and one suffers the anguish of knowing he will never be with God.

On Evil

EASTERN VIEW: There is no intrinsic evil. All is good. All is God. No force in the world or in man opposes God, though the veiling instinctive-intellectual mind keeps us from knowledge of Him.

WESTERN VIEW: There is indeed genuine evil in the world, a living force which opposes the will of God. This evil is embodied in Satan and his demons, and partially in man as one of his tendencies.

On Virtue and Salvation

EASTERN VIEW: Virtuous conduct and right belief are the foundation stones of religious life, the first step toward higher mystical communion. Liberation requires knowledge and personal attainment, not mere belief.

WESTERN VIEW: If one obeys God's commands for a moral and ethical life and believes in Him and in His Prophet—for example, Moses, Jesus, Mohammed or Zoroaster—salvation is assured.

On the Origin of Religion

EASTERN VIEW: Religion is cosmic, eternal, transcending human history, which is cyclical. Stress is placed on revelation of God's presence in the here and now.

WESTERN VIEW: Religion is historical, beginning with a prophet or event. Stress is placed on the past and on the rewards or punishments of the future. History is linear, never to be repeated.

Nature of Doctrines

EASTERN VIEW: Doctrines tend to be subtle, complex and

even paradoxical. Freedom to worship and to believe in a variety of ways is predominant. Other paths are accepted as God's divine will at work. Universal and tolerant.

WESTERN VIEW: Doctrines tend to be simple, clear and rational. Worship and belief are formalized, exacting and required. Other paths are endured, but not honored. Exclusivist and dogmatic.

On Liberation and Enlightenment

EASTERN VIEW: The goals of enlightenment and liberation are to be found in this life, within the context of time, within man himself. Schools may be dual or nondual, *dvaitic* or *advaitic.*

WESTERN VIEW: Salvation comes at the end of the world, the end of time, and has nothing to do with enlightenment. Strictly dualistic, *dvaitic.* Mystical sects, though minor, provide exceptions.

On the Path to Sainthood

EASTERN VIEW: Path to saintliness is through self-discipline, purification, concentration and contemplation. Value is placed on ascetic ideals, individual *sādhana, yoga* and superconscious awakening.

WESTERN VIEW: Path to saintliness is through self-sacrifice, submission to God and concern for the welfare of others. Value is placed on good works, social concerns and scriptural study, with little emphasis on *yoga* or asceticism.

On the Nature of Worship

EASTERN VIEW: Worship is individual, highly ritualistic and meditative, centering around the holy temple and the home shrine all days of the week.

WESTERN VIEW: Worship is congregational, simple in its rituals, centering around the church, synagogue or mosque, mostly on a Sabbath day.

SIMILARITIES

On God and Devas

EASTERN VIEW: Belief in a Supreme Deity, maker of all souls and all things, and in lesser Deities and Mahādevas.

WESTERN VIEW: Belief in a Supreme Deity, maker of all souls and all things, and in the angels and celestial hosts.

On Salvation and God's Will

EASTERN VIEW: Salvation is through strict obedience to God's will and the descent of His grace through the enlightened spiritual preceptor.

WESTERN VIEW: Salvation is through strict obedience to God's will, usually through a messiah, prophet or priest.

On Good Conduct

EASTERN VIEW: To live a virtuous and moral life is essential to further spiritual progress, for *adharmic* thoughts, deeds and words keep us from knowledge of God's closeness.

WESTERN VIEW: Religion must be based on ethical and moral conduct, for their opposite leads us away from God.

On the Destiny of the Soul

EASTERN VIEW: The purpose of life is to evolve, through experience, into our spiritual destiny. Things of the world are not the purpose of the world.

WESTERN VIEW: Man's destiny lies beyond this world, which is but an opportunity for earning eternal joy or suffering.

On the Nature of Reality

EASTERN VIEW: There is more to reality than we experience with the five senses. The soul is immortal, deathless and eternal, ultimately merging in God.

WESTERN VIEW: There is more to reality than the things of this world. The soul is immortal, deathless and eternal, living forever in God's presence or separated from Him.

Comparing Judaism, Christianity and Islam

The similarities between these three Abrahamic religions are stronger than their differences, though historically it is the differences that have been exalted. They each believe in a single life, followed by heaven or hell. They agree that God is opposed by evil, by Satan, who tempts and destroys sinners by causing disobedience to God's law. They are all prophet-oriented, though Christianity is the only one to make the prophet divine. They believe in their religion as the one and only true religion, and that nonbelievers are condemned, though Judaism is somewhat more tolerant or universal, believing God judges all men of all religions by their actions. These three Biblical religions are strongly monotheistic and dualistic, believing man is eternally separate from God and that man's highest destiny is in heaven. Together they rely not so much on inner experience or mystical contact and guidance, as on sacred rites, on faith and belief, and on good works to guide man Godward. Each believes that God has a special covenant with its members, though the terms differ. They each bury their dead, anticipating that the physical body will one day be resurrected on the earth, rising from the grave on Judgment Day.

On the True Religion

JUDAISM: There is but one true religion, Judaism, and one revealed scripture, the *Torah,* which includes the *Pentateuch* (the first five books of the *Old Testament)* and the *Talmud.*

CHRISTIANITY: There is but one true religion, Christianity, and one scripture—the *Holy Bible,* Old and New Testaments.

ISLAM: The one true faith is Islam, and the *Koran* is the highest revealed scripture, but other books are honored as revealed too, including the *Bible* and certain Hindu scriptures.

On Genesis and Original Sin

JUDAISM: Belief in Adam, his temptation and fall from grace and in original sin.

CHRISTIANITY: The same.

ISLAM: Same, but Allah forgave Adam. Therefore, there is no original sin.

On the Proof of God's Power

JUDAISM: Such proof can be seen in the historic Exodus.

CHRISTIANITY: Proof of God's power lies in Christ's resurrection.

ISLAM: Proof of God's power is in the *Koran* itself.

On Man's Obligation to God

JUDAISM: Jews are obligated exclusively to Yahweh, since He delivered them out of Egypt.

CHRISTIANITY: Man is obligated to God since He sacrificed His Son for man's sins.

ISLAM: There exists no special obligation; avoidance of hell is man's motivation.

On the Means to Salvation

JUDAISM: Salvation is through strict adherence to the Law as stated in the *Torah.*

CHRISTIANITY: Salvation is through acceptance of Christ as Lord and Savior.

ISLAM: Salvation is through total submission to Allah.

Comparing the Four Hindu Sects

The spectrum of Hindu religiousness is found within four major sects or denominations: Śaivism, Śāktism, Vaishṇavism and Smārtism. Among these four streams, there are certainly more similarities than differences. Many of the *ślokas* and *bhāshyas* of *Dancing with Śiva (Śivena saha Nartanam): Hinduism's Contemporary Catechism (Sanātana Dharma Praśnottaram)* have shown how they concur as well as differ.

All four believe in *karma* and reincarnation and in a Supreme Being who is both form and pervades form, who creates, sustains and destroys the universe only to create it again in unending cycles. They strongly declare the validity and importance of temple worship, in the three worlds of existence and the myriad Gods and *devas* residing in them. They concur that there is no intrinsic evil, that the cosmos is created out of God and is permeated by Him. They each believe in *māyā* (though their definitions differ somewhat), and in the liberation of the soul from rebirth, called *moksha,* as the goal of human existence. They believe in *dharma* and in *ahiṁsā,* noninjury, and in the need for a *satguru* to lead the soul toward Self Realization. They wear the sacred marks, *tilaka,* on their foreheads as sacred symbols, though each wears a distinct mark. Finally, they prefer cremation of the body upon death, believing that the soul will inhabit another body in the next life. While Hinduism has many sacred scriptures, all sects ascribe the highest authority to the *Vedas* and *Āgamas,* though their *Āgamas* differ somewhat. Here, now, is a brief comparison of these four denominations.

On the Personal God/Goddess

ŚAIVISM: Personal God and temple Deity is Śiva, neither male nor female. Lords Gaṇeśa and Kārttikeya are also worshiped.

ŚĀKTISM: Personal Goddess and temple Deity is Śrī Devī or Śakti, female, worshiped as Rājarājeśvarī, Pārvatī, Lakshmī, Sarasvatī, Kālī, Amman, etc. —the Divine Mother.

VAISHṆAVISM: Personal God and temple Deity is Vishṇu, male. His incarnations as Rāma and Kṛishṇa are also worshiped, as well as His divine consort, Rādhā Rāṇī.

SMĀRTISM: Personal God and temple Deity is Īśvara, male or female, worshiped as Vishṇu, Śiva, Śakti, Gaṇeśa and Sūrya or any Deity of devotee's choice, e.g., Kumāra or Kṛishṇa.

On the Nature of Śakti

ŚAIVISM: Śakti is God Śiva's inseparable power and manifest will, energy or mind.

ŚĀKTISM: Śakti is an active, immanent Being, separate from a quiescent and remote Śiva.

VAISHṆAVISM: No special importance is given to Śakti. However, there are parallels wherein the divine consorts are conceived as the inseparable powers of Vishṇu and His incarnations: e.g., Kṛishṇa's Rādhā Rāṇī and Rāma's Sitā.

SMĀRTISM: Śakti is a divine form of Īśvara. It is God's manifesting power.

On the Nature of Personal God

ŚAIVISM: God Śiva is pure love and compassion, immanent and transcendent, pleased by our purity and *sādhana.*

ŚĀKTISM: The Goddess Śakti is both compassionate and terrifying, pleasing and wrathful, assuaged by sacrifice and submission.

VAISHṆAVISM: God Vishṇu is loving and beautiful, the object of man's devotion, pleased by our service and surrender.

SMĀRTISM: Īśvara appears as a human-like Deity according to devotees' loving worship, which is sometimes considered a rudimentary self-purifying practice.

On the Doctrine of Avatāra

ŚAIVISM: There are no divine earthly incarnations.

ŚĀKTISM: The Divine Mother does incarnate in this world.

VAISHṆAVISM: Vishṇu has ten or more incarnations.

SMĀRTISM: All Deities may assume earthly incarnations.

On the Soul and God

ŚAIVISM: God Śiva is one with the soul. The soul must realize this *advaitic* Truth by God Śiva's grace.

ŚĀKTISM: The Divine Mother, Śakti, is mediatrix, bestowing *advaitic moksha* on those who worship Her.

VAISHṆAVISM: God and soul are eternally distinct. Through Lord Vishṇu's grace, the soul's destiny is to worship and enjoy God.

SMĀRTISM: Īśvara and man are in reality Absolute Brahman. Within *māyā,* the soul and Īśvara appear as two. *Jñāna* dispels the illusion.

Spiritual Practice

ŚAIVISM: With *bhakti* as a base, emphasis is placed on *sādhana, tapas* and *yoga.* Ascetic.

ŚĀKTISM: Emphasis is on *bhakti* and *tantra,* sometimes occult, practices. Ascetic-occult.

VAISHṆAVISM: Emphasis is on supreme *bhakti* or surrender, called *prapatti.* Generally devotional and nonascetic.

SMĀRTISM: Preparatory *sādhanas* are *bhakti, karma, rāja yoga.* Highest path is through knowledge, leading to *jñāna.*

Major Scriptures

ŚAIVISM: *Vedas, Śaiva Āgamas* and *Śaiva Purāṇas.*

ŚĀKTISM: *Vedas, Śākta Āgamas* (*Tantras*) and *Purāṇas.*

VAISHṆAVISM: *Vedas, Vaishṇava Āgamas, Purāṇas* and the *Itihāsas (Rāmāyaṇa* and *Mahābhārata,* especially the *Bhagavad Gītā*).

SMĀRTISM: *Vedas, Āgamas* and classical *smṛiti—Purāṇas, Itihāsas,* especially the *Bhagavad Gītā,* etc.

Regions of Influence

ŚAIVISM: Geographically widespread, strongest in South and North India, Nepal and Sri Lanka.

ŚĀKTISM: Geographically widespread, most prominent in North India, especially Bengal and Assam.

VAISHṆAVISM: Geographically widespread, especially strong throughout India, North and South.

SMĀRTISM: Geographically widespread, most prominent in North and South India.

CONCLUSION

This concludes our simple comparison of Hinduism's four prominent denominations, and of other religions, faiths and philosophies. There are many more indigenous, tribal groups who follow similar paths and call themselves by unique names, and there are many more paths yet to be discovered in the future. This chapter can be a complete study, conferring on those who read it carefully a simple overview of those intangible human beliefs which, in all their variety, are at the root of attitudes and behavior, that, over time, create culture. This chapter can also be more. It can be the beginning of discovering your own place in this grand scheme. Conversion is easy into any one of these forms of worship, practice and attainment. It is happening all the time. All souls on the path to perfection eventually commit themselves by choosing a preceptor, one who has gone before. Approaching life without a preceptor is like traversing the ocean without a map or a compass. Even climbing the slopes of the Himalayas, a Sherpa is needed to safely guide. Compare your beliefs, as they are today, with all those contained within this treatise, and come to terms with the supreme dedication that each of these paths demands of its followers. Having done this, declare boldly who you are to your own self. Claim your spiritual identity, your preceptor and the religious to faith to which you find you belong. Then follow your chosen path with all your heart. Give it your full devotion, energy and loyalty in fullfiling its goals. True seekers on the path hoping for genuine attainment do not wander from path to path, school to school, preceptor to preceptor, because it is known that indecision inhibits all spiritual growth.

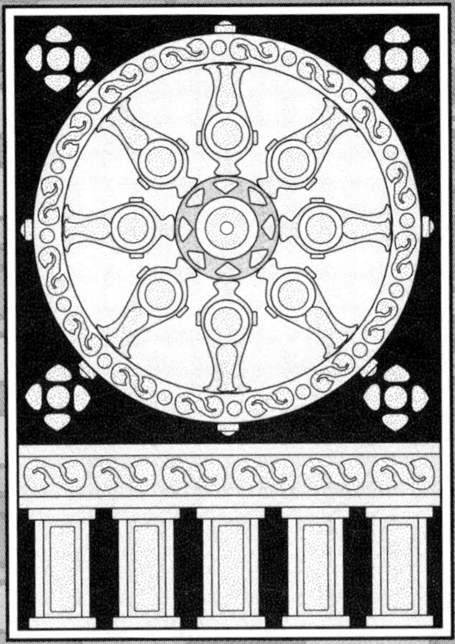

Bhārata Kālachakra

भारतकालचक्र

Hindu Timeline

Chakra, or "wheel," is the circle of time, symbol of perfect creation, of the cycles of existence. Time and space are interwoven, and eight spokes mark the directions, each ruled by a Deity and having a unique quality. Aum.

Hindu Timeline

MUCH OF WHAT INDIA AND HINDUISM ARE TODAY CAN BE UNDERSTOOD BY EXAMINING THEIR ORIGINS AND HISTORY. HERE IS A humble chronology that tells the story of the sages, kings, outside invaders and inside reformers who contributed to the world's oldest living civilization and largest democracy.

The emphasis on spirituality in India's thought and history is unparalleled in human experience. Life in India is spiritually centered, and history in India is the story of seeking. The king in his court, the sage on his hill and the farmer in one of India's 700,000 villages each pursues his *dharma* with a common ultimate purpose: spiritual enlightenment. This perspective is the source of Hinduism's resilience in the face of competing faiths and conquering armies. No other nation has faced so many invaders and endured. These invasions have brought the races of the world to a subcontinent one-third the size of the United States.

There are many feats of which the ancient Hindus could be proud, such as the invention of the decimal system of numbers, philosophy, linguistics, surgery, city planning and statecraft. And most useful to us in this particular timeline: their skill in astronomy. Dates in Hindu history after Buddha are subject to little dispute, while dates before Buddha have been decided as much by current opinion and politics as by scientific evidence. An overwhelming tendency of Western scholarship has been to deny the great antiquity of Hinduism.

Fortunately, Indian researchers such as S.B. Roy and their Western associates have developed new chronologies based on a highly reliable method: dating scriptural references by their relationship to the known precession of the equinoxes. Earth "wobbles" on its axis, causing constellations, as viewed from Earth, to drift at a constant rate and along a predictable course over a 25,000-year cycle. Thus, a *Rig Vedic* verse indicating winter solstice at Aries can be correlated to around 6500 BCE, for example. Roy confirms his findings by cross-referring other firmly established historical traditions and carbon-dated archaeological finds. Much of the dating in this timeline prior to 600 BCE derives from Roy's research (*Chronological Framework of Indian Protohistory—The Lower Limit*, published in *The Journal of the Baroda Oriental Institute*, March-June 1983).

Roy points out that the commonly accepted chronology of German linguist Max Müller (1823–1900) is based solely "on the ghost story of *Kathasaritasagara*." Historian Klaus K. Klostermaier agrees: "The chronology provided by Max Müller and accepted uncritically by most Western scholars is based on very shaky ground indeed." American Sanskṛit scholar David Frawley states, "Precessional changes are the hallmark of Hindu astronomy. We cannot ignore them in ancient texts just because they give us dates too early for our conventional view of human history." While doing many good things, Müller's also admitted his intention to undermine Hinduism. In a letter to his wife in 1886 he wrote: "The translation of the *Veda* will hereafter tell to a great extent on the fate of India and on the growth of millions of souls in that country. It is the root of their religion, and to show them what the root is, I feel sure, is the only way of uprooting all that has sprung from it during the last 3,000 years."

Professor Subhash Kak, Dr. N.R. Waradpande, Bhagwan Singh and others have helped develop a more accurate picture of ancient India. There is much to support the dates of these researchers, such as carbon-14 dating, the discovery of Indus Valley cities and the recent locating of the famed Sarasvati River, a prominent landmark of the Vedic writings.

Max Müller is the central figure in another, more invidious, dispute central to Hindu history, the "Āryan invasion" theory. Originally referring to the parent-language of Greek, Sanskṛit, Latin and German, the term *Āryan* soon referred to those who spoke it, a supposed race of light-skinned Āryans. The idea of a parent-race caught the imagination of 18th and 19th century European Christian scholars, who hypothesized elaborate Āryan migrations from Central Asia, west to Europe, south to India and east to China—conquering local primitive peoples and founding the world's great civilizations. According to this theory, the Āryans, the proposed authors of the *Vedas*, moved into India from the northwest, conquering and displacing indigenous dark-skinned Dravidian peoples to the south. This theory wrongly implies that the *Vedas* were brought to India by outsiders and not composed in India.

Although lacking supporting scientific evidence, this theory, and the Āryan-Dravidian racial split, was accepted and promulgated as fact for three main reasons. It provided a convenient precedent for Christian British subjugation of India. It reconciled ancient Indian civilization and religious scripture with the 4000 BCE Biblical date of Creation. It created division and conflict between the peoples of India, making them vulnerable to conversion by Christian missionaries.

Many scholars today of both East and West believe that the people of the *Ṛig Veda* who called themselves Āryan were indigenous to India, and there never was an Āryan invasion. The various languages of India have been shown to share common ancestry in ancient Sanskṛit and Tamil. Even these two apparently unrelated languages, according to current "super-family" research, have a common origin: an ancient language dubbed *Nostratic*. Finally, there is an ever-increasing amount of physical and scriptural evidence that describes a gradual evolution of religion and culture in India from prehistoric lifestyles to today's rich ethnic diversity.

This timeline is necessarily brief and not meant to convey the details of any one event. Interspersed with the Hindu history are major and minor corresponding world events.

How to Read the Timeline

The thick line represents the flow of time from the date on the top to dates on the bottom. The thinner lines to the left indicate the duration of major ruling dynasties. Not all are included, for at times India was divided into dozens of small independent kingdoms.

Approximate dates are preceded by the letters *ca,* an abbreviation of the word *circa,* which denotes "about," "around" or "in approximately." All dates prior to Buddha (624 BCE) are considered estimates.

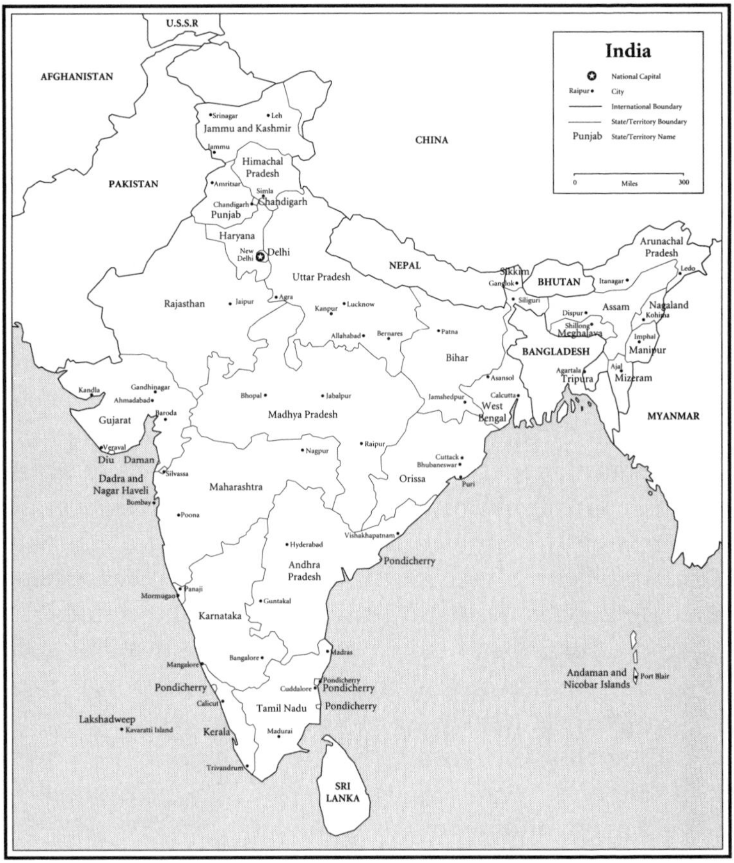

-2.5 M	Genus *Homo* originates in Africa.
-1.8 M	Stone artifacts are perhaps being manufactured and used for the first time by hominids in Northern India, an area rich in animal species, including the elephant.
-500,000	Stone hand axes, as well as other stone tools, are being made in Northern India.
-470,000	India's hominids are active in Tamil Nadu and Punjab.
-400,000	Soan culture in India is using primitive chopping tools.
-360,000	Fire is first controlled by *homo erectus* in China.
-300,000	*Homo sapiens* roams the earth, from Africa to Asia.
-100,000	*Homo sapiens sapiens* (humans) with same brain size that humans have today (1,450 cc) live in Eastern Africa. Populations separate. Migrations proceed from Africa to Asia via the Isthmus of Suez.
-75,000	Last ice age begins. Human population is 1.7 million.
-45,000	After mastery of marine navigation, migrations from Southeast Asia settle Australia and the Pacific islands.
-40,000	Groups of hunter-gatherers in Central India are living in painted rock shelters. Similar groups in Northern Punjab work at open sites protected by windbreaks.
-35,000	Migrations of separated Asian populations settle Europe.
-30,000	American Indians spread throughout the Americas.
-10,000	Last ice age ends; earliest signs of agriculture. World human population is four million. Population of India subcontinent is estimated at 100,000.
-7000	In a farming village of Mehrgarh, India, at the edge of the Indus Valley, residents grow barley, raise sheep and goats. They store grain, entomb their dead and construct buildings of sun-baked, mud bricks.
-6500	*Ṛig Veda* verses indicate winter solstice is at the beginning of the sign of Aries, placing composition of early Vedic hymns at this date, according to Western researcher David Frawley.
-6000	Śiva worship exists in the Indus Valley civilization (regarded by some scholars as Proto-Dravidian), according to archeological evidence, first historical signs of Śaivism.
-5500	Mehrgarh villagers are making baked pottery and small, clay female figurines, and are involved in long-distance trade in precious stones and sea shells.
-5500	Signs of folk Śāktism, earliest known form of Śākta worship, include thousands of female statuettes made by Mehrgarh villagers and references to several important Goddesses in the folk-narrative *Purāṇas* and the *Ṛig Veda.*
-5500	Date of astrological observations associated with ancient events later mentioned in the *Purāṇas.*

-2,500,000 · -100,000 · -10,000 · -5000 · MEHRGARH & INDUS VALLEY CIVILIZATION

-5000 World population reaches five million, and is doubling every 1,000 years.

-5000 Beginnings of the Indus Valley civilizations of Harappa and Mohenjo-daro. (Date arrived at by examining present-day archaeological sites, early layers of which are 25 feet beneath the water table, itself reached after excavating 45 feet.)

-4000 Excavations from this period at Sumerian sites of Kish and Susa reveal existence of Indian trade products.

-4000 India population is one million.

-4000 Date of creation of the world, based on genealogies in the *Old Testament.*

-3928 On July 25th occurs the earliest eclipse mentioned in the *Ṛig Veda* (according to modern Indian researcher P.C. Sengupta).

-3700 Indus Valley civilization reaches a height that it will sustain until 1700 BCE. Spreading from present-day Pakistan to Gujarat, Punjab and Uttar Pradesh, it is the largest of the world's three oldest civilizations.

-3500 People from Baluchistan (whose present-day descendants speak a Dravidian tongue) and Southern Afghanistan move into the Indus Valley.

-3200 There exists in India a special class of professional astronomers called *nakshatra-darśas* who observe with great care the full moon (Pūrṇimā) and the new moon (Darśa or Amāvāsya) with reference to fixed stars called *nakshatra.* Because the sun is 180° away when there is Pūrṇimā at a *nakshatra,* the exact position of the sun at the equinox can be calculated from these precise astronomical observations and recordings of the moon by the *nakshatra-darśas.* This method of observation sharply distinguishes Indian astronomy from the astronomy of all other countries.

-3167 Manu Vaivasvata is born, traditional "father of mankind," first in the Purāṇic list of kings and sages.

-3149 Nabhānedishṭha is born, son of Manu Vaivasvata (gleaned from *Ṛig Veda* hymns. 10.61.5–9, along with the observation that vernal equinox is occurring with full moon at Rohiṇī).

-3102 Traditional Hindu calendar starts at zero, the beginning of the Kali Yuga and end of the great war between the Pāṇḍavas and the Kauravas, as narrated in the *Mahābhārata.* (This ending date for the war contradicts the *Mahābhārata* text itself, in which winter solstice is observed at Dhanishṭha, which occurs around 1400 BCE.)

-5000 -4000 -3500 -3100

INDUS VALLEY

REIGN OF KINGS LISTED IN PURĀṆAS

-3100 Early Vedic Age (3100–2000) begins. Āryan people are in Iran, Iraq and western frontier of the Indus Valley and in extensive contact with the Indus Valley people. (This is according to some scholars, while others now believe 1) the Land of Seven Rivers (Sapta Sindhu) mentioned in the *Ṛig Veda* refers to India only, 2) that the people of Indus Valley and those of the *Ṛig Veda* are the same, and 3) there was no Āryan invasion. Others hold that the Indus people were Dravidian and moved out or were displaced by incoming Āryans.)

-3000 Weaving in Europe, Near East and Indus Valley is primarily coiled basketry, either spiraled or sewn.

-3000 People of Tehuacan, Mexico, are first to cultivate corn.

-3000 *Śaiva Āgamas* are recorded in the time of the earliest Tamil Saṅgam. (This strong traditional date is not yet historically proven.)

-2700 Seals of Indus Valley indicate the presence of Śiva worship, in depictions of Śiva as Paśupati, Lord of Animals.

-2609 Major part of *Vedic Saṁhitās* (hymns) is composed during the reign of Viśvāmitra I.

-2600 First Egyptian pyramid is under construction.

-2500 Hindu cities of Harappa and Mohenjo-Daro in Indus Valley (in present-day Pakistan), have populations of approximately 100,000.

-2400 Astronomical events are observed and recorded in the *Brāhmaṇas* of the *Yajur* and *Atharva Vedas*, establishing the earliest verifiable date of these scriptural texts.

-2393 Bharata is born (44th in Purāṇic list of kings and sages), a contemporary of Sargon of Akkad (2334–2279 BCE by Babylonian chronology).

-2350 Sage Gārgya (born 2285), 50th in Purāṇic list of kings and sages, son of Gārga, initiates method of describing

PURĀṆIC KINGS
INDUS VALLEY
-2000
-1500

successive centuries in relation to a *nakshatra* list he records in the *Atharva Veda* with Kṛittikā as the first star. Equinox occurs at Kṛittikā Pūrṇimā.

-2300 Sargon founds Mesopotamian kingdom of Akkad, trades with Indus Valley cities.

-2051 Divodāsa (reign 2051–1961) begins reign, has contact with Babylonian king Indatu (as dated in the Babylonian chronology).

-2051 Vedic people are living in Persia at this time. (Some scholars give this date for the invasion of Āryans into India and the beginning of their spread throughout Northern India over the next 500 years.)

ca -2040 Rāma is born at Ayodhya, site of future Rāma temple.

-2033 Reign of Daśaratha, father of Lord Rāma. King Rāvaṇa reigns in Sri Lanka.

-2015 Reign of Lord Rāma at Ayodhyā.

-2000 Probable date of first written *Śaiva Āgamas.* (However, Alain Daniélou and certain other scholars believe that the Vedic authors came into India from elsewhere and that the Āgamic, or *tantric,* scriptures reflect a tradition even more ancient than the *Vedas.*)

-2000 Date of astronomical events referred to in the sixth maṇḍala of the *Ṛig Veda*, approximately dating that portion of this scripture.

-2000 World population is 27 million. India population is five million: 22% of world.

-2000 Inuit (Eskimo) people near Arctic Circle develop stone and bone tools.

-1961 King Sudāsa II of North Panchāla is born, (68th in the Purāṇic list of kings and sages) victor of Dāśarājña, Battle of the Ten Kings.

-1930 Indus Valley metropolis of Harappa on the Parushni River, with its twelve granaries (total floor-space of 9,000 square feet), is destroyed in Dāśarājña, Battle of the Ten Kings, as related in the *Ṛig Veda.*

-1915 All Madurai Tamil Saṅgam is held at Thiruparankundram (according to traditional Tamil chronology).

-1792 Hammurabi (lived 1792–1750), sixth Amorite king of Babylonia, is born.

-1500 Egyptians bury their royalty in the Valley of the Kings.

-1500 Polynesians on islands off Southeast Asia begin migration throughout Pacific islands.

-1500 Indus Valley cities are abandoned due to flood, internal strife or invasion. (Western authors generally connect the decline of the Indus civilization with the invasion of

PURĀṆIC KINGS

-1500

the supposed Vedic Āryans, 1500–1200 BCE.)

-1500 Date of extensive archaeological finds at the large stone port of Dwarka, home of Lord Kṛishṇa, where Brāhmī script, the alphabet of ancient India is used.

-1500 Cinnamon is exported from Kerala to Middle East.

-1472 Reign of Dhṛitarāshṭra, father of the Kauravas. Reign of Yudhisṭhira, lifetime of sage Yājñavalkya. *Mahābhārata* mentions winter solstice observed at Dhanistha, which occurs around 1400 BCE.

-1450 End of *Ṛig Veda Saṁhitā* narration.

-1450 Early *Upanishads* are composed during the next 200 years, also *Vedāṅga* and *Sūtra* literature until 1250 BCE.

-1424 Bhārata battle is fought, as related in the *Mahābhārata.*

-1424 Birth of Parīkshit, grandson of Arjuna, and next king.

-1390 Vaiśampāyana writes the *Bhārata Saṁhitā.*

-1350 Date of an inscription at Boghaz Koi in Asia Minor of the name "In-da-ra," thought to be the Vedic Deity Indra.

-1326 K-Draconis is the pole star, observed and recorded by Patañjali, author of the *Yoga Sūtras,* first to mention Śaiva Pāśupata sect. (This date from Roy is compelling evidence in favor of the argument to place Patañjali around 1300 BCE, rather than the more traditionally accepted date of 250 BCE.)

-1316 *Mahābhārata* epic poem is written down.

-1300

-1300 Pāṇini composes his Sanskṛit grammar, the *Ashṭādhyāyī,* systematizing Sanskṛit grammar in 4,000 terse rules. (Date according to Roy.) Pāṇini was a contemporary of sages Patañjali, Vyāghrapāda, Vasishṭha and Nandikeśa (Maharishi Nandinātha), traditionally placed at 250 BCE).

-1300 Age of interpolations begins. Changes are made in the *Mahābhārata* and *Rāmāyaṇa* through 200 BCE. *Purāṇas* are edited up until 400 CE. Early *smṛiti* literature is com-

PURĀṆIC KINGS

-1200 -900 -700

posed over the next 400 years.

-1298 Śuchi of Magadha is born (103rd in Purāṇic list of kings and sages), son of Bibhu. He writes the *Jyotisha Vedāṅga,* including astronomical observations that date the creation of this scripture.

-1250 Vedic Age ends. Moses leads 600,000 Jews out of Egypt.

-1124 Elamite Dynasty of Nebuchadnezzar (1124–1103 BCE) moves capital to Babylon, the largest city in the world, covering 24,700 acres (10,000 hectares), slightly larger than present-day San Francisco.

-1000 World population is 50 million, doubling every 500 years.

-950 Jewish people first arrive in India in King Solomon's merchant fleet. Later Jewish colonies find a tolerant home in India.

-950 Gradual breakdown of Sanskṛit as a spoken language occurs over the next 200 years.

-925 Jewish King David forms an empire in what is present-day Israel and Lebanon.

-900 Use of iron supplements bronze in Greece.

-800 Iron-working is introduced into India from Iran, and rice cultivation is developed.

-776 First Olympic Games are held in Greece.

-750 Over the next 950 years, interpolations are added to the Hindu *smṛiti* scriptures.

-750 Prākṛits, vernacular or "natural" languages, develop among the common people of India. Already flourishing in 500, Pāli and other Prākṛits are chiefly known from Buddhist and Jain works composed at this time.

-750 Priestly Sanskṛit is gradually revived over next 500 years.

-700 Lifetime of Zoroaster, founder of Zoroastrianism, original religion of the Persians. *Zend Aveshṭa,* holy book of this faith, is closely related to the *Ṛig Veda,* sharing many verses. Zoroastrianism makes strong distinctions between good and evil, setting the dualist tone of God and devil which pervades all later Western religions.

-700 Earliest forms of Smārtism emerge from the Vedic *brāhminical* (priest caste) tradition.

-624 Siddhārta Gautama, the Buddha (624–544 BCE), is born into a Śaivite Hindu family in North India. (Date is according to Sri Lankan Buddhist tradition.)

ca-600 Lifetime of Vaidya Suśruta, Hindu surgeon of Varanasi (Banaras) considered the father of surgery. His extensive scientific treatises, considered āyurvedic scripture, cover pulse diagnosis, hernia, cataract and cosmetic surgery, medical ethics, definitions for 121 surgical im-

-600

plements, control of infection through antiseptics, use of drugs to control bleeding, toxicology, psychiatry, classification of burns, midwifery methods still used in the present day, surgical anesthesia, as well as a thesis on the therapeutic properties of garlic.

ca -600 Earliest records of the holy city of Varanasi (one of the world's oldest living cities) on the sacred river Ganges.

ca -600 The Ājīvika sect, an ascetic and atheistic group of naked *sādhus* with a reputation for fierce curses, is at its height, continuing in Mysore until the 14th century. They are adversaries of both Buddha and Mahāvīra. their philosophy is deterministic, holding that everything is inevitable.

ca -600 Lifetime of Lao-tzu, founder of Taoism, China's major indigenous religio-philosophical tradition. Its esoteric teachings shape Chinese life for the next 2,000 years, and permeate religions of Vietnam, Japan and Korea. Lao-tzu is traditionally credited with the authorship of the classic text *Tao-te Ching*. Other important Taoist writings include those of *Chuang-tzu* and *Lieh-tzu*.

-599 Mahāvīra (599–527 BCE) is born, 24th Tīrthaṅkara and famous promulgator of Jainism. His faith preaches strict codes of vegetarianism, asceticism and nonviolence.

-560 In Greece, Pythagoras teaches math, music, vegetarianism and yoga.

-551 Confucius (551–478 BCE) is born, founder of China's Confucianist faith. His teachings on social ethics are the basis of education, ruling-class ideology and religion in China for 2000 years.

-518 Darius I of Persia (present Iran) invades Indus Valley. This Zoroastrian king shows tolerance for local religions.

-500

ca -500 Lifetime of Kapila, founder of Sāṅkhya Darśana, one of six classical systems of Hindu philosophy.

ca -500 Dams to store water are constructed in India.

-500 World population is 100 million. India population is 25 million (15 million of whom live in the Ganges basin).

ca -500 Over the next 300 years numerous secondary Hindu scriptures *(smṛiti)* are composed: *Śrauta Sūtras, Gṛihya Sūtras, Dharma Sūtras, Mahābhārata, Rāmāyaṇa* and *Purāṇas* (according to the later dating of Müller).

ca -500 Tamil Saṅgam age (ca 500 BCE–500 CE) begins, earliest period of Tamil literature, during which Agastya writes *Agattiyam*, the first known Tamil Grammar, and Tolkappiyar writes *Tolkappiyam Purananuru*, also on grammar. The latter author states he is recording thoughts

-500

on poetry, rhetoric, etc., expressed by earlier grammarians, pointing to a highly developed state of language much prior to his day. He displays a familiarity with Sanskṛit, giving rules for absorbing Sanskṛit words into Tamil. Other famous works from the Saṅgam age are the poetical collections known as *Paripadal, Pattuppattu, Ettuthokai Purananuru, Akananuru, Aingurunuru, Padinenkilkanakku,* some of which contain references to worship of Vishṇu and Indra.

ca -486 Ajātaśatru (reign 486–458) ascends Magadha throne.

-480 Ajita, *nāstika* (atheist) who teaches a purely material explanation of life and that death is final, dies.

-478 Prince Vijaya sails from Bengal, India, to found a new Singhalese kingdom in Sri Lanka.

-450

-450 Athenian philosopher Socrates flourishes (ca 470–400).

-428 Plato (428–348) is born in Athens. Disciple of Socrates, this great philosopher founds Athens Academy in 387.

MAURYA

ca -400 Pāṇini composes his Sanskṛit grammar, the *Ashṭādhyāyī.* (Date accepted among most Western scholars.)

ca -400 Lifetime of Hippocrates, Greek physician and "Father of Medicine," formulates Hippocratic oath, code of medical ethics still pledged by present-day Western doctors.

ca -400 "Barbarian" period (ca 400 BCE–400 CE) begins. North India is ruled by invaders from Central Asia and Persia known as the Śaka (Scythian), the Pahlava (Parthian) and the Yueh-chi (Kushān). Most of the invaders convert to Buddhism and help spread Buddhist influence outside of India.

ca -350 Rainfall is measured by Indian scientists.

-326 Alexander of Macedonia conquers Northern India. His soldiers mutiny, and Alexander leaves India the same year. Greeks who stay behind in India intermarry with Indians and establish lineages, most of which are Śaiva. Interchanges of philosophy influence both civilizations. Greek sculpture dramatically impacts Hindu styles.

-317 King Chandragupta defeats Greek garrisons in India.

ca -302 Kauṭilya, chief minister to Chandragupta, writes *Arthaśāstra,* a singularly important manual on art of politics.

-302 Megasthenes, Greek ambassador to India, describes the glory of India in reports, marvelling that extensive areas are under engineered irrigation.

-300

ca -300 Chinese discover cast iron, known in Europe by 1300 CE.

ca -300 Pañcharātra Vaishṇava sect is prominent. All later Vaishṇava sects are based on the Pañcharātra beliefs (formalized by Śāṇḍilya around 100 CE).

ca-300 Pāṇḍya kingdom (ca-300–1700 CE) of South India is founded, constructs magnificent Mīnākshī temple at its capital city, Madurai. Pāṇḍya dynasty also builds temple of Śrīraṅgam and Rāmeśvaram temple, with its thousand-pillared hall (around 1700 CE).

-297 Chandragupta abdicates to become a Jain monk.

-273 Aśoka (273–232) is born, last Mauryan Emperor, grandson of Chandragupta. He converts to Buddhism after his brutal invasion of Kaliṅga. Aśoka excels at public works, sends Buddhist missionaries to Egypt, Macedonia, Sri Lanka, China and several other countries. He preserves his work and teachings in engravings, the Rock and Pillar Edicts (e.g., lion capital of the pillar at Sarnath, present-day India's national emblem).

-251 Emperor Aśoka sends his son, Mahendra (270–204BCE), to Sri Lanka to spread Buddhism. Present-day Sri Lankan Buddhists revere Mahendra as the founding missionary of Buddhism in Sri Lanka, its majority religion.

ca-250 Lifetime of Maharishi Nandinātha, first known *satguru* in the Kailāsa Paramparā of the Nandinātha Sampradāya. His eight disciples are Sanatkumār, Śanakar, Sanādanar, Sananthanar, Śivayogamuni, Patañjali, Vyāghrapāda and (Sundaranātha) Tirumular.

ca-221 Great Wall of China is built, ultimately 2,600 miles long, the only man-made object visible from the moon.

ca-200 Lifetime of Ṛishi Tirumular, *śishya* of Maharishi Nandinātha and author of the 3,047-verse *Tirumantiram,* a powerful summation of the *Śaiva Āgamas* and *Vedas,* and concise articulation of the Nātha Sampradāya teachings, founding the monistic Śaiva Siddhānta school in South India.

ca-200 Lifetime of Patañjali, *śishya* of Maharishi Nandinātha and brother *śishya* of Tirumular. Writes *Yoga Sūtras* at Chidambaram, South India (by Western dating).

-200
-150
50

SUṄGA
KUSHĀN
ĀNDHRA
PALLAVA (KĀÑCHIPURAM, SOUTH INDIA)

ca-200 Lifetime of Bhogar Ṛishi, one of the eighteen Tamil *siddhas.* He shapes from nine poisons the Palaniswāmī *mūrti* enshrined in present-day Palani Hills temple in South India. Bhogar is either from China or visits there.

ca-200 Lifetime of Saint Tiruvalluvar, poet-weaver who lived near present-day Madras, author of *Tirukural,* a classic Tamil work on ethics and statecraft (sworn on in today's South Indian law courts).

ca-200 Jaimini writes the *Mīmāṁsā Sūtras.*

-165 Kushān Empire begins (165 BCE–200 CE). At its height it will extend from China to Persia. Patrons of Buddhism, these Mongolians also rule large parts of North India.

ca-150 Ajantā Buddhist Caves begun near present-day Hyderabad. Construction of the 29 monasteries and galleries continues until approximately 650 CE. The famous murals are painted between 600 and 650 CE.

-145 Chola Empire (145–1300 CE) of Tamil Nadu is founded, rising from modest beginnings to a height of government organization and artistic accomplishment, including the development of enormous irrigation works.

-140 Emperor Wu begins three-year reign of China; worship of the Mother Goddess, Earth, attains importance.

-130 Reign ends of Menander, Indo-Greek king who converts to Buddhism.

-57 Sāmvat calendar of Hinduism begins.

ca-10 Ilangovadikal, son of King Cheralathan of the Tamil Saṅgam age, writes the outstanding epic *Silappathikaram,* classical Tamil treatise on music and dance.

-4 Jesus of Nazareth (4 BCE–30 CE), founder of Christianity, is born in Bethlehem (according to current Biblical scholarship).

Western calendar begins.

10 World population is 170 million. India population is 35 million: 20.5% of world.

ca 50 South Indians occupy Funan, Indo-China. Kauṇḍinya, a South Indian *brāhmin,* is regarded as its first king.

53 Saint Thomas dies in Madras, one of the 12 Christian Apostles and founder of the Church of the Syrian Malabar Christians (Syrian Rite) in Goa.

65 King Mingdi of China converts to Buddhism.

75 A Gujarat prince named Ajiśaka invades Java.

78 Śaka Hindu calendar begins.

80 Jains divide into the Śvetāmbara, "white-clad," and the Digambara, "sky-clad."

ĀNDHRA — KUSHĀN — PALLAVA — 100 — 200

ca 80 Chaka (ca 80–180) is born. Court physician of the Kushān king, he formulates a code of conduct for doctors of āyurveda and writes an early manual of medicine.

ca 100 Lifetime of Śāṇḍilya, first systematic promulgator of the ancient Pāñcharātra doctrines who composes several *bhakti sūtras,* or devotional aphorisms, on Vishṇu, bringing about a Vaishṇava rennaisance. The *saṁhitās* of Śāṇḍilya and his followers, known as the *Pañcharātra Āgama,* embody the chief doctrines of present-day Vaishṇavas. The sect acquires great popularity and by the 10th century CE has left a permanent mark on many other Hindu sects.

100 Zhang Qian of China establishes trade routes to India and as far west as Rome, later known as the "Silk Roads."

105 Paper is invented in China.

110 Buddhist council is held in Kashmir. Mahāyāna and Hīnayāna sects split off.

117 The Roman Empire reaches its greatest extent.

125 Śātakarṇī of the Āndhra dynasty destroys Śaka kingdom of Bengal.

ca 175 Greek astronomer Ptolemy is known as Asura Māyā in India, where he explains solar astronomy, Sūrya Siddhānta, to Indian astronomer pupils.

180 Mexican city of Teotihuacan has 100,000 population and covers 11 square miles. Grows to 250,000 by 500 CE.

ca 200 Lifetime of Lakulīśa, famed *guru* who leads a reformist movement within Pāśupata Śaivism.

ca 200 First Hindu kingdoms are established in present-day Cambodia and Malaysia.

205 Plotinus (205–270) is born in Egypt, monistic Greek philosopher and religious genius who transforms a revival of Platonism in the Roman Empire into what present-day scholars call Neoplatonism, which exercises a great influence on Islamic and European thought. He practices and teaches *ahiṁsā,* vegetarianism, *karma,* reincarnation and belief in a Supreme Being, both immanent and transcendent.

ca 250 Pallava dynasty (ca 250–750) is established in present-day Tamil Nadu. Capital is Kanchipuram, responsible for building the monuments at Mahābalipuram.

274 Catholic Council of Lyons affirms that souls go immediately to heaven, purgatory or hell. This is interpreted by subsequent Catholic fathers as a condemnation of the doctrine of reincarnation.

ca 275 Buddhist monastery Mahāvihāra is founded in Anurād-

300 ĀNDHRA GUPTA PALLAVA

hāpura, capital of Sri Lanka.

ca 300 Licchavi dynasty (ca 300–900) establishes Hindu rule of the small Himalayan kingdom of Nepal. During their rule, Nepal becomes the major intellectual and commercial center between South and Central Asia.

320 Gupta dynasty (320–499) is founded, flourishes until invading Huns conquer it in 499. At its height, the Guptas rule or receive tribute from nearly all of India. Buddhism also thrives under Gupta Hindus' zealous but tolerant rule. Considered a golden age of Indian history.

ca 350 Lifetime of Kālidāsa, the great Sanskṛit poet and dramatist, author of *Śākuntala* and *Meghadūta.*

358 Huns, excellent archers and horsemen of Chinese origin, invade Europe.

380 Chandragupta II (380–413) is born. Great Gupta monarch, he creates a rich and contented kingdom.

391 Roman Emperor Theodosius destroys pagan temples in favor of Christianity.

400

ca 400 *Laws of Manu* (*Manu Dharma Śāstra)* written in the Gupta period. Its 2,685 verses codify cosmogony, four *āśramas, kshatriya* duties, government, domestic affairs, caste and morality.

ca 400 Polynesians sailing in open outrigger canoes have reached as far as Hawaii and Easter Island.

ca 400 Shaturaṅga, Indian forerunner of chess, has evolved from Ashṭapāda, a board-based race game, to a four-handed war game played with a die. However, in deference to the *Laws of Manu,* which forbids gambling, Shaturaṅga players discard the die, and it becomes Shatrañj, a two-sided strategy game.

ca 400 Vātsyāyana writes *Kāmasūtra,* famous text on erotics.

419 Moche people of Peru build a Sun temple 150 feet high using 50 million bricks.

439 Christian Council of Florence strengthens Catholic stance against doctrine of reincarnation.

ca 440 Ajantā cave frescoes (long before Islam) depict Buddha as Prince Siddhārtha, wearing "chūḍīdara pyjama" and the prototype of the present-day "Nehru shirt."

450

450 Bodhidharma (450–535) is born, Buddhist founder of the *dhyāna,* or meditation, sect known in the present day as Zen. He travels to South India in 480 to gather scriptures and learn martial arts.

ca 450 Hun invasions (ca 450–565) of North India take a great toll. These Hephtalite Huns from China are probably not related to the Huns who invade Europe. The Turks and

450 500 590

GUPTA PALLAVA EARLY CHALUKYA

Persians defeat the Hephtalites in 565.

ca 450 Chālukya Dynasty (ca 450–1189) is founded by the "barbarian" Chulik, first in Gujarat, then later in larger areas of Western India.

ca 450 As the Gupta Empire declines, Indian medieval sculptural style evolves and continues roughly until the foundation of the Mogul Empire (16th century). The trend is a progressive movement away from the swelling modeled forms of the Gupta period toward increasing flatness and linearity.

453 Attila the Hun dies after lifetime of plundering Europe.

484 Gupta Empire, in decline since about 450 BCE, is overthrown by the Hephtalites from beyond the Oxus River.

ca 500 *Mahāvaṁsa,* chronicle of history and dynastic succession of Sri Lanka from 6th century BCE to early 4th century CE, is written in Pāli, probably by Buddhist monk Mahānāma. A sequel, known as the *Chulavaṁśa,* continues the history of Sri Lanka to the 16th century.

ca 500 Over the next millennium, earlier oral Purāṇic traditions are gathered and reduced to writing in the format of present-day *Purāṇas,* Hinduism's folk narratives.

500 World population is 190 million. India population is 50 million: 26.3% of world.

548 Emperor Kimmei officially recognizes Buddhism in Japan by accepting a gift image of Buddha from Korea.

553 Fifth Ecumenical Council held in Constantinople denies the doctrine of pre-existence of the soul before conception, and by implication, reincarnation, as incompatible with Christian belief.

570 Mohammed (570–632) is born, preacher of the Quraysh tribe of the Bedouin, founder of Islam. He begins to preach in Mecca, calling for an end to the "demons and idols" of Arab religion and conversion to the ways of the one God, Allah.

ca 590 Nayanar Śaiva saint and first Samayāchārya and Nalvar, Tirunavukkarasu (lived ca 590-671), is born Marul-nikki, "dispeller of darkness," into a farmer family at Āmur village, in present-day South Arcot, Tamil Nadu, writes 312 songs totalling 3,066 verses. Cleaning the grounds of every temple he visits, he emphasizes humble physical service to Śiva on the *dāsa mārga.* His junior contemporary, the child-saint Sambandar, addresses him affectionately as Appar, "father."

598 Brahmagupta (598–665) is born. Last and most accomplished of the ancient Indian astronomers, he writes on

EARLY CHALUKYA

PALLAVA

RASHṬRAKUTA

600

650

gravity and sets forth the Hindu astronomical system in the verses of his *Brāhma Sphuṭa Siddhānta,* with two chapters on advanced mathematics.

ca 600 Religiously tolerant Pallava King Narasiṅhavarman builds China Pagoda, a Buddhist temple, at Negapatam for the Chinese merchants and monks who frequently call at this chief port.

ca 600 Over the next 300 years, 12 Vaishṇava Alvar saints of Tamil Nadu flourish, writing 4,000 songs and poems (assembled in the Vaishṇava canon, *Nalayira Divya Prabandham)* in praise of Lord Nārāyaṇa and Rāma and of the love between Kṛishṇa and the gopīs. The Alvars are the forerunners of the Vaishṇava bhakti renaissance (12th to 16th centuries) in South India.

606 Harsha (606–644) is born, of the Vardhana dynasty. He establishes the first great kingdom after the Hun invasions, eventually ruling all of India to the Narmada River in the South. His is the last Buddhist kingdom of India.

ca 610 Lifetime of Vāgbhaṭa, author of the definitive *Ashṭāṅga Saṅgraha* on āyurveda.

630 For the next 14 years, Chinese pilgrim Hiuen-Tsang travels in India, recording his insightful and voluminous observations for posterity. When he studies at the Buddhist university of Nalanda (in present-day Bihar), he records that it has 3,000 students, 150 teachers, and thousands of manuscripts. In Varanasi, he records Pāśupata Śaiva population at around 10,000.

ca 650 Lifetime of Nayanar Śaiva saint and second Samayāchārya, Tirujñāna Sambandar. Born a *brāhmin* in Tanjavur, he writes 384 songs totalling 4,158 verses that make up first three books of *Tirumurai.* At 16, he disappears into the sanctum of Nallur temple, near Tiruchi.

ca 650 More than 60 Chinese monks have traveled to India and her colonies. Four hundred Sanskṛit works have been translated into Chinese, 380 survive to the present day.

ca 650 Lifetime of Bāṇa, Śākta master of Sanskṛit prose, author of the *Harshācharita* and *Kādambarī.*

686 Reign of Rājasiṅha (686–705) begins. He inherits the stone-carving legacy of Emperor Mahendra and his son, Narasiṅha, who began the extensive sculptural art in the thriving sea-port of Mahabalipuram.

ca 690 Nayanar Śaiva saint and third Samayāchārya, Sundarar (ca 690–708), is born into a family of temple priests in present-day South Arcot. One hundred of his songs in praise of Śiva, totalling 1,026 verses (the only ones sur-

PALLAVA — RASHṬRAKUTA — CHOLA

700 750 800

viving of his 38,000 songs), make up *Tirumurai* book 7. His famous poem, *Tirut-Tondat-tohai,* names the 63 Śaiva saints and is the basis for Sekkilar's *Periyapurāṇam.*

ca700 Over the next 100 years the 2095-square-mile island of Bali, one of the islands in Indonesia, receives Hinduism from its neighbor, Java.

712 Muslims conquer Sind region (present-day Pakistan).

725 *Mahāvairochana Sūtra,* Great Sun Sūtra, product of late *tantric* Buddhism and principal scripture of large Japanese sect of Shingon, receives a Chinese translation.

ca730 Lifetime of Bhavabhūti, Sanskṛit dramatist, second only to Kālidāsa. Writes *Mālatī Mādhava,* a Śākta work.

732 French barely prevent Muslim conquest of Europe.

ca750 Valmīki writes *Yoga Vasishṭha.*

ca750 A timepiece, *kadikaram* in Tamil, is worn by an Emperor on a chain around his neck (according to Tamil scholar M. Arunachalam).

760 Kailāsa temple is carved into a hill of rock at Ellora.

788 Ādi Śaṅkara (788–820) is born, native of Malabar and great philosopher of India. Writes commentaries on scripture, foremost of which is his *Viveka Chūḍāmaṇi,* and regularizes ten of India's many monastic orders. Preaches Māyāvādin Advaita philosophy within the Smārta tradition, emphasizing that the world is illusion and God is the only Reality.

ca800 Hindu revival from South India curtails Buddhist presence in India. In North India, Buddha is revered as the ninth incarnation of Vishṇu.

ca800 Lifetime of Nammalvar, greatest of the Vaishṇava Alvar saints. His poems shape the religious beliefs of the Southern Vaishṇavas to the present day.

ca800 Lifetime of Vasugupta, modern founder of Kashmīr

Śaivism, a monistic, meditative school.

ca 800 Lifetime of Matsyendranātha, exponent of the Nātha sect emphasizing *kuṇḍalinī yoga* practices.

ca 800 Lifetime of Andāl, woman saint of Tamil Nadu. Writes devotional poetry to Lord Kṛishṇa, disappears at age 16.

ca 800 Lifetime of Auvaiyar, woman saint of Tamil Nadu, great devotee of Lord Gaṇeśa and author of *Auvai Kural.* She is associated with the Lambika *kuṇḍalinī* school. (A second date for Auvaiyār of 200 BCE is from a story about Auvaiyar and Saint Tiruvalluvar as siblings. A third Auvaiyar reference is dated at approximately 1000. *(Auvaiyar* is a Tamil word meaning "old, learned woman;" some believe it may refer to three different persons.)

ca 800 Karaikkal Ammaiyar, one of the 63 Śaiva saints of Tamil Nadu. Her mystical and *yogic* hymns, preserved in *Tirumurai,* remain popular to the present day.

ca 825 Vasugupta discovers the rock-carved *Śiva Sūtras.*

846 Vijayālaya reestablishes his Chola dynasty, which, over the next 100 years, grows and strengthens into one of the greatest South Indian Empires ever known.

ca 850 Lifetime of Śaiva saint and fourth Samayāchārya (title synonymous with "Nalvar"), Manikkavasagar, born in Tiruvadavur near Madurai into a *brāhmin* family. He writes the famous Tamil work, *Tiruvasagam,* "holy utterances," 51 poems totalling 656 verses in 3,394 lines, chronicling the soul's evolution to God Śiva. *Tirupallieluchi* and *Tiruvembavai* are two classic examples of his innovative style of composing devotional songs.

875 Muslim conquests extend from Spain to Indus Valley.

885 Cholas kill Aparājita, king of the Pallavas, in battle.

ca 900 Lifetime of Gorakshanātha, Nātha *yogī* who founds the order of Kanphaṭha Yogīs and Gorakshanātha Śaivism, the philosophical school called Siddha Siddhānta.

ca 900 Under the Hindu Malla dynasty of Nepal (ca 900–1700), legal and social codes influenced by Hinduism are introduced; Nepal is broken into three major and several minor principalities.

ca 900 Sembiyan Mā Devī (ca 900–1001), queen of Gandarāditta Chola from 950–957 and great patron of Śaivism, builds ten temples and inspires and molds her grandnephew prince, son of Sundara Chola, into the great temple-builder, Emperor Rājarāja I.

900 Mataramas dynasty in Indonesia reverts to Śaivism after a century of Buddhism, building 150 Śaiva temples.

960 Chola King Vīra, after having a vision of Śiva Naṭarāja

800 850 900

RASHṬRAKUTA CHOLA CHALUKYA CHANDEL (BUNDHELKHAND)

dancing, commences enlargement of the Śiva temple at Chidambaram, including the construction of the gold-roofed shrine. The enlargement is completed in 1250 CE.

985 Rājarāja I (reign 985–1014) accedes the South Indian Chola throne and ushers in a new age of temple architecture including Tanjavur, Darasuram, Tirubhuvanam and Chidambaram. Pallava architectural influences (dominant *vimānas,* inconspicuous *gopuras*) fade.

ca 1000 Hindu communities from Rājput and other areas, the ancestors of present-day Romanī, or Gypsies, gradually move out of India to Persia and on to Europe.

ca 1000 Vikings reach North America, landing in Nova Scotia.

ca 1000 Polynesians arrive in New Zealand, last stage in the greatest migration and navigational feat in history, making them the most widely-spread race on Earth.

1000 World population is 265 million. India population is 79 million, 29.8% of world.

1008 Turkish Muslims sweep through India under Mahmud, defeating a Hindu confederacy at Peshawar.

ca 1010 *Tirumurai,* devotional hymns of Śaiva saints, is collected as an anthology by Nambiandar Nambi.

1017 Mahmud of Ghazni sacks Mathura, birthplace of Lord Kṛishṇa, and establishes a mosque on the site during one of his 17 invasions of India for plunder.

1017 Rāmānuja (1017–1137) is born in Kanchipuram in South India, Tamil founder of the Śrī Vaishṇava sect which continues the *bhakta* tradition of the South Indian Ālvārs. His *Viśishṭādvaita* philosophy is articulated in his *Śrī Bhāshya* (commentary) on the *Vedānta Sūtra,* and is a restating of the earlier Pañcharātra tradition. A major opponent of Śaṅkara's system, he propounds a strongly theistic dual-nondual form of Vedānta. Dies at age 120 while still head of the great Śrīraṅgam monastery.

1024 Turk Muslim Mahmud plunders Somanāth Śiva temple, destroying the Liṅga and killing 50,000 Hindu defenders. He later builds a mosque on the site.

ca 1040 Chinese invent the compass and moveable type and perfect the use of gunpowder, first invented and used in India as an explosive mixture of saltpetre, sulfur and charcoal to power guns, cannons and artillery.

ca 1050 *Siddha Siddhānta Paddhati,* "Tracks of the Doctrines of the Adepts," is written by Gorakshanātha. The nature of God and universe, structure of *chakras, kuṇḍalinī* force and methods for realization are explained in 353 esoteric verses.

CHALUKYA

ORISSA (FROM THE 5TH CENTURY)

CHOLA

1000

1050

1100 · 1200 · ORISSA · CHOLA · CHĀLUKYA · SLAVE SULTANS OF DELHI

ca 1100 Lifetime of Śrīkaṇṭha, founder of Śiva Advaita, a major philosophical school of Śaivism.

ca 1100 Lifetime of Sekkilar, Tamil chief minister under Chola Emperor Kulottunga II (reign 1133–1150) and author of *Periyapurāṇam,* 4,286-verse epic biography (hagiography) of the 63 Śaiva saints and 12th book of *Tirumurai.*

ca 1100 Lifetime of Meykandar, Śaiva saint who founds the Meykandar school of pluralistic Śaiva Siddhānta, of which his 12-*sūtra Śivajñānabodham,* becomes a core scripture.

ca 1130 Nimbārka (ca 1130–1200) is born, Telegu founder of the Vaishṇava Nimandi sect holding the philosophy of *dvaitādvaita,* dual-nondualism. He introduces the worship of Kṛishṇa together with His consort Rādhā. (Present-day Nimavats revere Vishṇu Himself, in the form of the *Haṁsa Avatāra,* as the originator their sect.)

ca 1150 Lifetime of Basavaṇṇa, renaissance guru of the Vīra Śaiva sect, stressing free will, equality of men, service to humanity and worship of the Śivaliṅga worn around the neck.

1150 King Sūryavarman II completes construction of his funeral temple in Angkor Wat, Khmer (present-day Cambodia). Dedicated to Vishṇu, it is the largest Hindu temple in Asia, measuring 12 miles in circumference with a 200-foot central tower.

ca 1162 Mahādevī is born, female Śaiva ascetic saint of Karnataka, writes 350 majestic and mystical poems.

1175 Toltec Empire of Mexico crumbles.

1185 Mohammed of Ghur takes Punjab and Lahore.

1191 Eisai founds Rinzai Zen sect in Japan after study in China.

1197 Buddhist university of Nalanda is destroyed by Muslims.

1200 All of North India is under Muslim domination.

1200 India population reaches 80 million.

ca 1200 An unknown author writes *Yoga Yājñavalkya.*

1206 Line of "Slave Kings" (1206–1290) is founded by Qutb ud-Din Aybak, first Muhammedan Sultan of Delhi.

1215 King John is forced to sign the Magna Carta, giving greater rights to citizens in England.

1227 Mongolian Emperor Genghis Khan, conqueror of a vast area from Beijing, China, to Iran and north of Tibet, the largest empire the world has yet seen, dies.

1238 Ānanda Tīrtha, Mādhva (1238–1317), is born Vasudeva near Udupi, Karnataka, great Vaishṇava exponent of dualism and opponent of Śaṅkara's *māyāvādin advaita* philosophy. He composes 37 works and founds the Dvaita school of Vedānta, the Brahma Vaishṇava Sam-

1250 — SLAVE SULTANS OF DELHI — CHOLA — ORISSA — 1300 — TUGHLAK

pradāya, and its eight monasteries, *ashṭamaṭha.*

1260 Meister Eckhart, the German mystic, is born.

1268 Vedānta Deśikar (1268–1369) is born, gifted Tamil scholar and poet, founds sect of Vaishṇavism, called Vadakalai, headquartered at Kanchipuram.

1270 Nāmadeva (1270–1350) is born, poet saint of Bengal and disciple of Jñānadeva. He and his family compose a million verses in praise of Lord Vishṇu.

1272 Marco Polo visits India en route to China.

1275 Jñānadeva (1275–1296) is born, Nātha-trained Śaiva saint who writes *Jñāneśvarī,* a commentary on the Bhagavad Gītā, which becomes the most popular book of Maharashtrian people.

1279 Muktābāī is born, Maharashtrian saint and Nātha *yoginī,* writes 100 sacred verses, founding Vakarī School.

1280 Mongol (Yuen) dynasty (1280–1368) begins in China, under which occurs the last of much translation work into Chinese from Sanskṛit.

1296 Ala-ud-din, sultan of Delhi, founds a dynasty that rules most of India.

ca 1300 Svātmarāma writes *Haṭha Yoga Pradīpikā.*

ca 1300 Lifetime of Janābāī, Maharashtrian Vaishṇava woman saint, writes a portion of Nāmadeva's 1,000,000 verses to Vithoba of the Vakarī tradition.

ca 1300 *Ānanda Samucçhaya* is written.

1300 Muslim conquerors reach Cape Comorin at the southernmost tip of India and build a mosque there.

1313 Lallā of Kashmir is born, Śaiva mystic and poetess who contributed greatly to the development of the Kashmiri language.

1336 Vijayanagara Empire (1336–1565) of South India is founded. European visitors are overwhelmed by the

1350 · 1400 · 1450

TUGHLAK SULTANS OF DELHI · VIJAYANAGARA · ORISSA · LODĪ SULTANS OF DELHI

wealth and advancement of the 17-square-mile main city.

1345 Aztecs establish great civilization in Mexico.

1347 Bubonic plague spreads, killing 75 million worldwide before it recedes in 1351.

ca1350 Lifetime of Appaya Dīkshita, great saint of South India who works heroically to reconcile Vaishṇavism and Śaivism and strengthen Śaivism, advances the Śiva Advaita school of Śaivism by his writings, as well as other schools of Śaiva philosophy and creates standard manual of Śaiva temple ritual (still in use in the present day).

1398 Tamerlane invades India with 90,000 cavalry and sacks Delhi because its Muslim rulers have become too tolerant of Hindu idolatry. A Mongolian follower of Sufism, he is one of the most ruthless of all conquerors.

1399 Hardwar, pilgrimage town on the upper Ganges, is sacked by Tamerlane.

ca1400 *Goraksha Upanishad* is written.

1414 Hindu prince Parameśvara of Malaysia converts to Islam.

1415 Bengali poet and singer Baru Chaṇḍidās writes *Śrī-kṛishṇakīrtan,* a collection of exquisite songs in praise of Lord Kṛishṇa.

1429 Joan of Arc, age 17, leads French to victory over English.

ca1433 China cloisters itself from the outside world by banning further voyages to the West.

1440 Kabīr (1440–1518) is born, Vaishṇava reformer who has both Muslim and Hindu followers. (His Hindi songs remain immensely popular to the present day.)

1468 Gutenberg invents the moveable-type printing press.

1469 Guru Nānak (1469–1538) is born, founder of Sikhism. Sikhism is originally a reformist Hindu sect stressing devotion, faith in the *guru,* repetition of God's name and rejection of caste. (Most Sikhs in the present day consider themselves members of a separate religion.)

1478 Spanish Inquisition begins. Over the next 20 years, Christians burn several thousand persons at the stake.

1479 Vallabha (1479–1531) is born. A married Telegu *brāhmin,* he founds the Rudrasampradāya, establishing a monotheistic Vaishṇava school in his name. He teaches what becomes known as *pushṭimārga,* which promises salvation to those who unconditionally follow the *guru.* His sect worships Lord Kṛishṇa in the form of Śrī Nāthjī.

1486 Chaitanya (1486–1534) is born, founder of a popular Vaishṇava sect in Bengal which proclaims Lord Kṛishṇa as Supreme God. Chaitanya emphasizes the chanting of the Lord's name in congregation, *sankīrtan.*

1492 Christopher Columbus lands in San Salvador island in the Caribbean, thus "discovering" the Americas and proving to doubting Europeans that the earth is round.

1498 Mīrābāī (1498–1546) is born, Vaishṇava woman saint of Rajasthan, writes numerous mystic hymns that are sung to the present day.

1498 Vasco da Gama of Portugal rounds Cape of Good Hope with four ships and arrives in Calcutta, as the first European to discover a sea route to India. Portuguese Catholics soon capture Goa (1510) and other territories, beginning conquest and exploitation of India by Europeans.

ca 1500 Lifetime of Arunagirināthar, Tamil saint, author of *Tiruppugal* songs (1,360 are known today of his 16,000 songs); emphasizes feeding the hungry during a time of heavy Muslim oppression of Hindus.

ca 1500 Buddhist and Śaiva Hindu princes are forced off the island of Java by invading Muslims. They resettle on neighboring Bali, bringing with them their overlapping priesthoods and vast royal courts—poets, dancers, musicians and artisans. Within 100 years they have constructed what many call a fairytale kingdom.

1500 World population is 425 million. India population is 105 million: 24.7% of world.

1503 Nostradamus (1503–1566) is born, famous, mysterious, talented European astrologer, prophet, doctor of medicine, herbalist, magician and noted inventor of fruit preservatives and cosmetics.

1506 Saint Francis Xavier (1506–1552) is born, most successful Roman Catholic missionary. First to train and employ a native clergy in conversion efforts, this Jesuit brings Christianity to India (centered in Madurai), the Malay Archipelago and Japan.

1509 Mahārāja Kṛishṇadevarāya ascends the throne of the Vijayanagara Empire.

1517 Luther begins Protestant reformation in Europe.

1526 Mongol conqueror Babur (1483–1530) defeats the Sultan of Delhi and captures the Koh-i-Nor diamond. He occupies Delhi, and by 1529 founds and becomes Emperor of the Mogul Empire in North India. Also a man of letters, his prose memoirs, the *Babur-nāmā*, are considered a present-day autobiographical classic.

1527 Tulasīdāsa (1527–1623) is born, author of the Hindi version of the *Rāmāyaṇa.*

1528 Babur destroys temple marking the birthplace of Lord Rāma at Ayodhyā.

VIJAYANAGARA · LODĪ SULTANS · MOGUL SULTANS · SIKH KINGDOMS · 1500 · 1520

1550 1600

VIJAYANAGARA — MOGUL SULTANS OF DELHI — SIKH KINGDOMS

1543 Copernicus proposes to the West that the Earth orbits the sun.

1556 Akbar (1542–1605), son of Babur, becomes second Emperor of Mogul Empire in India at the age of 13.

1560 Lifetime of Maharashtrian saint Ekanātha, who edits Jñānadeva's *Jñāneśvarī* and advances Marāṭhi language.

1565 Muslim neighbors defeat and completely destroy the Vijayanagara Empire, which falls in its 229th year.

1569 Akbar captures fortress of Ranthambor, ending Rājput independence.

1588 British ships defeat the Spanish Armada off the coast of Calais, to become rulers of the high seas.

1589 Akbar rules half of India, shows tolerance for all faiths.

1591 Kingdom of Jaffna comes under Portuguese Catholic control. In 1619, Sri Lanka's ruling dynasty is deposed.

1595 Construction is begun on Chidambaram Temple's Hall of a Thousand Pillars in South India, completed in 1685.

ca 1600 "Persian wheel" to lift water by oxen is adopted—one of the few agricultural innovations to occur since the time of the Indus Valley civilization.

1600 Royal Charter forms English East India Company, setting in motion a process that results in the ultimate subjugation of India under British rule.

1605 Akbar dies at age 63. His son Jahāngīr succeeds him as third Mogul Emperor.

1605 Sikh Golden Temple at Amritsar, Punjab, is finished, completely covered with gold leaf.

1607 Tukārām (1607–1649) is born, Marathi religious writer and devotee of Lord Kṛishṇa.

1610 Galileo invents the telescope.

1619 First black slaves from Africa are sold in the US.

1620 European pilgrims land and settle at Plymouth Rock, US.

1627 Śivaji is born (1627–1680), founds Maratha Empire, restores large areas of Muslim territory to Hindu control.

ca 1628 Kumaraguruparar (ca 1628–1688) is born, prolific poet-saint of Tamil Nadu, who founds monastery in Varanasi to propound Śaiva Siddhānta philosophy.

1630 Over the next two years, millions starve to death as Shah Jahan (1592–1666), fourth Mogul Emperor, empties the royal treasury to buy jewels for his "Peacock Throne."

SIKH KINGDOMS

MOGUL SULTANS OF DELHI

1650

1700

1639 First British trading post in India is opened.
1647 Shah Jahan completes Tāj Mahal in Agra beside Yamuna River. Its construction has taken 20,000 laborers 15 years, at a total cost equivalence of US$25 million.
1649 Red Fort is completed in Delhi by Shah Jahan.
ca1650 Dharmapuram Aadheenam, Śaiva monastery, founded at near Mayuram, South India, by Guru Jñānasambandar.
ca1650 Robert de Nobili, Jesuit missionary, arrives in Madurai, declares himself a *brāhmin* and composes a *Veda*-like scripture extolling Jesus.
ca1650 Two *yoga* classics, *Śiva Saṁhitā* and *Gheraṇḍa Saṁhitā,* are written.
1654 A Tamil *karttanam* is written and sung to celebrate recovery installation of the Tiruchendur Murugan *mūrti.*
1658 Zealous Muslim Aurangzeb (1618–1707) becomes Mogul Emperor. His discriminatory policies toward Hindus, Marāṭhas and the Deccan kingdoms contribute to the dissolution of the Mogul Empire by 1750.
1660 Frenchman François Bernier reports India's peasantry is living in misery under Mogul rule.
1675 Aurangzeb executes Sikh Guru Tegh Bahadur, beginning the Sikh-Muslim feud that continues to this day.
1679 Aurangzeb levies *Jizya* tax on non-believers, Hindus.
1686 Island of Mauritius, east of Africa, has 269 inhabitants. By 1728, Mauritius is under French administration and is receiving immigrating artisans from Tamil Nadu.
1688 Aurangzeb demolishes all temples of Mathura, said to have numbered 1,000. (Muslim rulers are said to have destroyed a total of 60,000 Hindu temples in India. Mosques were constructed on 3,000 of these sites.)
ca1700 *Śākta* songs of Bengali poets Rāmprasād Sen and Kamalakānta Bhattāchārya glorify Her as loving Mother and

Daughter and stimulate a rise in devotional Śāktism.

1700 World population is 610 million. India population is 165 million: 27% of world.

1705 Tayumanavar (1705–1742) is born, Tamil Śaiva poet saint of Tiruchirappalli.

1708 Govind Singh, tenth Sikh Guru is assassinated by Bahadur Shah, the next Mogul Emperor.

1722 Peter the Great rules in Russia.

1751 Robert Clive, age 26, seizes Arcot in Karnataka, as French and British fight for control of South India.

1760 Śaiva *sannyāsīs* fight Vaishṇava *vairāgīs* in a tragic battle for control of the Kumbha Mela area at Hardwar in which 18,000 monks are killed.

1760 Eliezer (Besht), liberal founder of Hasidic Judaism, dies. (Present-day Hasidism is unchanged, practices God-consciousness, selfless service and transcending the material world without messianic redemption.)

1761 Afghan army of Ahmed Shah Durrani annihilates the Hindu Marāṭhas, who are now allies of the Moguls.

1764 British defeat the weak Mogul Emperor to become rulers of Bengal, richest province of India.

1769 Pṛithivī Nārāyaṇ Shah, ruler of the Gorkha principality of Nepal, conquers Nepal Valley and moves his capital to Kathmandu, establishing the present-day Hindu state of Nepal (area: 54,362 square miles/population: 11.5 million, 88% Hindus).

ca 1770 Ṛishi from the Himalayas (ca 1770–1840) is born, first known *satguru* in recent history in the Kailāsa Paramparā of the Nandinātha Sampradāya.

1773 British East India Company obtains monopoly on the production and sale of opium in Bengal.

1781 George Washington defeats British at Yorktown, US.

1781 Sahajānandaswāmī (1781–1830) is born, Gujarati founder of the Swāminārāyaṇ sect (with 1.5 million followers in present-day India).

1786 British Christian judge and linguist William Jones uses the ancient Ṛig Vedic term *Āryan* to refer to the ancient parent-language of Sanskṛit, Greek, Latin and the Germanic languages. (Modern scholars call this root language Nostratic.)

1787 British Parliament impeaches Warren Hastings, Governor General of Bengal and effective ruler of British India, for misconduct.

1787 British Committee for the Abolition of the Slave Trade is formed, marking the beginning of the end of slavery.

SIKH KINGDOMS

MOGUL SULTANS OF DELHI

1800

1820

1789 French revolution begins with storming of the Bastille.

1792 Cornwallis defeats Tipu Sahib, Sultan of Mysore and most powerful ruler in South India, main bulwark of resistance to British expansion in India.

1793 Eli Whitney invents the cotton gin in the US, greatly affecting the institution of slavery.

1796 Over two million worshipers compete for sacred Ganges bath at Kumbha Mela in Hardwar. Five thousand Śaiva ascetics are killed in tragic clash with Sikh ascetics.

1799 Tipu Sahib is killed in battle against 5,000 British soldiers who storm and raze his capital, Seringapatam.

1803 British Christians capture Delhi and take control of much of India.

1803 India population is 200 million.

1803 Ralph Waldo Emerson (1803–1882) is born, American poet who helps popularize the *Bhagavad Gītā* and *Upanishads* in the US.

1807 Importation of slaves is banned in the US, through an act of Congress motivated by Thomas Jefferson.

1809 British strike a bargain with Rañjīt Singh for exclusive areas of influence.

ca1810 Siddha Kadaitswāmī (ca1810–1875) of Sri Lanka, is born near Bangalore, successor to Ṛishi from the Himalayas in the Nandinātha Sampradāya's Kailāsa Paramparā.

1812 Napoleon's army retreats from Moscow. Only 20,000 soldiers survive out of a 500,000-man invasion force.

1814 First practical steam locomotive is built.

1817 Bahaullah, Mirza Husayn 'Ali (1817–1892) is born, founds Baha'i faith, a major off-shoot religion of Islam, having stemmed from the Babi faith—founded in 1844 by Mirza'Ali Mohammed (Bab) of Shiraz.

1818 Śivadayāl (1818–1878) is born, founder of the Rādhāsoamī sect of Vaishṇavism.

1820 First Indian immigrants arrive in the US.

1822 Arumuga Navalar (1822-1879) is born in Nallur, Jaffna, Sri Lanka, a Champion reformer of Hinduism, propounds the Śaiva philosophy of Advaita Siddhānta, writes the first Hindu catechism and translates Christian *Bible* into Tamil to make its contents known to the Tamil people.

1823 Swāmī Rāmaliṅgam (1823–1874) of South India is born, author of 7,000 poems and founder of the universalist temple of light in Vadalur.

1824 Dayānanda Sarasvatī (1824–1883) is born, founder of the Ārya Samāj, a Hindu reformist movement stressing a return to the values and practices of the *Vedas.*

1825 First massive immigration of Indian workers from Madras is to Reunion and Mauritius. This immigrant Hindu community builds their first temple in 1854.

1828 Rām Mohan Roy (lived 1772–1833) founds Ādi Brāhmo Samāj, a quasi-Protestant, theistic, social reform movement. Influenced by Islam and Christianity, it denounces polytheism, idol worship, and abandons the *Vedas, avatāras, karma* and reincarnation.

1831 Madame H.P. Blavatsky (1831–1891) is born in Russia, founds Theosophical Society in 1875, instrumental in bringing Hindu mysticism and esoteric cosmology to the West.

1831 Sikh forces of Rañjīt Singh are defeated at Balakot in their attempt to establish a Sikh state in Northwest India.

1833 Slavery is formally abolished in all British Commonwealth countries, giving great impetus to abolitionists in the United States.

1835 Mauritius receives 19,000 immigrant indentured laborers from India. Last ship carrying workers arrives in 1922.

1836 Śrī Rāmakṛishṇa (1836–1886) is born, God-intoxicated Bengali Śākta saint, *guru* of Swāmī Vivekānanda. He stresses the *bhakti* dimension of the newly developing Śākta Universalism.

1837 Britain formalizes emigration of Indian indentured laborers to supply cheap labor under a system more morally acceptable to British Christian society than slavery, which has been illegal in the British Empire since 1833.

1837 Kālī-worshiping Thugees are suppressed by British.

1838 British Guyana receives its first 250 Indian laborers.

1838 Keshab Chandra Sen (1838–1884) is born, Hindu reformer, founds Brāhmo Samāj of India, a radical offshoot of the Ādi Brāhmo Samāj of Rām Mohan Roy.

1840 Satguru Chellappaswāmī (1840–1915) of Jaffna, Sri Lanka, is born. He is initiated at age 19 by Siddha Kadaitswāmī as the next *satguru* in the Nandinātha Sampradāya's Kailāsa Paramparā.

1840 Joseph de Goubineau (1816–1882), French scholar, writes *The Inequality of Human Races.* In this book, extrapolating from previous hypotheses, Gobineau proclaims the superiority of the "Āryan race" over other great strains and lays down the aristocratic class-doctrine of Āryanism in its fullness, differing greatly from earlier concepts of Āryan. Gobineau's theories are to provide the basis for Adolf Hitler's doctrine of Āryanism.

1843 British Christians conquer the Sind region (present-day Pakistan).

1845 Trinidad receives its first 197 Indian immigrant laborers.

1846 British forcibly separate Kashmir from the Sikhs and sell it to the Mahārāja of Jammu for £1,000,000.

1849 Sikh army is defeated by the British at Amritsar.

1853 Śrī Śāradā Devī (1853–1920) is born, saintly wife of Śrī Rāmakṛishṇa.

1853 Max Müller (1823–1900), German philologist and Orientalist, advocates the use of the term *Āryan* to refer to a hypothetical primitive people of Central Asia, the common ancestors of Hindus, Persians and Greeks. Müller speculates that this "Āryan race" divided and marched west to Europe and east to India and China around 1500 BCE. They spoke a language called Āryan, Müller continues, that developed into Sanskṛit, Greek, Latin, German, etc. Müller concludes that all ancient civilizations of the world, both European and Eastern, descended from this race.

1856 Catholic missionary Bishop Caldwell coins the term *Dravidian* to refer to South Indian Caucasian peoples.

1857 First Indian Revolution, called the Sepoy Mutiny, ends in a few months with the fall of Delhi and Lucknow.

1858 India has a total of 200 miles of railroad track. By 1869 more than 5,000 miles of steel track have been completed by British railroad companies. In 1900, total track is 25,000 miles, and by World War I, 35,000 miles. By 1970, the figure has doubled to 62,136 miles.

1858 British Queen Victoria, head of the Church of England, is proclaimed ruler of India.

1859 Charles Darwin, releases his then controversial book,

The Origin of Species, in which he propounds his "natural selection" theory of evolution, laying the foundations of modern biology.

1860 S.S. Truro and S.S. Belvedere dock in Durban, South Africa, carrying the first scores of indentured servants brought from Madras and Calcutta to work on sugar plantations. Bound by contracts of five years and up, thousands more emigrate over the next 51 years.

1861 American Civil War begins.

1861 Bengali poet Rabindranāth Tagore (1861–1941) is born, is awarded the Nobel Prize for Literature in 1913.

1863 Swāmī Vivekānanda (1863–1902) is born, Hindu missionary to the West and leader of Hindu revival in India.

1863 Emancipation Proclamation, signed by US President Lincoln, goes into effect, freeing slaves in all states still at war with the Union.

1863 President Lincoln delivers historic Gettysburg Address.

1869 Mohandās K. Gāndhi (1869–1948) is born in South Africa, later gains India's freedom through nonviolence and becomes a saint to the entire world.

1870 Papal doctrine of infallibility is asserted by the Vatican.

1872 Satguru Yogaswāmī (1872–1964) is born, Nātha sage of Sri Lanka, Chellappaswāmī's successor in the Kailāsa Paramparā of the Nandinātha Sampradāya.

1872 Śrī Aurobindo Ghosh (1872–1950) is born, Indian nationalist and *yoga* mystic philosopher. His 30-volume literary work propounds a philosophy which aims at producing the "superman," in whom the Divine transforms the individual soul.

1873 Rāma Tīrtha (1873–1906) is born, tours Japan and America spreading Vedānta.

1876 Alexander Graham Bell invents the telephone.

1876 For the next 24 years Max Müller, founder of comparative religion as a scholarly discipline, publishes the 50 volumes of the *Sacred Books of the East*, a massive English translation of Indian and Oriental scripture.

1877 Ānanda Coomaraswāmy (1877–1947) of Sri Lanka is born, foremost interpreter of Indian art and culture to the Western world.

1879 Thomas Edison invents the light bulb.

1879 At the request of Fiji's Governor, Sir Arthur Gordon, the "Leonidas," first emigrant ship to Fiji, adds 498 more Indian indentured laborers to the nearly 340,000 already working in other far-flung British colonies.

1879 Sādhu T.L. Vāswanī (1879–1966) is born, altruistic poet

1880

and man of God, founds several missions in India, and seven Mīrā Educational Institutions.

1879 Rāmana Maharshi (1879–1950) is born, great renunciate saint of Tiruvaṇṇāmalai, South India.

1882 Hazrat Inayat Khan (1882–1927) is born in India, instrumental in bringing Islamic mysticism, Sufism, to the West.

1884 Swāmī "Pāpā" Rāmdās (1884–1963) is born, Indian saint and great devotee of Lord Rāma.

1885 A group of middle class intellectuals in India, some of them British, found the Indian National Congress to be a voice of Indian opinion to the British government. This was the origin of the later Congress I.

1885 First automobile powered by an internal combustion engine is produced by Karl Benz in Mannheim, Germany. Henry Ford makes his first car in 1893 in the US and later invents assembly line production.

1886 René Guénon is born, French Vedāntist and first European philosopher to personally adopt Hindu Vedānta, according to his biographer, Robin Waterfield.

1887 Swāmī Śivānanda (1887–1963) is born, author of 200 books and founder of Divine Life Society, which has 400 branches worldwide in the present day.

1888 Max Müller revises his earlier position, writing, "*Āryan,* in scientific language, is utterly inapplicable to race. If I say *Āryas,* I mean neither blood nor bones, nor hair nor skull; I mean simply those who spoke the Āryan language."

1888 Sarvepalli Rādhākṛishṇan (1888–1975) is born, renowned Tamil panentheist Hindu philosopher, spokesman and first president of India.

1890

1891 Mahā Bodhi Society, an organization to encourage Buddhist studies in India and abroad, is founded in Sri Lanka by Buddhist monk Anagarika Dharmapāla.

BRITISH RULE

1893 Swāmī Vivekānanda represents Hinduism at the Parliament of Religions in Chicago, dramatically impacting and enlightening Western opinion as to the profundity of Hindu philosophy.

1893 Paramahaṁsa Yogānanda (1893–1952) is born, founds Self Realization Fellowship in 1925 in California, authors famed *Autobiography of a Yogī.*

1894 Gāndhi drafts first petition protesting the indentured servant system. Less than six months later, British announce the halt of indentured emigration from India.

1894 Swāmī Chandraśekarendra is born, venerated Śaṅkarā-

BRITISH RULE

charya of Kāñchi monastery in South India.

1894 Meher Bāba (1894–1969) is born in Poona, "Father of Compassion," silent sage whose mystical teachings stress divine love, self-inquiry and God consciousness.

1896 Ānandamayī Mā (1896–1982) is born, God-intoxicated woman saint of Bengal.

1896 Maharashtrian leader Tilak launches a Śivaji festival to fan Indian nationalism after the successful introduction of Gaṇeśa Visarjana for the same purpose.

1896 Bhaktivedānta Swāmī Prabhupāda (1896–1977) is born, founder of International Society for Kṛishṇa Consciousness (ISKCON).

1896 American humorist Mark Twain keeps a diary of his three-month stay in India, part of his globetrotting tour of Hawaii, Fiji, New Zealand, Australia, Sri Lanka, Mauritius, South Africa and England. According to him and his critics, the resulting book, *Following the Equator,* is one of his finest works.

1900

1900 World population is 1.6 billion. India population is 290 million: 17.8% of world.

1900 India's tea exports to Britain reach 137 million pounds.

1900 Uday Śaṅkar (1900–1977) is born in Udaipur, dancer and choreographer, adapts Western theatrical techniques to traditional Hindu dance, popularizing the ancient art form in India, Europe and the US.

1905 Lord Curzon (1859–1925), arrogant British Viceroy of India, resigns.

1905 Sage Yogaswāmī, age 33, is initiated by Chellappaswāmī at Nallur, Sri Lanka; later becomes the next preceptor in the Nandinātha Sampradāya's Kailāsa Paramparā.

1906 Muslim League political party is formed in India.

1906 Bali is forcibly brought under Dutch Christian control after terrible puputan massacres in which entire Hindu Balinese royal families and their retainers are murdered.

1908 Swāmī Muktānanda (1908–1982) is born, Kashmīr Śaiva *satguru* and founder of Siddha Yoga Dhām.

1909 Dādā Lekhrāj (1909–1969) is born in present-day Pakistan, founder of the Brahma Kumārīs, a Śaivite social reform movement stressing mediation and love of God within as Śiv Bāba.

1909 Gāndhi, with assistant Dr. Manilal Maganlāl, agitates for better working conditions and for abolition of indentured servant system in South Africa. Maganlāl continues Gāndhi's work in Fiji.

1910

1912 Anti-Indian racial riots on the US West Coast expel

large Hindu immigrant population.

1913 New law prohibits Indian immigration to South Africa, primarily in answer to white colonists' alarm at competition created by Indian merchants and by those whose labor contracts have expired.

1914 US government excludes Indian citizens from immigration. Restriction stands until 1965.

1914 Archduke Ferdinand of Austria is assassinated, catalyzing a chain reaction that produces World War I.

1914 Swāmī Satchidānanda is born, founder of Integral Yoga Institute and Light Of Truth Universal Shrine in the US.

1917 Bolshevik party takes control of Russia.

1917 Last Indian indentured laborers are brought to British Christian colonies of Fiji and Trinidad.

1917 Swāmī Chinmayānanda is born, founder of Chinmaya Mission and a co-founder of Viśva Hindu Parishad.

1918 World War I ends. Death toll is estimated at ten million.

1918 Spanish Influenza epidemic kills 12.5 million in India, 21.6 million worldwide.

1918 Śirdī Sāī Bāba, saint to both Hindus and Muslims, dies at approximately age 70.

1919 Brigadier Dyer orders Gurkhā troops to shoot unarmed demonstrators in Amritsar, killing 379. Massacre convinces Gāndhi that India must demand full independence from oppressive British Christian rule.

1920 Gāndhi formulates *satyagraha,* "firmness in truth," program of noncooperation and nonviolence against the British rulers of India. Later resolves to wear only loincloth in devotion to homespun cotton and simplicity.

1920 Indentured servant emigration system is abolished in India, following the agitation of Gāndhi.

1920 Ravi Shaṅkar is born in Varanasi, player of the sitār, composer and founder of National Orchestra of India, he is influential in stimulating Western appreciation of Indian music.

1922 Pramukh Swāmī is born, present-day head of Bochasanwasi Swāminārāyaṇ Sanstha Saṅgh.

1923 US law excludes citizens of India from naturalization.

1924 Sir John Marshall discovers relics of the Indus Valley Hindu civilization.

1925 K.V. Hedgewar founds the Rāshṭrīya Swayamsevak Sangh (RSS).

1926 Satya Sāī Bāba is born, worker of miracles and founder of a worldwide education and human values movement.

1927 Sivaya Subramuniyaswami is born, to become present-day *satguru* in the Nandinātha Sampradāya's Kailāsa Paramparā.

1928 Hindu leader Jawaharlal Nehru drafts plan for a free India; becomes president of Congress Party in 1929.

1929 Chellachiamman, woman saint of Sri Lanka, dies. She was mentor to Sage Yogaswāmī and Kandiah Chettiar.

1931 Śrī Chinmoy is born, *yogī*, artist, mystic and international "peace ambassador."

1931 Census report shows approximately 2.5 million Indians are residing overseas, with the largest communities in Sri Lanka, Malaya, Mauritius and South Africa.

1931 Dr. Karan Singh is born, son and heir apparent of Kashmir's last Mahārāja; becomes parliamentarian, ambassador to the US and global Hindu spokesman.

1936 Śrīmatī Rukminī Devī (1936–1991) founds Kalākshetra in Bangladesh, school of Hindu classical music, dancing, theatrical art, painting and handicrafts.

1939 World War II is declared as Germany invades France.

1939 Maria Montessori (1870–1952), first Italian female physician and "discoverer of the child," spends next nine years in India, teaching and refining her kindergarten method while learning about Hinduism through the Theosophical Society in Adyar.

1939 Muslim leader Mohammed Ali Jinnah calls for a separate Muslim state.

1942 Archaeologist Sir Aurel Stein finds shards with incised characters at sites along the lost Sarasvati River in Rajasthan, which are identical to incised characters appearing on Indus Valley seals.

1945 Germany surrenders to Allied forces. Ghastly concentration camps which killed millions are uncovered.

1945 United States drops atomic bombs on Japanese cities of Nagasaki and Hiroshima, ending World War II. Total war dead is estimated at 60 million.

1945 United Nations is founded to "save succeeding generations from the scourge of war."

1947 India gains independence from Britain on August 15. Pakistan emerges as a separate Islamic nation, and 600,000 die in violent clashes during subsequent population exchange of 14 million people between the two new countries.

1947 Britain grants Dominion status to Sri Lanka, permitting the former colony self-government under Commonwealth jurisdiction.

1930

1940

BRITISH RULE

INDEPENDENT INDIA

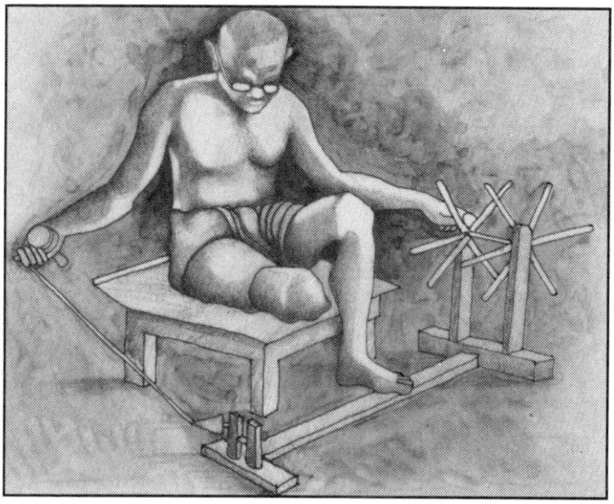

1948 Mahātmā Gāndhi is assassinated on January 30th by Nāthuram Godse, a fanatical RSS Hindu, in retaliation for Gāndhi's agreeing to the partitioning of India, granting 27% of its land to the new Islamic nation of Pakistan.

1949 In Columbuthurai, Sri Lanka, on the full-moon day in May, Sage Yogaswāmī initiates Sivaya Subramuniyaswami, age 22, as his successor in the Nandinātha Sampradāya's Kailāsa Paramparā. Subramuniyaswami founds Śaiva Siddhānta Church and Yoga Order the same year.

1949 India's new constitution, authored chiefly by B.R. Ambedkar, declares that there shall be no "discrimination" against any citizen on the grounds of caste, *varṇa,* and that the practice of "untouchability" is abolished.

1950 India is declared a secular republic, with Jawaharlal Nehru as its Prime Minister, with primary motivations to abolish casteism and industrialize the nation. New constitution goes into effect on January 26.

1955 Albert Einstein (1879–1955), brilliant German scientist who formulated the theory of relativity, dies. He once declared Śiva Naṭarāja to be the best metaphor for the workings of the universe.

1956 India government reorganizes states according to linguistic principles and inaugurates second Five-Year Plan.

1957 Sivaya Subramuniyaswami, age 30, formally begins his teaching mission, founds Himalayan Academy and opens Palaniswāmī Śivan Temple in California.

1959 Dalai Lama flees Tibet and finds refuge in North India as China invades the Buddhist nation.

1960 Since 1930, 5% of immigrants to US have been Asians, while European immigrants have constituted 58%.

1960 Border war with China shakes India's nonaligned policy.

1961 India forcibly reclaims Goa, Damao and Diu from Portuguese Catholic domination. Goa gains independence in Union in 1987.

1964 Viśva Hindu Parishad (VHP), a Hindu nationalist group, is founded in India.

1964 Popular Rock group, the *Beatles,* practice Transcendental Meditation (TM), bringing its founder, Maharshi Mahesh Yogī, into the public eye.

1965 US immigration cancels racial qualifications and restores naturalization rights. Welcomes 170,000 Asians yearly.

1966 Daughter of Jawaharlal Nehru, Indirā Gāndhi, of the Congress Party, becomes Prime Minister of India, world's largest democracy, succeeding Lal Bahadur Śāstrī who took office after Nehru's death in 1964.

1969 Neil Armstrong sets foot on the moon.

1970 Kauai Aadheenam is established February 5 on Hawaii's Garden Island, Hindu monastery and site of Kadavul Hindu Temple.

1971 India's Congress party government sides against West Pakistan on East Bengal issue and grants East Pakistan status as the independent nation of Bangladesh. Indian army later enters Bangladesh to protect Hindu minority. Ten million Hindus flee to India.

1972 Muslim dictator Idi Amin expels Indians from Uganda.

1973 Neem Karoli Bāba, mystic *siddha,* dies.

1973 Netherlands gives independence to Dutch Guyana, which becomes Surinam. One third of minority Hindus (descendants of plantation workers from India) immigrate to the Netherlands to escape native prejudice from Surinam's newly-formed government.

1974 India detonates a "nuclear device."

1977 One hundred thousand Tamil Hindu tea-pickers expatriated from Sri Lanka are shipped to Madras, South India.

1979 Sivaya Subramuniyaswami founds *Hinduism Today* international newspaper to promote Hindu solidarity.

1980 Grand South Indian counterpart to the Kumbha Mela of Prayag, the Mahāmagham religious festival attracts over two million participants. It is held every 12 years in Kumbhakonam, Tanjavur district, on the river Kaveri.

1981 India has about half of the world's cattle, a ratio of eight cattle for every ten persons.

1983 Violence between Hindu Tamils and Buddhist Singha-

1985

lese in Sri Lanka marks beginning of a Tamil rebellion by Tiger freedom fighters demanding an independent nation called Eelam. Prolonged civil war results.

1984 Bālasarasvatī, eminent classical *Karnatic* singer and *bharata nāṭyam* dancer of worldwide acclaim, dies.

1984 Since 1980, Asians have made up 48% of immigrants to the US, with the European portion shrinking to 12%.

1984 Indian soldiers under orders from Prime Minister Indirā Gāndhi storm Sikh Golden Temple in Amritsar to crush rebellion.

1984 Indirā Gāndhi is assassinated by her Sikh body guards in retaliation for Golden Temple attack. Her son Rajīv takes office.

1986 Swāmī Satchidānanda dedicates his newly-constructed Light of Truth Universal Shrine (LOTUS) at his Integral Yoga Institute āśram in Yogaville, Virginia.

1986 J. Kṛishṇamūrti, semi-existentialist philosophical lecturer and author, dies.

1986 World Religious Parliament, in New Delhi, bestows the title of Jagadāchārya, "world teacher," on five spiritual leaders outside India: Swāmī Chinmayānanda of Chinmaya Mission (Bombay, India); Satguru Sivaya Subramuniyaswami of Śaiva Siddhānta Church and Himalayan Academy (Hawaii-California, USA); Yogīrāj Amṛit Desāi of Kṛipālu Yoga Center (New York, USA); Paṇḍit Tej Rāmjī Sharma of Nepāli Bāba (Kathmandu, Nepal); Swāmī Jagpūrṇadās Mahārāj (Port Louis, Mauritius).

1988 General Hussain Ershad, declares Islam the state religion of Bangladesh, outraging the 12-million (about 11%) minority Hindu population.

1988 US immigration allows total annual influx of 270,000 persons from Asian countries.

1988 First Global Forum of Spiritual and Parliamentary Leaders on Human Survival is held at Oxford University, England. Hindu leaders join in discussions on international cooperation with 100 spiritual leaders and 100 parliamentarians from around the world.

1989 Christian missionaries are spending US$165 million per year to convert Hindus.

1990

1990 The Berlin Wall is taken down February 12. Germany is reunited over the next year. Warsaw Pact is dissolved.

1990 Under its new democratic constitution, Nepal remains the world's only Hindu country.

1990 Over 100 Hindu temples, built over the past two decades, are open for worship in the US.

1990 1991 1992

1990 Hindus flee Muslim persecution in Kashmir Valley.

1990 Foundation stones are laid in Ayodhyā for new temple at birthplace of Lord Rāma, as Hindu nationalism rises.

1990 Vatican's "Congregation for the Doctrine of the Faith" (former "Office of the Inquisition") condemns *yoga* in letter written by Cardinal Ratzinger and approved by Pope Paul II, in an attempt to purge Catholic monasteries and convents and thousands of clergy of involvement in Eastern meditation and mysticism.

1990 Second Global Forum of Spiritual Leaders and Parliamentarians for Human Survival, in Moscow and sponsored by the Supreme Soviet, gives world stage for Hindu thinking. Śṛiṅgerī Maṭha *sannyāsin* Paramānanda Bhārati, concludes Forum with Vedic prayer for peace in Kremlin Hall, leading 2,500 world leaders in chanting *Aum* three times together.

1990 Communist leadership of the United Soviet Socialist Republic (USSR) collapses, to be replaced by 12 independent democratic nations.

1991 Hindu Renaissance Award is founded by *Hinduism Today* and declares Swāmī Paramānanda Bhārati of Śṛīṅgeri Maṭha "1990 Hindu of the Year."

1991 Prime Minister Rajīv Gāndhi is assassinated in Tamil Nadu on May 21 by a Tamil separatist.

1991 Indian tribals, *ādivāsīs,* are 45 million strong.

1991 In Bangalore, India, Sivaya Subramuniyaswami authorizes renowned architect V. Gaṇapati Sthapati to begin carving the Chola-style, white-granite, *moksha* Iraivan Temple in a project guided by Śrī Śrī Trichy Swāmī, Śrī Śrī Balagangādaranāthaswāmi and Śrī Śivapuriswāmī. Shipped to Hawaii's Garden Island of Kauai and erected on San Mārga, Iraivan will be the first all-stone Āgamic temple in the Western Hemisphere. Enshrined as its Śivaliṅga will be the world's largest single-pointed, six-sided crystal (700 lbs.), known as the Earthkeeper.

1992 Swāmī Chidānanda Saraswatī, president of the Parmārth Niketan Trust and Parmārth Niketan 1,000-room *āśrama* in Ṛishikesh, is named 1991 Hindu of the Year by *Hinduism Today* for founding the historic *Encyclopedia of Hinduism* project.

1992 World population is 5.2 billion. Of this number, 17% or 895 million, live in India. Of these, 85%, or 760 million, are Hindu.

1992 Third Global Forum of Spiritual Leaders and Parliamentarians for Human Survival meets in Rio de Janeiro in conjunction with the June 1–12 Earth Summit (UNCED). Hindu views of nature, environment and traditional values expressed at the Forum help inform the gathering of 70,000 political delegates planning for the global future of environmental development.

1992 On December 6, Hindus demolish the Babri Masjid built in 1548 on the birthplace of Lord Rama in Ayodhya, India, by Muslim conqueror Babar after he destroyed a Hindu temple marking the site. This has been a major symbol of long-standing Hindu resentment toward the destruction of thousands of temples during the Muslim and Christian conquest of India.

1993 Swāmī Chinmayānanda is named 1992 Hindu of the Year, receiving the Rennaisance Award from *Hinduism Today* for his lifetime of dynamic service to the Sanātana Dharma worldwide.

1993 In April, the Fourth Global Forum of Spiritual and Parliamentary Leaders on Human Survival meets in Kyoto, Japan. Eminent Hindus join with spiritual and political leaders of the world and with artists, businessmen and members of the media to discuss the human dilemma and found the International Green Cross, an ecological institution for environmental relief and protection.

2000 World population is 6.2 billion. India population is 1.2 billion: 20% of world (projection by World Watch).

Bālaka Pustaka

बालकपुस्तक

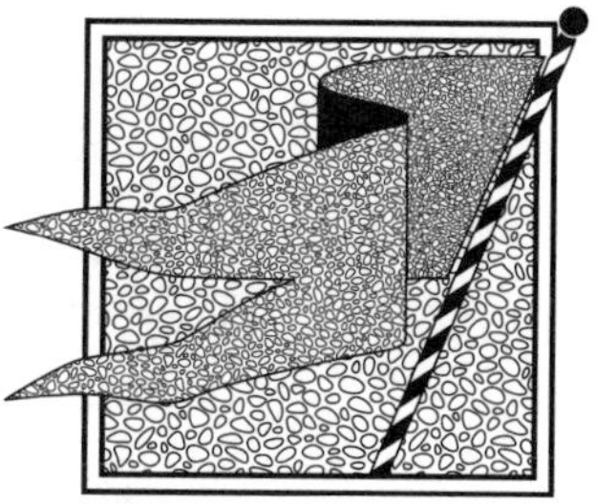

A Children's Primer

Dhvaja, "flag," is the orange or red banner flown above temples, at festivals and in processions. It is a symbol of victory, signal to all that "Sanātana Dharma shall prevail." Its color betokens the sun's life-giving glow. Aum.

A Children's Primer

Loving Hindu parents worldwide have called for a common religious code to teach their sons and daughters. They have asked, "What is the minimum I must do to dispatch my duty to my religion and my children?" The World Hindu Federation of Nepal discussed this need at its international conference in Bali in late 1992, and shared their concern with me at that time. In response, I told the Bali Mahāsaṅgha that I would work with my research staff to prepare the minimal duties for parents to pass on the Sanātana Dharma to the next generation. The result was ten *ślokas* summarizing the five essential Hindu beliefs, and the five corresponding observances performed in expression of those beliefs. *Āchāryas* concur that these are enough to know and follow to be a good Hindu. We first published these in *Hinduism Today*'s March, 1993, edition, along with the very popular primer for children covering Hinduism from A to Z. Both of these are assembled here as *A Children's Primer.*

In this section you will also find an illustrated summary of the essential Hindu *saṁskāras,* or rites of passage. These sacraments are vital to Hindus, for whom life is a sacred journey and every crucial step is acknowledged through traditional ceremony. There are many types of *saṁskāras,* from the rite prior to conception to the funeral ceremony. Each one, properly observed, empowers spiritual life, preserves religious culture and establishes bonds with inner worlds as the soul accepts and matures into the responsibilities of each succeeding stage of life.

The modern Hindu child raised up with these precepts, practices and sacraments will be a fully functioning human being, one who is tolerant, devotional, fair, fearless, obedient, secure, happy, selfless, detached and traditional.

Hinduism A to Z

Dharma Varṇamālā

धर्मवर्णमाला

A CHILDREN'S PRIMER ON HINDU THOUGHT AND IDEALS, COVERING DHARMA FROM A TO Z AND FEATURING A UNIQUE INITIAL ALPHABET DESIGNED WITH INDIAN MOTIFS.

A is for Aum, the three-syllabled mantra that represents the Sacred Mystery in sound and vibration.

B is for bhakti, deep devotion and love for the Divine which softens even hearts of stone.

C is for culture, the beauty of Hindu music, fine arts, drama, dance, literature and architecture.

D is for dharma, which is righteousness, cosmic order and duty, leading us on the right path.

E is for Earth, our lovely blue planet, which we treat as sacred, protecting all its wonderful creatures.

F is for family, the precious cornerstone of Hindu life, culture, service and tradition.

G is for guru, our enlightened master who, knowing Truth himself, can guide us there.

H is for haṭha yoga, healthful physical science for vitality, energy-balancing and meditation.

I is for India, Bhārata, Mother-land to one-sixth of humanity, Holy Land for Hindus everywhere.

J is for japa, repetitive, prayerful mantras which quiet emotion and empower the mind.

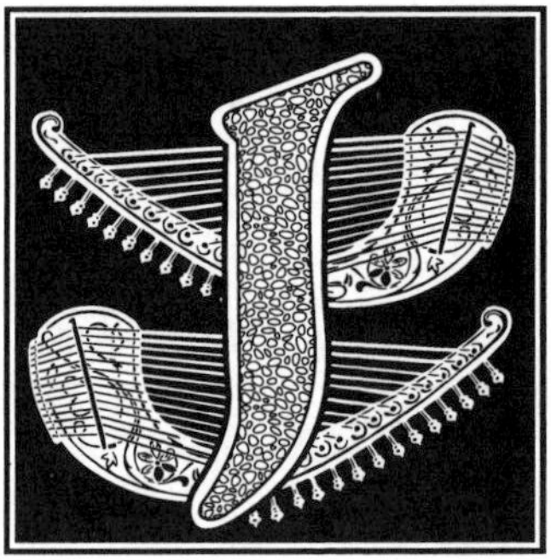

K is for karma, the law of cause and effect by which we determine our experience and destiny.

L is for lotus, the heart's inner shrine, where God dwells, ever serene, ever perfect.

M is for mauna, not talking, the inner silence known when words, thoughts and actions are stilled.

N is for non-attachment, the art of living the simple life, without too many needs or desires.

O is for open-mindedness, the Hindu's tolerant freedom of thought, inquiry and belief.

P is for pūjā, mystic worship of the Divine in our home shrine and holy temples and places.

Q is for quest, seeking to know, "Who am I? Where did I come from? Where am I going?"

R is for reincarnation, our immortal soul's journey from birth to rebirth. We do not fear death.

S is for saṁskāras, sacraments sanctifying life's passages: name-giving, marriage, death and more.

T is for tilaka, forehead marks worn in honor of our unique and varied lineages.

U is for utsava, our many home and temple festivals, full of bhakti, fun, feasting, and family sharing.

V is for Vedas, our oldest and holiest book, the word of God recorded in 100,000 Sanskṛit verses.

W is for wealth (artha), one of life's four goals, along with love, dharma and enlightenment.

X is for xerophily, the ability of certain plants and animals to thrive in India's hot, arid plains.

Y is for yoga, union of the soul with God which brings release from worldly bondage.

Z is for zeal, the fervor with which we perform service, go on pilgrimage and greet our holy religious leaders.

Five Precepts

Pañcha Śraddhā

पञ्चश्रद्धा

THESE FIVE ŚLOKAS CONSTITUTE THE MINIMAL HINDU BELIEFS. BY TEACHING THESE TO SONS AND DAUGHTERS, PARENTS WORLDWIDE PASS ON THE SANĀTANA DHARMA TO THEIR CHILDREN.

सर्व ब्रह्म 1. *Sarva Brahma:* God is All in all

The dear children are taught of one Supreme Being, all-pervasive, transcendent, creator, preserver, destroyer, manifesting in various forms, worshiped in all religions by many names, the immortal Self in all. They learn to be tolerant, knowing the soul's divinity and the unity of all mankind.

मन्दिर 2. *Mandira:* Holy Temples

The dear children are taught that God, other divine beings and highly evolved souls exist in unseen worlds. They learn to be devoted, knowing that temple worship, fire-ceremonies, sacraments and devotionals open channels for loving blessings, help and guidance from these beings.

कर्म 3. *Karma:* Cosmic Justice

The dear children are taught of *karma,* the divine law of cause and effect by which every thought, word and deed justly returns to them in this or a future life. They learn to be compassionate, knowing that each experience, good or bad, is the self-created reward of prior expressions of free will.

संसार मोक्ष 4. *Saṁsāra-Moksha:* Liberation

The dear children are taught that souls experience righteousness, wealth and pleasure in many births, while maturing spiritually. They learn to be fearless, knowing that all souls, without exception, will ultimately attain Self Realization, liberation from rebirth and union with God.

वेद गुरु 5. *Veda, Guru:* Scripture, Preceptor

The dear children are taught that God revealed the *Vedas* and *Āgamas,* which contain the eternal truths. They learn to be obedient, following the precepts of these sacred scriptures and awakened *satgurus,* whose guidance is absolutely essential for spiritual progress and enlightenment.

Five Practices

Pañcha Kriyā

पञ्चक्रिया

THESE FIVE ŚLOKAS OUTLINE THE MINIMAL HINDU PRACTICES THAT PARENTS TEACH THEIR CHILDREN IN ORDER TO NURTURE FUTURE CITIZENS WHO ARE STRONG, SECURE, RESPONSIBLE, TOLERANT AND TRADITIONAL.

उपासना 1. *Upāsanā:* Worship

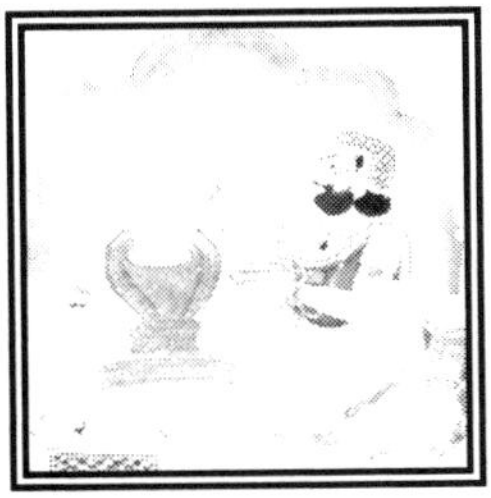

The dear children are taught daily worship in the family shrine room—rituals, disciplines, chants, *yogas* and religious study. They learn to be secure through devotion in home and temple, wearing traditional dress, bringing forth love of the Divine and preparing the mind for serene meditation.

उत्सव 2. *Utsava:* Holy Days

The dear children are taught to participate in Hindu festivals and holy days in the home and temple. They learn to be happy through sweet communion with God at such auspicious celebrations. *Utsava* includes fasting and attending the temple on Monday or Friday and other holy days.

धर्म 3. *Dharma:* Virtuous Living

The dear children are taught to live a life of duty and good conduct. They learn to be selfless by thinking of others first, being respectful of parents, elders and *swāmīs,* following divine law, especially *ahiṁsā,* mental, emotional and physical noninjury to all beings. Thus they resolve *karmas.*

तीर्थयात्रा 4. *Tīrthayātrā:* Pilgrimage

The dear children are taught the value of pilgrimage and are taken at least once a year for *darśana* of holy persons, temples and places, near or far. They learn to be detached by setting aside worldly affairs and making God, Gods and *gurus* life's singular focus during these journeys.

संस्कार 5. *Saṁskāra:* Rites of Passage

The dear children are taught to observe the many sacraments which mark and sanctify their passages through life. They learn to be traditional by celebrating the rites of birth, name-giving, head-shaving, first feeding, ear-piercing, first learning, coming of age, marriage and death.

Five Parenting Guidelines

Pañcha Kuṭumba Sādhana

पञ्चकुटुम्ब साधन

1. Good Conduct—*Dharmāchāra:* Loving fathers and mothers, knowing they are the greatest influence in a child's life, behave the way their dear children should when adults. They never anger or argue before young ones. Father in a *dhotī*, mother in a *sārī* at home, all sing to God, Gods and *guru*.

2. Home Worship—*Dharma Svagṛiha:* Loving fathers and mothers establish a separate shrine room in the home for God, Gods and guardian *devas* of the family. Ideally it should be large enough for all the dear children. It is a sacred place for scriptural study, a refuge from the *karmic* storms of life.

3. Talking About Religion—*Dharma Sambhāshana:* Loving fathers and mothers speak Vedic precepts while driving, eating and playing. This helps dear children understand experiences in right perspective. Parents know many worldly voices are blaring, and their *dharmic* voice must be stronger.

4. Continuing Self-Study—*Dharma Svādhyāya:* Loving fathers and mothers keep informed by studying the *Vedas*, *Āgamas* and sacred literature, listening to *swāmīs* and *paṇḍitas*. Youth face a world they will one day own, thus parents prepare their dear children to guide their own future progeny.

5. Following a Spiritual Preceptor—*Dharma Saṅga:* Loving fathers and mothers choose a preceptor, a traditional *satguru,* and lineage to follow. They support their lineage with all their heart, energy and service. He in turn provides them clear guidance for a successful life, material and religious.

Eight Rites of Passage

Ashṭa Saṁskāra

अष्टसंस्कार

SACRAMENTS ARE PERFORMED TO CELEBRATE AND SANCTIFY LIFE'S CRUCIAL JUNCTURES, INFORM FAMILY AND COMMUNITY, AND SECURE INNER-WORLD BLESSINGS. HERE ARE EIGHT OF THE ESSENTIAL RITES.

Nāmakaraṇa Saṁskāra
This is the Hindu name-giving ceremony, performed in the home or the temple 11 to 41 days after birth. The father whispers the auspicious new name in the infant's right ear.

Annaprāśana Saṁskāra
The first feeding of solid food is a sacred event performed by the father in the temple or home. The choice of food offered to a child at this crucial time is said to help forge his or her destiny.

Karṇavedha Saṁskāra
The ear-piercing ceremony, given to both boys and girls, performed in the temple or the home, generally on the child's first birthday. Health and wealth benefits derive from this ancient rite.

Chūḍākaraṇa Saṁskāra
The head is shaven and smeared with sandalwood paste in this rite performed in the temple or home before age four. It is a very happy day for the child. The shaven head denotes purity and egolessness.

Vidyārambha Saṁskāra
The official beginning of primary education. In this rite, performed in the home or temple, the child scribes his or her first letter of the alphabet in a tray of unbroken, uncooked, saffron rice.

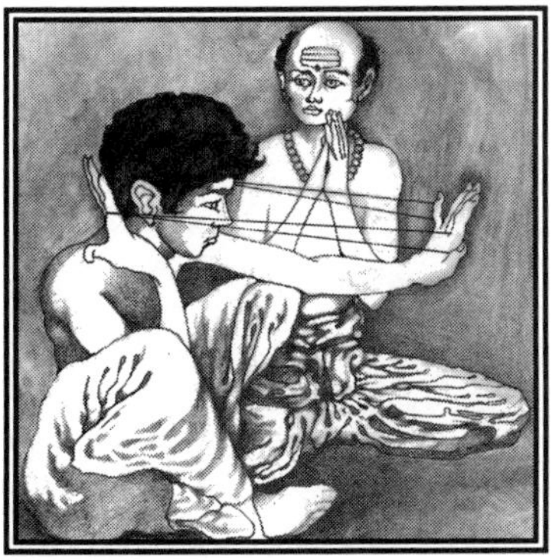

Upanayana Saṁskāra
The ceremonial investment of the "sacred thread" and inititation into Vedic study, performed in the home or temple, usually between the ages of 9 and 15, after which a youth is considered "twice born."

Vivāha Saṁskāra
The marriage ceremony, performed in a temple or wedding hall around the sacred *homa* fire. Lifetime vows, Vedic prayers and seven steps before God and Gods consecrate the union of husband and wife.

Antyeshṭi Saṁskāra
The funeral rite includes preparation of the body, cremation, home-cleansing and dispersal of ashes. The purifying fire releases the soul from this world that it may journey unhindered to the next.

Conclusion

Nirvahaṇa

निर्वहण

THERE IS NO COMING. THERE IS NO GOING. YOU AND I ARE EVER ONE. REMAIN SILENT AND KNOW THE SELF WITHIN. YOU WON'T FIND IT in books. You will find it deep within yourself, my *satguru* said. So, *Dancing with Śiva* is a signpost to point the way. It is a map to give direction. And it is five months of daily *sādhana*, reading one *śloka* a day, at night just before sleep, to remold the subconscious memory patterns of the base subjective mind into a brand new you. The wisdom of the *Vedas* will be yours when the old *saṁskāras* no longer fight with the new. The old impressions of how you were raised, whom and what you were taught to like and dislike will be erased by the eternal wisdom of the *Vedas* and *Āgamas*, amplified by the explanations above the verses in each of these daily lessons. All this will bring you new life and new hope. It will bring you solace, contentment and a deep, inner, growing knowledge of the creation of this universe, its preservation and dissolution. It will show you that, yes, you are the center of the universe, the Self, the infinite and supreme Paraśiva. With this goal well in mind, you will persist in working out the patterns of the past, living in the eternal present while being selective in the new patterns you create in the future. As you dance with Śiva from life to life, live with Śiva from life to life, and slowly merge with Śiva, you yourself will fulfill from within yourself the proclamations of the *ṛishis* who spoke forth the *Vedas*, the oldest scripture on our planet. You yourself will find, follow and in joyous discovery fulfill the path which all knowers of God tread. Aum Namaḥ Śivāya!

Lexicon

Śabda Kośa

शब्दकोश

aadheenam: ஆதீனம் "Ownership, possession, dependence; Śaiva monastery." A Śaivite Hindu monastery-temple complex in the South Indian, Śaiva Siddhānta tradition, as in "Dharmapuram Aadheenam." Also also known as *maṭha* or *pīṭha,* as in Kailāsa Pīṭha. The *aadheenam* head, or pontiff, is called the *guru mahāsannidhānam* or *aadheenakartar.*

ābhāsa: आभास "Shining out; manifestation, emanation." The means by which Śiva creates out of Himself, a concept central to monistic schools. See: *emanation, tattva.*

abhaya: अभय Fearlessness, one of the cardinal virtues. "Fearlessness is the fruit of perfect Self Realization—that is, the recovery of nonduality" *(Bṛihadāraṇyaka Upanishad* 1.4.2). Also names the *mudrā* (hand pose) common in Hindu icons, betokening "fear not," in which the fingers of the right hand are raised and the palm faces forward. See: *mudrā, mūrti.*

Abhinavagupta: अभिनवगुप्त Kashmīr Śaivite *guru* (ca 950–1015) scholar and adept in the lineage of Vasugupta. Among his philosophical writings, *Pratyabhijñā Vimarshiṇī* and *Tantrāloka* are an important basis of Kashmīr Śaivism. Also an influential theoretician of poetics, dance, drama and classical music, he is said to have disappeared into a cave near Mangam along with 1,200 disciples. See: *Kashmīr Śaivism.*

abhisheka: अभिषेक "Sprinkling; ablution." Ritual bathing of the Deity's image with water, curd, milk, honey, *ghee,* rosewater, etc. A special form of *pūjā* prescribed by Āgamic injunction. Also performed in the inauguration of religious and political monarchs and other special blessings. See: *pūjā.*

abhor (abhorrence): To detest, hate or find disgusting or repulsive and hence to pull back or shrink from.

abide: To stand firm, remain as one is. Not abandoning principles or qualities of character even in the face of difficulties.

abjuration: Renunciation, giving up by oath, as a *sannyāsin* gives up family life. See: *sannyāsa dharma.*

ablution: A washing of the body, especially as a religious ceremony.

abode: Home. Place where one lives or stays.

abortion: The deliberate termination of pregnancy. From the earliest times,

Hindu tradition and scriptures condemn the practice, except when the mother's life is in danger. It is considered an act against *ṛita* and *ahiṁsā*. Hindu mysticism teaches that the fetus is a living, conscious person, needing and deserving protection (a *Ṛig Vedic* hymn [7.36.9, RvP, 2469] begs for protection of fetuses). The *Kaushītakī Upanishad* (3.1 UpR, 774) describes abortion as equivalent to killing one's parents. The *Atharva Veda* (6.113.2 HE, 43) lists the fetus slayer, *brūnaghni*, among the greatest of sinners (6.113.2). The *Gautama Dharma Śāstra* (3.3.9 HD, 214) considers such participants to have lost caste. The *Suśruta Saṁhitā*, a medical treatise (ca 100), stipulates what is to be done in case of serious problems during delivery *(Chikitsāsthāna* Chapter, *Mūḍhagarbha*), describing first the various steps to be taken to attempt to save both mother and child. "If the fetus is alive, one should attempt to remove it from the womb of the mother alive..." (sūtra 5). If it is dead, it may be removed. In case the fetus is alive but cannot be safely delivered, surgical removal is forbidden for "one would harm both mother and offspring. In an irredeemable situation, it is best to cause the miscarriage of the fetus, for no means must be neglected which can prevent the loss of the mother" (sūtras 10-11).

Absolute: Lower case (absolute): real, not dependent on anything else, not relative. Upper case (Absolute): Ultimate Reality, the unmanifest, unchanging and transcendent Paraśiva—utterly nonrelational to even the most subtle level of consciousness. It is the Self God, the essence of man's soul. Same as *Absolute Being* and *Absolute Reality.* **—absolutely real:** A quality of God Śiva in all three perfections: Paraśiva, Parāśakti and Parameśvara. As such, He is uncreated, unchanging, unevolutionary. See: *Parameśvara, Parāśakti, Paraśiva.*

absolution (to absolve): Forgiveness. A freeing from guilt so as to relieve someone from obligation or penalty. **—atone:** to compensate or make up for a wrongdoing. *Atonement* can only be done by the person himself, while *absolution* is granted by others, such as a family head, judge or jury. *Exoneration,* the taking away of all blame and all personal *karmic* burden, can only be given by God Śiva. Society would naturally acknowledge and accept this inner transformation by forgiving and forgetting. See: *penance, sin.*

absorption: To take in and make part of an existent whole. Known in Sanskṛit as *saṁhāra,* absorption is one of God's five powers (*pañchakṛitya*), synonymous with *destruction* or *dissolution*, but with no negative or frightful implications. All form issues from God and eventually returns to Him. See: *Maheśvara, Naṭarāja.*

abstain: To hold oneself back, to refrain from or do without. To avoid a desire, negative action or habit. See: *yama-niyama.*

abyss: A bottomless pit. The dark states of consciousness into which one may fall as a result of serious misbehavior; the seven *chakras* (psychic centers), or *talas* (realms of consciousness), below the *mūlādhāra chakra,* which is located at the base of the spine. See: *chakra, Naraka, loka.*

accelerate: To increase the speed of a thing; to intensify its rate of progress.

accordant: In agreement or harmony with.

āchāra: **आचार** "Conduct, mode of action, behavior; good conduct." Also, custom, tradition; rule of conduct, precept.

āchārya: **आचार्य** A highly respected teacher. The wise one who practices what he preaches. A title generally bestowed through *dīkshā* and ordination, such as in the Śivāchārya priest tradition. See: *dīkshā.*

acosmic pantheism: "No-cosmos, all-is-God doctrine." A Western philosophical term for the philosophy of Śaṅkara. It is *acosmic* in that it views the world, or cosmos, as ultimately unreal, and *pantheistic* because it teaches that God (Brahman) is all of existence. See: *Śaṅkara, shaḍ darśana.*

actinic: Spiritual, creating light. From the Greek *aktis,* meaning "ray." Of or pertaining to consciousness in its pure, unadulterated state. Describes the extremely rarified superconscious realm of pure *bindu,* of quantum strings, the substratum of consciousness, *śuddha māyā,* from which light first originates. *Actinic* is the adjective form of *actinism,* defined in the *Oxford English Dictionary* as: "1) the radiation of heat or light, or that branch of philosophy that treats of it; 2) that property or force in the sun's rays by which chemical changes are produced, as in photography." See: *actinodic, kalā, kośa, odic, tattva.*

actinodic: Spiritual-magnetic. Describes consciousness within *śuddhāśuddha māyā,* which is a mixture of odic and actinic force, the spectrum of the *ājñā chakra,* and to a certain degree the *viśuddha chakra.* See: *tattva.*

adept: Highly skilled; expert. In religion, one who has mastered certain spiritual practices or disciplines. An advanced *yogī.*

adharma: **अधर्म** Opposite of *dharma.* Thoughts, words or deeds that transgress divine law. Unrighteousness, irreligiousness; demerit. See: *dharma, pāpa, sin.*

adhere: To remain attached or faithful, as to a leader, society, principle, etc.

adhyātma: **अध्यात्म** "Spiritual; soul." The inner, spiritual self or spirit. See: *ātman.*

adhyātma prasāra: **अध्यात्मप्रसार** "Spiritual evolution." The gradual maturation of the soul body, *ānandamaya kośa,* through many lives. *Prasāra* means, "coming forth, spreading; advance, progress. See: *evolution of the soul.*

adhyātma vikāsa: **अध्यात्मविकास** "Spiritual unfoldment." The blossoming of inner or higher *(adhi),* soul *(ātma)* qualities as a result of religious striving, *sādhana. Vikāsa* means, "becoming visible, shining forth, manifestation opening," as a flower unfolds its petals, or the *chakras* unfold theirs as a result of *kuṇḍalinī* awakening. See: *spiritual unfoldment.*

Ādi Granth: **आदिग्रन्थ** "First book." The central Sikh scripture, compiled 1603–1604 from the writings of Sikh, Moslem and Hindu holy men, most importantly the beautiful hymns of adoration, called *Japjī,* by Guru Nānak, the first Sikh Guru. In 1699, Gobind Singh, the tenth preceptor, decreed that the living succession would end with him, and this scripture would henceforth serve as Sikhism's *guru.* Its eloquent teachings are in harmony with Hinduism, but for the rejection of the *Vedas* and disavowal of image worship and caste. The *Ādi Granth* is enshrined in all Sikh temples *(gurudwaras).* See: *Sikhism.*

Ādinātha: **आदिनाथ** "First Lord." A sage considered the first great preceptor (date unknown) of the Ādinātha Sampradāya, a teaching tradition embodied in the Siddha Siddhānta sect of Śaivism. See: *Śaivism, Nātha.*

Ādinātha Sampradāya: **आदिनाथसंप्रदाय** See: *Nātha Sampradāya.*

Ādiśaiva: **आदिशैव** A hereditary priest and teacher of the South Indian Śaiva Siddhānta tradition; Śaivite *brāhmins* descended from the *gotras* of five *ṛishis* and who alone are entitled to conduct rites in Āgamic Śiva temples. *Ādiśaiva* and *Śivāchārya* are synonyms for this hereditary priest lineage. See: *Śivāchārya.*

adopt: To take an idea, principle, or even a religion and henceforth live with it and use it as one's own. See: *conversion to Hinduism.*

adore: To love greatly; to worship as divine. See: *pūjā.*

adorn: To put on ornaments or decorations to make more beautiful, attractive or distinguished. See: *kalā-64.*

adṛishṭa: **अदृष्ट** "Unseen potency; destiny." The unseen power of one's past *karma* influencing the present life. This power is known in the West as fate or destiny, generally not cognized as being of one's own making, but misunderstood as a mysterious, uncontrollable cosmic force. See: *karma, fate.*

adulate: To praise or admire greatly, even too much.

adultery: Sexual intercourse between a married man and a woman not his wife, or between a married woman and a man not her husband. Adultery is spoken of in Hindu *śāstras* as a serious breach of *dharma.* See: *sexuality.*

advaita: **अद्वैत** "Non dual; not two." Nonduality or monism. The philosophical doctrine that Ultimate Reality consists of a one principle substance, or God. Opposite of *dvaita,* dualism. Advaita is the primary philosophical stance of the Vedic *Upanishads,* and of Hinduism, interpreted differently by the many *ṛishis, gurus, paṇḍitas* and philosophers. See: *dvaita-advaita, Vedānta.*

Advaita Īśvaravāda: **अद्वैत ईश्वरवाद** "Nondual and Personal-God-as-Ruler doctrine." The Sanskṛit equivalent of *monistic theism.* A general term that describes the philosophy of the *Vedas* and *Śaiva Āgamas,* which believes simultaneously in the ultimate oneness of all things and in the reality of the personal Deity. See: *Advaita, Advaita Siddhānta, monistic theism.*

Advaita Īśvaravādin: **अद्वैत ईश्वरवादिन्** A follower of Advaita Īśvaravāda.

Advaita Siddhānta: **अद्वैत सिद्धान्त** "Nondual perfect conclusions." Śaivite philosophy codified in the *Āgamas* which has at its core the nondual (*advaitic*) identity of God, soul and world. This monistic-theistic philosophy, unlike the Śaṅkara, or Smārta view, holds that *māyā* (the principle of manifestation) is not an obstacle to God Realization, but God's own power and presence guiding the soul's evolution to perfection. While Advaita Vedānta stresses *Upanishadic* philosophy, Advaita Siddhānta adds to this a strong emphasis on internal and external worship, *yoga sādhanas* and *tapas. Advaita Siddhānta* is a term used in South India to distinguish Tirumular's school from the pluralistic Siddhānta of Meykandar and Aghoraśiva. This unified Vedic-Āgamic doctrine is also known as *Śuddha Śaiva Siddhānta.* It is the philosophy of this contemporary Hindu catechism. See: *Advaita Īśvaravāda, dvaita-advaita, monistic theism, Śaiva Siddhānta.*

Advaita Vedānta: **अद्वैत वेदान्त** "Nondual end (or essence) of the *Vedas.*" Names the monistic schools, most prominently that of Śaṅkara, that arose from the *Upanishads* and related texts. See: *Vedānta.*

adversity: A condition of misfortune, poverty or difficulty.

advocate: To write or speak in support of an idea, action or practice.

affirmation: *Dṛidhavāchana* ("firm statement"). A positive declaration or assertion. A statement repeated regularly while concentrating on the meaning and mental images invoked, often used to attain a desired result.

affirmation of faith: A brief statement of one's faith and essential beliefs. See: *anbe Sivamayam Satyame Parasivam.*

aftermath: A result or consequence of a happening. The events or repercussions following an experience.

Āgama: **आगम** "That which has come down." An enormous collection of Sanskṛit scriptures which, along with the *Vedas,* are revered as *śruti* (revealed scripture). Dating is uncertain. They were part of an oral tradition of unknown antiquity which some experts consider as ancient as the earliest *Vedas,* 5000 to 6000 BCE. The *Āgamas* are the primary source and authority for ritual, *yoga* and temple construction. Each of the major denominations—Śaivism, Vaishṇavism and Śāktism—has its unique *Āgama* texts. Smārtas recognize the *Āgamas,* but don't necessarily adhere to them and rely mainly on the *smṛiti* texts. See: *Śaiva Āgamas, śruti.*

Agastya: **अगस्त्य** One of 18 celebrated Śaiva *siddhas* (adepts), and accepted as the first grammarian of Tamil language. He is said to have migrated from North India to the South. His name appears in the *Mahābhārata, Rāmāyaṇa* and the *Purāṇas* and was known to ancient Indonesians. See: *siddha.*

Aghora: **अघोर** "Nonterrifying." An aspect of Śiva which, like Rudra, is the personification of His power of dissolution or reabsorption. *Ghora* means "terrific, frightful, terrible, etc." See: *Sadāśiva.*

Aghoraśiva: **अघोरशिव** A Śaivite philosopher of South India who in the 12th century founded a Siddhānta school emphasizing dualistic passages of the *Āgamas* and other early texts. The later Meykandar pluralistic philosophy is based partly on Aghoraśiva's teachings. See: *dvaita-advaita, dvaita Siddhānta, Śaiva Siddhānta.*

***Aghorī:* अघोरी** "Nonterrifying." An order of Śaiva ascetics thought to be derived from the Kāpālika order (ca 14th century). Following the *vāmāchāra,* "left-hand ritual of the *tantras,*" they are widely censured for radical practices such as living in cemeteries and using human skulls as eating bowls.

***agni:* अग्नि** "Fire." 1) One of the five elements, *pañchabhūta.* 2) God of the element fire, invoked through Vedic ritual known as *yajña, agnikāraka, homa* and *havana.* The God *Agni* is the divine messenger who receives prayers and oblations and conveys them to the heavenly spheres. See: *yajña.*

***agnihotra:* अग्निहोत्र** "Fire sacrifice." Household rite traditionally performed daily, in which an oblation of milk is sprinkled on the fire. See: *yajña.*

***agnikāraka:* अग्निकारक** "Fire ritual." The *Āgamic* term for *yajña.* See: *yajña.*

***Aham Brahmāsmi:* अहं ब्रह्मास्मि** "I am God." Famous phrase often repeated in the *Upanishads.* In this ecstatic statement of enlightenment, "I" does not refer to the individuality or outer nature, but to the essence of the soul which is ever identical to God Śiva (or Brahman, the Supreme Being) as Satchidānanda and Paraśiva. One of four Upanishadic "great sayings," *mahāvākya.*

***ahaṁkāra:* अहंकार** "I-maker." Personal ego. The mental faculty of individuation; sense of duality and separateness from others. Sense of I-ness, "me" and "mine." *Ahaṁkāra* is characterized by the sense of I-ness *(abhimāna),* sense of mine-ness, identifying with the body *(madīyam),* planning for one's own happiness *(mamasukha),* brooding over sorrow *(mamaduḥkha),* and possessiveness *(mama idam).* See: *āṇava, ego, mind (individual).*

***ahiṁsā:* अहिंसा** "Noninjury," nonviolence or nonhurtfulness. Refraining from causing harm to others, physically, mentally or emotionally. *Ahiṁsā* is the first and most important of the *yamas* (restraints). It is the cardinal virtue upon which all others depend. See: *yama-niyama.*

***aikya:* ऐक्य** "Union, oneness." See: *Vīra Śaivism.*

***Aitareya Brāhmaṇa:* ऐतरेयब्राह्मण** Part of the *Ṛig Veda* dealing principally with worship and ceremonies of royal inauguration. See: *Ṛig Veda, Vedas.*

***Aitareya Upanishad:* ऐतरेय उपनिषद्** Three chapters of the *Aitareya Āraṇyaka* of the *Ṛig Veda* expounding the esoterics of ritual, revealing the means of preparing oneself for the deepest spiritual attainments.

***Ajita Āgama:* अजित आगम** Among the 28 *Śaiva Siddhānta Āgamas,* this scripture especially elucidates temple construction, worship and rules for installation of various Śiva icons *(mūrti).* See: *mūrti, Śaiva Āgamas.*

***ājñā chakra:* आज्ञाचक्र** "Command wheel." The third-eye center. See: *chakra.*

***ākāśa:* आकाश** "Space." The sky. Free, open space. Ether, the fifth and most subtle of the five elements—earth, air, fire, water and ether. Empirically, the rarified space or ethereal fluid plasma that pervades the universes, inner and outer. Esoterically, mind, the superconscious strata holding all that exists and all that potentially exists, wherein all happenings are recorded and can be read by clairvoyants. It is through psychic entry into this transcendental *ākāśa* that cosmic knowledge is gathered, and the entire circle of time—past, present and future—can be known. Space, *ākāśa,* in this concept is a positive substance, filled with unseen energies and intelligences, in contrast with the Western conception that space is the absence of everything and is therefore nothing in and of itself. The *Advayatāraka Upanishad* (2.1.17) describes five levels of *ākāśa* which can be *yogically* experienced: *guṇa rahita ākāśa* (space devoid of qualities); *parama ākāśa* (supreme space), *mahā ākāśa* (great space), *tattva ākāśa* (space of true existence) and *sūrya ākāśa* (space of the sun). See: *mind (universal).*

akshata: **अक्षत** "Unbroken." Unmilled, uncooked rice, often mixed with turmeric, offered as a sacred substance during *pūjā,* or in blessings for individuals at weddings and other ceremonies. This, the very best food, is the finest offering a devotee can give to God or a wife can give to her husband. See: *pūjā.*

Allama Prabhu: **अल्लमप्रभु** A contemporary of *Basavaṇṇa* and central figure of Vīra Śaivism (ca 1150), the head of an order of 300 enlightened beings which included 60 women. Initially a temple drummer, he became an extraordinary *siddha,* mystic and poet. The *Mantra Gopya* are his collected writings. See: *Basavaṇṇa, Vīra Śaivism.*

allegory: A story in which the character, places and events have symbolic meaning, used to teach ideas and moral principles. See: *Itihāsa, Purāṇa.*

all-pervasive: Diffused throughout or existing in every part of the universe. See: *Satchidānanda.*

aloof: Distant, reserved, withdrawn, drawn back; cool in attitude, not sympathetic with or interested in an idea, project or group of people.

altruistic: Unselfish. Showing more concern for others than oneself.

Alvar: ஆழ்வார் "One who rules the Lord through bhakti." A group of renowned saints of the Vaishṇava religion (7th–9th century), devotional mystics whose lives and teachings catalyzed to a resurgence of Vaishṇavism in Tamil Nadu. Their devotional poems are embodied in the *Nalayiram Divya Prabandham,* containing about 4,000 hymns. Among the 12 most famous Alvars are Poykai, Pudam, Tirumalisai, Nammalvar, Kulaśekhara, Andal, Tiruppan and Tirumangai. A term not to be confused with *Nalvar,* naming the four Samayāchārya Śaivite saints: Appar, Sundarar, Sambandar and Manikkavasagar, who were their contemporaries. See: *Nalvar, Nayanar.*

Āmardaka Order: **आमर्दक** An order of *Śaiva sannyāsins* founded by Āmardaka Tīrthanātha in Andhra Pradesh (ca 775).

Āmardaka Tīrthanātha: **आमर्दक तीर्थनाथ** See: *Āmardaka Order.*

Ambikā: **अम्बिका** "Mother." A benign form of the Goddess, one of the central Deities of the Śākta religion, along with Durgā, Kālī and Pārvatī. See: *Śakti.*

amends: To make amends, to make up for injury or loss that one has caused to another. This is done through sincere apology, expressing contrition, public penance, such as *kavadi,* and the abundant giving of gifts. See: *pāpa, penance.*

amid (amidst, amongst): In the middle of, among.

Amman: அம்மன் "Mother." Usually refers to Mariyamman, the "smallpox Goddess," protectress from plagues, a popular *grāmadevatā* ("village Deity" or tutelary Deity of a locale). There are many Mariyamman temples and shrines in Malaysia, Mauritius and rural areas of South India. In the Tamil tradition, *amman* is often appended to the names of various Goddesses, as in Kālī Amman or Draupadī Amman (deified heroine of the *Mahābhārata*). One of the distinguishing features of *grāmadevatā* shrines is that they are not served by *brāhmin* priests. See: *Śakti, Śāktism.*

amorphous: Of no definite shape or form. See: *formless.*

amṛitātman: अमृतात्मन् "Immortal soul." See: *ātman, jīva, purusha, soul.*

amṛita: अमृत "Immortality." Literally, "without death *(mṛita)*." The nectar of divine bliss which flows down from the *sahasrāra chakra* when one enters very deep states of meditation. This word is apparently the source of the Greek *amrotos*, the ambrosia, food or drink, of the Gods, which has its Vedic equivalent in the legendary elixir called *soma,* a central element in Vedic rites in which it is venerated as a Divinity.

anāhata chakra: अनाहतचक्र "Wheel of unstruck [sound]." The heart center. See: *chakra.*

analogy: An explanation of a thing made by comparing it point by point with another thing. For example, in the analogy of the potter, the potter represents God and the clay represents the primal substance, or "matter."

analytical: Prone to looking closely at things, intellectually studying them to understand their nature, meaning and component parts.

ānanda: आनन्द "Bliss." The pure joy—ecstasy or enstasy—of God-consciousness or spiritual experience. In its highest sense, *ānanda* is expressed in the famous Vedic description of God: *sat-chit-ānanda,* "existence-consciousness-bliss"—the divine or superconscious mind of all souls. See: *God consciousness, God Realization, Satchidānanda.*

ānandamaya kośa: आनन्दमयकोश "Bliss body." The body of the soul, which ultimately merges with Śiva. See: *soul, kośa.*

ānanda tāṇḍava: आनन्दताण्डव "Violent dance of bliss." See: *Naṭarāja, tāṇḍava.*

āṇava mala: आणवमल "Impurity of smallness; finitizing principle." The individualizing veil of duality that enshrouds the soul. It is the source of finitude and ignorance, the most basic of the three bonds *(āṇava, karma, māyā)* which temporarily limit the soul. *Āṇava mala* has the same importance in Āgamic philosophy that *māyā-avidyā* has in Vedāntic philosophy. The presence of *āṇava mala* is what causes the misapprehension about the nature of God, soul and world, the notion of being separate and distinct from God and the universe. *Āṇava* obscures the natural wisdom, light, unity and humility of the soul and allows spiritual ignorance, darkness, egoity and pride to manifest. It is inherent in a maturing soul, like the shell of a seed. When *āṇava* is ripe, *anugraha,* "grace," comes, and *āṇava* falls away. *Āṇava* is the root *mala* and the last bond to be dissolved. See: *evolution of the soul, grace, mala, soul.*

āṇavopāya: **आणवोपाय** "Minute or individual means." See: *upāya.*

Anbe Sivamayam Satyame Parasivaṁ: அன்பே சிவமயம் சத்தியமே பரசிவம் Tamil for "God Śiva is Immanent Love and transcendent Reality." The affirmation of faith which capsulizes the entire creed of the monistic Śaiva Siddhāntin. In the Sanskṛit language it is *Premaiva Śivamaya, Satyam eva Paraśivaḥ.*

anchorite: "Hermit." A monk or aspirant who lives alone and apart from society, as contrasted with *cenobite,* a member of a religious order living in a monastery or convent. See: *monk, nunk.*

ancillary: Auxiliary. Aiding or supporting. Supplementary; secondary.

Andal: ஆண்டாள் Famed Vaishṇava saint of Tamil Nadu. One of the Alvars, she lived in the early 9th century and today is venerated as one of South India's greatest *bhakta* poetesses. See: *Alvar, Vaishṇavism.*

Andhra Pradesh (Pradeśa): **आन्ध्रप्रदेश** Modern Indian state located on the southeast coast of India north of Tamil Nadu. The capital is Hyderabad. Language: Telegu. Dominant faith: Vaishṇavism. Area: 106,000 square miles. Population 54 million. Famous for its opulent Tirupati Vaishṇava temple.

anekavāda: **अनेकवाद्** "Pluralism," or "not-one theology." See: *pluralism.*

anekavādin: **अनेकवादिन्** A follower of *anekavāda.*

anew: Again.

aṅga: **अङ्ग** "Part; limb." Term for the individual soul in Vīra Śaivism. The *aṅga* is of finite intelligence, while Śiva is of infinite intelligence. See: *Vīra Śaivism.*

aniconic: "Without likeness; without image." When referring to a Deity image, *aniconic* denotes a symbol which does not attempt an anthropomorphic (humanlike) or representational likeness. An example is the Śivaliṅga, "mark of God." See: *mūrti, Śivaliṅga.*

animate-inanimate: From the Latin *animatus,* "to make alive, fill with breath." These terms indicate the two poles of manifest existence, that which has movement and life (most expressly animals and other "living" beings) and that which is devoid of movement (such as minerals and, to a lesser degree, plants). From a deeper view, however, all existence is alive with movement and possessed of the potent, divine energy of the cosmos. See: *tattva.*

añjali mudrā: **अञ्जलिमुद्रा** "Reverence gesture." Also called *praṇāmāñjali.* A gesture of respect and greeting, in which the two palms are held softly together and slightly cupped. Often accompanied by the verbal salutation "*namaskāra,*" meaning "reverent salutation." The *añjali mudrā* has various forms, including held near the chest in greeting equals, at eye level in greeting one's *guru,* and above the head in salutation to God. One form is with the open hands placed side by side, as if by a beggar to receive food, or a worshiper beseeching God's grace in the temple. See: *mudrā, namaskāra.*

aṅkuśa: **अंकुश** Goad, symbol of Lord Gaṇeśa's power to remove obstacles from the devotee's path, and to spur the dullards onward.

annamaya kośa: **अन्नमयकोश** "Food sheath." The physical body. See: *kośa.*

annaprāśana: **अन्नप्राशन** "Feeding." The childhood sacrament of first solid food. See: *saṁskāras of childhood.*

annihilate: To destroy completely, to reduce to nothing.

antagonism: Opposition, hostility.

antaḥkaraṇa: **अन्तःकरण** "Inner faculty." The mental faculty of the astral body, *manomaya kośa,* comprising intellect, instinct and ego—in Sanskṛit, *buddhi, manas* and *ahaṁkāra*—which are a three-fold expression of *chitta,* consciousness. *Chitta* is sometimes listed as a *tattva,* or part of a *tattva,* at the Prakṛiti level, in Śaiva Siddhānta. In Vedānta, *chitta,* "mind stuff," is often understood as a part of *antaḥkaraṇa;* while in the Śaiva Siddhānta, Yoga and Sāṅkhya Darśanas, it is generally viewed as the total mind, of which *manas, buddhi* and *ahaṁkāra* are the inner faculties. Thus, while Vedānta describes *antaḥkaraṇa* as four-fold, Sāṅkhya and Yoga discuss it as three-fold. Siddha Siddhānta views *antaḥkaraṇa* as five-fold, with the inclusion of *chaitanya* as "higher consciousness." See: *consciousness, mind (individual), tattva.*

Antarloka: **अन्तर्लोक** "Inner or in-between world." The astral plane. See: *loka.*

anthology: A choice collection of prose or poetry excerpts.

antyaśabda: **अन्त्यशब्द** "Final word." Colophon.

antyeshṭi: **अन्त्येष्टि** "Last rites." Funeral. See: *death, saṁskāra.*

anu: **अनु** A common prefix conveying the meanings: "after, near to, under, secondary or subordinate to."

anubhava: **अनुभव** "Perception, apprehension; experience." Personal experience; understanding; impressions on the mind not derived from memory.

anugraha śakti: **अनुग्रहशक्ति** "Graceful or favoring power." Revealing grace. God Śiva's power of illumination, through which the soul is freed from the bonds of *āṇava, karma* and *māyā* and ultimately attains liberation, *moksha.* Specifically, *anugraha* descends on the soul as *śaktipāta,* the *dīkshā* (initiation) from a *satguru. Anugraha* is a key concept in Śaiva Siddhānta. It comes when *āṇava mala,* the shell of finitude which surrounds the soul, reaches a state of ripeness, *malaparipāka.* See: *āṇava, grace, Naṭarāja, śaktipāta.*

anukramaṇī: **अनुक्रमणी** "Succession, arrangement." A table of contents.

anupāya: **अनुपाय** "Without means." A term used in Kashmīr Śaivism to mean spontaneous Self Realization without effort. See: *upāya.*

anxiety: State of uneasiness, worry or apprehension. See: *manas.*

Apasmārapurusha: **अपस्मारपुरुष** "Forgetful person." The soul under Śiva's foot of obscuring grace, depicted in numerous icons. He represents ignorance and heedlessness. (Sometimes simply *Apasmāra.*) See: *Naṭarāja.*

apatya: **अपत्य** "Offspring; child; descendant."

apex: Highest point, peak.

apex of creation: The highest or initial movement in the mind that will eventually manifest a creation. The quantum level of manifestation. See: *microcosm-macrocosm, quantum, tattva.*

Appar: அப்பர் "Father." Endearing name for Tirunavukarasu (ca 700), one of four Tamil saints, Samayāchāryas, who reconverted errant Śaivites who had embraced Jainism. Calling himself the servant of God's servants, he composed magnificent hymns in praise of Śiva that are reverently sung to this day. See: *Nalvar, Nayanar, Śaiva Siddhānta.*

apparent: Appearing, but not necessarily real or true. Seeming to be.

Appaya Dīkshita: अप्पयदीक्षित Philosophical genius of South India (1554-1626) who worked to reconcile Vaishṇavism and Śaivism, advancing the Śiva Advaita school of Śaivism by his writings, and bolstering other schools by his brilliant summations of their philosophies. He is best known for his commentaries on the teachings of Śrīkaṇṭha. Appaya Dīkshita also created a manual of Śaiva temple ritual still in use today. See: *Śiva Advaita.*

apprehend: To mentally seize and hold, to see or understand; to physically detain.

Āraṇyaka: आरण्यक "Forest treatise." Third section of each of the four *Vedas.* Texts containing esoteric, mystical knowledge, largely on the inner meanings and functions of the Vedic *yajña,* or fire ceremonies. See: *Vedas.*

ārati: आरती "Light." The circling or waving of a lamp—usually fed with *ghee,* camphor or oil—before a holy person or the temple Deity at the high point of *pūjā.* The flame is then presented to the devotees, each passing his or her hands through it and bringing them to the eyes three times, thereby receiving the blessings. *Āratī* can also be performed as the briefest form of *pūjā.* See: *archana, pūjā.*

Arbhuta Tiru Antadi: அற்புதத் திரு அந்தாதி A poem of 100 verses in praise of Lord Śiva composed in Tamil by the woman Saint Karaikkal Ammaiyar (ca 5th century). See: *Nayanar.*

archana: अर्चन A special, personal, abbreviated *pūjā* done by temple priests in which the name, birthstar and family lineage of a devotee are recited to invoke individual guidance and blessings. *Archana* also refers to chanting the names of the Deity, which is a central part of every *pūjā. See: pūjā.*

Ardhanārī Naṭeśvara Stotram: अर्धनारीनटेश्वरस्तोत्रम् A short hymn alternately praising Śiva and Śakti as merged in the androgynous image of Ardhanārīśvara. See: *Ardhanārīśvara.*

Ardhanārīśvara: अर्धनारीश्वर "Half-female Lord." Lord Śiva in androgynous form, male on the right side and female on the left, indicating that: 1) Śiva (like all Mahādevas) is genderless; 2) Śiva is All, inseparable from His energy, Śakti; 3) in Śiva the *iḍā* (feminine) and the *piṅgalā* (masculine) *nāḍīs* (psychic nerve currents) are balanced so that *sushumṇā* is ever active. The meditator who balances these through *sādhana* and *yoga* becomes like Śiva.

In the unity of Ardhanārīśvara all opposites are reconciled; duality vanishes back into the one source. This icon especially represents Śiva's second perfection: Pure Consciousness (Satchidānanda or Parāśakti). See: *kuṇḍalinī, nāḍī, Śakti, Śiva.*

Ārdrā Darśana: **आर्द्रादर्शन** A ten-day festival ending on Ārdrā *nakshatra,* near the full moon of December-January honoring Śiva Naṭarāja. In Tamil Nadu, each morning at 4 AM, the mystical songs of Saint Manikkavasagar, *Tiruvembavai,* are sung or recited. Unmarried girls to go to the temple in small groups to pray for rains, for the welfare of the land and for fine, spiritual husbands. At the famed temple of Chidambaram in Tamil Nadu, Lord Naṭarāja, the presiding Deity, is taken out for a grand procession in a chariot pulled through the streets by thousands of devotees. See: *darśana, Naṭarāja.*

arduous: Strenuous, laborious. Difficult to climb, do or accomplish.

arena: Any place where an event, usually involving struggle or conflict, takes place. The earth is the arena of the soul's evolution. See: *evolution of the soul.*

Aristotle: Greek philosopher (384–322 BCE) who left a profound legacy of writings on metaphysics, ethics, logic and law. A disciple of Plato.

ārjava: **आर्जव** "Steadfastness." See: *yama-niyama.*

Arjuna: **अर्जुन** A hero of the *Mahābhārata* and central figure of the *Bhagavad Gītā.* See: *Bhagavad Gītā.*

artha: **अर्थ** "Goal or purpose; wealth, property, money." Also has the meaning of utility, desire. See: *dharma, purushārtha.*

Arthaveda: **अर्थवेद्** "Science of statecraft." A class of ancient texts, also called *Nītiśāstras,* on politics, statecraft and much more, forming the *Upaveda* of the *Ṛig Veda.* The most important text of this group is Kauṭilīya's *Arthaśāstra* (ca 300 BCE) which gives detailed instructions on all areas of government. It embodies the *kshatriya* perspective of rulership and society. See: *Upaveda.*

Arunagirinathar: அருணகிரிநாதர் South Indian Śaivite poet saint (ca 1500). See: *Kandar Anubhuti.*

Āruṇeya Upanishad: **आरुणेय उपनिषद्** A short *Upanishad* dealing with *sannyāsa.* See: *sannyāsa.*

Aryaman: **अर्यमन्** "Close friend; matchmaker; Sun God." A Vedic Deity who personifies hospitality, the household and *gṛihastha* life. He presides over matrimonial alliances, and protects tradition, custom and religion. He is also invoked during *śrāddha* (funeral-memorial) ceremonies.

āsana: **आसन** "Seat; posture." In *haṭha yoga, āsana* refers to any of numerous poses prescribed to balance and tune up the subtle energies of mind and body for meditation and to promote health and longevity. Examples are the shoulder-stand *(sarvāṅgāsana,*"whole body pose") and the lotus pose *(padmāsana).* Each *āsana* possesses unique benefits, affecting the varied inner bodies and releasing energies in different parts of the nervous system. While the physical science of *haṭha yoga* can dramatically influence health and general well-being, it is primarily a preparation for the deeper *yogas* and meditations. Sivaya Subramuniyaswami has provided a system of 27 *āsanas* to tune the nervous system for meditation and contemplation and to mitigate the burdensome *karmas,* known by the modern term "stress," built up through the interaction with other people. His 27 *āsanas* are performed in a meditative sequence, not unlike a serene dance, accompanied by certain visualizations and *prāṇāyāmas.* See: *haṭha yoga, rāja yoga, yoga.*

ascent: Rising or climbing higher. A path that leads upward.

ascetic: A person who leads a life of contemplation and rigorous self-denial, shunning comforts and pleasures for religious purposes. See: *monk, nunk.*

asceticism: The austerities of an ascetic. See: *sādhana, tapas.*

ash: See: *vibhūti.*

ashṭāṅga praṇāma: **अष्टाङ्गप्रणाम** "Eight-limbed salutation." See: *praṇāma.*

ashṭāvaraṇam: **अष्टावरणम्** "Eight shields." Vīra Śaivism's eight aids to faith: *guru,* Liṅga, *jaṅgama* (monk), *vibhūti, rudrāksha, pādukā, prasāda* (bathing water from Śivaliṅga or *guru's* feet), and Pañchākshara Mantra (Namaḥ Śivāya). See: *Vīra Śaivism.*

āśrama: **आश्रम** "Place of striving." From *śram,* "to exert energy." Hermitage; order of the life. Holy sanctuary; the residence and teaching center of a *sādhu,* saint, *swāmī,* ascetic or *guru;* often includes lodging for students. Also names life's four stages. See: *āśrama dharma, sādhana.*

āśrama dharma: **आश्रमधर्म** "Laws of each order of life." Meritorious way of life particular to each of the four stages *(āśramas)* of life, following which one lives in harmony with nature and life, allowing the body, emotions and mind to develop and undergo their natural cycles in a most positive way. The four stages are as follows. —***brahmacharya:*** Studentship, from age 12 to 24. —***gṛihastha:*** Householder, from 24 to 48. —***vānaprastha:*** Elder advisor, from 48 to 72. —***sannyāsa:*** Religious solitaire, from 72 onward. The first two *āśramas* make up the *pravṛitti mārga,* the way of going toward the world through the force of desire and ambition. The last two are the *nivṛitti mārga,* moving away from the world through introspection and renunciation. See: *dharma, gṛihastha dharma, sannyāsa dharma.*

Assam: **अस्सम** Indian state in the northeast corner of the country, south of Bhutan, almost separated from the rest of India by Bangladesh. Area 30,000 square miles, population 21 million.

assuage: To lessen pain or distress; to calm passions or desires.

asteya: **अस्तेय** "Nonstealing." See: *yama-niyama.*

āstikya: **आस्तिक्य** "Faith." See: *faith, śraddhā, yama-niyama.*

astral body: The subtle, nonphysical body *(sūkshma śarīra)* in which the soul functions in the astral plane, the inner world also called Antarloka. The astral body includes the *prāṇic* sheath *(prāṇamaya kośa),* the instinctive-intellectual sheath *(manomaya kośa)* and the cognitive sheath *(vijñānamaya kośa)*—with the *prāṇic* sheath dropping off at the death of the physical body. See: *kośa, soul.*

astral plane: The subtle world, or Antarloka, spanning the spectrum of consciousness from the *viśuddha chakra* in the throat to the *pātāla chakra* in the soles of the feet. The astral plane includes: 1) the higher astral plane, ***Maharloka,*** "plane of balance;" 2) mid-astral plane, ***Svarloka,*** "celestial plane;" 3) lower astral plane, ***Bhuvarloka,*** "plane of atmosphere," a counterpart or subtle duplicate of the physical plane (consisting of the Pitṛiloka and Pretaloka); and 4) the sub-astral plane, ***Naraka,*** consisting of seven hellish realms corresponding to the seven *chakras* below the base of the spine. In the astral plane, the soul is enshrouded in the astral body, called *sūkshma śarīra.* See: *astral body, loka, Naraka, three worlds.*

astrology: Science of celestial influences. See: *jyotisha, Vedāṅga.*

asura: **असुर** "Evil spirit; demon." (Opposite of *sura:* "deva; God.") A being of the lower astral plane, Naraka. *Asuras* can and do interact with the physical plane, causing major and minor problems in people's lives. *Asuras* do evolve and are not permanently in this state. See: *Naraka.*

Aśvaghosha: **अश्वघोष** Buddhist scholar, pantheist philosopher (ca 80 BCE–150 CE), and one of the great poets of Indian history. A principal architect of the *Mahāyana* school. See: *pantheism.*

Aśvin: **अश्विन्** Vedic heroes—twins, young, handsome, brilliant and agile—who embody the dawn, the transition from darkness to light, and from disease to health. They are physicians of the Gods, and honey is one of their symbols. They also represent duality acting in unison. See: *Vedas, Ṛig Veda.*

atala: **अतल** "Bottomless region." The first *chakra* below the *mūlādhāra,* centered in the hips. Region of fear and lust. Corresponds to the first astral netherworld beneath the earth's surface, called Put ("childless") or Atala, the first of seven hellish regions of consciousness. See: *chakra, loka, Naraka.*

atattva: **अतत्त्व** "Noncategory; beyond existence." *Atattva* is the negation of the term *tattva,* and is used to describe the indescribable Reality—the Absolute, Paraśiva, the Self God—which transcends all 36 categories *(tattvas)* of manifestation. It is beyond time, form and space. And yet, in a mystery known only to the knower—the enlightened mystic—Parāśakti-*nāda,* the first *tattva,* ever comes out of Paraśiva. If it were not for Paraśiva, nothing could be. Paraśiva does not exist to the outer dimensions of cosmic consciousness, but without it, the mind itself would not exist. See: *tattva.*

atha: **अथ** "Now; then; certainly." An inceptive particle and mark of auspiciousness used to begin sacred works. For example, the first *sūtra* of the *Yoga Sūtras* reads, "Now then *(atha),* an exposition on *yoga.*"

Atharvaśikhā Upanishad: **अथर्वशिखा उपनिषद्** A minor *Upanishad* dealing with the interpretation of *Aum.* See: *Upanishad, Vedas.*

Atharva Veda: **अथर्ववेद** From "*Atharva,*" the name of the *ṛishi* said to have compiled this fourth *Veda.* The *Atharva* consists of 20 books and 720 hymns. Considered the last *Veda* recorded, it consists of mostly original hymns (rather than replications from the *Ṛig Veda*). It is known as the *Veda* of prayer, in recognition of its abundant magical charms and spells. It also contains many *Āgama*-like cosmological passages that bridge the earlier Vedic hymns and formulas with the metaphysics of the *Upanishads*. See: *Vedas*.

atheism: The rejection of all religion or religious belief, or simply the belief that God or Gods do not exist. See: *chārvāka, materialism, nāstika*.

ātman: आत्मन् "The soul; the breath; the principle of life and sensation." The soul in its entirety—as the soul body *(ānandamaya kośa)* and its essence (Parāśakti and Paraśiva). One of Hinduism's most fundamental tenets is that we are the *ātman,* not the physical body, emotions, external mind or personality. In Hindu scriptures, *ātman* sometimes refers to the ego-personality, and its meaning must be determined according to context. The *Ātma Upanishad* (1–3) describes *ātman,* or *purusha,* as threefold: *bāhyātman,* the outer or physical person; *antarātman,* the inner person, excluding the physical form, who perceives, thinks and cognizes; and Paramātman, the transcendent Self God within. See: *Paramātman, kośa, soul.*

ātmārtha pūjā: आत्मार्तपूजा "Personal worship rite." Home *pūjā*. See: *pūjā*.

ātmasvarūpa: आत्मस्वरूप "Nature of the soul." See: *ātman, soul.*

atmosphere: The pervading or surrounding spirit or influence. General mood or environment. See: *sānnidhya.*

atone: To make amends or reconcile. See: *absolution, penance, sin.*

attainment: Something which has been acquired, achieved or reached through effort. Spiritual accomplishment. Śaiva Siddhānta notes four primary levels of attainment: *sālokya* (sharing God's world, the goal of *charyā), sāmīpya* (nearness to God, the goal of *kriyā*), *sārūpya* (likeness to God, the goal of *yoga)* and *sāyujya* (union with God, the state of *jñāna).* See: *pāda.*

attitude: Disposition. State of mind. Manner of carrying oneself. Manner of acting, thinking or feeling which reveals one's disposition, opinions and beliefs. See: *conscience.*

augural: Having to do with divination, prediction or interpreting omens.

Augustine: Catholic bishop saint (354–430) and highly influential theologian.

Aum: ॐ or ओम् Often spelled *Om*. The mystic syllable of Hinduism, placed at the beginning of most sacred writings. As a *mantra,* it is pronounced *aw* (as in *law*), *oo* (as in *zoo*), *mm.* Aum represents the Divine, and is associated with Lord Gaṇeśa, for its initial sound "aa," vibrates within the *mūlādhāra,* the *chakra* at the base of the spine upon which this God sits. The second sound of this *mantra,* "oo," vibrates within the throat and chest *chakras,* the realm of Lord Murugan, or Kumāra, known by the Hawaiian people as the God Ku. The third sound, "mm," vibrates within the cranial *chakras, ājñā* and *sahasrāra,* where the Supreme God reigns. The dot above, called *anusvāra,* represents the Soundless Sound, Paranāda. Aum is explained in the *Upanishads* as standing for the whole world and its parts, including past, present and future. It is from this primal vibration that all manifestation issues forth. Aum is the primary, or *mūla mantra,* and often precedes other *mantras.* It may be safely used for chanting and *japa* by anyone of any religion. Its three letters represent the three worlds and the powers of creation, preservation and destruction. In common usage in several Indian languages, *aum* means "yes, verily" or "hail." See: *nāda, Praṇava, sound.*

aura: The luminous colorful field of subtle energy radiating within and around the human body, extending out from three to seven feet. The colors of the aura change constantly according to the ebb and flow of one's state of consciousness, thoughts, moods and emotions. Higher, benevolent feelings create bright pastels; base, negative feelings are darker in color. Thus, auras can be seen and "read" by clairvoyants. The general nature of auras varies according to individual unfoldment. Great mystics have very bright auras, while instinctive persons are shrouded in dull shades. The aura consists of two aspects, the outer aura and the inner aura. The outer aura extends beyond the physical body and changes continuously, reflecting the individual's moment-to-moment panorama of thought and emotion. The inner aura is much more constant, as it reflects deep-seated subconscious patterns, desires, repressions and tendencies held in the sub-subconscious mind. Those colors which are regularly and habitually reflected in the outer aura are eventually recorded more permanently in the inner aura. The colors of the inner aura permeate out through the outer aura and either shade with sadness or brighten with happiness the normal experiences of daily life. The inner aura hovers deep within the astral body in the chest and torso and looks much like certain "modern-art" paintings, with heavy strokes of solid colors here and there. In Sanskṛit, the aura is called *prabhāmaṇḍala,* "luminous circle," or *dīptachakra,* "wheel of light." See: *mind (five states), pāpa, puṇya.*

Aurobindo Ghosh: A prolific Bengali writer and poet, pantheistic philosopher and *yoga* mystic, widely known as Śrī Aurobindo (1872–1950). He perceived the modern global crisis as marking a period of transition from a dark age to a more enlightened one, when Hinduism will play a preponderant role. He founded the Auroville community in Pondichery, based on *purṇa* (integral) *yoga* and contributed much to this century's Hindu revival.

auspicious: Favorable, of good omen, foreboding well. *Maṅgala.* One of the central concepts in Hindu life. Astrology defines a method for determining times that are favorable for various human endeavors. Much of daily living and religious practice revolves around an awareness of auspiciousness. Endowed with great power and importance, it is associated with times, places and persons. See: *jyotisha, muhūrta, swastika, Tai Pongal.*

austerity: Self-denial and discipline, physical or mental, performed for various reasons including acquiring powers, attaining grace, conquering the instinctive nature and burning the seeds of past *karmas.* Ranging from simple deprivations, such as foregoing a meal, to severe disciplines, called *tapas,* such as always standing, never sitting or lying down, even for sleep. See: *penance, tapas.*

authenticity: Quality of being authentic, or genuine, trustworthy. Reliable.

authority: Influence, power or right to give commands, enforce obedience, take action or make final decisions.

Auvaiyar: ஔவையார் A woman saint of Tamil Nadu (ca 200 BCE), a contemporary of Saint Tiruvalluvar, devotee of Lord Gaṇeśa and Kārttikeya, or Murugan, and one of the greatest literary figures in ancient India. As a young girl, she prayed to have her beauty removed so she would not be forced into marriage and could devote her full life to God. She was a great *bhakta* who wrote exquisite ethical works, some in aphoristic style and some in four-line verse. Among the most famous are *Atti Chudi, Konrai Ventan, Ulaka Niti, Muturai,* and *Nalvali.* Her Tamil primer is studied by children to this day. A second Saint Auvaiyar may have lived around the seventh century.

Avantīvarman: अवन्तीवर्मन् King of Kashmir (855–883) during whose reign lived Kallaṭa, one of the great exponents of Kashmīr Śaivism.

avatāra: अवतार "Descent." A God born in a human (or animal) body. A central concept of Śāktism, Smārtism and Vaishṇavism. See: *incarnation, Ishṭa Devatā, Vaishṇavism.*

avidyā: अविद्या "Spiritual ignorance." Wrongful understanding of the nature of reality. Mistaking the impermanent for the everlasting.

awareness: *Sākshin,* or *chit.* Individual consciousness, perception, knowing; the witness of perception, the "inner eye of the soul." The soul's ability to sense, see or know and to be conscious of this knowing. When awareness is indrawn *(pratyak chetana),* various states of *samādhi* may occur. Awareness is known in the Āgamas as *chitśakti,* the "power of awareness," the inner self and eternal witness. See: *consciousness, sākshin.*

āyurveda: आयुर्वेद "Science of life." A holistic system of medicine and health native to ancient India. This sacred Vedic science is an *Upaveda* of the *Atharva Veda.* Three early giants in this field who left voluminous texts are Charaka, Suśruta and Vāgbhata. *Āyurveda* covers many areas, including: 1) *chikitsā,* general medicine, 2) *śalya,* surgery, 3) *dehavṛitti,* physiology, 4) *nidāna,* diagnosis, 5) *dravyavidyā,* medicine and pharmacology, 6) *agada tantra,* antidote method, 7) *strītantra,* gynecology, 8) *paśu vidyā,* veterinary science, 9) *kaumāra bhṛitya,* pediatrics, 10) *ūrdhvāṅga,* diseases of the organs of the head, 11) *bhūta vidyā,* demonology, 12) *rasayana,* tonics, rejuvenating, 13) *vājīkaraṇa,* sexual rejuvenation. Among the first known surgeons was Suśruta (ca 600 BCE), whose *Suśruta Saṁhitā* is studied to this day. (Hippocrates, Greek father of medicine, lived two centuries later.) The aims of *āyurveda* are *āyus,* "long life," and *ārogya,* "diseaselessness," which facilitate progress toward ultimate spiritual goals. Health is achieved by balancing energies (especially the *doshas,* bodily humors) at all levels of being, subtle and gross, through innumerable methods, selected according to the individual's constitution, lifestyle and nature. Similar holistic medical systems are prevalent among many communities, including the Chinese, American Indians, Africans and South Americans. See: *doshas.*

āyurveda vaidya: आयुर्वेद वैद्य A practitioner, or physician, of *āyurveda.*

Ayyappan: ஐயப்பன் The popular God of a recently formed sect that focuses on pilgrimage to the top of Sabarimalai, a sacred hill in Kerala, where He is said to appear at night as a divine light. Ayyappan is revered as a son of Vishṇu and Śiva (Hari-Hara *putra).* His *vāhana* is the tiger.

axiom: A rule or maxim that is universally accepted as true.

axis: A real or imaginary straight line around which a planet rotates. More generally, *axis* means a central line of development.

backbiting: Speaking maliciously or slanderously about a person who is absent.

Bādarāyaṇa: बादरायण Author of the *Brahma Sūtras.* See: *Brahma Sūtra.*

balipīṭha: बलिपीठ "Offering place." An inverted lotus-shaped stone atop a pedestal situated near the temple flagpole, *dhvajastambha.* Here devotees are to leave all negative thoughts as they enter the temple.

bard: A singer or reciter of epic poems.

Basavaṇṇa: बसवण्ण A 12th-century philosopher, poet and prime minister who reformed and revived Vīra Śaivism in Karnataka. See: *Vīra Śaivism.*

Batara: A name of Śiva used in Indonesia. See: *Śiva.*

Baudhāyana Dharma Śāstra: बौधायनधर्मशास्त्र A book of laws associated with the *Kṛishṇa Yajur Veda* and governing studentship, marriage, household rituals, civil law, etc. It is followed by *brāhmins* of Southwest India. See: *Dharma Śāstra, Kalpa Vedāṅga.*

bce: Abbreviation for "before common era," referring to dating prior to the year zero in the Western, or Gregorian calendar, system. Thus, 300 BCE was 300 years before the turn of the millennium. Cf: *ce.*

Being: When capitalized *being* refers to God's essential divine nature—Pure Consciousness, Absolute Reality and Primal Soul (God's nature as a divine Person). Lower case *being* refers to the essential nature of a person, that within which never changes; existence. See: *Śiva.*

benediction: A blessing, especially a spoken one. See: *blessing.*

benevolence: Inclination to do good; charitable, kindly. See: *yama-niyama.*

benign: Good, kindly, doing no harm. See: *ahiṁsā.*

beseech: To ask of someone earnestly. To solicit with fervor.

bestow: To offer as a gift. See: *dāna.*

betoken: To indicate, show; offer as a sign of the future. Symbolize.

betrothal: Mutual pledge to marry; engagement. In Sanskṛit, *vāgdāna* or *niśchitārtha.* See: *saṁskāras of adulthood.*

bewilder: To baffle or confuse through something complicated or involved.

bhaga: भग "Good fortune; happiness." A God of the *Ṛig Veda;* Lord of wealth, prowess and happiness. See: *purushārtha, Ṛig Veda, wealth.*

Bhagavad Gītā: भगवद् गीता "Song of the Lord." One of the most popular of Hindu writings, a conversation between Lord Kṛishṇa and Arjuna on the brink of the great battle at Kurukshetra. In this central episode of the epic *Mahābhārata* (part of the sixth book), Kṛishṇa illumines the warrior-prince Arjuna on *yoga,* asceticism, *dharma* and the manifold spiritual path. See: *Itihāsa, Mahābhārata.*

Bhāgavata: भागवत "Relating to God or a God holy; sacred, divine." Pertaining to Vishṇu or Kṛishṇa. From *bhaga,* "Gracious lord; patron; good fortune." The name of a sect of Vaishṇavism which arose in the Western part of India after 600 BCE. A highly devotional monotheistic faith worshiping God as Kṛishṇa, Vāsudeva or Vāsudeva-Kṛishṇa. It is believed by scholars to have been one of five religions (along with the Ekāntika, Nārāyaṇīya, Vaikhānasa and Sātvata) that blended to form what was called the Pañcharātra religion in the vicinity of Mathura around 300 BCE. Today, the term *Bhāgavata* is often used to refer to the Vaishṇavite religion as a whole. See: *Pañcharātra, Vaishṇavism.*

Bhāgavata Purāṇa: भागवतपुराण Also known as *Śrīmad Bhāgavatam,* a work of 18,000 stanzas. A major *Purāṇa* and primary *Vaishṇava* scripture, from oral tradition, written down ca 800. It provides the stories of all incarnations of Vishṇu, filled with the *bhakti,* inner current of devotion. See: *Purāṇa.*

Bhairava: भैरव "Terrifying." Lord Śiva as the fiery protector. He carries and is represented by a *triśūla* (trident), a symbol often enshrined as guardian at the entrance to Śiva temples. See: *Śiva, triśūla.*

bhajana: भजन Spiritual song. Individual or group singing of devotional songs, hymns and chants. See: *congregational worship, kīrtana.*

bhakta: भक्त "Devotee." A worshiper. One who is surrendered in the Divine.

bhakti: भक्ति "Devotion." Surrender to God, Gods or *guru. Bhakti* extends from the simplest expression of devotion to the ego-decimating principle of *prapatti,* which is total surrender. *Bhakti* is the foundation of all sects of Hinduism, as well as *yoga* schools throughout the world. See: *bhakti yoga, darśana, prapatti, prasāda, sacrifice, surrender, yajña.*

bhakti yoga: भक्तियोग "Union through devotion." *Bhakti yoga* is the practice of devotional disciplines, worship, prayer, chanting and singing with the aim of awakening love in the heart and opening oneself to God's grace. *Bhakti* may be directed toward God, Gods or one's spiritual preceptor. *Bhakti yoga* seeks communion and ever closer rapport with the Divine, developing qualities that make communion possible, such as love, selflessness and purity. Saint Sambandar described *bhakti* as religion's essence and the surest means to divine union and liberation. He advised heartfelt worship, unstinting devotion and complete surrender to God in humble, committed service. From the beginning practice of *bhakti* to advanced devotion, called *prapatti,* self-effacement is an intricate part of Hindu, even all Indian, culture. *Bhakti yoga* is embodied in Patañjali's Yoga Darśana in the second limb, *niyamas* (observances), as devotion (Īśvarapraṇidhāna). *Bhakti yoga* is practiced in many Hindu schools, and highly developed in Vaishṇavism as a spiritual path in itself, leading to perfection and liberation. In Śaiva Siddhānta, its cultivation is the primary focus during the *kriyā pāda* (stage of worship). See: *bhakti yoga, prapatti, sacrifice, surrender, yajña.*

Bhārata: भारत Ancient and original name of India.

bhāshya: भाष्य "Speech, discussion." Commentary on a text, especially scripture. Hindu philosophies are largely founded upon the various interpretations, or *bhāshyas,* of primary scripture. Other types of scriptural commentaries include: *vṛitti,* a brief commentary on aphorisms, less extensive than a *bhāshya; tippani,* which is like a *vṛitti* but less formal, explains difficult words or phrases; *vārttika,* a critical study and elaboration of a *bhāshya;* and *tika* or *vyakhyana,* an explanation of a *bhāshya* or *śāstra* in simpler language.

Bhāskara: भास्कर Philosopher (ca 950). His *Bhāskarabhāshya,* a commentary on the *Brahma Sūtras,* was the first elaborate criticism of Śaṅkara's *Advaitic* doctrine of *avidyā-māyā.* See: *Śaṅkara, Vedānta, Viśishṭādvaita.*

Bhāvaliṅga: भावलिङ्ग "Mark of existence." Śiva beyond space and time. See: *atattva, Paraśiva, Śivaliṅga, Vīra Śaivism.*

bhedābheda: भेदाभेद् "Difference-nondifference." A term in Vedānta which means that soul and world are identical with and yet different from God, in the same way that the waves of an ocean can be seen as being nondifferent from the ocean, yet they are not the ocean, only a part of it. See: *Vedānta.*

Bhogaṛishi: भोगऋषि One of the 18 *siddhas* of Śaiva tradition, an alchemist and *tantrika yogī,* associated with the Palani Hills Murugan temple in South India, who created the Daṇḍayūthapaniswāmī *mūrti* from nine poisonous metals. He is thought by some to still reside there in a cave. Chinese historical records suggest that he came from China. See: *siddha, siddhi, tantric.*

Bhojadeva Paramāra: भोजदेव परमार Śaivite king, poet, artist and theologian of Gujarat (1018-1060). Author of *Tattvaprakāśa.* Renowned for establishing a systematic, monistic Śaiva Siddhānta, and creating India's then largest artificial lake, 250 miles in length, called Bhojpur. See: *Tātparyadīpikā.*

bhṛityāchāra: भृत्याचार "Servant's way." One of the five Vīra Śaiva codes of conduct. See: *Pañchāchāra, Vīra Śaivism.*

Bhūloka: भूलोक "Earth world." The physical plane. See: *loka.*

bhūmikā: भूमिका "Earth; ground; soil." Preface; introduction to a book. From *bhū,* "to become, exist; arise, come into being."

Bhuvarloka: भुवर्लोक "Plane of atmosphere." The second of the seven upper worlds, realm of *svādhishṭāna chakra,* consisting of the two astral regions closest to the physical plane: Pitṛiloka, "world of ancestors," and Pretaloka, "world of the departed." See: *loka.*

***Bijjala*:** बिज्जल A king in Karnataka associated with the life of *Basavaṇṇa.*

bilva: बिल्व Wood-apple (or bael) tree, *Aegle marmelos,* sacred to Lord Śiva. Its leaves, picked in threes, are offered in the worship of the Śivaliṅga. The delicious fruit when unripe is used medicinally.

bindu: बिन्दु "A drop, small particle, dot." 1) The seed or source of creation. In the 36 *tattvas,* the nucleus or first particle of transcendent light, technically called Parābiṇḍu, corresponding to the Śakti *tattva.* Scientists say the whole universe just before the big bang could fit on the head of a pin—a tremendous point of energy—that is Parabindu. 2) Small dot worn on the forehead between the eyebrows, or in the middle of the forehead, made of red powder *(kuṅkuma),* sandalpaste, clay, cosmetics or other substance. It a sign that one is a Hindu. Mystically, it represents the "third eye," or the "mind's eye," which sees things that the physical eyes cannot see. The forehead dot is a reminder to use and cultivate one's spiritual vision, to perceive and understand life's inner workings, as well as to look into the past to see the future. The *bindu* is also a beauty mark worn by Hindu women, the color red generally a sign of marriage, black often worn before marriage to ward off the evil eye, *kudṛishṭi* or *pāpadṛishṭi.* The *bindu* is known as *pottu* in Tamil. *Bindu* is also a term for semen. See: *tattva, tilaka.*

birth chart: An astrological map of the sky drawn for a person's moment and place of birth. The birth chart is also known as *rāśi chakra* or zodiac wheel. It is the basis for interpreting the traits of individuals and the experiences, *prarabdha karmas,* they will go through in life. See: *jyotisha, karma.*

birthstar: See: *nakshatra.*

bi-sexual: Of or characterized by sexual attraction for members of both genders. See: *heterosexual, homosexual, sexuality.*

blessing: Good wishes; benediction. Seeking and giving blessings is extremely central in Hindu life, nurtured in the precepts of *kāruṇya* (grace), *śakti* (energy), *darśana* (seeing the divine), *prasāda* (blessed offerings), *pūjā* (invocation), *tīrthayātrā* (pilgrimage), *dīkshā* (initiation), *śaktipāta* (descent of grace), *saṁskāras* (rites of passage), *sānnidhya* (holy presence) and *sādhana* (inner-attunement disciplines).

bodhaka: बोधक "Teacher." One who awakens or catalyzes knowing; a religious instructor or catalyst.

bodhi tantra: बोधितन्त्र "Wise methods; ways of wisdom." See: *sādhana, tantra.*

bodies: See: *kośa, śarīra, soul.*

bodily humor: Commonly, the fluids of the body, but in this text used as the English equivalent of the *āyurvedic* term *dosha,* which names three fundamental interbalancing principles or constituents of the human constitution. See: *āyurveda, dosha.*

bond (bondage): See: *evolution of the soul, mala, pāśa.*

bone-gathering: Part of Hindu funeral rites. About twelve hours after cremation, family men return to the cremation site to collect the remains. Water is first sprinkled on the ashes, which separates the black ash of the wood from the fine, white ash of the body. The white ash and bones (up to four inches long, called flowers) are collected in a tray or brass pot. Some Hindus return the ashes and bones to India for deposition in the Ganges. Or they may be put into any ocean or river. Arrangements can be made with crematoriums in the East or West for the family to personally gather the ash and flowers. See: *cremation, death, reincarnation, saṁskāras of adulthood.*

boon: A welcome blessing, a benefit received. An unexpected benefit or bonus. See: *blessing, grace.*

bountiful: Giving abundantly and without restraint; plentiful.

Brahmā: ब्रह्मा The name of God in His aspect of Creator. Śaivites consider Brahmā, Vishṇu and Rudra to be three of five aspects of Śiva. Smārtas group Brahmā, Vishṇu and Śiva as a holy trinity in which Śiva is the destroyer. *Brahmā* the Creator is not to be confused with 1) *Brahman,* the Transcendent Supreme of the *Upanishads;* 2) *Brāhmaṇa,* Vedic texts; 3) *brāhmaṇa,* the Hindu priest caste (also spelled *brāhmin*). See: *Brahman, Parameśvara.*

brahmachārī: ब्रह्मचारी An unmarried male spiritual aspirant who practices continence, observes religious disciplines, including *sādhana,* devotion and service and who may be under simple vows. Also names one in the student stage, age 12–24, or until marriage. See: *āśrama dharma, monk.*

brahmachāriṇī: ब्रह्मचारिनी Feminine counterpart of *brahmachārī.* See: *nunk.*

brahmacharya: ब्रह्मचर्य See: *yama-niyama.*

brahmacharya āśrama: ब्रह्मचर्य आश्रम See: *āśrama dharma.*

brāhma muhūrta: ब्रह्मामुहूर्त "Time of God." A very favorable time for *sādhana.* It is traditional to arise before this period, bathe and begin one's morning worship. *Brāhma muhūrta* is defined as roughly 1.5 hours, the last *muhūrta* of the night in the 8-*muhūrta* system. It is understood as comprising the final three *muhūrtas* of the night in 15 or 16-*muhūrta* systems, equalling 144 minutes or 135 minutes respectively. See: *muhūrta.*

Brahman: ब्रह्मन् "Supreme Being; expansive spirit." From the root *bṛih,* "to grow, increase, expand." Name of God or Supreme Deity in the *Vedas,* where He is described as the 1) Transcendent Absolute, 2) the all-pervading energy and 3) the Supreme Lord or Primal Soul. These three correspond to Śiva in His three perfections. Thus, Śaivites know Brahman and Śiva to be one and the same God. —***Nirguṇa Brahman:*** God "without qualities (*guṇa*)," i.e., formless, Absolute Reality, Parabrahman, or Paraśiva—totally transcending *guṇa* (quality), manifest existence and even Parāśakti, all of which exhibit perceivable qualities. —***Saguṇa Brahman:*** God "with qualities;" Śiva in His perfections of Parāśakti and Parameśvara—God as superconscious, omnipresent, all-knowing, all-loving and all-powerful. The term Brahman is not to be confused with 1) *Brahmā,* the Creator God; 2) *Brāhmaṇa,* Vedic texts, nor with 3) *brāhmaṇa,* Hindu priest caste (English spelling: *brāhmin*). See: *Parameśvara, Parāśakti, Paraśiva.*

***Brāhmaṇa:* ब्राह्मण** 1) One of four primary sections of each *Veda;* concerned mainly with details of *yajña*, or sacrificial fire worship, and specific duties and rules of conduct for priests, but also rich in philosophical lore. 2) The first of the four *varṇas,* or social classes, comprising pious souls of exceptional learning, including priests, educators and humanity's visionary guides. Also spelled *brāhmin.* See: *brāhmin, varṇa dharma, Vedas.*

***Brahmāṇḍa:* ब्रह्माण्ड** "Egg of God." The cosmos; inner and outer universe. See: *loka, three worlds, world.*

***brahmarandhra:* ब्रह्मरन्ध्र** "Door of Brahman." See: *door of Brahman.*

***Brahma Sūtra(s):* ब्रह्मसूत्र** Also known as the *Vedānta Sūtras,* composed by Bādarāyaṇa (ca 400 BCE) as the first known systematic exposition of Upanishadic thought. Its 550 aphorisms are so brief as to be virtually unintelligible without commentary. It was through interpretations of this text, as well as the *Upanishads* themselves and the *Bhagavad Gītā,* that later schools of Vedānta expressed and formulated their own views of the Upanishadic tenets. A third name for this important work is *Śārīraka Sūtras,* "aphorisms on the embodied soul." See: *Upanishad, Vedānta.*

***Brahma Sūtra Bhāshya:* ब्रह्मसूत्रभाष्य** A lengthy 13th-century commentary on the *Brahma Sūtras* by Śrīkaṇṭha to establish a Vedic base for the Śaivite qualified nondualism called Śiva Advaita. See: *Śiva Advaita, Vedānta.*

***Brahma Sūtra, Śaṅkara Bhāshya:* ब्रह्मसूत्र शाङ्करभाष्य** Śaṅkara's explanation of one of the three major treatises on Vedānta philosophy. See: *Smārta.*

***brāhmin (brāhmaṇa):* ब्राह्मण** "Mature or evolved soul." The class of pious souls of exceptional learning. From *Brāhman,* "growth, expansion, evolution, development, swelling of the spirit or soul." The mature soul is the exemplar of wisdom, tolerance, forbearance and humility. See: *varṇa dharma.*

brāhminical tradition: The hereditary religious practices of the Vedic *brāhmins,* such as reciting *mantras,* and personal rules for daily living.

***Brahmotsava:* ब्रह्मोत्सव** "God's festival, or foremost festival." Each temple has one festival of the year which is its major celebration. This is called Brahmotsava, often a ten-day event. See: *festival, temple.*

***Bṛihadāraṇyaka Upanishad:* बृहदारण्यक उपनिषद्** One of the most important *Upanishads,* part of the *Śatapatha Brāhmaṇa* of the *Yajur Veda.* Ascribed to Sage Yājñavalkya, it teaches modes of worship, meditation and the identity of the individual self with the Supreme Self. See: *Upanishad.*

***Bṛihaspati:* बृहस्पति** "Lord of Prayer." Vedic preceptor of the Gods and Lord of the Word, sometimes identified with Lord Gaṇeśa. Also names a great exponent of Śaiva Siddhānta (ca 900). See: *Gaṇeśa.*

***bṛihatkuṭumba:* बिृहत्कुटुम्ब** "Extended family." Also called *mahākuṭumba.* See: *extended family, joint family.*

***Buddha:* बुद्ध** "The enlightened." Usually refers to Siddhārtha Gautama (ca 624–544 BCE), a prince born of the Śākya clan—a Śaivite Hindu tribe that lived in eastern India on the Nepalese border. He renounced the world and became a monk. After his enlightenment he preached the doctrines upon which followers later founded Buddhism. See: *Buddhism.*

buddhi: **बुद्धि** "Intellect, reason, logic." The intellectual or disciplined mind. *Buddhi* is characterized by discrimination *(viveka),* voluntary restraint *(vairāgya),* cultivation of calmness *(śānti),* contentment *(santosha)* and forgiveness *(kshamā).* It is a faculty of *manomaya kośa,* the instinctive-intellectual sheath. See: *intellectual mind, kośa, mind (individual).*

buddhi chitta: **बुद्धिचित्त** "Intellectual mind." See: *buddhi, intellectual mind.*

Buddhism: The religion based on the teachings of Siddhārtha Gautama, known as the Buddha (ca 624–544 BCE). He refuted the idea of man's having an immortal soul and did not preach of any Supreme Deity. Instead he taught that man should seek to overcome greed, hatred and delusion and attain enlightenment through realizing the Four Noble Truths and following the Eightfold Path. Prominent among its holy books is the *Dhammapada.* Buddhism arose out of Hinduism as an inspired reform movement which rejected the caste system and the sanctity of the *Vedas.* It is thus classed as *nāstika,* "unbeliever," and is not part of Hinduism. Buddhism eventually migrated out of India, the country of its origin, and now enjoys a following of over 350 million, mostly in Asia. See: *Buddha.*

ca: Abbreviation for *circa*—Latin for "approximately"—used with dates that are not precise, e.g., ca 650 means "around the year 650."

callous: Unfeeling, not sensitive, lacking compassion or pity. See: *yama-niyama.*

camphor: *Karpura.* An aromatic white crystalline solid derived from the wood of camphor trees (or prepared synthetically from pinene), prized as fuel in temple *āratī* lamps. See: *āratī, pūjā.*

canon: The religious laws governing a sect or a religion. Body of accepted or authorized scriptures.

caste: A hierarchical system, called *varṇa dharma* (or *jāti dharma),* established in India in ancient times, which determined the privileges, status, rights and duties of the many occupational groups, wherein status is determined by heredity. There are four main classes *(varṇas)—brāhmin, kshatriya, vaiśya* and *śūdra*—and innumerable castes, called *jāti.* See: *varṇa dharma.*

catalyst: A person or thing acting as a stimulus upon another, whose presence brings about change. Difficulties can be a catalyst for spiritual unfoldment. *Catalyst* is sometimes used to name a teacher or facilitator.

causal body: *Kāraṇa śarīra,* the inmost body; the soul form, also called *ānandamaya kośa,* "bliss sheath," and actinic causal body. See: *kośa, soul.*

causal plane: Highest plane of existence, Śivaloka. See: *loka.*

cause: *Kāraṇa.* Anything which produces an effect, a result. **—efficient cause:** *(nimitta kāraṇa)* That which directly produces the effect; that which conceives, makes, shapes, etc., such as the potter who fashions a clay pot, or God who creates the world. **—material cause:** *(upādāna kāraṇa)* The matter from which the effect is formed, as the clay which is shaped into a pot, or God as primal substance becoming the world. **—instrumental cause:** *(sahakāri kāraṇa)* That which serves as a means, mechanism or tool in producing the effect, such as the potter's wheel, necessary for making a pot, or God's generative Śakti. See: *māyā, tattva.*

ce: Abbreviation for "common era." Equivalent to the abbreviation AD. Following a date, it indicates that the year in question comes after the year zero in the Western, or Gregorian calender, system. E.g., 300 CE is 300 years after the turn of the millennium. Cf: *bce.*

celestial: "Of the sky or heavens." Of or relating to the heavenly regions or beings. Highly refined, divine.

celibacy: Complete sexual abstinence. Also the state of a person who has vowed to remain unmarried. See: *brahmachārī, brahmacharya.*

centillion: The number 1 followed by 600 zeros. An unimaginably large figure.

ceremony: A formal rite established by custom or authority as proper to special occasions. From the Latin *caerimonia,* "awe; reverent rite."

cf: An abbreviation for "compare." A scholastic notation.

chaitanya: **चैतन्य** "Spirit, consciousness, especially higher consciousness; Supreme Being." A widely used term, often preceded by modifiers, e.g., *sākshī chaitanya,* "witness consciousness," or *bhakti chaitanya,* "devotional consciousness," or Śivachaitanya, "God consciousness." See: *chitta, consciousness, mind (five states), Śiva consciousness.*

Chaitanya: **चैतन्य** A renowned Vaishṇava saint (1485–1534), revered today especially in Bengal and Orissa, remembered for his ecstatic states of devotion. He taught a dualistic philosophy in which *bhakti* (devotion) to the divine couple Rādhā and Kṛishṇa is the only means to liberation. Practice revolves mainly around *kīrtana,* devotional singing and dancing. He gave prominence to the Gaudiya Vaishṇava sect, of which several branches thrive today, including ISKCON. See: *Kṛishṇa, Vaishṇavism, Vedānta.*

chakra: **चक्र** "Wheel." Any of the nerve plexes or centers of force and consciousness located within the *inner bodies* of man. In the physical body there are corresponding nerve plexuses, ganglia and glands. The seven principle *chakras* can be seen psychically as colorful, multi-petaled wheels or lotuses. They are situated along the spinal cord from the base to the cranial chamber. Additionally, seven *chakras,* barely visible, exist below the spine. They are seats of instinctive consciousness, the origin of jealousy, hatred, envy, guilt, sorrow, etc. They constitute the lower or hellish world, called *Naraka* or *pātāla.* Thus, there are 14 major *chakras* in all.

The seven upper chakras, from lowest to highest, are: 1) ***mūlādhāra*** (base of spine): memory, time and space; 2) ***svādhishṭhāna*** (below navel): reason; 3) ***maṇipūra*** (solar plexus): willpower; 4) ***anāhata*** (heart center): direct cognition; 5) ***viśuddha*** (throat): divine love; 6) ***ājñā*** (third eye): divine sight; 7) ***sahasrāra*** (crown of head): illumination, Godliness.

The seven lower chakras, from highest to lowest, are 1) ***atala*** (hips): fear and lust; 2) ***vitala*** (thighs): raging anger; 3) ***sutala*** (knees): retaliatory jealousy; 4) ***talātala*** (calves): prolonged mental confusion; 5) ***rasātala*** (ankles): selfishness; 6) ***mahātala*** (feet): absence of conscience; 7) ***pātāla*** (located in the soles of the feet): murder and malice. See: *pradakshiṇa, Naraka (also: individual chakra entries).*

Chālukya: **चालुक्य** Indian dynasty (450–1189) in the Punjab area. Buddhism and Śaivism were prominent. This dynasty completed the Buddhist Ajanta Cave frescoes and advanced the art of Hindu temple building.

chandana: **चन्दन** "Sandalwood paste." One of the sacred substances offered during *pūjā* and afterwards distributed to devotees as a sacrament *(prasāda).*

Çhandas Vedāṅga: **छन्दस् वेदाङ्ग** Auxiliary Vedic texts on the metrical rules of poetic writing. *Çhanda,* meter, is among four linguistic skills taught for mastery of the *Vedas* and the rites of *yajña. Çhandas* means "desire; will; metrical science." The most important text on Çhandas is the *Çhanda Śāstra,* ascribed to Piṅgala (ca 200 BCE). See: *Vedāṅga.*

Çhāndogya Upanishad: **छान्दोग्य उपनिषद्** One of the major *Upanishads,* it consists of eight chapters of the *Çhāndogya Brāhmaṇa* of the *Sāma Veda.* It teaches the origin and significance of *Aum,* the importance of the *Sāma Veda,* the Self, meditation and life after death. See: *Upanishad.*

chandra: **चन्द्र** "The moon." Of central importance in Hindu astrology and in the calculation of the festival calendar. Considered the ruler of emotion.

Chārvāka: **चार्वाक** "Good or sweet voice or word." Indian philosopher (ca 600 BCE) who fashioned the school of pure materialism bearing his name. One of the great skeptics of all time. See: *nāstika.*

charyā pāda: **चर्यापाद** "Conduct stage." Stage of service and character building. See: *pāda, Śaiva Siddhānta, Śaivism.*

chaturdharma: **चतुर्धर्म** "Four *dharmas:*" *ṛita, āśrama dharma, varṇa dharma* and *svadharma.* See: *dharma.*

chelā: **चेला** "Disciple." (Hindi.) A disciple of a *guru;* synonym for *śishya.* The feminine equivalent is *chelinā* or *chelī.*

Chellappaswāmī: செல்லப்பாசுவாமி "Wealthy father." Reclusive *siddha* and *satguru* (1840-1915) of the Nandinātha Sampradāya's Kailāsa Paramparā who lived on Sri Lanka's Jaffna peninsula near the Nallur Kandaswāmī Temple, in a small hut where today there is a small *samādhi* shrine. Among his disciples was Sage Yogaswāmī, whom he trained intensely for five years and initiated as his spiritual successor. See: *Kailāsa Paramparā, Nātha Sampradāya.*

Chennabasavaṇṇa: **चेन्नबसवण्ण** "Little Basavaṇṇa." The 12th-century theologian who systematized the religious doctrine of Vīra Śaivism.

Chidambaram: சிதம்பரம் "Hall of Consciousness." A very famous South Indian Śiva Naṭarāja temple. See: *Naṭarāja.*

Chinna Bomman: சின்ன பொம்மன் King of Vellore, near Madras (1559–1579), patron and disciple of Appaya Dīkshita.

chit: **चित्** "Consciousness," or "awareness." Philosophically, "pure awareness; transcendent consciousness," as in *Sat-chit-ānanda.* In mundane use, *chit* means "to perceive; be conscious." See: *awareness, chitta, consciousness, mind (universal), sākshin.*

chitsabhā: **चित्सभा** "Hall of consciousness." See: *Naṭarāja.*

chitta: **चित्त** "Mind; consciousness." Mind-stuff. On the personal level, it is that in which mental impressions and experiences are recorded. Seat of the conscious, subconscious and superconscious states, and of the three-fold mental faculty, called *antaḥkaraṇa,* consisting of *buddhi, manas* and *ahaṁkāra.* See: *awareness, consciousness, mind (individual), mind (universal), sākshin.*

chūḍākaraṇa: **चूडाकरण** Head-shaving sacrament. See: *saṁskāra.*

circumambulate: *Pradakshiṇa.* To walk around, usually clockwise. See: *pradakshiṇa, pūjā.*

citadel: Fortress, usually situated on a height.

clairaudience: "Clear-hearing." Psychic or divine hearing, *divyaśravana.* The ability to hear the inner currents of the nervous system, the *Aum* and other mystic tones. Hearing in one's mind the words of inner-plane beings or earthly beings not physically present. Also, hearing the *nādanāḍī śakti* through the day or while in meditation. See: *clairvoyance, nāda.*

clairvoyance: "Clear-seeing." Psychic or divine sight, *divyadṛishṭi.* The ability to look into the inner worlds and see auras, *chakras, nāḍīs,* thought forms, non-physical people and subtle forces. The ability to see from afar or into the past or future—*avadhijñāna,* "knowing beyond limits." Also the ability to separate the light that illumines one's thoughts from the forms the light illumines. Also, *dūradarśana,* "far-seeing," the modern Sanskṛit term for television in India. *Dūradarśin* names a seer or prophet. See: *ākāśa.*

coarse: Of poor quality; gross, rough cut. Not fine or refined.

coexistent: "Existing together."

cognition: Knowing; perception. Knowledge reached through intuitive, superconscious faculties rather than through intellect alone.

cognitive body: *Vijñānamaya kośa.* The most refined sheath of the astral, or subtle, body *(sūkshma śarīra).* It is the sheath of higher thought and cognition. See: *astral body, kośa.*

cohesive: Remaining together; not disintegrating.

coined: Made up; invented.

commemorative: Anything that honors the memory of a departed person or past event. See: *śrāddha.*

commencement: Beginning.

commission: To give an order or power for something to be made or done.

commitment: Dedication or engagement to a long-term course of action.
commune: To communicate closely, sharing thoughts, feelings or prayers in an intimate way. To be in close rapport.
compatible: Capable of combining well; getting along, harmonious.
compensate: To make up for; counteract; recompense.
component: An element; one of the parts constituting a whole.
comprehend: Understand.
comprehensive: Including much or all.
comprise: To consist of; be composed of.
concealing grace: See: *grace, tirodhāna śakti.*
conceive: To form or develop an idea, thought, belief or attitude.
concentration: Uninterrupted and sustained attention. See: *rāja yoga.*
concept: An idea or thought, especially a generalized or abstract idea.
conception: Power to imagine, conceive or create. Moment when a pregnancy is begun, a new earthly body generated. **—the point of conception; the apex of creation:** The simple instant that precedes any creative impulse and is therefore the source and summit of the powers of creation or manifestation. To become conscious of the point of conception is a great *siddhi.*
concomitant: Accompanying a condition or circumstance.
concord: Harmony and agreement; peaceful relations.
condone: To forgive, pardon or overlook.
confer: To give or grant, especially an honor or privilege.
confession: An admission of guilt or acknowledgement of wrongdoing.
confidentiality: The ability to keep confidences or information told in trust; not divulging private or secret matters.
confine(s): Boundary, limits, border. To restrict or keep within limits.
conflagration: A large, destructive fire.
conform: To be in accord or agreement with.
conformity: Action in accordance with customs, rules, prevailing opinion.
congregational worship: Worship done as a group, such as synchronized singing, community prayers or other participatory worship by individuals sharing a strict membership to a particular organization, with no other religious affiliations. Hindu worship is strongly congregational within *āśramas* and tightly organized societies, but usually noncongregational in the general sphere. See: *bhajana, kīrtana, pūjā, yajña.*
conquest: Act or process of overcoming.
conscience: The inner sense of right and wrong, sometimes called "the knowing voice of the soul." However, the conscience is affected by the individual's training and belief patterns, and is therefore not necessarily a perfect reflection of *dharma.* In Sanskṛit the conscience is known as *antaryamin,* "inner guide," or *dharmabuddhi,* "moral wisdom." Other terms are *sadasadvichāra śakti* "good-bad reflective power" and *saṁjñāna,* "right conception." It is the subconscious of the person—the sum total of past impres-

sions and training—that defines the creedal structure and colors the conscience and either clearly reflects or distorts superconscious wisdom. If the subconscious has been impressed with Western beliefs, for example, of Christianity, Judaism, existentialism or materialism, the conscience will be different than when schooled in the Vedic *dharma* of Śāktism, Smārtism, Śaivism or Vaishṇavism. This psychological law has to do with the superconscious mind working through the subconscious (an interface known as the subsuperconscious) and explains why the *dharma* of one's *sampradāya* must be fully learned as a young child for the conscience to be free of conflict. The Sanātana Dharma, fully and correctly understood provides the purest possible educational creedal structure, building a subconscious that is a clear, unobstructing channel for superconscious wisdom, the soul's innate intelligence, to be expressed through the conscience. Conscience is thus the sum of two things: the superconscious knowing (which is the same in all people) and the creedal belief structure through which the superconscious flows. This explains why people in different cultures have different consciences. See: *creed, dharma, mind (individual).*

conscious mind: The external, everyday state of consciousness. See: *mind.*

consciousness: *Chitta* or *chaitanya.* 1) A synonym for mind-stuff, *chitta;* or 2) the condition or power of perception, awareness, apprehension. There are myriad gradations of consciousness, from the simple sentience of inanimate matter to the consciousness of basic life forms, to the higher consciousness of human embodiment, to omniscient states of superconsciousness, leading to immersion in the One universal consciousness, Parāśakti. *Chaitanya* and *chitta* can name both individual consciousness and universal consciousness. Modifiers indicate the level of awareness, e.g., *vyashṭi chaitanya,* "individual consciousness;" *buddhi chitta,* "intellectual consciousness;" Śivachaitanya, "God consciousness." Five classical "states" of awareness are discussed in scripture: 1) wakefulness *(jāgrat),* 2) "dream" *(svapna)* or astral consciousness, 3) "deep sleep" *(sushupti)* or subsuperconsciousness, 4) the superconscious state beyond *(turīya* "fourth") and 5) the utterly transcendent state called *turīyātita* ("beyond the fourth"). See: *awareness, chitta, chaitanya, mind (all entries).*

consecrate: To declare holy, or designate for sacred or religious use.

consecrated temple: A temple duly and fully established in all three worlds through formal religious ceremony known as *kumbhābisheka.*

consent: Accord; agreement; approval, especially for a proposed act.

console: To make someone feel less sad or disappointed. To comfort.

consolidate: To make stronger by bringing several things into a single whole.

consort: Spouse, especially of a king or queen, God or Goddess. Among the Gods there are actually no sexes or sexual distinctions, though Hinduism traditionally portrays these great beings in elaborate human-like depictions in mythological folk narratives. Matrimony and human-like family units among the Gods are derived from educational tales designed to illustrate the way people should and should not live. See: *Śakti.*

contemplation: Religious or mystical absorption beyond meditation. See: *enstasy, rāja yoga, samādhi.*

contend: To hold as a belief or assert as fact.

continence (continent): Restraint, moderation or, most strictly, total abstinence from sexual activity. See: *brahmacharya.*

conversely: A word used to introduce a concept with terms similar to a previous one, but in reversed order.

conversion to Hinduism: Entering Hinduism has traditionally required little more than accepting and living the beliefs and codes of Hindus. This remains the basic factor of adoption, although there are, and always have been, formal ceremonies recognizing an individual's entrance into the religion, particularly the *nāmakaraṇa,* or naming rite. The most obvious sign of true sincerity of adoption or conversion is the total abandoning of the former name and the choosing of the Hindu name, usually the name of a God or Goddess, and then making it legal on one's passport, identity card, social security card and driver's license. This name is used at all times, under all circumstances, particularly with family and friends. This is severance. This is adoption. This is embracing Hinduism. This is conversion. This is true sincerity and considered by born members as the most honorable and trusted testimony of those who choose to join the global congregation of the world's oldest religion. Many temples in India and other countries will ask to see the passport or other appropriate identification before admitting devotees of non-Indian origin for more than casual worship. It requires nothing more than one's own commitment to the process. Belief is the keynote of religious conviction, and the beliefs vary greatly among the different religions of the world. What we believe forms our attitudes, shapes our lives and molds our destiny. To choose one's beliefs is to choose one's religion. Those who find themselves at home with the beliefs of Hinduism are, on a simple level, Hindu. Formally entering a new religion, however, is a serious commitment. Particularly for those with prior religious ties it is sometimes painful and always challenging.

The acceptance of outsiders into the Hindu fold has occurred for thousands of years. As Swāmī Vivekānanda once said, "Born aliens have been converted in the past by crowds, and the process is still going on." Dr. S. Rādhākṛishṇan confirms the *swāmī's* views in a brief passage from his well known book *The Hindu View of Life:* "In a sense, Hinduism may be regarded as the first example in the world of a missionary religion. Only its missionary spirit is different from that associated with the proselytizing creeds. It did not regard it as its mission to convert humanity to any one opinion. For what counts is conduct and not belief. Worshipers of different Gods and followers of different rites were taken into the Hindu fold. The ancient practice of *vrātyastoma,* described fully in the *Taṇḍya Brāhmaṇa,* shows that not only individuals but whole tribes were absorbed into Hinduism. Many modern sects accept outsiders. *Dvala's Smṛiti* lays down rules for the simple purification of people forcibly converted to other faiths, or of womenfolk defiled and confined for years, and even of people who, for worldly advantage, embrace other faiths (p. 28-29)." See: *Hindu, Hinduism.*

cope: To successfully contend with on equal terms. To face or deal with the difficulties of life.

cosmic: Universal; vast. Of or relating to the cosmos or entire universe.

cosmic cycle: One of the infinitely recurring periods of the universe, comprising its creation, preservation and dissolution. These cycles are measured in periods of progressive ages, called *yugas.* Satya (or Kṛita), Tretā, Dvāpara and Kali are the names of these four divisions, and they repeat themselves in that order, with the Satya Yuga being the longest and the Kali Yuga the shortest. The comparison is often made of these ages with the cycles of the day: Satya Yuga being morning until noon, the period of greatest light or enlightenment, Tretā Yuga afternoon, Dvāpara evening, and Kali Yuga the darkest part of the night. Four *yugas* equal one *mahāyuga.* Theories vary, but by traditional astronomical calculation, a *mahāyuga* equals 4,320,000 solar years (or 12,000 "divine years;" one divine year is 360 solar years)—with the Satya Yuga lasting 1,728,000 years, Tretā Yuga 1,296,000 years, Dvāpara Yuga 864,000 years, and Kali Yuga 432,000 years. Mankind is now experiencing the Kali Yuga, which began at midnight, February 18, 3102 BCE (year one on the Hindu calendar [see Hindu Timeline]) and will end in approximately 427,000 years. (By another reckoning, one *mahāyuga* equals approximately two million solar years.)

A dissolution called *laya* occurs at the end of each *mahāyuga,* when the physical world is destroyed by flood and fire. Each destructive period is followed by the succession of creation *(sṛishṭi),* evolution or preservation *(sthiti)* and dissolution *(laya).* A summary of the periods in the cosmic cycles:

1 *mahāyuga* = 4,320,000 years
71 *mahāyugas* = 1 *manvantara* or *manu* (we are in the 28th *mahayuga*)
14 *manvantaras* = 1 *kalpa* or day of Brahmā (we are in the 7th *manvantara*)
2 *kalpas* = 1 *ahoratra* or day and night of Brahmā
360 *ahoratras* = 1 year of Brahmā
100 Brahmā years = lifespan of Brahmā (or the universe), now in "year" 51.

At the end of every kalpa or day of Brahmā a greater dissolution, called *pralaya* (or *kalpanta,* "end of an eon"), occurs when both the physical and subtle worlds are absorbed into the causal world, where souls rest until the next *kalpa* begins. This state of withdrawal or "night of Brahmā," continues for the length of an entire kalpa until creation again issues forth. After 36,000 of these dissolutions and creations there is a total, universal annihilation, *mahāpralaya,* when all three worlds, all time, form and space, are withdrawn into God Śiva. After a period of total withdrawal a new universe or lifespan of Brahmā begins. This entire cycle repeats infinitely. This view of cosmic time is recorded in the *Purāṇas* and the *Dharma Śāstras.* See: *mahāpralaya.*

Cosmic Dance: See: *Naṭarāja.*

Cosmic Soul: Purusha or Parameśvara. Primal Soul. The Universal Being; Personal God. See: *Parameśvara, Primal Soul, purusha, Śiva.*

cosmology: "Cosmos-knowledge." The area of metaphysics pertaining to the origin and structure of the universe. Hindu cosmology includes both inner and outer worlds of existence. See: *tattva.*

cosmos: The universe, or whole of creation, especially with reference to its order, harmony and completeness. See: *Brahmāṇḍa, loka, three worlds, tattva.*

covenant: A binding agreement to do or keep from doing certain things.

covet: To want ardently, especially something belonging to another. To envy.

cranial *chakras:* The *ājñā,* or third-eye center, and the *sahasrāra,* at the top of the head near the pineal and pituitary glands. See: *chakra.*

creation: The act of creating, especially bringing the world into ordered existence. Also, all of created existence, the cosmos. Creation, according to the monistic-theistic view, is an emanation or extension of God, the Creator. It is Himself in another form, and not inherently something other than Him. See: *cause, tattva.*

creator: He who brings about creation. Śiva as one of His five powers. See: *creation, Naṭarāja, Parameśvara.*

creed: *Śraddhādhāraṇā.* An authoritative formulation of the beliefs of a religion. Historically, creeds have arisen to protect doctrinal purity when religions are transplanted into foreign cultures. See: *conscience.*

cremation: *Dahana.* Burning of the dead. Cremation is the traditional system of disposing of bodily remains, having the positive effect of releasing the soul most quickly from any lingering attachment to the earth plane. In modern times, cremation facilities are widely available in nearly every country, though gas-fueled chambers generally take the place of the customary wood pyre. Embalming, commonly practiced even if the body is to be cremated, is ill-advised, as it injures the astral body and can actually be felt by the departed soul, as would an autopsy. Should it be necessary to preserve the body a few days to allow time for relatives to arrive, it is recommended that hot ice surround the body and that the coffin be kept closed. Arrangements for this service should be made well in advance with the mortuary. Note that the remains of enlightened masters are sometimes buried or sealed in a special tomb called a *samādhi.* This is done in acknowledgement of the extraordinary attainment of such a soul, whose very body, having become holy, is revered as a sacred presence, *sānnidhya,* and which not infrequently becomes the spiritual seed of a temple or place of pilgrimage. See: *bone-gathering, death, reincarnation, sānnidhya.*

cringe: To retreat, bend or crouch in an attitude of fear, especially from something dangerous or painful.

crown *chakra*: *Sahasrāra chakra.* The thousand-petaled cranial center of divine consciousness. See: *chakra.*

crucial: Of supreme importance; decisive; critical.

crude: Raw. Not prepared or refined. Lacking grace, tact or taste. Uncultured.

crux: The essential or deciding point.

culminate: To reach the highest point or climax. Result.

culture: Development or refinement of intellect, emotions, interests, manners, and tastes. The ideals, customs, skills and arts of a people or group that are transmitted from one generation to another. Culture is refined living that arises in a peaceful, stable society. Hindu culture arises directly out of worship in the temples. The music, the dance, the art, the subtleties of mannerism and interraction between people all have their source in the humble devotion to the Lord, living in the higher, spiritual nature, grounded in the security of the immortal Self within.

Dakshiṇāmūrti: दक्षिणामूर्ति "South-facing form." Lord Śiva depicted sitting under a *pīpala* (bo) tree, silently teaching four *ṛishis* at His feet.

dampatī: दम्पती "House lord(s)." A term for husband and wife as the dual masters and sovereign guides of the Hindu home *(dama).* See: *gṛihastha dharma.*

dāna: दान Generosity, giving. See: *yama-niyama.*

dance: See: *tāṇḍava, Naṭarāja.*

***daṇḍa*:** दण्ड "Staff of support." The staff carried by a *sādhu* or *sannyāsin*, representing the *tapas* which he has taken as his only support, and the vivifying of *sushumṇā* and consequent Realization he seeks. *Daṇḍa* also connotes "penalty or sanction." See: *sādhu, sannyāsin.*

darśana: दर्शन "Vision, sight." Seeing the Divine. Beholding, with inner or outer vision, a temple image, Deity, holy person or place, with the desire to inwardly contact and receive the grace and blessings of the venerated being or beings. Even beholding a photograph in the proper spirit is a form of *darśana.* Not only does the devotee seek to see the Divine, but to be seen as well, to stand humbly in the awakened gaze of the holy one, even if for an instant, such as in a crowded temple when thousands of worshipers file quickly past the enshrined Lord. Gods and *gurus* are thus said to "give" *darśana,* and devotees "take" *darśana,* with the eyes being the mystic locus through which energy is exchanged. This direct and personal two-sided apprehension is a central and highly sought-after experience of Hindu faith. Also: "point of view," doctrine or philosophy. See: *shaḍ darśana, sound.*

Darwin's theory: Theory of evolution developed by Charles Darwin (1809–1882) stating that plant and animal species develop or evolve from earlier forms due to hereditary transmission of variations that enhance the organism's adaptability and chances of survival. See: *evolution of the soul, nonhuman birth.*

daśama bhāga vrata: दशमभागव्रत "One-tenth-part vow." A promise that tithers make before God, Gods and their family or peers to tithe regularly each month—for a specified time, or for life, as they wish. See: *daśamāṁśa.*

daśamāṁśa: दशमांश "One-tenth sharing." The traditional Hindu practice of tithing, giving one-tenth of one's income to a religious institution. It was formerly widespread in India. In ancient times the term *makimai* was used in Tamil Nadu. See: *daśama bhāga vrata, purushārtha.*

dāsa mārga: दासमार्ग "Servant's path." See: *pāda.*

Daśanāmī: दशनामी "Ten names." Ten monastic orders organized by Ādi Śaṅkara (ca 800): Āraṇya, Vāna, Giri, Pārvata, Sāgara, Tīrtha, Āśrama, Bhārati, Pūrī and Sarasvatī. Also refers to *sannyāsins* of these orders, each of whom bears his order's name, with *ānanda* often attached to the religious name. For example, Rāmānanda Tīrtha. Traditionally, each order is associated with one of the main Śaṅkarāchārya pīṭhas. See: *Śaṅkarāchārya pīṭha, Smārta Sampradāya, Śaṅkara.*

daurmanasya: दौर्मनस्य "Mental pain, dejection, sorrow, melancholy and despair." See: *chakra.*

dayā: दया "Compassion." See: *yama-niyama.*

death: Death is a rich concept for which there are many words in Sanskṛit, such as: *mahāprasthāna,* "great departure;" *samādhimaraṇa,* dying consciously while in the state of meditation; *mahāsamādhi,* "great merger, or absorption," naming the departure of an enlightened soul. Hindus know death to be the soul's detaching itself from the physical body and continuing on in the subtle body *(sūkshma śarīra)* with the same desires, aspirations and occupations as when it lived in a physical body. Now the person exists in the in-between world, the subtle plane, or Antarloka, with loved ones who have previously died, and is visited by earthly associates during their sleep. Hindus do not fear death, for they know it to be one of the most glorious and exalted experiences, rich in spiritual potential. Other terms for death include *pañchatvam* (death as dissolution of the five elements), *mṛityu* (natural death), *prāyopaveśa* (self-willed death by fasting), *māraṇa* (unnatural death, e.g., by murder). See: *reincarnation, suicide, videhamukti.*

deceit (deception): The act of representing as true what is known to be false. A dishonest action.

decentralized: Whose administrative agencies, power, authority, etc., are distributed widely, rather than concentrated in a single place or person. In Hinduism, authority is decentralized.

decked: Covered with fine clothing or ornaments.

defiled: Polluted, made dirty, impure.

deformity: Condition of being disfigured or made ugly in body, mind or emotions.

***deha:* देह** "Body." From the verb *dih,* "to plaster, mold; anoint, fashion." A term used in the *Upanishads, yoga* texts, *Śaiva Āgamas, Tirumantiram* and elsewhere to name the three bodies of the soul: gross or physical *(sthula),* astral or subtle *(sūkshma)* and causal *(kāraṇa).* A synonym for *śarīra.* See: *śarīra.*

Deism: A doctrine which believes in the existence of God based on purely rational grounds; a particular faith prominent in the 17th and 18th centuries adhered to by several founding fathers of the United States, including Benjamin Franklin and Thomas Jefferson. It holds that God created the world and its natural laws but is not involved in its functioning.

Deity: "God." Can refer to the image or *mūrti* installed in a temple or to the Mahādeva the *mūrti* represents. See: *mūrti, pūjā.*

delineate: To mark or trace out the boundaries of a thing, concept, etc.

delude: To fool as by false promises or improper concepts or thinking.

delusion: *Moha.* False belief, misconception.

denial: Saying "no." Opposing or not believing in the existence of something.

denomination: A name for a class of things, especially for various religious groupings, sects and subsects. See: *paramparā, sampradāya.*

denote: To indicate, signify or refer to.

deplore: To be regretful or sorry about; to lament, disapprove.

deploy: To spread out; rearrange into an effective pattern.

deportment: The manner of bearing or conducting oneself; behavior.

depraved: Immoral; corrupt; bad; perverted.

desirous: Having a longing or desire; motivated by desire.

despair: The state of having lost or given up hope.

despise: To strongly dislike; look down upon with contempt or scorn.

destiny: Final outcome. The seemingly inevitable or predetermined course of events. See: *adṛishṭa, fate, karma.*

Destroyer: Term for God Śiva in His aspect of Rudra. See: *Naṭarāja.*

***deva:* देव** "Shining one." A being living in the higher astral plane, in a subtle, nonphysical body. *Deva* is also used in scripture to mean "God or Deity." See: *Mahādeva.*

***Devaloka:* देवलोक** "Plane of radiant beings." A synonym of Maharloka, the higher astral plane, realm of *anāhata chakra.* See: *loka.*

***devamandira:* देवमन्दिर** "Abode of celestial beings." From *mand,* "to stand or tarry." A Hindu temple; also simply *mandira.* See: *temple.*

***Devanāgarī:* देवनागरी** "Divine writing of townspeople." The alphabetic script in which Sanskṛit, Prākṛit, Hindi and Marāṭhi are written. A descendant of the Northern type of the Brāhmī script. It is characterized by the connecting, horizontal line at the top of the letters. See: *Sanskṛit.*

***Devī:* देवी** "Goddess." A name of Śakti, used especially in Śāktism. See: *Śakti, Śāktism.*

***Devī Bhāgavata Purāṇa:* देवीभागवतपुराण** A subsidiary text of the Śiva

Purāṇas.

Devī Gītā: देवीगीता Twelve chapters (29 to 40) from the 7th book of *Śrīmad Devī Bhāgavatam,* a Śākta scripture. It teaches external worship of the Deity with form and meditation on the Deity beyond form.

Devīkālottara Āgama: देवीकालोत्तर आगम One recension (version) of the *Sārdha Triśati Kālottara Āgama,* a subsidiary text of *Vātula Āgama.* Also known as *Skanda Kālottara.* Its 350 verses are in the form of a dialog between Kārttikeya and Śiva and deal with esoterics of *mantras,* initiations, right knowledge, faith and worship of Śiva. See: *Śaiva Āgamas.*

Devī Upanishad: देवी उपनिषद् A Śākta *Upanishad* dealing with the nature and worship of the Goddess. See: *Śāktism.*

devoid: Completely without; empty.

devonic: Of or relating to the *devas* or their world. See: *deva.*

devotee: A person strongly dedicated to something or someone, such as to a God or a *guru.* The term *disciple* implies an even deeper commitment. See: *guru bhakti.*

Dhammapada: धम्मपद The holy book of Buddhism. See: *Buddhism.*

Dhanurveda: धनुर्वेद "Science of archery." A class of ancient texts on the military arts, comprising the *Upaveda* of the *Yajur Veda. Dhanurveda* teaches concentration, meditation, *haṭha yoga,* etc., as integral to the science of warfare. See: *Upaveda.*

dhāraṇā: धारणा "Concentration." From *dṛi,* "to hold." See: *meditation, rāja yoga, śraddādhāraṇā, yoga.*

dharma: धर्म From *dhṛi,* "to sustain; carry, hold." Hence *dharma* is "that which contains or upholds the cosmos." *Dharma* is a complex and all-inclusive term with many meanings, including: divine law, law of being, way of righteousness, religion, duty, responsibility, virtue, justice, goodness and truth. Essentially, *dharma* is the orderly fulfillment of an inherent nature or destiny. Relating to the soul, it is the mode of conduct most conducive to spiritual advancement, the right and righteous path. There are four principal kinds of *dharma,* as follows. They are known collectively as ***—chatur-dharma:*** "four religious laws." 1) ***—ṛita:*** "Universal law." The inherent order of the cosmos. The laws of being and nature that contain and govern all forms, functions and processes, from galaxy clusters to the power of mental thought and perception. 2) ***—varṇa dharma***: "Law of one's kind." Social duty. *Varṇa* can mean "race, tribe, appearance, character, color, social standing, etc." *Varṇa dharma* defines the individual's obligations and responsibilities within the nation, society, community, class, occupational subgroup and family. An important part of this *dharma* is religious and moral law. See: *jāti, varṇa dharma.* 3) ***—āśrama dharma:*** "Duties of life's stages." Human *dharma.* The natural process of maturing from childhood to old age through fulfillment of the duties of each of the four stages of life—*brahmachārī* (student), *gṛihastha* (householder), *vānaprastha* (elder advisor) and *sannyāsa* (religious solitaire)—in pursuit of the four human goals: *dharma* (righteousness), *artha* (wealth), *kāma* (pleasure) and *moksha* (liberation). See: *āśrama dharma.* 4) ***—svadharma***: "Personal law." One's perfect individual pattern through life, according to one's own particular physical, mental and emotional nature. *Svadharma* is determined by the sum of past *karmas* and the cumulative effect of the other three *dharmas.* It is the individualized application of *dharma,* dependent on personal *karma,* reflected on one's race, community, physical characteristics, health, intelligence, skills and aptitudes, desires and tendencies, religion, *sampradāya,* family and *guru.*

Within *āśrama dharma,* the unique duties of man and woman are respectively called *strī dharma* and *purusha dharma.* ***—purusha dharma:*** "Man's duty." Man's proper pattern of conduct; traditional observances, vocation, behavior and attitudes dictated by spiritual wisdom. Characterized by leadership, integrity, accomplishment, sustenance of the family. Notably, the married man works in the world and sustains his family as abundantly as he can. ***—strī dharma:*** "Woman's duty." Traditional conduct, observances, vocational and spiritual patterns which bring spiritual fulfillment and societal stability. Characterized by modesty, quiet strength, religiousness, dignity and nurturing of family. Notably, she is most needed and irreplaceable as the maker of the home and the educator of their children as noble citizens of tomorrow. See: *gṛihastha dharma.*

A part of the *varṇa dharma* of each person is *sādhārana dharma*—the principles of good conduct applicable to all people regardless of age, gender or class. ***—sādhāraṇa dharma:*** "Duties applicable to all." Listed in the *Manu Śāstras* as: *dhairya* (steadfastness), *kshamā* (forgiveness), *dama* (self-restraint), *chauryābhāva* (nonstealing), *śaucha* (cleanliness), *indriyanigraha* (sense control), *dhī* (high-mindedness), *vidyā* (learning), *satya* (veracity), *akrodha* (absence of anger). Another term for such virtues is — ***sāmānya dharma:*** "general duty," under which scriptures offer similar lists of ethical guidelines. These are echoed and expanded in the *yamas* and *niyamas,* "restraints and observances." See: *yama-niyama.*

One other important division of *dharma* indicates the two paths within Hinduism, that of the family person, the *gṛihastha dharma,* and that of the monastic, the *sannyāsa dharma.* ***—gṛihastha dharma:*** "Householder duty." The duties, ideals and responsibilities of all nonmonastics, whether married or unmarried. This *dharma,* which includes the vast majority of Hindus, begins when the period of studentship is complete and extends until the end of life. See: *gṛihastha dharma.* ***—sannyāsa dharma:*** "Monastic duty." Above and beyond all the other *dharmas ("ati-varṇāśrama dharma")* is *sannyāsa dharma*—the ideals, principles and rules of renunciate monks. It is the highest *dharma.* See: *sannyāsa dharma.*

—āpad dharma: "Emergency conduct." This *dharma* embodies the principle that the only rigid rule is wisdom, and thus exceptional situations may require deviating from normal rules of conduct, with the condition that such exceptions are to be made only for the sake of others, not for personal advantage. These are notable exceptions, made in cases of extreme distress or calamity.

—***adharma:*** "Unrighteousness." Thoughts, words or deeds that transgress divine law in any of the human expressions of *dharma.* It brings the accumulation of demerit, called *pāpa,* while *dharma* brings merit, called *puṇya. Varṇa adharma* is violating the ideals of social duty, from disobeying the laws of one's nation to squandering family wealth. *Āśrama adharma* is failure to fulfill the duties of the stages of life. *Sva adharma* is understood as not fulfilling the patterns of *dharma* according to one's own nature. The *Bhagavad Gītā* states (18.47), "Better one's *svadharma* even imperfectly performed than the *dharma* of another well performed. By performing the duty prescribed by one's own nature *(svabhāva)* one incurs no sin *(kilbisha).*" See: *puṇya, pāpa, purity-impurity, varṇa dharma.*

dharmasabhā: धर्मसभा "Religious assembly, congregation." A church.

Dharma Śāstra: धर्मशास्त्र "Religious law book." A term referring to all or any of numerous codes of Hindu civil and social law composed by various authors. The best known and most respected are those by Manu and Yajñavalkya, thought to have been composed as early as 600 BCE. The *Dharma Śāstras,* along with the *Artha Śāstras,* are the codes of Hindu law, parallel to the Muslim Sharia, the Jewish *Talmud,* each of which provides guidelines for kings, ministers, judicial systems and law enforcement agencies. These spiritual-parliamentary codes differ from British and American law, which separate religion from politics. (Contemporary British law is influenced by Anglican Christian thought, just as American democracy was, and is, profoundly affected by the philosophy of its non-Christian, Deistic founders.) The *Dharma Śāstras* also speak of much more, including creation, initiation, the stages of life, daily rites, duties of husband and wife, caste, Vedic study, penances and transmigration. The *Dharma Śāstras* are part of the *Smṛiti* literature, included in the *Kalpa Vedāṅga,* and are widely available today in many languages. See: *Deism, Manu Dharma Śāstras.*

dhotī: धोती (Hindi) A long, unstitched cloth wound about the lower part of the body, and sometimes passed between the legs and tucked into the waist. A traditional Hindu apparel for men. See: *veshti.*

dhṛiti: धृति "Steadfastness." See: *yama-niyama.*

dhvaja: ध्वज "Flag." Part of the pageantry of Hinduism, orange or red flags and banners, flown at festivals and other special, occasions symbolize the victory of *Sanātana Dharma.* See: *festival.*

dhvajastambha: ध्वजस्तम्भ "Flag tree, flagpole." (*Kodimaram* in Tamil.) A tall cylindrical post usually behind the *vāhana* in Āgamic temples. Metaphysically, it acts as the complementary pole to the enshrined *mūrti.* These two together create an energy field to contain the temple's power. See: *temple.*

dhyāna: ध्यान "Meditation." See: *internalized worship, meditation, rāja yoga.*

dichotomy: A division into two parts, usually sharply distinguished or contradictory. See: *paradox.*

Dieu Siva est amour omniprésent et Réalité transcendante: French for "God Śiva is Immanent Love and Transcendent Reality." It is an affirmation of faith which capsulizes the entire creed of monistic Śaiva Siddhānta.

differentiation: State or condition of making or perceiving a difference.

dīkshā: दीक्षा "Initiation." Action or process by which one is entered into a new realm of spiritual knowledge and practice by a teacher or preceptor through the transmission of blessings. Denotes initial or deepened connection with the teacher and his lineage and is usually accompanied by ceremony. Initiation, revered as a moment of awakening, may be bestowed by a touch, a word, a look or a thought. As the aspirant matures, he may receive deeper initiations, each one drawing him further into his spiritual being. Most Hindu schools, and especially Śaivism, teach that only with initiation from a *satguru* is enlightenment attainable. Sought after by all Hindus is the *dīkshā* called *śaktipāta,* "descent of grace," which, often coming unbidden, stirs and arouses the mystic *kuṇḍalinī* force. Central Śaivite *dīkshās* include *samaya, vishesha, nirvāṇa* and *abhiśeka.* See: *grace, śaktipāta, sound.*

Dīpāvalī: दीपावली "Row of Lights." A very popular home and community festival during which Hindus of all denominations light oil or electric lights and set off fireworks in a joyful celebration of the victory of good or evil, light over darkness. It is a Hindu solidarity day and is considered the greatest national festival of India. In several countries, including Nepal, Malaysia, Singapore, Sri Lanka and Trinidad and Tobago, it is an inter-religious event and a national holiday. It occurs in October-November.

dipolar: Relating to two poles instead of only one. A philosophy is said to be dipolar when it embraces both of two contradictory (or apparently contradictory) propositions, concepts, tendencies, etc. For example, panentheism is dipolar in that it accepts the truth of God's being (and being in) the world, and also the truth that He transcends the world. Instead of saying "it is either this or that," a dipolar position says "it is both this and that." See: *dvaita-advaita.*

discordant: Not in accord. Disagreeing; clashing; out of harmony.

discrimination: *Viveka.* Act or ability to distinguish or perceive differences. In spirituality, the ability to distinguish between right and wrong, real and apparent, eternal and transient, as in the Upanishadic maxim, *Neti, neti,* "It is not this, it is not that." See: *conscience.*

disheveled: Untidy hair, clothing or general appearance. Rumpled.

dismay: Loss of courage or confidence before danger. Fearful worry.

dispassionate: Free from emotion or passion. Calm; impartial; detached.

dispatch: To send off promptly, especially on an errand. To finish quickly.

dispel: To cause to go in various directions. To scatter and drive away; disperse.

dissolution: Dissolving or breaking up into parts. An alternative term for destruction. See: *absorption, mahāpralaya, Naṭarāja.*

distort: To twist out of shape. To misrepresent.

divergent: Going off in different directions; deviating or varying.

Divine Mother: Śakti, especially as Personal Goddess, as conceived of and worshiped by Śāktas. See: *Śakti, Śaktism.*

dominion: Rulership; domain. **—hold dominion over:** To be king, ruler, lord, or master of (a world, realm, etc).

don: To put on (a piece of clothing).

door of Brahman: *Brahmarandhra;* also called *nirvāna chakra.* An aperture in the crown of the head, the opening of *sushumṇā nāḍī* through which *kuṇḍalinī* enters in ultimate Self Realization, and the spirit escapes at death. Only the spirits of the truly pure leave the body in this way. *Saṁsārīs* take a downward course. See: *jñāna, kuṇḍalinī, videhamukti.*

dormant: Sleeping; inactive; not functioning.

dosha: दोष "Bodily humor; individual constitution." Refers to three bodily humors, which according to *āyurveda* regulate the body, govern its proper functioning and determine its unique constitution. These are *vāta,* the air humor; *pitta,* the fire humor; and *kapha,* the water humor. *Vāta* has its seat in the intestinal area, *pitta* in the stomach, and *kapha* in the lung area. They govern the creation, preservation and dissolution of bodily tissue. *Vāta* humor is metabolic, nerve energy. *Pitta* is the catabolic, fire energy. *Kapha* is the anabolic, nutritive energy. The three *doshas (tridosha)* also give rise to the various emotions and correspond to the three *guṇas,* "qualities:" *sattva* (quiescence—*vāta*), *rajas* (activity—*pitta*) and *tamas* (inertia—*kapha*). See: *āyurveda, kapha, pitta, vāta.*

dross: Waste matter; useless byproduct.

dual: Having or composed of two parts or kinds. **—duality:** A state or condition of being dual. **—realm of duality:** The phenomenal world, where each thing exists along with its opposite: joy and sorrow, etc. **—dualism:** See: *dvaita-advaita.*

duly: At the proper time, in the proper manner; as required.

Durgā: दुर्गा "She who is incomprehensible or difficult to reach." A form of Śakti worshiped in Her gracious as well as terrifying aspect. Destroyer of demons, She is worshiped during an annual festival called Durgā *pūjā,* especially popular among Bengalis. See: *Śakti, Śāktism.*

Durvāsas: दुर्वासस् A great sage (date unknown) who, according to Kashmīr Śaivism, was commissioned by Lord Śiva to revive the knowledge of the *Śaiva Āgamas,* whereupon he created three "mind-born" sons—Tryambaka to disseminate *advaita,* Śrīnātha to teach monistic theism, and Āmardaka to postulate dualism.

dvaita-advaita: द्वैत अद्वैत "Dual-nondual; twoness-not twoness. Among the most important terms in the classification of Hindu philosophies. *Dvaita* and *advaita* define two ends of a vast spectrum. ***—dvaita:*** The doctrine of dualism, according to which reality is ultimately composed of two irreducible principles, entities, truths, etc. God and soul, for example, are seen as eternally separate. **—dualistic:** Of or relating to dualism, concepts, writings, theories which treat dualities (good-and-evil, high-and-low, them-and-us) as fixed, rather than transcendable. **—pluralism:** A form of dualism which emphasizes three or more eternally separate realities, e.g., God, soul and world. ***—advaita:*** The doctrine of nondualism or monism, that reality is ultimately composed of one whole principle, substance or God, with no independent parts. In essence, all is God. **—monistic theism:** A dipolar view which encompasses both monism and dualism. See: *anekavāda, dipolar, monistic theism, pluralistic realism.*

dvaitic (dvaita) Siddhānta: द्वैतसिद्धान्त "Dualistic final conclusions." Refers to schools of Śaiva Siddhānta that postulate God, soul and world as three eternally distinct and separate realities. See: *Pati-paśu-pāśa, Śaiva Siddhānta.*

earrings: Decorative jewelry worn in the ears by Hindu women and many men. *Yogīs,* especially those of the Nātha tradition, wear large earrings to stimulate the psychic *nāḍīs* connected to the ears. Traditionally, the ascetic Kanphaṭis ("split-eared ones") split the cartilage of their ears to accommodate massive earrings. Ear-piercing for earrings is said to bring health (right ear) and wealth (left ear). See: *Kanphaṭi, saṁskāras of childhood.*

ecclesiastical: "Of the church or clergy." By extension, relating to the authoritative body of any religion, sect or lineage. Having to do with an assembly of spiritual leaders and their jurisdiction.

ecology: The science of relations between organisms and their environment.

ecstasy (ecstatic): State of being overtaken by emotion such as joy or wonder. Literally, "standing outside oneself." See: *enstasy, samādhi.*

ecumenical: Universal. **—ecumenism:** the principles or practices of promoting cooperation and better understanding among differing faiths.

efficacious: Producing or capable of producing the desired effect.

efficient cause: *Nimitta kāraṇa.* That which directly produces the effect; that which conceives, makes, shapes, etc. See: *cause.*

effulgent: Bright, radiant; emitting its own light.

egalitarian: Equalitarian. Characterized by the belief in the equal sharing of powers, rights or responsibility among all people.

ego: The external personality or sense of "I" and "mine." Broadly, individual identity. In Śaiva Siddhānta and other schools, the ego is equated with the *tattva* of *ahaṁkāra,* "I-maker," which bestows the sense of I-ness, individuality and separateness from God. See: *ahaṁkāra, āṇava.*

eligible: Qualified; suitable; desirable.
eliminate: To remove; get rid of; reject.
elixir: Hypothetical substance that would change any metal into gold or prolong life indefinitely. An English term for *soma,* a magical beverage celebrated in ancient Vedic hymns and which played an important role in worship rites. See: *amṛita.*
elliptical: Having the shape of an ellipse (more or less egg-shaped).
elusive: Tending to escape one's grasp or understanding. Hard to capture.
emanation: To "flow out from." *Ābhāsa.* To come forth from a source, to be emitted or issued from. A monistic doctrine of creation whereby God issues forth manifestation like rays from the sun or sparks from a fire. See: *ābhāsa.*
emancipator: That which, or one who, liberates.
eminent: High; above others in stature, rank or achievement. Renowned or distinguished; prominent, conspicuous. Not to be confused with: 1) *imminent,* about to happen; 2) *emanate,* to issue from; 3) *immanent,* inherent or indwelling.
empower: To give power or authority to a person or society. Strengthen.
emulate: To imitate. To attempt to equal or surpass someone, generally by copying his ways, talents or successes.
encompass: To surround or encircle; to include.
endow: To give. To provide with a quality or characteristic.
enhance: To improve, make better.
enlightened: Having attained enlightenment, Self Realization. A *jñānī* or *jīvanmukta.* See: *jīvanmukta, jñāna, Self Realization.*
enlightenment: For Śaiva monists, Self Realization, *samādhi* without seed *(nirvikalpa samādhi);* the ultimate attainment, sometimes referred to as Paramātma *darśana,* or as *ātma darśana,* "Self vision" (a term which appears in Patañjali's *Yoga Sūtras).* Enlightenment is the experience-nonexperience resulting in the realization of one's transcendent Self—Paraśiva—which exists beyond time, form and space. Each tradition has its own understanding of enlightenment, often indicated by unique terms. See: *God Realization, kuṇḍalinī, nirvikalpa samādhi, Self Realization.*
enshrine: To enclose in a shrine. To hold as sacred and worthy of worship.
enstasy: A term coined in 1969 by Mircea Eliade to contrast the Eastern view of bliss as "standing inside oneself" (enstasy) with the Western view as ecstasy, "standing outside oneself." A word chosen as the English equivalent of *samādhi.* See: *ecstasy, samādhi, rāja yoga.*
enthrall: To hold in a spell; captivate; fascinate.
entourage: A group of accompanying attendants, associates or assistants.
entreat: To ask earnestly; to beseech, implore, plead or beg.
epic history: Long narrative poem in a high style about grand exploits of Gods and heroes. The *Rāmāyaṇa* and *Mahābhārata* are India's two great epic histories, called *Itihāsa.* See: *Itihāsa, Mahābhārata, Rāmāyaṇa.*

equanimity: The quality of remaining calm and undisturbed. Evenness of mind; composure.

equilibrium: Evenly balanced. A quality of good spiritual leadership. "Having attained an equilibrium of *iḍā* and *piṅgalā*, he becomes a knower of the known." See: *jñāna.*

equivalent: Equal, or nearly so, in quantity, volume, force, meaning, etc.

erotic: "Of love (from the Greek *eros*)." Of or arousing sexual passion.

erroneous: Containing or based on error; wrong.

eschew: To shun, avoid, stay away from.

esoteric: Hard to understand or secret. Teaching intended for a chosen few, as an inner group of initiates. Abtruse or private.

essence (essential): The ultimate, real and unchanging nature of a thing or being. **—essence of the soul:** See: *ātman, soul.*

esteem: To respect highly; to value.

estranged: "Made a stranger." Set apart or divorced from.

eternity: Time without beginning or end.

ether: *Ākāśa.* Space, the most subtle of the five elements. See: *ākāśa, tattva.*

ethics: The code or system of morals of a nation, people, religion, etc. See: *dharma, pañcha nitya karmas, puṇya, purity-impurity.*

etymology: The science of the origin of words and their development. The history of a word. See: *Nirukta Vedāṅga, Sanskṛit.*

evil: That which is bad, morally wrong, causing harm, pain, misery. In Western religions, evil is often thought of as a moral antagonism with God. This force is the source of sin and is attached to the soul from its inception. Whereas, for Hindus, evil is not a conscious, dark force, such as Satan. It is situational rather than ontological, meaning it has its basis in relative conditions, not in ultimate reality. Evil (badness, corruption) springs from ignorance *(avidyā)* and immaturity. Nor is one fighting with God when he is evil, and God is not standing in judgment. Within each soul, and not external to it, resides the principle of judgment of instinctive-intellectual actions. God, who is ever compassionate, blesses even the worst sinner, the most depraved *asura*, knowing that individual will one day emerge from lower consciousness into the light of love and understanding. Hindus hold that evil, known in Sanskṛit as *pāpa, pāpman* or *dushṭā,* is the result of unvirtuous acts *(pāpa* or *adharma*) caused by the instinctive-intellectual mind dominating and obscuring deeper, spiritual intelligence. (Note: both *pāpa* and *pāpman* are used as nouns and adjectives.) The evil-doer is viewed as a young soul, ignorant of the value of right thought, speech and action, unable to live in the world without becoming entangled in *māyā.* **—intrinsic evil:** Inherent, inborn badness. Some philosophies hold that man and the world are *by nature* imperfect, corrupt or evil. Hinduism holds, on the contrary, that there is no intrinsic evil, and the real nature of man is his divine, soul nature, which is goodness. See: *hell, karma, pāpa, Satan, sin.*

evoke: To call forth; to conjure up; to summon, as to summon a Mahādeva, a God. See: *pūjā, yajña.*

evolution of the soul: *Adhyātma prasāra.* In Śaiva Siddhānta, the soul's evolution is a progressive unfoldment, growth and maturing toward its inherent, divine destiny, which is complete merger with Śiva. In its essence, each soul is ever perfect. But as an individual soul body emanated by God Śiva, it is like a small seed yet to develop. As an acorn needs to be planted in the dark underground to grow into a mighty oak tree, so must the soul unfold out of the darkness of the *malas* to full maturity and realization of its innate oneness with God. The soul is not created at the moment of conception of a physical body. Rather, it is created in the Śivaloka. It evolves by taking on denser and denser sheaths—cognitive, instinctive-intellectual and *prāṇic*—until finally it takes birth in physical form in the Bhūloka. Then it experiences many lives, maturing through the reincarnation process. Thus, from birth to birth, souls learn and mature.

Evolution is the result of experience and the lessons derived from it. There are young souls just beginning to evolve, and old souls nearing the end of their earthly sojourn. In Śaiva Siddhānta, evolution is understood as the removal of fetters which comes as a natural unfoldment, realization and expression of one's true, self-effulgent nature. This ripening or dropping away of the soul's bonds *(mala)* is called *malaparipāka.* The realization of the soul nature is termed *svānubhuti* (experience of the Self).

Self Realization leads to *moksha,* liberation from the three *malas* and the reincarnation cycles. Then evolution continues in the celestial worlds until the soul finally merges fully and indistinguishably into Supreme God Śiva, the Primal Soul, Parameśvara. In his *Tirumantiram,* Ṛishi Tirumular calls this merger *viśvagrāsa,* "total absorption. The evolution of the soul is not a linear progression, but an intricate, circular, many-faceted mystery. Nor is it at all encompassed in the Darwinian theory of evolution, which explains the origins of the human form as descended from earlier primates. See: *Darwin's theory, mala, moksha, reincarnation, saṁsāra, viśvagrāsa.*

exalt: To make high. To raise in status, glorify or praise.

excel: To stand out as better, greater, finer than others. To do well at something.

exclusive: Excluding all others. Śaivites believe that there is no exclusive path to God, that no spiritual path can rightly claim that it alone leads to the goal.

exemplar: One regarded as worthy of imitation; a model. An ideal pattern to be followed by others.

exhaustive: "Drawn out." Very thorough; covering all details; leaving nothing out.

existence: "Coming or standing forth." Being; reality; that which is.

experience: From the Latin *experior,* "to prove; put to the test." Living through an event; personal involvement. In Sanskṛit, *anubhava.*

expound: To explain or clarify, point by point.
extended family: *Bṛihatkuṭumba* or *mahākuṭumba.* One or more joint families plus their broader associations and affiliations. Unlike the joint family, whose members live in close proximity, the extended family is geographically widespread. The extended family is headed by the patriarch, called *bṛihatkuṭumba pramukha* (or *mukhya),* recognized as the leader by each joint family. He, in turn is under the guidance of the *kulaguru,* or family preceptor. It includes the following, in order of their precedence: priests of one's faith; elder men and women of the community; in-laws of married daughters; married daughters, granddaughters, great-granddaughters, and the spouses and children of these married girls; members of the staff and their families and those closely associated with the joint family business or home; maternal great-grandparents and grandparents, parents, uncles and their spouses, aunts and their spouses, children and grandchildren of these families; very close friends and their children; members of the community at large. See: *gṛihastha, gṛihastha dharma, joint family.*
extol: To praise highly.
exultant: Rejoicing greatly. Immensely happy or triumphant.

fable: Myth or legend. A story, usually with animal characters, meant to illustrate moral principles. See: *mythology, Pañchatantra.*
faith: Trust or belief. Conviction. From the Latin *fidere,* "to trust." *Faith* in its broadest sense means "religion, *dharma.*" More specifically, it is the essential element of religion—the belief in phenomena beyond the pale of the five senses, distinguishing it sharply from rationalism. Faith is established through intuitive or transcendent experience of an individual, study of scripture and hearing the testimony of the many wise *ṛishis* speaking out the same truths over thousands of years. This inner conviction is based in the divine sight of the third eye center, *ājñā chakra.* Rightly founded, faith transcends reason, but does not conflict with reason. Faith also means confidence, as in the testimony and reputation of other people. The Sanskṛit equivalent is *śraddhā.* Synonyms include *āstikya, viśvāsa, dharma* and *mati.*
family life: See: *gṛihastha āśrama, extended family, joint family.*
far-seeing: *Dūradarśana.* Having the power of clairvoyance, also known as *divyadṛishṭi,* "divine sight." See: *clairvoyance, siddhi.*
fast: To abstain from all or certain foods, as in observance of a vow or holy day. Hindus fast in various ways. A simple fast may consist of merely avoiding certain foods for a day or more, such as when vegetarians avoid *tamasic* or *rajasic* foods or when nonvegetarians abstain from fish, fowl and meats. A moderate fast would involve avoiding heavier foods, or taking only juices, teas and other liquids. Such fasts are sometimes observed only

during the day, and a normal meal is permitted after sunset. Serious fasting, which is done under supervision, involves taking only water for a number of days and requires a cessation of most external activities.

fate: From the Latin *fatum,* "prophetic declaration, oracle." In Western thought, fate is the force or agency, God or other power, outside man's control, believed to determine the course of events before they occur. According to Hindu thought, man is not ruled by fate but shapes his own destiny by his actions, which have their concomitant reactions. The Hindu view acknowledges fate only in the limited sense that man is subject to his own past *karmas,* which are a driving force in each incarnation, seemingly out of his own control. But they can be mitigated by how he lives life, meaning how he faces and manages his *prārabdha* ("begun, undertaken") *karmas* and his *kriyamāna* ("being made") *karmas.* See: *adṛishṭa, karma, destiny.*

fellowship: Companionship. Mutual sharing of interests, beliefs or practice. A group of people with common interests and aspirations.

festival: A time of religious celebration and special observances. Festivals generally recur yearly, their dates varying slightly according to astrological calculations. They are characterized by acts of piety (elaborate *pūjās,* penance, fasting, pilgrimage) and rejoicing (songs, dance, music, parades, storytelling and scriptural reading). See: *sound, teradi.*

fetch: Retrieve. To go get a thing and bring it back.

finesse: Ability to handle situations with skill and delicacy.

firewalking: The trance-inducing ceremonial practice of walking over a bed of smoldering, red-hot coals as an expression of faith and sometimes as a form of penance. Participants describe it as a euphoric experience in which no pain is felt and no burns received. Many lose body consciousness during the walk. Firewalking is associated with folk-shamanic Śāktism and is popular among Hindu communities inside and outside India. See: *folk-shamanic, penance, Śāktism.*

five acts of Śiva: *Pañchakṛitya.* Creation, preservation, destruction, veiling and revealing. See: *Naṭarāja, Parameśvara.*

flux: Continuous movement or change.

folk narratives: Community or village stories which are passed from generation to generation through verbal telling—often a mixture of fact and fiction, allegory and myth, legend and symbolism, conveying lessons about life, character and conduct. The most extensive and influential of India's folk narratives are the *Purāṇas.* While these stories are broadly deemed to be scriptural fact, this contemporary Hindu catechism accepts them as important mythology—stories meant to capture the imagination of the common peoples and to teach them moral living. See: *fable, kathā, mythology, Purāṇa.*

folk-shamanic: Of or related to a tribal or village tradition in which the mystic priest, shaman, plays a central role, wielding powers of magic and spirituality. Revered for his ability to influence and control nature and people, to cause good and bad things to happen, he is the intermediary between man and divine forces. The term *shaman* is from the Sanskṛit *śramaṇa,* "ascetic," akin to *śram,* "to exert." See: *Śāktism, shamanism.*

forbearance: Self-control; responding with patience and compassion, especially under provocation. Endurance; tolerance. See: *yama-niyama.*

formerly: At an earlier time; in the past.

formless: Philosophically, *atattva,* beyond the realm of form or substance. Used in attempting to describe the wondersome, indescribable Absolute, which is "timeless, formless and spaceless." God Śiva has form and is formless. He is the immanent Pure Consciousness or pure form. He is the Personal Lord manifesting as innumerable forms; and He is the impersonal, transcendent Absolute beyond all form. Thus we know Śiva in three perfections, two of form and one formless. This use of the term *formless* does not mean *amorphous,* which implies a form that is vague or changing. Rather, it is the absence of substance, sometimes thought of as a void, an emptiness beyond existence from which comes the fullness of everything. In describing the Self as formless, the words *timeless* and *spaceless* are given also to fully indicate this totally transcendent noncondition. See: *atattva, Paraśiva, Satchidānanda, void.*

fortress: A fortified place; a fort.

foster: To help grow or develop.

fountainhead: A spring that is the source of a stream. The source of anything.

fruition: The bearing of fruit. The coming to fulfillment of something that has been awaited or worked for.

funeral rites: See: *cremation, bone-gathering, saṁskāras of later life.*

gaja: गज The elephant, king of beasts, representative of Lord Gaṇeśa and sign of royalty and power. Many major Hindu temples keep one or more elephants.

galactic: Of or pertaining to our galaxy, the Milky Way (from the Greek *gala,* "milk") and/or other galaxies.

gaṇa(s): गण "Multitude, troop; number; a body of followers or attendants." A troop of demigods—God Śiva's attendants, devonic helpers under the supervision of Lord Gaṇeśa. See: *Gaṇapati, Gaṇeśa.*

gaṇāchāra: गणाचार Loyalty to the community. One of five Vīra Śaiva codes of conduct. Also, name of a Vīra Śaiva saint. See: *pañchāchāra, Vīra Śaivism.*

Gaṇapati: गणपति "Leader of the *gaṇas.*" A name of *Gaṇeśa.*

Gaṇapati Upanishad: गणपति उपनिषद् A later *Upanishad* on Lord Gaṇeśa, not connected with any *Veda;* date of composition is unknown. It is a major scripture for the Gaṇapatians, a minor Hindu sect which reveres Gaṇeśa as Supreme God and is most prevalent in India's Maharashtra state. See:

Gaṇeśa.

Gāndharvaveda: गान्धर्ववेद् "Science of music." A class of ancient texts on music, song and dance. It is the *Upaveda* of the *Sāma Veda.* See: *Upaveda.*

Gaṇeśa: गणेश "Lord of Categories." (From *gaṇ,* "to count or reckon," and *Īśa,* "lord.") Or: "Lord of attendants *(gaṇa),*" synonymous with *Gaṇapati.* Gaṇeśa is a Mahādeva, the beloved elephant-faced Deity honored by Hindus of every sect. He is the Lord of Obstacles (Vighneśvara), revered for His great wisdom and invoked first before any undertaking, for He knows all intricacies of each soul's *karma* and the perfect path of *dharma* that makes action successful. He sits on the *mūlādhāra chakra* and is easy of access. Lord Gaṇeśa is sometimes identified with the Ṛig Vedic God Bṛihaspati ("Lord of Prayer, the Holy Word)" *Ṛig Veda* 2.23.1. See: *gaṇa, Ganapati, Mahādeva.*

Gaṇeśa Chaturthī: गणेश चतुर्थी Birthday of Lord Gaṇeśa, a ten-day festival of August-September that culminates in a spectacular parade called *Gaṇeśa Visarjana.* It is a time of rejoicing, when all Hindus worship together.

Gaṇeśa Visarjana: गणेश विसर्जन "Gaṇeśa departure." A parade occurring on the 11th day after Gaṇeśa Chaturthī, in which the Gaṇeśa *mūrtis* made for the occasion are taken in procession to a body of water and ceremoniously immersed and left to dissolve. This represents Gaṇeśa's merging with the ocean of consciousness. See: *Gaṇeśa.*

Ganges *(Gaṅgā)*: गंगा India's most sacred river, 1,557 miles long, arising in the Himalayas above Hardwar under the name Bhagīratha, and being named Gaṅgā after joining the Alakanada (where the Sarasvatī is said to join them underground). It flows southeast across the densely populated Gangetic plain, joining its sister Yamunā (or Jumnā) at Prayaga (Allahabad) and ending at the Bay of Bengal. See: *Gangetic Plain.*

Gangetic Plain: The densely populated plain surrounding India's most sacred river, the Ganges (Gaṅga), an immense, fertile area of 300,000 square miles, 90 to 300 miles wide. See: *Ganges.*

garbha: गर्भ "Womb; interior chamber." The inside or middle of anything.

garbhādhāna: गर्भाधान "Womb-placing." The rite of conception. See: *reincarnation, saṁskāras of birth.*

garbhagṛiha: गर्भगृह The "innermost chamber," sanctum sanctorum, of a Hindu temple, where the primary *mūrti* is installed. It is a small, cave-like room, usually made of granite stone, to which only priests are permitted access. Esoterically it represents the cranial chamber. See: *temple.*

gārgya: गार्ग्य One of the known disciples of Lakulīśa. See: *Lakulīśa.*

Gautama: गौतम The name of the founder of the Nyāya school of Śaivism, author of the *Nyāya Sūtras.* Also, the Buddha (Siddhārtha Gautama). See: *Buddha, Buddhism, shaḍ darśana.*

gay: Homosexual, especially a male homosexual, though may also refer to females. See: *bisexual, homosexual, heterosexual, sexuality.*

gāyatrī: गायत्री According with the *gāyatrī* verse form, an ancient meter of

24 syllables, generally as a triplet with eight syllables each. From *gāya*, "song." —***Gāyatrī:*** The Vedic Gāyatrī Mantra personified as a Goddess, mother of the four *Vedas.*

Gāyatrī Mantra: **गायत्रीमन्त्र** 1) Famous Vedic *mantra* used in *pūjā* and personal chanting. *Om [bhūr bhuvaḥ svaḥ] tatsavitur vareṇyam, bhargo devasya dhīmahi, dhiyo yo naḥ prachodayāt.* "[O Divine Beings of all three worlds,] we meditate upon the glorious splendor of the Vivifier divine. May He Himself illumine our minds." *(Ṛig Veda* 3.62.10 VE). This sacred verse is also called the Sāvitrī Mantra, being addressed to Savitṛi, the Sun as Creator, and is considered a universal mystic formula so significant that it is called Vedamātṛi, "mother of the Vedas. 2) Any of a class of special *tantric mantras* called Gāyatrī. Each addresses a particular Deity. The Śiva Gāyatrī Mantra is: *Tryambakam yajāmahe sugandhim pushṭivardhanam, urvārukamiva bandhanān mṛtyormukshīya māmṛtāt.* "We adore the fragrant three-eyed one who promotes prosperity. May we be freed from the bondage of death as a cucumber from its stalk, but not from immortality." This is a famous verse of *Yajur Veda* (from *Rudranāmaka,* or *Śrī Rudram),* considered an essential *mantra* of Śiva worship used in all Śiva rites.

germinate: To sprout. To begin to develop.

ghaṇṭā: **घण्टा** "Bell." Akin to *ghaṇṭ,* "to speak." An important implement in Hindu worship *(pūjā),* used to chase away *asuras* and summon *devas* and Gods. See: *pūjā.*

ghee: **घी** Hindi for clarified butter; *ghṛita* in Sanskṛit. Butter that has been boiled and strained. An important sacred substance used in temple lamps and offered in fire ceremony, *yajña.* It is also used as a food with many virtues and *āyurvedic* virtues. See: *yajña.*

Gheraṇḍa Saṁhitā: **घेरण्डसंहिता** A Vaishṇava manual on *haṭha yoga* (ca 1675), still influential today, presented as a dialog between Sage Gheraṇḍa and a disciple. See: *haṭha yoga.*

gloom: Darkness. Deep sadness or despair.

go: **गो** The cow, considered especially sacred for its unbounded generosity and usefulness to humans. It is a symbol of the earth as the abundant provider. For the Hindu, the cow is a representative of all living species, each of which is to be revered and cared for.

Goddess: Female representation or manifestation of Divinity; Śakti or Devī. *Goddess* can refer to a female perception or depiction of a causal-plane being (Mahādeva) in its natural state, which is genderless, or it can refer to an astral-plane being residing in a female astral body. To show the Divine's transcendence of sexuality, sometimes God is shown as having qualities of both sexes, e.g., Ardhanārīśvara, "half-woman God;" or Lord Naṭarāja, who wears a feminine earring in one ear and a masculine one in the other.

Godhead: God; Divinity. A term describing the essence or highest aspect of the Supreme Being.

God Realization: A term naming the direct and personal experience of the Divine within oneself. It can refer to either 1) *savikalpa samādhi* ("enstasy with form") in its various levels, from the experience of inner light to the realization of Satchidānanda, the pure consciousness or primal substance flowing through all form, or 2) *nirvikalpa samādhi* ("enstasy without form"), union with the transcendent Absolute, Paraśiva, the Self God, beyond time, form and space. In *Dancing with Śiva,* the term *God Realization* is used to name both of the above *samādhis,* whereas *Self Realization* refers only to *nirvikalpa samādhi.* See: *rāja yoga, samādhi, Self Realization.*

Gods: Mahādevas, "great beings of light." In *Dancing with Śiva,* the plural form of *God* refers to extremely advanced beings existing in their self-effulgent soul bodies in the causal plane. The meaning of *Gods* is best seen in the phrase, "God and the Gods," referring to the Supreme God—Śiva—and the Mahādevas who are His creation. See: *Mahādeva.*

God's power: See: *Śakti.*

gopura: गोपुर South Indian temple entrance tower, often quite tall with ornate carvings. See: *balipīṭha, temple.*

Gorakshanātha: गोरक्षनाथ Profound *siddha yoga* master of the Ādinātha Sampradāya (ca 1000). Expounder and foremost *guru* of Siddha Siddhānta Śaivism. He traveled and extolled the greatness of Śiva throughout North India and Nepal where he and his *guru,* Matsyendranātha, are still highly revered. See: *haṭha yoga, Siddha Siddhānta, Siddha Siddhānta Paddhati.*

Gorakhnātha Śaivism: गोरख्नाथशैव One of the six schools of Śaivism, also called Siddha Siddhānta. See: *Siddha Siddhānta, siddha yoga.*

Gorakshapantha: गोरक्षपन्थ "Path of Gorakshanātha." A synonym for Siddha Siddhānta. See: *Śaivism. Siddha Siddhānta.*

Gorakshaśataka: गोरक्षशतक A text by Gorakshanātha, which along with *Siddha Siddhānta Pradīpikā,* extols the path of "Śiva *yoga,*" which is *haṭha-kuṇḍalinī yoga* emphasizing control over body and mind, awakening of higher *chakras* and *nāḍī* nerve system with the intent of realizing the Absolute, Parāsamvid, and residing in the *sahasrāra chakra* in perfect identity with Śiva. See: *Gorakshanātha, Siddha Siddhānta.*

gotra: गोत्र "Cowshed." Family lineage or subcaste stemming from a *ṛishi* or *satguru* and bearing his name. Originally described as several joint families sharing a common cowshed. See: *caste, jāti, varṇa dharma.*

grace: "Benevolence, love, giving," from the Latin *gratus,* "beloved, agreeable." God's power of revealment, *anugraha śakti* ("kindness, showing favor"), by which souls are awakened to their true, Divine nature. Grace in the unripe stages of the spiritual journey is experienced by the devotee as receiving gifts or boons, often unbidden, from God. The mature soul finds himself surrounded by grace. He sees all of God's actions as grace, whether they be seemingly pleasant and helpful or not. For him, his very love of God, the power to meditate or worship, and the spiritual urge which drives his life are entirely and obviously God's grace, a divine endowment, an intercession, unrelated to any deed or action he did or could perform.

In Śaiva Siddhānta, it is grace that awakens the love of God within the devotee, softens the intellect and inaugurates the quest for Self Realization. It descends when the soul has reached a certain level of maturity, and often comes in the form of a spiritual initiation, called *śaktipāta,* from a *satguru.*

Grace is not only the force of illumination or revealment. It also includes Śiva's other four powers—creation, preservation, destruction and concealment—through which He provides the world of experience and limits the soul's consciousness so that it may evolve. More broadly, grace is God's ever-flowing love and compassion, *karuṇā,* also known as *kṛipā* ("tenderness, compassion") and *prasāda* (literally, "clearness, purity").

To whom is God's grace given? Can it be earned? Two famous analogies, that of the monkey *(markaṭa)* and that of the cat *(mārjāra)* express two classical viewpoints on salvation and grace. The *markaṭa* school, perhaps represented more fully by the *Vedas,* asserts that the soul must cling to God like a monkey clings to its mother and thus participate in its "salvation." The *mārjāra* school, which better reflects the position of the *Āgamas,* says that the soul must be like a young kitten, totally dependent on its mother's will, picked up in her mouth by the scruff of the neck and carried here and there. This crucial state of loving surrender is called *prapatti.* See: *anugraha śakti, prapatti, śaktipāta, tirodhāna śakti.*

grandeur: Greatness, magnificence; of lofty character; noble.

grantha: **ग्रन्थ** Literally, "knot," a common name for book—a term thought to refer to the knot on the cord that bound ancient palm-leaf or birch-bark manuscripts. Books are afforded deep respect in Hinduism, always carefully treated, never placed directly on the floor. Special books are not uncommonly objects of worship. *Grantha* also names an ancient literary script developed in South India. See: *olai.*

granthavidyā: **ग्रन्थविद्या** "Book knowledge." Bibliography; booklist, recommended reading.

gṛihastha: **गृहस्थ** "Householder." Family man or woman. Family of a married couple and other relatives. Pertaining to family life. The purely masculine form of the word is *gṛihasthi.* The feminine form is *gṛihasthin. Gṛihasthi* also names the home itself. See: *āśrama dharma, extended family, gṛihastha dharma, joint family.*

gṛihastha āśrama: **गृहस्थ आश्रम** "Householder stage." See: *āśrama dharma.*

gṛihastha dharma: **गृहस्थधर्म** "Householder law." The virtues and ideals of family life. This *dharma* includes all nonmonastics, whether married, single or gay. In general, *gṛihastha dharma* begins with the completion of the period of studentship and extends throughout the period of raising a family (called the *gṛihastha āśrama).* Specific scriptures, called *Dharma Śāstras* and *Gṛihya Śāstras,* outline the duties and obligations of family life. In Hinduism, family life is one of serving, learning and striving within a close-knit community of many relatives forming a joint family and its broader connections as an extended family under the aegis of a spiritual *guru.* Each is expected to work harmoniously to further the wealth and happiness of the family and the society, to practice religious disciplines and raise children of strong moral fiber to carry on the tradition. Life is called a *jīvayajña,* "self-sacrifice," for each incarnation is understood as an opportunity for spiritual advancement through fulfilling one's *dharma* of birth, which is the pattern one chose before entering this world, a pattern considered by many as bestowed by God. In the majority of cases, sons follow in the footsteps of their father, and daughters in those of their mother. All interrelate with love and kindness. Respect for all older than oneself is a keynote. Marriages are arranged and the culture is maintained.

The householder strives to fulfill the four *purushārthas,* "human goals" of righteousness, wealth, pleasure and liberation. While taking care of one's own family is most central, it is only part of this *dharma's* expectations. *Gṛihasthas* must support the religion by building and maintaining temples, monasteries and other religious institutions, supporting the monastics and disseminating the teachings. They must care for the elderly and feed the poor and homeless. Of course, the duties of husband and wife are different. The *Tirukural* describes the householder's central duties as serving these five: ancestors, God, guests, kindred and himself. The *Dharma Śāstras,* similarly, enjoin daily sacrifice to *ṛishis,* ancestors, Gods, creatures and men. See: *āśrama dharma, extended family, joint family, yajña.*

gṛiheśvara* and *gṛihiṇī: गृहेश्वर गृहिणी From *gṛiha,* "home," hence "lord and lady of the home." The family man, *gṛiheśvara* (or *gṛihapati),* and family woman, *gṛihiṇī,* considered as master and mistress of their respective realms, so they may fulfill their *purusha* and *strī dharmas.* Implies that both of their realms are equally important and inviolable. See: *dharma.*

Gṛihya Sūtras: गृह्यसूत्र "Household maxims or codes." An important division of classical *smṛiti* literature, designating rules and customs for domestic life, including rites of passage and other home ceremonies, which are widely followed to this day. The *Gṛihya Sūtras (or Śāstras)* are part of the *Kalpa Sūtras,* "procedural maxims" *(or Kalpa Vedāṅga),* which also include the *Śrauta* and *Śulba Śāstras,* on public Vedic rites, and the *Dharma Śāstras* (or *Sūtras),* on domestic-social law. Among the best known *Gṛihya Sūtras* are *Āśvalāyana's Gṛihya Sūtras* attached to the *Ṛig Veda, Gobhila's Sūtras* of the *Sāma Veda,* and the *Sūtras* of *Pāraskara* and *Baudhāyana* of the *Yajur Veda.* See: *Kalpa Vedāṅga, Vedāṅga.*

gross plane: The physical world. See: *loka, world, tattva.*

Guha: गुह An epithet of Kārttikeya. "The interior one." —***guhā:*** "Cave." See: *Kārttikeya.*

Guhāvāsī Siddha: गुहावासीसिद्ध A *guru* of central India (ca 675) credited with the modern founding of Śaiva Siddhānta in that area, based fully in Sanskṛit. *Guhāvāsī*—literally "cave-dweller; he who is hidden"—is also a name of Lord Śiva.

Guheśvara: गुहेश्वर "Lord of the cave." A name for Lord Śiva implying His presence in the heart or the interior of all beings.

Gujarāt: गुजरात State of West India. Capital is Ahmedabad, population 40,000,000, area 75,670 square miles.

guṇa: गुण "Strand; quality." The three constituent principles of *prakṛiti*, primal nature. The three *guṇas* are as follows. ***—sattva:*** Quiescent, rarified, translucent, pervasive, reflecting the light of Pure Consciousness. ***—rajas:*** "Passion," inherent in energy, movement, action, emotion, life. ***—tamas:*** "Darkness," inertia, density, the force of contraction, resistance and dissolution. The *guṇas* are integral to Hindu thought, as all things are composed of the combination of these qualities of nature, including *āyurveda*, arts, environments and personalities. See: *āyurveda, prakṛiti, tattva.*

Gurkhā: गुर्खा A Rajput people of the mountains of Nepal; famed warriors.

guru: गुरु "Weighty one," indicating a being of great knowledge or skill. A term used to describe a teacher or guide in any subject, such as music, dance, sculpture, but especially religion. For clarity, the term is often preceded by a qualifying prefix. Hence, terms such as *kulaguru* (family teacher), *vīnaguru (vīna* teacher) and *satguru* (spiritual preceptor). In Hindu astrology, *guru* names the planet Jupiter, also known as Bṛihaspati. According to the *Advayatāraka Upanishad* (14–18), *guru* means "dispeller *(gu)* of darkness *(ru)*." See: *guru-śishya system, satguru.*

guru bhakti: गुरुभक्ति Devotion to the teacher. The attitude of humility, love and ideation held by a student in any field of study. In the spiritual realm, the devotee strives to see the *guru* as his higher Self. By attuning himself to the *satguru's* inner nature and wisdom, the disciple slowly transforms his own nature to ultimately attain the same peace and enlightenment his *guru* has achieved. *Guru bhakti* is expressed through serving the *guru,* meditating on his form, working closely with his mind and obeying his instructions. See: *guru, satguru, guru-śishya system, Kulārṇava Tantra.*

Gurudeva: गुरुदेव "Divine or radiant preceptor." An affectionate, respectful name for the *guru.* See: *guru.*

Guru Gītā: गुरु गीता "Song of the guru." A popular 352-verse excerpt from the *Skanda Purāṇa*, wherein Lord Śiva tells Pārvatī of the *guru*-disciple relationship. See: *guru.*

Guru Jayantī: गुरु जयन्ती Preceptor's birthday, celebrated as an annual festival by devotees. A *pādapūjā*, ritual bathing of his feet, is usually performed. If he is not physically present, the *pūjā* is done to the *śrī pādukā,* "holy sandals," which represent the guru and hold his vibration. See: *pādapūjā.*

gurukula: गुरुकुल A training center where young boys live and learn in residence with their teacher. *Kula* means "family." See: *āśrama, brahmacharya.*

guru paramparā: गुरुपरंपरा "Preceptorial succession" (literally, "from one to another"). A line of spiritual *gurus* in authentic succession of initiation; the chain of mystical power and authorized continuity, passed from *guru* to *guru.* Cf: *sampradāya.*

Guru Pūrṇimā: गुरु पूर्णिमा Occurring on the full moon of July, Guru Pūrṇimā is for devotees a day of rededication to all that the *guru* represents. It is occasioned by *pādapūjā*—ritual worship of the *guru's* sandals, which represent his holy feet. See: *guru-śishya system.*

guru-śishya system: गुरुशिष्य "Master-disciple system." An important education system of Hinduism whereby the teacher conveys his knowledge and tradition to a student. Such knowledge, whether it be Vedic-Āgamic art, architecture or spirituality, is imparted through the developing relationship between *guru* and disciple. The principle of this system is that knowledge, especially subtle or advanced knowledge, is best conveyed through a strong human relationship based on ideals of the student's respect, commitment, devotion and obedience, and on personal instruction by which the student eventually masters the knowledge the *guru* embodies. See: *guru, guru bhakti, satguru.*

gush: To flow out suddenly and plentifully.

hallowed: Sacred.

haṁsa: हंस "Swan;" more accurately, the high-flying wild goose *Anser indicus.* The *vāhana,* vehicle, of the God Brahmā. It has various meanings, including Supreme Soul and individual soul. It is a noble symbol for an adept class of renunciates *(paramahaṁsa)*—winging high above the mundane, driving straight toward the goal, or of the discriminating *yogī* who—like the graceful swan said to be able to extract milk from water—can see the Divine and leave the rest. The *haṁsa mantra* indicates the sound made by the exhalation *(ha)* and inhalation *(sa)* of the breath. See: *paramahaṁsa.*

Harihara: हरिहर "Vishṇu-Śiva." Also known as Śaṅkaranārāyaṇa, an icon of the Supreme One, in which the right half is Śiva and left half is Vishṇu. It symbolizes the principle that Śiva and Vishṇu are not two separate Deities. See: *Brahmā, mūrti, Parameśvara, Vishṇu.*

haṭha yoga: हठयोग "Forceful yoga." *Haṭha yoga* is a system of physical and mental exercise developed in ancient times as a means of rejuvenation by *ṛishis* and *tapasvins* who meditated for long hours, and used today in preparing the body and mind for meditation. Its elements are 1) postures *(āsana),* 2) cleansing practices *(dhauti* or *shodhana),* 3) breath control *(prāṇāyāma),* 4) locks *(bandha,* which temporarily restrict local flows of *prāṇa)* and 5) hand gestures *(mudrā),* all of which regulate the flow of *prāṇa* and purify the inner and outer bodies. *Haṭha yoga* is broadly practiced in many traditions. It is the third limb *(aṅga)* of Patañjali's *rāja yoga*. It is integral to the Śaiva and Śākta *tantra* traditions, and part of modern *āyurveda* treatment. In the West, *haṭha yoga* has been superficially adopted as a health-promoting, limbering, stress-reducing form of exercise, often included in aerobic routines. Esoterically, *ha* and *ṭha*, respectively, indicate the microcosmic sun *(ha)* and moon *(ṭha)*, which symbolize the masculine current, *piṅgalā nāḍī*, and feminine current, *iḍā nāḍī*, in the human body. The most popular *haṭha yoga* manuals are *Haṭha Yoga Pradīpikā* and the *Gheraṇḍa Saṁhitā*. See: *āsana, kuṇḍalinī, nāḍī, yoga, rāja yoga*.

Haṭha Yoga Pradīpikā: **हठयोगप्रदीपिका** "Light on *haṭha yoga*." A 14th-century text of 389 verses by Svātmārāma Yogin which describes the philosophy and practices of *haṭha yoga*. It is widely used in *yoga* schools today.

havana: **हवन** "Fire pit for sacred offering; making oblations through fire." Synonymous with *homa*. *Havis* and *havya* name the offerings. See: *Agni, homa, yajña*.

heart chakra: *Anāhata chakra*. Center of direct cognition. See: *chakra*.

heaven: The celestial spheres, including the causal plane and the higher realms of the subtle plane, where souls rest and learn between births, and mature souls continue to evolve after *moksha*. Heaven is often used by translators as an equivalent to the Sanskṛit *Svarga*. See: *loka*.

heed: To pay close attention to, especially to follow instructions carefully.

hell: *Naraka*. An unhappy, mentally and emotionally congested, distressful area of consciousness. Hell is a state of mind that can be experienced on the plane of physical existence or in the sub-astral plane (Naraka) after the death of the physical body. It is accompanied by the tormented emotions of hatred, remorse, resentment, fear, jealousy and self-condemnation. However, in the Hindu view, the hellish experience is not permanent, but a temporary condition of one's own making. See: *asura, loka, Naraka, purgatory, Satan*.

hereditary: Ancestral. Passed down through family lines. For example, it is Hindu family *dharma* for the son to be taught everything that the father knows and the daughter to learn everything the mother knows. Thus they inherit knowledge, control of mind and emotions, as well as property.

heresy: Belief, thought or opinion that opposes official or established views. Rejecting orthodox doctrines, especially those of a church or religion.

heterodox: "Different opinion." Opposed to or departing from established doctrines or beliefs. Opposite of *orthodox*, "straight opinion." See: *nāstika*.

heterosexual: Of or characterized by sexual attraction for only members of the opposite sex. See: *bisexual, homosexual, sexuality*.

hierarchy: A group of beings arranged in order of rank or class; as a hierarchy of God, Gods and *devas*.

higher-nature, lower nature: Expressions indicating man's refined, soulful qualities on the one hand, and his base, instinctive qualities on the other.

See: *kośa, mind (five states), soul.*

high soul: See: *soul.*

Himālayas: **हिमालय** "Abode of snow." The mountain system of South-Central Asia extending along the India-Tibet border and through Pakistan, Nepal and Bhutan.

hiṁsā: **हिंसा** "Injury; harm; hurt." Injuriousness, hostility—mental, verbal or physical. See: *ahiṁsā.*

Hindu: **हिन्दु** A follower of, or relating to, Hinduism. Generally, one is understood to be a Hindu by being born into a Hindu family and practicing the faith, or by declaring oneself a Hindu. Acceptance into the fold is recognized through the name-giving sacrament, a temple ceremony called *nāmakaraṇa saṁskāra,* given to born Hindus shortly after birth, and to self-declared Hindus who have proven their sincerity and been accepted by a Hindu community. Full conversion is completed through disavowal of previous religious affiliations and legal change of name. While traditions vary greatly, all Hindus rely on the *Vedas* as scriptural authority and generally attest to the following nine principles: 1) There exists a one, all-pervasive Supreme Being who is both immanent and transcendent, both creator and unmanifest Reality. 2) The universe undergoes endless cycles of creation, preservation and dissolution. 3) All souls are evolving toward God and will ultimately find *moksha,* spiritual knowledge and liberation from the cycle of rebirth. Not a single soul will be eternally deprived of this destiny. 4) *Karma* is the law of cause and effect by which each individual creates his own destiny by his thoughts, words and deeds. 5) The soul reincarnates, evolving through many births until all *karmas* have been resolved. 6) Divine beings exist in unseen worlds, and temple worship, rituals, sacraments, as well as personal devotionals, create a communion with these *devas* and Gods. 7) A spiritually awakened master or *satguru* is essential to know the Transcendent Absolute, as are personal discipline, good conduct, purification, self-inquiry and meditation. 8) All life is sacred, to be loved and revered, and therefore one should practice *ahiṁsā,* nonviolence. 9) No particular religion teaches the only way to salvation above all others. Rather, all genuine religious paths are facets of God's pure love and light, deserving tolerance and understanding. See: *Hinduism.*

Hindu cosmology: See: *loka, three worlds.*

Hinduism (Hindu Dharma): **हिन्दुधर्म** India's indigenous religious and cultural system, followed today by nearly one billion adherents, mostly in India, but with large populations in many other countries. Also called Sanātana Dharma, "eternal religion" and Vaidika Dharma, "religion of the *Vedas.*" Hinduism is the world's most ancient religion and encompasses a broad spectrum of philosophies ranging from pluralistic theism to absolute monism. It is a family of myriad faiths with four primary denominations: Śaivism, Vaishṇavism, Śāktism and Smārtism. These four hold such divergent beliefs that each is a complete and independent religion. Yet, they share a vast heritage of culture and belief—*karma, dharma,* reincarnation, all-pervasive Divinity, temple worship, sacraments, manifold Deities, the *guru-śishya* tradition and a reliance on the *Vedas* as scriptural authority. From the rich soil of Hinduism long ago sprang various other traditions. Among these were Jainism, Buddhism and Sikhism, which rejected the *Vedas* and thus emerged as completely distinct religions, disassociated from Hinduism, while still sharing many philosophical insights and cultural values with their parent faith.

Though the genesis of the term is controversial, the consensus is that the term *Hindu* or *Indu* was used by the Persians to refer to the Indian peoples of the Indus Valley as early as 500 BCE. Additionally, Indian scholars point to the appearance of the related term *Sindhu* in the ancient *Ṛig Veda Saṁhitā.*

Janaki Abhisheki writes *(Religion as Knowledge: The Hindu Concept,* p. 1): "Whereas today the word *Hindu* connotes a particular faith and culture, in ancient times it was used to describe those belonging to a particular region. About 500 BCE we find the Persians referring to 'Hapta Hindu.' This referred to the region of Northwest India and the Punjab (before partition). The *Ṛig Veda* (the most ancient literature of the Hindus) uses the word *Sapta Sindhu* singly or in plural at least 200 times. Sindhu is the River Indus. Panini, the great Sanskṛit grammarian, also uses the word *Sindhu* to denote the country or region. While the Persians substituted *h* for *s*, the Greeks removed the *h* also and pronounced the word as 'Indoi.' *Indian* is derived from the Greek *Indoi.*"

Dr. S. Rādhākṛishṇan similarly observed, "The Hindu civilization is so called since its original founders or earliest followers occupied the territory drained by the Sindhu (the Indus) River system corresponding to the Northwest Frontier Province and the Punjab. This is recorded in the *Ṛig Veda,* the oldest of the *Vedas,* the Hindu scriptures, which give their name to this period of Indian history. The people on the Indian side of the Sindhu were called Hindus by the Persians and the later Western invaders. That is the genesis of the word *Hindu*" *(The Hindu View of Life,* p. 12). See: *Hindu.*

Hindu solidarity: Hindu unity in diversity. A major theme in contemporary Hinduism according to which the various Hindu denominations are mutually supportive and work together in harmony, while taking care not to obscure or lessen their distinctions or unique virtues. The underlying belief is that Hinduism will be strong if each of its sects, denominations and lineages is individually vibrant. See: *Hinduism.*

Hiuen Tsang: Chinese pilgrim who toured India about 630. The diary of his remarkable travels is a rare and colorful source of information about the India of his day.

hoard: To get and store away things such as money, goods, usually secretly.

holy feet: The feet of God, a God, *satguru* or any holy person, often represented by sacred sandals, called *śrī pādukā* in Sanskṛit and *tiruvadi* in Tamil. The feet of a divine one are considered especially precious as they represent the point of contact of the Divine and the physical, and are thus revered as the source of grace. The sandals or feet of the *guru* are the object of worship on his *jayantī* (birthday), on Guru Pūrṇimā and other special occasions. See: *pādapūjā, pādukā, satguru.*

holy orders: A divine ordination or covenant, giving religious authority. Vows that members of a religious body make, especially a monastic body or order, such as the vows (holy orders of renunciation) given a *sannyāsin* at the time of his initiation *(sannyāsa dīkshā),* which establish a covenant with the ancient holy order of *sannyāsa. Sannyāsins,* the wearers of the ocher robe, are the ordained religious leaders of Hinduism. See: *sannyāsa dīkshā.*

homa: होम "Fire-offering." A sacred ceremony in which the Gods are offered oblations through the medium of fire in a sanctified fire pit, *homakuṇḍa,* usually made of earthen bricks. *Homa* rites are enjoined in the *Vedas, Āgamas* and *Dharma* and *Gṛihya Śāstras.* Many domestic rites are occasions for *homa,* including *upanayana* and *vivāha.* Major *pūjās* in temples are often preceded by a *homa.* See: *agni, havana, yajña.*

homosexual: Of or characterized by sexual attraction for members of one's own gender. A modern synonym is *gay,* especially for males, while female homosexuals are termed *lesbian.* See: *bisexual, gay, heterosexual, sexuality.*

hrī: ह्री "Remorse; modesty." See: *yama-niyama.*

hued: Having specific color.

human *dharma:* The natural growth and expression through four stages of life. Known as *āśrama dharma.* See: *āśrama dharma, dharma.*

humors (or bodily humors): See: *āyurveda, bodily humor, dosha.*

icçhā śakti: इच्छाशक्ति "Desire; will." See: *Śakti, triśūla.*

icon: A sacred image, usually of God or a God. English for *mūrti.* See: *aniconic, mūrti.*

iconoclastic: Opposed to widely accepted ideas, beliefs and customs. Also [but not used as such in this text], opposed to the worship or use of religious icons, or advocating their destruction.

iḍā nāḍī: इडानाडी "Soothing channel." The feminine psychic current flowing along the spine. See: *kuṇḍalinī, nāḍī, odic, piṅgalā.*

illusion (illusory): A belief, opinion or observation that appears to be, but is not in accord with the facts, truth or true values, such as the illusion created by a magician. See: *avidyā.*

illustrious: Very luminous or bright; distinguished, famous; outstanding.

immanent: Indwelling; present and operating within. Relating to God, the term *immanent* means present in all things and throughout the universe, not aloof or distant. Not to be confused with *imminent,* about to happen;

emanate, to issue from; *eminent*, high in rank.

immature: Not ripe; not fully grown, undeveloped. Still young. **—immature soul:** See: *ātman, evolution of the soul, soul.*

immemorial (from time immemorial): From a time so distant that it extends beyond history or human memory.

immutable: Never changing or varying. See: *Absolute Reality, relative.*

impasse: A dead end; a passage with no escape. A difficulty with no solution.

impede: To obstruct or delay something; make difficult to accomplish. (Noun form: *impediment.*)

impediment: "That which holds the feet." Hindrance; obstacle. Anything that inhibits or slows progress.

impending: That which is about to happen; threatening.

imperishable: That which cannot die or decay; indestructible; immortal. With capital *I*, *imperishable* refers to God—the Eternal, Beginningless and Endless.

impermanence: The quality of being temporary and nonlasting.

impersonal: Not personal; not connected to any person.

impersonal being: One's innermost nature, at the level of the soul's essence, where one is not distinguished as an individual, nor as separate from God or any part of existence. The soul's essential being—Satchidānanda and Paraśiva. See: *ātman, essence, evolution of the soul, soul.*

impersonal God: God in His perfections of Pure Consciousness (Parāśakti*)* and Absolute Reality beyond all attributes (Paraśiva*)* wherein He is not a person. (Whereas, in His third perfection, Parameśvara, Śiva *is* someone, has a body and performs actions, has will, dances, etc.)

impetus: Anything that stimulates activity. Driving force; motive, incentive.

implore: To ask or beg for earnestly.

impoverished: Poor; reduced to a condition of severe deprivation.

inanimate: See: *animate-inanimate.*

inauspicious: Not favorable. Not a good time to perform certain actions or undertake projects. Ill-omened. See: *auspiciousness, muhūrta.*

incandescent: Glowing with heat; white-hot. Radiant; luminous; very bright.

incantation: *Mantraprayoga.* The chanting of prayers, verses or formulas for magical or mystical purposes. Also refers to such chants *(mantra). Vaśakriyā* is the subduing or bewitching by charms, incantation or drugs. Incantation for malevolent purposes (black magic) is called *abhichāra.* See: *mantra.*

incarnation: From *incarnate,* "to be made flesh." The soul's taking on a human body. **—divine incarnation:** The concept of *avatāra.* The Supreme Being's (or other Mahādeva's) taking of human birth, generally to reestablish *dharma.* This doctrine is important to several Hindu sects, notably Vaishṇavism, but not held by most Śaivites. See: *avatāra, Vaishṇavism.*

incense: *Dhūpa.* Substance that gives off pleasant aromas when burned, usually made from natural substances such as tree resin. A central element in Hindu worship rites, waved gently before the Deity as an offering, especially after ablution. Hindi terms include *sugandhi* and *lobāna.* A popular term for stick incense is *agarbatti* (Gujarati). See: *pūjā.*

incisive: "Cutting into." Sharp or keen, such as a penetrating and discriminating mind. See: *discrimination.*

incognito: Without being recognized; keeping one's true identity unrevealed or disguised.

increment: An amount of increase, usually small and followed by others; a measure of growth or change.

individual soul: A term used to describe the soul's nature as a unique entity, emanated by God Śiva (the Primal Soul), as a being which is evolving and not yet one with God. See: *ātman, essence, kośa, Parameśvara, soul.*

individuality: Quality that makes one person or soul other than, or different from, another. See: *ahaṁkāra, ego, āṇava, soul.*

indomitable: Not easily discouraged, defeated or subdued. Unconquerable.

Indra: **इन्द्र** "Ruler." Vedic God of rain and thunder, warrior king of the *devas.*

indriya: **इन्द्रिय** "Agent, sense organ." The five agents of perception (*jñānendriyas*), hearing (*śrotra*), touch (*tvak*), sight (*chakshus*), taste (*rasana*) and smell (*ghrāṇa*); and the five agents of action (*karmendriyas*), speech (*vāk*), grasping, by means of the hands (*pāṇi*), movement (*pāda*), excretion (*pāyu*) and generation (*upastha*). See: *kośa, soul, tattva.*

induce: To bring about, cause, persuade.

Indus Valley: Region of the Indus River, now in Pakistan, where in 1924 archeologists discovered the remains of a high civilization which flourished between 5000 and 1000 BCE. There, a "seal" was found with the effigy of Śiva as Paśupati, "lord of animals," seated in a *yogic* posture. Neither the language of these people nor their exact background is known. They related culturally and carried on an extensive trade with peoples of other civilizations, far to the West, using sturdy ships that they built themselves. For centuries they were the most advanced civilization on earth. See: *Śaivism.*

indwell: To dwell or be in. "The priest asks the Deity to indwell the image," or come and inhabit the *mūrti* as a temporary physical body. See: *mūrti.*

I-ness: The conceiving of oneself as an "I," or ego, which Hinduism considers a state to be transcended. See: *ahaṁkāra, āṇava, mind (individual).*

inexhaustible: Cannot be exhausted, used up or emptied. Tireless.

inexplicable: Beyond explaining or accounting for.

inextricable: Cannot be disentangled or separated from another thing.

infatuation: The magnetic condition of being captured by a foolish or shallow love or affection.

infinitesimal: Infinitely small; too small to be measured.

inflict: To give or cause pain, wounds, etc.

infuse: To transmit a quality, idea, knowledge, etc., as if by pouring. To impart, fill or inspire.

ingest: To take food, medicine, etc., into the body by swallowing or absorbing.

inherent (to inhere in): Inborn. Existing in someone or something as an essential or inseparable quality. **—inherent sin:** See: *sin.*

inherit: To receive from an ancestor, as property, title, etc.—or to reap from our own actions: "...seed *karmas* we inherit from this and past lives."

initiation (to initiate): To enter into; to admit as a member. In Hinduism, initiation from a qualified preceptor is considered invaluable for spiritual progress. See: *dīkshā, śaktipāta, sannyāsa dīkshā.*

injunction: An urging; an order or firm instruction.

inmost: Located deepest within.

innate: Naturally occurring; not acquired. That which belongs to the inherent nature or constitution of a being or thing.

inner (innermost): Located within. Of the depths of our being. **—inner advancement (or unfoldment):** Progress of an individual at the soul level rather than in external life. **—inner bodies:** The subtle bodies of man within the physical body. **—inner discovery:** Learning from inside oneself, experiential revelation; one of the benefits of inner life. **—inner form (or nature) of the *guru*:** The deeper levels of the *guru*'s being that the disciple strives to attune himself to and emulate. **—inner law:** The principles or mechanism underlying every action or experience, often hidden. *Karma* is one such law. **—inner life:** The life we live inside ourselves, at the emotional, mental and spiritual levels, as distinguished from outer life. **—inner light:** A moonlight-like glow that can be seen inside the head or throughout the body when the *vṛittis,* mental fluctuations, have been sufficiently quieted. To be able to see and bask in the inner light is a milestone on the path. See: *vṛitti.* **—inner mind:** The mind in its deeper, intuitive functions and capacities—the subsuperconscious and superconscious. **—innermost body:** The soul body. **—inner planes:** Inner worlds or regions of existence. **—inner self:** The real, deep Self; the essence of the soul, rather than the outer self with which we usually identify. **—inner sky:** The area of the mind which is clear inner space, free of mental images, feelings, identifications, etc. Tranquility itself. The superconscious mind, Satchidānanda. See: *ākāśa.* **—inner truth:** Truth of a higher order. **—inner universes (or worlds):** The astral and causal worlds. See: *kośa.*

innumerable: So many as to be beyond counting.

inscrutable: That cannot be analyzed or understood. Mysterious; beyond examining.

insignia: Sign or symbol of identity, rank or office, such as a badge or emblem.

instinctive: "Natural or innate." From the Latin *instinctus,* "to impel, instigate." The drives and impulses that order the animal world and the physical and lower *astral* aspects of humans—for example, self-preservation, procreation, hunger and thirst, as well as the emotions of greed, hatred, anger, fear, lust and jealousy. The first steps on the spiritual path consist in learning to harness these tendencies and impulses and transmute their energies into the higher nature. See: *manas, mind (individual), mind (three phases), yama-niyama.*

instinctive mind: *Manas chitta.* The lower mind, which controls the basic faculties of perception, movement, as well as ordinary thought and emotion. *Manas chitta* is of the *manomaya kośa.* See: *manas, manomaya kośa, yama-niyama.*

instrumental cause: *Sahakāri kāraṇa.* Cosmologically, the means of implementing creation. See: *cause.*

intellect: The power to reason or understand; power of thought; mental acumen. See: *buddhi, intellectual mind.*

intellectual mind: *Buddhi chitta.* The faculty of reason and logical thinking. It is the source of discriminating thought, rather than the ordinary, impulsive thought processes of the lower or instinctive mind, called *manas chitta. Buddhi chitta* is of the *manomaya kośa.* See: *buddhi, mind (individual).*

internalize: To take something inside of oneself.

internalized worship: *Yoga.* Worship or contact with God and Gods via meditation and contemplation rather than through external ritual. This is the *yogī*'s path, preceded by the *charyā* and *kriyā pādas.* See: *meditation, yoga.*

interplay: Interaction between two or more things.

intervene: To come between, especially two people or parties, with the intent to effect a change between them. See: *mediatrix.*

interweave (interwoven): To weave together like threads into cloth. To closely interrelate; to blend.

intimacy: The state of being intimate or very close. Having a close rapport.

intrigue: Secret plotting or scheming.

intrinsic: Essential; inherent. Belonging to the real nature of a being or thing. **—intrinsic evil:** See: *evil.*

intuition (to intuit): Direct understanding or cognition, which bypasses the process of reason. Intuition is a far superior source of knowing than reason, but it does not contradict reason. See: *cognition, mind (five states).*

invigorate: To give vigor, life or energy.

invocation (to invoke): A "calling or summoning," as to a God, saint, etc., for blessings and assistance. Also, a formal prayer or chant. See: *mantra.*

Iraivan: இறைவன் "Worshipful one; divine one." One of the most ancient Tamil names for God. See: *San Mārga Sanctuary.*

Iraivan Temple: See: *San Mārga Sanctuary.*

Īśa: ईश "Lord, master of all; superior, commanding, reigning." *Īśa* and its derivative *Īśāna* are very old names for God Śiva found in the *Ṛig Veda.*

Īśānyaguru: ईशान्यगुरु Śaivite *brāhmin* of the Kālāmukha sect who Basavaṇṇa, principal founding teacher of Vīra Śaivism, received instruction from in his youth. See: *Basavaṇṇa, Vīra Śaivism.*

***Īśa Upanishad:* ईश उपनिषद्** Last of the 40 chapters of *Vājasaneyi Saṁhitā* of the *Yajur Veda.* A short, highly mystical scripture. See: *Upanishad.*

***Ishṭa Devatā:* इष्टदेवता** "Cherished or chosen Deity." The Deity that is the object of one's special pious attention. *Ishṭa Devatā* is a concept common to all Hindu sects. Vaishṇavas may choose among many Divine forms, most commonly Vishṇu, Bālāji, Kṛishṇa, Rādhā, Rāma, Lakshmī, Hanumān and Narasiṁha, as well as the aniconic *śālagrāma,* a sacred river rock. Traditionally, Smārtas choose from among six Deities: Śiva, Śakti, Vishṇu, Sūrya, Gaṇeśa and Kumāra (or any of their traditional forms). For Śaktas, the Divine is worshiped as the Goddess, *Śakti,* in Her many fierce forms and benign forms, invoking the furious power of Kālī or Durgā, or the comforting grace of Pārvatī, Ambikā and others. Śaivites direct their worship primarily to Śiva as represented by the aniconic Śiva Liṅga, and the human-like *mūrtis,* Naṭarāja and Ardhanārīśvara. In temples and scriptural lore, Śiva is venerated in a multitude of forms, including the following 23 additional anthropomorphic images: Somāskanda, Ṛishabarudra, Kalyānasundara, Chandraśekhara, Bhikshātana, Kāmadahanamūrti, Kālāri, Jalandara, Tripurari, Gajari, Vīrabhadra, Dakshināmūrti, Kirātamūrti, Nīlakaṇṭha, Kaṅkāla, Chakradāna, Gajamukhānugraha, Chandesānugraha, Ekapāda, Liṅgodbhava, Sukhāsana, Umā Maheśvara and Haryardha. See: *mūrti, Śakti, Śiva.*

***Ishṭaliṅga:* इष्टलिङ्ग** "Cherished, chosen or personal mark of God." *(Ishṭa:* "sought, desired.") For Vīra Śaivites it is the personal Śivaliṅga, ceremonially given by a priest shortly after birth, and worn on a chain or cord around the neck thereafter. See: *Śivaliṅga, Vīra Śaivism.*

Islam: The religion founded by Prophet Muhammed in Arabia about 625 CE. Islam connotes submission to Allah, the name for God in this religion. Adherents, known as Moslems, follow the "five pillars" found in their scripture, the *Koran:* faith in Allah, praying five times daily facing Mecca, giving of alms, fasting during the month of Ramadan, and pilgrimage. One of the fastest growing religions, Islam has over one billion followers, mostly in the Middle East, Pakistan, Africa, China, Indochina, Russia and neighboring countries. See: *Koran, Mohammed.*

issue forth: To come out; be created. To start existing as an entity. E.g., creation issues forth from Naṭarāja's drum. See: *emanation, Naṭarāja, tattva.*

***Īśvara:* ईश्वर** "Highest Lord." Supreme or Personal God. See: *Parameśvara.*

***Īśvarapūjana:* ईश्वरपूजन** "Worship." See: *yama-niyama.*

***Itihāsa:* इतिहास** "So it was." Epic history, particularly the *Rāmāyaṇa* and *Mahābhārata* (of which the famed *Bhagavad Gītā* is a part). This term sometimes refers to the *Purāṇas,* especially the *Skānda Purāṇa* and the *Bhāgavata Purāṇa* (or *Śrīmad Bhāgavatam).* See: *Mahābhārata, Rāmāyaṇa, Smṛiti.*

itinerant: Traveling from place to place, with no permanent home. Wandering. See: *monk, sādhu, vairāgī.*

Jābāla Upanishad: जाबाल उपनिषद् Belongs to the *Atharva Veda.* This short scripture teaches of knowledge attained in renunciation. See: *Upanishad.*

Jagadāchārya: जगदाचार्य "World teacher." In 1986 the World Religious Parliament of New Delhi named five world leaders who were most active in spreading Sanātana Dharma outside India. The five are: H.H. Swāmi Chinmayānanda of Chinmaya Missions, India; Satguru Sivaya Subramuniyaswami of Śaiva Siddhānta Church and Himalayan Academy, USA; Yogīrāj Amṛit Desai of Kṛipālu Yoga Center, USA; Pandit Tej Rāmji Sharma of Nepāli Baba, Nepal; and Swāmī Jagpurṇadās Mahārāj, Mauritius.

Jaimini: जैमिनि Founder of the *Mīmāṁsā Darśana.* See: *shaḍ darśana.*

Jaiminīya Brāhmaṇa Upanishad: जैमिनीय ब्राह्मण उपनिषद् A philosophical discourse of the *Sāma Veda* dealing with death, passage to other worlds and reincarnation. See: *Upanishad.*

Jainism: (Jaina) जैन An ancient non-Vedic religion of India made prominent by the teachings of Mahāvīra ("great hero"), ca 500 BCE. The Jain *Āgamas* teach reverence for all life, vegetarianism and strict renunciation for ascetics. Jains focus great emphasis on the fact that all souls may attain liberation, each by his own effort. Their worship is directed toward their great historic saints, called Tīrthaṅkaras ("ford-crossers"), of whom Mahāvīra was the 24th and last. Jains number about six million today, living mostly in India. See: *Mahāvīra.*

Janaloka: जनलोक "Plane of creativity, or of liberated mortals." The third highest of the seven upper worlds, realm of *viśuddha chakra.* See: *loka.*

jaṅgama: जङ्गम "Moving; wanderer." A term used by Vīra Śaivites, originally to name their mendicant, renunciates who walked as homeless *sādhus,* uplifting others. Now an order of Vīra Śaivite teachers. See: *Vīra Śaivism.*

japa: जप "Recitation." Practice of concentratedly repeating a *mantra,* often while counting the repetitions on a *mālā* or strand of beads. It may be done silently or aloud. Sometimes known as *mantra yoga.* A major *sādhana* in Hindu spiritual practice, from the simple utterance of a few names of God to extraordinary feats of repeating sacred syllables millions of times for years on end. It is recommended as a cure for pride and arrogance, anger and jealousy, fear and confusion. It harmonizes the *doshas* and quiets the *vṛittis.* Filling the mind with divine syllables, awakening the divine essence of spiritual energies in the physical body, *japa* brings forth the *amṛita.* For Śaivites, Namaḥ Śivāya in its various forms is the most treasured *mantra* used in *japa.* The *mantra* Hare-Rāma-Hare-Kṛishṇa is among the foremost Vaishṇava *mantras. Japa yoga* is said to be of 14 kinds: daily *(nitya),* circumstantial *(naimittika),* the *japa* of desired results *(kāmya),* forbidden *(nishiddha),* penitential *(prāyaśchitta),* unmoving *(achala),* moving *(chala),* voiced *(vāchika),* whispered *(upānśu),* bee, or murmured *(bhramara),* mental *(mānasa)*, uninterrupted *(akhanda)*, nonuttered *(ajapa)* and circumambulatory *(pradakshina)*. See: *amṛita, mantra, yama-niyama, yoga.*

jātakarma: **जातकर्म** "Rite of birth." See: *saṁskāras of birth.*

jāti: **जाति** "Birth; genus; community or caste." See: *varṇa dharma.*

jayantī: **जयन्ती** "Birthday." See: *Guru Jayantī.*

jīva: **जीव** "Living, existing." From *jīv*, "to live." The individual soul, *ātman*, during its embodied state, bound by the three *malas (āṇava, karma* and *māyā)*. The *jīvanmukta* is one who is "liberated while living." See: *ātman, evolution of the soul, jīvanmukta, purusha, soul.*

jīvanmukta: **जीवन्मुक्त** "Liberated soul." A being who has attained *nirvikalpa samādhi*—the realization of the Self, Paraśiva—and is liberated from rebirth while living in a human body. (Contrasted with *videhamukta*, one liberated at the point of death.) This attainment is the culmination of lifetimes of intense striving, *sādhana* and *tapas*, requiring total renunciation, *sannyāsa* (death to the external world, denoted in the conducting of one's own funeral rites), in the current incarnation. While completing life in the physical body, the *jīvanmukta* enjoys the ability to reenter *nirvikalpa samādhi* again and again. At this time, *siddhis* can be developed which are carried to the inner worlds after *mahāsamādhi.* Such an awakened *jñānī* benefits the population by simply being who he is. When he speaks, he does so without forethought. His wisdom is beyond reason, yet it does not conflict with reason. Nor does he arrive at what he says through the process of reason, but through the process of *ājñā-chakra* sight. See: *jīvanmukti, jñāna, kaivalya, moksha, Self Realization, Śivasāyujya, videhamukti.*

jīvanmukti: **जीवन्मुक्ति** "Liberation while living." The state of the *jīvanmukta.* Contrasted with *videhamukti*, liberation at the point of death. See: *death, jīvanmukta, moksha, reincarnation, videhamukti.*

jīvayajña: **जीवयज्ञ** "Self sacrifice." See: *yajña.*

jñāna: **ज्ञान** "Knowledge; wisdom." The matured state of the soul. It is the wisdom that comes as an aftermath of the *kuṇḍalinī* breaking through the door of *Brahman* into the realization of Paraśiva, Absolute Reality. The repeated *samādhis* of Paraśiva ever deepen this flow of divine knowing which establishes the knower in an extraordinary point of reference, totally different from those who have not attained this enlightenment. *Jñāna* is the awakened, superconscious state *(kāraṇa chitta)* working within the ordinary experience of the world, flowing into daily life situations. It is the fruition of the progressive stages of *charyā, kriyā* and *yoga* in the Śaiva Siddhānta system of spiritual unfoldment. *Jñāna* is sometimes misunderstood as book knowledge, as a maturity or awakening that comes from simply understanding a complex philosophical system or systems. Those who define *jñāna* in this way deny that the path is a progression of *charyā-kriyā-yoga-jñāna* or of *karma-bhakti-rāja-jñāna.* Rather, they say that one can choose his or her path, and that each leads to the ultimate goal. See: *God Realiza-*

tion, door of Brahman, Self Realization, samādhi.

Jñānāmṛita: **ज्ञानामृत** A treatise of poems by Gorakshanātha on the duties of a *yogī.* See: *Gorakshanātha.*

jñāna pāda: **ज्ञानपाद्** "Stage of wisdom." According to the Śaiva Siddhānta *ṛishis, jñāna* is the last of the four successive *pādas* (stages) of spiritual unfoldment. It is the culmination of the third stage, the *yoga pāda.* Also names the knowledge section of each *Āgama.* See: *jñāna, pāda.*

jñāna śakti: **ज्ञानशक्ति** "Power of wisdom." One of Śiva's three primary *śaktis.* Also a name for Lord Kārttikeya's *vel.* See: *Kārttikeya. śakti, triśūla.*

jñāna yoga: **ज्ञानयोग** "Union of knowledge." Describes the esoteric spiritual practices of the fully enlightened being, or *jñānī.* An alternative meaning, popularized by Swāmī Vivekānanda, is the quest for cognition through intellectual religious study, as one of four alternate paths to truth, the other three being *bhakti yoga, karma yoga* and *rāja yoga.* See: *jñāna, yoga.*

Jñāneśvarī: **ज्ञानेश्वरी** Foremost religious treatise in the Marāṭhi language. Written by the Nātha saint Jñāneśvar (or Jñānadeva) about 1290. It is a verse-by-verse commentary on the *Bhagavad Gītā.*

jñānī: **ज्ञानी** "Sage." One who possesses *jñāna.* See: *jīvanmukta, jñāna.*

joint family: *Kuṭumba* or *kula.* The Hindu social unit consisting of several generations of kindred living together under the same roof or in a joining compound. Traditionally, joint families live in a large single home, but in modern times accommodations are often in individual, nuclear homes within a shared compound. The joint family includes the father and mother, sons, grandsons and great-grandsons with their spouses, as well as the daughters, granddaughters and great-granddaughters until they are married—thus often comprising several married couples and their children. The head of the joint family, called *kuṭumba mukhya* (also *mukhya* or *kartṛi),* is the father, supported by the mother, and in his absence, the elder son, guided by his mother and supported by his spouse. From an early age, the eldest son is given special training by his father to assume this future responsibility as head of the family. In the event of the father's death, sacred law does allow for the splitting of the family wealth between the sons. Division of family assets may also be necessary in cases where sons are involved in different professions and live in different towns, when there is an inability for all to get along under one roof, or when the family becomes unmanageably large.

The main characteristics of the joint family are that its members 1) share a common residence, 2) partake of food prepared in the same kitchen, 3) hold their property in common and, 4) ideally, profess the same religion, sect and *sampradāya.* Each individual family of husband, wife and children is under the guidance of the head of the joint family. All work together unselfishly to further the common good. Each joint family extends out from its home to include a second level of connections as an "extended family (*bṛihatkuṭumba* or *mahākuṭumba*)." See: *extended family, gṛihastha dharma.*

juncture: A critical point in the development of events.

jyotisha: ज्योतिष From *jyoti,* "light." "The science of the lights (or stars)." Hindu astrology, the knowledge and practice of analyzing events and circumstances, delineating character and determining auspicious moments, according to the positions and movements of heavenly bodies. In calculating horoscopes, *jyotisha* uses the sidereal (fixed-star) system, whereas Western astrology uses the tropical (fixed-date) method.

jyotisha śāstrī: ज्योतिषशास्त्री "Astrologer." A person well versed in the science of *jyotisha.* See: *jyotisha.*

Jyotisha Vedāṅga: ज्योतिषवेदाङ्ग "Veda-limb of celestial science (astronomy-astrology)." Ancient texts giving knowledge of astronomy and astrology, for understanding the cosmos and determining proper timing for Vedic rites. (*Jyoti* means light [of the sun, fire, etc.]) See: *jyotisha, Vedāṅga.*

Kadaitswāmī: கடையிற்சுவாமி "Marketplace *swāmī.*" A *satguru* of the Nandinātha Sampradāya's Kailāsa Paramparā. Born ca 1820; died 1875. Renouncing his career as a judge in Bangalore, South India, Kadaitswāmī became a *sannyāsin* and trained under the "Ṛishi from the Himālayas," who then sent him on mission to Sri Lanka. He performed severe *tapas* on an island off the coast of Jaffna, awakening many *siddhis.* For decades he spurred the Sri Lankan Śaivites to greater spirituality through his inspired talks and demonstration of *siddhis.* He initiated Chellappaswāmī as the next *satguru* in the *paramparā.* Kadaitswāmī's name given at his initiation was Muthyānandaswāmī. See: *Kailāsa Paramparā, Nātha Sampradāya.*

Kadavul: கடவுள் "Beyond and within." An ancient Tamil name for Lord Śiva meaning, "He who is both immanent and transcendent, within and beyond." See: *Śiva.*

Kailāsa: कैलास "Crystalline" or "abode of bliss." The four-faced Himalayan peak in Western Tibet; the earthly abode of Lord Śiva. Associated with Mount Meru, the legendary center of the universe, it is an important pilgrimage destination for all Hindus, as well as for Tibetan Buddhists. Kailāsa is represented in Śāktism by a certain three-dimensional form of the *Śrī Chakra yantra* (also called *kailāsa chakra*). See: *Śrī Chakra.*

Kailāsa Paramparā: कैलासपरंपरा A spiritual lineage of *siddhas,* a major stream of the Nandinātha Sampradāya, proponents of the ancient philosophy of monistic Śaiva Siddhānta. The first of these masters that history recalls was Maharishi Nandinātha (or Nandikeśvara) 2,250 years ago, *satguru* to the great Tirumular, ca 200 BCE, and seven other disciples (as stated in the *Tirumantiram*): Patañjali, Vyāghrapāda, Sanatkumāra, Śivayogamuni, Sanakar, Sanadanar and Sananthanar. Tirumular had seven disciples:

Malaṅgam, Indiran, Soman, Brahman, Rudran, Kalaṅga, and Kañjamalayam, each of whom established one or more monasteries and propagated the Āgamic lore. In the line of Kalaṅga came the sages Ṛighama, Māligaideva, Nādāntar, Bhogadeva and Paramānanda. The lineage continued down the centuries and is alive today—the first recent *siddha* known being the Ṛishi from the Himalayas, so named because he descended from those holy mountains. In South India, he initiated Kadaitswāmī (ca 1810–1875), who in turn initiated Chellappaswāmī (1840–1915). Chellappan passed the mantle of authority to sage Yogaswāmī (1872–1964), who in 1949 initiated the current *satguru,* Sivaya Subramuniyaswami. See: *Chellapaswāmī, Kadaitswāmī, Nātha Sampradāya, Patañjali, Subramuniyaswami, Tirumular, Vyāghrapāda, Yogaswāmī.*

kaivalya: **कैवल्य** "Absolute oneness, aloneness; perfect detachment, freedom." Liberation. *Kaivalya* is the term used by Patañjali and others in the *yoga* tradition to name the goal and fulfillment of *yoga,* the state of complete detachment from transmigration. It is virtually synonymous with *moksha. Kaivalya* is the perfectly transcendent state, the highest condition resulting from the ultimate realization. It is defined uniquely according to each philosophical school, depending on its beliefs regarding the nature of the soul. See: *moksha, samarasa, Śivasāyujya, jñāna.*

Kaivalya Upanishad: **कैवल्य उपनिषद्** A philosophical text of the *Atharva Veda.* This treatise teaches how to reach Śiva through meditation.

kāla: **काल** 1) "Time; to calculate." 2) "Black; of a black or dark blue color; death."

kalā: **कला** "Part, segment; art or skill." 1) Cultural arts. (See: *kalā–64*). 2) A five-fold division of the cosmos based on the 36 *tattvas,* as explained in the *Śaiva Āgamas.* The five *kalās*—spheres, or dimensions of consciousness—are: 1) Śāntyatītakalā, "sphere beyond peace," the extremely rarified level of *śuddha māyā* (actinic energy) in which superconsciousness is expanded into endless inner space, the realm of God Śiva and the Gods; 2) Śāntikalā, "sphere of peace," the level within *śuddha māyā* where forms are made of inner sounds and colors, where reside great *devas* and *ṛishis* who are beyond the reincarnation cycles; 3) Vidyākalā, "sphere of knowing," the level within *śuddhāśuddha māyā* (actinodic energy) of subsuperconscious awareness of forms in their totality in progressive states of manifestation, and of the interrelated forces of the actinodic energies; 4) Pratishṭākalā, "sphere of resting, tranquility," the level within *aśuddha māyā* (odic energy) of intellect and instinct; 5) Nivṛittikalā, "sphere of perdition, destruction; returning," the level within *aśuddha māyā* of physical and near-physical existence, conscious, subconscious and sub-subconscious mind. See: *tattva.*

kalā–64 (chatuḥ shashṭi kalā): **चतुः षष्टिकला** "Sixty-four arts." A classical curriculum of sacred sciences, studies, arts and skills of cultured living listed in various Hindu *śāstras.* Its most well-known appearance is in the

Kāma Sūtra, an extensive manual devoted to sensual pleasures. The *Kāma Sūtra* details as its primary subject matter the 64 secret arts, *abhyantara kalā,* of erotic love. In addition to these it lists 64 *bāhya kalās,* or practical arts, as required study for cultured persons. They are: 1) singing, 2) instrumental music, 3) dancing, 4) painting, 5) forehead adornments, 6) making decorative floral and grain designs on the floor, 7) home and temple flower arranging, 8) personal grooming, 9) mosaic tiling, 10) bedroom arrangements, 11) creating music with water, 12) splashing and squirting with water, 13) secret *mantras,* 14) making flower garlands, 15) head adornments, 16) dressing, 17) costume decorations, 18) perfumery, 19) jewelry making, 20) magic and illusions, 21) ointments for charm and virility, 22) manual dexterity, 23) skills of cooking, eating and drinking, 24) beverage and dessert preparation, 25) sewing (making and mending garments), 26) embroidery, 27) playing *vīna* and drum, 28) riddles and rhymes, 29) poetry games, 30) tongue twisters and difficult recitation, 31) literary recitation, 32) drama and story telling, 33) verse composition game, 34) furniture caning, 35) erotic devices and knowledge of sexual arts, 36) crafting wooden furniture, 37) architecture and house construction, 38) distinguishing between ordinary and precious stones and metals, 39) metal-working, 40) gems and mining, 41) gardening and horticulture, 42) games of wager involving animals, 43) training parrots and mynas to speak, 44) hairdressing, 45) coding messages, 46) speaking in code, 47) knowledge of foreign languages and dialects, 48) making flower carriages, 49) spells, charms and omens, 50) making simple mechanical devices, 51) memory training, 52) game of reciting verses from hearing, 53) decoding messages, 54) the meanings of words, 55) dictionary studies, 56) prosody and rhetoric, 57) impersonation, 58) artful dressing, 59) games of dice, 60) the game of *akarsha* (a dice game played on a board), 61) making dolls and toys for children, 62) personal etiquette and animal training, 63) knowledge of *dharmic* warfare and victory, and 64) physical culture.

These are among the skills traditionally taught to both genders, while emphasizing masculinity in men and femininity in women. Their subject matter draws on such texts as the *Vedāṅgas* and *Upavedas,* and the *Śilpa Śāstras,* or craft manuals. Through the centuries, writers have prescribed many more skills and accomplishments. These include sculpture, pottery, weaving, astronomy and astrology, mathematics, weights and measures, philosophy, scriptural study, agriculture, navigation, trade and shipping, knowledge of time, logic, psychology and *āyurveda.* In modern times, two unique sets of 64 *kalās* have been developed, one for girls and one for boys. See: *hereditary, Śilpa Śāstra.*

Kālāmukha: **कालामुख** "Black-faced"(probably for a black mark of renunciation worn on the forehead). A Śaiva sect issued from Pāśupata Śaivism at its height (ca 600–1000). As no Kālāmukha religious texts exist today, this sect is known only indirectly. They were said to be well organized in temple construction and worship, as well as eccentric and unsocial: eating from human skulls, smearing their bodies with ashes from the cremation ground, carrying a club, wearing matted hair, etc. See: *left-handed, Pāśupata Śaivism, Tantrism.*

kalaśa: **कलश** "Water pot; pitcher; jar." In temple rites, a pot of water, *kalaśa,* topped with mango leaves and a husked coconut represents the Deity during special *pūjās. Kalaśa* also names the pot-like spires that adorn temple roofs.

Kālī: **काली** "Black." Goddess. A form of Śakti in Her fierce aspect worshiped by various sects within Śāktism. She is dark, nude, primordial and fiercely powerful, as of a naked energy untamed. But from the perspective of devotees, She is the incomparable protectress, champion of *sādhana* and mother of liberation. The Goddess Durgā, seated on a tiger, has similar characteristics and is often identified with Kālī. See: *Śakti, Śāktism.*

Kali Yuga: **कलियुग** "Dark Age." The Kali Yuga is the last age in the repetitive cycle of four phases of time the universe passes through. It is comparable to the darkest part of the night, as the forces of ignorance are in full power and many of the subtle faculties of the soul are obscured. See: *cosmic cycle, mahāpralaya, yuga.*

Kallaṭa: **कल्लट** An exponent of Kashmīr Śaivism (ca 875) who wrote the *Spaṇda Kārikās.* Kallaṭa was a disciple of Vasugupta. See: *Kashmīr Śaivism.*

kalpa: **कल्प** From *kṛlip,* "arranged, ordered." 1) Rules for ceremony or sacred living, as in the *Kalpa Vedāṅga.* 2) Determination or resolve, as in *saṅkalpa.* 3) A vast period of time also known as a day of *Brahmā,* equaling 1,000 *mahāyugas,* or 4,320,000,000 years. See: *cosmic cycle, Kalpa Vedāṅga, saṅkalpa, yuga.*

Kalpa Vedāṅga: **कल्पवेदाङ्ग** "Procedural or ceremonial Veda-limb." Also known as the *Kalpa Sūtras*—a body of three groups of auxiliary Vedic texts: 1) the *Śrauta Sūtras* and *Śulba Sūtras,* on public Vedic rites (*yajña*), 2) the *Gṛihya Sūtras* (or *Śāstras*), on domestic rites and social custom, and 3) the *Dharma Śāstras* (or *Sūtras*), on religious law. There are numerous sets of *Kalpa Sūtras,* composed by various *ṛishis.* Each set is associated with one of the four *Vedas.* See: *Dharma Śāstra, Gṛihya Sūtras, Śulba Śāstras, Śrauta Sūtras, Vedāṅgas.*

Kalyāna: **कल्यान** A town in Karnataka, South India.

kāma: **काम** "Pleasure, love; desire." Cultural, intellectual and sexual fulfillment. One of four human goals, *purushārtha.* See: *Kāma Sūtras, purushārtha.*

kamaṇḍalu: **कमण्डलु** "Vessel, water jar." Traditionally earthen or wooden, carried by *sannyāsins,* it symbolizes the renunciate's simple, self-contained life. The tree from which *kamaṇḍalus* are traditionally made is the *kamaṇḍalutaru.* See: *sannyāsa dharma, sannyāsin.*

Kāma Sūtra(s): **कामसूत्र** "Aphorisms on pleasure." A fifth-century text by Vātsyāyana on erotics. The *Kāma Śūtra* and other *Kāma Śāstras* are sometimes classed as an *Upaveda.* See: *Upaveda.*

Kāmika Āgama: कामिक आगम An important scripture among the 28 *Śaiva Siddhānta Āgamas,* widely available today. The verses from its *kriyā pāda,* on ritual and temple construction, are a crucial reference for South Indian priests. See: *Śaiva Āgamas.*

Kaṇāda: कणाद् Founder of the Vaiśeshika Darśana, author of the *Vaiśeshika Sūtras.* See: *shaḍ darśana.*

Kandar Anubhuti: கந்தர் அனுபூதி A highly mystical 51-verse poem in praise of Lord Kārttikeya-Murugan composed by the Tamil saint, Arunagirināthar (ca 1500). It describes the narrator's arduous path to Ultimate Reality.

Kannada: One of four modern Dravidian languages, and principal medium for Vīra Śaivism. It is spoken by 20 million people, mostly in Karnataka.

Kanphaṭi: कन्फटि (Hindi.) "Split eared," from the custom of splitting the cartilage of the ear to insert large earrings. The name of the ascetic order of men and women founded by Gorakshanātha (ca 950), proponents of *kuṇḍalinī-haṭha yoga* still today. See: *earrings, Gorakshanātha, Siddha Siddhānta.*

Kāpālika: कापालिक An ascetic sect which developed out of the Pāśupatas around 500 CE and largely vanished around 1400. They earned a reputation for extreme practices. Possible predecessors of Gorakshanātha Siddha Siddhānta *yogīs.* See: *Pāśupata Śaivism.*

kapha: कफ "Biological water." One of the three bodily humors, called *dosha, kapha* is known as the water humor. Principle of cohesion. *Kapha* gives bodily structure and stability, lubricates, heals and bestows immunity. See: *āyurveda, dosha.*

Kapila: कपिल Founder (ca 500 BCE) of the Sāṅkhya philosophy, one of the six *darśanas* of Hinduism. See: *shaḍ darśana.*

Kāraṇa Āgama: कारण आगम One of the 28 *Śaiva Siddhānta Āgamas* widely available today. Its *kriyā pāda* forms the basis for temple rituals performed in nearly all South Indian Śiva temples. See: *Śaiva Āgamas.*

kāraṇa chitta: कारणचित्त "Causal mind." The intuitive-superconscious mind of the soul. It corresponds to the *ānandamaya kośa,* bliss sheath, also called *kāraṇa śarīra,* causal body. See: *kośa, mind (five states), soul.*

Karaṇa Hasuge: करणहसुगे A central Vīra Śaiva scripture authored by Chennabasavaṇṇa. See: *Chennabasavaṇṇa.*

kāraṇa śarīra: कारणशरीर "Causal body," the actinic body or soul body. See: *actinic, actinodic, kośa, odic, soul, subtle body.*

Karavaṇa Māhātmya: करवणमाहात्म्य See: *Pāśupata Śaivism.*

karma: कर्म "Action, deed." One of the most important principles in Hindu thought, *karma* refers to 1) any act or deed; 2) the principle of cause and effect; 3) a consequence or "fruit of action" *(karmaphala)* or "after effect" *(uttaraphala),* which sooner or later returns upon the doer. What we sow, we shall reap in this or future lives. Selfish, hateful acts *(pāpakarma* or *kukarma)* will bring suffering. Benevolent actions *(puṇyakarma* or *sukarma)* will bring loving reactions. *Karma* is a neutral, self-perpetuating law of the inner cosmos, much as gravity is an impersonal law of the outer cosmos. In fact, it has been said that gravity is a small, external expression of the greater law of *karma.* The impelling, unseen power of one's past actions is called *adṛishṭa.*

The law of *karma* acts impersonally, yet we may meaningfully interpret its results as either positive *(puṇya)* or negative *(pāpa)*—terms describing actions leading the soul either toward or away from the spiritual goal. *Karma* is further graded as: white *(śukla),* black *(kṛishṇa),* mixed *(śukla-kṛishṇa)* or neither white nor black *(aśukla-akṛishṇa).* The latter term describes the *karma* of the *jñānī,* who, as Ṛishi Patañjali says, is established in *kaivalya,* freedom from *prakṛiti* through realization of the Self. Similarly, one's *karma* must be in a condition of *aśukla-akṛishṇa,* quiescent balance, in order for liberation to be attained. This equivalence of *karma* is called *karmasāmya,* and is a factor that brings *malaparipāka,* or maturity of *āṇava mala.* It is this state of resolution in preparation for *samādhi* at death that all Hindus seek through making amends and settling differences.

Karma is threefold: *sañchita, prārabdha* and *kriyamāna.* ***—sañchita karma:*** "Accumulated actions." The sum of all *karmas* of this life and past lives. ***—prārabdha karma:*** "Actions begun; set in motion." That portion of *sañchitta karma* that is bearing fruit and shaping the events and conditions of the current life, including the nature of one's bodies, personal tendencies and associations. ***—kriyamāna karma:*** "Being made." The *karma* being created and added to *sañchita* in this life by one's thoughts, words and actions, or in the inner worlds between lives. *Kriyamāna karma* is also called *āgāmi,* "coming, arriving," and *vartamāna,* "living, set in motion." While some *kriyamāna karmas* bear fruit in the current life, others are stored for future births. Each of these types can be divided into two categories: *ārabdha* (literally, "begun, undertaken;" *karma* that is "sprouting"), and *anārabdha* ("not commenced; dormant"), or "seed *karma.*"

In a famed analogy, *karma* is compared to rice in its various stages. *Sañchita karma,* the residue of one's total accumulated actions, is likened to rice that has been harvested and stored in a granary. From the stored rice, a small portion has been removed, husked and readied for cooking and eating. This is *prārabdha karma,* past actions that are shaping the events of the present. Meanwhile, new rice, mainly from the most recent harvest of *prārabdha karma,* is being planted in the field that will yield a future crop and be added to the store of rice. This is *kriyamāna karma,* the consequences of current actions.

In Śaivism, *karma* is one of three principal bonds of the soul, along with *āṇava* and *māyā. Karma* is the driving force that brings the soul back again and again into human birth in the evolutionary cycle of transmigration called *saṁsāra.* When all earthly *karmas* are resolved and the Self has been realized, the soul is liberated from rebirth. This is the goal of all Hindus.

For each of the three kinds of *karma* there is a different method of resolution. Nonattachment to the fruits of action, along with daily rites of worship and strict adherence to the codes of *dharma,* stops the accumulation of *kriyamāna. Prārabdha karma* is resolved only through being experienced and lived through. *Sañchita karma,* normally inaccessible, is burned away only through the grace and *dīkshā* of the *satguru,* who prescribes *sādhana* and *tapas* for the benefit of the *śishya.* Through the sustained *kuṇḍalinī* heat of this extreme penance, the seeds of unsprouted *karmas* are fried, and therefore will never sprout in this or future lives. See: *dīkshā, grace.*

Like the four-fold edict of *dharma,* the three-fold edict of *karma* has both individual and impersonal dimensions. Personal *karma* is thus influenced by broader contexts, sometimes known as family *karma,* community *karma,* national *karma,* global *karma* and universal *karma.* See: *āṇava, fate, māyā, moksha, pāpa, pāśa, puṇya, sin, soul.*

karmasāmya: **कर्मसाम्य** "Balance or equipoise of *karma.*" See: *karma.*

karmāśaya: **कर्माशय** "Holder of *karma.*" Describes the body of the soul, or *ānandamaya kośa.* See: *karma, kośa.*

karma yoga: **कर्मयोग** "Union through action." The path of selfless service. See: *yoga.*

Karṇāṭaka: **कर्णाटक** Southwest state of modern India, where Vijayanagara flourished. Vīra Śaivism is centered here. Population 25 million, area 74,043 square miles.

karṇavedha: **कर्णवेध** "Ear-piercing." See: *saṁskāras of childhood.*

Kārttikeya: **कार्त्तिकेय** Child of the Pleiades, from *Kṛittikā,* "Pleiades." A son of Śiva. A great Mahādeva worshiped in all parts of India and the world. Also known as Murugan, Kumāra, Skanda, Shaṇmukhanātha, Subramaṇya and more, He is the God who guides that part of evolution which is religion, the transformation of the instinctive into a divine wisdom through the practice of *yoga.* He holds the holy *vel* of *jñāna śakti,* which is His Power to vanquish darkness or ignorance.

Kārttikeya Stotram: **कार्त्तिकेयस्तोत्रं** A subdivision *(Rudrāyamala Tantra)* of the *Śākta Tantras* dedicated to God Kārttikeya. See: *Kārttikeya.*

karuṇā: **करुणा** "Compassionate; loving, full of grace."

Kāruṇa Āgama: **कारुण आगम** One of the 28 *Āgamas* of Śaiva Siddhānta. See: *Śaiva Āgamas.*

Kāruṇākarak Kadavul: கருணைகரக் கடவுள் Hymn by the Tamil saint, Tayumanavar (1705–1742), in praise of Lord Śiva. See: *Tayumanavar.*

kāruṇya: **कारुण्य** "Compassion, kindness, love." In Śaivism, an alternate term for Śiva's revealing grace, *anugraha śakti.* See: *anugraha śakti, grace.*

kāshāya: **काषाय** "Brownish-red." The color of *sannyāsins'* robes. See: *kavi.*

Kashmir (Kaśmīra): **कश्मीर** The Northernmost area of India, part of the present-day state of Jammu and Kashmir. It figures prominently in the history of Śaivism. Area 115,000 square miles, under dispute between India and Pakistan. Population is six million in the Indian sector.

Kashmīr Śaivism: कश्मीरशैव In this mildly theistic and intensely monistic school founded by Vasugupta around 850, Śiva is immanent and transcendent. Purification and *yoga* are strongly emphasized. Kashmīr Śaivism provides an extremely rich and detailed understanding of the human psyche, and a clear and distinct path of *kuṇḍalinī-siddha yoga* to the goal of Self Realization. The Kashmīr Śaivite is not so much concerned with worshiping a personal God as he is with attaining the transcendental state of Śiva consciousness. *Sādhana* leads to the assimilation of the object (world) in the subject (I) until the Self (Śiva) stands revealed as one with the universe. The goal—liberation—is sustained recognition *(pratyabhijñā)* of one's true Self as nothing but Śiva. There are three *upāya,* or stages of attainment of God consciousness: *āṇavopāya (yoga), śāktopāya* (spiritual discrimination), *śāmbhavopāya* (attainment through the guru's instruction) and *anupāya,* or "no means" (spontaneous realization without effort). Kashmīr Śaivite literature is in three broad divisions: *Āgama Śāstras, Spanda Śāstras* and *Pratyabhijñā Śāstras.* Today various organizations promulgate the esoteric teachings. While the number of Kashmīr Śaivite formal followers is uncertain, the school remains an important influence in India. See: *Śaivism, upāya.*

kathā: कथा "Story; discussion." Also, the literary form involving the telling of stories. *Kathakas* are bards, storytellers. See: *folk-narratives, mythology.*

Kaṭha Upanishad: कठ उपनिषद् One of the major *Upanishads,* belonging to the *Taittirīya Brāhmaṇa* of the *Yajur Veda.* This scripture contains the famous story of Nachiketas who extracts from Yama, Lord of Death, the knowledge of liberation to be had through realization of the Supreme.

Kathirgāma Purāṇa: कथिर्गामपुराण A secondary scripture regarding the famous central Sri Lankan abode of Lord Murugan (Kārttikeya).

Kauṇḍinya: कौण्डिन्य Author of a commentary on the *Pāśupata Sūtras* (ca 500). See: *Pāśupata Śaivism, Pāśupata Sūtras.*

Kaurusha: कौरुष One of four known disciples of *Lakulīśa.* See: *Lakulīśa, Pāśupata Śaivism.*

Kaushītakī Upanishad: कौषीतकी उपनिषद् A major *Upanishad* belonging to the *Ṛig Veda.* It discusses: 1) the course of souls after death, 2) the doctrine of *prāṇa* as related to the *ātman* and 3) the attainment of *moksha.*

kavadi: காவடி A penance offered to Lord Murugan-Kārttikeya, especially during Tai Pusam, consisting of carrying in procession a heavy, beautifully decorated, wooden object from which pots of milk hang which are to be used for His *abhisheka.* The participant's tongue and other parts of the body are often pierced with small silver spears or hooks. See: *penance.*

kavi: காவி "Ocher-saffron color." A Tamil term referring to the color taken on by robes of *sādhus* who sit, meditate or live on the banks of the Ganges.

Names the color of the *sannyāsin's* robes. The Sanskṛit equivalent is *kāshāya.*

Kāyavarohaṇa: **कायवरोहण** Birthplace of *Lakulīśa,* most prominent *guru* of *Pāśupata Śaivism,* in India's present-day state of Baroda. See: *Lakulīśa.*

kāya siddhi: **कायसिद्धि** In Siddha Siddhānta, as well as Śaiva Siddhānta and other *yoga* traditions, the process by which a *yogī* transforms his body from physical to spiritual substance to attain deathlessness. See: *siddhi.*

***Kedāreśvara* Temple: केदारेश्वर** A temple in Karnataka which belonged to the Kālāmukha sect of Śaivism. Inscriptions upon it (1162) are a main source of knowledge about this now nearly extinct sect. See: *Kālāmukha.*

Kena Upanishad: **केन उपनिषद्** Belongs to the *Talavakāra Brāhmaṇa* of the *Sāma Veda.* It is a discourse upon Brahman, Absolute Reality and His worship as personal God. See: *Upanishad.*

Kerala: **केरल** The small Indian state, formerly called Koṅkaṇ, along the southwestern tip of India. Area 15,000 square miles, population 25 million.

keśānta: **केशान्त** "Beard-shaving." See: *saṁskāras of adulthood.*

kindred: Family, relatives, kin. See: *joint family, extended family.*

kīrtana: **कीर्तन** "Praising." Devotional singing and dancing in celebration of God, Gods and *guru.* An important form of congregational worship in many Hindu sects. See: *congregational worship, bhajana.*

knower: One who knows. In philosophy, that within conscious beings which understands or is conscious. See: *awareness, jñāna, sākshin, chit.*

konrai: கொன்றை The Golden Shower tree, *Cassia fistula*; symbol of Śiva's cascading, abundant, golden grace.

Koran: The Islamic religion's sacred book, God's word transmitted through the angel Gabriel to Mohammed, the prophet of Islam. Its official version appeared around 650, 18 years after Mohammed's death. See: *Mohammed.*

kośa: **कोश** "Sheath; vessel, container; layer." Philosophically, five sheaths through which the soul functions simultaneously in the various planes or levels of existence. They are sometimes compared to the layers of an onion. The *kośas,* in order of increasing subtlety, are as follows. ***—annamaya kośa:*** "Sheath composed of food." The physical or odic body, coarsest of sheaths in comparison to the faculties of the soul, yet indispensable for evolution and Self Realization, because only within it can all fourteen *chakras* fully function. See: *chakra.* ***—prāṇamaya kośa:*** "Sheath composed of *prāṇa* (vital force)." Also known as the *prāṇic* or health body, or the etheric body or etheric double, it coexists within the physical body as its source of life, breath and vitality, and is its connection with the astral body. *Prāṇa* moves in the *prāṇamaya kośa* as five primary currents or *vayus,* "vital airs or winds." *Prāṇamaya kośa* disintegrates at death along with the physical body. See: *prāṇa* ***—manomaya kośa:*** "Mind-formed sheath." The astral body, from *manas,* "thought, will, wish." The instinctive-intellectual sheath of ordinary thought, desire and emotion. It is the seat of the *indriyas,* sensory and motor organs, respectively called *jñānendriyas* and *karmendriyas.* The *manomaya kośa* takes form as the physical body develops and is discarded in the inner worlds before rebirth. It is understood in two layers: 1) the odic-causal sheath *(buddhi)* and 2) the odic-astral sheath *(manas).* See: *indriya, manas.* ***—vijñānamaya kośa:*** "Sheath of cognition." The mental or cognitive-intuitive sheath, also called the actinodic sheath. It is the vehicle of higher thought, *vijñāna*—understanding, knowing, direct cognition, wisdom, intuition and creativity. ***—ānandamaya kośa:*** "Body of bliss." The intuitive-superconscious sheath or actinic-causal body. This inmost soul form *(svarūpa)* is the ultimate foundation of all life, intelligence and higher faculties. Its essence is Parāśakti (Pure Consciousness) and Paraśiva (the Absolute). *Ānandamaya kośa* is not a sheath in the same sense as the four outer *kośas.* It is the soul itself, a body of light, also called *kāraṇa śarīra,* causal body, and *karmāśaya,* holder of *karmas* of this and all past lives. *Kāraṇa chitta,* "causal mind," names the soul's superconscious mind, of which Parāśakti (or Satchidānanda) is the rarified substratum. *Ānandamaya kośa* is that which evolves through all incarnations and beyond until the soul's ultimate, fulfilled merger, *viśvagrāsa,* in the Primal Soul, Parameśvara. Then *ānandamaya kośa* becomes Śivamayakośa, the body of God Śiva.

The physical body *(annamaya kośa)* is also called *sthūla śarīra,* "gross body." The soul body *(ānandamaya kośa)* is also called *kāraṇa śarīra,* "causal body." The *prāṇamaya, manomaya* and *vijñānamaya kośas* together comprise the *sūkshma śarīra,* "subtle body," with the *prāṇamaya* shell disintegrating at death. See: *actinic, actinodic, manomaya kośa, niyati, odic, śarīra, soul, subtle body.*

Kṛishṇa: **कृष्ण** "Black." Also related to *kṛishṭiḥ,* meaning "drawing, attracting." One of the most popular Gods of the Hindu pantheon. He is worshiped by Vaishṇavas as the eighth *avatāra,* incarnation, of Vishṇu. He is best known as the Supreme Personage depicted in the *Mahābhārata,* and specifically in the *Bhagavad Gītā.* For Gauḍīya Vaishṇavism, Kṛishṇa is the Godhead.

Kṛittikā Dīpa: **कृत्तिकादीप** A joyous one-day festival on the Kṛittikā *nakshatra* (Pleiades constellation), in November-December, when God Śiva is worshiped as an infinite pillar of light. Great bonfires are lit at night on hills and in villages in India and elsewhere to represent the divine, all-permeating light of Parāśakti. See: *festival.*

kriyā: **क्रिया** "Action." In a general sense, *kriyā* can refer to doing of any kind. Specifically, it names religious action, especially rites or ceremonies. In *yoga* terminology, *kriyā* names involuntary physical movements caused by the arousal of the *kuṇḍalinī.* See: *pāda.*

Kriyākramadyotikā: **क्रियाक्रमद्योतिका** A manual by Aghoraśiva (ca 1050) detailing Āgamic Śaiva ritual. It is used widely by South Indian priests today.

kriyamāna karma: **क्रियमानकर्म** "Actions being made." See: *karma.*

kriyā pāda: **क्रियापाद्** "Stage of religious action; worship." The stage of worship and devotion, second of four progressive stages of maturation on the Śaiva Siddhānta path of attainment. See: *pāda.*

kriyā śakti: क्रियाशक्ति "Action power." The universal force of doing. See: *Śakti, triśūla.*

kshamā: क्षमा "Patience." See: *yama-niyama.*

kshatriya: क्षत्रिय "Governing; sovereign." The social class of lawmakers, lawenforcers and military. See: *varṇa dharma.*

Kūḍala Saṅgamadeva: कूडलसङ्गमदेव A name of Śiva meaning "Lord of rivers' confluence."

kula: कुल "Family; home; group of families." See: *extended family, joint family.*

kula guru: कुलगुरु The spiritual preceptor of the family or extended family.

Kulārṇava Tantra: कुलार्णवतन्त्र A leading scripture of the Kaula school of Śāktism. It comprises 17 chapters totaling 2,058 verses which focus on ways to liberation, with notable chapters on the *guru-śishya* relationship.

Kumāra: कुमार "Virgin youth; ever-youthful." A name of Lord Kārttikeya as an eternal bachelor. See: *Kārttikeya.*

kumbha: कुम्भ "Jar or pot; water vessel."

kuṇḍalinī: कुण्डलिनी "She who is coiled; serpent power." The primordial cosmic energy in every individual which, at first, lies coiled like a serpent at the base of the spine and eventually, through the practice of *yoga,* rises up the *sushumṇā nāḍī.* As it rises, the *kuṇḍalinī* awakens each successive *chakra. Nirvikalpa samādhi,* enlightenment, comes as it pierces through the door of Brahman at the core of the *sahasrāra* and enters! *Kuṇḍalinī śakti* then returns to rest in any one of the seven *chakras.* Śivasāyujya is complete when the *kuṇḍalinī* arrives back in the *sahasrāra* and remains coiled in this crown *chakra.* See: *chakra, door of Brahman, samādhi, nāḍī, tantrism.*

kuṅkuma: कुंकुम "Saffron; red." The red powder, made of turmeric and lime, worn by Hindus as the *pottu,* dot, at the point of the third eye on the forehead. Names the saffron plant, *Crocus sativus,* and its pollen.

Kūrma Purāṇa: कूर्मपुराण "Tortoise story." One of the six *Śiva Purāṇas,* it glorifies the worship of Śiva and Durgā.

Kurukshetra: कुरुक्षेत्र An extensive plain near Delhi, scene of the great war between the Kauravas and Pāṇḍavas. See: *Mahābhārata, Bhagavad Gītā.*

Kuśika: कुशिक One of four known disciples of Lakulīśa.

kuttuvilaku: குத்துவிளக்கு A standing lamp found in the temple, shrine room or home. It is made of metal, with several wicks fed by *ghee* or special oils. Used to light the home and used in *pūjā.* Part of temple and shrine altars, the standing lamp is sometimes worshiped as the divine light, Parāśakti or Parajyoti. Returning from the temple and lighting one's *kuttuvilaku* courts the accompanying *devas* to remain in the home and channels the vibration of the temple sanctum sanctorum into the home shrine. Called *dīpastambha* in Sanskṛit.

kuṭumba: कुटुम्ब "Joint family." See: *extended family, joint family.*

Lakshmī: **लक्ष्मी** "Mark or sign," often of success or prosperity. Śakti, the Universal Mother, as Goddess of wealth. The mythological consort of Vishṇu. Usually depicted on a lotus flower. Prayers are offered to Lakshmī for wealth, beauty and peace. See: *Goddess, Śakti.*

Lakulīśa: **लकुलीश** The most prominent *guru* (ca 200) of the ancient Pāśupata school of Śaivism. The *Pāśupata Sūtras* are attributed to him. See: *Śaivism.*

Lallā: (*Lalāsa* **ललास** in Sanskṛit.) A woman *Kashmīr Śaivite* saint (ca 1300) whose intensely mystical poems, *Lalla Vākyāni,* describe her inner experiences of oneness with Śiva. See: *Kashmīr Śaivism.*

lance: A spear. See: *vel, Kārttikeya.*

larder: Pantry; room in a house where food supplies are kept.

laud: To praise. To sing, chant or speak the qualities or glories of.

lavish: Very abundant or generous in giving or spending.

left-handed: *Vāma mārga.* A term describing certain *tantric* practices where the instincts and intellect are transcended, and detachment is sought through practices and behavior which are contrary to orthodox social behavior. See: *tantra, tantrika, tantrism.*

legend: A story of uncertain historical basis, transmitted from generation to generation. See: *folk narratives, kathā, mythology.*

legislate: To make or pass laws.

legitimate: According to the rules or the law. Authentic; reasonable.

lekhaprārtha havana: **लेखप्रार्थहवन** "Written-prayer-burning rite." A coined term for the ancient practice of sending written prayers to the Gods by burning them in a sanctified fire in a temple or shrine. Alternately this rite can be performed at other appropriate sites, with four persons sitting around a fire and chanting to create a temporary temple. Prayers can be written in any language, but should be clearly legible, in black ink on white paper. The *devas* have provided a special script, called Tyaf, especially for this purpose. Its letters, from A to Z, which replace the letters of the Roman script, looks like this:

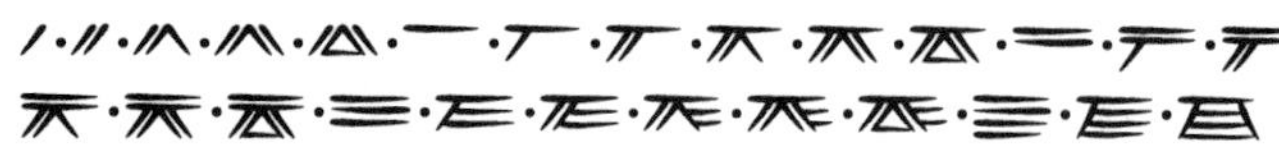

lest: For fear that a thing might happen.

liberal Hinduism: A synonym for Smārtism and the closely related neo-Indian religion. See: *neo-Indian religion, Smārtism, universalist.*

liberation: *Moksha,* release from the bonds of *pāśa,* after which the soul is liberated from *saṁsāra* (the round of births and deaths). In Śaiva Siddhānta, *pāśa* is the three-fold bondage of *āṇava, karma* and *māyā,* which limit and confine the soul to the reincarnational cycle so that it may evolve. *Moksha* is freedom from the fettering power of these bonds, which do not cease to exist, but no longer have the power to fetter or bind the soul. See: *mala, jīvanmukti, moksha, pāśa, reincarnation, satguru, Self Realization, soul.*

licentious: Morally unrestrained, especially in sexual behavior.

light: In an ordinary sense, a form of energy which makes physical objects visible to the eye. In a religious-mystical sense, light also illumines inner objects (i.e., mental images). **—inner light:** light perceived inside the head and body, of which there are varying intensities. When the *karmas* have been sufficiently quieted, the meditator can see and enjoy inner light independently of mental images. **—moon-like inner light:** Inner light perceived at a first level of intensity, glowing softly, much like the moon. The meditator's first experience of it is an important milestone in unfoldment. **—clear white light:** Inner light at a high level of intensity, very clear and pure. When experienced fully, it is seen to be permeating all of existence, the universal substance of all form, inner and outer, pure consciousness, Satchidānanda. This experience, repeated at regular intervals, can yield "a knowing greater than you could acquire at any university or institute of higher learning." See: *Śiva consciousness, tattva.*

Liṅga: लिङ्ग "Mark." See: *Śivaliṅga, svayambhū Liṅga.*

Liṅgāchāra: लिङ्गाचार Daily worship of the Śivaliṅga. One of the five essential codes of conduct for Vīra Śaivites. See: *Pañchāchāra, Vīra Śaivism.*

Liṅga Dīkshā: लिङ्गदीक्षा The Vīra Śaiva initiation ceremony in which the *guru* ties a small Śivaliṅga (Ishṭaliṅga) around the neck of the devotee and enjoins him-her to worship it twice daily. This initiation replaces the sacred thread ceremony, *upanayana.* See: *Vīra Śaivism.*

Liṅga Purāṇa: लिङ्ग पुराण One of the six principal *Śiva Purāṇas.* This text explains the *purushārthas* (the four goals of life) and the significance of Śivaliṅga worship. See: *Purāṇa.*

Liṅgāshṭakam: लिङ्गाष्टकम् A short hymn of eight verses in praise of the Śivaliṇga.

Liṅgavanta: लिङ्गवन्त "Wearer of the Liṅga." (Hindi: Liṅgāyat.) Alternate term for Vīra Śaivite. See: *Vīra Śaivism.*

liturgy: The proper, prescribed forms of ritual.

livelihood: Subsistence, or the means of obtaining it. One's profession, trade or employment. See: *dharma, caste.*

loka: लोक "World, habitat, realm, or plane of existence." From *loc,* "to shine, be bright, visible." A dimension of manifest existence; cosmic region. Each *loka* reflects or involves a particular range of consciousness. The three primary *lokas* are 1) ***—Bhūloka:*** "Earth world." The world perceived through the five senses, also called the gross plane, as it is the most dense of the worlds. 2) ***—Antarloka:*** "Inner or in-between world." Known in English as the subtle or astral plane, the intermediate dimension between the physical and causal worlds, where souls in their astral bodies sojourn between incarnations and when they sleep. 3) ***—Śivaloka:*** "World of Śiva," and of the Gods and highly evolved souls. The causal plane, also called Kāraṇaloka, existing deep within the Antarloka at a higher level of vibration, it is a world of superconsciousness and extremely refined energy. It is the plane of creativity and intuition, the quantum level of the universe, where souls exists in self-effulgent bodies made of actinic particles of light. It is here that God and Gods move and lovingly guide the evolution of all the worlds and shed their ever-flowing grace. Its vibratory rate is that of the *viśuddha, ājñā* and *sahasrāra chakras* and those above. From the perspective of the seven worlds, the Śivaloka is of three levels: Janaloka, "creative plane" *(viśuddha chakra);* Tapoloka, "plane of austerity" *(ājñā chakra);* and Satyaloka, "plane of reality" *(sahasrāra chakra);* also called Brahmaloka.

The Antarloka and Śivaloka are the ever-present substratum of physical existence, most frequently experienced by humans during sleep and deep meditation. Each *loka* is a microcosm of the next higher world, which is its macrocosm, e.g., the physical plane is a microcosm (a smaller and less-refined version) of the Antarloka. See: *Hindu cosmology, three worlds.*

lotus *āsana:* The most famous of *haṭha yoga* poses and the optimum position for meditation. It is known as the *padmāsana* (lotus pose), as the legs are crossed, turning the soles of the feet up, which then resemble a lotus flower. See: *āsana, haṭha yoga.*

lute: A stringed instrument of highly pleasant sound.

macrocosm: "Great world or universe." See: *microcosm-macrocosm, piṇḍa, three worlds.*

Madhumateya: मधुमतेय A Śaiva Siddhānta monastic order founded by Pavanaśiva, preceptor of the Kalachuri kings of Central India.

Mādhva: माध्व South Indian Vaishṇava saint (1197–1278) who expounded a purely dualistic (pluralistic) Vedānta in which there is an essential and eternal distinction between God, soul and world, and between all beings and things. He is also one the few Hindus to have taught the existence of an eternal hell where lost souls would be condemned to suffer forever. See: *dvaita-advaita, Vedānta.*

mahā: महा A prefix meaning "great."

Mahābhārata: महाभारत "Great Epic of India." The world's longest epic poem. It revolves around the conflict between two kingdoms, the Pāṇḍavas and Kauravas, and their great battle of Kurukshetra near modern Delhi in approximately 1424 BCE. Woven through the plot are countless discourses on philosophy, religion, astronomy, cosmology, polity, economics and many stories illustrative of simple truths and ethical principles. The *Bhagavad Gītā* is one section of the work. The *Mahābhārata* is revered as scripture by Vaishṇavites and Smārtas. See: *Bhagavad Gītā, Itihāsa.*

Mahādeva: महादेव "Great shining one; God." Referring either to God Śiva or any of the highly evolved beings who live in the Śivaloka in their natural, effulgent soul bodies. God Śiva in His perfection as Primal Soul is one of the Mahādevas, yet He is unique and incomparable in that He alone is uncreated, the Father-Mother and Destiny of all other Mahādevas. He is called Parameśvara, "Supreme God." He is the Primal Soul, whereas the other Gods are individual souls. It is said in scripture that there are 330 million Gods. See: *Gods, monotheism, Parameśvara, Śiva.*

***Mahādeva* Mountain:** See: *Vasugupta.*

***Mahākāla:* महाकाल** "Great time," or "dissolver of time." One of the names and forms of Śiva. Mahākāla is Time beyond time, who devours all things and forms and, by so doing, helps the soul transcend all dualities. Mystically, time devours itself and thus the timeless state is achieved. See: *tattva.*

***mahākuṭumba:* महाकुटुम्ब** "Great or extended family." See: *extended family.*

***mahāmaṇḍapa:* महामण्डप** "Great hall." Main, outer assembly hall in the temple where devotees gather for ceremony. See: *maṇḍapa, temple.*

***Mahānārāyaṇa Upanishad:* महानारायण उपनिषद्** A philosophical text of the *Kṛishṇa Yajur Veda.*

***Mahānirvāṇa Tantra:* महानिर्वाणतन्त्र** "Treatise on the great emancipation." An 11th-century *advaita* scripture dealing with *mantra* and esoteric rituals.

***mahāpralaya:* महाप्रलय** "Great dissolution." Total annihilation of the universe at the end of a *mahākalpa.* It is the absorption of all existence, including time, space and individual consciousness, all the *lokas* and their inhabitants into God Śiva, as the water of a river returns to its source, the sea. Then Śiva alone exists in His three perfections, until He again issues forth creation. During this incredibly vast period there are many partial dissolutions, *pralayas,* when either the Bhūloka or the Bhūloka and the Antarloka are destroyed. See: *cosmic cycle, pralaya.*

***mahāprasthāna:* महाप्रस्थान** "Great departure." Death. See: *death, transition.*

***mahārāja:* महाराज** "Great king." Indian monarch. Title of respect for political or (in modern times) spiritual leaders.

***Mahārāshṭra:* महाराष्ट्र** Central state of modern India whose capital is Bombay. Area 118,717 square miles, population 63 million.

***maharishi (mahārshi):* महर्षि** "Great seer." Title for the greatest and most influential of *siddhas.*

***Maharloka:* महर्लोक** "Plane of greatness." From *mahas,* "greatness, might, power, glory." Also called the Devaloka, this fourth highest of the seven upper worlds is the mental plane, realm of *anāhata chakra.* See: *loka.*

***mahāsākāra-piṇḍa:* महासाकार पिण्ड** "Great manifest body." In Siddha Siddhānta Śaivism, the first manifestation of Śiva out of the transcendent state. From it all of existence issues forth. See: *piṇḍa.*

***mahāsamādhi:* महासमाधि** "Great enstasy." The death, or dropping off of the physical body, of a great soul, an event occasioned by tremendous blessings. Also names the shrine in which the remains of a great soul are entombed.

***mahāsamādhi* day:** Anniversary of the transition of a great soul. See: *cremation, death, reincarnation, samādhi, transition.*

***Mahāśivarātri:* महाशिवरात्रि** "Śiva's great night." Śaivism's foremost festival, celebrated on the night before the new moon in February-March. Fasting and an all-night vigil are observed as well as other disciplines: chanting, praying, meditating and worshiping Śiva as the Source and Self of all that exists. See: *festival.*

***mahātala:* महातल** Sixth netherworld. Region of consciencelessness. See: *chakra.*

***mahātma:* महात्म** "Great soul." Honorific title given to people held in high esteem, especially saints. See: *ātman.*

***mahāvākya:* महावाक्य** "Great saying." A profound aphorism from scripture or a holy person. Most famous are four Upanishadic proclamations: *Prajanam Brahma* ("Pure consciousness is God"—*Aitareya U.), Aham Brahmāsmi* ("I am God"—*Bṛihadāraṇyaka U.), Tat tvam asi* ("Thou art That"—*Çhandogya U.)* and *Ayam ātma Brahma* ("The soul is God"—*Māṇḍūkya U.).*

***maheśa:* महेश** "Great God." Term used by Vīra Śaivites to mean charity, seeing all as God. See: *shaṭsthala.*

***Maheśvara:* महेश्वर** "Great Lord." In Śaiva Siddhānta, the name of Śiva's energy of veiling grace, one of five aspects of Parameśvara, the Primal Soul. *Maheśvara* is also a popular name for Lord Śiva as Primal Soul and personal Lord. See: *Cosmic Dance, Naṭarāja, Parameśvara.*

***Maitreya:* मैत्रेय** One of four known disciples of *Lakulīśa.* See: *Pāśupata Śaivism.*

***Maitrī Upanishad:* मैत्री उपनिषद्** Belongs to the *Maitrāyaṇīya* branch of the *Kṛishṇa Yajur Veda.* A later *Upanishad* covering *Aum,* outer nature, the Self, control of the mind, etc.

***mala:* मल** "Impurity." An important term in Śaivism referring to three bonds, called *pāśa—āṇava, karma,* and *māyā*—which limit the soul, preventing it from knowing its true, divine nature. See: *liberation, pāśa.*

***mālā:* माला** "Garland." A strand of beads for holy recitation, *japa,* usually made of *rudrāksha, tulasī,* sandalwood or crystal. Also a flower garland.

***malaparipāka:* मलपरिपाक** "Maturing of the malas." See: *āṇava, karma, mala.*

***Mālatī-Mādhava:* मालतीमाधव** A Sanskṛit play by Bhavabhūti (ca 500). Primarily a love story, it contains incidental descriptions of the Kāpālika Śaivite sect of ascetics.

malice: Ill will; desire or intent to do harm to another, generally without conscience. See: *mahātala.*

***manana:* मनन** "Thinking; deep reflection." See: *self-reflection.*

***manas:* मनस्** "Mind; understanding." The lower or instinctive mind, seat of desire and governor of sensory and motor organs, called *indriyas. Manas* is termed the undisciplined, empirical mind. *Manas* is characterized by desire, determination, doubt, faith, lack of faith, steadfastness, lack of steadfastness, shame, intellection and fear. It is a faculty of *manomaya kośa,* the lower astral or instinctive-intellectual sheath. See: *awareness, indriya, instinctive mind, manomaya kośa, mind (individual).*

manas chitta: मनस् चित्त "Instinctive mind." See: *manas, manomaya kośa, instinctive mind.*

maṇḍala: मण्डल "Circular; orb; mystic diagram." A circle. Name of the chapters of the *Ṛig Veda Saṁhitā.* A circular diagram without beginning or end—which indicates the higher and the lower and other possibilities—upon which one meditates. A tapestry, picture or grouping of words used in meditation to enter the realms depicted.

maṇḍapa: मण्डप From *maṇḍ,* "to deck, adorn." Temple precinct; a temple compound, open hall or chamber. In entering a large temple, one passes through a series of *maṇḍapas,* each named according to its position, e.g., *mukhamaṇḍapa,* "facing chamber." In some temples, *maṇḍapas* are concentrically arranged. See: *mahāmaṇḍapa, temple.*

mandira: मन्दिर Temple; abode." See: *devamandira, temple.*

Māṇḍūkya Upanishad: माण्डूक्य उपनिषद् A "principal" *Upanishad* (belonging to the *Atharva Veda*) which, in 12 concise verses, teaches of Aum and the four states *(avasthā)* of awareness: waking *(viśva),* dreaming *(taijasa),* dreamless sleep *(prājña)* and transcendent, spiritual consciousness *(turīya).*

maṅgala kriyā: मङ्गलक्रिया "Auspicious action or practice." Hindu culture.

Maṅgalavede: मङ्गलवेदे A town in Karnataka, South India.

manifest: To show or reveal. Perceivable or knowable, therefore having form. The opposite of unmanifest or transcendent. See: *formless, tattva.*

manifold: Varied. Having many forms, aspects, parts.

Manikkavasagar: மாணிக்கவாசகர் "He of ruby-like utterances." Tamil saint who contributed to the medieval Śaivite renaissance (ca 850). He gave up his position as prime minister to follow a renunciate life. His poetic *Tiruvasagam,* "holy utterances"—a major Śaiva Siddhānta scripture (part of the eighth *Tirumurai)* and a jewel of Tamil literature—express his aspirations, trials and *yogic* realizations. See: *Nalvar, Tirumuṛai.*

maṇipūra chakra: मणिपूरचक्र "Wheeled city of jewels." Solar-plexus center of willpower. See: *chakra.*

mankolam: மாங்கோலம் "Mango design." The paisley, a stylized image of the mango, symbol of auspiciousness, associated with Lord Gaṇeśa.

manomaya kośa: मनोमयकोश "Mind-made sheath." The astral or instinctive-intellectual aspect of the soul's subtle body *(sūkshma śarīra),* also called the odic-astral sheath. It is the sheath of ordinary thought, desire and emotion. The *manomaya kośa* is made up of odic *prāṇa* and is almost an exact duplicate of the physical body. However, changes that appear upon the physical body, such as aging, first occur within the structure of this sheath of the astral body. This is the sheath of the subconscious mind; it can be easily disturbed and is sometimes called the emotional body. See: *astral body, in-*

stinctive mind, kośa, odic, soul, subtle body, vāsanā.

mānsāhāra: **मांसाहार** "Meat-eating."

mānsāhārī: **मांसाहारी** "Meat-eater." Those who follow a non-vegetarian diet. See: *meat-eater, vegetarian.*

mantra: **मन्त्र** "Mystic formula." A sound, syllable, word or phrase endowed with special power, usually drawn from scripture. *Mantras* are chanted loudly during *pūjā* to invoke the Gods and establish a force field. Certain *mantras* are repeated softly or mentally for *japa,* the subtle tones quieting the mind, harmonizing the inner bodies and stimulating latent spiritual qualities. Hinduism's universal *mantra* is Aum. To be truly effective, such *mantras* must be given by the preceptor through initiation. See: *Aum, incantation, japa, pūjā, yajña.*

Mantra Gopya: **मन्त्रगोप्य** The collected writings of Allama Prabhu. See: *Allama Prabhu.*

Manu Dharma Śāstra: **मनुधर्मशास्त्र** "Sage Manu's law book." An encyclopedic treatise of 2,685 verses on Hindu law assembled as early as 600 BCE. Among its major features are the support of *varṇa dharma, āśrama dharma, strī dharma* and seeing the Self in all beings. Despite its caste-based restrictions, which determine one's life unrelentlingly from birth to death, it remains the source of much of modern Hindu culture and law. These "Laws of Manu" are the oldest and considered the most authoritative of the greater body of *Dharma Śāstras.* Even during the time of the British Raj in India, law was largely based on these texts. The text is widely available today in several languages. (Bühler's English translation is over 500 pages.) See: *caste, dharma, Dharma Śāstras, Kalpa Vedāṅga.*

mārga: **मार्ग** "Path; way." From *mārg,* "to seek." See: *pāda.*

marital: Having to do with marriage. See: *gṛihastha, gṛiheśvara and gṛihaṇī.*

Mariyamman: மாரியம்மன் "Smallpox Goddess," protectress from plagues. See: *Amman, Śakti, Śāktism.*

marriage covenant: The written (or verbal) statements of bride and groom expressing the promises and expectations of their marriage. Known in Sanskṛit as *vāṅniśchaya,* "settlement by word."

Mātaṅga Parameśvara Āgama: **मातङ्गपरमेश्वर आगम** Among the 28 *Śaiva Siddhānta Āgamas,* containing 3,500 verses, deals at length with the categories of existence *(tattvas).* The Angkor Wat temple in Cambodia is thought to have been built using the temple section of this scripture. See: *Śaiva Āgamas.*

material cause: *Upādāna kāraṇa.* The substance of creation, *māyā,* Śiva's "mirific energy." In Śaivism, material cause, *māyā,* is threefold: *śuddha* ("pure") *māyā, śuddhāśuddha* ("pure-impure") *māyā* and *aśuddha* ("impure") *māyā. Śuddha māyā,* or *bindu,* is the material cause of the causal plane. *Śuddhāśuddha māyā* is the material cause of the subtle plane. *Aśuddhamāyā* (or Prakṛiti) is the material cause of the gross plane. See: *cause, māyā, tattva.*

materialism (materialistic): The doctrine that matter is the only reality, that all life, thought and feelings are but the effects of movements of matter, and that there exist no worlds but the physical. Materialists usually hold that there is no God—a cosmic, material, prime mover perhaps, but no personal God. An Indian school of thought which propounded this view was the Chārvāka. See: *atheism, Chārvāka, nāstika, worldly.*

mati: **मति** "Cognition, understanding; conviction." See: *yama-niyama.*

matrimonial: Related to marriage.

Matsyendranātha: **मत्स्येन्द्रनाथ** A patron saint of Nepal, *guru* of Gorakshanātha and a mystic in the Nātha tradition (ca 900). Some consider him to have been the foremost human teacher of *haṭha yoga.* See: *haṭha yoga.*

Mattamayūra Order: **मत्तमयूर** A Śaiva Siddhānta monastic order founded by Purandara (successor to Rudraśambhu), centered in the Punjab. Members of this order served as advisors to the king.

matter: Substance, especially of the physical world. May also refer to all of manifest existence, including the subtle, nonphysical dimensions. See: *māyā.*

mature: Ripe; fully grown or developed.

maya: **मय** "Consisting of; made of," as in *manomaya,* "made of mind."

māyā: **माया** "She who measures;" or "mirific energy." The substance emanated from Śiva through which the world of form is manifested. Hence all creation is also termed *māyā.* It is the cosmic creative force, the principle of manifestation, ever in the process of creation, preservation and dissolution. *Māyā* is a key concept in Hinduism, originally meaning "supernatural power; God's mirific energy," often translated as "illusion." The *Upanishads* underscore *māyā's* captivating nature, which blinds souls to the transcendent Truth. In Śaṅkara's Vedāntic interpretation, *māyā* is taken as pure illusion or unreality. In Śaivism it is one of the three bonds *(pāśa)* that limit the soul and thereby facilitate its evolution. For Śaivites and most other nondualists, it is understood not as illusion but as relative reality, in contrast to the unchanging Absolute Reality. In the Śaiva Siddhānta system, there are three main divisions of *māyā,* the pure, the pure-impure and the impure realms. Pure or *śuddha māyā* consists of the first five *tattvas*—Śiva *tattva,* Śakti *tattva,* Sadāśiva *tattva,* Īśvara *tattva* and Śuddhavidyā *tattva.* The pure-impure realm consists of the next seven *tattvas.* The impure realm consists of the *māyā tattva* and all of its evolutes—from the *kāla tattva* to *pṛithivī,* the element earth. Thus, in relation to the physical universe, *māyā* is the principle of ever-changing matter. In Vaishṇavism, *māyā* is one of the nine Śaktis of Vishṇu. See: *loka, mind (universal), mirific, tattva, world.*

mayūra: **मयूर** "Peacock." The *vāhana,* or mount, of Lord Kārttikeya, symbolizing effulgent beauty and religion in full glory. The peacock is able to control powerful snakes, such as the cobra, symbolizing the soulful domination of the instinctive elements—or control of the *kuṇḍalinī,* which is *yoga.* See: *Kārttikeya, vāhana.*

mean: As a verb: "to signify." As an adjective: base, low-minded; selfish.

meat-eater: *Mānsāhārī.* Those who follow a nonvegetarian diet. They are described in the following passage from the obscure *Mānsāhāra Parihāsajalpita Stotram.* "Those who eat the flesh of other creatures are nothing less than gristle-grinders, blood-drinkers, muscle-munchers, sinew-chewers, carcass-crunchers, flesh-feeders—those who make their throat a garbage pit and their stomach a graveyard—mean, angry, loathsomely jealous, confused and beset by covetousness, who without restraint would lie, deceive, kill or steal to solve immediate problems. They are flesh-feeders, loathsome to the Gods, but friendly to the *asuras,* who become their Gods and Goddesses, the blood-sucking monsters who inhabit Naraka and deceptively have it decorated to look like the *pitṛiloka,* the world of the fathers. To such beings the deluded meat-eaters pay homage and prostrate while munching the succulent flesh off bones." See: *vegetarianism.*

mediatrix: A go-between, intermediary or reconciler between two parties. The feminine form of the term *mediator.*

meditation: *Dhyāna.* Sustained concentration. Meditation describes a quiet, alert, powerfully concentrated state wherein new knowledge and insights are awakened from within as awareness focuses one-pointedly on an object or specific line of thought. See: *internalized worship, rāja yoga, Satchidānanda.*

mediumship: Act or practice of serving as a channel through which beings of inner worlds communicate with humans. See: *folk-shamanic, trance.*

mendicant: A beggar; a wandering monk, or *sādhu,* who lives on alms.

menses: A woman's monthly menstruation period, during which, by Hindu tradition, she rests from her usual activities and forgoes public and family religious functions.

mental body (sheath): The higher-mind layer of the subtle or astral body in which the soul functions in Maharloka of the Antarloka or subtle plane. In Sanskṛit, the mental body is *vijñānamaya kośa,* "sheath of cognition." See: *intellectual mind, kośa, subtle body.*

mental plane: Names the refined strata of the subtle world. It is called Maharloka or Devaloka, realm of *anāhata chakra.* Here the soul is shrouded in the mental or cognitive sheath, called *vijñānamaya kośa.*

merge: To lose distinctness or identity by being absorbed. To unite or become one with.

merger of the soul: See: *evolution of the soul, viśvagrāsa.*

meritorious: Having merit, deserving of praise or reward. See: *puṇya.*

mesmerizing: Hypnotizing; spell-binding; fascinating.

metamorphosis: Complete transformation, as in a caterpillar's becoming a butterfly. See: *kuṇḍalinī, reincarnation.*

metaphysics: 1) The branch of philosophy dealing with first causes and nature of reality. 2) The science of mysticism. See: *darśana, mysticism.*

Meykandar: மெய்கண்டார் "Truth seer." The 13th-century Tamil theologian, author (or translator from the *Raurava Āgama*) of the *Śivajñānabodham.* Founder of the Meykandar Sampradāya of pluralistic Śaiva Siddhānta. See: *Śaiva Siddhānta, Śivajñānabodham.*

Meykandar Śāstras: Fourteen Tamil works on Śaiva Siddhānta written during the 13th and 14th centuries by seven authors—Meykandar, Arulnandi, Uyyavanda Deva I and II, Umapati, Śivajñāna Yogin and Manavasagam Kadandar. See: *Śaiva Siddhānta, Śivajñānabodham.*

microcosm-macrocosm: "Little world" or "miniature universe" as compared with "great world." *Microcosm* refers to the internal source of something larger or more external (macrocosm). In Hindu cosmology, the outer world is a macrocosm of the inner world, which is its microcosm and is mystically larger and more complex than the physical universe and functions at a higher rate of vibration and even a different rate of time. The microcosm precedes the macrocosm. Thus, the guiding principle of the Bhūloka comes from the Antarloka and Śivaloka. Consciousness precedes physical form. In the *tantric* tradition, the body of man is viewed as a microcosm of the entire divine creation. "Microcosm-macrocosm" is embodied in the terms *piṇḍa* and *aṇḍa.* See: *apex of creation, piṇḍa, quantum, tattva, tantra.*

milestone: An event which serves as a significant marker in the progress of a project, history, etc.

milieu: Environment; social or cultural setting.

millennium: A period of 1,000 years. **millennia:** Plural of millenium.

Mīmāṁsā: मीमांसा "Inquiry." See: *shaḍ darśana.*

mind (five states): A view of the mind in five parts. **—conscious mind:** *Jāgrat chitta* ("wakeful consciousness"). The ordinary, waking, thinking state of mind in which the majority of people function most of the day. **—subconscious mind:** *Saṁskāra chitta* ("impression mind"). The part of mind "beneath" the conscious mind, the storehouse or recorder of all experience (whether remembered consciously or not)—the holder of past impressions, reactions and desires. Also, the seat of involuntary physiological processes. **—subsubconscious mind:** *Vāsanā chitta* ("mind of subliminal traits"). The area of the subconscious mind formed when two thoughts or experiences of the same rate of intensity are sent into the subconscious at different times and, intermingling, give rise to a new and totally different rate of vibration. This subconscious formation later causes the external mind to react to situations according to these accumulated vibrations, be they positive, negative or mixed. **—superconscious mind:** *Kāraṇa chitta.* The mind of light, the all-knowing intelligence of the soul. The psychological term is *turīya,* "the fourth," meaning the condition beyond the states of wakefulness *(jāgrat),* "dream" *(svapna),* and "deep sleep" *(sushupti).* At its deepest level, the superconscious is Parāśakti, or Satchidānanda, the Divine Mind of God Śiva. In Sanskṛit, there are numerous terms for the various levels and states of superconsciousness. Specific superconscious states such as: *viśvachaitanya* ("universal consciousness"), *advaita chaitanya* ("nondual consciousness"), *adhyātma chetanā* ("spiritual consciousness"). **—subsuperconscious mind:** *Anukāraṇa chitta.* The superconscious mind working through the conscious and subconscious states, which brings forth intuition, clarity and insight. See: *chitta, consciousness, saṁskāra, Satchidānanda, vāsanā.*

mind (individual): At the microcosmic level of individual souls, mind is consciousness and its faculties of memory, desire, thought and cognition. Individual mind is *chitta* (mind, consciousness) and its three-fold expression is called *antaḥkaraṇa,* "inner faculty" composed of: 1) *buddhi* ("intellect, reason, logic," higher mind); 2) *ahaṁkāra* ("I-maker," egoity); 3) *manas* ("lower mind," instinctive-intellectual mind, the seat of desire). From the perspective of the 36 *tattvas* (categories of existence), each of these is a *tattva* which evolves out of the one before it. Thus, from *buddhi* comes *ahaṁkāra* and then *manas. Manas, buddhi* and *ahaṁkāra* are faculties of the *manomaya kośa* (astral or instinctive-intellectual sheath). *Anukāraṇa chitta,* subsuperconsciousness, the knowing mind, is the mind-state of the *vijñānamaya kośa* (mental or intuitive-cognitive sheath). The aspect of mind corresponding directly to the *ānandamaya kośa* (causal body) is *kāraṇa chitta,* superconsciousness. See: *ahaṁkāra, antaḥkaraṇa, buddhi, chitta, manas, mind (universal).*

mind (three phases): A perspective of mind as instinctive, intellectual and superconscious. **—instinctive mind.** *Manas chitta,* the seat of desire and governor of sensory and motor organs. **—intellectual mind.** *Buddhi chitta,* the faculty of thought and intelligence. **—superconscious mind:** *Kāraṇa chitta,* the strata of intuition, benevolence and spiritual sustenance. Its most refined essence is Parāsakti, or Satchidānanda, all-knowing, omnipresent consciousness, the One transcendental, self-luminous, divine mind common to all souls. See: *awareness, consciousness, mind (five states).*

mind (universal): In the most profound sense, mind is the sum of all things, all energies and manifestations, all forms, subtle and gross, sacred and mundane. It is the inner and outer cosmos. Mind is *māyā.* It is the material matrix. It is everything but That, the Self within, Paraśiva, which is timeless, formless, causeless, spaceless, known by the knower only after Self Realization. The Self is the indescribable, unnameable, Ultimate Reality. Mind in its subtlest form is undifferentiated Pure Consciousness, primal substance (called Parāśakti or Satchidānanda), out of which emerge the myriad forms of existence, both psychic and material. See: *chitta, consciousness, māyā, tattva, world.*

minister: Someone charged with a specific function on behalf of a religious or political body, especially in serving the spiritual needs of the people. In Hinduism, this term may be applied to temple priests, monks, preceptors, scriptural scholars and others.

minutiae: Small or relatively unimportant details.

Mīrābāī: **मीराबाई** A Vaishṇava saint (ca 1420), poetess and mystic, said to be a Rajput princess who abandoned the world in total surrender to Lord Kṛishṇa. Her life story and songs are popular today, especially in Gujarat.

mirific: "Wonder-making; magical; astonishing." See: *māyā, material cause.*

misconception: A wrong idea or concept; misunderstanding, *avidyā.* See: *avidyā, illusion.*

mitāhāra: **मिताहार** "Measured eating; moderate appetite." A requisite to good health and an essential for success in *yoga.* The ideal portion per meal is described as no more than would fill the two hands held side by side and slightly cupped piled high, an amount called a *kuḍava.* All the six tastes should be within these foods (sweet, salty, sour, pungent, bitter and astringent), and the foods should be well cooked and highly nutritious. See: *yama-niyama.*

modaka: **मोदक** "Sweets." A round lemon-sized sweet made of rice, coconut, sugar, etc. It is a favorite treat of Gaṇeśa. Esoterically, it corresponds to *siddhi* (attainment or fulfillment), the gladdening contentment of pure joy, the sweetest of all things sweet. See: *Gaṇeśa.*

moksha: **मोक्ष** "Liberation." Release from transmigration, *saṁsāra,* the round of births and deaths, which occurs after *karma* has been resolved and *nirvikalpa samādhi*—realization of the Self, Paraśiva—has been attained. Same as *mukti.* See: *jīvanmukta, kaivalya, kuṇḍalinī, nirvikalpa samādhi, Paraśiva, rāja yoga, videhamukti.*

monastic: A monk or nunk (based on the Greek *monos,* "alone"). A man or woman who has withdrawn from the world and lives an austere, religious life, either alone or with others in a monastery. (Not to be confused with *monistic,* having to do with the doctrine of monism.) Terms for Hindu monastics include *sādhaka, sādhu, muni, tapasvin, vairāgī, ūdāsin* and *sannyāsin. (Feminine: sādhikā, sādhvī, munī, tapasvinī, vairāginī,* and *sannyāsinī.)* A monastery-dweller is a *maṭhavāsi,* and *sādhu* is a rough equivalent for mendicant. See: *monk, nunk, sannyāsin, sannyāsinī, vairāgī.*

monism: "Doctrine of oneness." 1) The philosophical view that there is only one ultimate substance or principle. 2) The view that reality is a unified whole without independent parts. See: *dvaita-advaita, pluralism.*

monistic theism: Advaita Īśvaravāda. Monism is the doctrine that reality is a one whole or existence without independent parts. Theism is the belief that God exists as a real, conscious, personal Supreme Being. Monistic theism is the dipolar doctrine, also called panentheism, that embraces both monism and theism, two perspectives ordinarily considered contradictory or mutually exclusive, since theism implies dualism. Monistic theism simultaneously accepts that God has a personal form, that He creates, pervades and *is* all that exists—and that He ultimately transcends all existence and that the soul is, in essence, one with God. Advaita Siddhānta (monistic Śaiva Siddhānta, or Advaita Īśvaravāda Śaiva Siddhānta) is a specific form of monistic theism. See: *advaita, Advaita Īśvaravāda, Advaita Siddhānta, dvaita-advaita, panentheism, theism.*

monk: A celibate man wholly dedicated to religious life, either cenobitic (residing with others in a monastery) or anchoritic (living alone, as a hermit or mendicant). Literally, "one who lives alone" (from the Greek *monos,* "alone"). Through the practice of *yoga,* the control and transmutation of the masculine and feminine forces within himself, the monk is a complete being, free to follow the contemplative and mystic life toward realization of the Self within. Benevolent and strong, courageous, fearless, not entangled in the thoughts and feelings of others, monks are affectionately detached from society, defenders of the faith, kind, loving and ever-flowing with timely wisdom. A synonym for *monastic.* Its feminine counterpart is *nunk.* See: *monastic, sannyāsin, nunk.*

monotheism: "Doctrine of one God." Contrasted with polytheism, meaning belief in many Gods. The term *monotheism* covers a wide range of philosophical positions, from exclusive (or pure) monotheism, which recognizes only one God (such as in Semitic faiths), to inclusive monotheism, which also accepts the existence of other Gods. Generally speaking, the sects of Hinduism are inclusively monotheistic in their belief in a one Supreme God, and in their reverence for other Gods, or Mahādevas. However, such terms which arose out of Western philosophy do not really describe the fullness of Hindu thinking. Realizing this, the author of *The Vedic Experience,* Raimundo Panikkar, has offered a new word: *cosmotheandrism,* "world-God-man doctrine," which describes a philosophy that views God, soul and world (Pati, *paśu, pāśa)* as an integrated, inseparable unity. See: *Advaita Īśvaravāda, monistic theism, Pati-paśu-pāśa.*

mortal: Subject to death. Opposite of *immortal.* See: *amṛita, death.*

mortal sin: See: *sin.*

Mṛigendra Āgama: मृगेन्द्र आगम First subsidiary text *(Upāgama)* of the *Kāmika Āgama,* one of the 28 *Śaiva Siddhānta Āgamas.* It is especially valuable because its *jñāna pāda* (philosophical section) is complete and widely available. Other noted sections are on hand gestures *(mudrā)* used in *pūjā* and on establishing temporary places *(yāgaśālā)* of special worship. See: *pāda, Śaiva Āgamas.*

mudrā: मुद्रा "Seal." Esoteric hand gestures which express specific energies or powers. Usually accompanied by precise visualizations, *mudrās* are a vital element of ritual worship *(pūjā),* dance and *yoga.* Among the best-known *mudrās* are: 1) *abhaya mudrā* (gesture of fearlessness), in which the fingers are extended, palm facing forward; 2) *añjali mudrā* (gesture of reverence); 3) *jñāna mudrā* (also known as *chin mudrā* and *yoga mudrā*), in which the thumb and index finger touch, forming a circle, with the other fingers extended; 4) *dhyāna mudrā* (seal of meditation), in which the two hands are open and relaxed with the palms up, resting on the folded legs, the right hand atop the left with the tips of the thumbs gently touching. See: *abhaya mudrā, añjali mudrā, haṭha yoga, namaskāra.*

muhūrta: मुहूर्त "Moment." 1) A period of time. 2) A certain division of a day or night. *Muhūrtas* vary slightly in length as the lengths of days and nights change through the year. There are at least three *muhūrta* systems. The first defines one *muhūrta* as 1/8th of a day or night (= 1.5 hours in a 12-hour night), the second as 1/15th of a day or night (= 48 minutes), and the third as 1/16th of a day or night (= 45 minutes). 3) *Muhūrta* also refers to the astrological science of determining the most auspicious periods for specific activities. See: *brāhma muhūrta, auspiciousness, sandhyā upāsanā.*

mukhya: मुख्य "Head; foremost." From *mukha*, "face, countenance." Leader, guide; such as the family head, *kuṭumba mukhya* (or *pramukha*). See: *extended family, joint family.*

mukti: मुक्ति "Release." A synonym for *moksha*. See: *moksha.*

Mukti Upanishad: मुक्ति उपनिषद् A 14th-century writing dealing in part with *yoga.*

mūla: मूल "Root." The root, base or bottom or basis of anything, as in *mūlādhāra chakra*. Foundational, original or causal, as in *mūlagrantha*, "original text."

mūla mantra: मूलमन्त्र "Root mystic formula." See: *Aum.*

mūlādhāra chakra: मूलाधारचक्र "Root-support wheel." Four-petaled psychic center at the base of the spine; governs memory. See: *chakra.*

multitude: A very large number of things or people.

Muṇḍaka Upanishad: मुण्डक उपनिषद् Belongs to the *Atharva Veda* and teaches the difference between the intellectual study of the *Vedas* and their supplementary texts and the intuitive knowledge by which God is known.

muni: मुनि "Sage." A sage or *sādhu*, especially one vowed to complete silence or who speaks but rarely and who seeks stillness of mind. A hermit. The term is related to *mauna*, "silence." In the hymns of the *Ṛig Veda*, *munis* are mystic shamans associated with the God Rudra.

mūrti: मूर्ति "Form; manifestation, embodiment, personification." An image or icon of God or a God used during worship. *Mūrtis* range from aniconic *(avyakta*, "nonmanifest"), such as the Śivaliṅga, to *vyakta* "fully manifest," e.g., anthropomorphic images such as Naṭarāja. In-between is the partially manifest *(vyaktāvyakta)*, e.g., the *mukha liṅga*, in which the face of Śiva appears on the Śivaliṅga. Other Deity representations include symbols, e.g., the banyan tree, and geometric icons such as *yantras* and *maṇḍalas*. Another important term for the Deity icon or idol is *pratimā*, "reflected image." See: *aniconic, Ishṭa Devatā, teradi.*

Murugan: முருகன் "Beautiful one," a favorite name of Kārttikeya among the Tamils of South India, Sri Lanka and elsewhere. See: *Kārttikeya.*

muse: To think deeply.

***Mūshika:* मूषिक** From *mūsh,* "to steal." The mouse, Lord Gaṇeśa's mount, traditionally associated with abundance. Symbolically, the mouse carries Lord Gaṇeśa's grace into every corner of the mind. See: *Gaṇeśa, vāhana.*

Muslim: "True believer." A follower of Islam. See: *Islam.*

mutual: Said of something which is thought, done or felt by two or more people toward each other. Shared.

mysticism: Spirituality; the pursuit of direct spiritual or religious experience. Spiritual discipline aimed at union or communion with Ultimate Reality or God through deep meditation or trance-like contemplation. From the Greek *mystikos,* "of mysteries." Characterized by the belief that Truth transcends intellectual processes and must be attained through transcendent means. See: *clairaudient, clairvoyance, psychic, trance.*

myth: Traditional story, usually ancient and of no known author, involving Gods, *devas* and heroes, and serving to illustrate great principles of life, customs, the origin of the universe, etc. See: *folk narratives, kathā.*

mythology: Body of tales and legends. All the myths of a specific people, culture or religion. India's mythology is among the world's most bountiful. See: *folk narratives, kathā.*

***nāda:* नाद्** "Sound; tone, vibration." Metaphysically, the mystic sounds of the Eternal, of which the highest is the transcendent or Soundless Sound, Paranāda, the first vibration from which creation emanates. Paranāda is so pure and subtle that it cannot be identified to the denser regions of the mind. From Paranāda comes Praṇava, Aum, and further evolutes of *nāda.* These are experienced by the meditator as the *nādanāḍī śakti,* "the energy current of sound," heard pulsing through the nerve system as a constant high-pitched *hum,* much like a *tambura,* an electrical transformer, a swarm of bees or a *śruti* box. Listening to the inner sounds is a contemplative practice, called *nāda upāsanā,* "worship through sound," *nāda anusandhāna,* "cultivation of inner sound," or *nāda yoga.* The subtle variations of the *nādanāḍī śakti* represent the psychic wavelengths of established *guru* lineages of many Indian religions. *Nāda* also refers to other psychic sounds heard during deep meditation, including those resembling various musical instruments. Most commonly, *nāda* refers to ordinary sound. See: *Aum, nāḍī, praṇava, sound.*

***nādanāḍī śakti:* नाद्नाडीशक्ति** "Energy current of sound." See: *nāda.*

nāḍī:* नाडी** "Conduit." A nerve fiber or energy channel of the subtle (inner) bodies of man. It is said there are 72,000. These interconnect the *chakras.* The three main *nāḍīs* are named *iḍā, piṅgalā* and *sushumṇā.* **—*iḍā: Also known as *chandra* ("moon") *nāḍī,* it is pink in color and flows downward, ending on the left side of the body. This current is feminine in nature and is the channel of physical-emotional energy. —***piṅgalā:*** Also known as *sūrya* ("sun") *nāḍī*, it is blue in color and flows upward, ending on the right side of the body. This current is masculine in nature and is the channel of intellectual-mental energy. —***sushumṇā:*** The major nerve current which passes through the spinal column from the *mūlādhāra chakra* at the base to the *sahasrāra* at the crown of the head. It is the channel of *kuṇḍalinī*. Through *yoga*, the *kuṇḍalinī* energy lying dormant in the *mūlādhāra* is awakened and made to rise up this channel through each *chakra* to the *sahasrāra chakra*. See: *chakra, kuṇḍalinī, rāja yoga, tantrism.*

nāga: **नाग** "Snake," often the cobra; symbol of the *kuṇḍalinī* coiled on the four petals of the *mūlādhāra chakra*. See: *kuṇḍalinī, mūlādhāra chakra.*

naivedya: **नैवेद्य** Food offered to the Deity at the temple or home altar. An important element in *pūjā*. See: *prasāda, pūjā.*

nakshatra: **नक्षत्र** "Star cluster." Central to astrological determinations, the *nakshatras* are 27 star-clusters, constellations, which lie along the ecliptic, or path of the sun. An individual's *nakshatra*, or birth star, is the constellation the moon was aligned with at the time of birth. See: *jyotisha.*

Nalvar: நால்வர் "Four devout beings." Four renowned saints of the Śaiva religion (7th to 9th century): Appar, Sundarar, Sambandar and Manikkavasagar—devotional mystics whose lives and teachings helped catalyze a resurgence of Śaivism in Tamil Nadu. All but Manikkavasagar are among the Nayanars, 63 saints canonized by Sekkilar in his *Periyapurāṇam* (ca 1140). These four are also known as the Samayāchāryas, "teachers of the faith." Their devotional poems are embodied in the *Tirumurai*, along with the writings of other Nayanars. Numerous South Indian temples celebrate their historic pilgrimages from shrine to shrine where they beseeched the grace of Śiva through heartfelt song. *Nalvar* is a term not to be confused with *Alvar*, naming certain Vaishṇava saints of the same period. See: *Alvar, Nayanar, Tirumurai.*

nāmadīkshā: **नामदीक्षा** "Name initiation." Also known as *nāmakaraṇa saṁskāra*. See: *saṁskāras of childhood.*

Namaḥ Śivāya: **नमः शिवाय** "Adoration (or homage) to Śiva." The supreme *mantra* of Śaivism, known as the *Pañchākshara* or "five letters." *Na* is the Lord's veiling grace; *Ma* is the world; *Śi* is Śiva; *Vā* is His revealing grace; *Ya* is the soul. The letters also represent the physical body: *Na* the legs, *Ma* the stomach, *Śi* the shoulders, *Vā* the mouth and *Ya* the eyes. Embodying the essence of Śaiva Siddhānta, it is found in the center of the central *Veda* (the *Yajur*) of the original three *Vedas* (*Ṛig, Yajur* and *Sāma*). *Namastārāya namaḥ śaṁbhave cha mayobhave cha, namaḥ śaṅkarāya cha mayaskarāya cha, namaḥ śivāya cha śivayatarāya cha.* "Homage to the source of health and to the source of delight. Homage to the maker of health and to the maker of delight. Homage to the Auspicious, and to the more Auspicious" (*Kṛishṇa Yajur Veda, Taittirīya Saṁhitā* 4.5.8). See: *mantra, japa.*

nāmakaraṇa: **नामकरण** "Name giving." See: *saṁskāras of childhood.*

namaskāra: **नमस्कार** "Reverent salutations." Traditional Hindu verbal greeting and *mudrā* where the palms are joined together and held before the heart or raised to the level of the forehead. The *mudrā* is also called *añjali.* It is a devotional gesture made equally before a temple Deity, holy person, friend or momentary acquaintance. The hands held together connects the right side of the body with the left, and brings the nerve and *nāḍī* currents into poised balance, into a consciousness of the *sushumṇā,* awakening the third eye within the greeter to worship God in the greeted. See: *añjali mudrā, praṇāma.*

namaste: **नमस्ते** "Reverent salutations to you." A traditional verbal greeting. A form of *namas,* meaning "bowing, obeisance." See: *namaskāra.*

Namo Nārāyaṇāya: **नमो नारायणाय** "Salutations to Lord Vishṇu." The great *mantra* of the Vaishṇava faith. Also a popular greeting among Vaishṇavites and Smārtas. See: *Vaishṇavism, Vishṇu.*

Nandi: **नन्दि** "The joyful." A white bull with a black tail, the *vāhana,* or mount, of Lord Śiva, symbol of the powerful instinctive force tamed by Him. Nandi is the perfect devotee, the soul of man, kneeling humbly before God Śiva, ever concentrated on Him. The ideal and goal of the Śiva *bhakta* is to behold Śiva in everything. See: *vāhana.*

Nandikeśvara: **नन्दिकेश्वर** "Lord of Nandi." A name of Śiva. Also another name for Nandinātha, the first historically known *guru* of the Nandinātha Sampradāya. See: *Kailāsa Paramparā, Nātha Sampradāya.*

Nandikeśvara Kāśikā: **नन्दिकेश्वरकाशिका** The only surviving work of Nandikeśvara (ca 250 BCE). Its 26 verses are the earliest extant exposition of advaitic Śaivism, aside from the *Śaiva Āgamas.*

Nandinātha: **नन्दिनाथ** A synonym of *Nandikeśvara.* See: *Kailāsa Paramparā.*

Nandinātha Sampradāya: **नन्दिनाथसंप्रदाय** See: *Nātha Sampradāya.*

Nārada Sūtra(s): **नारदसूत्र** A Vaishṇava text of 84 aphorisms in which Sage Nārada explains *bhakti yoga* (ca 1200).

Nārada Parivrājaka: **नारदपरिव्राजक** An *Upanishad* of the *Aṭharva Veda* which teaches of asceticism, *sannyāsa,* true *brāhminhood,* and more.

Naraka: **नरक** Abode of darkness. Literally, "pertaining to man." The lower worlds. Equivalent to the Western term *hell,* a gross region of the Antarloka. Naraka is a congested, distressful area where demonic beings and young souls may sojourn until they resolve the darksome *karmas* they have created. Here beings suffer the consequences of their own misdeeds in previous lives. *Naraka* is understood as having seven regions, called *tala,* corresponding to the states of consciousness of the seven lower *chakras* as follows: 1) Put, "childless"—*atala chakra,* "wheel of the bottomless region." Fear and lust (located in the hips). 2) Avīchi, "joyless"—*vitala chakra:* "wheel of negative region." Center of anger (thighs). 3) Saṁhāta, "abandoned"—*sutala chakra:* "Great depth." Region of jealousy (knees). 4) Tāmisra, "darkness"—*talātala chakra:* "wheel of the lower region." Realm of confused thinking (calves). 5) Ṛijīsha, "expelled"—*rasātala chakra:* "wheel of subterranean region." Selfishness (ankles). 6) Kuḍmala, "leprous"—*mahātala chakra:* "wheel of the great lower region." Region of consciencelessness (feet). The intensity of "hell" begins at this deep level. 7) Kākola, "black poison"—*pātāla chakra,* "wheel of the fallen or sinful level." Region of malice (soles of the feet).

The seven-fold hellish region in its entirety is also called *pātāla,* "fallen region." Scriptures offer other lists of hells, numbering 7 or 21. They are described as places of torment, pain, darkness, confusion and disease, but none are places where souls reside forever. Hinduism has no eternal hell. See: *hell, loka, purgatory (also, individual tala entries).*

Narasiṁha Pūrvatāpanīya: नरसिंहपूर्वतापनीय "The ascetic's surrender to Narasiṁha (incarnation of Vishṇu as half-man, half-lion)." An *Upanishad* of the *Atharva Veda* which deals with worship of Vishṇu.

Nārāyaṇa: नारायण "Abode of men." A name of Lord Vishṇu. See: *Vishṇu.*

Nārāyaṇakaṇṭha: नारायणकण्ठ Great exponent of Śaiva Siddhānta (ca 1050).

nāstika: नास्तिक "One who denies; unbeliever." Opposite of *āstika,* "one who asserts." The terms *āstika* (orthodox) and *nāstika* (unorthodox) are a traditional classification of Indian schools of thought. *Nāstika* refers to all traditions that reject and deny the scriptural authority of the *Vedas.* This includes Sikhism, Jainism, Buddhism, the Chārvāka materialists and others. *Āstika* refers to those schools that accept the revealed authority of the *Vedas* as supreme scripture. This includes the four major sects: Śaivism, Śāktism, Vaishṇavism and Smārtism. See: *atheism, Chārvāka, materialism.*

Naṭarāja: नटराज "King of Dance, or King of Dancers." God as the Cosmic Dancer. Perhaps Hinduism's richest and most eloquent symbol, Naṭarāja represents Śiva, the Primal Soul, Parameśvara, as the power, energy and life of all that exists. This is Śiva's intricate state of Being in Manifestation. The dance of Śiva as Naṭeśa, Lord of Dancers, is the dance of the entire cosmos, the rhythmic movements in all. All that is, whether sentient or insentient, pulsates in His body. Naṭarāja is art and spirituality in perfect oneness, chosen to depict the Divine because in dance that which is created is inseparable from its creator, just as the universe and soul cannot be separated from God. Naṭarāja is also stillness and motion wrought together. The stillness speaks of the peace and poise that lies within us all, at the center. The intense motion, depicted by His hair flying wildly in all directions, is an intimation of the fury and ferocity, the violent vigor, which fills this universe wherein we dwell. The implication of these opposites is that God contains and allows them both, that there is divine purpose at work in our life, whether we find ourselves engaged in its beauty or its "madness." Dance and dancer are one; not an atom moves on any plane of existence but by His Will. Thus, this elegant symbol embodies the underlying unity of all.

Śiva's Dance, or all that happens, is composed of an ever-flowing combination of His five potent actions, *pañchakṛitya:* 1) ***sṛishṭi:*** creation, or emanation, represented by His upper right hand and the *ḍamaru* (drum), upon which he beats Paranāda, the Primal Sound from which issue forth the rhythms and cycles of creation; 2) ***sthiti:*** preservation, represented by His lower right hand in a gesture of blessing, *abhaya mudrā,* saying "fear not;" 3) ***saṁhāra:*** destruction, dissolution or absorption, represented by the fire in His upper left hand, posed in *ardhachandra mudrā,* "half-moon gesture;" 4) ***tirobhāva:*** obscuring grace, the power which hides the truth, thereby permitting experience, growth and eventual fulfillment of destiny, represented by His right foot upon the prostrate person (Apasmārapurusha), the principle of ignorance, or *āṇava;* 5) ***anugraha:*** revealing grace—which grants knowledge and severs the soul's bonds—represented by Śiva's raised left foot, and by His lower left hand, held in *gajahasta* ("elephant trunk") *mudrā,* inviting approach. These five cosmic activities are sometimes personalized respectively as Brahmā, Vishṇu, Rudra, Maheśvara and Sadāśiva—or as Sadyojāta (creation), Vāmadeva (preservation), Aghora (reabsorption), Tatpurusha (obscuration) and Īśāna (granting grace).

The ring of fire *(prabhāmaṇḍala),* in which Śiva dances is the hall of consciousness, *chitsabhā;* in other words, the light-filled heart of man, the central chamber of the manifest cosmos. Śiva dances the universe into and out of existence, veiling Ultimate Reality for most, unveiling it for devotees who draw near and recognize Paraśiva, Ultimate Reality, in the chamber of their own inner being. Yea, all are dancing with Śiva. See: *nāda, Parameśvara, Parāśakti, Paraśiva, Sadāśiva.*

Natchintanai: நற்சிந்தனை The collected songs of Sage Yogaswāmī (1872–1964) of Jaffna, Sri Lanka, extolling the power of the *satguru,* worship of Lord Śiva, the path of *dharma* and the attainment of Self Realization. See: *Kailāsa Paramparā.*

Nātha: नाथ "Master, lord; adept." Names an ancient Himalayan tradition of Śaiva-yoga mysticism, whose first historically known exponent was Nandikeśvara (ca 250 BCE). *Nātha*—Self-Realized adept—refers to the extraordinary ascetic masters of this school. Through their practice of *siddha yoga* they have attained tremendous powers, *siddhis,* and are sometimes referred to as *siddha yogīs* (accomplished or fully enlightened ones). The words of such beings naturally penetrate deeply into the psyche of their devotees, causing mystical awakenings. Like all *tantrics,* Nāthas have refused to recognize caste distinctions in spiritual pursuits. Their *satgurus* initiate from the lowest to the highest, according to spiritual worthiness. *Nātha* also refers to any follower of the Nātha tradition. The *Nāthas* are considered the source of *haṭha* as well as *rāja yoga.* See: *Kailāsa Paramparā, Nātha Sampradāya, siddha yoga.*

Nātha Maṭha: नाथमठ "Adepts' monastery." As a proper noun, a synonym for

Siddha Siddhānta. See: *Siddha Siddhānta.*

Nātha Sampradāya: नाथसंप्रदाय "Traditional doctrine of knowledge of masters." *Sampradāya* means a living stream of tradition or theology. Nātha Sampradāya is a philosophical and *yogic* tradition of Śaivism whose origins are unknown. This oldest of Śaivite *sampradāyas* existing today consists of two major streams: the Nandinātha and the Ādinātha. The Nandinātha Sampradāya has had as exemplars Maharishi Nandinātha and his disciples: Patañjali (author of the *Yoga Sūtras)* and Tirumular (author of *Tirumantiram).* Among its representatives today are the successive *siddhars* of the Kailāsa Paramparā. The Ādinātha lineage's known exemplars are Maharishi Ādinātha, Matsyendranātha and Gorakshanātha, who founded a well-known order of *yogīs.* See: *Kailāsa Paramparā, Nātha, Śaivism, sampradāya.*

Nayanar: நாயனார் "Teacher." The 63 canonized Tamil saints of South India, as documented in the *Periyapurāṇam* by Sekkilar (ca 1140). All but a few were householders, recognized as outstanding exemplars of devotion to Lord Śiva. Several contributed to the Śaiva Siddhānta scriptural compendium called *Tirumurai.* See: *Nalvar, Tirumurai.*

neo-Indian religion: *Navabhārata Dharma.* A modern form of liberal Hinduism that carries forward basic Hindu cultural values—such as dress, diet and the arts—while allowing religious values to subside. It emerged after the British Raj, when India declared itself an independent, secular state. It was cultivated by the Macaulay education system, implanted in India by the British, which aggressively undermined Hindu thought and belief. Neo-Indian religion encourages Hindus to follow any combination of theological, scriptural, *sādhana* and worship patterns, regardless of sectarian or religious origin. Extending out of and beyond the Smārta system of worshiping the Gods of each major sect, it incorporates holy icons from all religions, including Jesus, Mother Mary and Buddha. Many Navabhāratis choose to not call themselves Hindus but to declare themselves members of all the world's religions. See: *pañchāyatana pūjā, Smārtism, Smārta Sampradāya, syncretism, universalist.*

Nepāl: नेपाल Ancient land between India and Tibet—50,000 square miles, population 14 million. It was the birthplace of Buddha and Sātā, the original home of Matsyendranātha and is renowned for its Pāśupatinātha Śiva temple. Hinduism is the state religion.

neti neti: नेति नेति "Not this, not that." An Upanishadic formula connoting, through negation, the undefinable and inconceivable nature of the Absolute. It is an affirmation which the meditating *yogī* applies to each thought and phase of the mind as he penetrates deeper and deeper in his quest for Truth. Ultimately he transcends all "this-ness" to realize That which is beyond the mind. See: *kuṇḍalinī, samādhi, rāja yoga.*

neuter: Having no sex or gender.

neutron star: A star which has collapsed in on itself and is extremely dense.

A neutron star the size of an orange would weigh more than the entire earth.

new age: According to *Webster's New World Dictionary:* "Of or pertaining to a cultural movement popular in the 1980s [and 90s] characterized by a concern with spiritual consciousness, and variously combining belief in reincarnation and astrology with such practices as meditation, vegetarianism and holistic medicine."

New Year: The majority of Hindus in India celebrate the New Year according to traditional, pre-colonial calendars, several of which are still in use. There are, therefore, various New Year's days in different states of India, the two major ones being Dīpāvalī in October-November, observed in North India, and the day when the sun enters Mesha (Aries) in April, celebrated in Tamil Nadu, Bengal and Nepal.

Nimbārka: निम्बार्क Mystic, philosopher and founder of the Minandi Vaishṇava school of Vedānta (ca 1150). He acclaimed the *guru's* grace as the only true means to salvation. See: *Vedānta.*

Nirguṇa Brahman: निर्गुणब्रह्मन् "God without qualities." See: *Brahman.*

Nirukta Vedāṅga: निरुक्तवेदाङ्ग "Etymology *Veda*-limb." Auxiliary Vedic texts which discuss the origin and development of words; among the four linguistic skills taught for mastery of the *Vedas* and the rites of *yajña.* Nirukta relies upon ancient lexicons, *nighaṇṭu,* as well as detailed hymn indices, *anukramaṇi.* Five *nighaṇṭus* existed at the time of Yāska (320 BCE), whose treatise is regarded a standard work on Vedic etymology. See: *Vedāṅga.*

nirvahaṇa: निर्वहण "End; completion." Conclusion.

nirvāṇī* and *upadeśī: निर्वाणी उपदेशी *Nirvāṇī* means "extinguished one," and *upadeśī* means "teacher." In general, *nirvāṇi* refers to a liberated soul, or to a certain class of monk. *Upadeśī* refers to a teacher, generally a renunciate. In *Dancing with Śiva,* these two terms have special meaning, similar to the Buddhist *arhat* and *bodhisattva,* naming the two earthly modes of the realized, liberated soul. After full illumination, the *jīvanmukta* has the choice to return to the world to help others along the path. This is the way of the *upadeśī* (akin to *bodhisattva),* exemplified by the benevolent *satguru* who leads seekers to the goal of God Realization. He may found and direct institutions and monastic lineages. The *nirvāṇī* (akin to *arhat)* abides at the pinnacle of consciousness, shunning all worldly involvement. He is typified by the silent ascetic, the reclusive sage. See: *satguru, viśvagrāsa.*

nirvikalpa samādhi: निर्विकल्पसमाधि "Enstasy *(samādhi)* without form or seed." The realization of the Self, Paraśiva, a state of oneness beyond all change or diversity; beyond time, form and space. *Vi* means "to change, make different." *Kalpa* means "order, arrangement; a period of time." Thus *vikalpa* means "diversity, thought; difference of perception, distinction." *Nir* means "without." See: *enstasy, kalpa, rāja yoga, samādhi.*

niśchitārtha: निश्चितार्थ "Engagement (to be married); resolution of aim." Synonym for *vāgdāna.* See: *marriage covenant, saṁskāras of adulthood.*

nivedana: **निवेदन** "Announcement." The dedication of a book.
niyama: **नियम** "Restraint." See: *yama-niyama.*
niyati: **नियति** "Necessity, restriction; the fixed order of things, destiny." A synonym for *karma, niyati* is the eighth *tattva.* It is part of the soul's five-fold "sheath," *pañcha kañchuka* (or *vijñānamaya kośa),* along with *kāla* (time), *kalā* (creativity), *vidyā* (knowing) and *rāga* (attachment, desire). The soul thus encased is called *purusha.* See: *karma, tattva.*
nondual (nondualism): See: *dvaita-advaita, monistic theism, Vedānta.*
nonhuman birth: The phenomenon of the soul being born as an animal or other nonhuman life forms during the course of its reincarnational cycles, explained in various Hindu scriptures. For example, Saint Manikkavasagar's famous hymn *(Tiruvasagam* 8.14): "I became grass and herbs, worm and tree. I became many beasts, bird and snake. I became stone and man, goblins and sundry celestials. I became mighty demons, silent sages and the Gods. Taken form in life, moveable and immovable, born in all, I am weary of birth, my Great Lord." The *Upanishads,* too, contain similar references, describing the soul's course after death and later taking a higher or lower birth according to its merit or demerit of the last life *(Kaushītakī Upanishad* 1.2, *Çhandogya Upanishad* 5.3–5.10, *Bṛihadāraṇyaka Upanishad* 6.2).

These statements are sometimes misunderstood to mean that each soul must slowly, in sequential order incarnate as successively higher beings, beginning with the lowest organism, to finally obtain a human birth. In fact, as the *Upanishads* explain, after death the soul, reaching the inner worlds, reaps the harvest of its deeds, is tested and then takes on the appropriate incarnation—be it human or nonhuman—according to its merit or demerit. Souls destined for human evolution are human-like from the moment of their creation in the Śivaloka. This is given outer expression in the Antarloka and Bhūloka, on earth or other similar planets, as the appropriate sheaths are developed. However, not all souls are human souls. There are many kinds of souls, such as genies, elementals and certain Gods, who evolve toward God through different patterns of evolution than do humans.

One cause of unclarity is to confuse the previously mentioned scriptural passages with the theory of biological evolution developed by Charles Darwin (1809–1882), which states that plant and animal species develop or evolve from earlier forms due to hereditary transmission of variations that enhance the organism's adaptability and chances of survival. These principles are now considered the kernel of biology. Applying this theory to man, modern scientists argue that the human form is the result of the development of earlier primates, including apes and monkeys. The Darwinian theory is reasonable but necessarily incomplete as it is based in a materialistic conception of reality that does not encompass the existence of the soul. While the Upanishadic evolutionary vision speaks of the individual soul's development and progress through reincarnation, the Darwinian theory focuses on evolution of the biological organism, with no relation to a soul or individual being. See: *evolution of the soul, kośa, reincarnation, soul.*

noninjurious: Which does not cause harm or injury. **—noninjuriousness:** A translation of *ahiṁsā,* the principle of not causing harm or injury to living beings, whether by thought, word or deed. See: *ahiṁsā.*

nonperseverance: The act, practice or attitude of not persisting, giving up too easily. See: *yama-niyama.*

nonviolence: See: *ahiṁsā.*

Northern Śaivism: A name for Kashmīr Śaivism. See: *Kashmīr Śaivism.*

notable: Worthy of being noted. Remarkable.

novelty: Newness. The constant changes and enchantments of life.

novitiate: Same as *novice.* A newcomer to a monastic or religious community, on probation, before taking final vows.

nucleus of the soul: See: *ātman, impersonal being, soul.*

nunk: A contemporary word coined by Catholic theologian Raimundo Panikkar to describe women contemplatives or female monks, in contrast to the word *nun* which commonly describes a religious teacher or service-oriented woman under vows. A nunk is a celibate woman following strict, perhaps austere and usually solitary, spiritual disciplines and lifestyle. By balancing the masculine and feminine energies within herself through *sādhana* and *yoga,* she is a complete being, detached from the thoughts and feelings of others, free to follow the contemplative and mystical life in pursuit of the Self within. To accomplish this, she works to permanently conquer her feminine instincts and the emotional tendencies of a woman's body. She strives to transmute her sexuality into the Divine, giving up her womanliness so thoroughly that she is indistinguishable from a monk. In Hinduism, nunks may be *sannyāsinīs, yoginīs* or *sādhikās.* See: *monastic, sannyāsin, monk.*

nurturance: Same as nurture, to nourish. The act or process or furnishing the essentials to growth, development or education.

Nyāya: न्याय "System; rule; logic." See: *Gautama, shaḍ darśana.*

objective: 1) Quality of thinking or perception relating to the object as it truly is. Not biased or colored by one's personal point of view or prejudices, which then would be subjective thinking. 2) A target, goal or anything sought for or aimed at. Cf: *subjective.*

oblation: An offering or sacrifice ceremoniously given to a God or *guru.* See: *sacrifice, yajña.*

obscuration: Same as obscuring grace. See: *grace, Naṭarāja.*

obscuring grace: See: *grace, Naṭarāja.*

obstacle: See: *upasarga.*

obstinate (obstinacy): Overly determined to have one's own way. Stubborn.

occult: Hidden, or kept secret; revealed only after initiation. See: *mysticism.*

odic: Magnetic—of or pertaining to consciousness within *aśuddha māyā,* the realm of the physical and lower astral planes. Odic force in its rarified state is *prakṛiti,* the primary gross energy of nature, manifesting in the three *guṇas: sattva, rajas* and *tamas.* It is the force of attraction and repulsion between people, people and their things, and manifests as masculine (aggressive) and feminine (passive), arising from the *piṅgalā* and *iḍā* currents. These two currents *(nāḍī)* are found within spine of the subtle body. Odic force is a magnetic, sticky, binding substance that people seek to develop when they want to bind themselves together, such as in partnerships, marriage, *guru-śishya* relationships and friendships. Odic energy the combined emanation of the *prāṇamaya* and *annamaya kośas.* The term o*dic* is the adjective form of *od* (pronounced like *mode),* defined in the *Oxford English Dictionary* as "a hypothetical force held by Baron von Reichenbach (1788–1869) to pervade all nature, manifesting itself in certain persons of sensitive temperament (streaming from their fingertips), and exhibited especially by magnets, crystals, heat, light and chemical action; it has been held to explain the phenomena of mesmerism and animal magnetism." See: *actinic, actinodic, guṇa, kośa, odic, subtle body, tattva.*

offset: Made up for, compensated for, counterbalanced by.

offspring: The young of animals. Children. Sanskṛit: *apatya.*

olai: ஓலை "Leaf." An ancient form of Indian books used in South India, made of strips of fronds from the palmyra *(triṇḍruma)* and talipot (*tālapatra,* "fan-leaf") palms. Prepared birch bark *(bhūrja pattra)* was the medium in the North. The pages were loosely tied, with cord passed between one or two holes and usually bound between wooden covers. Ink, made from lampblack or charcoal, was applied with a reed pen. Or, more commonly in the South, the letters were scribed with a stylus, then rubbed with powdered lampblack. These books are small in size, averaging about 2 inches high and 8 inches wide and up to 11 or 12 inches thick, wound with string and generally protected in colored cloth. See: *grantha.*

old soul: One who has reincarnated many times, experienced much and is therefore further along the path. Old souls may be recognized by their qualities of compassion, self-effacement and wisdom. See: *evolution of the soul, soul.*

Om: ओम् "Yes, verily." The most sacred *mantra* of Hinduism. An alternate transliteration of *Aum* (the sounds A and U blend to become O). See: *Aum.*

ominous: Foreboding; frightening, sinister.

omnipotent: All-powerful. Able to do anything.

omnipresent: Present everywhere and in all things.

omniscient: Having infinite knowledge, all-knowing.

oneness: Quality or state of being one. Unity, identity, especially in spite of appearances to the contrary—e.g., the oneness of soul and God. See: *monism.*

ontology: The branch of metaphysics dealing with the nature of reality.
orbit: The path taken by a celestial object gravitating around another.
ordain (ordination): To give someone the duties and responsibilities, authority and spiritual power of a religious office, such as priest, minister or *satguru,* through religious ceremony or mystical initiation. See: *dīkshā.*
original sin: See: *sin.*
orthodox: "Straight opinion." Conforming to established doctrines or beliefs. Opposite of *heterodox,* "different opinion." See: *āstika.*
outgrow (outgrown): To grow faster or larger than and, therefore, to lose or be rid of in the process of growing.
outstretch: To extend, to stretch out, as one's arms or a large cloth.
overshadow: To cast a shadow over or be more important than; to dominate.
overwhelm: To overcome or overpower as with great force or emotion.

pada: पद "A step, pace, stride; footstep, trace."
pāda: पाद "The foot (of men and animals); quarter-part, section; stage; path." Names the major sections of the Āgamic texts and the corresponding stages of practice and unfoldment on the path to *moksha.* According to Śaiva Siddhānta, there are four *pādas,* which are successive and cumulative; i.e. in accomplishing each one the soul prepares itself for the next. (In Tamil, Śaiva Siddhānta is also known as Nalu-pāda, "four-stage," Śaivam.)—***charyā pāda:*** "Good conduct stage." The first stage where one learns to live righteously, serve selflessly, performing *karma yoga.* It is also known as *dāsa mārga,* "path of the slave," a time when the aspirant relates to God as a servant to a master. Traditional acts of *charyā* include cleaning the temple, lighting lamps and collecting flowers for worship. Worship at this stage is mostly external. —***kriyā pāda:*** "Religious action; worship stage." Stage of *bhakti yoga,* of cultivating devotion through performing *pūjā* and regular daily *sādhana.* It is also known as the *satputra mārga,* "true son's way," as the soul now relates to God as a son to his father. A central practice of the *kriyā pāda* is performing daily *pūjā.* —***yoga pāda:*** Having matured in the *charyā* and *kriyā pādas,* the soul now turns to internalized worship and *rāja yoga* under the guidance of a *satguru.* It is a time of *sādhana* and serious striving when realization of the Self is the goal. It is the *sakhā mārga,* "way of the friend," for now God is looked upon as an intimate friend. —***jñāna pāda:*** "Stage of wisdom." Once the soul has attained Realization, it is henceforth a wise one, who lives out the life of the body, shedding blessings on mankind. This stage is also called the San Mārga, "true path," on which God is our dearest beloved. The *Tirumantiram* describes the fulfillment of each stage as follows. In *charyā,* the soul forges a kindred tie in "God's world" *(sālokya).* In *kriyā* it attains "nearness" *(sāmīpya)* to Him. In *yoga* it attains

"likeness" *(sārūpya)* with Him. In *jñāna* the soul enjoys the ultimate bliss of identity *(sāyujya)* with Śiva. See: *jñāna, nirvāṇī and upadeśī.*

pādapūjā: **पादपूजा** "Foot worship." Ceremonial worship of the *guru's* sandals or holy feet, often through ablution with precious substances and offering of fruit and flowers. After the ceremony, the water of the bath, the fruit and other precious substances are partaken of as *prasāda* by the devotees. See: *guru, guru bhakti, pādukā, prasāda, ucçhishṭa.*

padārtha: **पदार्थ** "Constituent substance." Primary categories or essential elements of existence, defined differently or uniquely by each philosophical school. For example, in the Sāṅkhya Darśana, the *padārthas* are *purusha* (spirit) and *prakṛiti* (matter). According to Advaita Vedānta, they are *chit* (spirit) and *achit* (nonspirit), which from an absolute perspective are taken as the One *padārtha,* Brahman. In Śākta and Śaiva traditions, the *padārthas* are Pati (God), *paśu* (soul) and *pāśa* (world, or bonds).

paddhati: **पद्धति** "Foot-path; track; guide." The name of a class of expository writings, e.g., Gorakshanātha's *Siddha Siddhānta Paddhati,* and the many *paddhatis* that are guidebooks for ritual temple rites. There are *paddhatis* for the *Vedas* and for the *Āgamas.*

padma: **पद्म** The lotus flower, *Nelumbo nucifera,* symbol of spiritual development and the *chakras.* Because it grows out of mud and rises to perfect purity and glory, it is an apt representation of spiritual unfoldment.

Padma Purāṇa: **पद्मपुराण** One of the six main *Vishṇu Purāṇas.*

pādukā: **पादुका** "Sandals." *Śrī Pādukā* refers to the sandals of the preceptor, the traditional icon of the *guru,* representing his holy feet and worshiped as the source of grace. *Pādukā* also names one of Vīra Śaivism's eight aids *(ashṭāvaraṇa)* to faith—the practice of drinking the water from the ceremonial washing of the Śivaliṅga or the *guru's* feet. See: *guru bhakti, pādapūjā, prasāda, satguru, ucçhishṭa.*

pagan: Term used negatively by Semitic faiths to indicate a follower of another religion, or of no religion. Also names the pre-Christian religion of Europe, akin to shamanism and other of the world's indigenous faiths, which have survived to this day despite organized persecution. Pagans are gradually surfacing again, and have acknowledged their kinship with Hinduism. See: *mysticism, shamanism.*

pageantry: A spectacular and grand representation, elaborately decorated show, procession, drama, etc. See: *festival.*

Paiṅgala Upanishad: **पैङ्गल उपनिषद्** Belongs to the *Śukla Yajur Veda.* A 12-verse dialog between Sage Yājñavalkya and his disciple Paiṅgala covering a wide range of topics, including liberation and the five sheaths of man.

pañchabhūta: **पञ्चभूत** "Five elements." Earth, water, fire, air and ether. Also called *mahābhūta.* See: *indriya, tattva.*

pañchāchāra: **पञ्चाचार** "Five rules." The five Vīra Śaivite codes of conduct. —***Liṅgāchāra:*** Daily worship of the Śivaliṅga. —***sadāchāra:*** attention to vocation and duty. —***Śivāchāra:*** Acknowledging Śiva as the one God and observing equality among members. —***bhṛityāchāra:*** Humility toward all creatures. —***gaṇāchāra:*** defense of the community and its tenets.

Pañcha Gaṇapati Utsava: पञ्चगणपतिउत्सव "Five-fold Gaṇapati festival." A modern five-day festival observed from the 21st through 25th of December. *Pañcha* (five) denotes Gaṇeśa's five faces, each representing a specific power *(śakti)*. One face is worshiped each day, creating 1) harmony in the home, 2) concord among relatives, neighbors and friends, 3) good business and public relations, 4) cultural upliftment and 5) heartfelt charity and religiousness. The festival, a favorite among children, was conceived in 1985 by Satguru Sivaya Subramuniyaswami along with elders of various Hindu sects. It is a time of sharing gifts, renewing ties of family and friendship while focusing inwardly on this great God of abundance. See: *Gaṇeśa.*

Pañchākshara Mantra: पञ्चाक्षरमन्त्र "Five-lettered chant." Śaivism's most sacred *mantra.* See: *Namaḥ Śivāya.*

Pañchamukha Gaṇapati: पञ्चमुखगणपति "Five-faced Gaṇapati." A special form of Lord Gaṇeśa with five faces; similar to Siddhi Gaṇapati.

pañcha nitya karma(s): पञ्चनित्यकर्म "Five constant duties." A traditional regimen of religious practice for Hindus: 1) *dharma* (virtuous living), 2) *upāsanā* (worship), 3) *utsava* (holy days), 4) *tīrthayātrā* (pilgrimage) and 5) *saṁskāras* (sacraments.) See: *dharma, festival, saṁskāra, tīrthayātrā.*

Pañcharātra: पञ्चरात्र An ancient name of Vaishṇavism. The term literally means "five nights," but may be a corruption of *pañcharatha* ("five vehicles, ways or paths"), thought to indicate five ancient sects in the vicinity of Mathura that eventually merged into one with the worship of Kṛishṇa.

Pāñcharātra Āgama(s): पाञ्चरात्र आगम The most popular of the two major groups of *Vaishṇava Āgamas* (the other being the *Vaikāsana Āgamas).*

Pañchārtha Bhāshya: पञ्चार्थभाष्य Commentary by Kauṇḍinya (ca 100) on Lakulīśa's *Pāśupata Sūtras,* one of the few extant philosophical texts of Pāśupata Śaivism. It was rediscovered in 1930. See: *Pāśupata Śaivism.*

pañcha śraddhā: पञ्चश्रद्धा "Five faiths." A concise summary of Hindu belief exactly correlated to the "five constant practices," *pañcha nitya karmas.* The *pañcha śraddhā* are 1) *sarva* Brahman: God is All in all, soul is divine; 2) *maṇḍira:* belief in temples and divine beings; 3) *karma:* cosmic justice; 4) *saṁsāra–moksha:* rebirth brings enlightenment and liberation; 5) *Vedas* and *satguru:* the necessity of scripture and preceptor. See: *pañcha nitya karma.*

Pañchatantra: पञ्चतन्त्र The collection of animal stories used by sage Vishṇu Sharma to teach the king's sons the "art of practical life." They were written down in Sanskṛit in about 200 BCE, but existed previously as part of oral tradition. The engaging stories have migrated all over the world to reappear in *Aesop's Fables, Arabian Nights, Canterbury Tales* and in ancient Chinese and Japanese works. See: *folk-narratives, mythology.*

pañchāyatana pūjā: पञ्चायतनपूजा "Five-shrine worship." A system of personal worship, thought to have developed after the 7th century, in the Smārta *brāhminical* tradition, and which is now part of orthodox daily practice for Smārtas. The ritual involves the worship of five Deities: Vishṇu, Śiva, Sūrya, Gaṇeśa and Śakti. The five are represented by small *mūrtis,* or by five kinds of stones, or by five marks drawn on the floor. One is placed in the center as the devotee's preferred God, Ishṭa Devatā, and the other four in a square around it. Kumāra, often added as a sixth Deity, is generally situated behind the Ishṭa Devatā. Philosophically, all are seen by Smārtas as equal reflections of the one Saguṇa Brahman, rather than as distinct beings. This arrangement is also represented in Smārta temples, with one in a central sanctum, and the others installed in smaller shrines. Each God may be worshiped in any of His/Her traditional aspects or incarnations, allowing for much variety (e.g., Śakti as Lakshmī, Vishṇu as Rāma, and Śiva as Bhairava). With the addition of the sixth Deity, Kumāra, the system is known as *shaṇmata,* "six-fold path." This system has laid the foundation for the modern secular or neo-Indian religion, in which Hindus freely add Jesus, mother Mary, Mohammed, Buddha or any other holy personage to their altars. This modern approach has no basis in traditional scripture of any kind. See: *Ishṭa Devatā, neo-Indian religion, shaṇmata sthāpanāchārya, Smārtism.*

paṇḍita: पण्डित See: *pundit.*

panentheism: "All-in-God doctrine." The view that the universe is part of the being of God, as distinguished from *pantheism* ("all-is-God doctrine"), which identifies God with the total reality. In contrast, panentheism holds that God pervades the world, but is also beyond it. He is immanent and transcendent, relative and Absolute. This embracing of opposites is called dipolar. For the panentheist, God is in all, and all is in God. Panentheism is the technical term for monistic theism. See: *Advaita Īśvaravāda, dvaita-advaita, monistic theism, pantheism.*

pantheism: "All-is-God doctrine." A term applied to a variety of philosophical position in which God and the world are identical. To the pantheist, God is not a Personal Lord, nor a transcendent or formless Being, but is the totality of all existence, including universal laws, movement, matter, etc. See: *monistic theism, panentheism.*

pāpa: पाप "Wickedness; sin, crime." 1) Bad or evil. 2) Wrongful action. 3) Demerit earned through wrongdoing. Pāpa includes all forms of wrongdoing, from the simplest infraction to the most heinous crime, such as premeditated murder. Each act of *pāpa* carries its karmic consequence, *karmaphala,* "fruit of action," for which scriptures delineate specific penance for expiation. Those who have awakened psychic sight can clearly see *pāpa* in the inner subconscious aura as a colorful, sticky, astral substance. *Pāpa* is seen as dark unrelated colors, whereas its counterpart, *puṇya,* is seen as pastels. The color arrangements are not unlike modern art murals. *Pāpa* colors can produce disease, depression, loneliness and such, but can be dissolved through penance *(prāyaśchitta)*, austerity *(tapas)* and good deeds *(sukṛityā)*.

There are specific consequences, *karmaphala*, "fruit of action," that result from each type of transgression of *dharma*. For example, a man who steals from his neighbors creates a cosmic debt which may be repaid later by having his own possessions taken away. There are also specific penances, *prāyaśchitta*, that can be performed for atonement and the accrual of *puṇya* (merit) to balance out the *pāpa*, the negative *karma* of the wrongful act. Such disciplines are provided in the various *Dharma Śāstras* and prescribed by knowing preceptors, *paṇḍitas, śāstrīs, swāmīs, yogīs* and village elders according to the *varṇa* and education of the individual.

For example, the *Laws of Manu* give several types of penance for the crime of murder, including 1) making a forest hut and subsisting there on alms for twelve years and using a human skull as one's emblem; or 2) walking 100 *yojanas* (900 miles), while reciting the *Vedas*, eating little and remaining continent. A contemporary example: if a man fells a large healthy tree, he may atone by planting ten trees and ensuring that at least one grows to replace it.

The degree of *pāpa* accrued from an action depends on various factors, including the *karma, dharma* and spiritual advancement of the individual, the intent or motivation, as well as the time and place of the action (for example, unvirtuous deeds carry great demerit when performed in holy places). *Pāpa* is the opposite of *puṇya* (merit, virtue). See: *evil, karma, penance, puṇya, sin.*

pāpa-duḥkha: **पापदुःख** "Sin and suffering." See: *karma, pāpa, sin.*

pāpman: **पाप्मन्** "Evil; sin." See: *evil, pāpa, Satan, sin.*

para: **पर** "Supreme; beyond." A term referring to the highest dimension of whatever it precedes—as in *Paraśiva* or *Parabrahman.* (Sometimes *parā*, as in Parāśakti.)

parable: A short, simple story illustrating a moral or religious principle.

Parabrahman: **परब्रह्मन्** "Supreme (or transcendent) God." A synonym for Nirguṇa Brahman, Absolute Reality, beyond time, form and space. Same as Paraśiva. See: *Brahman, Paraśiva.*

paradox: "Side-by-side opinion or thought." An apparent contradiction according to conventional logic and reason.

Parākhya Āgama: **पराख्य आगम** A subsidiary Śaiva Āgamic text (*Upāgama).*

parama: **परम** "Highest; supreme." See: *para.*

paramaguru: **परमगुरु** "Senior preceptor." The *guru* of a disciple's *guru.*

paramahaṁsa: **परमहंस** "Supreme swan." From *haṁsa*, meaning swan or, more precisely, the high-flying Indian goose, Anser Indicus. A class of liberated renunciates. See: *haṁsa.*

Paramātman: परमात्मन् "Supreme Self," or "transcendent soul." Paraśiva, Absolute Reality, the one transcendent Self of every soul. Contrasted with *ātman,* which includes all three aspects of the soul: *Paraśiva, Parāśakti* and *ānandamaya kośa.* See: *ātman, kośa, soul.*

Parameśvara: परमेश्वर "Supreme Lord or Ruler." God Śiva in the third perfection as Supreme Mahādeva, Śiva-Śakti, mother of the universe. In this perfection as Personal, father-mother God, Śiva is a person—who has a body, with head, arms and legs, etc.—who acts, wills, blesses, gives *darśana,* guides, creates, preserves, reabsorbs, obscures and enlightens. In Truth, it is Śiva-Śakti who does all. The term *Primal Soul,* Paramapurusha, designates Parameśvara as the original, uncreated soul, the creator of all other souls. Parameśvara has many other names and epithets, including those denoting the five divine actions—Sadāśiva, the revealer; Maheśvara, the obscurer; Brahmā, the creator; Vishṇu the preserver; and Rudra the destroyer. See: *Naṭarāja, Sadāśiva.*

paramparā: परंपरा "Uninterrupted succession." A lineage. See: *guru paramparā.*

parārtha pūjā: परार्थपूजा "Public liturgy and worship." See: *pūjā.*

Parāśakti: पराशक्ति "Supreme power; primal energy." God Śiva's second perfection, which is impersonal, immanent, and with form—the all-pervasive, Pure Consciousness and Primal Substance of all that exists. There are many other descriptive names for Parāśakti—Satchidānanda ("existence-consciousness-bliss"), light, silence, divine mind, superconsciousness and more. Parāśakti can be experienced by the diligent *yogī* or meditator as a merging in, or identification with, the underlying oneness flowing through all form. The experience is called *savikalpa samādhi.* See: *rāja yoga, Śakti, Satchidānanda, tattva.*

Parāsamvid: परासंविद् In Siddha Siddhānta the highest, transcendental state of Śiva. A synonym of *Paraśiva.*

Paraśiva: परशिव "Transcendent Śiva." The Self God, Śiva in His first perfection, Absolute Reality. God Śiva as *That* which is beyond the grasp of consciousness, transcends time, form and space and defies description. To merge with Him in mystic union is the goal of all incarnated souls, the reason for their living on this planet, and the deepest meaning of their experiences. Attainment of this is called Self Realization or *nirvikalpa samādhi.* See: *samādhi, Śiva.*

Pārvatī: पार्वती "Mountain's daughter." One of many names for the Universal Mother. Prayers are offered to Her for strength, health and eradication of impurities. Mythologically, Pārvatī is wedded to Śiva. See: *Goddess, Śakti.*

pāśa: पाश "Tether; noose." The whole of existence, manifest and unmanifest. That which binds or limits the soul and keeps it (for a time) from manifesting its full potential. *Pāśa* refers to the soul's three-fold bondage of *āṇava, karma* and *māyā.* See: *liberation, mala, Pati-paśu-pāśa.*

***paśu:* पशु** "Cow, cattle, kine; fettered individual." Refers to animals or beasts, including man. In philosophy, the soul. Śiva as lord of creatures is called Paśupati. See: *pāśa, Pati-paśu-pāśa.*

***paśupālaka:* पशुपालक** "Herdsman." A person who protects, nourishes and guards. A name for a Hindu chaplain or missionary.

***Pāśupata Śaivism:* पाशुपतशैव** Monistic and theistic, this school of Śaivism reveres Śiva as Supreme Cause and Personal Ruler of soul and world, denoted in His form as Paśupati, "Lord of souls." This school centers around the ascetic path, emphasizing *sādhana,* detachment from the world and the quest for "internal *kuṇḍalinī* grace." The *Kāravaṇa Māhātmya* recounts the birth of Lakulīśa (ca 200 BCE), a principal Pāśupata *guru,* and refers to the temple of Somanātha as one of the most important Pāśupata centers. Lakulīśa propounded a Śaiva monism, though indications are that Pāśupata philosophy was previously dualistic, with Śiva as efficient cause of the universe but not material cause. It is thought to be the source of various ascetic streams, including the Kāpālikas and the Kālāmukhas. This school is represented today in the broad *sādhu* tradition, and numerous Pāśupata sites of worship are scattered across India. See: *Śaivism.*

***Pāśupata Sūtra(s):* पाशुपतसूत्र** The recently rediscovered (1930) central scripture of the Pāśupata school of Śaivism, attributed to Lakulīśa. It covers asceticism at great length, and the five subjects of Pāśupata theology: effect, cause, meditation, behavior and dissolution of sorrow. It urges the ascetic to go unrecognized and even invite abuse. See: *Pāśupata Śaivism.*

***Paśupati:* पशुपति** "Herdsman; lord of animals." An ancient name for Śiva, first appearing in the *Atharva Veda.* This form of Śiva, seated in *yogic* pose, was found on a seal from the 6,000-year-old Indus Valley civilization. See: *Pāśupata Śaivism, Śaivism.*

***Pāśupatinātha mandira*: पाशुपतिनाथमन्दिर** Foremost temple of Nepal, linked to the ancient Pāśupata sect of Śaivism.

***pātāla:* पाताल** "Fallen or sinful region." The seventh *chakra* below the *mūlādhāra,* centered in the soles of the feet. Corresponds to the seventh and lowest astral netherworld beneath the earth's surface, called Kākola ("black poison") or Pātāla. This is the realm in which misguided souls indulge in destruction for the sake of destruction, of torture, and of murder for the sake of murder. *Pātāla* also names the netherworld in general, and is a synonym for *Naraka.* See: *chakra, loka, Naraka.*

***Patañjali:* पतञ्जलि** A Śaivite Nātha *siddha* (ca 200 BCE) who codified the ancient *yoga* philosophy which outlines the path to enlightenment through purification, control and transcendence of the mind. One of the six classical philosophical systems *(darśanas)* of Hinduism, known as Yoga Darśana. His great work, the *Yoga Sūtras,* comprises 200 aphorisms delineating *ashṭāṅga* (eight-limbed), *rāja* (kingly) or *siddha* (perfection) *yoga.* Still today it is the foremost text on meditative *yoga.* See: *Kailāsa Paramparā, rāja* *yoga, shaḍ darśana, yoga.*

path: *Mārga* or *pantha.* A trail, road or way. In Hinduism there are various ways that the term *path* is used. **—path of enlightenment/salvation/*moksha:*** The way to the ultimate goals of Self Realization and liberation. **—universal path:** The spiritual path conceived as being followed by all of existence, marching on its way to Godhood. **—path of *dharma:*** Following principles of good conduct and virtue. **—the two paths:** The way of the monk and that of the householder, a choice to be made by each Hindu young man. **—peerless/highest path:** The spiritual path (or the path of renunciation) as the noblest of human undertakings. **—the straight path:** The way that goes directly to the goal, without distraction or *karmic* detour. **—on the path:** someone who is seriously studying, striving and performing *sādhana* to perfect the inner and outer nature. **—our right path in life:** The best way for us personally to proceed; personal *dharma, svadharma.* **—"Truth is one, paths are many:"** Hinduism's affirmation for tolerance. It accepts that there are various ways to proceed toward the ultimate goal. See: *dharma, pāda.*

pāṭhaka: **पाठक** "Reader, reciter." An inspired reader of scripture and sacred literature.

Pati: **पति** "Master; lord; owner." A name for God Śiva indicating His commanding relationship with souls as caring ruler and helpful guide. In Śaiva Siddhānta the term is part of the analogy of cowherd *(pati),* cows *(paśu,* souls) and the tether *(pāśa—āṇava, karma* and *māyā)* by which cows are tied. See: *Pati-paśu-pāśa, Śiva.*

Pati-paśu-pāśa: **पति पशु पाश** Literally: "master, cow and tether." These are the three primary elements *(padārtha,* or *tattvatrayī)* of Śaiva Siddhānta philosophy: God, soul and world—Divinity, man and cosmos—seen as a mystically and intricately interrelated unity. Pati is God, envisioned as a cowherd. *Paśu* is the soul, envisioned as a cow. *Pāśa* is the all-important force or fetter by which God brings souls along the path to Truth. The various schools of Hinduism define the rapport among the three in varying ways. For pluralistic Śaiva Siddhāntins they are three beginningless verities, self-existent, eternal entities. For monistic Śaiva Siddhāntins, *paśu* and *pāśa* are the emanational creation of Pati, Lord Śiva, and He alone is eternal reality. See: *pāśa, Śaiva Siddhānta, soul.*

Paushkara Āgama: **पौष्कर आगम** Subsidiary text *(Upāgama)* of the *Mataṅga Parameśvara Śaiva Āgama,* containing 977 verses divided into 90 chapters. A mostly philosophic treatise dealing with God, soul and world and the instruments of knowledge.

penance: *Prāyaśchitta.* Atonement, expiation. An act of devotion *(bhakti),* austerity *(tapas)* or discipline *(sukṛitya)* undertaken to soften or nullify the anticipated reaction to a past action. Penance is uncomfortable *karma* inflicted upon oneself to mitigate one's *karmic* burden caused by wrongful actions *(kukarma)*. It includes such acts as prostrating 108 times, fasting, self-denial, or carrying *kavadi (public penance)*, as well as more extreme austerities, or *tapas*. Penance is often suggested by spiritual leaders and elders. Penitence or repentance, suffering regret for misdeeds, is called *anutāpa*, meaning "to heat." See: *evil, kavadi, pāpa, prāyaśchitta, sin, tapas.*

pendant: An ornament or piece of jewelry attached to a necklace. See: *wedding pendant.*

perfections: Describes a quality, nature or dimension that is perfect. God Śiva's three perfections are Paraśiva, Parāśakti and Parameśvara. Though spoken of as three-fold for the sake of understanding, God Śiva ever remains a one transcendent-immanent Being. See: *Śiva.*

Periyapurāṇam: பெரிய புராணம் Twelfth book of the *Tirumurai*. Story of the 63 Śaiva Nayanar saints of Tamil Nadu, written by Sekkilar (CA 1140). See: *Tirumurai.*

personal *dharma:* *Svadharma*. An individual's unique path in life in conformance with divine law. See: *dharma.*

Personal God: See: *Ishṭa Devatā, Parameśvara.*

perspective: Point of view in understanding or evaluation.

pilgrimage: *Tīrthayātrā*. Journeying to a holy temple, near or far, performed by all Hindus at least once each year. See: *tīrthayātrā.*

piṇḍa: पिण्ड "Roundish mass; body; part of the whole, individual; microcosm." In worship rites, small balls of rice set aside daily in remembrance of ancestors. Philosophically, and emphasized in Siddha Siddhānta, the human body as a replica of the macrocosm, *mahāsākāra piṇḍa*, also called Brahmāṇḍa (cosmic egg), or simply *aṇḍa* (egg). Within the individual body of man is reflected and contained the entire cosmos. Each *chakra* represents a world or plane of consciousness with the highest locus in the head and the lowest in the feet. "Microcosm-macrocosm" is embodied in the terms *piṇḍa-aṇḍa. Siddha Siddhānta Paddhati* lists six *piṇḍas*, from the *garbhapiṇḍa*, "womb-born body," to *parapiṇḍa*, "transcendental body." See: *Brahmāṇḍa, microcosm-macrocosm.*

piṅgalā: पिंगला "Tawny channel." The masculine psychic current flowing along the spine. See: *kuṇḍalinī, nāḍī, rāja yoga.*

pir: "Holy father." Muslim title for a religious leader; applied to leaders of a few Gorakshanātha monasteries.

pīṭha: पीठ "Seat; pedestal." 1) The base or pedestal of the Śivaliṅga, or of any Deity idol. 2) A religious seat, such as the throne of the abbot of a monastery. 3) An *aadheenam, āśrama* or *maṭha* established around such a seat of spiritual authority. See: *Śivaliṅga.*

Pitṛiloka: पितृलोक "World of ancestors." The upper region of Bhuvarloka. See: *loka.*

pitta: पित्त "Bile; fire." One of the three bodily humors, called *doshas, pitta* is known as the fire humor. It is the *āyurvedic* principle of bodily heat-energy.

Pitta dosha governs nutritional absorption, body temperature and intelligence. See: *āyurveda, dosha.*

plague: To distress, afflict, trouble or torment.

plane: A stage or level of existence; e.g., the causal plane (Śivaloka). See: *loka.*

Pleiades: A cluster of stars in the Taurus constellation, six of which are now visible from Earth. This group of stars is known in Sanskṛit as Kṛittikā, an important *nakshatra* for Lord Kārttikeya and believed to be this Deity's place of origin before He came to the star system of Earth. See: *Kārttikeya.*

pliant: Flexible, adaptable, not rigid.

Plotinus: Egyptian-born philosopher (205–270), one of the Western world's greatest known mystics, who extended and revived the work of the Greek philosopher Plato in the Roman Empire. His philosophy, known as Neo-Platonism, posits concentric levels of reality, not unlike the Hindu cosmology of *lokas,* with a central source of sublime existence and values and an outer sheath of physical matter. Man, he said, is a microcosm of this system, capable of attaining the sublime inner state through enstasy. He practiced and taught *ahiṁsā,* vegetarianism, *karma,* reincarnation and belief in Supreme Being as both immanent and transcendent. His writings, in six volumes, are called the *Ennead.* He was apparently familiar with Hindu wisdom through reading *Life of Apollonius,* a biography which narrated a young Greek renunciate's travels through India.

pluralism (pluralistic): Doctrine that holds existence to be composed of three or more distinct and irreducible components, such as God, souls and world. See: *dvaita-advaita.*

pluralistic realism: A term for pluralism used by various schools including Meykandar Śaiva Siddhānta, emphasizing that the components of existence are absolutely real in themselves and not creations of consciousness or God.

polygamy: Practice of having more than one spouse.

polytheism: Belief in or worship of many Gods. See: *monotheism.*

pomp: A dignified or brilliant display. Splendor and pageantry.

pontifical: Having to do with pontiffs, or high priests. Having all the dignity, respect, and influence of a spiritual leader endowed with great authority. See: *ordination, Śaṅkarāchārya pīṭha.*

potent: Having power, authority. Effective, able.

potentialities: A state of latency, something that has power but is not developed or manifest, such as a talent yet to be matured.

pradakshiṇa: **प्रदक्षिण** "Moving to the right." Worshipful circumambulation, walking clockwise around the temple sanctum or other holy place, with the intention of shifting the mind from worldly concerns to awareness of the Divine. *Clockwise* has esoteric significance in that the *chakras* of *mūlādhāra* and above spin clockwise, while those below spin counterclockwise, taking one down into the lower regions of selfishness, greed, conflict and turmoil.

pradosha: **प्रदोष** The auspicious 3-hour period, 1½ hours before and after sunset. *Pradosha* especially refers to this period on the 13th *(trayodaśī) tithi* of each fortnight, an optimum time of the month for meditation. Its observance, prepared for by fasting, is called *pradosha vrata.* See: *fast, tithi.*

pragmatic: Practical. Concerned with application, not theory or speculation.

***prakṛiti:* प्रकृति** "Primary matter; nature." In the 25-*tattva* Sāṅkhya system—which concerns itself only with the tangible spectrum of creation—*prakṛiti,* or *pradhāna,* is one of two supreme beginningless realities: matter and spirit, *prakṛiti* and *purusha,* the female and male principles. *Prakṛiti* is the manifesting aspect, as contrasted with the quiescent unmanifest—*purusha,* which is pure consciousness. In Śāktism, *prakṛiti,* the active principle, is personified as Devī, the Goddess, and is synonymous with Māyā. Prakṛiti is thus often seen, and depicted so in the *Purāṇas,* as the Divine Mother, whose love and care embrace and comfort all beings. In Śaivite cosmology, *prakṛiti* is the 24th of 36 *tattvas,* the potentiality of the physical cosmos, the gross energy from which all lower *tattvas* are formed. Its three qualities are *sattva, rajas* and *tamas.* See: *odic, purusha, tattva.*

***pralaya:* प्रलय** "Dissolution, reabsorption; destruction; death." A synonym for *saṁhāra,* one of the five functions of Śiva. Also names the partial destruction or reabsorption of the cosmos at the end of each eon or *kalpa.* There are three kinds of periods of dissolution: 1) *laya,* at the end of a *mahāyuga,* when the physical world is destroyed; 2) *pralaya,* at the end of a *kalpa,* when both the physical and subtle worlds are destroyed; and 3) *mahāpralaya* at the end of a *mahākalpa,* when all three worlds (physical, subtle and causal) are absorbed into Śiva. See: *cosmic cycle, mahāpralaya.*

***pramukha:* प्रमुख** "Turning the face toward." Head; foremost." Leader, guide; such as the family head, *kuṭumba pramukha.* See: *joint family.*

***prāṇa:* प्राण** Vital energy or life principle. Literally, "vital air," from the root *praṇ,* "to breathe." *Prāṇa* in the human body moves in the *prāṇamaya kośa* as five primary life currents known as *vāyus,* "vital airs or winds." These are *prāṇa* (outgoing breath), *apāṇa* (incoming breath), *vyāṇa* (retained breath), *udāṇa* (ascending breath) and *samāṇa* (equalizing breath). Each governs crucial bodily functions, and all bodily energies are modifications of these. Usually *prāṇa* refers to the life principle, but sometimes denotes energy, power or the animating force of the cosmos. See: *kośa, tattva.*

***Prāṇāgnihotra Upanishad:* प्राणाग्निहोत्र उपनिषद्** A minor *Upanishad* which explains how to transform the external ritual of the fire sacrifice into *prāṇāgnihotra,* "the sacrifice offered in the *prāṇa* fire" of one's own being.

***Prāṇaliṅga:* प्राणलिङ्ग** "Living mark." Personally experiencing God in the Śivaliṅga. A term used especially in Vīra Śaivism. See: *Śivaliṅga, Vīra Śaivism.*

***prāṇamaya kośa:* प्राणमयकोश** "Life-energy sheath." See: *kośa, prāṇa.*

praṇāma:* प्रणाम** "Obeisance; to bow down." Reverent salutation in which the head or body is bowed. ***—ashṭāṅga praṇāma: "Eight-limbed obeisance." The full body form for men, in which the hands, chest, forehead, knees and feet touch the ground. (Same as *śashṭāṅga praṇāma.*) —***pañchāṅga praṇāma:*** "Five-limbed obeisance." The woman's form of prostration, in which the hands, head and legs touch the ground (with the ankles crossed, right over the left). A more exacting term for prostration is *praṇipāta,* "falling down in obeisance." See: *bhakti, namaskāra, prapatti.*

***prāṇatyāga:* प्राणत्याग** "Abandoning life force." A term for suicide but without the connotation of violence expressed in the more common terms *svade-haghāta,* "murdering one's body," and *ātmaghāta,* "self-murder." See: *death, suicide.*

***Praṇava:* प्रणव** "Humming." The mantra *Aum,* denoting God as the Primal Sound. It can heard as the sound of one's own nerve system, like the sound of an electrical transformer or a swarm of bees. The meditator is taught to inwardly transform this sound into the inner light which lights the thoughts, and bask in this blissful consciousness. Praṇava is also known as the sound of the *nādanāḍī śakti.* See: *Aum, Śiva Consciousness.*

***prāṇāyāma:* प्राणायाम** "Breath control." See: *rāja yoga.*

prāṇic body: The subtle, life-giving sheath called *prāṇamaya kośa.* See: *kośa.*

***prapatti:* प्रपत्ति** "Throwing oneself down." *Bhakti*—total, unconditional submission to God, often coupled with the attitude of personal helplessness, self-effacement and resignation. A term especially used in Vaishṇavism to name a concept extremely central to virtually all Hindu schools. In Śaiva Siddhānta, *bhakti* is all important in the development of the soul and its release into spiritual maturity. The doctrine is perhaps best expressed in the teachings of the four Samayāchārya saints, who all shared a profound and mystical love of Śiva marked by 1) deep humility and self-effacement, admission of sin and weakness; 2) total surrender in God as the only true refuge and 3) a relationship of lover and beloved known as bridal mysticism, in which the devotee is the bride and Śiva the bridegroom. The practice of *yoga,* too, is an expression of love of God in Śaiva Siddhānta, and it is only with God's grace that success is achieved. Ṛishi Tirumular states: "Unless your heart melts in the sweet ecstasy of love—my Lord, my treasure-trove, you can never possess" *(Tirumantiram* 272). It is in this concept of the need for self-effacement and total surrender, *prapatti,* that the members of all sects merge in oneness, at the fulfillment of their individual paths. Similarly, they all meet in unity at the beginning of the path with the worship of Lord Gaṇeśa. See: *bhakti, grace, pāda, surrender.*

***prārabdha karma:* प्रारब्धकर्म** "Action that has been unleashed or aroused." See: *karma.*

***prasāda:* प्रसाद** "Clarity, brightness; grace." 1) The virtue of serenity and graciousness. 2) Food offered to the Deity or the *guru,* or the blessed remnants of such food. 3) Any propitiatory offering. See: *sacrament, Vīra Śaivism.*

***Praśna Upanishad:* प्रश्न उपनिषद्** Belongs to the *Atharva Veda* and is divided into six sections addressing six questions asked of sage Pippalāda by his disciples, regarding life, Realization and the *mantra Aum.*

praśnottaram: **प्रश्नोत्तरम्** "Question-answer *(praśna-uttaram).*" A term used in *Dancing with Śiva* for *catechism,* an interrogatory summation of religious doctrine.

Pratyabhijñā: **प्रत्यभिज्ञा** "Recognition or recollection," from "knowledge" *(jñāna)* which "faces" *(abhi)* the knower and toward which he eventually "turns" *(prati).* A concept of Kashmīr Śaivism which denotes the devotee's recognition, as a result of the *guru's* grace, of the Truth that ever was—that Śiva is indeed everywhere, and the soul is already united with Him.

Pratyabhijñā Darśana: **प्रत्यभिज्ञादर्शन** The philosophical name for Kashmīr Śaivism.

Pratyabhijñā Sūtra(s): **प्रत्यभिज्ञासूत्र** A foundational Kashmīr Śaiva scripture, 190 *sūtras.*

pratyāhāra: **प्रत्याहार** "Withdrawal." The drawing in of forces. In *yoga,* the withdrawal from external consciousness. (Also a synonym for *pralaya.)* See: *rāja yoga, mahāpralaya, meditation.*

prāyaśchitta: **प्रायश्चित्त** "Predominant thought or aim." Penance. Acts of atonement. See: *penance, pāpa, puṇya.*

prayojaka: **प्रयोजक** "Facilitator; employer; manager." A person who instigates, promotes. Also a name for a coordinator of religious outreach activities and literature distribution.

prāyopaveśa: **प्रायोपवेश** "Resolving to die through fasting." Self-willed death by fasting. See: *death, suicide.*

precede: To come before in time, importance, influence or rank.

precinct: An enclosed or delimited area. Also the grounds surrounding a religious edifice.

precursor: Forerunner. A person or thing that goes before.

Premaiva Śivamaya, Satyam eva Paraśivaḥ: **प्रेमैव शिवमय सत्यम् एव परशिवः** "God Śiva is immanent love and transcendent Reality." A Śaivite Hindu affirmation of faith. See: *affirmation.*

prenatal: Existing or occurring before physical birth, or relating to the time before birth. See: *saṁskāras of birth.*

preservation: The act of maintaining or protecting. One of the five cosmic powers. See: *Naṭarāja.*

preside: To be chairman at a gathering, in a position of authority within a group. To have charge of; to dominate.

Pretaloka: **प्रेतलोक** "World of the departed." The realm of the earth-bound souls. This lower region of Bhuvarloka is an astral duplicate of the physical world. See: *loka.*

prevail: To be strong and victorious; overcome all obstacles. To exist widely.

Primal Soul: The uncreated, original, perfect soul—Śiva Parameśvara—who emanates from Himself the inner and outer universes and an infinite plurality of individual souls whose essence is identical with His essence. God in His personal aspect as Lord and Creator, depicted in many forms: Naṭarāja by Śaivites, Vishṇu by Vaishṇavites, Devī by Śāktas. See: *Naṭarāja, Parameśvara.*

Primal Sound: In Hinduism, sound is the first manifestation, even before light, in the creative scheme of things. The Primal Sound is also known as *Praṇava,* the sound of the *mula mantra,* "Aum." See: *sound.*

Primal Substance: The fundamental energy and rarified form from which the manifest world in its infinite diversity is derived. See: *Parāśakti.*

principle: An essential truth, law or rule upon which others are based.

pristine: Pure, unspoiled; original condition.

procreation: The process of begetting offspring.

procurer: Provider.

progeny: Offspring, children; descendants.

prohibit (prohibition): To forbid or prevent by authority.

prominent: Conspicuous, noticeable at once. Widely known.

promiscuity: The state or character of engaging in sex indiscriminantly or with many persons.

prone: Tending or inclined toward.

pronged: Having one or several pointed ends.

propel: To push, impel, or drive forward.

prophecy: Divination. Act or practice of predicting the future.

propound: To set forth. To put forward for consideration.

protocol: Customs of proper etiquette and ceremony, especially in relation to religious or political dignitaries.

protrude: To jut out or project.

province: Sphere, area or division.

prow: The forward part of a ship; any similar projecting or leading part.

prudent: Careful. Showing wisdom and good judgment in practical matters.

psalm: A sacred hymn, song or poem.

psychic: "Of the psyche or soul." Sensitive to spiritual processes and energies. Inwardly or intuitively aware of nonphysical realities; able to use powers such as clairvoyance, clairaudience and precognition. Nonphysical, subtle; pertaining to the deeper aspects of man. See: *mysticism, odic.*

pūjā: पूजा "Worship, adoration." An Āgamic rite of worship performed in the home, temple or shrine, to the *mūrti, śrī pādukā,* or other consecrated object, or to a person, such as the *satguru.* Its inner purpose is to purify the atmosphere around the object worshiped, establish a connection with the inner worlds and invoke the presence of God, Gods or one's *guru.* During *pūjā,* the officiant *(pujārī)* recites various chants praising the Divine and beseeching divine blessings, while making offerings in accordance with established traditions. *Pūjā,* the worship of a *mūrti* through water, lights and flowers in temples and shrines, is the Āgamic counterpart of the Vedic *yajña* rite, in which offerings are conveyed through the sacred *homa* fire. These are the two great streams of adoration and communion in Hinduism. Central steps of *pūjā* include: 1) *āchamana,* water sipping for purification; 2) *Gaṇapati prārthanā,* prayers to Gaṇeśa; 3) *saṅkalpa,* declaration of intent; 4) *ghaṇṭā,* ringing bell, inviting *devas* and dismissing *asuras*; 5) *āvāhana,* inviting the Deity ; 6) *mantras* and *dhyāna,* meditating on the Deity; 7) *svāgata,* welcoming; 8) *namaskāra,* obeisance; 9) *arghyam,* water offerings; 10) *pradakshiṇa,* circumambulation; 11) *abhisheka,* bathing the *mūrti;* 12) *dhūpa,* incense-offering; 13) *dīpa,* offering lights; 14) *naivedya,* offering food; 15) *archana,* chanting holy names; 16) *āratī,* final offering of lights; 17) *prārthanā,* personal requests; 18) *visarjana,* dismissal-farewell. Also central are *prāṇāyāma* (breath control), *guru vandana* (adoration of the preceptor), *nyāsa* (empowerment through touching) and *mudrā* (mystic gestures). *Pūjā* offerings also include *pushpa* (flowers), *arghya* (water), *tāmbūla* (betel leaf) and *chandana* (sandalpaste). ***—ātmārtha pūjā:*** *Kāraṇa Āgama,* v. 2, states: *Ātmārtha cha parārtha cha pūjā dvividhamuchyate,* "Worship is two-fold: for the benefit of oneself and for the benefit of others." *Ātmārtha pūjā* is done for oneself and immediate family, usually at home in a private shrine. ***—parārtha pūjā:*** "*Pūjā* for others." *Parārtha pūjā* is public *pūjā,* performed by authorized or ordained priests in a public shrine or temple. See: *pujārī, yajña.*

pujārī: पुजारी "Worshiper." A general term for Hindu temple priests, as well as anyone performing *pūjā. Pujārī* (sometimes *pūjārī)* is the Hindi form of the Sanskṛit *pūjaka; pūsārī* in Tamil. *Archaka* is another term for priest used in the southern tradition. *Purohita* is a Smārta *brāhmin* priest who specializes in domestic rites. See: *pūjā.*

pulsate: To beat or throb in rhythm, as the heart.

pundit *(paṇḍita):* पण्डित A Hindu religious scholar or theologian, a man well versed in philosophy, liturgy, religious law and sacred science.

punarjanma: पुनर्जन्म "Reincarnation." From *punaḥ,* "again and again," and *janma,* "taking birth." See: *reincarnation.*

Puñjāb: पंजाब The area of ancient India between the Indus and Sutlej, below Kashmir. It is now divided between India and Pakistan. It was a center of Śaivism until Muslim invasions. The modern Indian state is 19,445 square miles in area with a population of 18 million.

punsavana: पुंसवन "Male rite; bringing forth a male." Traditional sacrament performed during early pregnancy in prayer of a son. See: *saṁskāras of birth.*

puṇya: पुण्य "Holy; virtuous; auspicious." 1) Good or righteous. 2) Meritorious action. 3) Merit earned through right thought, word and action. *Puṇya* includes all forms of doing good, from the simplest helpful deed to a lifetime of conscientious beneficence. Each act of *puṇya* carries its *karmic* consequence, *karmaphala,* "fruit of action"—the positive reward of actions, words and deeds that are in keeping with *dharma.* Awakened psychics who have developed clairvoyant sight can clearly see the *puṇya* accrued in the inner subconscious aura as a colorful, free-flowing, astral, light-energy, *prāṇic* substance. *Puṇya* is seen as light-hued, pastel colors, whereas its counterpart, *pāpa*, is seen as shades of darker colors which are usually static and immovable. These arrangements of the *pāpa* shades and *puṇya* hues are not unlike the free-expression paintings found in modern art. *Puṇya* colors produce inner contentment, deep joy, the feeling of security and fearlessness. *Pāpa* can be dissolved and *puṇya* created through penance *(prāyaśchitta)*, austerity *(tapas)* and good deeds *(sukṛityā)*. *Puṇya* is earned through virtuous living, following the multi-faceted laws of *dharma*. *Puṇya* depends on purity of acts according to various factors including 1) the *karma* and evolution of the individual, 2) degree of sacrifice and unselfish motivation and 3) time and place. For example, virtuous deeds, *sādhana*, *tapas* and penance have greater merit when performed in holy places and at auspicious times. The *Tirukural* (105) states that "Help rendered another cannot be measured by the extent of the assistance given. Its true measure is the worth of the recipient." In other words, a small act done for a great and worthy soul carries more *puṇya* that even a large act performed for a lesser person. (Opposite of *pāpa*.) See: *aura, karma, pāpa, penance.*

Purāṇa: पुराण "Ancient." Hindu folk narratives containing ethical and cosmological teachings relative to Gods, man and the world. They revolve around five subjects: primary creation, secondary creation, genealogy, cycles of time and history. There are 18 major *Purāṇas* which are designated as either Śaivite, Vaishṇavite or Śākta. See: *folk narratives, mythology.*

Pure Consciousness: See: *Parāśakti, Satchidānanda, tattva.*

purgatory: A state or place of temporary punishment or expiation. A hellish condition that is not eternal. *Purgatory* is actually more fitting than the term *hell* as an equivalent for the Sanskṛit *Naraka*. See: *hell, loka, Naraka.*

puritan: A person who is overly strict or rigid regarding morals and religion.

purity-impurity: *Śaucha-aśaucha.* Purity and its opposite, pollution, are a fundamental part of Hindu culture. While they imply a strong sense of physical cleanliness, their more important meanings extend to social, ceremonial, mental, emotional, psychic and spiritual contamination. Freedom from all forms of contamination is a key to Hindu spirituality, and is one of the *yamas*. Physical purity requires a clean and well-ordered environment, *yogic* purging of the internal organs and frequent cleansing with water. Mental purity derives from meditation, right living and right thinking. Emotional purity depends on control of the mind, clearing the subconscious and keeping good company. Spiritual purity is achieved through following the *yamas* and *niyamas*, study of the *Vedas* and other scriptures, pilgrimage, meditation, *jāpa, tapas* and *ahiṁsā*. Ritual purity requires the observance of certain *prāyaśchittas*, or penances, for defilement derived from foreign travel, contact with base people or places, conversion to other faiths, contact with bodily wastes, attending a funeral, etc. Purity is of three forms—purity in mind, speech and body, or thought, word and deed. Purity is the pristine and natural state of the soul. Impurity, or pollution, is the obscuring of this state by adulterating experience and beclouding conceptions. In daily life, the Hindu strives to protect this innate purity by wise living, following the codes of *dharma.* This includes harnessing the sexual energies, associating with other virtuous Hindu devotees, never using harsh, angered or indecent language, and keeping a clean and healthy physical body. See: *dharma, pāpa, penance, puṇya, yama-niyama.*

pūrṇimā: **पूर्णिमा** "Full." Full moon. See: *Guru Pūrṇimā.*

purohita: **पुरोहित** "Front-most; leader; family priest." A Smārta *brāhmin* priest who specializes in home ceremonies. See: *Smārta, pujārī.*

pursue (pursuit): To go with determination after a goal. To follow.

purusha: **पुरुष** "The spirit that dwells in the body/in the universe." Person; spirit; man. Metaphysically, the soul, neither male nor female. Also used in Yoga and Sāṅkhya for the transcendent Self. A synonym for *ātman. Purusha* can also refer to the Supreme Being or Soul, as it sometimes does in the *Upanishads.* In the *Ṛig Veda* hymn "Purusha Sūkta," Purusha is the cosmic man, having a thousand heads, a thousand eyes, a thousand feet and encompassing the earth, spreading in all directions into animate and inanimate things. In the Sāṅkhya system, *purusha* is one of two supreme, beginningless realities: spirit and matter, *purusha* and *prakṛiti,* the male and female principles. It is the quiescent unmanifest, pure consciousness, contrasted with *Prakṛiti,* the manifesting, primal nature from which the cosmos unfolds. In Śaiva cosmology, *purusha* is the 25th of 36 *tattvas,* one level subtler than *prakṛiti.* Beyond these lie the subtle realms of *śuddha māyā.* Transcending all the *tattvas* is Paraśiva. See: *ātman, jīva, prakṛiti, soul, tattva.*

purusha dharma: **पुरुषधर्म** "A man's code of duty and conduct." See: *dharma.*

purushārtha: **पुरुषार्थ** "Human wealth or purpose." The four pursuits in which humans may legitimately engage, also called *chaturvarga,* "four-fold good"—a basic principle of Hindu ethics. ***—dharma:*** "Righteous living." The fulfillment of virtue, good works, duties and responsibilities, restraints and observances—performing one's part in the service and upliftment of society. This includes pursuit of truth under a *guru* of a particular *paramparā* and *sampradāya. Dharma* is of four primary forms. It is the steady guide for *artha* and *kāma.* See: *dharma.* ***—artha:*** "Wealth." Material welfare and abundance, money, property, possessions. *Artha* is the pursuit of wealth, guided by *dharma.* It includes the basic needs—food, money, clothing and shelter—and extends to the wealth required to maintain a comfortable home, raise a family, fulfill a successful career and perform religious duties. The broadest concept of wealth embraces financial independence, freedom from debt, worthy children, good friends, leisure time, faithful servants, trustworthy employees, and the joys of giving, including tithing (*daśamāmsha),* feeding the poor, supporting religious mendicants, worshiping devoutly, protecting all creatures, upholding the family and offering hospitality to guests. *Artha* measures not only riches but quality of life, providing the personal and social security needed to pursue *kāma, dharma* and *moksha.* It allows for the fulfillment of the householder's five daily sacrifices, *pañcha mahāyajña:* to God, ancestors, *devas,* creatures and men. See: *yajña.* **—*kāma:*** "Pleasure, love; enjoyment." Earthly love, aesthetic and cultural fulfillment, pleasures of the world (including sexual), the joys of family, intellectual satisfaction. Enjoyment of happiness, security, creativity, usefulness and inspiration. See: *Kāma Sūtras.* **—*moksha:*** "Liberation." Freedom from rebirth through the ultimate attainment, realization of the Self God, Paraśiva. The spiritual attainments and superconscious joys, attending renunciation and *yoga* leading to Self Realization. *Moksha* comes through the fulfillment of *dharma, artha* and *kāma* (known in Tamil as *aram, porul* and *inbam,* and explained by Tiruvalluvar in *Tirukural)* in the current or past lives, so that one is no longer attached to worldly joys or sorrows. It is the supreme goal of life, called *paramārtha.* See: *liberation, moksha.*

qualified nondualism: See: *Viśishṭādvaita.*

quantum: Quantity or amount. In science's quantum theory: a fixed basic unit, usually of energy. **—quantum particles of light:** Light understood not as a continuum, but as traveling bundles each of a same intensity. Deeper still, these particles originate and resolve themselves in a one divine energy. **—at the quantum level (of the mind):** Deep within the mind, at a subtle energy level. See: *apex of creation, microcosm-macrocosm, tattva.*

quell: To put an end to, subdue or make quiet.

race: Technically speaking, each of the five races of man (Caucasoid, Congoid, Mongoloid, Australoid and Capoid) is a *Homo sapiens* subspecies. A subspecies is a branch showing slight but significant differences from another branch living in a different area. Few traits are unique to any one race. It is the combination of several traits that indicate racial identity. Accurate race determination can be made by blood analysis or by measuring and comparing certain body dimensions. Ninety-eight percent of all Hindus belong to the Caucasoid race. There are also large numbers of Hindu Mongoloids in Nepal and Assam and some Australoids, such as the Gond and Bhil tribes of India. North and South Indians are among Earth's 2.5 billion Caucasoids, whose traits include straight to wavy hair, thin lips, small to medium teeth, blue to dark brown eyes and a high incident of A_2-Rh and Gm blood genes. Skin color, often erroneously attached to the idea of race, is now known to be adaptation to climate: over generations, people in northern climates have developed lighter complexions than their southern brothers.

Rādhākrishnan, Dr. S.: **राधाकृष्णन्** (1888-1975) The president of India from 1962 to 1967, a scholar, philosopher, prolific writer, compelling speaker and effective spokesman of Hinduism. Along with Vivekānanda, Tagore, Aurobindo and others, he helped bring about the current Hindu revival. He made Hinduism better known and appreciated at home and abroad, especially in the intellectual world. He was a foremost proponent of panentheism. See: *Vedānta.*

rage: Uncontrolled anger. Fuming fit of fury. See: *vitala chakra.*

Rāhu: **राहु** "The seizer." In Hindu astrology, Rāhu is one of the nine important planets *(graha),* but is an invisible or "astral" one, along with its counterpart, Ketu. Physically speaking, it is one of two points in the heavens where the moon crosses the ecliptic or path of the sun. The point where the moon crosses the ecliptic moving from south to north is Rāhu, the north node. The south node is Ketu. Rāhu and Ketu are depicted as a serpent demon who encircles the earth. Ketu is the dragon's tail and Rāhu is the head. Both are believed to cause general consternation among people. See: *jyotisha.*

rājanya: **राजन्य** "Ruling." A synonym for *kshatriya.* See: *varṇa dharma.*

rajas: **रजस्** "Passion; activity." See: *guṇa.*

rāja yoga: **राजयोग** "King of *yogas.*" Also known as *ashṭāṅga yoga,* "eight-limbed *yoga.*" The classical *yoga* system of eight progressive stages to Illumination as described in various *yoga Upanishads,* the *Tirumantiram* and, most notably, the *Yoga Sūtras* of Patañjali. The eight limbs are as follows. 1) ***—yama:*** "Restraint." Virtuous and moral living, which brings purity of mind, freedom from anger, jealousy and subconscious confusion which would inhibit the process of meditation. 2) ***—niyama***: "Observance." Religious practices which cultivate the qualities of the higher nature, such as devotion, cognition, humility and contentment—giving the refinement of nature and control of mind needed to concentrate and ultimately plunge into *samādhi.* 3) ***—āsana:*** "Seat or posture." A sound body is needed for success in meditation. This is attained through *haṭha yoga,* the postures of which balance the energies of mind and body, promoting health and serenity, e.g., *padmāsana,* the "lotus pose," for meditation. The *Yoga Sūtras* indicate that *āsanas* make the *yogī* impervious to the impact of the pairs of opposites *(ḍvanḍva),* heat-cold, etc. 4) ***—prāṇāyāma:*** "Mastering life force." Breath control, which quiets the *chitta* and balances *iḍā* and *piṅgalā.* Science of controlling *prāṇa* through breathing techniques in which lengths of inhalation, retention and exhalation are modulated. *Prāṇāyāma* prepares the mind for deep meditation. 5) ***—pratyāhāra:*** "Withdrawal." The practice of withdrawing consciousness from the physical senses first, such as not hearing noise while meditating, then progressively receding from emotions, intellect and eventually from individual consciousness itself in order to merge into the Universal. 6) ***—dhāraṇā:*** "Concentration." Focusing the mind on a single object or line of thought, not allowing it to wander. The guiding of the flow of consciousness. When concentration is sustained long and deeply enough, meditation naturally follows. 7) —***dhyāna:*** "Meditation." A quiet, alert, powerfully concentrated state wherein new knowledge and insight pour into the field of consciousness. This state is possible once the subconscious mind has been cleared or quieted. 8) —***samādhi:*** "Enstasy," which means "standing within one's self." "Sameness, contemplation." The state of true *yoga,* in which the meditator and the object of meditation are one. See: *āsana, samādhi, yoga.*

Rāma: **राम** Venerated hero of the *Rāmāyaṇa* epic, and one of the two most popular incarnations of Vishṇu, along with Kṛishṇa. His worship is almost universal among Vaishṇavas, and extensive among Smārtas and other liberal Hindus. He was a great worshiper of Śiva, and a Śiva temple, called Rāmeśvaram, was built in his name at the southern tip of India.

Rāmakaṇṭha I: **रामकण्ठ** A great exponent of Śaiva Siddhānta, ca 950. In the lineage of Aghoraśiva.

Rāmakaṇṭha II: **रामकण्ठ** Great exponent of Śaiva Siddhānta, ca 1150. Aghoraśiva's teacher.

Rāmakṛishṇa: **रामकृष्ण** (1836–1886) One of the great saints and mystics of modern Hinduism, and an exemplar of monistic theism—fervent devotee of Mother Kālī and staunch monist who taught oneness and the pursuit of *nirvikalpa samādhi,* realization of the Absolute. He was *guru* to the great Swāmī Vivekānanda (1863–1902), who internationalized Hindu thought and philosophy.

Rāmānuja: **रामानुज** Philosopher (1017–1137), saint, great *bhakta,* founder of one of five major Vaishṇava schools, and considered the greatest critic of *advaita.* In his famous *Śrī Bhāshya* on the *Brahma Sūtras,* he countered Śaṅkara's absolute monism point-by-point with his qualified monism, called *Viśishṭādvaiṭa Vedānta.* See: *shaḍ darśana, Vedānta.*

Rāmarāja: **रामराज** (1478–1565). The last king of South India's Vijayanagara empire.

Rāmāyaṇa: **रामायण** "Life of Rāma." One of India's two grand epics *(Itihāsa)* along with the *Mahābhārata.* It is Valmiki's tragic love story of Rāma and Sītā, whose exemplary lives have helped set high standards of dignity and nobility as an integral part of Hindu *dharma.* Astronomical data in the story puts Rāma's reign at about 2015 BCE. See: *Rāma.*

Rāmprasād: **रामप्रसाद्** Great Bengali devotional saint-poet (1718–1775) who wrote hymns to Śakti.

rasātala: **रसातल** "Subterranean region." The fifth *chakra* below the *mūlādhāra,* centered in the ankles. Corresponds to the fifth astral netherworld beneath the earth's surface, called Ṛijīsha ("expelled") or Rasātala. Region of selfishness, self-centeredness and possessiveness. *Rasā* means "earth, soil; moisture." See: *chakra, loka, Naraka.*

rationalize: To excuse through reason. To make plausible explanations for.

***Raurava Āgama:* रौरव आगम** Among the 28 *Śaiva Siddhānta Āgamas,* this scripture was conveyed by Lord Śiva to sage Ruru (hence the name). Its extensive *kriyā pāda* section details the structure of the Śiva temple and its annexes.

***Rāvaṇa:* रावण** Villain of the *Rāmāyaṇa* epic. A legendary king of Sri Lanka, adversary of Rāma, eventually defeated by Rāma and his armies.

reabsorption (reabsorb): Taking in again, as water is squeezed from and then drawn back into a sponge. See: *cosmic cycle, mahāpralaya, pralaya.*

reaction: A response to an action.

reaffirmation: A new affirming or a declaration about a thing as being true or still pertinent. See: *affirmation.*

reality: See: *Absolute Reality, relative.*

realm: A kingdom, region or area. See: *loka.*

reap: To cut for harvest. To gain as a result of actions or effort.

rebellious: Resisting authority or any form of control.

rebound: To bounce back.

recluse: A person who retreats from the world and lives in seclusion.

reconcile (reconciliation): To settle or resolve, as a dispute. To make consistent or compatible, e.g., two conflicting ideas.

redeem: To recover, to set free from penalty or deliver from sin. **—redemption:** Act of redeeming. See: *absolution, penance.*

reembody: To come into a body again. To reincarnate.

reincarnation: "Re-entering the flesh." *Punarjanma;* metempsychosis. The process wherein souls take on a physical body through the birth process. Reincarnation is one of the fundamental principles of Hindu spiritual insight, shared by the mystical schools of nearly all religions, including Jainism, Sikhism, Buddhism (and even by Christianity until it was cast out by the Nicene Council in 787). It is against the backdrop of this principle of the soul's enjoying many lives that other aspects of Hinduism can be understood. It is a repetitive cycle, known as *punarjanma,* which originates in the subtle plane (Antarloka), the realm in which souls live between births and return to after death. Here they are assisted in readjusting to the "in-between" world and eventually prepared for yet another birth. The quality and nature of the birth depends on the merit or demerit of their past actions *(karma)* and on the needs of their unique pattern of development and experience *(dharma).* The mother, the father and the soul together create a new body for the soul. At the moment of conception, the soul connects with and is irrevocably bound to the embryo. As soon as the egg is fertilized, the process of human life begins. It is during the mid-term of pregnancy that the full humanness of the fetus is achieved and the soul fully inhabits the new body, a stage which is acknowledged when the child begins to move and kick within the mother's womb. (*Tirumantiram,* 460: "There in the pregnant womb, the soul lay in primordial quiescence [*turīya*] state. From that state, Māyā [or Prakṛiti] and Her tribe aroused it and conferred consciousness and *māyā's* evolutes eight—desires and the rest. Thus say scriptures holy and true.") Finally, at birth the soul emerges into earth consciousness, veiled of all memory of past lives and the inner worlds. The cycle of reincarnation ends when *karma* has been resolved and the Self God (Paraśiva) has been realized. This condition of release is called *moksha*. Then the soul continues to evolve and mature, but without the need to return to physical existence. How many earthly births must one have to attain the unattainable? Many thousands to be sure, hastened by righteous living, *tapas*, austerities on all levels, penance and good deeds in abundance. See: *evolution of the soul, karma, moksha, nonhuman birth, saṁsāra, soul.*

relative: Quality or object which is meaningful only in relation to something else. Not absolute. —**relative reality:** *Māyā*. That which is ever changing and changeable. Describes the nature of manifest existence, indicating that it is not an illusion but is also not Absolute Reality, which is eternal and unchanging. See: *Absolute Reality, māyā.*

religion: From Latin *religare*, "to bind back." Any system which advocates the belief in and worship of a Supreme Being or Power. Religion is a structured vehicle for soul advancement which often includes theology, scripture, spiritual and moral practices, priesthood and liturgy. See: *Hinduism.*

relinquish: To give up, let go of or abandon. See: *sacrifice, tyāga.*

remorse: Deep, painful regret or guilt over a wrong one has done. Moral anguish. See: *absolution, hrī, penance.*

remote: Distant, secluded; hidden away or difficult to reach.

renaissance: "Rebirth or new birth." A renewal, revival or reawakening.

render: To cause to be or to become.

renowned: Famous.

renunciation: See: *sannyāsa, tyāga, vairāgya.*

Reṇukāchārya: रेणुकाचार्य A Vīra Śaiva philosopher and saint.

replenish: To fill up or cause to be full again.

repose: To rest peacefully. —**to repose in one's realization:** To cease outward activity and enjoy communion with the Divine.

repudiation: The act of publicly rejecting a thing, habit or way of being.

rescind: To cancel or revoke.

resemble: To look like, or have similar traits and qualities.

resent (resentment): A feeling of ill-will, indignation or hostility from a sense of having been wronged.

residue: Remainder. That which is left over after a process.

resplendence: Radiance; brilliance.

restive: Nervous, unruly, eager to go forward; hard to control.

restraints: See: *yama-niyama.*

retaliation: Paying back an injury, returning like for like, hurt for hurt. Getting even; vengeance.

revealing grace: See: *anugraha śakti, grace.*

rigorous: Very strict or severe.

Ṛig Veda: ऋग्वेद् "*Veda* of verse *(ṛik).*" The first and oldest of the four *Veda* compendia of revealed scriptures *(śruti),* including a hymn collection *(Saṁhitā),* priestly explanatory manuals *(Brāhmaṇas),* forest treatises *(Āraṇyakas)* elaborating on the Vedic rites, and philosophical dialogs *(Upanishads).* Like the other *Vedas,* the *Ṛig Veda* was brought to earth consciousness not all at once, but gradually, over a period of perhaps several thousand years. The oldest and core portion is the *Saṁhitā,* believed to date back, in its oral form, as far as 8,000 years, and to have been written down in archaic Sanskṛit some 3,000 years ago. It consists of more than 10,000 verses, averaging three or four lines *(ṛiks),* forming 1,028 hymns *(sūktas),* organized in ten books called *maṇḍalas.* It embodies prayerful hymns of praise and invocation to the Divinities of nature and to the One Divine. They are the spiritual reflections of a pastoral people with a profound awe for the powers of nature, each of which they revered as sacred and alive. The *ṛishis* who unfolded these outpourings of adoration perceived a well-ordered cosmos in which *dharma* is the way of attunement with celestial worlds, from which all righteousness and prosperity descends. The main concern is man's relationship with God and the world, and the invocation of the subtle worlds into mundane existence. Prayers beseech the Gods for happy family life, wealth, pleasure, cattle, health, protection from enemies, strength in battle, matrimony, progeny, long life and happiness, wisdom and realization and final liberation from rebirth. The *Ṛig Veda Saṁhitā,* which in length equals Homer's *Iliad* and *Odyssey* combined, is the most important hymn collection, for it lends a large number of its hymns to the other three *Veda Saṁhitās* (the *Sāma, Yajur* and *Atharva).* Chronologically, after the *Saṁhitās* came the *Brāhmaṇas,* followed by the *Āraṇyakas,* and finally the *Upanishads,* also called the *Vedānta,* meaning "*Veda's* end." See: *śruti, Vedas.*

ṛishi: ऋषि "Seer." A term for an enlightened being, emphasizing psychic perception and visionary wisdom. In the Vedic age, *ṛishis* lived in forest or mountain retreats, either alone or with disciples. These *ṛishis* were great souls who were the inspired conveyers of the *Vedas.* Seven particular *ṛishis* (the *sapta-ṛishis)* mentioned in the *Ṛig Veda* are said to still guide mankind from the inner worlds. See: *śṛuti.*

ṛita: ऋत "Sacred order, cosmic law; truth." See: *dharma.*

rite (or ritual): A religious ceremony. See: *sacrament, sacrifice, saṁskāra.*

rites of passage: Sacraments marking crucial stages of life. See: *saṁskāra.*

ṛitukāla: ऋतुकाल "Fit or proper season." Time of menses. A traditional ceremony marking a young lady's coming of age. *Ṛitu* also carries the meaning of "fertile time." See: *saṁskāras of adulthood.*

Rudra: **रुद्र** "Controller of terrific powers;" or "red, shining one." The name of Śiva as the God of dissolution, the universal force of reabsorption. *Rudra-Śiva* is revered both as the "terrifying one" and the "lord of tears," for He wields and controls the terrific powers which may cause lamentation among humans. See: *Naṭarāja.*

rudrāksha: **रुद्राक्ष** "Eye of Rudra; or red-eyed." Refers to the third eye, or *ājñā chakra.* Marble-sized, multi-faced, reddish-brown seeds from the *Eleocarpus ganitrus,* or blue marble tree, which are sacred to Śiva and a symbol of His compassion for humanity. Garlands, *rudrāksha mālā,* of larger seeds are worn around the neck by monks, and nonmonastics often wear a single bead on a cord at the throat. Smaller beads (usually numbering 108) are strung together for *japa* (recitation). See: *japa, mantra.*

Rudraśambhu: **रुद्रशम्भु** Principal *guru* in the Āmardaka order of Śaiva monastics, about 775 in Ujjain, one of Śaivism's holiest cities. The sect served as advisors to the king until Muslim domination around 1300.

Rudrāyamala Tantra: **रुद्रयामलतन्त्र** Little known text dealing with worship.

śabda kośa: **शब्दकोश** "Sheath of sounds, or words." Vocabulary; a dictionary or glossary of terms.

sacrament: 1) Holy rite, especially one solemnized in a formal, consecrated manner which is a bonding between the recipient and God, Gods or *guru.* This includes rites of passage *(saṁskāra),* ceremonies sanctifying crucial events or stages of life. 2) *Prasāda.* Sacred substances, grace-filled gifts, blessed in sacred ceremony or by a holy person. See: *prasāda, saṁskāra.*

sacred thread: *Yajñopavīta.* See: *upanayana.*

sacrifice: *Yajña.* 1) Giving offerings to a Deity as an expression of homage and devotion. 2) Giving up something, often one's own possession, advantage or preference, to serve a higher purpose. The literal meaning of *sacrifice* is "to make sacred," implying an act of worship. It is the most common translation of the term *yajña,* from the verb *yuj,* "to worship." In Hinduism, all of life is a sacrifice—called *jīvayajña,* a giving of oneself—through which comes true spiritual fulfillment. *Tyāga,* the power of detachment, is an essential quality of true sacrifice. See: *tyāga, yajña.*

sadāchāra: **सदाचार** "Good conduct; virtue, morality." It is embodied in the principles of *dharma.* See: *dharma, yama-niyama, pāda.*

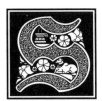

Sadāśiva: **सदाशिव** "Ever-auspicious." A name of the Primal Soul, Śiva, a synonym for Parameśvara, which is expressed in the physical being of the *satguru. Sadāśiva* especially denotes the power of revealing grace, *anugraha śakti,* the third *tattva,* after which emerge Śiva's other four divine powers. This five-fold manifestation or expression of God's activity in the cosmos is depicted in Hindu *mantras,* literature and art as the five-faced Sadāśivamūrti. Looking upward is Īśāna, "ruler" (the power of revealment). Facing east is Tatpurusha, "supreme soul" (the power of obscuration). Westward-looking is Sadyojāta, "quickly birthing" (the power of creation). Northward is Vāmadeva, "lovely, pleasing" (the power of preservation). Southward is Aghora, "nonterrifying" (the power of reabsorption). The first four faces revealed the *Vedas.* The fifth face, Īśana, revealed the *Āgamas.* These five are also called Sadāśiva, the revealer; Maheśvara, the obscurer; Brahmā, the creator; Vishṇu, the preserver; and Rudra, the destroyer. See: *Parameśvara, tattva.*

sādhaka: **साधक** "Accomplished one; a devotee who performs *sādhana.*" A serious aspirant who has undertaken spiritual disciplines, is usually celibate and under the guidance of a *guru.* He wears white and may be under vows, but is not a *sannyāsin.* See: *sādhana.*

sādhana: **साधन** "Effective means of attainment." Religious or spiritual disciplines, such as *pūjā, yoga,* meditation, *japa,* fasting and austerity. The effect of *sādhana* is the building of willpower, faith and confidence in oneself and in God, Gods and *guru. Sādhana* harnesses and transmutes the instinctive-intellectual nature, allowing progressive spiritual unfoldment into the superconscious realizations and innate abilities of the soul. See: *purity-impurity, pāda, rāja yoga, sādhana mārga, spiritual unfoldment.*

sādhana mārga: **साधनमार्ग** "The way of *sādhana.*" A term used by Sage Yogaswāmī to name his prescription for seekers of Truth—a path of intense effort, spiritual discipline and consistent inner transformation, as opposed to theoretical and intellectual learning. See: *mysticism, pāda, sādhana, spiritual unfoldment.*

sādhu: **साधु** "Virtuous one; straight, unerring." A holy person dedicated to the search for God. A *sādhu* may or may not be a *yogī* or a *sannyāsin,* or be connected in any way with a *guru* or legitimate lineage. *Sādhus* usually have no fixed abode and travel unattached from place to place, often living on alms. There are countless *sādhus* on the roads, byways, mountains, riverbanks, and in the *āśramas* and caves of India. They have, by their very existence, a profound, stabilizing effect on the consciousness of India and the world. See: *vairāgī.*

sādhvī: **साध्वी** Feminine counterpart of *sādhu.* See: *sādhu.*

Saguṇa Brahman: **सगुणब्रह्मन्** "God with qualities." The Personal Lord. See: *Brahman, Parameśvara.*

sahasra lekhana sādhana: **सहस्रलेखनसाधन** "Thousand-times writing discipline." The spiritual practice of writing a sacred *mantra* 1,008 times.

sahasrāra chakra: **सहस्रारचक्र** "Thousand-spoked wheel." The cranial psychic force center. See: *chakra.*

Śaiva: **शैव** Of or relating to Śaivism or its adherents, of whom there are about 400 million in the world today. Same as *Śaivite.* See: *Śaivism.*

Śaiva Āgamas: **शैव आगम** The sectarian revealed scriptures of the *Śaivas.*

Strongly theistic, they identify Śiva as the Supreme Lord, immanent and transcendent. They are in two main divisions: the 64 *Kashmīr Śaiva Āgamas* and the 28 *Śaiva Siddhānta Āgamas.* The latter group are the fundamental sectarian scriptures of Śaiva Siddhānta. Of these, ten are of the *Śivabheda* division and are considered dualistic: 1) *Kāmika,* 2) *Yogaja,* 3) *Chintya,* 4) *Kāraṇa,* 5) *Ajita,* 6) *Dīpta,* 7) *Sūkshma,* 8) *Sāhasraka,* 9) *Amśumat* and 10) *Suprabheda.* There are 18 in the *Rudrabheda* group, classed as dual-nondual: 11) *Vijaya,* 12) *Niḥśvāsa,* 13) *Svāyambhuva,* 14) *Aṇala,* 15) *Vīra (Bhadra),* 16) *Raurava,* 17) *Makuṭa,* 18) *Vimala,* 19) *Chandrajñāna* (or *Chandrahāsa),* 20) *Mukhabimba* (or *Bimba),* 21) *Prodgītā* (or *Udgītā),* 22) *Lalita,* 23) *Siddha,* 24) *Santāna,* 25) *Sarvokta (Narasiṁha),* 26) *Parameśvara,* 27) *Kiraṇa* and 28) *Vātula* (or *Parahita).* Ṛishi Tirumular, in his *Tirumantiram,* refers to 28 *Āgamas* and mentions nine by name. Eight of these—*Kāraṇa, Kāmika, Vīra, Chintya, Vātula, Vimala, Suprabheda* and *Makuṭa*—are in the above list of 28 furnished by the French Institute of Indology, Pondicherry. The ninth, *Kalottāra,* is presently regarded as an *Upāgama,* or secondary text, of *Vātula.* The *Kāmika* is the *Āgama* most widely followed in Tamil Śaiva temples, because of the availability of Aghoraśiva's manual-commentary *(paddhati)* on it. Vīra Śaivites especially refer to the *Vātula* and *Vīra Āgamas.* The *Śaiva Āgama* scriptures, above all else, are the connecting strand through all the schools of Śaivism. The *Āgamas* themselves express that they are entirely consistent with the teachings of the *Veda,* that they contain the essence of the *Veda,* and must be studied with the same high degree of devotion. See: *Āgamas, Vedas.*

Śaiva Siddhānta: **शैवसिद्धान्त** "Final conclusions of Śaivism." The most widespread and influential Śaivite school today, predominant especially among the Tamil people in Sri Lanka and South India. It is the formalized theology of the divine revelations contained in the twenty-eight *Śaiva Āgamas.* The first known *guru* of the Śuddha ("pure") Śaiva Siddhānta tradition was Maharishi Nandinātha of Kashmir (ca BCE 250), recorded in Pāṇini's book of grammar as the teacher of *ṛishis* Patañjali, Vyāghrapāda and Vasishṭha. Other sacred scriptures include the *Tirumantiram* and the voluminous collection of devotional hymns, the *Tirumurai,* and the masterpiece on ethics and statecraft, the *Tirukural.* For Śaiva Siddhāntins, Śiva is the totality of all, understood in three perfections: Parameśvara (the Personal Creator Lord), Parāśakti (the substratum of form) and Paraśiva (Absolute Reality which transcends all). Souls and world are identical in essence with Śiva, yet also differ in that they are evolving. A pluralistic stream arose in the middle ages from the teachings of Aghoraśiva and Meykandar. For Aghoraśiva's school (ca 1150) Śiva is not the material cause of the universe, and the soul attains perfect "sameness" with Śiva upon liberation. Meykandar's (ca 1250) pluralistic school denies that souls ever attain perfect sameness or unity with Śiva. See: *Śaivism.*

Śaiva Viśishṭādvaita: शैवविशिष्टाद्वैत The philosophy of Śiva Advaita. See: *Śiva Advaita.*

Śaivism (Śaiva): शैव The religion followed by those who worship Śiva as supreme God. Oldest of the four sects of Hinduism. The earliest historical evidence of Śaivism is from the 8,000-year-old Indus Valley civilization in the form of the famous seal of Śiva as Lord Paśupati, seated in a *yogic* pose. In the *Rāmāyaṇa,* dated astronomically at 2000 BCE, Lord Rāma worshiped Śiva, as did his rival Rāvaṇa. Buddha in 624 BCE was born into a Śaivite family, and records of his time speak of the Śaiva ascetics who wandered the hills looking much as they do today. There are many schools of Śaivism, six of which are Śaiva Śiddhānta, Pāśupata Śaivism, Kashmīr Śaivism, Vīra Śaivism, Siddha Siddhānta and Śiva Advaita. They are based firmly on the *Vedas* and *Śaiva Āgamas,* and thus have much in common, including the following principle doctrines: 1) the five powers of Śiva—creation, preservation, destruction, revealing and concealing grace; 2) The three categories: Pati, *paśu* and *pāśa* ("God, souls and bonds"); 3) the three bonds: *āṇava, karma* and *māyā;* 4) the three-fold power of Śiva: *icçhā śakti, kriyā śakti* and *jñāna śakti;* 5) the thirty-six *tattvas,* or categories of existence; 6) the need for initiation from a *satguru;* 7) the power of *mantra;* 8) the four *pādas* (stages): *charyā* (selfless service), *kriyā* (devotion), *yoga* (meditation), and *jñāna* (illumination); 9) the belief in the Pañchākshara as the foremost *mantra,* and in *rudrāksha* and *vibhūti* as sacred aids to faith; 10) the beliefs in *satguru* (preceptor), Śivaliṅga (object of worship) and *saṅgama* (company of holy persons). See: *individual school entries, Śaivism (six schools).*

Śaivism (six schools): Through history Śaivism has developed a vast array of lineages. Philosophically, six schools are most notable: Śaiva Siddhānta, Pāśupata Śaivism, Kashmīr Śaivism, Vīra Śaivism, Siddha Siddhānta and Śiva Advaita. Śaiva Siddhānta first distinguished itself in the second century BCE through the masterful treatise of a Himalayan pilgrim to South India, Ṛishi Tirumular. It is Śaivism's most widespread and influential school. Pāśupata Śaivism emerged in the Himalayan hills over 25 centuries ago. Ancient writings chronicle it as a Śiva ascetic *yoga* path whose most renowned *guru* was Lakulīśa. Kashmīr Śaivism, a strongly monistic lineage, arose from the revelatory aphorisms of Śrī Vasugupta in the tenth century. Vīra Śaivism took shape in India's Karnataka state in the 12th-century under the inspiration of Śrī Basavaṇṇa. It is a dynamic, reformist sect, rejecting religious complexity and stressing each devotee's personal relationship with God. Siddha Siddhānta, also known as Gorakshanātha Śaivism, takes its name from the writings of the powerful 10th-century *yogī,* Śrī Gorakshanātha, whose techniques for Śiva identity attracted a large monastic and householder following in North India and Nepal. Śiva Advaita is a Śaivite interpretation of the Vedānta Sūtras, based on the writings of Śrikaṇṭha, a 12th-century scholar who sought to reconcile the *Upanishads* with the

Āgamas. See: *individual school entries.*

Śaivite (Śaiva): शैव Of or relating to Śaivism or its adherents, of whom there are about 400 million in the world today. See: *Śaivism.*

śākāhāra: शाकाहार "Vegetarian diet." From *śāka,* "vegetable;" and *āhāra,* "eating; taking food." See: *meat-eater, vegetarian, yama-niyama.*

sakhā mārga: सखामार्ग "Friend's path." See: *attainment, pāda.*

sākshin: साक्षिन् "Witness." Awareness, the witness consciousness of the soul. Known as *nef* in the mystical Nātha language of Shum. See: *awareness, consciousness (individual), chit, Shum, soul.*

Śākta: शाक्त Of or relating to *Śāktism.* See: *Śāktism.*

Śākta Tantrism: शक्ततन्त्र See: *tantrism.*

Śakti: शक्ति "Power, energy." The active power or manifest energy of Śiva that pervades all of existence. Its most refined aspect is Parāśakti, or Satchidānanda, the pure consciousness and primal substratum of all form. This pristine, divine energy unfolds as *icçhā śakti* (the power of desire, will, love), *kriyā śakti* (the power of action) and *jñāna śakti* (the power of wisdom, knowing), represented as the three prongs of Śiva's *triśūla,* or trident. From these arise the five powers of revealment, concealment, dissolution, preservation and creation.

In Śaiva Siddhānta, Śiva is All, and His divine energy, Śakti, is inseparable from Him. This unity is symbolized in the image of Ardhanārīśvara, "half-female God." In popular, village Hinduism, the unity of Śiva and Śakti is replaced with the concept of Śiva and Śakti as separate entities. Śakti is represented as female, and Śiva as male. In Hindu temples, art and mythology, they are everywhere seen as the divine couple. This depiction has its source in the folk-narrative sections of the *Purāṇas,* where it is given elaborate expression. Śakti is personified in many forms as the consorts of the Gods. For example, the Goddesses Pārvatī, Lakshmī and Sarasvatī are the respective mythological consorts of Śiva, Vishṇu and Brahmā. Philosophically, however, the caution is always made that God and God's energy are One, and the metaphor of the inseparable divine couple serves only to illustrate this Oneness.

Within the Śākta religion, the worship of the Goddess is paramount, in Her many fierce and benign forms. Śakti is the Divine Mother of manifest creation, visualized as a female form, and Śiva is specifically the Unmanifest Absolute. The fierce or black *(asita)* forms of the Goddess include Kālī, Durgā, Chaṇḍī, Chamuṇḍī, Bhadrakālī and Bhairavī. The benign or white *(sita)* forms include Umā, Gaurī, Ambikā, Pārvatī, Maheśvarī, Lalitā and Annapūrṇā. As Rājarājeśvarī ("divine queen of kings"), She is the presiding Deity of the Śrī Chakra *yantra.* She is also worshiped as the ten Mahāvidyās, manifestations of the highest knowledge—Kālī, Tārā, Shoḍaśi, Bhuvaneśvarī, Chinnamastā, Bhairavī, Dhūmāvatī, Bagatā, Mātaṅgi and Kamalā. While some Śāktas view these as individual beings, most revere them as manifestations of the singular Devī. There are also numerous minor Goddess forms, in the category of *grāmadevatā* ("village Deity"). These include Piṭāri, "snake-catcher" (usually represented by a simple stone), and Mariyamman, "smallpox Goddess."

In the *yoga* mysticism of all traditions, divine energy, *śakti*, is experienced within the human body in three aspects: 1) the feminine force, *iḍā śakti*, 2) the masculine force, *piṅgalā śakti*, and 3) the pure androgynous force, *kuṇḍalinī śakti*, that flows through the *sushumṇā nāḍī*.

Śakti is most easily experienced by devotees as the sublime, bliss-inspiring energy that emanates from a holy person or sanctified Hindu temple. See: *Amman, Ardhanārīśvara, Goddess, Parāśakti, Śāktism.*

śaktipāta: शक्तिपात "Descent of grace." *Guru dīkshā*, initiation from the preceptor; particularly the first initiation, which awakens the *kuṇḍalinī* and launches the process of spiritual unfoldment. See: *anugraha śakti, dīkshā, grace, kuṇḍalinī.*

Śāktism (Śākta): शाक्त "Doctrine of power." The religion followed by those who worship the Supreme as the Divine Mother—Śakti or Devī—in Her many forms, both gentle and fierce. Śāktism is one of the four primary sects of Hinduism. Śāktism's first historical signs are thousands of female statuettes dated ca 5500 BCE recovered at the Mehrgarh village in India. In philosophy and practice, Śāktism greatly resembles Śaivism, both faiths promulgating, for example, the same ultimate goals of *advaitic* union with Śiva and *moksha.* But Śāktas worship Śakti as the Supreme Being exclusively, as the dynamic aspect of Divinity, while Śiva is considered solely transcendent and is not worshiped. There are many forms of Śāktism, with endless varieties of practices which seek to capture divine energy or power for spiritual transformation. Geographically, Śāktism has two main forms, the Śrīkula "family of the Goddess Śrī (or Lakshmī)," which respects the *brāhminical* tradition (a mainstream Hindu tradition which respects caste and purity rules) and is strongest in South India; and the Kālīkula, "family of Kālī," which rejects *brāhminical* tradition and prevails in Northern and Eastern India. Four major expressions of Śāktism are evident today: folk-shamanism, *yoga*, devotionalism and universalism. Among the eminent *mantras* of Śāktism is: *Aum Hṛim Chaṇḍikāyai Namaḥ*, "I bow to Her who tears apart all dualities." There are many varieties of folk Śāktism gravitating around various forms of the Goddess, such as Kālī, Durgā and a number of forms of Amman. Such worship often involves animal sacrifice and fire-walking, though the former is tending to disappear. See: *Amman, Goddess, Ishṭa Devatā, Kālī, Śakti, tantrism.*

Śakti Viśishṭādvaita: शक्तिविशिष्टाद्वैत The philosophy of Vīra Śaivism. See: *Vīra Śaivism.*

śāktopāya: शाक्तोपाय "Way of power." See: *upāya.*

Śākya: शाक्य Name of the Śaivite dynasty into which Buddha, also called

Śākyamuni, was born (in what is now Nepal). See: *Buddha.*

samādhi: **समाधि** "Enstasy," which means "standing within one's Self." "Sameness; contemplation; union, wholeness; completion, accomplishment." *Samādhi* is the state of true *yoga,* in which the meditator and the object of meditation are one. *Samādhi* is of two levels. The first is *savikalpa samādhi* ("enstasy with form or seed"), identification or oneness with the essence of an object. Its highest form is the realization of the primal substratum or pure consciousness, Satchidānanda. The second is *nirvikalpa samādhi* ("enstasy without form or seed"), identification with the Self, in which all modes of consciousness are transcended and Absolute Reality, Paraśiva, beyond time, form and space, is experienced. This brings in its aftermath a complete transformation of consciousness. In Classical Yoga, *nirvikalpa samādhi* is known as *asamprajñāta samādhi,* "supraconscious enstasy"—*samādhi,* or beingness, without thought or cognition, *prajñā. Savikalpa samādhi* is also called *samprajñāta samādhi,* "conscious enstasy." (Note that *samādhi* differs from *samyama*—the continuous meditation on a single subject or mystic key [such as a *chakra*] to gain revelation on a particular subject or area of consciousness. As explained by Patañjali, it consists of *dhāranā, dhyāna* and *samādhi.)* See: *enstasy, kuṇḍalinī, Paraśiva, rāja yoga, samarasa, Satchidānanda, Self Realization, trance.*

samarasa: **समरस** "Even essence" or "same taste." In Siddha Siddhānta, a term describing the state attained by a *yogī* in which he consciously experiences the world and daily life while never losing his perspective of the essential unity of God, soul and world. Similar in concept to *sāyujya samādhi.* See: *jñāna, kaivalya, samādhi, Siddha Siddhānta, Śivasāyujya.*

samāvartana: **समावर्तन** "Returning home." The ceremony marking a youth's completion of Vedic studies. See: *saṁskāras.*

Sāma Veda: **सामवेद्** "Song of wisdom." Third of the four *Vedas.* Ninety percent of its 1,875 stanzas are derived from the *Ṛig Veda.* It is a collection of hymns specially arranged and notated for chanting with a distinctive melody and cadence by the Udgātā priests during *yajña,* fire ceremony, together with stanzas from the *Yajur Veda.* This *Veda* forms the oldest known form of Indian music. See: *Śruti, Vedas.*

Sambandar: சம்பந்தர் Child saint of the 7th-century Śaivite renaissance. Composed many *Devaram* hymns in praise of Śiva, reconverted at least one Tamil king who had embraced Jainism, and vehemently sought to counter the incursion of Buddhism, bringing the Tamil people back to Śaivism. See: *Nalvar, Nayanar, Tirumurai.*

Śāmbhavopāya: **शाम्भवोपाय** "Way of Śambhu (Śiva)." See: *upāya.*

saṁhāra: **संहार** "Dissolution; destruction." See: *mahāpralaya, Naṭarāja.*

saṁhitā: **संहिता** "Collection." 1) Any methodically arranged collection of texts or verses. 2) The hymn collection of each of the four *Vedas.* 3) A common alternate term for Vaishṇava *Āgamas.* See: *Vedas.*

***sampradāya:* संप्रदाय** "Traditional doctrine of knowledge." A living stream of tradition or theology within Hinduism, passed on by oral training and initiation. The term derives from the verb *sampradā,* meaning "to give, grant, bestow or confer on; to hand down by tradition; to bequeath." *Sampradāya* is thus a philosophy borne down through history by verbal transmission. It is more inclusive than the related term *paramparā* which names a living lineage of ordained *gurus* who embody and carry forth a *sampradāya.* Each *sampradāya* is often represented by many *paramparās.* See: *paramparā.*

***saṁsāra:* संसार** "Flow." The phenomenal world. Transmigratory existence, fraught with impermanence and change. The cycle of birth, death and rebirth; the total pattern of successive earthly lives experienced by a soul. A term similar to *punarjanma* (reincarnation), but with broader connotations. See: *evolution of the soul, karma, punarjanma, reincarnation.*

***saṁsārī:* संसारी** "One in *saṁsāra;* wanderer." A soul during transmigration, immersed in or attached to mundane existence, hence not striving for liberation (*moksha*). A *saṁsārī* is someone who is not "on the path." See: *materialism, saṁsāra, San Mārga, worldly.*

***saṁskāra:* संस्कार** "Impression, activator; sanctification, preparation." 1) The imprints left on the subconscious mind by experience (from this or previous lives), which then color all of life, one's nature, responses, states of mind, etc. 2) A sacrament or rite done to mark a significant transition of life. These make deep and positive impressions on the mind of the recipient, inform the family and community of changes in the lives of its members and secure inner-world blessings. The numerous *saṁskāras* are outlined in the *Gṛihya Śāstras.* Most are accompanied by specific *mantras* from the *Vedas.* See: *mind (five states), sacrament.*

saṁskāras* of birth:** From the rite of conception to the blessings of the newborn child. ***—garbhādhāna: "Womb-placing." Rite of conception, where physical union is consecrated with the intent of bringing into physical birth an advanced soul. ***—punsavana:*** "Male rite; bringing forth a male." A rite performed during the third month of pregnancy consisting of prayers for a son and for the well-being of mother and child. A custom, found in all societies, based on the need for men to defend the country, run the family business and support the parents in old age. The need for male children in such societies is also based on the fact that women outlive men and leave the family to join their husband's family. ***—sīmantonnayana:*** "Hair-parting." A ceremony held between the fourth and seventh months in which the husband combs his wife's hair and expresses his love and support. ***—jātakarma:*** "Rite of birth." The father welcomes and blesses the new-born child and feeds it a taste of *ghee* and honey. See: *saṁskāra.*

saṁskāras* of childhood:** From naming to education. ***—nāmakaraṇa: "Name-giving" and formal entry into one or another sect of Hinduism, performed 11 to 41 days after birth. The name is chosen according to astrology, preferably the name of a God or Goddess. At this time, guardian *devas* are assigned to see the child through life. One who converts to or adopts Hinduism later in life would receive this same sacrament. ***—annaprāśana:*** "Feeding." The ceremony marking the first taking of solid food, held at about six months. (Breast-feeding generally continues). ***—karṇavedha:*** "Ear-piercing." The piercing of both ears, for boys and girls, and the inserting of gold earrings, held during the first, third or fifth year. See: *earrings.* ***—chūḍākaraṇa:*** "Head-shaving." The shaving of the head, for boys and girls, between the 31st day and the fourth year. ***—vidyārambha:*** Marks the beginning of formal education. The boy or girl ceremoniously writes his/her first letter of the alphabet in a tray of uncooked rice. ***—upanayana:*** Given to boys at about 12 years of age, marks the beginning of the period of *brahmacharya* and formal study of scripture and sacred lore, usually with an *āchārya* or *guru.* ***—samāvartana:*** Marks the end of formal religious study. See: *saṁskāra.*

saṁskāras* of adulthood:** From coming-of-age to marriage. ***—ṛitukāla: "Fit or proper season." Time of menses. A home blessing marking the coming of age for girls. ***—keśānta:*** Marking a boy's first beard-shaving, at about 16 years. Both of the above are home ceremonies in which the young ones are reminded of their *brahmacharya*, given new clothes and jewelry and joyously admitted into the adult community as young adults. ***—niśchitārtha*** "Settlement of aim." Also called *vāgdāna*, "word-giving." A formal engagement or betrothal ceremony in which a couple pledge themselves to one another, exchanging rings and other gifts. ***—vivāha:*** Marriage." An elaborate and joyous ceremony performed in presence of God and Gods, in which the *homa* fire is central. To conclude the ceremony, the couple take seven steps to the Northeast as the groom recites: "One step for vigor, two steps for vitality, three steps for prosperity, four steps for happiness, five steps for cattle, six steps for seasons, seven steps for friendship. To me be devoted (*Hiranyakeśi Gṛihya Sūtras* 1.6.21.2 VE)." See: *saṁskāra.*

saṁskāras* of later life:** ***—vānaprastha āśrama: Age 48 marks the entrance into the elder advisor stage, celebrated in some communities by special ceremony. ***—sannyāsa āśrama vrata:*** The advent of withdrawal from social duties and responsibilities at age 72 is sometimes ritually acknowledged (different from *sannyāsa dīkshā*). See: *sannyāsa dharma.* ***—antyeshṭi:*** The various funeral rites performed to guide the soul in its transition to inner worlds, including preparation of the body, cremation, bone-gathering, dispersal of ashes, home purification. See: *cremation, death, piṇḍa, śrāddha, bone-gathering, saṁskāra, shashṭyabda pūrti, transition.*

Sanātana Dharma: **सनातनधर्म** "Eternal religion" or "everlasting path." It is a traditional name for the Hindu religion. See: *Hinduism.*

Sanatkumāra: **सनत्कुमार** "Ever-youthful; perpetual virgin boy." See: *Kārttikeya.*

sañchita karma: **सञ्चितकर्म** "Accumulated action." The accumulated consequence of an individual's actions in this and past lives. See: *karma.*

sanctify: To make holy.

sanctum sanctorum: "Holy of holies." *Garbhagṛiha.* The most sacred part of a temple, usually a cave-like stone chamber, in which the main icon is installed. See: *darśana, garbhagṛiha, temple.*

sandalwood: *Chandana.* The Asian evergreen tree *Santalum album.* Its sweetly fragrant heartwood is ground into the fine, tan-colored paste distributed as *prasāda* in Śaivite temples and used for sacred marks on the forehead, *tilaka.* Sandalwood is also prized for incense, carving and fine cabinetry.

sandhyā upāsanā: **सन्ध्या उपासना** "Worship at time's junctures." Drawing near to God at the changes of time—worship and *sādhana* performed in the home at dawn, noon and dusk. See: *sādhana.*

Śāṇḍilya Upanishad: **शाण्डिल्य उपनिषद्** Belongs to the *Atharva Veda.* Discusses eight forms of *yoga,* restraints, observances, breath control, meditation and the nature of Truth.

saṅgama: **सङ्गम** "Association; fellowship." Coming together in a group, especially for religious purposes. Also a town in Karnataka, South India, where the *Kṛishṇa* and *Malaprabhā* rivers meet; an ancient center of Kālāmukha Śaivism where the Vīra Śaivite preceptor Basavaṇṇa lived and studied as a youth. See: *congregational worship.*

saṅkalpa: **संकल्प** "Will; purpose; determination." A solemn vow or declaration of purpose to perform any ritual observance. Most commonly, *saṅkalpa* names the mental and verbal preparation made by a temple priest as he begins rites of worship. During the *saṅkalpa,* he informs all three worlds what he is about to do. He recites the name of the Deity, and the present time and place according to precise astrological notations and announces the type of ritual he is about to perform. Once the *saṅkalpa* is made, he is bound to complete the ceremony. See: *pūjā.*

Śaṅkara: **शङ्कर** "Conferring happiness; propitious." A name of Śiva.

Śaṅkara: **शङ्कर** One of Hinduism's most extraordinary monks (788–820) and preeminent *guru* of the Smārta Sampradāya. He is noted for his monistic philosophy of Advaita Vedānta, his many scriptural commentaries, and establishing ten orders of *sannyāsins* with pontifical headquarters at strategic points across India. He only lived 32 years, but traveled throughout India and transformed the Hindu world in that time. See: *Daśanāmi, Śaṅkarāchārya pīṭha, shaṇmata sthāpanāchārya, Smārta Sampradāya, Vedānta.*

Śaṅkarāchārya pīṭha: **शङ्कराचार्यपीठ** Advaita monasteries established by Śaṅkara (ca 788–820) as centers of Smārta authority in India, each with a distinct *guru paramparā* and a reigning pontiff entitled Śaṅkarāchārya, and one of the four Upanishadic *mahāvākyas* as a *mantra.* East coast: Govardhana Maṭha, in Puri (center of the Āraṇya and Vāna orders). Himalayas: Jyotiḥ Maṭha, near Badrināṭh (Giri, Pārvata and Sāgara orders). West coast:

Śārada Maṭha, in Dvāraka (Tīrtha and Āśrama orders). South: Śṛingeri Maṭha (Bhārati, Pūrī and Sarasvatī orders). A fifth prominent *pīṭha*, associated with Sṛingeri Maṭha, is in Kanchipuram, also in the South. See: *Daśanāmī, Smārta, Śaṅkara.*

Sāṅkhya: सांख्य "Enumeration, reckoning." See: *prakṛiti, purusha, shaḍ darśana, tattva.*

San Mārga: सन्मार्ग "True path." A term especially important in *Śaiva Siddhānta.* 1) In general, the straight spiritual path leading to the ultimate goal, Self Realization, which does not detour into unnecessary psychic exploration or pointless development of *siddhis. San Mārgī* names a person who is "on the path," as opposed to *saṁsārī,* one engrossed in worldliness. 2) *San Mārga* is also an alternate term for the *jñāna pāda.* See: *liberation, pāda, sādhana mārga, saṁsārī.*

San Mārga Sanctuary: An 11-acre sanctuary at Kauai Aadheenam on the Garden Island of Kauai, Hawaii, centered around a ½-mile straight path to the Supreme God, Śiva (Parameśvara-Parāśakti-Paraśiva) enshrined as a massive 700-pound, single-pointed earthkeeper quartz crystal in Iraivan Temple. See: *Subramuniyaswami.*

sannidhāna: सन्निधान "Nearness; proximity; taking charge of." A title of heads of monasteries: Guru Mahāsannidhāna. See: *sānnidhya.*

sānnidhya: सान्निध्य "(Divine) presence; nearness, proximity." The radiance and blessed presence of divine *śakti* within and around a temple or a holy person.

sannyāsa: संन्यास "Renunciation." "Throwing down or abandoning." *Sannyāsa* is the repudiation of the *dharma,* including the obligations and duties, of the householder and the acceptance of the even more demanding *dharma* of the renunciate. The ancient *śāstras* recognize four justifiable motivations for entering into *sannyāsa: vidvat, vividishā, mārkaṭa* and *ātura. Vidvat* ("knowing; wise") *sannyāsa* is the spontaneous withdrawal from the world in search for Self Realization which results from *karma* and tendencies developed in a previous life. *Vividishā* ("discriminating") *sannyāsa* is renunciation to satisfy a yearning for the Self developed through scriptural study and practice. *Mārkaṭa sannyāsa* is taking refuge in *sannyāsa* as a result of great sorrow, disappointment or misfortune in worldly pursuits. *(Mārkaṭa* means "monkey-like," perhaps implying the analogy of a monkey clinging to its mother.) *Ātura* ("suffering or sick") *sannyāsa* is entering into *sannyāsa* upon one's deathbed, realizing that there is no longer hope in life. See: *sannyāsa dharma, sannyāsa dīkshā, videhamukti.*

sannyāsa āśrama: संन्यास आश्रम "Renunciate stage." The period of life after age 72. See: *āśrama.*

sannyāsa dharma: संन्यासधर्म "Renunciate life." The life, way and traditions of those who have irrevocably renounced duties and obligations of the householder path, including personal property, wealth, ambitions, social position and family ties, in favor of the full-time monastic quest for divine awakening, Self Realization and spiritual upliftment of humanity. Traditionally, this *dharma* is available to those who are under age 25 and who otherwise meet strict qualifications. Alternately, the householder may embrace *sannyāsa dharma* by entering the *sannyāsa āśrama* after age 72 through the customary initiatory rites given by a *sannyāsin* and then diligently pursuing his spiritual *sādhana* in a state of genuine renunciation and not in the midst of his family. These two forms of *sannyāsa* are not to be confused with simply entering the *sannyāsa āśrama,* the last stage of life. See: *sannyāsa, sannyāsa dīkshā, sannyāsin, videhamukti.*

sannyāsa dīkshā: **संन्यासदीक्षा** "Renunciate initiation." This *dīkshā* is a formal rite, or less often an informal blessing, entering the devotee into renunciate monasticism, binding him for life to certain vows which include chastity, poverty and obedience, and directing him on the path to Self Realization. Strictest tradition requires that lifetime renunciates be single men and that they enter training in their order before age 25. However, there are certain orders which accept men into *sannyāsa* after age 25, provided they have been in college and not in the world after that time. Others will accept widowers; and a few initiate women. Such rules and qualifications apply primarily to cenobites, that is, to those who will live and serve together in an *āśrama* or monastery. The rules pertaining to homeless anchorites are, for obvious reasons, more lenient. See: *sannyāsa dharma, videhamukti.*

Sannyāsa Upanishad: **संन्यास उपनिषद्** An *Upanishad* of the *Atharva Veda.* It deals with the transition from the *gṛihastha* to the *vānaprastha* and *sannyāsa āśramas.*

sannyāsin: **संन्यासिन्** "Renouncer." One who has taken *sannyāsa dīkshā.* A Hindu monk, *swāmī,* and one of a world brotherhood (or holy order) of *sannyāsins.* Some are wanderers and others live in monasteries. The seasoned *sannyāsin* is truly the liberated man, the spiritual exemplar, the disciplined *yogī* and ultimately the knower of Truth, freed to commune with the Divine and bound to uplift humanity through the sharing of his wisdom, his peace, his devotion and his illumination, however great or small. The *sannyāsin* is the guardian of his religion, immersed in it constantly, freed from worldliness, freed from distraction, able to offer his work and his worship in unbroken continuity and one-pointed effectiveness. He undertakes certain disciplines including the purification of body, mind and emotion. He restrains and controls the mind through his *sādhana, tapas* and meditative regimen. He unfolds from within himself a profound love of God and the Gods. His practice of *upāsanā,* worship, is predominantly internal, seeking God Śiva within. The term *sannyāsin* is usually synonymous with *swāmī,* though the term *swāmī* is sometimes used less specifically to refer to nonrenunciate persons who are doing spiritual work. See: *sannyāsa, sannyāsa dharma, sannyāsa dīkshā, swāmī.*

***Sanskṛit:* संस्कृत** "Well-made; perfected." The classical sacerdotal language of ancient India, considered a pure vehicle for communication with the celestial worlds. It is the primary language in which Hindu scriptures are written, including the *Vedas* and *Āgamas.* Employed today as a liturgical, literary and scholarly language, but no longer used as a spoken tongue.

***sant:* सन्त** "Saint." A Hindi or vernacular term derived from the Sanskṛit *sat,* meaning "truth; reality."

***santosha:* सन्तोष** "Contentment." See: *yama-niyama.*

***śaraṇa:* शरण** "Refuge." See: *Śivaśaraṇā, Vīra Śaivism.*

***Sarasvatī:* सरस्वती** "The flowing one."Śakti, the Universal Mother; Goddess of the arts and learning, mythological consort of the God Brahmā. Sarasvatī, the river Goddess, is usually depicted wearing a white *sārī* and holding a *vīna,* sitting upon a swan or lotus flower. Prayers are offered to her for refinements of art, culture and learning. *Sarasvatī* also names one of seven sacred rivers (Sapta Sindhu) mentioned in the *Ṛig Veda,* but which now flows underground. In addition, one of the ten *daśanāmī swāmī* orders is the *Sarasvatī.* See: *Goddess, Śakti.*

***Śaravaṇa:* शरवण** "Thicket of reeds." Mythologically, a sacred Himalayan pond where Lord Kārttikeya was nurtured; esoterically understood as the lake of divine essence, or primal consciousness. See: *Kārttikeya.*

sārī: (Hindi, साड़ी) The traditional outer garment of a Hindu woman, consisting of a long, unstitched piece of cloth, usually colorful cotton or silk, wrapped around the body, forming an ankle-length skirt, and around the bosom and over the shoulder.

***śarīra:* शरीर** "Body; husk." Three bodies of the soul: 1) *sthūla śarīra,* "gross or physical body" (also called *annamaya kośa),* the odic body; 2) *sūkshma śarīra,* "subtle body" (also called *liṅga śarīra,* it includes the *prāṇamaya, manomaya* and *vijñānamaya kośas);* 3) *kāraṇa śarīra,* "causal body" (also called *ānandamaya kośa),* the actinic causal body. Another term for *śarīra* is *deha.* See: *deha, kośa, subtle body.*

***sarvabhadra:* सर्वभद्र** "All is auspicious; the goodness of all." *Bhadra* indicates that which is "blessed, auspicious, dear, excellent." *Sarva* ("all") *bhadra* thus denotes the cognition that everything in the universe is a manifestation of Divinity, that it is holy, good and purposeful. See: *auspiciousness, grace, Śivamaya, world.*

***Sarvajñānottara Āgama:* सर्वज्ञानोत्तर आगम** This text is not among the traditional list of *Āgamas* and subsidiary scriptures. But it is thought to be a second version of *Kalajñām,* a subsidiary text of *Vātula Āgama.* The available sections deal with right knowledge.

***śāstra:* शास्त्र** "Sacred text; teaching." 1) Any religious or philosophical treatise, or body of writings. 2) A department of knowledge, a science; e.g., the *Dharma Śāstras* on religious law, *Artha Śāstras* on politics.

***śāstrī:* शास्त्री** One who is knowledgeable in *śāstra,* or scriptures.

***sat:* सत्** "True, existing, real, good; reality, existence, truth." See: *Satchidānanda.*

Satan: The devil; evil personified. A being who in Christian and other Semitic religions opposes God's will and tempts souls into wickedness. In Hinduism, all is seen as the manifestation of God, and there is no Satan. See: *asura, hell, Naraka.*

***Śatapatha Brāhmaṇa:* शतपथब्राह्मण** "Priest manual of 100 paths." A priestly manual of the *Śukla Yajur Veda,* dealing with theology, philosophy and modes of worship.

***Satchidānanda (Sachchidānanda):* सच्चिदानन्द** "Existence-consciousness-bliss." A synonym for *Parāśakti.* Lord Śiva's Divine Mind and simultaneously the pure superconscious mind of each individual soul. It is perfect love and omniscient, omnipotent consciousness, the fountainhead of all existence, yet containing and permeating all existence. It is also called pure consciousness, pure form, substratum of existence, and more. One of the goals of the meditator or *yogī* is to experience the natural state of the mind, Satchidānanda, holding back the *vṛittis* through *yogic* practices. In Advaita Vedānta, Satchidānanda is considered a description of the Absolute (Brahman). Whereas in monistic, or *śuddha,* Śaiva Siddhānta it is understood as divine form—pure, amorphous matter or energy—not as an equivalent of the Absolute, formless, *"atattva,"* Paraśiva. In this latter school, Paraśiva is radically transcendent, and Satchidānanda is known as the primal and most perfectly divine form to emerge from the formless Paraśiva. See: *atattva, Parāśakti, tattva.*

***satguru (sadguru):* सद्गुरु** "True weighty one." A spiritual preceptor of the highest attainment—one who has realized the ultimate Truth, Paraśiva, through *nirvikalpa samādhi*—a *jīvanmukta* able to lead others securely along the spiritual path. He is always a *sannyāsin,* an unmarried renunciate. All Hindu denominations teach that the grace and guidance of a living *satguru* is a necessity for Self Realization. He is recognized and revered as the embodiment of God, Sadāśiva, the source of grace and of liberation. See: *guru bhakti, guru, guru-śishya relationship, pādapūjā.*

***satgurunātha:* सद्गुरुनाथ** "Lord and true *guru.*" A highly respectful and honorific term for one's preceptor. See: *satguru.*

***sattva guṇa:* सत्त्वगुण** "Purity." The quality of goodness or purity. See: *guṇa.*

***satya:* सत्य** "Truthfulness." See: *yama-niyama.*

***Satyaloka:* सत्यलोक** "Plane of reality, truth." Also called Brahmaloka; the realm of *sahasrāra chakra,* it is the highest of the seven upper worlds. See: *loka.*

***śaucha:* शौच** "Purity." See: *purity-impurity, yama-niyama.*

***saumanasya:* सौमनस्य** "Benevolence, causing gladness or cheerfulness of mind, right understanding (related to the term *soma).* See: *chakra.*

***savikalpa samādhi:* सविकल्पसमाधि** "Enstasy with form or seed." See: *enstasy, rāja yoga, samādhi.*

sāyujya: सायुज्य "Intimate union." Perpetual God Consciousness. See: *Śivasāyujya, viśvagrāsa.*

scarlet: The color red with orange tint.

scepter: *Rājadaṇḍa.* The staff and insignia of royal or imperial authority and power held by spiritual monarchs or kings. Traditionally, the scepters of Indian kings are prepared and empowered by respected heads of traditional Hindu religious orders through esoteric means. See: *daṇḍa.*

scripture (scriptural): "A writing." A sacred text or holy book having authority for a given sect or religion. See: *śāstra, smṛiti, śruti.*

secluded (seclusion): Isolated; hidden. Kept apart from others. See: *muni.*

seed *karma:* Dormant or *anārabdha karma.* All past actions which have not yet sprouted. See: *karma.*

seer: Visionary; *ṛishi.* A wise being or mystic who sees beyond the limits of ordinary perception. See: *ākāśa, clairvoyance, muni, ṛishi, shamanism.*

Self (Self God): God Śiva's perfection of Absolute Reality, Paraśiva—That which abides at the core of every soul. See: *atattva, Paramātman, Paraśiva.*

self-assertive: Quality of one who makes himself, his ideas, opinions, etc., dominant. Demanding recognition.

self-conceit: Too high an opinion of oneself; vanity, vain pride.

self-luminous: Producing its own light; radiating light.

Self Realization: Direct knowing of the Self God, Paraśiva. Self Realization is known in Sanskṛit as *nirvikalpa samādhi;* "enstasy without form or seed;" the ultimate spiritual attainment (also called *asamprajñata samādhi).* Esoterically, this state is attained when the mystic *kuṇḍalinī* force pierces through the *sahasrāra chakra* at the crown of the head. This transcendence of all modes of human consciousness brings the realization or "nonexperience" of That which exists beyond the mind, beyond time, form and space. But even to assign a name to Paraśiva, or to its realization is to name that which cannot be named. In fact, it is "experienced" only in its aftermath as a change in perspective, a permanent transformation, and as an intuitive familiarity with the Truth that surpasses understanding. See: *God Realization, enstasy, liberation, kuṇḍalinī, Paraśiva, rāja yoga, samādhi.*

self-reflection: Observation of, or meditation upon, oneself, one's mind, emotions, thinking. Introspection. Playing back memories and impressions locked within the subconscious, endeavoring to deal with them. It is anticipating one's future and how the past will react upon it, enhance or detract from it. See: *spiritual unfoldment.*

servitude: Condition of a slave subject to a master.

sevā: सेवा "Service." *Karma yoga.* An integral part of the spiritual path, where the aspirant strives to serve without thought of reward or personal gain. The central practice of the *charyā pāda.* See: *yoga.*

seval: சேவல் The large, red, fighting rooster *(kukkuṭa* in Sanskṛit) that adorns Lord Murugan's flag, heralding the dawn of wisdom and the conquest of the forces of ignorance. See: *Kārttikeya.*

sexuality: Hinduism has a healthy, unrepressed outlook on human sexuality, and sexual pleasure is part of *kāma,* one of the four goals of life. On matters such as birth control, sterilization, masturbation, homosexuality, bisexuality, petting and polygamy, Hindu scripture is tolerantly silent, neither calling them sins nor encouraging their practice, neither condemning nor condoning. The two important exceptions to this understanding view of sexual experience are adultery and abortion, both of which are considered to carry heavy *karmic* implications for this and future births. See: *abortion, bisexuality, homosexuality.*

shaḍ darśana: **षड् दर्शन** "Six views or insights; six philosophies." Among the hundreds of Hindu *darśanas* known through history are six classical philosophical systems: Nyāya, Vaiśeshika, Sāṅkhya, Yoga, Mīmāṁsā and Vedānta. Each was tersely formulated in *sūtra* form by its "founder," and elaborated in extensive commentaries by other writers. They are understood as varied attempts at describing Truth and the path to it. Elements of each form part of the Hindu fabric today. —***Nyāya:*** "System, rule; logic." A system of logical realism, founded sometime around 300 BCE by Gautama, known for its systems of logic and epistemology and concerned with the means of acquiring right knowledge. Its tools of enquiry and rules for argumentation were adopted by all schools of Hinduism. —***Vaiśeshika:*** "Distinctionism." From *"viśesha,"* differences. Philosophy founded by Kaṇāda (ca 300 BCE) teaching that liberation is to be attained through understanding the nature of existence, which is classified in nine basic realities *(dravyas)*: earth, water, light, air, ether, time, space, soul and mind. Nyāya and Vaiśeshika are viewed as a complementary pair, with Nyāya emphasizing logic, and Vaiśeshika analyzing the nature of the world. —***Sāṅkhya:*** "Enumeration, reckoning." A philosophy founded by the sage Kapila (ca 500 BCE), author of the *Sāṅkhya Sūtras.* Sāṅkhya is primarily concerned with "categories of existence," *tattvas,* which it understands as 25 in number. The first two are the unmanifest *purusha* and the manifest primal nature, *prakṛiti*—the male-female polarity, viewed as the foundation of all existence. Prakṛiti, out of which all things evolve, is the unity of the three *guṇas: sattva, rajas* and *tamas.* Sāṅkhya and Yoga are considered an inseparable pair whose principles permeate all of Hinduism. See: *prakṛiti, purusha.*—***Yoga:*** "Yoking; joining." Ancient tradition of philosophy and practice codified by Patañjali (ca 200 BCE) in the *Yoga Sūtras.* It is also known as *rāja yoga,* "king of *yogas,*" or *ashṭāṅga yoga,* "eight-limbed *yoga.*" Its object is to achieve, at will, the cessation of all fluctuations of consciousness, and the attainment of Self Realization. Yoga is wholly dedicated to putting the high philosophy of Hinduism into practice, to achieve personal transformation through transcendental experience, *samādhi.* See: *yoga.* —***Mīmāṁsā:*** "Inquiry" (or Pūrva, "early," Mīmāṁsā). Founded by Jaimini (ca 200 BCE), author of the *Mīmāṁsā Sūtras,* who taught the correct performance of Vedic rites as the means to salvation. —***Vedānta*** (or Uttara "later" Mīmāṁsā): "End (or culmination) of the *Vedas.*" For Vedānta, the main basis is the *Upanishads* and *Āraṇyakas* (the "end," *anta,* of the *Vedas),* rather than the hymns and ritual portions of the *Vedas.* The teaching of Vedānta is that there is one Absolute Reality, Brahman. Man is one with Brahman, and the object of life is to realize that truth through right knowledge, intuition and personal experience. The *Vedānta Sūtras* (or *Brahma Sūtras)* were composed by Ṛishi Bādarāyaṇa (ca 400 BCE). See: *Brahma Sūtra, padārtha, tattva, Vedānta, yoga.*

shamanism (shamanic): From the Sanskṛit *śramaṇa,* "ascetic," akin to *śram,* meaning to exert." Generally refers to any religion based on the belief that good or evil spirits can be influenced by priests, or shamans. Descriptive of many of the world's tribal, indigenous faiths. See: *folk-shamanic, pagan, incantation, mysticism, Śāktism.*

shaṇmata sthāpanāchārya: षण्मतस्थापनाचार्य "Founder-teacher of the sixfold system." A title conferred upon Ādi Śaṅkara while he was living. It refers to his attempt to consolidate the six main sects of Hinduism in nonsectarian unity, as represented by its altar of five (or six) Deities. See: *Smārtism, pañchāyatana pūjā, Śaṅkara.*

Shaṇmukha: षण्मुख "Six-faced." A name for Lord Murugan or Kārttikeya, denoting the multiplicity of His divine functions. See: *Kārttikeya.*

Shaṇmukha Gāyatrī: षण्मुखगायत्री A Vedic Gāyatrī chant, the Sāvitrī Gāyatrī modified to address Lord Kārttikeya as Shaṇmukha "He of six faces."

shashṭyabda pūrti: षष्ट्यब्दपूर्ति "Sixtieth birthday celebration." Done for the couple on the husband's birthday, usually with many family and friends attending. It consists in a *homa,* retaking of marriage vows and retying the wedding pendant.

shaṭkoṇa: षट्कोण "Six-pointed star," formed by two interlocking triangles, the upper one representing Śiva's transcendent Being, and the lower one Śiva's manifest energy, Śakti. The *shaṭkoṇa* is part of Lord Kārttikeya's *yantra.* See: *Ardhanārīśvara Kārttikeya.*

shaṭsthala: षट्स्थल "Six stages." Vīra Śaivism's six stages to union with Śiva. See: *Vīra Śaivism.*

shatter: To break into many pieces suddenly, as if struck.

sheath: A covering or recepticle, such as the husk surrounding a grain of rice. In Sanskṛit, it is *kośa,* philosophically the bodily envelopes of the soul. See: *kośa, soul, subtle body.*

Shum: A Nātha mystical language of meditation revealed in Switzerland in 1968 by Sivaya Subramuniyaswami. Its primary alphabet looks like this:

shuttle: An instrument that carries a spool of thread in the weaving of cloth.

siddha: **सिद्ध** A "perfected one" or accomplished *yogī*, a person of great spiritual attainment or powers. See: *siddhi, siddha yoga, siddha yogī.*

Siddha Mārga: **सिद्धमार्ग** Another term for *Siddha Siddhānta.* See: *Siddha Siddhānta, siddha yoga.*

siddhānta: **सिद्धान्त** "Final attainments or conclusions." Siddhānta refers to ultimate understanding arrived at in any given field of knowledge.

Siddha Siddhānta Paddhati: **सिद्धसिद्धान्तपद्धति** "Tracks on the doctrines of the adepts." A text of 353 highly mystical verses ascribed to Gorakshanātha, founder of the Siddha Siddhānta school of Śaivism. Deals with the esoteric nature of the inner bodies and the soul's union with Supreme Reality. See: *Gorakshanātha, Siddha Siddhānta.*

Siddha Siddhānta: **सिद्धसिद्धान्त** Siddha Siddhānta, also called Gorakhnātha Śaivism, is generally considered to have come in the lineage of the earlier ascetic orders of India. Its most well-known preceptor was Gorakshanātha (ca 1000) a disciple of Matsyendranātha, patron saint of Nepal, revered by certain esoteric Buddhist schools as well as by Hindus. The school systematized and developed the practice of *haṭha yoga* to a remarkable degree. Indeed, nearly all of what is today taught about *haṭha yoga* comes from this school. Among its central texts are *Haṭha Yoga Pradīpikā* by Svātmarāma, *Gheraṇḍa Saṁhitā, Śiva Saṁhitā* and *Jñānāmṛita.* Siddha Siddhānta theology embraces both transcendent Śiva (being) and immanent Śiva (becoming). Śiva is both the efficient and material cause of the universe. Devotion is expressed through temple worship and pilgrimage, with the central focus on internal worship and *kuṇḍalinī yoga,* with the goal of realizing Parāsamvid, the supreme transcendent state of Śiva. Today there are perhaps 750,000 adherents of Siddha Siddhānta Śaivism, who are often understood as Śāktas or *advaita tantrics.* The school fans out through India, but is most prominent in North India and Nepal. Devotees are called *yogīs,* and stress is placed on world renunciation—even for householders. This sect is also most commonly known as Nātha, the Gorakshapantha and Siddha Yogī Sampradāya. Other names include Ādinātha Sampradāya, Nāthamaṭha and Siddhamārga. See: *Gorakshanātha.*

siddha yoga: **सिद्धयोग** "*Yoga* of perfected attainment, or of supernatural powers." 1) A term used in the *Tirumantiram* and other Śaiva scriptures to describe the *yoga* which is the way of life of adepts after the attainment of Paraśiva. *Siddha yoga* involves the development of magical or mystical powers, or *siddhis,* including some or all of the eight classical powers. It is a highly advanced *yoga* which seeks profound transformation of body, mind and emotions and the ability to live in a flawless state of God Consciousness. 2) The highly accomplished practices of certain alchemists. See: *siddha yogī, siddhi.*

siddha yogī: **सिद्धयोगी** "*Yogī* of perfection." A perfected one, adept, a realized being who is the embodiment of the most profound *yogic* states and has attained magical or mystical powers. See: *siddha yoga, siddhi.*

Siddha Yogī Sampradāya: सिद्धयोगीसंप्रदाय Another term for *Siddha Siddhānta.* See: *Siddha Siddhānta.*

siddhānta śravaṇa (or śrāvaṇa): सिद्धान्तश्रवण "Scriptural listening." See: *yama-niyama.*

siddhi: सिद्धि "Power, accomplishment; perfection." Extraordinary powers of the soul, developed through consistent meditation and deliberate, grueling, often uncomfortable *tapas,* or awakened naturally through spiritual maturity and *yogic sādhana.* Through the repeated experience of Self Realization, *siddhis* naturally unfold according to the needs of the individual. Before Self Realization, the use or development of *siddhis* is among the greatest obstacles on the path, because it develops the *ahaṁkāra,* I-ness, and militates against the attainment of *prapatti,* complete submission to the will of God, Gods and *guru.* Six *siddhis* in particular are considered primary obstacles in the way of *samādhi:* clairvoyance *(ādarśa siddhi* or *divya siddhi),* clairaudience *(śravana siddhi* or *divyaśravana),* divination *(pratibhā siddhi),* super-feeling (*vedana siddhi)* and super-taste *(āsvādana siddhi),* super-smell *(vārtā siddhi).* The supreme *siddhi (parasiddhi)* is realization of the Self, Paraśiva. See: *siddha yoga.*

śikhara: शिखर "Summit or crest." The towering superstructure above the *garbhagṛiha* in North Indian style temples. In Southern temples, *śikhara* refers to the top stone of the superstructure, or *vimāna.*

Sikhism: "Disciple." Religion of nine million members founded in India about 500 years ago by the saint Guru Nānak. A reformist faith which rejects idolatry and the caste system, its holy book is the *Ādi Granth,* and main holy center is the Golden Temple of Amritsar. See: *Ādi Granth.*

Śikshā Vedāṅga: शिक्षावेदाङ्ग Auxiliary Vedic texts on Sanskṛit phonetics (pronunciation, articulation and accent), among four linguistic skills taught for mastery of the *Vedas* and the rites of *yajña. Śikshā* literally means "wish to accomplish; learning, method of study." The *Prātiśākhyas,* phonetic handbooks developed by ancient Vedic schools, and a later text by Pāṇini are of this class. See: *Vedāṅga.*

Śilpa Śāstra: शिल्पशस्त्र "Art or craft manual." 1) A particular class of works which formed the primary teachings on any of the fine arts or sacred sciences, such as architecture, dance, painting, jewelry-making, pottery, weaving, and basketry, garlandry, metal-working, acting, cooking and horsemanship. The earliest *Śilpa Śāstras* are thought to date to 200 BCE. Many were written between the 5th and 14th centuries. See: *kalā–64, Sthāpatyaveda.*

sīmantonnayana: सीमन्तोन्नयन "Hair-parting rite." See: *saṁskāras of birth.*

sin: Intentional transgression of divine law. Akin to the Latin *sous,* "guilty." Hinduism does not view sin as a crime against God, but as an act against *dharma*—moral order—and one's own self. It is thought natural, if unfortunate, that young souls act wrongly, for they are living in nescience, *avidya,* the darkness of ignorance. Sin is an *adharmic* course of action which automatically brings negative consequences. The term *sin* carries a double meaning, as do its Sanskṛit equivalents: 1) a wrongful act, 2) the negative consequences resulting from a wrongful act. In Sanskṛit the wrongful act is known by several terms, including *pātaka* (from *pat*, "to fall") *pāpa, enas, kilbisha, adharma, anṛita* and *ṛiṇa* (transgress, in the sense of omission). The residue of sin is called *pāpa*, sometimes conceived of as a sticky, astral substance which can be dissolved through penance *(prāyaśchitta)*, austerity *(tapas)* and good deeds *(sukṛityā)*. This astral substance can be psychically seen within the inner, subconscious aura of the individual. Note that *pāpa* is also accrued through unknowing or unintentional transgressions of *dharma*, as in the term *aparādha* (offense, fault, mistake). **—inherent (or original) sin:** A doctrine of Semitic faiths whereby each soul is born in sin as a result of Adam's disobedience in the Garden of Eden. Sometimes mistakenly compared to the Śaiva Siddhānta concept of the three *malas*, especially *āṇava*. See: *pāśa*. **—mortal sin:** According to some theologies, sins so grave that they can never be expiated and which cause the soul to be condemned to suffer eternally in hell. In Hinduism, there are no such concepts as *inherent* or *mortal sin*. See: *aura, evil, karma, pāpa.*

śishya: **शिष्य** "A pupil or disciple," especially one who has proven himself and has formally been accepted by a *guru*.

Śiva: **शिव** "The auspicious, gracious or kindly one." Supreme Being of the Śaivite religion. God Śiva is All and in all, simultaneously the creator and the creation, both immanent and transcendent. As personal Deity, He is creator, preserver and destroyer. He is a one being, perhaps best understood in three perfections: Parameśvara (Primal Soul), Parāśakti (pure consciousness) and Paraśiva (Absolute Reality). See: *Ishṭa Devatā, Parameśvara, Parāśakti, Paraśiva, Naṭarāja, Sadāśiva, Śaivism, Satchidānanda.*

Śiva Advaita: **शिवाद्वैत** Also called Śiva Viśishṭādvaita, or Śaivite "qualified nondualism," Śiva Advaita is the philosophy of Śrīkaṇṭha (ca 1050) as expounded in his commentary on the *Brahma Sūtras* (ca 500-200 BCE). Patterned after the Vaishṇavite Viśishṭādvaita of Rāmānuja, this philosophy was later amplified by Appaya Dīkshita. Brahman, or Śiva, is transcendent and the efficient and material cause of the world and souls. Souls are not identical to Him and never merge in Him, even after liberation. As a school Śiva Advaita remained exclusively intellectual, never enjoying a following of practitioners. Purification, devotion and meditation upon Śiva as the Self—the *ākāśa* within the heart—define the path. Meditation is directed to the Self, Śiva, the One Existence that evolved into all form. Liberation depends on grace, not deeds. See: *Appaya Dīkshita, Śaivism, Śrīkaṇṭha.*

Śivachaitanya: **शिवचैतन्य** "God consciousness." See: *Śiva consciousness.*

Śivāchāra: **शिवाचार** "Treating all as God." See: *Vīra Śaivism.*

Śivāchārya: **शिवाचार्य** The hereditary priests of the Śaiva Siddhānta tradition.

The title of Ādiśaiva Brāhmins. An Ādiśaiva priest who has received the necessary training and *dīkshās* to perform public Śiva temple rites known as Āgamic *nitya parārtha pūjā*. A fully qualified Śivāchārya is also known as *archaka*. *Śivāchārya*, too, names the family clan of this priest tradition. See: *Ādiśaiva. brāhmin.*

Śiva consciousness: Śivachaitanya. A broad term naming the experience or state of being conscious of Śiva in a multitude of ways, such as in the five expressed in the following meditation. **Vital Breath: *prāṇa.*** Experience the inbreath and outbreath as Śiva's will within your body. Become attuned to the ever-present pulse of the universe, knowing that nothing moves but by His divine will. **All-Pervasive Energy: *śakti.*** Become conscious of the flow of life within your body. Realize that it is the same universal energy within every living thing. Practice seeing the life energy within another's eyes. **Manifest Sacred Form: *darśana.*** Hold in your mind a sacred form, such as Naṭarāja, Śivaliṅga or your *satguru*—who is Sadāśiva—and think of nothing else. See every form as a form of our God Śiva. **Inner Light: *jyoti.*** Observe the light that illumines your thoughts. Concentrate only on that light, as you might practice being more aware of the light on a TV screen than of its changing pictures. **Sacred Sound: *nāda.*** Listen to the constant high-pitched *ee* sounding in your head. It is like the tone of an electrical transformer, a hundred *tamburas* distantly playing or a humming swarm of bees.

These five constitute the "Śivachaitanya Pañchatantra," five simple experiences that bring the Divine into the reach of each individual. Śivachaitanya, of course, applies to deeper states of meditation and contemplation as well. See: *jñāna, mind (five states), Śivasāyujya.*

Śiva Dṛishṭi: **शिवदृष्टि** A scripture of Kashmīr Śaivism, now lost, written by Somānanda, a disciple of Vasugupta. See: *Kashmīr Śaivism.*

Śivajñānabodham: **शिवज्ञानबोधम्** "Treatise on Śiva Wisdom." A work authored (or, some believe, a portion of the *Raurava Āgama* translated into Tamil) by Meykandar, ca 1300, consisting of 12 *sūtras* describing the relationship between God, soul and world. The Meykandar Sampradāya revere it as their primary philosophical text, and consider it a pluralistic exposition. For others, it is monistic in character, the pluralistic interpretation being introduced by later commentators. Included in this important text is an acute commentary on each of the 12 *sūtras*. See: *Meykandar Śāstras.*

Śivakarṇāmṛita: **शिवकर्णामृत** A text by Appaya Dīkshita (1554–1626) written to reestablish the superiority of God Śiva in the face of widespread conversion to Vaishṇavism. See: *Appaya Dīkshita.*

Śivālaya: **शिवालय** The holy Śiva temple. "Śiva's house or dwelling *(ālaya).*" See: *temple.*

Śivaliṅga: **शिवलिङ्ग** "Mark, or sign, of Śiva." The most prevalent icon of Śiva, found in virtually all Śiva temples. A rounded, elliptical, aniconic image, usually set on a circular base, or *pīṭha*. The Śivaliṅga is the simplest and most ancient symbol of Śiva, especially of Paraśiva, God beyond all forms and qualities. The *pīṭha* represents Parāśakti, the manifesting power of God. Liṅgas are usually of stone (either carved or naturally existing, *svayambhū,* such as shaped by a swift-flowing river), but may also be of metal, precious gems, crystal, wood, earth or transitory materials such as ice. According to the *Kāraṇa Āgama* (6), a transitory Śivaliṅga may be made of 12 different materials: sand, rice, cooked food, river clay, cow dung, butter, *rudrāksha* seeds, ashes, sandalwood, *dharba* grass, a flower garland or molasses. See: *mūrti, Śaivism, svayambhū Liṅga.*

Śivaloka: **शिवलोक** "Realm of Śiva." See: *loka.*

Śivamaya: **शिवमय** "Formed, made, consisting of or full of Śiva." Denotes that all of existence—all worlds, all beings, all of manifestation, that which undergoes creation, preservation and destruction, all dualities and paradoxes—consists of and is pervaded by Śiva. An important concept of monistic Śaivism. See: *sarvabhadra, world, tattva.*

Śivamayakośa: **शिवमयकोश** "Sheath composed of Śiva." Names the Primal Soul form, Parameśvara—the body of God Śiva—into which the individual soul merges as the fulfillment of its evolution. See: *kośa, Parameśvara, viśvagrāsa.*

Sivanadiyar: **சிவனடியார்** "Slave of Śiva." Conveys a mystic relationship between the devotee and Śiva in which all spiritual, mental and physical actions are perceived as fulfilling the will and design of Śiva. See: *karma yoga.*

Śivaness: Quality of being Śiva or like Śiva, especially sharing in His divine state of consciousness. See: *samarasa, Śiva consciousness, Śivasāyujya.*

Śivānubhava Maṇḍapa: **शिवानुभवमण्डप** The "hall of Śiva experience," where the Vīra Śaivites gathered to develop the basic doctrines of the movement in the 12th century.

Śiva Purāṇa: **शिवपुराण** "Ancient [lore] of Śiva." 1) A collection of six major scriptures sacred to Śaivites. 2) The name of the oldest of these six texts, though some consider it a version of the *Vāyu Purāṇa.*

Śiva Rakshāmaṇi Dīpikā: **शिवरक्षामणिदीपिका** A purely nondual commentary and interpretation by Appaya Dīkshita (1554–1626) on the writings of Śrīkaṇṭha. See: *Śaivism.*

Śivarātri: **शिवरात्रि** "Night of Śiva." See: *Mahāśivarātri.*

Śiva-Śakti: **शिवशक्ति** Father-Mother God, both immanent and transcendent. A name for God Śiva encompassing His unmanifest Being and manifest energy. See: *Ardhanārīśvara, Parameśvara, Primal Soul, Śiva.*

Śiva Saṁhitā: **शिवसंहिता** Text from the Gorakshanātha school of Śaivism, ca 1700. In 212 *sūtras* it discusses anatomy, *āsanas,* energy, breathing and philosophy. It is available in various languages and widely studied as a valuable overview of *yoga* practice.

Śivaśaraṇā: **शिवशरणा** "One surrendered in God." See: *Vīra Śaivism.*

Śivasāyujya: **शिवसायुज्य** "Intimate union with Śiva." Becoming one with

God. The state of perpetual Śiva consciousness; simultaneous perception of the inner and the outer. A permanent state of oneness with Śiva, even in the midst of ordinary activities, the aftermath or plateau which comes after repeated Self Realization experiences. Ṛishi Tirumular says: "*Sāyujya* is the state of *jagrātita*—the 'Beyond Consciousness.' *Sāyujya* is to abide forever in *upaśanta*, the peace that knows no understanding. *Sāyujya* is to become Śiva Himself. *Sāyujya* is to experience the infinite power of inward bliss forever and ever (*Tirumantiram* 1513)." In many Hindu schools of thought it is defined as the highest attainment. Esoterically, it dawns when the *kuṇḍalinī* resides coiled in the *sahasrāra chakra.* See: *jīvanmukti, kaivalya, kuṇḍalinī, moksha.*

Śiva's five faces: See: *Sadāśiva.*

Śiva Sūtra(s): **शिवसूत्र** The seminal or seed scripture of Kashmīr Śaivism, 77 aphorisms revealed to Sage Vasugupta (ca 800). See: *Vasugupta.*

Sivathondan: சிவதொண்டன் "Servant of Śiva." Conveys the same mystic meaning as Sivanadiyar, denoting a devotee who regularly performs actions dedicated to God Śiva; selfless work in service to others. See: *karma yoga.*

Sivathondu: சிவதொண்டு "Service to Śiva." Akin to the concept of *karma yoga.* See: *karma yoga.*

Śivāya Namaḥ: **शिवाय नमः** "Adoration to Śiva." Alternate form of *Namaḥ Śivāya.* See: *Namaḥ Śivāya.*

Śivena saha Nartanam: **शिवेन सह नर्तनम्** "Dancing with Śiva."

Skanda: **स्कन्द** "Quicksilver; leaping one." One of Lord Kārttikeya's oldest names, and His form as scarlet-hued warrior God. See: *Kārttikeya.*

Skanda Shashṭhī: **स्कन्दषष्ठी** A six-day festival in October-November celebrating Lord Kārttikeya's, or Skanda's, victory over the forces of darkness.

slaughter: The killing of animals for food; the murder of many people.

śloka: **श्लोक** A verse, phrase, proverb or hymn of praise, usually composed in a specified meter. Especially a verse of two lines, each of sixteen syllables. *Śloka* is the primary verse form of the Sanskṛit epics, *Mahābhārata* and *Rāmāyaṇa.* See: *bhāshya, sūtra.*

Smārta: **स्मार्त** "Of or related to *smṛiti,*" the secondary Hindu scriptures. See: *Smārtism, smṛiti.*

Smārta Sampradāya: **स्मार्तसंप्रदाय** The teaching tradition of Hinduism's Smārta sect, formalized by Ādi Śaṅkara in the 9th century. See: *Smārtism.*

Smārtism: **स्मार्त** "Sect based on the secondary scriptures *(smṛiti).*" The most liberal of the four major denominations of Hinduism, an ancient Vedic *brāhminical* tradition (ca 700 BCE) which from the 9th century onward was guided and deeply influenced by the Advaita Vedānta teachings of the reformist Ādi Śaṅkara. Its adherents rely mainly on the classical *smṛiti* literature, especially the *Itihāsas (Rāmāyana* and *Mahābhārata,* the latter of which includes the *Bhagavad Gītā), Purāṇas* and *Dharma Śāstras.* These are regarded as complementary to and a means to understanding the *Vedas.*

Smārtas adhere to Śaṅkara's view that all Gods are but various depictions of Saguṇa Brahman. Thus, Smārtas are avowedly eclectic, worshiping all the Gods and discouraging sectarianism. The Smārta system of worship, called *pañchāyatana pūjā,* reinforces this outlook by including the major Deity of each primary Hindu sect of ancient days: Gaṇeśa, Sūrya, Vishṇu, Śiva and Śakti. In order to encompass a sixth important lineage, Śaṅkara recommended the addition of a sixth Deity, Kumāra. Thus he was proclaimed *shaṇmata sthapanāchārya,* founder of the six-fold system. One among the six is generally chosen as the devotee's preferred Deity, Ishṭa Devatā. For spiritual authority, Smārtas look to the regional monasteries established across India by Śaṅkara, and to their pontiffs. These are the headquarters of ten orders of renunciate monks who spread the Advaita Vedānta teachings far and wide. Within Smārtism three primary religious approaches are distinguished: ritualistic, devotional and philosophical. See: *daśanāmi, pañchāyatana pūjā, Śaṅkara.*

smṛiti: **स्मृति** "That which is remembered; the tradition." Hinduism's nonrevealed, secondary but deeply revered scriptures, derived from man's insight and experience. *Smṛiti* speaks of secular matters—science, law, history, agriculture, etc.—as well as spiritual lore, ranging from day-to-day rules and regulations to superconscious outpourings. 1) The term *smṛiti* refers to a specific collection of ancient Sanskṛitic texts as follows: the six or more *Vedāṅgas,* the four *Upavedas,* the two *Itihāsas,* and the 18 main *Purāṇas.* Among the *Vedāṅgas,* the *Kalpa Vedāṅga* defines codes of ritual in the *Śrauta* and *Śulba Śāstras,* and domestic-civil laws in the *Gṛihya* and *Dharma Śāstras.* Also included as classical *smṛiti* are the founding *sūtras* of six ancient philosophies called *shaḍ darśana* (Sāṅkhya, Yoga, Nyāya, Vaiśeshika, Mīmaṁsā and Vedānta). 2) In a general sense, *smṛiti* may refer to any text other than *śruti* (revealed scripture) that is revered as scripture within a particular sect. From the vast body of sacred literature, *śāstra,* each sect and school claims its own preferred texts as secondary scripture, e.g., the *Rāmāyaṇa* of Vaishṇavism and Smārtism, or the *Tirumurai* of Śaiva Siddhānta. Thus, the selection of *smṛiti* varies widely from one sect and lineage to another. See: *Mahābhārata, Rāmāyaṇa, Tirumurai.*

snare: A trap for catching animals.

social *dharma:* *(varṇa dharma).* See: *dharma.*

solace: A comforting or easing of distress, pain or sorrow.

solemn: Observed or performed according to ritual or tradition. Formal, serious, inspiring feelings of awe. **—solemnize:** To consecrate with formal ceremony. See: *sacrament, saṁskāra.*

soliloquy: An act of speaking to oneself.

solitaire (solitary): A hermit. One who lives alone and away from all human company.

Somānanda: **सोमानन्द** Disciple of Vasugupta and author of *Śivadṛishṭi* (ca

850–900), which was said to be a highly influential explanation and defense of the Kashmīr Śaiva philosophy. See: *Kashmīr Śaivism.*

***Somanāth* Temple: सोमनाथ** Ancient center of Pāśupata Śaivism located in modern Gujarat state and mentioned in the *Mahābhārata.* The first recorded temple was built there before 100. In 1026 the then fabulously wealthy temple was sacked by Muslim invaders, the Śivaliṅga smashed and 50,000 *brāhmins* slaughtered. The temple was rebuilt several times and finally demolished by the Moghul emperor Aurangzeb (ca 1700). Sardar Patel, deputy prime minister of India, spearheaded its reconstruction in 1947.

soul: The real being of man, as distinguished from body, mind and emotions. The soul—known as *ātman* or *purusha*—is the sum of its two aspects, the form or body of the soul and the essence of the soul (though many texts use the word *soul* to refer to the essence only). **—essence or nucleus of the soul:** Man's innermost and unchanging being—Pure Consciousness *(Parāśakti* or *Satchidānanda)* and Absolute Reality *(Paraśiva).* This essence was never created, does not change or evolve and is eternally identical with God Śiva's perfections of Parāśakti and Paraśiva. **—soul body:** *ānandamaya kośa* ("sheath of bliss"), also referred to as the "causal body" *(kāraṇa śarīra),* "innermost sheath" and "body of light." *Body of the soul,* or *soul body,* names the soul's manifest nature as an individual being—an effulgent, human-like form composed of light (quantums). It is the emanational creation of God Śiva, destined to one day merge back into Him. During its evolution, the soul functions through four types of outer sheaths that envelope the soul form—mental, instinctive-intellectual, vital and physical—and employs the mental faculties of *manas, buddhi* and *ahaṁkāra,* as well as the five agents of perception *(jñānendriyas),* and five agents of action *(karmendriyas).* The "soul body" is not a body in sense of a case, a vessel, vehicle or enclosure for something else. The soul body is the soul itself—a radiant, self-effulgent, human-like, super-intelligent being. Its very composition is Satchidānanda in various subtle levels of manifestation. It is the finest of subatomic forms, on the quantum level. The soul form evolves as its consciousness evolves, becoming more and more refined until finally it is the same intensity or refinement as the Primal Soul, Parameśvara. The experiences of life, in all the various planes of consciousness, are "food for the soul," reaping lessons that actually raise the level of intelligence and divine love. Thus, very refined souls, whether embodied or in the disembodied, *ajīva,* state, are like walking intelligences with inventive creativeness and powers of preservation, beaming with love and luminosity in their self-effulgent bodies of quantum light particles. See: *ātman, evolution of the soul, indriya, kośa, Parāśakti, Paraśiva, purusha, quantum, Satchidānanda, spiritual unfoldment.*

sound: *Śabda.* As the *darśana,* or "seeing," of the Divine is a central article of faith for Hindus, similarly, *hearing* the Divine is spiritually indispensable.

The ears are a center of many *nāḍīs* connected to inner organs of perception. *Gurus* may when imparting initiation whisper in the ear of disciples to stimulate these centers and give a greater effect to their instructions. During temple *pūjā,* bells ring loudly, drums resound, conches and woodwinds blare to awaken worshipers from routine states of consciousness. Meditation on inner sound, called *nāda-anusandhāna,* is an essential *yoga* practice. Listening to the *Vedas* or other scripture is a contemplative, mystical process. Traditional music is revered as the nectar of the Divine. See: *Aum, nāda, Śiva consciousness.*

Soundless Sound: Paranāda. See: *nāda.*

sovereign: Greatest; above or superior to all others. Ruling; supreme in rank or authority.

sow: To scatter or plant, as seeds for cultivation; disseminate; propagate.

span: To stretch across or over, as a bridge spans a river. To cover or take in the whole of something.

***Spanda Kārikā:* स्पन्दकारिका** A commentary of 52 verses by Vasugupta on the *Śiva Sūtras.* Also called the *Spanda Sūtras.* See: *Vasugupta, Vīra Śaivism.*

spark: A small burning piece of matter, usually thrown off by a fire. A tiny beginning. To stir or activate.

spectrum: A series of colored bands which blend one into the other so as to include the entire range of colors, as a rainbow. The entire range of variations of anything, as in the spectrum of all possible emotions.

speculate (speculation): To conjecture, reflect, think or meditate on a subject. See: *meditation, self-reflection.*

***sphaṭika:* स्फटिक** "Quartz crystal." From *sphaṭ,* "to expand; blossom; to burst open or into view." See: *sphaṭika Śivaliṅga.*

***sphaṭika Śivaliṅga:* स्फटिकशिवलिङ्ग** "Crystal mark of God." A quartz-crystal Śivaliṅga. See: *San Mārga Sanctuary, Śivaliṅga, Svayambhū Liṅga.*

sphere: A world. The area, place; the extent or range or action, experience or influence. See: *loka, world.*

Spinoza, Baruch: German philosopher (1632-1677) who taught a monistic pantheism of one infinite substance, God or nature.

spiritual evolution: *Adhyātma prasāra.* See: *adhyātma prasāra, evolution of the soul.*

spiritual unfoldment: *Adhyātma vikāsa.* The unfoldment of the spirit, the inherent, divine soul of man. The very gradual expansion of consciousness as *kuṇḍalinī śakti* slowly rises through the *sushumṇā.* The term *spiritual unfoldment* indicates this slow, imperceptible process, likened to a lotus flower's emerging from bud to effulgent beauty. Contrasted with *development,* which implies intellectual study; or *growth,* which implies character building and *sādhana.* Sound intellect and good character are the foundation for spiritual unfoldment, but they are not the unfoldment itself. When philosophical training and *sādhana* is complete, the *kuṇḍalinī* rises safely and imperceptively, without jerks, twitches, tears or hot flashes. Brings greater willpower, compassion and perceptive qualities. See: *adhyātma vikāsa, kuṇḍalinī, liberation, pāda, sādhana, sādhana mārga, San Mārga, tapas.*

splendor (splendid): Great brightness, magnificent in richness, beauty or character. Grandeur.

spouse: A partner in a marriage; a husband or wife.

śraddhā: **श्रद्धा** "Faith; belief." See: *pañcha śraddhā.*

śrāddha: **श्राद्ध** Relating to commemorative ceremonies for the deceased, held one week, one month after death, and annually thereafter, according to tradition. See: *death, bone-gathering, piṇḍa, saṁskāras of later life.*

śraddhādhāraṇā: **श्रद्धाधारणा** "Collection or concentration of faith or belief." A term used in *Dancing with Śiva* for *creed,* a concise synopsis of religious doctrine. See: *creed, faith.*

śrauta: **श्रौत** "Related to hearing; audible." That which is prescribed by or conforms with the *Vedas.*

Śrauta Śāstra: **श्रौतशात्र** "Texts on the revelation." 1) Refers to scriptures or teachings that are in agreement with the *Vedas.* 2) A specific group of texts of the *Kalpa Vedāṅga,* and part of the essential study for Vedic priests. The *Śrauta Śāstras* offer explanation of the *yajña* rituals. See: *Vedāṅga.*

śrī: **श्री** "Radiant, beautiful, majestic; prosperous." An honorific prefix meaning "sacred, holy," often attached to the names of Deities (as in Śrī Gaṇeśa); to the names of scriptural works; and to the names of eminent persons, similar to the English *reverend* or, more commonly, *Mr.* (the feminine equivalent is *śrīmātī).*

Śrī Chakra: **श्रीचक्र** See: *yantra.*

Śrī Laṅkā **श्रीलङ्का** ஸ்ரீ லங்கா "Venerable lion." Island country off the southeast tip of India, formerly called Ceylon, 80% Buddhist, home to several million Tamil Śaivites who live mostly in the arid north. It was a British colony until independence in 1948 as a member of the Commonwealth; became a republic in 1972; 25,000 square miles, 15 million population.

Śrīkaṇṭha: **श्रीकण्ठ** A saint and philosopher (ca 1050) who promoted a Śaivite theology which embraced monism and dualism. Founder of the Śaiva school called Śiva Advaita, or Śiva Viśishṭādvaita, teaching a "Śaivite qualified nondualism," resembling Rāmānuja's Vaishṇavite Viśishṭādvaita. He was also known as Nīlakaṇṭha Śivāchārya. See: *Śiva Advaita.*

Śrīkumāra: **श्रीकुमार** Monistic Śaiva Siddhānta philosopher (ca 1050) who refuted the Śaṅkaran Vedānta doctrine of *māyā* as illusion and expounded that Śiva is both material cause *(upādāna kāraṇa)* and efficient cause *(nimitta kāraṇa).*

Śrīnagara: **श्रीनगर** A principal city of Kashmir.

Śrīnātha: **श्रीनाथ** A great Kashmīr Śaivite teacher of monistic theism. See: *Durvāsas.*

śrī pādukā: **श्रीपादुका** The *guru's* holy sandals. See: *pādukā.*

Śrī Rudram: **श्रीरुद्रम्** "Hymn to the wielder of terrific powers." Preeminent Vedic hymn to Lord Śiva as the God of dissolution, chanted daily in Śiva temples throughout India. It is in this long prayer, located in the *Yajur Veda, Taittirīya Saṁhitā,* in the middle of the first three *Vedas,* that the Śaivite *mantra* Namaḥ Śivāya first appears.

sṛishṭi**:** **सृष्टि** "Creation." See: *Naṭarāja.*

śruti: **श्रुति** "That which is heard." Hinduism's revealed scriptures, of supreme theological authority and spiritual value. They are timeless teachings transmitted to *ṛishis,* or seers, directly by God thousands of years ago. *Śruti* is thus said to be *apaurusheya,* "impersonal." *Śruti* consists of the *Vedas* and the *Āgamas,* preserved through oral tradition and eventually written down in Sanskṛit. Among the many sacred books of the Hindus, these two bodies of knowledge are held in the highest esteem. For countless centuries *śruti* has been the basis of philosophical discussion, study and commentary, and this attention has given rise to countless schools of thought. It is also the subject of deep study and meditation, to realize the wisdom of the ancients within oneself. Most *mantras* are drawn from *śruti,* used for rites of worship, both public and domestic, as well as personal prayer and *japa.* It is a remarkable tribute to Hindu culture that so much of *śruti* was preserved for thousands of years without alteration by means of oral instruction from *guru* to *śishya,* generation after generation. In the *Veda* tradition this was accomplished by requiring the student to learn each verse in eleven different ways, including backwards. Traditionally *śruti* is not read, but chanted according to extremely precise rules of grammar, pitch, intonation and rhythm. This brings forth its greatest power. In the sacred language of *śruti,* word and meaning are so closely aligned that hearing these holy scriptures properly chanted is magical in its effect upon the soul of the listener. See: *Āgamas, smṛiti, Vedas.*

stave off: To push back, impede, keep from happening.

steadfast: Constant. Firm, fixed, established, secure. Not wavering or changeable.

sthapati: **स्थपति** From *stha,* "building or place," and *pati,* "lord or father." A master architect of Āgamic temples. A *sthapati* must be well versed in the *Śilpa Śāstras,* experienced in all aspects of temple construction, pious, mystically trained, and a good administrator, for he has a team of *śilpīs* working under him, stone cutters, carvers, sculptors, wood workers, etc. See: *Śilpa Śāstras, Stāpatyaveda.*

Sthāpatyaveda: **स्थापत्यवेद्** "Science of architecture." A class of writings on architecture, sometimes classed as one of the *Upavedas.* It embodies such works as the *Mānasāra,* the *Vāstu Śāstras* and the architectural *Śilpa Śāstra.* See: *Upaveda.*

sthiti: **स्थिति** "Preservation." See: *Naṭarāja.*

sthūla śarīra: **स्थूलशरीर** "Gross or physical body." The odic body. See: *actinic,* *actinodic, kośa, odic, subtle body.*

stingy (stinginess): Miserly. Unwilling or reluctant to give or spend.

Stoics: Ancient Greek philosophers who held that all things are governed by natural laws and that the wise follow virtue and remain aloof from the external world and its passions.

straits: A narrow waterway; a difficult, dangerous experience or passage in life.

stranglehold: Any action that suppresses freedom or cuts off life.

stratification: "Making layers." The process of organizing or arranging in layers or levels.

strī dharma: **स्त्रीधर्म** "Womanly conduct." See: *dharma.*

Subāla Upanishad: **सुबाल उपनिषद्** Belongs to the *Śukla Yajur Veda.* A dialog between sage Subāla and Brahmā about the Supreme Being as Nārāyaṇa.

subatomic: Of the inner parts of atoms; anything smaller than an atom.

subconscious mind: *Saṁskāra chitta.* See: *aura, conscience, mind (five states).*

śubha muhūrta: **शुभमुहूर्त** "Auspicious time." A range of time when specified activities are most likely to thrive and succeed. See: *muhūrta.*

subjective: Personal. Of or colored by the personality, state of mind etc., of the observer (subject). Opposite of objective. Cf: *objective.*

sublime: Noble, grand. Inspiring awe or reverence.

subliminal: Below the threshold of consciousness or apprehension, such as an attitude of which one is not aware. Subconscious. See: *mind (five states).*

Subramaṇya: **सुब्रमण्य** "Very pious; dear to holy men." A Name of Lord Kārttikeya. See: *kārttikeya.*

Subramuniyaswami: சுப்பிரமுனியசுவாமி Current *satguru* (1927–) of the Nandinātha Sampradāya's Kailāsa Paramparā. He was ordained Sivaya Subramuniyaswami by Sage Yogaswāmī on the full-moon day of May 12, 1949, in Jaffna, Sri Lanka, at 6:21 PM. This was just days after he had attained *nirvikalpa samādhi* in the caves of Jalani. Yogaswāmī, then 77, ordained the 22-year old *yogī* with a tremendous slap on the back, saying, "This will be heard in America," and conferring upon him the mission to bring the fullness of Śaivism to the West. That same year, while still in Sri Lanka, Subramuniyaswami founded the Śaiva Siddhānta Yoga Order and Śaiva Siddhānta Church at the Śrī Subramuniya Āśrama in Alaveddy. Returning to America, he spent the next six years preparing for his teaching mission through intense *sādhana* and *tapas.* He began actively teaching in 1957 when he founded the Himalayan Academy. In 1970, he established his international headquarters and monastery complex, Kauai Aadheenam, on Hawaii's Garden Island of Kauai. Five years later, he designated a portion of the 51-acre holy site as the San Mārga Sanctuary, future site of Iraivan Temple, carved of white granite stone in Bangalore, India. To spearhead a growing Hindu renaissance, he founded the international newspaper *Hinduism Today* in 1979. Now franchised in several countries, the journal has become known worldwide as the Hindu family newspaper.

In August of 1986, the World Religious Parliament in New Delhi honored Subramuniyaswami as one of five Hindu spiritual leaders outside of India who had most dynamically promoted Sanātana Dharma in the past 25 years. He was given the title Jagadāchārya, "World Teacher." In April of 1988, he was selected to represent Hinduism at the five-day Global Forum of Spiritual and Parliamentary Leaders for Human Survival, held in England at Oxford University, and again at the Global Forum on Human Survival in Moscow from January 11 to 15, 1990; in Brazil, June 5–7, 1992; and in Kyoto, Japan, April 15–18, 1993.

Over the years Subramuniyaswami has written hundreds of tracts and books, which have been distributed in the tens of thousands in many languages. Especially in the 1980s, he lectured worldwide and established the worship in numerous Hindu temples. Gurudeva teaches the traditional Śaivite Hindu path to enlightenment, a path that leads the soul from simple service to worshipful devotion to God, from the disciplines of meditation and *yoga* to the direct knowing of Divinity within. His insights into the nature of consciousness provide a key for quieting the external mind and revealing to aspirants their deeper states of being, which are eternally perfect, full of light, love, serenity and wisdom. He urges all seekers to live a life of *ahiṁsā,* harmlessness towards nature, people and creatures, an ethic which includes vegetarianism. From his *āśrama* in Hawaii, Gurudeva continues to follow his *satguru's* instruction to bring Śaivism to the Western world by teaching others to "know thy Self by thyself" and thus "see God Śiva everywhere." Through the ordained *swāmīs* of the Śaiva Siddhānta Yoga Order, he trains young men in the ancient path of *brahmacharya,* enlightenment and service to humanity. Over 30 full-time monks, along with family groups in eight countries, have joined to fulfill this *paramparā's* mission of furthering monistic Śaiva Siddhānta and Hindu solidarity.

The name *Subramuniya* is a Tamil spelling of the Sanskṛit *Śubhramunya* (not to be confused with *Subramaṇya).* It is formed from *śubhra* meaning "light; intuition," and *muni,* "silent sage." *Ya* means "restraint; religious meditation." Thus, *Subramuniya* means a self-restrained soul who remains silent or, when he speaks, speaks out from intuition.

subside: To become less active or less intense. To abate.

substance: Essence; real nature.

substratum: "Layer underneath." In geology, the layer of rock or other matter forming the foundation of a particular landscape and acting as its support. In philosophy, that which is "underneath," not visible but the support for all of existence, the substance or underlying force which is the foundation of any and all manifestation: Satchidānanda. See: *Parāśakti, Satchidānanda, tattva.*

sub-subconscious mind: *Vāsanā chitta.* See: *mind (five states).*

subsuperconscious mind: *Anukāraṇa chitta.* See: *kalā, mind (five states),* *tattvas.*

subtle body: *Sūkshma śarīra,* the nonphysical, astral body or vehicle in which the soul encases itself to function in the Antarloka, or subtle world. The subtle body includes the *prāṇamaya, manomaya* and *vijñānamaya kośas* if the soul is physically embodied. It consists of only *manomaya* and *vijñānamaya* after death, when *prāṇamaya kośa* disintegrates. And it consists of only *vijñānamaya kośa* when *manomaya kośa* is dropped off just before rebirth or when higher evolutionary planes are entered. Also part of the subtle body are the *antaḥkaraṇa* (mental faculty: intellect, instinct and ego—*buddhi, manas* and *ahaṁkāra),* the five *jñānendriyas* (agents of perception: hearing, touch, sight, taste and smell); *and* the five *karmendriyas* (agents of action: speech, grasping, movement, excretion and generation). See: *indriya, jīva, kośa.*

subtle plane: See: *loka, three worlds.*

successor: A person who follows another, in office or title, as the successor to a *satguru* or king. —**succession:** A number of persons or things coming one after another in order; e.g., a spiritual succession. See: *guru paramparā.*

sūchī: सूची "Needle; sharp point." An index: that which reveals a book.

Śuddha Śaiva Siddhānta: शुद्धशैवसिद्धान्त "Pure Śaiva Siddhānta," a term first used by Tirumular in the *Tirumantiram* to describe his monistic Śaiva Siddhānta and distinguish it from pluralistic Siddhānta and other forms of Siddhānta that do not encompass the ultimate monism of Vedānta.

Śuddhavidyā: शुद्धविद्या "Pure Knowledge." The fifth *tattva* in the Śaiva Siddhānta system. See: *tattva.*

śūdra: शूद्र "Worker, servant." The social class of skilled artisans, workers and laborers. See: *varṇa dharma.*

suicide: "Self-killing." In Sanskṛit, *prāṇatyāga,* "abandoning life force." Intentionally ending one's own life through poisoning, drowning, burning, jumping, shooting, etc. Suicide has traditionally been condemned in Hindu scripture because, being an abrupt escape from life, it creates unseemly *karma* to face in the future. However, in cases of terminal disease or great disability, religious self-willed death through fasting—*prāyopaveśa*—is permitted. The person making such a decision declares it publicly, which allows for community regulation and distinguishes the act from suicide performed privately in traumatic emotional states of anguish and despair. Ancient lawgivers cite various stipulations: 1) inability to perform normal bodily purification; 2) death appears imminent or the condition is so bad that life's pleasures are nil; 3) the action must be done under community regulation. The gradual nature of *prāyopaveśa* is a key factor distinguishing it from sudden suicide, *svadehaghata* ("murdering one's body"), for it allows time for the individual to settle all differences with others, to ponder life and draw close to God, as well as for loved ones to oversee the person's gradual exit from the physical world. In the ideal, highly ritualized practice, one begins by obtaining forgiveness and giving forgiveness. Next a formal vow, *mahāvrata-marana,* "great vow of death," is given to one's *guru,* following a full discussion of all *karmas* of this life, especially fully and openly confessing one's wrongdoings. Thereafter, attention is to be focused on scripture and the *guru's* noble teachings. Meditation on the innermost, immortal Self becomes the full focus as one gradually abstains from food. At the very end, as the soul releases itself from the body, the sacred *mantra* is repeated as instructed by the preceptor. See: *death, penance, reincarnation, soul, prāyopaveśa.*

Śukla Yajur Veda: शुक्लयजुर्वेद See: *Yajur Veda.*

sūkshma śarīra: सूक्ष्मशरीर "Subtle body," or astral body. See: *actinic, actinodic, kośa, odic, soul, subtle body.*

Śulba Śāstra(s): शुल्बशास्त्र Practical manuals giving the measurements and procedures for constructing the sites of Vedic *yajña* rites. A division of the *Kalpa Vedāṅga (Veda* limb on rituals), these *sūtras* employ sophisticated geometry and are India's earliest extant mathematical texts. *Śulba* means "string or cord," denoting the use of string for measuring. See: *Vedāṅga.*

sully (sullied): To make dirty, or impure. See: *purity-impurity.*

Sundaranāthar: சுந்தரநாதர் Original name of Nātha Siddha Tirumular before he trekked to South India from the Himalayas. See: *Tirumular.*

Sundarar: சுந்தரர் One of the four Tamil Samayāchāryas (ca 800), and composer of devotional hymns to God Śiva, which form the seventh book of the *Tirumurai.* In these, he pleads forth-rightly to Śiva for material as well as spiritual abundance. See: *Nalvar, Nayanar, Tirumurai.*

Śūnya Sampādane: शून्यसंपादने "Gaining of Nothingness." A primary text of Vīra Śaivism (ca 1550) consisting of debates and writings of the Śiva Śaraṇās. *Śūnya:* "the void, the distinctionless absolute;" *sampādana:* "attainment, realization, enlightenment."

superconscious mind: *Kāraṇa chitta.* See: *kalā, mind (five states), mind (three phases), Satchidānanda, tattva.*

supernatural: Beyond or transcending the natural laws of the physical cosmos. Of or relating to an order of existence beyond the visible universe, referring to events, agencies or knowledge superseding or mystically explaining the laws of nature. See: *mysticism, shamanism.*

supplicate (supplication): To ask for humbly. To earnestly pray for.

Suprabheda Āgama: सुप्रभेद आगम One of the 28 *Śaiva Siddhānta Āgamas,* this scripture discusses temple worship, especially personal devotions, festivals, practices and initiations for each stage of life. A total of 4,666 verses have been preserved from the original scripture.

supreme: Highest in rank, power, authority.

Supreme God: Highest God, the source or creator of all other Gods, beings and all manifestation.

Sūrdās: सूरदास Blind North-Indian Vaishṇava poet (ca 1550), famous for his devotional hymns to Lord Kṛishṇa. His massive writing *Sūrsagar*, "Sur's Ocean," is widely read.

surpass: To excel; to be superior to.

surrender: Giving up or yielding. Surrender to the Divine is called *prapatti*, a complete giving over of oneself to God's will in total trust and abandonment. See: *bhakti, prapatti, sacrifice.*

Sūrya: सूर्य "Sun." One of the principal Divinities of the *Vedas*, also prominent in the epics and *Purāṇas*. Śaivites revere Sūrya, the Sun God each morning as Śiva Sūrya. Smārtas and Vaishṇavas revere the golden orb as Sūrya Nārāyaṇa. As the source of light, the sun is the most readily apparent image of Divinity available to man. As the giver of life, Sūrya is worshiped during harvest festivals everywhere. Esoterically, the sun represents the point where the manifest and unmanifest worlds meet or unite. In *yoga*, the sun represents the masculine force, *piṅgalā*. Sūrya also signifies the Self within. In the Vedic description of the course of souls after death, the "path of the sun" leads liberated souls to the realm of Brahman; while the path of the moon leads back to physical birth.

sushumṇā nāḍī: सुषुम्णानाडी "Most gracious channel." Central psychic nerve current within the spinal column. See: *kuṇḍalinī, nāḍī, samādhi.*

sustainable: Maintainable; able to be kept up or continued consistently over a period of time.

sustenance (to sustain): Support. That which preserves life, or gives strength. Nourishment.

sutala: सुतल "Great depth." Region of obsessive jealousy and retaliation. The third *chakra* below the *mūlādhāra*, centered in the knees. Corresponds to the third astral netherworld beneath the earth's surface, called Saṁhāta ("abandoned") or Sutala. See: *chakra, loka, Naraka.*

Sūta Saṁhitā: सूतसंहिता A chapter of the *Skānda Purāṇa* dealing in part with philosophy.

sūtra: सूत्र "Thread." An aphoristic verse; the literary style consisting of such maxims. From 500 BCE, this style was widely adopted by Indian philosophical systems and eventually employed in works on law, grammar, medicine, poetry, crafts, etc. Each *sūtra* is often accompanied by a commentary called *bhāshya* and sometimes subcommentary called *tika, vyakhyana* or *tippani.* Through the media of short, concise, easily memorized *sūtras*, vast amounts of knowledge were preserved. Reciting relevant *sūtra* texts from memory is a daily *sādhana* in various Hindu arts and sciences. *Sūtra* also names the wife's wedding pendant *(maṅgala sūtra)*. See: *bhāshya, wedding pendant.*

svadharma: स्वधर्म "One's own way." See: *dharma.*

svādhishṭhāna: स्वाधिष्ठान "One's own base." See: *chakra.*

svādhyāya: स्वाध्याय "Self-reflection; scriptural study." See: *yama-niyama.*

svarga: स्वर्ग "Abode of light." An intermediate realm of the Antarloka; a term essentially synonymous with *Svarloka.* See: *loka.*

***Svarloka:* स्वर्लोक** "Celestial or bright plane." The third of the seven upper worlds, the mid-astral region (equated in some texts with Svarga), realm of *maṇipūra chakra.* See: *loka.*

***Svātmarāma:* स्वात्मराम** See: *Haṭha Yoga Pradīpikā.*

***svayambhū Liṅga:* स्वयम्भूलिङ्ग** "Self-existent mark or sign of God." Names a Śivaliṅga discovered in nature and not carved or crafted by human hands; often a smooth cylindrical stone, called *bāṇaliṅga,* such as found in India's Narmada River. See: *Śivaliṅga.*

***Svāyambhuva Āgama:* स्वायम्भुव आगम** One of the 28 *Śaiva Siddhānta Āgamas.* See: *Śaiva Āgama.*

***Svāyambhuva Sūtra(s):* स्वायम्भुवसूत्र** A subsidiary text of the *Śaiva Āgamas.*

***Śvetāśvatara Upanishad:* श्वेताश्वतर उपनिषद्** An *Upanishad* of the *Yajur Veda* that speaks of personal God and devotion, and at the same time of the unity of God, soul and world. It is a major *Upanishads,* among the greatest monistic writings, especially valued by Śaivite schools.

***swāmī:* स्वामी** "Lord; owner." He who knows or is master of himself. A respectful title for a Hindu monk, usually a *sannyāsin.* The term *swāmī* is sometimes applied more broadly to include nonmonastics dedicated to spiritual work. See: *monk, sannyāsin.*

***swāminī:* स्वामिनी** The feminine form of *swāmī.* See: *nunk, sannyāsa, swāmī.*

***Swāmī Nityānanda:* स्वामीनित्यानन्द** Kashmīr Śaivite *satguru* (?–1961), whose successor, Swāmī Muktānanda (1908–1982), founded the Siddha Yoga Dhām.

***Swāmī Śivānanda:* स्वामीशिवानन्द** One of Hinduism's most influential modern-day saints (1887–1963). He was born in South India, practiced medicine in Malaysia, published a medical journal, became administrator of a hospital and later renounced the world. He was initiated by Swāmī Viśvānanda Sarasvatī at Rishikesh in 1924, and founded the Divine Life Society in 1939, which has branches in many countries today. He has been a powerful force in spreading Hindu teachings in India and abroad through his many books and the travels of his numerous *swāmīs.* Emphasized *haṭha* and *rāja yoga* and a broad, universal form of Hinduism.

***swastika:* स्वस्तिक** "It is well." The ancient Hindu symbol of auspiciousness and good fortune, representing the sun. The right-angled arms of the swastika denote the indirect way in which Divinity is reached—through intuition and not by intellect. It has been a prominent icon in many cultures. See: *mūrti.*

swirl: To move in a whirling, circular motion, like a whirlpool.

symbolism: The representation of one thing by something else. E.g., the *ḍamaru,* Śiva's drum, is a symbol of creation.

syncretism: A combination of various beliefs and practices, often of opposing views formed into a one creed or system of belief, typically marked by inconsistencies. See: *universalist.*

synonymous: Having the same or similar meaning. Quality of two words or phrases whose meanings are identical.

synthesis: A combining of various parts to make a whole.

Tagore, Rabīndranāth: One of India's most highly acclaimed modern-day writers and poets (1861–1941), son of Devendranāth Tagore. He wrote in Bengali and in English. His most famous poetic religious work is *Gītāñjali,* which centers around dialogs between the soul and God Vishṇu. He received the Nobel Prize for literature in 1913.

tainted: Sullied, spoiled or stained. Morally corrupt or depraved.

Tai Pongal: தைப்பொங்கல் A four-day home festival held in the Tamil month of Tai (January-February), celebrating the season's first harvest. Sūrya, the Sun God, is honored at this time as the giver of all good fortune and as the visible Divine One. Newly harvested rice is ceremoniously cooked outdoors over an open fire in a giant pot (hence *pongal,* from *pongu,* "to cook"). The direction of the overflow of boiling milk is an augury for the coming year.

Tai Pusam: தைப்பூசம் A festival held on the Pushya *nakshatra* near the full-moon day of January-February to worship Lords Śiva or Kārttikeya, depending on the locality. It is an important holiday, especially dear to the Tamil people, celebrated with great pomp, fervor and intensity in India, Sri Lanka, Malaysia, Fiji, South Africa and Réunion, often marked by the carrying of *kavadi.* In Mauritius and Singapore it is a national holiday. See: *kavadi, Kārttikeya.*

Taittirīya Āraṇyaka: तैत्तिरीय आरण्यक A forest treatise of *Kṛishṇa Yajur Veda.* See: *Veda.*

Taittirīya Saṁhitā: तैत्तिरीयसंहिता See: *Yajur Veda.*

Taittirīya Upanishad: तैत्तिरीय उपनिषद् Belongs to the *Taittirīya Brāhmaṇa* of the *Yajur Veda* and is divided into three sections called *valli(s).* The first deals with phonetics and pronunciation, the second and third with Brahman and the attainment of bliss.

tala: तल "Plane or world; level; base, bottom." Root of the name of the seven realms of lower consciousness centered in the seven *chakras* below the *mūlādhāra.* See: *chakra, hell, purgatory, loka, Naraka.*

talātala chakra: तलातल "Lower region." The fourth *chakra* below the *mūlādhāra,* centered in the calves. Region of chronic mental confusion and unreasonable stubbornness. Corresponds to the fourth astral netherworld beneath the earth's surface, called Tāmisra ("darkness") or Talātala. This state of consciousness is born of the sole motivation of self-preservation. See: *chakra, loka, Naraka.*

tamas(ic): तमस् "Force of inertia." See: *guṇa.*

Tamil: தமிழ் The ancient Dravidian language of the Tamils, a Caucasoid people of South India and Northern Sri Lanka, who have now migrated throughout the world. The official language of the state of Tamil Nadu, India. See: *race.*

Tamil Nadu: தமிழ் நாடு State in South India, 50,000 square miles, population 55 million. Land of countless holy scriptures, saints, sages and over 40,000 magnificent temples, including Chidambaram, Madurai, Palani Hills and Rāmeśvaram.

tāṇḍava: ताण्डव "Violent dance." Any vigorous dance sequence performed by a male dancer. There are many forms of *tāṇḍava.* Its prototype is Śiva's dance of bliss, *ānanda tāṇḍava.* The more sublime, female dance is called *lāsya,* from *lasa,* "lively." Dance in general is *nartana.* See: *Naṭarāja.*

tantra: तन्त्र "Loom, methodology." 1) Most generally, a synonym for *śāstra,* "scripture." 2) A synonym for the Āgamic texts, especially those of the Śākta faith, a class of Hindu scripture providing detailed instruction on all aspects of religion, mystic knowledge and science. The *tantras* are also associated with the Śaiva tradition. 3) A specific method, technique or spiritual practice within the Śaiva and Śākta traditions. For example, *prāṇāyāma* is a *tantra. Tantra* generally involves a reversal of the normal flow of energies. Its perspective is that the inner self is most important, and outer life is secondary. *Tantra* causes the life force to flow up through the *sushumṇā.* Many are the methods for overcoming the unovercomeable. Fallen into the hands of the unscrupulous, these techniques become black magic *(abhichāra).*

Tantrāloka: तन्त्रालोक One of the most comprehensive and authoritative expositions of Kashmīr Śaivism, written by Abhinavagupta. See: *Abhinavagupta, Kashmīr Śaivism.*

tantrika: तन्त्रिक (Anglicized: *tantric.)* Adjectival form for practices prescribed in the Tantra traditions. The name of a follower of any of the *tantric* traditions. See: *tantra, tantrism.*

tantrism: The enlightenment path outlined in the *Tantra* scriptures. 1) Tantrism is sometimes considered a parallel stream of history and tradition in Hinduism, running alongside and gradually interweaving with the Vedic *brāhminical* tradition. 2) Tantrism refers to traditions, mainly within Śaivism and Śāktism, that focus on the arousal of the *kuṇḍalinī* force, and which view the human body as a vehicle of the Divine and an instrument for liberation. Tantrism's ultimate aim is a channeling of the *kuṇḍalinī* life force through the *sushumṇā,* the gracious channel, upwards into the *sahasrāra chakra* and beyond, through the door of *brahman (brahmarandhra)* into Paraśiva, either before or at the time of death. The stress is on the transformation of all spheres of consciousness, spiritual, psychic, emotional and material. It is a path of *sādhana.* 3) ***—Śākta Tantrism:*** Brings a strong emphasis on the worship of the feminine force. Depending on the school, this may be symbolic or literal in rites involving sexual intercourse, etc. Śākta

Tantrism's main principle is the use of the material to gain the spiritual. In certain schools, historically, this implies embracing that which is normally forbidden and manipulating the forces to attain transcendent consciousness rather than lower consciousness. There are three main streams: 1) the right-hand path *(dakshiṇa mārga* or *dakshiṇāchāra)* of conservative Hindu practice, 2) the left-hand path *(vāma mārga* or *vāmāchāra)* involving the use of things normally forbidden such as taking intoxicants, meat, ritual sex, etc., and 3) the *yogic* path of the Kaula sect. Gorakshanātha followers are sometimes grouped with the latter. See: *Śāktism, kuṇḍalinī, rāja yoga, tantra.*

Tao: "The way." The central concept of the Chinese religion called Taoism. Though traditionally considered impossible to translate, *Tao* is often rendered as "cosmic order," akin to the Sanskṛit *ṛita.* See: *dharma.*

tapas: **तपस्** "Heat, fire." 1) Purificatory spiritual disciplines, severe austerity, penance and sacrifice. The endurance of pain, suffering, through the performance of extreme penance, religious austerity and mortification. By comparison, *sādhana* is austerity of a simple, sustained kind, while *tapas* is austerity of a severe, psyche-transforming nature. *Tapas* is extreme bodily mortification, long term *sādhanas,* such as meditating under a tree in one place for 12 years, taking a lifetime vow of silence and never speaking or writing, or standing on one leg for a prescribed number of years. Scriptures generally warn against extreme asceticism which would bring harm to the body. 2) On a deeper level, *tapas* is the intense inner state of *kuṇḍalinī* "fire" which stimulates mental anguish and separates the individual from society. Life does not go on as usual when this condition occurs. The association with a *satguru,* Sadāśiva, brings the devotee into *tapas,* and it brings him out of it. The fire of *tapas* burns on the dross of *sañchita karmas.* This is the source of heat, dismay, depression and striving until the advent of final and total surrender, *prapatti.* The individual can *mollify* this heated condition by continuing his regular *sādhana* as outlined by the *guru.* The fires of self-transformation may be stimulated by the practice of *tapas,* or come unbidden. One can "do" *tapas,* but the true *tapas* is a condition of being and consciousness which is a state of grace, bringing positive change, transformation and purification of one's nature. *Guru bhakti* is the only force that can cool the fires of *tapas.* See: *kuṇḍalinī, penance, sādhana.*

tapasvin: **तपस्विन्** One who performs *tapas* or is in the state of *tapas.* See: *tapas.*

Tapoloka: **तपोलोक** "Plane of austerity." The second highest of the seven upper worlds, realm of *ājñā chakra.* See: *loka.*

tarnished: Dulled, sullied, spoiled, lacking luster.

Tat: **तत्** "That; the indescribable Absolute; supreme."

Tātparyadīpikā: **तात्पर्यदीपिका** A commentary by Śrīkumāra (ca 1100) on the *Tattvaprakāśa* of Śrī Bhojadeva Paramāra (1018–1060), a philosopher-king in Central India who expounded Śaiva Siddhānta. Śrīkumāra upheld the monistic basis of Bhojadeva's work, while later commentator Aghoraśiva reinterpreted it in dualistic terms. See: *Aghoraśiva, Śaiva Siddhānta.*

Tat Sat: **तत् सत्** "That is Truth." A terse phrase pointing to the inexpressible truth of which nothing more can be said.

tattva: **तत्त्व** "That-ness" or "essential nature." *Tattvas* are the primary principles, elements, states or categories of existence, the building blocks of the universe. Lord Śiva constantly creates, sustains the form of and absorbs back into Himself His creations. Ṛishis describe this emanational process as the unfoldment of *tattvas,* stages or evolutes of manifestation, descending from subtle to gross. At *mahāpralaya,* cosmic dissolution, they enfold into their respective sources, with only the first two *tattvas* surviving the great dissolution. The first and subtlest form—the pure consciousness and source of all other evolutes of manifestation—is called Śiva *tattva,* or Parāśakti-*nāda.* But beyond Śiva *tattva* lies Paraśiva—the utterly transcendent, Absolute Reality, called *attava.* That is Śiva's first perfection. The Sāṅkhya system discusses 25 *tattvas.* Śaivism recognizes these same 25 plus 11 beyond them, making 36 *tattvas* in all. These are divided into three groups: 1) First are the five *śuddha* (pure) *tattvas.* These constitute the realm of *śuddha māyā.* 2) Next are the seven *śuddha-aśuddha* (pure-impure) *tattvas.* These constitute the realm of *śuddhāśuddha māyā.* 3) The third group comprises the 24 *aśuddha* (impure) *tattvas.* These constitute the realm of *aśuddha māyā.*

—THE ŚUDDHA TATTVAS: **Actinic or spiritual energy.** This is the superconscious realm, also known as *śuddha* (pure) *māyā* or *mahāmāyā. Bindu,* transcendent light, is the "material" cause of this pure sphere. This is the Śivaloka, the region of the 330 million Gods, the myriad *ṛishis* and other beings who have attained freedom from the triple bondage.

1) ***Śiva tattva:*** "auspiciousness," of two parts: the higher is Parāśakti, "Supreme Energy," from which emerges primal sound, *nāda* (more precisely Paranāda, soundless sound). Though most often referred to as sound, *nāda* is more mystically known as movement, the first impulse arising from perfect quiescence, the first "thing" out of the motionless Self. This is Śiva's second perfection, Parāśakti, superconsciousness, the mind of God. The Śiva *tattva* pervades all other 35 categories and possesses the powers of will, knowledge and action *(icçhā, jñāna, kriyā).*

2) ***Śakti tattva:*** energy, corresponds to *bindu,* light, the cause of form (more precisely Parabindu, primal nucleus). This is the *tattva* of Parameśvara, the Primal Soul, father-mother God, Śiva's third perfection, who after *mahāpralaya* remains transfixed in deep *samādhi,* until He again emanates the universe through His Cosmic Dance.

3) ***Sadāśiva tattva:*** the power of revealing grace. In this realm the energies of knowledge and action are in perfect equilibrium. This is the realm of the *ānandamaya kośa.*

4) ***Īśvara tattva:*** the energy of concealment, concealing grace. The energy of action prevails over that of knowledge in order to arouse cosmic activity

in its subtle form.

5) ***śuddhavidyā tattva:*** pure knowledge, *dharma.* This is a level of manifestation in which the energy of action is in abeyance and the energy of knowledge prevails. *Śuddhavidyā tattva* includes Śiva's other three powers or aspects: Rudra (destruction), Vishṇu (preservation) and Brahmā (creation).

—***THE ŚUDDHĀŚUDDHA TATTVAS:*** **Actinodic, or spiritual-magnetic, energy.** The seven *tattvas* from *māyā* to *purusha* make up the *śuddhāśuddha* (pure-impure) realm.

6) ***māyā tattva:*** mirific energy, the "material" cause of the "impure sphere." The category of *māyā* brings into being as its immediate aids the following five *tattvas,* known as the "five sheaths," *pañcha kañchuka,* of the individual soul, *purusha.* Collectively they make up the *vijñānamaya kośa,* or mental body.

7) ***kāla tattva:*** the phenomenon of time, which divides all experience into past, present and future.

8) ***niyati tattva:*** *karmic* destiny; necessity; order; law of cause and effect; restraint.

9) ***kalā tattva:*** creativity, aptitude, the power which draws the soul toward spiritual knowledge. Its energy partially removes the veil of *āṇava* which clouds the inherent powers of the soul.

10) ***vidyā tattva:*** limited knowledge, the power which gives the soul practical knowledge in accord with its present life experiences.

11) ***rāga tattva:*** attachment, the arousal of desire, without which no experience of the objective world is possible.

12) ***purusha tattva:*** soul identity; soul connected with subjectivity. Through identification with the five above "sheaths," the soul, *ātman,* becomes a *purusha,* or bound soul, capable of experiencing the higher Antarloka as a limited individual. This five-fold sheath is called the *pañcha kañchuka,* or *vijñānamaya kośa* (mental body).

—***AŚUDDHA TATTVAS: Odic, or magnetic, energy.*** These 24 categories make up the "world" of *aśuddha* (impure) *māyā.* This is the realm of the astral and physical planes, in which souls function through the *manomaya, prāṇamaya* and *annamaya kośas,* depending on their level of embodiment.

13) ***prakṛiti tattva:*** primal nature, the gross energy of which all lower *tattvas* are formed. *Prakṛiti,* also called *pradhāna,* is expressed as three *guṇas* (qualities)—*sattva, rajas* and *tamas.* These manifest as light, activity and inertia, respectively; and on the subtle level as pleasure, sorrow and delusion. These *guṇas* dominate the soul's powers of knowledge, action and desire *(jñāna, kriyā* and *icçhā),* and form the *guṇa* body, *manomaya kośa.*

—*antaḥkaraṇa:* the mental faculty. 14) ***buddhi tattva:*** judgment, intellect, the faculty of discrimination. 15) ***ahaṁkāra tattva:*** egoism, sense of I-ness in the external form. It is the fundamental principle of individuality. 16) ***manas tattva:*** the instinctive mind, the receiving and directing link between the outer senses and the inner faculties.

—*jñānendriya:* the five cognitive senses, of the nature of *sattva guṇa.* Each has a subtle and physical aspect. 17) ***śrotra tattva:*** hearing (ears). 18) ***tvak tattva:*** touching (skin). 19) ***chakshu tattva:*** seeing (eyes). 20) ***rasanā tattva:*** tasting (tongue). 21) ***ghrāṇa tattva:*** smelling (nose).

—*karmendriya:* the five organs of action, of the nature of *rajaguṇa.* Each has a subtle and physical aspect. 22) ***vāk tattva:*** speech (voice). 23) ***pāṇi tattva:*** grasping (hands). 24) ***pāda tattva:*** walking (feet). 25) ***pāyu tattva:*** excretion (anus). 26) ***upastha tattva:*** procreation (genitals).

—*tanmatra:* the five subtle elements, of the nature of *tamaguṇa.* 27) ***śabda tattva:*** sound. 28) ***sparśa tattva:*** feel. 29) ***rūpa tattva:*** form. 30) ***rasa tattva:*** taste. 31) ***gandha tattva:*** odor. These are the subtle characteristics of the five gross elements, *ākāśa, vāyu, tejas, āpas* and *pṛithivī,* respectively.

—*pañchabhūta:* the five gross elements. 32) ***ākāśa tattva:*** ether or space. 33) ***vāyu tattva:*** air. 34) ***tejas tattva:*** fire. 35) ***āpas tattva*** (or *jāla):* water. 36) ***pṛithivī tattva:*** earth. See: *atattva, antaḥkaraṇa, guṇa, kośa, Śiva (also, charts at end of lexicon).*

Tattva Prakāśa: तत्त्वप्रकाश "Illumination of the categories." Text of 76 verses by the philosopher-king Bhoja Paramāra which systematized and consolidated monistic Śaiva Siddhānta in the 11th century.

tattvatrayī: तत्त्वत्रयी "Essential triad." Names the primary categories of Śaiva and Śākta schools, Pati (God), *paśu* (soul) and *pāśa* (world, or bonds). See: *padārtha, Pati-paśu-pāśa.*

Tayumanavar: தாயுமானவர் A Tamil Śaivayogī, devotional mystic and poet saint (ca 17th century) whose writings are a harmonious blend of philosophy and devotion. In his poem "Chinmayānanda Guru," Tayumanavar places himself in the genealogy of Ṛishi Tirumular. See: *Tirumular.*

temper: To reduce in intensity or moderate by the addition of other qualities. Also, the quality of anger, or the propensity to become angry. See: *chakra.*

temple: A place consecrated for, and dedicated to, the worship of God or Gods. Hindus revere their temples as sacred, magical places in which the three worlds most consciously commune—structures especially built and consecrated to channel the subtle spiritual energies of inner-world beings. The temple's psychic atmosphere is maintained through regular worship ceremonies *(pūjā)* invoking the Deity, who uses His installed image *(mūrti)* as a temporary body to bless those living on the earth plane. In Hinduism, the temple is the hub of virtually all aspects of social and religious life. It may be referred to by the Sanskṛit terms *mandira, devālaya* (or Śivālaya, a Śiva temple), as well as by vernacular terms such as *koyil* (Tamil). See: *garbhagṛiha, darśana, maṇḍapa, pradakshiṇa, sound, teradi, tīrthayātrā.*

temporal: Referring to time; subject to time. Passing, existing only for a time.

tend: Having a tendency or inclination to do something.

teradi: தேரடி "Chariot shed." Tamil term for the building that houses the temple cart or chariot *(ter)* in which the parade Deity, *utsava mūrti*, is taken in procession on festival days.

terminable: Which can be ended. Not lasting forever.

terminal: Concluding, ending, final.

terminal illness: Incurable disease, ending in death. See: *death, suicide.*

That: When capitalized, this simple demonstrative refers uniquely to the Ultimate, Indescribable or Nameless Absolute. The Self God, Paraśiva. It is the English equivalent of *Tat,* as in, *Tat tvam asi,* "You are That!"

theism: Belief that God exists as a real, conscious, personal Supreme Being, creator and ruler of the universe. May also include belief in the Gods.

theology: The study of religious doctrines, specifically of the nature of God, soul and world. —**theologians:** Those who study, are expert in or formulate theology. Cf: *metaphysics.*

thither: Toward that place; there. Farther.

thou/thy: Poetic, Old English alternates for *you/your. Thy* is the possessive form of *thou.* Often used in religious writing or translation of devotional scripture as an expression of respect and veneration not conveyed in the ordinary pronouns *you* and *your.*

three worlds: The three worlds of existence, *triloka,* are the primary hierarchical divisions of the cosmos. 1) Bhūloka: "Earth world," the physical plane. 2) Antarloka: "Inner or in-between world," the subtle or astral plane. 3) Śivaloka: "World of Śiva," and of the Gods and highly evolved souls; the causal plane, also called Kāraṇaloka.

The three-world cosmology is readily found in Hindu scriptures. In the major *Upanishads* of the *Vedas* we find numerous citations, with interesting variations. Verse 1.5.17 of the *Bṛihadāraṇyaka Upanishad* states, "Now, there are, verily, three worlds, the world of men (Manushyaloka), the world of the fathers (Pitṛiloka) and the world of the Gods (Devaloka)..." Later, verse 6.2.15 refers to the two higher worlds as the Devaloka and the Brahmaloka. The *Katha Upanishad,* verse 2.3.8, omitting the world of men, lists the Pitṛiloka, the Gandharvaloka (world of genies or elementals) and the Brahmaloka (world of God). Another perspective of three worlds is offered in the Praśna *Upanishad* 3.8, which lists the world of good (Puṇyaloka), the world of evil (Pāpaloka) and the world of men (Manushyaloka).

Scriptures offer several other cosmological perspectives, most importantly seven upper worlds *(sapta urdhvaloka)* and seven lower worlds *(sapta adholoka),* which correspond to the 14 *chakras* and make up the "world-egg of God," the universe, called *Brahmāṇḍa.* The seven upper worlds are Bhūloka, Bhuvarloka, Svarloka, Maharloka, Janaloka, Tapoloka and Satyaloka. The second, third and fourth comprise the subtle plane. The highest three comprise the causal plane. The seven lower worlds, collectively known as Naraka or Pātāla, are (from highest to lowest) Put, Avīchi, Saṁhāta, Tāmisra, Ṛijīsha, Kuḍmala and Kākola.

From the Śaiva Āgamic perspective of the 36 *tattvas,* the pure sphere, *śuddha māyā*—the first five *tattvas*—is subdivided into 33 planes of existence. The "pure-impure" realm, *śuddhāśuddha māyā*—the seven *tattvas* from *māyā tattva* to *purusha*—contains 27 planes of existence. The *aśuddha* ("impure") *realm*—of 24 *tattvas*—has 56 planes of existence. See: *chakra, loka, Naraka, tattva (also: individual loka entries).*

thwart: To hinder, obstruct or frustrate.

thy: See: *thou/thy.*

tilaka: **तिलक** Marks made on the forehead or the brow with clay, ashes or sandalwood paste as an indication of sectarian affiliation. Vaishṇavas wear a vertical v-shaped *tilaka* made from clay. The Śaivite *tilaka,* called *tripuṇḍra,* consists of three horizontal strips of holy ash with a dot near the middle, or between the eyebrows. Wearing the *tilaka* is an expression of religious affiliation and pride in one's beliefs, not unlike the Christian's cross or the Jew's *yarmulke.* Elaborate *tilakas* are worn by Hindus today mainly at religious events and when on pilgrimage, though many Hindus wear the simple dot *(bindu)* on the forehead, indicating that they are Hindu, even when moving in the general public. See: *bindu, Hinduism, tripuṇḍra.*

timeless: Outside the condition of time, or not measurable in terms of time.

tirobhāva: **तिरोभाव** "Concealment," same as *tirodhāna.* See: *Naṭarāja, tirodhāna śakti.*

tirodhāna śakti: **तिरोधानशक्ति** "Concealing power." Veiling grace, or God's power to obscure the soul's divine nature. *Tirodhāna śakti* is the particular energy of Śiva that binds the three bonds of *āṇava, karma, māyā* to the soul. It is a purposeful limiting of consciousness to give the opportunity to the soul to grow and mature through experience of the world. See: *evolution of the soul, grace.*

tīrthayātrā: **तीर्थयात्रा** "Journeying to a holy place." Pilgrimage. One of the five sacred duties *(pañcha nitya karmas)* of the Hindu is to journey periodically to one of the innumerable holy spots in India or other countries. Preceded by fasting and continence, it is a time of austerity and purification, when all worldly concerns are set aside and God becomes one's singular focus. Streams of devout pilgrims are received daily at the many ancient holy sites *(tīrthas)* in India, and tens of thousands at festival times. See: *pañcha nitya karma, pañcha śraddhā.*

tiru: திரு "Sacred; holy." The exact Tamil equivalent of *śrī.* Feminine equivalent is *tirumati.* See: *śrī.*

Tirukural: திருக்குறள் "Holy couplets." A treasury of Hindu ethical insight and a literary masterpiece of the Tamil language, written by Śaiva Saint Tiruvalluvar (ca 200 BCE) near present-day Madras. Its nonsectarian wisdom has been adopted by Christians, Muslims, Jains and even atheists. The text focuses primarily on the first three goals of life—*artha* (wealth), *dharma* (conduct) and *kāma* (desire)—but also includes 13 chapters on renunciate *dharma,* relating to life's fourth goal, *moksha* (liberation). In an extraordinarily compact verse form of 14 syllables, the poet presents 133 subjects of ten verses each on relationships, human strengths and foibles, statecraft and more. One of the world's earliest ethical texts, the *Tirukural* could well be considered a bible on virtue for the human race. In fact, it is sworn on in South Indian courts of law. See: *Tiruvalluvar.*

Tirumantiram: திருமந்திரம் "Holy incantation." The Nandinātha Sampradāya's oldest Tamil scripture; written ca 200 BCE by Ṛishi Tirumular. It is the earliest of the *Tirumurai,* and a vast storehouse of esoteric *yogic* and *tantric* knowledge. It contains the mystical essence of *rāja yoga* and *siddha yoga,* and the fundamental doctrines of the 28 *Śaiva Siddhānta Āgamas,* which in turn are the heritage of the ancient pre-historic traditions of Śaivism. As the *Āgamas* themselves are now partially lost, the *Tirumantiram* is a rare source of the complete *Āgamanta* (collection of Āgamic lore). Its 3047 verses were, as legend has it, composed in a rather extraordinary way. Before writing each verse, Tirumular would meditate for an entire year, then summarize his meditation in a four-line Tamil verse. He did this for 3,000 years! The allegory is said to mean that 3,000 years of knowledge is compacted in this one book. The text is organized in nine parts, called *tantras,* summarized as follows: 1) basic rules of religious morality; 2) allegorical explanations of Śaiva mythological stories; five powers of Śiva, three classifications of souls; 3) a complete treatise on *rāja yoga;* 4) *mantras* and *tantras;* 5) the essential features of the Śaiva religion; the four forms of Śaivism, four stages, unorthodox paths, conduct to be avoided; 6) the Śivaguru, grace, renunciation, sin, penance, *jñāna,* worthy and unworthy persons; 7) *siddha yoga,* more on grace, *mudrās,* control of *iḍā* and *piṅgalā,* worlds reached by different classes of *yogīs* after death, refinements of *yoga,* the *satguru;* 8) essential theology: five sheaths, eleven states, three *padārthas* (Pati-*paśu-pāśa),* 36 *tattvas,* four states of consciousness, three *malas,* three *guṇas,* ten *kāraṇas,* etc.; 9) the fruits of realization, liberation, *jñāna,* Śiva's dances, meeting of the *guru.* See: *Tirumurai, Tirumular.*

Tirumular: திருமூலர் An illustrious *siddha yogī* and *ṛishi* of the Nandinātha Sampradāya's Kailāsa Paramparā who came from the Himalayas (ca 200 BCE) to Tamil Nadu to compose the *Tirumantiram.* In this scripture he recorded the tenets of Śaivism in concise and precise verse form, based upon his own realizations and the supreme authority of the *Śaiva Āgamas* and the *Vedas.* Tirumular was a disciple of Maharishi Nandinātha. See: *Tirumantiram, Kailāsa Paramparā, Vedānta.*

Tirumurai: திருமுறை "Holy book." A twelve-book collection of hymns and writings of South Indian Śaivite saints, compiled by Saint Nambiyandar Nambi (ca 1000). Of these, books 1-3 are the hymns of Saint Tirujñāna Sambandar (ca 600). Books 4-6 are the hymns of Saint Tirunavakarasu (Appar), a contemporary of Sambandar. Book 7 contains the hymns of

Saint Sundaramūrti (ca 800). Book 8 contains the two works of Saint Manikkavasagar (9th century)—*Tiruvasagam* and *Tirukovaiyar.* Book 9 is the *Tiruvisaippa* and *Tiruppallandu,* which together comprise the works of nine saints. Book 10 is the *Tirumantiram* of Saint Tirumular (ca 200 BCE). Book 11 contains the hymns of ten saints, including Saint Nakkirar and Nambiyandar Nambi, the compiler. Book 12 is the *Periyapurāṇam* by Saint Sekkilar (11th century), narrating the life story of the 63 Śaiva Nayanar saints. The first seven books are known as *Devarams.*

Tiruvalluvar: திருவள்ளுவர் "Holy weaver." Tamil weaver and householder saint (ca 200 BCE) who wrote the classic Śaivite ethical scripture Tirukural. He lived with his wife Vasuki, famed for her remarkable loyalty and virtues, near modern-day Madras. There a memorial park, the Valluvar Kottam, enshrines his extraordinary verses in marble. See: *Tirukural.*

Tiruvasagam: திருவாசகம் "Holy Utterances." The lyrical Tamil scripture by Saint Manikkavasagar (ca 850). Considered one of the most profound and beautiful devotional works in the Tamil language, it discusses every phase of the spiritual path from doubt and anguish to perfect faith in God Śiva, from earthly experience to the *guru-disciple* relationship and freedom from rebirth. The work is partly autobiographical, describing how Manikkavasagar, the prime minister to the Pandyan King, renounced the world after experiencing an extraordinary vision of Śiva seated beneath a tree. The 658 hymns of *Tiruvasagam* together with the 400 hymns of *Tirukovaiyar* by the same author make up the eighth *Tirumurai* of Śaiva Siddhānta scripture. See: *Manikkavasagar, Tirumurai.*

tithe (tithing): The spiritual discipline, often a *vrata,* of giving one tenth of one's gainful and gifted income to a religious organization of one's choice, thus sustaining spiritual education and upliftment on earth. The Sanskṛit equivalent is *daśamāṁśa,* called *makimai* in the Tamil tradition. Tithing is given not as an offering, but as "God's money." In olden days it was a portion of one's crops, such as one coconut out of ten. Immediately setting aside the tithe as soon as income is received sanctifies the remaining portion and reaps the greatest *puṇya.* It is an acknowledgement by faithful Hindus of God's providential care, bringing a greater awareness of God's power in the world. Because tithers are thus uplifted to a purer, spiritual consciousness, abundance naturally floods into their lives. Additional offerings should be given after this minimal obligation is paid. See: *daśamāṁśa.*

tithi: तिथि A lunar day, approximately one-thirtieth of the time it takes the moon to orbit the earth. Because of their means of calculation (based on the difference of the longitudinal angle between the position of sun and the moon), *tithis* may vary in length. There are 15 *tithis* in each fortnight (half month). The names of the *tithis* are Prathamā (new moon), Dvitīyā, Tritīyā, Chaturthī, Pañchamī, Shashṭhī, Saptamī, Ashṭamī, Navamī, Daśamī, Ekādaśī, Dvādaśī, Trayodaśī, Chaturdaśī, and lastly either Pūrṇimā (full moon) or Amāvasyā (new moon). These are sometimes prefixed to indicate either the dark *(kṛishṇa)* fortnight—when the moon is waning—or the light *(śukla)* fortnight—when the moon is waxing—e.g., Śukla-Navamī. Most Hindu festivals are calculated according to the *tithis.*

touchstone: A test or criterion for determining value or authenticity.

trait: A quality or distinguishing peculiarity of character.

trance: In general, a condition of altered consciousness, accompanied by a lack of awareness to physical surroundings, neither a state of wakefulness nor sleep. In a religious sense it is a state of intense concentration, introspection or meditation. In such a state, called *samādhi,* body consciousness is completely lost as the energies are drawn up the spine into the *sahasrāra chakra* at the crown of the head. Great prophets have gone into trance and spoken out predictions of the future and in their waking state later had no memory of what they had said. In spiritualism, trance describes the phenomenon in which an individual leaves the physical body, and a disincarnate being enters or takes control of the body, often giving forth verbal messages to others in attendance, as in a seance. Trance can be either voluntary or involuntary. See: *mediumship, samādhi.*

tranquil: Quiet, peaceful.

transcend: To go beyond one's limitations, e.g., "to transcend one's ego." Philosophically, to go beyond the limits of this world, or more profoundly, beyond time, form and space into the Absolute, the Self God.

transcendent: Surpassing the limits of experience or manifest form. In Śaiva Siddhānta, a quality of God Śiva as Absolute Reality, Paraśiva, the Self. Distinguished from immanent. See: *atattva, Paraśiva.*

transfix: To render motionless.

transgress: To overstep or break a law or ethical principle.

transient: That which is temporary, fleeting. Passing, not permanent.

transition: Passing from one condition or place to another. A synonym of *death* which implies, more correctly, continuity of the individual rather than his annihilation. See: *death.*

traverse: To move across or extend over.

treacherous: Dangerous, unreliable. Giving a false sense of safety.

tread: To walk on or across.

treatise: An article or book which systematically discusses a subject.

trepidation: Anxiety; fearful uncertainty. Trembling.

tribal: Relating to, or having the character of a tribe, a group, clan or village often related by ancestry, race or allegiance to a common leader or lineage. A term often used derogatorily to refer to so-called primitive peoples, but more accurately seen as the natural human social structure into which all villages and communities, ancient or modern, naturally organize. A term often used in reference to indigenous peoples, mostly shamanic in conviction, found worldwide from ancient times. See: *pagan.*

trickery: Deception, fraud. Creating illusion, such as by magic.

trident: Three-pronged spear. See: *triśūla.*

Trikaśāsana: **त्रिकशासन** "Three teachings." Also, *Trikaśāstra.* A name for Kashmīr Śaivism based on its various philosophical triads including: Śiva, Śakti and Nara (bound soul); Pati, *paśu and pāśa*; three energies: highest *(parā)*, lowest *(aparā)*, and in-between *(parāparā)*; and three sets of scriptures. See: *Kashmīr Śaivism.*

trikoṇa: **त्रिकोण** A triangle; symbol of God Śiva as Absolute Reality. Also represents the element fire.

triloka: **त्रिलोक** "Three worlds." The physical, astral and causal planes (Bhūloka, Antarloka and Śivaloka). See: *world, loka.*

Trimūrti: **त्रिमूर्ति** A classic representation of God as the three-fold Deity image—Brahmā, Vishṇu and Rudra. See: *Brahmā.*

triple bondage: See: *mala, pāśa.*

tripuṇḍra: **त्रिपुण्ड्र** "Three marks." The Śaivite sectarian mark, consisting of three horizontal lines of *vibhūti* (holy ash) on the brow, often with a dot *(bindu)* at the third eye. The three lines represent the soul's three bonds: *āṇava, karma* and *māyā.* Holy ash, made of burnt cow dung, is a reminder of the temporary nature of the physical body and the urgency to strive for spiritual attainment and closeness to God. See: *bindu, tilaka, vibhūti.*

Triśūla: **त्रिशूल** A three-pronged spear or trident wielded by Lord Śiva and certain Śaivite ascetics. Symbolizes God's three fundamental *śaktis* or powers—*icçhā* (desire, will, love), *kriyā* (action) and *jñāna* (wisdom).

Truth: When capitalized, ultimate knowing which is unchanging. Lower case (truth): honesty, integrity; virtue.

Tryambaka: **त्र्यम्बक** "Three-eyed one." A name of Rudra-Śiva, one of the Ekādaśa ("eleven") Rudras. His emblems include a water pot, *chakra,* drum, bow, goad, snake and trident. The grace of Tryambaka is beseeched in the famous Mṛituñjāya Mantra, or Śiva Gāyatrī. Also the name of a disciple of Durvāsās who disseminated *advaita.* See: *Durvāsās, Gāyatrī Mantra.*

Tukārām: **तुकाराम** Among the most beloved and widely-read of Maharashtrian Sant poets (1598–1649) who wrote passionate songs urging devotees to seek the grace of Lord Vishṇu.

Tulasīdāsa: **तुलसीदास** Vaishṇava *sannyāsin* poet (ca 1532–1623) whose *Śrī Rāmacharitamānasa,* a Hindi rendering of Valmiki's Sanskṛit epic, *Rāmāyaṇa,* is acclaimed one of the world's greatest literary works. See: *Rāmāyaṇa.*

tumult: Noise, uproar, disturbance; agitation, confusion.

turbulent: Violently agitated. Marked by turmoil or wildly irregular motions.

turmeric: A plant of India, *Curcuma longa,* of the ginger family whose powdered rhyzome is a prized seasoning and yellow dye. It has rich *āyurvedic* properties, is used in holy ritual and serves also to make *kuṅkuma.*

tyaf: A special bamboo-like script used for writing prayers to be conveyed to the inner worlds through the sacred fire. See: *lekhaprārtha havana.*

tyāga: **त्याग** "Letting go, detachment, renunciation." Described in the *Bhagavad Gītā* as the basic principle of *karma yoga,* detachment from the fruits of one's actions. See: *sacrifice, sannyāsa, vairāgya.*

ucchāraṇa vyākhyā: **उच्चारणव्याख्या** "Pronunciation key or explanation."

ucçhishṭa: **उच्छिष्ट** "Leavings; remainder." Religiously, the precious leavings from the *guru's* food plate or the waters from the bathing of his feet or sandals which are ingested by devotees as *prasāda.* Partaking of the *satguru's ucçhishṭa* is an important means of receiving his vibration and thus creating a psychic connection and harmony with him, being in touch with his grace in a physical way. See: *prasāda, satguru, pādapūjā.*

Ujjain: **उज्जैन** A city on the Sipra River, one of the seven sacred Hindu cities; a traditional holy place of Śaivism. See: *Rudraśambhu.*

ultimate: Final, last. —**Ultimate Reality:** Final, highest Truth. God Śiva's Absolute Reality, Paraśiva.

Umā: **उमा** "O do not." A name for Śakti said to derive from the exclamation addressed to Pārvatī by her mother in the *Śiva Purāṇa,* beseeching her to not practice austerities.

unconnectedness: The quality of being separate, unrelated to or uninvolved.

uncreated: Not created, without origin. An attribute of God.

undecaying: Not decaying or deteriorating.

undifferentiated: Uniform. Same. Not having distinct or different elements.

unerring: Not making an error, sure. Exacting.

unevolutionary perfection: A term describing God Śiva as eternally complete and flawless and therefore not changing or developing.

unfold: To open gradually, especially in stages. See: *spiritual unfoldment.*

unharness: To take a harness off, to loosen restraints and make free.

unhindered: Free of obstacles. Not restrained.

universal *dharma:* Cosmic order, *ṛita.* See: *dharma.*

universal dissolution: The final stage in the recurring cosmic cycles of creation in which all manifestation is reabsorbed into God. See: *mahāpralaya.*

universalist: Applicable to all; including everyone or all groups. Any doctrine that emphasizes principles, beliefs or theologies that are or could be acceptable to many or all people, especially as contrasted with sectarian, denominational perspectives. Such schools are often syncretic in nature, but firmly based around a core of the original faith of the founder, and usually viewed by adherents as enlightened substitutes to traditional, established faiths. See: *neo-Indian religion, syncretism.*

unleash: To release, as by removing a tether or rope.

unmanifest: Not evident or perceivable. Philosophically, akin to *transcen-*

dent. God Śiva is unmanifest in His formless perfection, Paraśiva. See: *formless.*

unoriginated: Never begun or created. God Śiva is unoriginated as He has no beginning. See: *atattva, Paraśiva, Primal Soul.*

unpretentiousness: Modesty, humility. Not having false pride about oneself.

unrepressed: Open and honest, not marked by thoughts or feelings that are hidden or held back. Not repressed, pushed back or controlled to excess. Free of subconscious impulses, compulsions and inhibitions.

unshrouded: Uncovered. Made visible or knowable.

unwind: To undo something wound, as to unwind the thread from a spool.

upa: **उप** A common prefix conveying the meanings: "towards, near to (as opposed to *apa,* away), by the side of, with, below."

upadeśa: **उपदेश** "Advice; religious instruction." Often given in question-and-answer form from *guru* to disciple. The *satguru's* spiritual discourses.

upadeśī: **उपदेशी** A liberated soul who chooses to teach, actively helping others to the goal of liberation. Contrasted with *nirvāṇī.* See: *nirvāṇī* and *upadeśī, satguru.*

Upāgama: **उपागम** Secondary *Āgama.* A large body of texts and similar in character to the principle *Āgamas.* Each of the 28 Siddhānta *Śaiva Āgamas* has as many as 16 *Upāgamas* associated with it, giving more specific or elaborate information on the basic text; their total number is given as 207 or 208.

upagrantha: **उपग्रन्थ** "Secondary text." Appendices or additional resources of a book. See: *Grantha.*

upanayana: **उपनयन** "Bringing near." A youth's formal initiation into Vedic study under a *guru,* traditionally as a resident of his *āśrama,* and the investiture of the sacred thread *(yajñopavīta or upavīta),* signifying entrance into one of the three upper castes. The *upanayana* is among twelve *saṁskāras* prescribed in the *Dharma Śāstras* and explained in the *Gṛihya Sūtras.* It is prescribed between ages 8-16 for *brāhmins* (who received a white thread), 11-22 for *kshatriyas* (red thread), and 12-24 for *vaiśyas* (yellow thread). At present the color white for the sacred thread has been adopted universally. The *upanayana* is regarded as a second or spiritual birth, and one so initiated is known as *dvija,* "twice-born." Until about the beginning of the common era, the *upanayana* was also afforded to girls. Great value was placed on their learning the *Vedas* in preparation for the duties of married life. See: *saṁskāras of childhood.*

Upanishad: **उपनिषद्** "Sitting near devotedly." The fourth and final portion of the *Vedas,* expounding the secret, philosophical meaning of the Vedic hymns. The *Upanishads* are a collection of profound texts which are the source of Vedānta and have dominated Indian thought for thousands of years. They are philosophical chronicles of *ṛishis* expounding the nature of God, soul and cosmos, exquisite renderings of the deepest Hindu thought.

Traditionally, the number of *Upanishads* is given as 108. Ten to 16 are classified as "major" or "principle" *Upanishads,* being those which philosophers have commented on through the centuries. The *Upanishads* are generally dated later than the *Saṁhitās* and *Brāhmaṇas,* though some are actually portions of the *Brāhmaṇas.* It is thought that most were written down in Sanskṛit between 1500 and 600 BCE. In content, these popular and approachable texts revolve around the identity of the soul and God, and the doctrines of reincarnation, of *karma* and of liberation through renunciation and meditation. They are widely available in many languages. Along with the *Bhagavad Gītā* ("song of God") they were the primary scripture to awaken the Western world to the wealth of Hindu wisdom. See: *śruti, Vedas, Vedānta.*

upāsanā: **उपासना** "Sitting near." Worship or contemplation of God. One of the *pañcha nitya karmas.* "five constant duties." See: *sandhyā upāsanā.*

upasarga: **उपसर्ग** "Trouble, obstacle." Difficulties, challenges or distractions which retard one's progress on the spiritual path. Numerous lists are given in scripture under the Sanskṛit terms *upasarga, dosha* (defect; blemish), *klesha, vighna* and *antarāya.* The *Yogatattva Upanishad* lists twenty *doshas* including hunger, thirst, excitement, grief, anger and greed; as well as five *vighnas:* sloth, boastfulness, bad company, cultivation of *mantras* for wrong reasons and longing for women. Patañjali names nine *antarāyas* to success in *yoga,* including sickness, doubt, sloth, nonattainment and instability. Spiritually, all these obstacles unless overcome lead to a dead end of unhappiness and despair, often affording steps which can only be retraced through reincarnating again. See: *purity-impurity.*

Upaveda: **उपवेद** "Secondary *Vedas.*" A class of texts on sacred sciences, composed by *ṛishis* over the course of time to amplify and apply the Vedic knowledge. The four prominent *Upavedas* (each encompassing numerous texts) are: *Arthaveda* (statecraft), *Āyurveda* (health), *Dhanurveda* (military science) and *Gāndharvaveda* (music and the arts). Also sometimes classed as *Upavedas* are the *Sthāpatyaveda* (on architecture) and the *Kāma Śāstras* (texts on erotic love). See: *Arthaveda, Āyurveda, Dhanurveda, Kāma Sūtra, Gāndharvaveda, purushārtha, Stāpatyaveda.*

upāya: **उपाय** "Means." A term used in Kashmīr Śaivism to describe the means to move from individual into universal consciousness. ***—āṇavopāya:*** "Individual, or limited means." Also called *kriyopāya,* the way of ritual worship, *haṭha yoga,* concentration and *yogic* breathing. ***—śāktopāya:*** "Way of power." Active inquiry through mental effort, emphasizing control of awareness, *japa* and meditation. ***—śāmbhavopāya:*** "Way of Śambhu (Śiva)." Also called *icçhopāya,* "Way of will." Seeing Śiva everywhere; surrender in God. ***—anupāya:*** "No-means." Not really a means, but the goal of the first three *upāyas*—the transcendent condition of Śiva Consciousness. The spontaneous realization of the Self without effort. Also called *pratyabhijñā upāya,* "way of recognition." See: *Kashmīr Śaivism.*

upbringing: Childhood education and training.

utmost: To the highest degree, the very greatest.

Utpaladeva: **उत्पलदेव** Disciple (ca 900-950) of *Somānanda* and author of *Pratyabhijñā Sūtras* (also called *Pratyabhijñā Darśana)* and other works. See: *Kashmīr Śaivism.*

utsava: **उत्सव** "Festival." Religious celebrations or holy days and their observance in the home and temple. *Utsava* is one of the five constant duties, *pañcha nitya karmas.* See: *festival.*

utsavaka: **उत्सवक** "Festival maker." A person who coordinates arrangements for religious festivals.

Vachana: **वचन** "Utterance." Short, insightful devotional poems written by the early Vīra Śaiva *śaraṇā* saints. Full of wit and brilliant philosophy, they are the basis for Liṅgāyat philosophy and practice.

vāgdāna: **वाग्दान** "Word-giving." Marriage engagement ceremony. See: *saṁskāras of adulthood.*

vāhana: **वाहन** "Bearing, carrying or conveying." Each Hindu God is depicted as riding an animal or bird *vāhana,* which is symbolic of a function of the God. For example, Śiva rides the bull, a symbol of strength and potency. Kārttikeya rides the peacock, *mayūra,* emblem of beauty and regality.

vaidya: **वैद्य** "Versed in science; learned; a doctor." See: *āyurveda vaidya.*

Vaikāsi Viśākham: வைகாசி விசாகம் A festival held on Viśākha *nakshatra,* near the full moon day of the Tamil month of Vaikāsi, May-June, to celebrate the creation, or "birth," of Lord Kārttikeya. It is a time of gift-giving to *paṇḍitas* and great souls, weddings, feedings for the poor, caring for trees, spiritual initiation and conclaves of holy men.

Vaikuṇṭha: **वैकुण्ठ** "Vishṇu's heaven." See: *Vaishṇavism.*

vairāgī: **वैरागी** "Dispassionate one." An ascetic who lives by the principle of *vairāgya.* Also names a particular class of mendicants, generally Vaishṇavas, of North India who have freed themselves from worldly desires. See: *monk, sannyāsa, tyāga.*

vairāgya: **वैराग्य** "Dispassion; aversion." Freedom from passion. Distaste or disgust for worldliness because of spiritual awakening. Also, the constant renunciation of obstacles on the path to liberation. Ascetic or monastic life.

Vaiśeshika: **वैशेषिक** "Distinctionism." A philosophical school (ca 600 BCE) that focuses on understanding the categories of existence. See: *shaḍ darśana.*

Vaishṇava: **वैष्णव** Of or relating to Vishṇu; same as Vaishṇavite. A follower of Lord Vishṇu or His incarnations. See: *Vishṇu, Vaishṇavism.*

Vaishṇavism (Vaishṇava): **वैष्णव** One of the four major religions, or denominations of Hinduism, representing roughly half of the world's one billion

Hindus. It gravitates around the worship of Lord Vishṇu as Personal God, His incarnations and their consorts. The doctrine of *avatāra* (He who descends), especially important to Vaishṇavism, teaches that whenever *adharma* gains ascendency in the world, God takes a human birth to reestablish "the way." There are either 10, 22 or 34 *avatāras* of Vishṇu, according to various scriptures. The most renowned *avatāras* were Rāma and Kṛishṇa. The last to come will be Kalki, the harbinger of a golden age on Earth. Vaishṇavism stresses the personal aspect of God over the impersonal, and *bhakti* (devotion) as the true path to salvation. The goal of Vaishṇavism is the attainment of *mukti*, defined as blissful union with God's body, the loving recognition that the soul is a part of Him, and eternal nearness to Him in Vaikuṇṭha, heaven. Foremost among Vaishṇava scriptures are the *Vaishṇava Āgamas, Bhagavad Gītā* and *Bhāgavata Purāṇa.* Among the earliest schools were the Pañcharātras and the Bhāgavatas. The five major contemporary schools (founded between 1000 and 1500) are those of Rāmānuja (Śrī Vaishṇavism), Mādhva, Nimbarka, Vallabha and Chaitanya. Philosophically they range from Mādhva's pure dualism to Vallabha's lofty monistic vision.

Vaishṇavite: Of or relating to Vishṇu; same as Vaishṇava. A follower of Vishṇu or His incarnations. See: *Vaishṇavism, Vishnu.*

vaiśya: **वैश्य** "Landowner; merchant." The social class of bankers, businessmen, industrialists; employers. Merchant class, originally those whose business was trade as well as agriculture. See: *varṇa dharma.*

valipadu: வழிபாடு "Ritual worship; revering, following." The acts of adoration of the divine, expressed in many practices and ways.

Vallabhāchārya: **वल्लभाचार्य** "Beloved." Vaishṇava saint (ca 1475-1530) whose panentheistic Śuddha Advaita (pure nondualism) philosophy became the essential teaching of the nonascetic Vaishṇava sect that bears his name. He composed 17 works, most importantly commentaries on the *Vedānta* and *Mīmāṁsā Sūtras* and the *Bhāgavata Purāṇa.* The stories of his 84 disciples are often repeated on festive occasions by followers. The sect is strongest in Bombay and Gujarat. See: *Vedānta.*

vāma: **वाम** 1) "Pleasant; beautiful; benignant; striving after"—as in Vāmadeva, a name of Śiva. 2) "Left; crooked; acting in the opposite way"—as in *vāma mārga,* the left-handed *tantric* path." See: *left-handed, tantrism.*

vānaprastha āśrama: **वानप्रस्थ आश्रम** "Forest-dweller stage." See: *āśrama dharma, shashṭyābda pūrti.*

vanquish: To defeat or conquer in conflict or competition. See: *victors and vanquished.*

Vārāṇasī: **वाराणसी** Also known as Kāśī or Banāras. One of the most holy of Śaivite cities, and among the oldest cities in the world. Located in North India on the Ganges River. Hindus consider it highly sanctifying to die in Kāśī, revering it as a gateway to *moksha.*

varṇa: वर्ण "External appearance, covering; type, species, kind, color; caste. See: *varṇa dharma.*

varṇa dharma: वर्णधर्म "The way of one's kind." The hereditary social class system, generally referred to as *caste,* established in India in ancient times. Within *varṇa dharma* are the many religious and moral codes which define human virtue. *Varṇa dharma* is social duty, in keeping with the principles of good conduct, according to one's community, which is generally based on the craft or occupation of the family. Strictly speaking it encompasses two interrelated social hierarchies: 1) *varṇa,* which refers to the four classes: *brāhmin, kshatriya, vaiśya* and *śūdra;* and 2) *jāti,* the myriad occupational subgroups, or guilds, which in India number over 3,000. Hence this *dharma* is sometimes called *jāti dharma.* The class-caste system is still very much a part of Indian life today. Many modern Hindus propose that social status is now (and was originally) more properly determined by a person's skills and accomplishments than by birth. Mobility between *jātis,* or castes, within Hindu communities worldwide is limited but not impossible, and is accomplished through marrying into a new *jāti,* or changing professions through persistence, skill and education. *Śāstrīs* say that once a person breaks out of his *varṇa* or *jāti* of birth and changes "caste," it takes three generations for his family to become fully established in that new strata of society, provided the continuity is unbroken.

—***varṇa:*** The four *varṇas* are as follows. —***brāhmin (brāhmaṇa):*** "Mature, evolved soul." Scholarly, pious souls of exceptional learning. Hindu scriptures traditionally invest the *brāhmin* class with the responsibility of religious leadership, including teaching and priestly duties. —***kshatriya***: "Governing; endowed with sovereignty." Lawmakers and law enforcers and military, also known as *rājanya.* —***vaiśya***: "Landowner, merchant." Businessmen, financiers, industrialists; employers. Those engaged in business, commerce and agriculture. —***śūdra***: "Worker, servant." Skilled artisans and laborers. It is in keeping with *varṇa dharma* that sons are expected to follow the occupation of their father, as that is the occupation that was chosen prior to birth.

—***jāti:*** "Birth; position assigned by birth; rank, caste, family, race, lineage." *Jāti,* more than *varṇa,* is the specific determinant of one's social community. Traditionally, because of rules of purity each *jāti* is excluded from social interaction with the others, especially from interdining and intermarriage. In modern times there is also a large group (one-seventh of India's population in 1981) outside the four *varṇas.* These are called unscheduled classes, untouchables, *jātihīta* ("outcaste"), *chandālas* (specifically those who handle corpses) and *harijan,* a name given by Mahātma Gāndhi, meaning "children of God." Untouchable *jātis* included the *nishāda* (hunter), *kaivarta* (fisherman) and *kārāvara* (leather worker).

The *varṇa dharma* system—despite its widespread discrimination against *harijans,* and the abuse of social status by higher castes—ensures a high standard of craftsmanship, a sense of community belonging, family integrity and religio-cultural continuity. Caste is not unique to Hinduism and India. By other names it is found in every society. The four *varṇas,* or classes, and myriad *jātis,* occupational castes, or guilds, form the basic elements of human interaction. See: *jāti.*

varṇāśrama dharma: वर्णाश्रमधर्म "The way of one's caste and stage of life." Names the social structure of four classes *(varṇa),* hundreds of castes *(jāti)* and four stages of life *(āśramas).* It is the combined principles of *varṇa dharma* and *āśrama dharma.* See: *āśrama dharma, dharma, varṇa dharma.*

vāsanā: वासना "Subconscious inclination." From *vās,* "living, remaining." The subliminal inclinations and habit patterns which as driving forces, color and motivate one's attitudes and future actions. *Vāsanās* are the conglomerate results of subconscious impressions *(saṁskāras)* created through experience. *Saṁskāras,* experiential impressions, combine in the subconscious to form *vāsanās,* which thereafter contribute to mental fluctuations, called *vṛitti.* Taken as a whole, *vāsanās* form a dimension of the mind called the sub-subconscious, or *vāsanā chitta.* See: *saṁskāra, manomaya kośa, mind (five states), vṛitti.*

Vasishṭha: वसिष्ठ Disciple of Maharishi Nandikeśvara (Nandinātha) (ca 250 BCE) along with Patañjali and Vyāghrapāda (as recorded in Pāṇini's book of grammar). Also the name of several other famous sages, including the *ṛishi* attributed with composing the hymns of the *Ṛig Veda's* seventh maṇḍala, another who plays a central role in the epics and certain *Purāṇas* and *Upanishads,* and a third who expounds the ancient *yogic* wisdom to Lord Rāma in the 29,000-verse *Yoga Vāsishṭha.*

Vasugupta: वसुगुप्त Celebrated preceptor (ca 800) whose finding of the *Śiva Sūtras* catalyzed the reemergence of the ancient Kashmīr Śaiva tradition. It is said that he discovered the 77 *sūtras* carved in a rock on Mahādeva mountain after a visionary dream in which Lord Śiva told him of their location. The sacred rock, named Śaṅkarpal, is revered to this day. See: *Kashmīr Śaivism, Śiva Sūtras.*

vaṭa: वट The banyan tree, *Ficus indicus* sacred to Śiva. Thought to derive from *vaṭ,* "to surround, encompass"—also called *nyagrodha,* "growing downwards." Ancient symbol of the Sanātana Dharma. Its relative, the *aśvattha,* or *pīpal* tree, is given in the *Upanishads* as a metaphor for creation, with the "roots above and the branches below."

vāta: वात "Movement." *Vāyu,* "air-ether." One of the three bodily humors, called *dosha, vāta* is known as the air humor. Principle of movement in the body. *Vāta dosha* governs such functions as breathing and movement of the muscles and tissues. See: *āyurveda, dosha.*

vault: An arched roof, ceiling or chamber.

Veda: वेद "Wisdom." Sagely revelations which comprise Hinduism's most authoritative scripture. They, along with the *Āgamas,* are *śruti,* "that which is heard." The *Vedas* are a body of dozens of holy texts known collectively as the *Veda,* or as the four *Vedas: Ṛig, Yajur, Sāma* and *Atharva.* In all they include over 100,000 verses, as well as additional prose. The knowledge imparted by the *Vedas* is highly mystical or superconscious rather than intellectual. Each *Veda* has four sections: *Saṁhitās* (hymn collections), *Brāhmaṇas* (priestly manuals), *Āraṇyakas* (forest treatises) and *Upanishads* (enlightened discourses). The *Saṁhitās* and *Brāhmaṇas* (together known as the *karmakāṇḍa,* "ritual section") detail a transcendent-immanent Supreme-Being cosmology and a system of worship through fire ceremony and chanting to establish communication with the Gods. The *Āraṇyakas* and *Upanishads* (the *jñānakāṇḍa,* "knowledge section") outline the soul's evolutionary journey, providing *yogic*-philosophic training and propounding a lofty, nondual realization as the destiny of all souls. The oldest portions of the *Vedas* are thought to date back as far as 6,000 BCE, written down in Sanskṛit in the last few millennia, making them the world's most ancient scriptures. See: *Āraṇyaka, Brāhmaṇa, śruti, Upanishad.*

Vedāṅga: **वेदाङ्ग** "*Veda-limb.*" Six branches of post-Vedic studies revered as auxiliary to the *Vedas.* Four *Vedāṅgas* govern correct chanting of the *Vedas:* 1) *Śikshā* (phonetics), 2) *Çhandas* (meter), 3) *Nirukta* (etymology), 4) *Vyākaraṇa* (grammar). The two other *Vedāṅgas* are 5) *Jyotisha Vedāṅga* (astronomy-astrology) and 6) *Kalpa Vedāṅga* (procedural canon) which includes the *Śrauta* and *Śulba Śāstras* (ritual codes), *Dharma Śāstras* (social law) and *Gṛihya Śāstras* (domestic codes). See: *Kalpa Vedāṅga and individual entries.*

Vedānta: **वेदान्त** "Ultimate wisdom" or "final conclusions of the *Vedas.*" Vedānta is the system of thought embodied in the *Upanishads* (ca 1500-600 BCE), which give forth the ultimate conclusions of the *Vedas.* Through history there developed numerous Vedānta schools, ranging from pure dualism to absolute monism. The first and original school is Advaita Īsvaravāda, "monistic theism" or panentheism, exemplified in the Vedānta-Siddhānta of Ṛishi Tirumular (ca 250 BCE) of the Nandinātha Sampradāya in his *Tirumantiram,* which is a perfect summation of both the *Vedas* and the *Āgamas.* This is a dipolar reconciliation of monism and dualism which, as philosopher-statesman Dr. S. Rādhākṛishṇan (1888–1975) declared, best depicts the philosophy of the *Upanishads.* After about 700 CE, many other schools developed, each establishing itself through written commentaries on the major *Upanishads,* the *Bhagavad Gītā* and the *Brahma Sūtras.* The latter text, authored by Bādarāyaṇa (ca 400 BCE), is the earliest known systematization of Vedānta, but its extremely terse aphorisms are philosophically illusive without further commentary. During the "scholastic era" (700–1700), three main variations of the original Vedānta were developed: 1) Advaita Vedānta, or pure nondualism, exemplified by Śaṅkara (788–820);

2) Viśishṭādvaita Vedānta, or qualified nondualism, most fully expressed by Rāmānuja (1017–1137); and 3) Dvaita Vedānta, expounded by Mādhva (1197–1278).

Panentheism is embodied in those qualified nondual Vedānta schools that accept the ultimate identity of the soul and God. Examples are the Viśishṭādvaita of Bhāskara (ca 950), the Śuddha Advaita, "pure nondualism," of Vallabha (ca 1475–1530) and, to a lesser degree, the Viśishṭādvaita of Rāmānuja.

In summary: Mādhva, the dualist, conceives Brahman to be the Personal God. In his philosophy, the universe, souls and God are all separate from one another and real. Rāmānuja, the qualified nondualist, also conceives Brahman to be the Personal God. In his philosophy, God must not be considered apart from the world and souls, for the three together form a one whole. The world and souls are real as the body of God, and the individual soul feels himself to be part of God. Śaṅkara, the strict *advaitist*, conceives Brahman to be the Impersonal God, the Absolute. Śaṅkara does not deny the existence of the Personal God, known as Īśvara, but declares Īśvara to be equally as unreal as the universe and the individuality of the soul. In truth, the only Reality is the Absolute, and man *is* that Absolute. To Ṛishi Tirumular, the panentheist, there is an eternal oneness of God and man at the level of their inner Being, but a difference is acknowledged during the evolution of the soul. Ultimately even this difference merges in identity. Thus, there is perfectly beginningless oneness and a temporary difference which resolves itself in perfect identity.

The great Bengali saint, Śrī Rāmakṛishṇa (1836–1886), further summarized the three medieval Vedānta schools with characteristically profound simplicity: Dvaita: "When I think of myself as identified with the body, I am Thy servant and Thou art my Master. My will is controlled by Thy will." Viśishṭādvaita: "When I think of myself as a soul as distinct from the body, I am the part and Thou art the Whole." Advaita: "When I recognize the spiritual principle in me as distinct from body, mind and soul, I realize that I am one with the Divine." To complete the analysis, we would say that the enlightened unification of all three views is Advaita Īśvaravāda, or panentheism.

Vedānta is one of the six classical philosophies *(shaḍ darśanas)* along with Nyāya, Vaiśeshika, Sāṅkhya, Yoga and Mīmāṁsā. Vedānta is also called Uttara Mīmāṁsā, "upper or later examination," as distinguished from Pūrva Mīmāṁsā, which concerned itself solely with the earlier portions of the *Veda.* Other important schools of Vedānta include the Dvaitādvaita, "dual-nondualism,"of Nimbārka (ca 1150), and the Achintya Bhedābheda, "unthinkable difference-nondifference," of Chaitanya (1485–1534). See: *acosmic pantheism, Advaita Īśvaravāda, dvaita-advaita, monistic theism, Mādhva, panentheism, Rāmānuja, Tirumantiram, Vallabha.*

Vedic-Āgamic: Simultaneously drawing from and complying with both of Hinduism's revealed scriptures *(śruti), Vedas* and *Āgamas,* which represent two complimentary, intertwining streams of history and tradition. The difference between Siddhānta and Vedānta is traditionally described in the following way. While the *Vedas* depict man looking for God, the *Āgamas* hold the perspective of God looking to help man. This is reflected in the fact that while the *Vedas* are voiced by *ṛishis,* God or the Goddess is the giver of truth in the *Āgama* texts. See: *grace, śruti.*

vegetarian: *Śakāhāra.* Of a diet which excludes meat, fish, fowl and eggs. Vegetarianism is a principle of health and environmental ethics that has been a keystone of Indian life for thousands of years. Vegetarian foods include grains, fruits, vegetables, legumes and dairy products. Natural, fresh foods, locally grown, without insecticides or chemical fertilizers, are preferred. The following foods are minimized: frozen and canned foods, highly processed foods, such as white rice, white sugar and white flour; and "junk" foods and beverages (those with abundant chemical additives, such as artificial sweeteners, colorings, flavorings and preservatives). A person following a vegetarian diet is called a *śakāhārī.* See: *guṇa, mānsāhārī, yama-niyama.*

veil: A piece of cloth used to conceal. To cover or hide.

veiling grace: *Tirobhāva śakti.* The divine power that limits the soul's perception by binding or attaching the soul to the bonds of *āṇava, karma,* and *māyā*— enabling it to grow and evolve as an individual being. See: *grace.*

vel: வேல் "Spear, lance." The symbol of Lord Kārttikeya's divine authority as Lord of *yoga* and commander of the *devas.* (Known as *śūla* in Sanskṛit.) See: *Kārttikeya.*

Vellore: வேலூர் See: *Chinna Bomman.*

venerate: To love or consider with respect and admiration; to revere. From the Latin *veneratus,* to worship, reverence.

vengeful: Desiring or seeking to return injury for injury. Wanting revenge.

venture: To risk. To express in words at the risk of criticism.

veracity: Honesty, truthfulness; accuracy.

vermillion: Bright red.

veshti: வேஷ்டி A long, unstitched cloth like a sarong, wound about the waist and reaching below the ankles. Traditional Hindu apparel for men. It can be wrapped in many different styles. A Tamil word derived from the Sanskṛit *veshṭana,* "encircling." Also called *vetti* (Tamil) or *dhoti* (Hindi).

vestments: The clothing, especially official robes or other garb, worn by religious persons, often as a sign of their spiritual position or ordination.

vibhūti: विभूति "Resplendent, powerful." Holy ash, prepared by burning cow dung along with other precious substances, milk, *ghee,* honey, etc. It symbolizes purity and is one of the main sacraments given at *pūjā* in all Śaivite temples and shrines. Śaivites wear three stripes on the brow as a distinct sectarian mark, as do many Smārtas. *Vibhūti* is also a synonym for *siddhi,* supernormal powers developed through *yoga* practice. It is the title of the third chapter of Patañjali's *Yoga Sūtras,* which discusses *siddhis.* See: *tilaka. tripuṇḍra.*

vice: Fault or failing. Corrupt habits; depravity. From the Sanskṛit *vishu,* meaning, "adverse; in opposite directions."

victors and vanquished: Those who triumph and those who are defeated in battle, debate or any competition. A concept or attitude about winning and losing derived from dualistic beliefs, which can lead to *adharma, hiṁsā,* etc.

vid: **विद्** "To know." Verbal root of *Veda* and *vidyā,* "knowledge."

videhamukti: **विदेहमुक्ति** "Disembodied liberation." Release from reincarnation through *nirvikalpa samādhi*—the realization of the Self, Paraśiva—at the point of death. Blessed are those who are aware that departure, *mahāsamādhi,* is drawing near. They settle all affairs, make amends and intensify personal *sādhana.* They seek the silver channel of *sushumṇā* which guides *kuṇḍalinī* through the door of *Brahman* into the beyond of the beyond. They seek total renunciation as the day of transition looms strongly in their consciousness. Those who know that Lord Yama is ready to receive them, seek to merge with Śiva. They seek *nirvikalpa samādhi* as the body and earthly life fall away. Those who succeed are the *videhamuktas,* honored as among those who will never be reborn. Hindu tradition allows for vows of renunciation, called *ātura sannyāsa dīkshā,* to be taken and the orange robe donned by the worthy *sādhaka* or householder in the days prior to death. See: *jīvanmukti, kaivalya, moksha, Paraśiva, Self Realization.*

vidyā: **विद्या** "Knowledge, learning, science." The power of understanding gained through study and meditation. Contrasted with *avidyā,* ignorance.

vidyārambha: **विद्यारंभ** "Commencement of learning." See: *saṁskāras of childhood.*

Vighneśvara: **विघ्नेश्वर** "Lord of Obstacles." A name for Lord Gaṇeśa describing His power to both remove and create obstacles to guide souls along the right path. See: *Gaṇeśa.*

Vijayanagara: **विजयनगर** "City of Victory." Opulent city and last Indian empire, centered in present-day Karnataka state, which extended as far as Malaysia, Indonesia and the Philippines. It flourished from 1336 to 1565, at which time it began to disintegrate following defeat at the hand of Muslim armies. However, its existence and strength did serve to prevent Muslim expansion into South India. Awed visitors recounted its fabulously rich culture and great wealth. Site of extensive recent archeological renovation.

vijñānamaya kośa: **विज्ञानमयकोश** "Sheath of cognition." The soul's mental or cognitive-intuitive sheath, also called the actinodic sheath. See: *kośa, mental body, soul.*

Vināyaka: **विनायक** "Remover." A name of Lord Gaṇeśa, meaning the remover of obstacles (sometimes preceded by *vighna,* "obstacle"). See: *Gaṇeśa.*

Vināyaka Ahaval: விநாயகர் அகவல் "Poem to Vināyaka." Famous Tamil poem in praise of Gaṇeśa by the 8th-century woman saint, Auvaiyar.

Vināyaka Vratam: விநாயகவிரதம் A 21-day festival to Lord Gaṇeśa beginning on the full-moon day of November-December. An important festival in Tamil Nadu and in Tamil communities worldwide, when special *pūjās* are conducted in Gaṇeśa temples, and devotees make a vow *(vrata)*, such as to attend the daily *pūjā*, or to fast by taking only one meal a day.

Vīra Śaivism (Śaiva): **वीरशैव** "Heroic Śaivism." Made prominent by Basavaṇṇa in the 12th century. Also called Liṅgāyat Śaivism. Followers, called Liṅgāyats, Liṅgavantas or Śivaśaraṇās, always wear a Śivaliṅga on their person. Vīra Śaivites are proudly egalitarian and emphasize the personal relationship with Śiva, rather than temple worship. Vīra Śaiva priests, *jaṅgamas,* conduct marriages and other domestic rites and also act as *gurus* or teachers. Among the most central texts are Basavaṇṇa's *Vachanas,* Allama Prabhu's *Mantragopya,* Chennabasavaṇṇa's *Kāraṇa Hasuge,* and the collected work called *Śūnya Sampādane.* The monistic-theistic doctrine of Vīra Śaivism is called Śakti Viśishṭādvaita—a version of qualified nondualism which accepts both difference and nondifference between soul and God, like rays are to the sun. In brief, Śiva and the cosmic force or existence are one ("Śiva are you; you shall return to Śiva."). Yet, Śiva is beyond His creation, which is real, not illusory. God is both efficient and material cause. In Vīra Śaivism, Śiva divides from His Absolute state into Liṅga (Supreme Lord) and *āṅga,* individual soul, the two eventually reuniting in undifferentiated oneness. There are three aspects of Śivaliṅga. 1) Ishṭaliṅga, personal form of Śiva, in which He fulfills desires and removes afflictions—God as bliss or joy; 2) Bhāvaliṅga, Śiva beyond space and time, the highest divine principle, knowable through intuition; 3) Prāṇaliṅga, the reality of God which can be apprehended by the mind. The soul merges with Śiva by a progressive, six-stage path called *shaṭsthala,* consisting of *bhakti* (devotion), *maheśa* (charity and selfless service), *prasāda* (seeking Śiva's grace), Prāṇaliṅga (experience of all as Śiva), *śaraṇā* (egoless refuge in Śiva) and *aikya* (oneness with Śiva). Today Vīra Śaivism is a vibrant faith, particularly strong in its religious homeland of Karnataka, South Central India. Roughly 40 million people live here, of which perhaps 25% are members of the Vīra Śaiva religion. Early on, they rejected *brāhminical* authority, and along with it the entire caste system and the *Vedas.* By rejecting the *Vedas,* they continue to stand outside mainstream Hinduism, but in their profound love of Śiva and acceptance of certain *Śaiva Āgamas,* as well as the main truths of the Vedic wisdom, they have identified themselves as a unique Śaiva sect. Though they have established their faith as a distinct and independent religion in Indian courts of law, they are still widely embraced as devout brothers and sisters of the Hindu *dharma.* See: *Liṅgavanta, Śaivism.*

virginal: Characteristic of a virgin. Pure. —**virginal God:** Reference to Lord

Kārttikeya, the perpetual bachelor, descriptive of His inherent purity.

visarjana: **विसर्जन** "Departure." See: *Gaṇeśa Chaturthī.*

Vishṇu: **विष्णु** "All-pervasive." Supreme Deity of the Vaishṇavite religion. God as personal Lord and Creator, the All-Loving Divine Personality, who periodically incarnates and lives a fully human life to reestablish *dharma* whenever necessary. In Śaivism, Vishṇu is Śiva's aspect as Preserver. See: *Vaishṇavism.*

visionary: Characteristic of one who has visions; a prophet, evolved seer.

Viśishṭādvaita: **विशिष्टाद्वैत** "Qualified nondualism." Best known as the term used by Rāmānuja (ca 1017-1137) to name his Vaishṇava Vedānta philosophy, which is nondualistic in that the ultimate truth or reality is one, not two, and souls are in fact part of God. And it is "qualified" in that souls are *fully* one with God, but not identical. Thus there is a full union which is somewhat shy of total merger. *Śiva Viśishṭādvaita* was the term chosen by Bhāskara (ca 950) to name his philosophy. See: *Śiva Advaita, Vedānta.*

visualize (visualization): To imagine, create mental images. Exercising the power of thought to create the future.

viśuddha chakra: **विशुद्धचक्र** "Wheel of purity." The fifth *chakra.* Center of divine love. See: *chakra.*

viśvagrāsa: **विश्वग्रास** "Total absorption." The final merger of the soul in Śiva at the fulfillment of its evolution. It is ultimate union of the individual soul body with the body of Śiva—Parameśvara—within the Śivaloka, from whence the soul was first emanated. This occurs at the end of the soul's evolution, after the four outer sheaths—*annamaya kośa, prāṇamaya kośa, manomaya kośa* and *vijñāmaya kośa*—have been dropped off. Finally, *ānandamaya kośa,* the soul form itself, merges in the Primal Soul. Individuality is lost as the soul becomes Śiva, the creator, preserver, destroyer, veiler and revealer. Individual identity expands into universality. Having previously merged in Paraśiva and Parāśakti in states of *samādhi,* the soul now fully merges into Parameśvara and is one with all three of Śiva's perfections. *Jīva* has totally become Śiva—not a new and independent Śiva, as might be construed, for there is and can only be one Supreme God Śiva. This fulfilled merger can happen at the moment the physical body is dropped off, or after eons of time following further unfoldment of the higher *chakras* in the inner worlds—all depending on the maturity, ripeness and intentions of the soul, by which is meant the advanced soul's choice to be either an *upadeśī* or a *nirvāṇī.* See: *ātman, evolution of the soul, nirvāṇī and upadeśī, samādhi, soul.*

vitala: **वितल** "Region of negation." Region of raging anger and viciousness. The second *chakra* below the *mūlādhāra,* centered in the thighs. Corresponds to the second astral netherworld beneath the earth's surface, called Avīchi ("joyless") or Vitala. See: *chakra, loka, Naraka.*

vivāha: **विवाह** "Marriage." See: *saṁskāras.*

Viveka Chūḍāmaṇi: विवेकचूडामणि "Crest jewel of discrimination." A famous text by Śaṅkara (788-820) on discipline and discrimination between the real and the unreal as the way to God.

Viveka Mārtaṇḍa: विवेकमार्तण्ड A philosophic treatise of the Siddha Siddhānta school of Śaivism ascribed to Gorakshanātha (ca 900).

Vivekānanda, Swāmī: विवेकानन्द् Disciple of Śrī Rāmakṛishṇa who was overtaken by an ardent love of Hinduism and a missionary zeal that drove him onward. He attained *mahāsamādhi* at age 39 (1863–1902). Most notable among his achievements was a trip around the world on which he gave brilliant lectures, especially in Europe and America, that created much respect for Hinduism. In India he founded the Rāmakṛishṇa Mission which thrives today internationally with over 100 centers and nearly 1,000 *sannyāsins.* He is credited, along with Tagore, Aurobindo, Rādhākṛishṇan and others, with sparking the modern Hindu revival. See: *jñāna yoga, Rāmakṛishṇa.*

vivify: To give life to, or make more active, influential, etc.

void: An empty space. Philosophically, emptiness itself. The absence of time, form and space. God Śiva in His perfection as Paraśiva, as a sacred void, but not "like the emptiness inside of an empty box....[It] is the fullness of everything." See: *Paraśiva.*

votary: A person committed by a vow. A devotee; a monk or nunk.

vrata: व्रत "Vow, religious oath." Often a vow to perform certain disciplines over a period of time, such as penance, fasting, specific *mantra* repetitions, worship or meditation. *Vratas* extend from the simplest personal promise to irrevocable vows made before God, Gods, *guru* and community. See: *marriage covenant, sannyāsa dīkshā, Vināyaka Vratam.*

vṛitti: वृत्ति "Whirlpool." In *yoga* psychology, names the fluctuations of consciousness, the waves of mental activities *(chitta vṛitti)* of thought and perception. A statement from Patañjali's *Yoga Sūtras* (1.2) reads, "*Yoga* is the restraint *(nirodha)* of mental activity *(chitta vṛitti)*." In general use, *vṛitti* means: 1) course of action, mode of life; conduct, behavior; way in which something is done; 2) mode of being, nature, kind, character. See: *mind (individual), rāja yoga.*

Vyāghrapāda: व्याघ्रपाद् "Tiger feet." Famous Nandinātha Sampradāya *siddha* (ca 200 BCE), trained under Maharishi Nandinātha, was a brother disciple of *ṛishis* Tirumular and Patañjali. He pilgrimaged south from Kashmir, settling at Tamil Nadu's Chidambaram Śiva Temple to practice *yoga.* See: *Kailāsa Paramparā.*

Vyākaraṇa Vedāṅga: व्याकरणवेदाङ्ग Auxiliary Vedic texts on Sanskṛit grammar. Vyākaraṇa is among four linguistic skills taught for mastery of the *Vedas* and the rites of *yajña.* The term literally means "separation, or explanation." The most celebrated *Vyākaraṇa* work is Pāṇini's 4,000-*sūtra Ashṭādhyāyī,* which set the linguistic standards for classical Sanskṛit (ca 400 BCE). See: *Vedāṅga.*

wane: To decrease. "*On the wane:*" in the process of decreasing or disappearing.

warp and woof: In the art of weaving, *warp* names the lengthwise threads that give structure to the cloth; *woof* denotes the crossing threads that give design and color. Taken together, the expression "warp and woof" means the very fiber or essence of a thing.

waver: To vacillate, showing doubt or indecision. Characteristic of not being firm-minded. To be unsure of oneself. See: *conversion to Hinduism.*

wealth: *Artha.* Abundance; financial stability. See: *purushārtha.*

wedding pendant: A gold ornament worn by the Hindu wife around the neck representing her vows of matrimony. Known as *maṅgala sūtra* in Sanskṛit, and *tali* in Tamil. She reveres it as an image of her husband and ritually worships it during her morning devotions.

whence: From where. Whence does it come? Where does it come from?

whirling: To move rapidly in a circular motion.

wield: To hold and use with skill.

wisdom: The timely application of knowledge. The power of judging the best course of action, based on understanding, knowledge and experience.

withholding: To refrain from giving. Not granting.

woeful: Sad, pitiful, full of sorrow. —**woeful birth:** An unfavorable birth; a life of difficulties resulting from negative *karmas* accrued in previous lives.

wondrous: Inspiring awe, extraordinary, mirific.

woodwind: A wind instrument such as the flute or the Indian *nāgasvara.*

woof: See: *warp and woof.*

Words of Our Master: A collection of sayings and inspiring statements of Sage Yogaswāmī of Sri Lanka—compiled from the notes and recollections of devotees.

world: In Hindu theology, *world* refers to 1) ***loka:*** a particular region of consciousness or plane of existence. 2) ***māyā:*** The whole of manifest existence; the phenomenal universe, or cosmos. In this sense it transcends the limitations of physical reality, and can include emotional, mental and spiritual, physical realms of existence, depending on its use. Also denoted by the terms *prakṛiti* and Brahmāṇḍa. 3) ***pāśa:*** In Śaivism, the term *world* is often used to translate the term *pāśa* in the Āgamic triad of fundamentals—Pati, *paśu, pāśa,* "God, soul, world." It is thus defined as the "fetter" *(pāśa)* that binds the soul, veiling its true nature and enabling it to grow and evolve through experience as an individual being. In this sense, the world, or *pāśa,* is three-fold, comprising *āṇava* (the force of individuation), *karma* (the principle of cause and effect) and *māyā* (manifestation, the principle of matter, Śiva's mirific energy, the sixth *tattva).* See: *Brahmāṇḍa, microcosm-macrocosm, sarvabhadra, Śivamaya, tattva.*

worldly: Materialistic, unspiritual. Devoted to or concerned with the affairs or pleasures of the world, especially excessive concern to the exclusion of religious thought and life. Connoting ways born of the lower *chakras:* jealousy, greed, selfishness, anger, guile, etc. —**worldliness:** The state or quality of being worldly. —**worldly wise:** Knowledgeable in the ways of the world. Street wise. Sophisticated. See: *materialism, saṁsārī.*
wrath: Intense anger. Rage.
written prayers: See: *lekhaprārtha havana.*
wrought: Formed, fashioned, crafted, built.

yajña: यज्ञ "Worship; sacrifice." One of the most central Hindu concepts—sacrifice and surrender through acts of worship, inner and outer. 1) A form of ritual worship especially prevalent in Vedic times, in which oblations—*ghee,* grains, spices and exotic woods—are offered into a fire according to scriptural injunctions while special *mantras* are chanted. The element fire, *Agni,* is revered as the divine messenger who carries offerings and prayers to the Gods. The ancient *Veda Brāhmaṇas* and the *Śrauta Śāstras* describe various types of *yajña* rites, some so elaborate as to require hundreds of priests, whose powerful chanting resounds for miles. These major *yajñas* are performed in large, open-air structures called *yāgaśālā.* Domestic *yajñas,* prescribed in the *Gṛihya Śāstras,* are performed in the family compound or courtyard. *Yajña* requires four components, none of which may be omitted: *dravya,* sacrificial substances; *tyāga,* the spirit of sacrificing all to God; *devatā,* the celestial beings who receive the sacrifice; and *mantra,* the empowering word or chant.

While *pūjā* (worship in temples with water, lights and flowers) has largely replaced the *yajña,* this ancient rite still continues, and its specialized priestly training is carried on in schools in India. *Yajñas* of a grand scale are performed for special occasions, beseeching the Gods for rain during drought, or for peace during bloody civil war. Even in temples, *yajña* has its Āgamic equivalent in the *agnikāraka,* the *homa* or *havana* ceremony, held in a fire pit *(homakuṇḍa)* in an outer *maṇḍapa* of a temple as part of elaborate *pūjā* rites.

2) Personal acts of worship or sacrifice. Life itself is a ***jīvayajña.*** The *Upanishads* suggest that one can make "inner *yajñas*" by offering up bits of the little self into the fires of *sādhana* and *tapas* until the greater Self shines forth. The five daily *yajñas,* ***pañcha mahāyajña,*** of the householder (outlined in the *Dharma Śāstras)* ensure offerings to *ṛishis,* ancestors, Gods, creatures and men. They are as follows. —***brahma yajña:*** (also called *Veda yajña* or *ṛishi yajña*) "Homage to the seers." Accomplished through studying and teaching the *Vedas.* —***deva yajña:*** "Homage to Gods and elementals."

Recognizing the debt due to those who guide nature, and the feeding of them by pouring into the fire. This is the *homa* sacrifice. ***—pitṛi yajña:*** "Homage to ancestors." Offering of cakes *(piṇḍa)* and water to the family line and the progenitors of mankind. ***—bhūta yajña:*** "Homage to beings." Placing food-offerings, *bali,* on the ground, intended for animals, birds, insects, wandering outcastes and beings of the invisible worlds. ("Let him gently place on the ground [food] for dogs, outcastes, *svapachas,* those diseased from sins, crows and insects" *Manu Dharma Śāstras* 3.92). —***manushya yajña:*** "Homage to men." Feeding guests and the poor, the homeless and the student. *Manushya yajña* includes all acts of philanthropy, such as tithing and charity. The Vedic study is performed in the morning. The other four *yajñas* are performed just before taking one's noon meal. *Manu Dharma Śāstras* (3.80) states, "Let him worship, according to the rule, the *ṛishis* with *Veda* study, the *devas* with *homa,* the *pitṛis* with *śrāddha,* men with food, and the *bhūtas* with *bali.*" Mystics warn that all offerings must be tempered in the fires of *kuṇḍalinī* through the power of inner *yajña* to be true and valuable, just as the fire of awareness is needed to indelibly imprint ideas and concepts on one's own *ākāśic* window. See: *dharma, havana, homa, pūjā, sacrifice.*

Yājñavalkya Smṛiti: **याज्ञवल्क्यस्मृति** A Hindu code of law, one of the *Dharma Śāstras,* regarded second in authority only to the earlier *Manu Dharma Śāstras.* See: *Dharma Śāstra, smṛiti.*

Yājñavalkya Upanishad: **याज्ञवल्क्य उपनिषद्** A metrical rendering of the *Jābāla Upanishad,* which expounds on *sannyāsa,* renunciation of worldly life in the quest for liberation.

Yajñopavīta: **यज्ञोपवीत** "Sacred thread." See: *upanayana.*

Yajur Veda: **यजुर्वेद** "Wisdom of sacrificial formulas." One of the four compendia of revelatory texts called *Vedas (Ṛig, Sāma, Yajur* and *Atharva).* When used alone, the term *Yajur Veda* generally refers to this *Veda's* central and oldest portion—the *Saṁhitā,* "hymn collection." Of this there are two recensions: 1) the *Kṛishṇa* ("black") *Yajur Veda* (so-called because the commentary, *Brāhmaṇa,* material is mixed with the hymns); and 2) the *Śukla* ("white or clear") *Yajur Veda* (with no commentary among the hymns). The contents of these two recensions are also presented in different order. The *Yajur Veda Saṁhitā* is divided into 40 chapters and contains 1,975 stanzas. About 30 percent of the stanzas are drawn from the *Ṛig Veda Saṁhitā* (particularly from chapters eight and nine). This *Veda* is a special collection of hymns to be chanted during *yajña.* The *Kṛishṇa Yajur Veda Saṁhitā* exists today in various recensions, most importantly the *Taittirīya Saṁhitā* and the *Maitrāyaṇī Saṁhitā.* The *Śukla Yajur Veda Saṁhitā* is preserved most prominently as the *Vājasaneyi Saṁhitā.* See: *Vedas.*

Yama: **यम** "The restrainer." Hindu God of death; oversees the processes of death transition, guiding the soul out of its present physical body. See: *death.*

yama-niyama: **यम नियम** The first two of the eight limbs of *rāja yoga,* constituting Hinduism's fundamental ethical codes, the *yamas* and *niyamas* are the essential foundation for all spiritual progress. They are codified in numerous scriptures including the *Śāṇḍilya* and *Varuha Upanishads, Haṭha Yoga Pradīpikā* by Gorakshanātha, the *Tirumantiram* of Tirumular and the *Yoga Sūtras* of Patañjali. All the above texts list ten *yamas* and ten *niyamas,* with the exception of Patañjali's classic work, which lists only five of each. The *yamas* are the ethical restraints; the *niyamas* are the religious practices. Because it is brief, the entire code can be easily memorized and reviewed daily by the spiritual aspirant. Here are the ten traditional *yamas* and ten *niyamas.* —***yamas:*** 1) ***ahiṁsā:*** "Noninjury." Not harming others by thought, word, or deed. 2) ***satya:*** "Truthfulness." Refraining from lying and betraying promises. 3) ***asteya:*** "Nonstealing." Neither stealing, nor coveting nor entering into debt. 4) ***brahmacharya:*** "Divine conduct." Controlling lust by remaining celibate when single, leading to faithfulness in marriage. 5) ***kshamā:*** "Patience." Restraining intolerance with people and impatience with circumstances. 6) ***dhṛiti:*** "Steadfastness." Overcoming nonperseverance, fear, indecision and changeableness. 7) ***dayā:*** "Compassion." Conquering callous, cruel and insensitive feelings toward all beings. 8) ***ārjava:*** "Honesty, straightforwardness." Renouncing deception and wrongdoing. 9) ***mitāhāra:*** "Moderate appetite." Neither eating too much nor consuming meat, fish, fowl or eggs. 10) ***śaucha:*** "Purity." Avoiding impurity in body, mind and speech. —***niyamas:*** 1) ***hrī:*** "Remorse." Being modest and showing shame for misdeeds. 2) ***santosha:*** "Contentment." Seeking joy and serenity in life. 3) ***dāna:*** "Giving." Tithing and giving generously without thought of reward. 4) ***āstikya:*** "Faith." Believing firmly in God, Gods, *guru* and the path to enlightenment. 5) **Īśvarapūjana:** "Worship of the Lord." The cultivation of devotion through daily worship and meditation. 6) ***siddhānta śravaṇa:*** "Scriptural listening." Studying the teachings and listening to the wise of one's lineage. 7) ***mati:*** "Cognition." Developing a spiritual will and intellect with the *guru's* guidance. 8) ***vrata:*** "Sacred vows." Fulfilling religious vows, rules and observances faithfully. 9) ***japa:*** "Recitation." Chanting *mantras* daily. 10) ***tapas:*** "Austerity." Performing *sādhana,* penance, *tapas* and sacrifice. Patañjali lists the *yamas* as: *ahiṁsā, satya, asteya, brahmacharya* and *aparigraha* (noncovetousness)*;* and the *niyamas* as: *śaucha, santosha, tapas, svādhyāya* (self-reflection, scriptural study) and Īśvarapraṇidhāna (worship). See: *rāja yoga.*

yantra: **यन्त्र** "Vessel; container." A mystic diagram composed of geometric and alphabetic figures—usually etched on small plates of gold, silver or copper. Sometimes rendered in three dimensions in stone or metal. The purpose of a *yantra* is to focus spiritual and mental energies according to computer-like *yantric* pattern, be it for health, wealth, childbearing or the invoking of one God or another. It is usually installed near or under the temple Deity. Psychically seen, the temple *yantra* is a magnificent three-dimensional edifice of light and sound in which the *devas* work. On the astral plane, it is much larger than the temple itself. —***Śrī Chakra:*** The most well known *yantra* and a central image in Śākta worship. Consisting of nine interlocking triangles, it is the design of Śiva-Śakti's multidimensional manifestations. *Yantras* are also used for meditation and *sādhana*, especially in the Śākta tradition. Installing them beneath Deities is a fairly modern practice, while the *Āgamas* prescribe the placement of precious gems. For Śaivites the Tiru-ambala *chakra*, representing Lord Naṭarāja, is most sacred. See: *mūrti.*

yea: Yes, indeed, truly.

yield: To produce as a result of cultivation, such as fruit. To profit or give.

yoga: योग "Union." From *yuj*, "to yoke, harness, unite." The philosophy, process, disciplines and practices whose purpose is the yoking of individual consciousness with transcendent or divine consciousness. One of the six *darśanas*, or systems of orthodox Hindu philosophy. *Yoga* was codified by Patañjali in his *Yoga Sūtras* (ca 200 BCE) as the eight limbs *(ashṭāṅga)* of *rāja yoga*. It is essentially a one system, but historically, parts of *rāja yoga* have been developed and emphasized as *yogas* in themselves. Prominent among the many forms of *yoga* are *haṭha yoga* (emphasizing bodily perfection in preparation for meditation), *kriyā yoga* (emphasizing breath control), as well as *karma yoga* (selfless service) and *bhakti yoga* (devotional practices) which could be regarded as an expression of *rāja yoga's* first two limbs *(yama* and *niyama)*. See: *bhakti yoga, haṭha yoga, shaḍ darśana, karma yoga, rāja yoga, siddha yoga.*

yoga pāda: योगपाद् The third of the successive stages in spiritual unfoldment in Śaiva Siddhānta, wherein the goal is realization of the Self. See: *pāda, yoga.*

Yoga Sampradāya: योगसंप्रदाय Another term for Siddha Siddhānta. See: *Śaivism.*

Yogaswāmī: யோகசுவாமி "Master of *yoga*." See: *Kailāsa Paramparā.*

yoga tapas: योगतपस् "Fiery union." Relentless, sustained *yoga* practice that awakens the fiery *kuṇḍalinī*, bringing the transforming heat of *tapas* and ultimately the repeated experience of the Self God, leading to *jñāna*, the wisdom state. See: *jñāna, tapas, yoga.*

Yogatattva Upanishad: योगतत्त्व उपनिषद् Scripture of 142 verses based on Advaita Vedānta and *yoga* practices, ca 1400.

Yoga Vāsishṭha: योगवासिष्ठ Poetic work of over 29,000 verses attributed to Vālmīki. It is a dialog between Prince Rāma and his teacher, Sage Vasishṭha, in the form of 50 intriguing stories which present *advaita* and the concepts and ideals of *yoga* in elegant Sanskṛit. (Variously dated between 500 and 1000 CE.)

yogī: योगी One who practices *yoga*, especially *kuṇḍalinī* or *rāja yoga.*

***yoginī:* योगिनी** Feminine counterpart of *yogī.*

yon: That or those (at a distance).

***yoni:* योनि** "Source, origin; female genitals, womb." In some *tantric* sects the Śivaliṅga is depicted as a phallic symbol, and the base as a vulva, or *yoni.* While the *liṅga* represents the unmanifest or static Absolute, the *yoni* represents the dynamic, creative energy of God, the womb of the universe.

yore: Of yore: a long time ago, in a distant past.

young soul: A soul who has gone through only a few births, and is thus inexperienced or immature. See: *evolution of the soul, soul.*

***yuga:* युग** "Period, age." One of four ages which chart the duration of the world according to Hindu thought. They are: Satya (or Kṛita), Tretā, Dvāpara and Kali. In the first period, *dharma* reigns supreme, but as the ages revolve, virtue diminishes and ignorance and injustice increases. At the end of the Kali Yuga, which we are in now, the cycle begins again with a new Satya Yuga. It is said in the *Mahābhārata* that during the Satya Yuga all are *brāhmins,* and the color of this *yuga* is white. In the Tretā Yuga, righteousness decreases by one-fourth and men seek reward for their rites and gifts; the color is red and the consciousness of the *kshatriya,* sovereignty, prevails. In the Dvāpara Yuga, the four *varṇas* come fully into existence. The color is yellow. In the Kali Yuga, the color is black. Righteousness is one-tenth that of the Satya Yuga. True worship and sacrifice cease, and base, or *śūdra,* consciousness is prominent. Calamities, disease, fatigue and faults such as anger and fear prevail. People decline and their motives grow weak. See: *cosmic cycle.*

zenith: Highest point; apex; summit.

Zoroastrian: Of or related to Zoroastrianism, a religion founded in Persia by Spenta Zarathustra (ca 600 BCE). It has roughly 150,000 adherents today, mostly near Bombay, where they are called Parsis. The faith stresses monotheism while recognizing a universal struggle between the force of good (led by Ahura Mazda) and evil (led by Ahriman). The sacred fire, always kept burning in the home, is considered the only worshipful symbol. Scripture is the *Zend Avesta.*

Charts

Vedic-Āgamic Cosmology, Tattvas and Chakras

Three charts are given on the following pages. The first shows Hindu cosmology, correlating the various divisions and categories of manifestation, as well as the bodies, sheaths, *chakras* and states of consciousness of the soul. It is organized with the highest consciousness, or subtlest level of manifestation, at the top, and the lowest, or grossest at the bottom. In studying the chart, it is important to remember that each level includes within itself all the levels above it. Thus, the element earth, the grossest or outermost aspect of manifestation, contains all the *tattvas* above it on the chart. They are its inner structure. Similarly, the soul encased in a physical body also has all the sheaths named above—*prāṇic,* instinctive-intellectual, cognitive and causal. Here, now, is a brief description of the major parts of the cosmology chart.

lokas (3 worlds & 14 planes): These are the classical divisions of consciousness, traditionally numbering 14, as listed. A simpler breakdown, shown in column one, is three *lokas,* causal, subtle and gross. The 14 *lokas* correspond directly to the *chakras,* psychic force centers within the inner bodies of the soul, also listed in column two. The 14 *chakras* are "doorways" within man to each of the 14 planes.

kalā (5 spheres): The center of the chart lists the five *kalās,* which are vast divisions of consciousness or "dimensions" of the mind. Note that the five states of mind—superconscious, subsuperconscious, conscious, subconscious and sub-subconscious—are also listed in this column.

tattva (36 evolutes): The 36 *tattvas,* listed to the right of the *kalās,* are the basic "building blocks" of the universe, successively grosser evolutes of consciousness. These are in three groups, as shown.

kośa & śarīra (3 bodies & 5 sheaths): The sheaths or bodies of the soul are given in the two right-hand columns. Note the correlation of these and the worlds by reading across the chart to the left to the two columns named "three worlds," and "14 planes."

On the second chart, the 14 *chakras* and their attributes are listed, and on the third, a complete list of all 36 *tattvas* is given. For more insights on the subjects in the chart, please refer to the lexicon.

ॐ Vedic-Āgamic Cosmology

३ लोक 3 WORLDS		१४ लोक 14 PLANES		५ लोक 5 SPHERES
3rd World Śivaloka, "plane of God," and the Gods, or Kāraṇaloka, the "causal plane"		**7. Satyaloka,** "plane of reality," also called Brahmaloka, ***sahasrāra chakra***		**5. Śāntyatītakalā** Śivānanda, superconsciousr panded into endless inner s
		6. Tapoloka, "plane of austerity," ***ājñā chakra***		**4. Śāntikalā** *kāraṇa chitta,* superconscio forms made of inner sound colors.
		5. Janaloka, "creative plane"		
		viśuddha chakra		• LIBERATE • BOUND
2nd World Antarloka, subtle or astral plane	higher astral plane	**4. Maharloka,** "plane of greatness," ***anāhata chakra***	Devaloka	**3. Vidyākalā** *anukāraṇa chitta,* • subsuperconscious aware forms in their totality in pr sive states of manifestation. • subsuperconscious cognit the interrelated forces of th tual and magnetic energies.
		maṇipūra chakra		
cycle of reincarnation, *saṁsāra*	mid-astral	**3. Svarloka,** "celestial plane"	Pitṛiloka	**2. Pratishṭhākalā** *buddhi chitta and manas ch* realm of intellect and instir
	lower astral	**2. Bhuvarloka,** "plane of atmosphere," ***svādhishṭhāna chakra*** — Pitṛiloka, "world of ancestors"		
		Pretaloka, "world of the departed," earth-bound souls. Astral duplicate of Bhūloka	Pretaloka	**1. Nivṛittikalā** *jāgrat chitta, saṁskāra chit vāsanā chitta*—the conscic subconscious and sub-subc scious mind, the interrelate magnetic forces between p people and their possessior
1st World Bhūloka		**1. Bhūloka,** "earth plane," ***mūlādhāra chakra***		
Antarloka's netherworld, Naraka	sub-astral	**Naraka (7 hellish planes of lower consciousness,** in descendi order): –1) Put *(atala chakra),* –2) Avīchi *(vitalā chakra),* –3) *(sutala chakra),* –4) Tāmisra *(talātala chakra),* –5) Ṛijīsha *(ra chakra),* –6) Kuḍmala *(mahātala chakra),* –7) Kākola *(pātāla*		

ब्रह्माण्ड The Inner and Outer Universe

Paraśiva *(atattva,* "beyond existence") **३६ तत्त्व 36 EVOLUTES**	**३ शरीर** **3 BODIES**		**५ कोश** **5 SHEATHS**
***ldha māyā:* pure spiritual energy** *Śiva tattva:* Parāśakti-*nāda,* Satchidānanda, pure consciousness *Śakti tattva:* Parameśvara-*bindu,* Personal God	***viśvagrāsa:*** final merger of *ānandamaya kośa* in Parameśvara		
Sadāśiva tattva: power of revealment *Īśvāra tattva:* power of concealment *Śuddhavidyā tattva: dharma,* pure knowing, the powers of dissolution, preservation and creation—Rudra, Vishṇu and Brahmā	***kāraṇa śarīra – ānandamaya kośa*** "causal body"– "sheath of bliss" the body of the soul, also called the actinic causal body		
***ldhāśuddha māyā:* spiritual-magnetic** *māyā tattva:* mirific energy *kāla tattva:* time *niyati tattva: karma* *kalā tattva:* creativity, aptitude *vidyā tattva:* knowledge *rāga tattva:* attachment, desire *purusha tattva:* shrouded soul	***sūkshma śarīra*** "subtle body," also called the astral body	refined astral body	***vijñānamaya kośa*** "sheath of cognition," the mental or actinodic causal sheath
***uddha māyā:* magnetic-gross energy** *prakṛiti tattva:* primal nature -16) *antaḥkaraṇa:* mental faculties -21) *karmendriyas:* organs of perception -26) *jñānendriyas:* organs of action -35) *ākāśa tattva* (ether), *vāyu tattva* (air), *tejas tattva* (fire), *āpas tattva* (water)		gross astral body	***manomaya kośa*** intellectual (odic causal) sheath and instinctive (odic-astral) sheath
			prāṇamaya kośa "sheath of vitality," which enlivens the physical body
) *pṛithivī tattva:* earth	***sthūla śarīra – annamaya kośa*** "gross body"– " food-made sheath" the physical body, or odic body		

14 Chakras, Force Centers of Consciousness

Name	Location	Attribute	Plane	Planet	Element/sense	Petals	Letter
7) ***sahasrāra***	crown of head	illumination	Satyaloka	Neptune	Śūnya (void)	1008	
6) ***ājñā***	third eye	divine sight	Tapoloka	Uranus	*mahātattva*	2	AUM
5) ***viśuddha***	throat	divine love	Janaloka	Saturn	ether/hearing	16	YA
4) ***anāhata***	heart center	direct cognition	Maharloka	Jupiter	air/touch	12	VĀ
3) ***maṇipūra***	solar plexus	willpower	Svarloka	Mars	fire/sight	10	ŚI
2) ***svādhishṭhāna***	navel	reason	Bhuvarloka	Venus	water/taste	6	MA
1) ***mūlādhāra***	base of spine	memory/time/space	Bhūloka	Mercury	earth/smell	4	NA
1) ***atala***	hips	fear and lust	Put				
2) ***vitala***	thighs	raging anger	Avīchi				
3) ***sutala***	knees	retaliatory jealousy	Saṁhāta				
4) ***talātala***	calves	prolonged confusion	Tāmisra				
5) ***rasātala***	ankles	selfishness	Ṛijīsha				
6) ***mahātala***	feet	absence of conscience	Kuḍmala				
7) ***pātāla***	soles of feet	malice and murder	Kākola				

The *chakras* are nerve plexuses or centers of force and consciousness located within the inner bodies of man. In the physical body there are corresponding nerve plexuses, ganglia and glands. The seven principle *chakras* can be seen psychically as colorful, multi-petalled wheels or lotuses situated along the spinal cord. The seven lower *chakras*, barely visible, exist below the spine.

See: *Cosmology chart, Naraka, and individual chakra entries.*

The 36 Tattvas: Categories of Existence

ŚUDDHA TATTVAS
Actinic or Pure Spiritual Energy

1) *Śiva tattva:* Parāśakti-*nāda* (Satchidānanda, pure consciousness)
2) *Śakti tattva:* Parameśvara-*bindu* (Naṭarāja, Personal God), energy, light and love
3) *Sadāśiva tattva:* the power of revealment (Sadāśiva)
4) *Īśvāra tattva:* the power of concealment (Maheśvara)
5) *Śuddhavidyā tattva: dharma,* pure knowing, the powers of dissolution (Rudra), preservation (Vishṇu) and creation (Brahmā)

ŚUDDHĀŚUDDHA TATTVAS
Actinodic or Spiritual-Magnetic Energy

6) *māyā tattva:* mirific energy
7) *kāla tattva:* time
8) *niyati tattva: karma*
9) *kalā tattva:* creativity, aptitude
10) *vidyā tattva:* knowledge
11) *rāga tattva:* attachment, desire
12) *purusha tattva:* the soul shrouded by the above five *tattvas*

AŚUDDHA TATTVAS
Odic or Gross-Magnetic Energy

13) *prakṛiti tattva:* primal nature
14) *buddhi tattva:* intellect
15) *ahaṁkāra tattva:* external ego
16) *manas tattva:* instinctive mind
17) *śrotra tattva:* hearing (ears)
18) *tvak tattva:* touching (skin)
19) *chakshu:* seeing (eyes)
20) *rasanā tattva:* tasting (tongue)
21) *ghrāṇa tattva:* smelling (nose)
22) *vāk tattva:* speech (voice)
23) *pāṇi tattva:* grasping (hands)
24) *pāda tattva:* walking (feet)
25) *pāyu tattva:* excretion (anus)
26) *upastha tattva:* procreation (genitals)
27) *śabdha tattva:* sound
28) *sparśa tattva:* feel
29) *rūpa tattva:* form
30) *rasa tattva:* taste
31) *gandha tattva:* odor
32) *ākāśa tattva:* ether
33) *vāyu tattva:* air
34) *tejas tattva:* fire
35) *āpas tattva:* water
36) *pṛithivī tattva:* earth

Index

Sūchi

सूची

Aadheenam: def., 675; home of *guru,* 343
Abhāsa: creation, 511; def., 675
Abhaya: def., 675; *mudrā,* 159
Abide: def., 675
Abhinavagupta: influence and works, 675; Kashmīr Śaiva *guru,* 510
Abhisheka: aftermath, 333; def., 675
Abhisheki, Janaki: genesis of word Hindu, 731
Abhor: def., 675
Abjuration: def., 675; at age 60, 277
Ablution: def., 675
Abode: def., 675
Abortion: def., 675; prohibition, 217
Abraham: founder of Judaism, 564
Absolute: def., 676
Absolute Being: description, 51; belief, 465; see also *All-pervasive God; God; Pati; Śiva; Supreme Being*
Absolute Reality: def., 676; Paraśiva, 781; Self Realization, 13; is Śiva, 49; in worship, 57
Absolutely real: def., 676
Absolution: def., 676; sin, 153; *tantras* for, 255
Absolve: See *Absolution*
Absorption: def., 676
Abstain: def., 676; from injuring others, 195
Abyss: def., 676; hell, 155; Naraka, 65
Accelerate: def., 677; time, 439
Acceptance: attitude, 197; what is, 9
Accordant: def., 677
Āchāra: def., 677; description, 361
Acorn: analogy of soul, 81, 718
Acosmic pantheism: def., 677; Śaṅkara, 417
Actinic: def., 677
Actinodic: def., 677
Adept: def., 677; Nātha, 447
Adharma: def., 677; description, 712; and evil, 717; God, 139; against divine law, 167, sin, 818
Adhere: def., 677
Adhyātma: def., 677
Adhyātma prasāra: def., 677
Adhyātma vikāśa: def., 677
Ādi Granth: concepts of, 677-678; Sikh scripture, 542; and *Vedas,* 377
Ādinātha: def., 678
Ādinātha Sampradāya: Gorakshanātha, 447, 495; Nātha Sampradāya, 447
Ādiśaiva: lineage, 678; priests of Śaivism, 319
Adopt: children, 239; def., 678; religion of wife, 227
Adore: def., 678
Adorn: def., 678
Adṛishṭa: def., 678; karma, 746
Adulate: def., 678
Adultery: avoiding thought of, 219; def., 678; scripture prohibits, 217
Adulthood: nurturing children to, 239; rites of passage, 273
Advaita: Appaya Dīkshita, 514-515; def., 678; philosophy, 417; Śaivism,

33; Siddha Siddhānta, 518
Advaita Īśvaravāda: def., 678; monistic theism, 421; theology of Śaivism, 33
Advaita Īśvaravādins: authority, 431; def., 678
Advaita Siddhānta: philosophy, 395, 678-679
Advaita tantrics: of Gorakshanātha, 518
Advaita Vedānta: monistic schools, 679; Vedānta, 852-853
Adversity: def., 679; dancing with Śiva, 9; obstacle on path, 255
Advocate: def., 679
Affectionate detachment: from world, 145
Affirmation: def., 678
Affirmation of faith: def., 679; description, 407, 409
Aftermath: def., 679; of pūjā, 333
Āgama Śāstra: Kashmīr Śaivism, 510
Āgamas: discussion, 379-381; authority, 379, xxvi; familiarity, 493; Hindu scripture, 528; Namaḥ Śivāya in, 401; *olai* leaves, 493; philosophy, 492; realizing truth, xxv; ritual authority, 679; Śaiva, 800-801; Śaivism, 493; scripture, 373; significance, 381; structure, 379; temple construction, 301; veneration of, xx; worship, 313
Agarbatti: incense, stick, 734
Agastya: profile, 679; *siddha*, 496
Age: for marriage, 225; fidelity until old, 215; marriage compatibility, 229; old age, death through, 101; periods of life, 173; priest training, 319; profession of father taught when young, 245; sacraments, 271-277; *sannyāsa* taken while young, 87, 349
Aged: caring for, 263
Aghora: def., 679
Aghoraśiva: Paddhatis and pluralistic theism, 431; profile, 679; Śaiva ritual, 498; Śaiva Siddhānta, changed, 497; Tirumular comparison, 431
Aghorī: ascetic order, 680
Agni: burning written prayers, 331; created by Śiva, 63; def., 680
Agnihotra: def., 680; *Vedas* on, 322
Agnikāraka: def., 680; *yajña*, 860
Agreement: marriage contract, 211; marriage, husband and wife, 225; Siddhānta's two schools, 431
Agriculture: in *Purāṇas*, 391
Aham Brahmāsmi: meaning, 680; *Vedas*, 425
Ahaṁkāra: def., 680; ego, 11
Ahaṁkāra tattva: chart, 869; def., 837
Ahiṁsā: def., 680, 862; discussion, 195-203; guide, 187; Jain view of, 538; and Pāśupata, 499; practice, xxi; scripture, 204-205; *sannyāsa* vow, 351; source, 197
Aikya: def., 680
Aitareya Brāhmaṇa: use, 680
Ajantā Buddhist Caves: beginnings, 620; frescoes of Buddha, 622
Ajātaśatru: reign, 618
Ajīvika sect: dates, 617
Ajiśaka: invasion of Java, 620
Ajita: death, 618
Ajita Āgama: use, 680
Ājñā chakra: and causal plane, 129; def., 680, 700; faith and, 719
Ākāśa: def., 680-681; Namaḥ Śivāya Mantra, 401
Ākāśa tattva: chart, 866-867, 869; def., 838; Śiva Advaita, 513
Akbar: captures Ranthambor, 632; death, 632; reign, 632; tolerance of faiths, 632
Akrodha: in *sādhāraṇa dharma*, absence of anger, 711
Akshata: def., 681
Ala-ud-din: dynasty, 629
Alexander of Macedonia: conquers Northern India, 618

Alien influences: and children, 261
All-pervasive: def., 681
All-pervasive God: belief of Hindus, 19, 197; cognizing through *japa,* 403; pure consciousness, 53; see also *Absolute Being; God; Pati; Śiva; Supreme Being*
All-pervasive energy: def., 819
Allama Prabhu: Vīra Śaivism, 506; works, 681
Allegory: def., 681; epics, myths, 391
Aloof: def., 681; sages, 359
Altruistic: def., 681; service, 109
Alvar: famous listed, 681; hymns, 393; lives and works, 681
Amardaka: and dualistic Śaivism, 509; monastic order, 496, 681
Ambitiousness: obstacle, 255
Amardaka Tīrthanātha: Amardaka Order, 681
Ambikā: profile, 681; Śakti, 803; Śāktism, 23
Amends: def., 681; before death, 101
Amid: def., 681
Amman: features, 682; Śakti, 803; in Śāktism, 23
Amorphous: def., 682; formless, 721; soul according to pluralists, 435
Amṛita: def., 682; elixir, 716
Amṛitātman: def., 682
Amritsar: massacre, 641; rebellion crushed, 645; Sikh defeat by British, 637; Sikh Golden Temple completed, 632
Anāhata chakra: def., 682, 700
Analects: Confucian scripture, 550
Analogy: def., 682; fire and creation, 419, 433, 494; grace (monkey and cat), 725; *karma* and rice, 745; 725; ocean and monism, 433, 435, 494, 508; potter and clay, creation, 433; river and sea (God and soul), 81, 435; wheel and monism, 275, 377
Analytical: def., 682; thinking, 141
Ānanda: def., 682
Ānandamayī Mā: life of, 640
Ānanda Samucçhaya: written, 629
Ānanda tāṇḍava: def., 682
Ānandamaya kośa: creation by Śiva, 435; def., 682, 750; *śarīra,* 811; soul body, 79
Āṇava: Āgamas, 492; apparent suffering, 137; def., 682; *kalā tattva,* 837; pluralists on, 433, 437; at *pralayas,* 439; soul's bond, 85; and *tripuṇḍra,* 31
Āṇavopāya: def., 683, 847; Kashmīr Śaivism, 511
Anbe Sivamayam Satyame Parasivam: def., 683; discussion, 407
Ancestors: not neglecting, 181; *piṇḍa,* 784; Pitṛiloka, 784; *pitṛi yajña,* 861
Anchorite: def., 683; Lakulīśa, 501; monk, 343, 764
Ancillary: def., 683
Andal: life and work, 626; mystic poetess, 393; profile, 683
Andhra: timeline, 620
Andhra Pradesh: Amardaka order, 496; location, 683
Anekavāda: def., 683
Anekavādin: def., 683; Siddhānta, 431
Aṅga: def., 683
Anger: astral realm of, 155, 868; *chakra* of, 868, forbidden in *guru's* presence, 363; instinct, 141; *japa,* 403, 738; maturing out of, 7; obstacle, 255; refraining from, 183; *sannyāsin* protects mind from; 351; violence reflects, 199
Anguttara-Nikaya: Buddhist scripture, 534
Aniconic: def., 683; *mūrti,* 765
Animal kingdom: violence against, 201
Animal sacrifice: in Śāktism, 23; rejected by Vīra Śaivites, 504
Animate-inanimate: def., 683; manifestations of His grace, *Tirumantiram,* 437; Śiva created all, 123; Śiva

is within all, 53
Añjali mudrā: description, 683; *namaskāra,* 768; symbol, 179; in worship, 305
Aṅkuśa: def., 684; symbol, 165
Annamaya kośa: chart, 867; def., 684, 749; physical body, 79; *śarīra,* 811; soul, 823
Annaprāśana: childhood rite, 271, 669
Annihilate: def., 684; ego, 365; *mahāpralaya,* 439
Antagonism: def., 684; dualistic beliefs generate, 199; suppressed feelings, 155
Antaḥkaraṇa: def., 684; *prakṛiti tattva,* 837; mind (individual), 762; subtle body, 823
Antarloka: creation, 123; and death, 798; def., 684, 753; description, 127, 807; *devas,* 63; soul, 87
Antaryamin: conscience, 702
Anthology: def., 684
Antyaśabda: colophon, 959; def., 684
Antyeshṭi: def., 684; description, 807, 671; funeral 277
Anu: def., 684
Anubhava: def., 684
Anugraha: def., 684, 724-725; Naṭarāja, 770; revelation, *Āgamas,* 55
Anukāraṇa chitta: subsuperconscious mind, 762; Vidyākalā, 866
Anukramaṇi: def., 684
Anupāya: def., 684, 848; Kashmīr Śaivism, 511
Anxiety: and affirmation of faith, 407; def., 684; obstacle, 255
Apad dharma: description, 711-712
Aparājita: killed, 626
Apasmārapurusha: def., 684; and Naṭarāja, 41, 770
Āpas tattva: chart, 867, 869; def., 838
Apatya: def., 684
Apaurusheya: śruti, impersonal, 826
Apex: of creation, 129, 702; def., 685
Appar: and *bhakti* movement, 495; date, 623; profile, 685
Apparent: def., 685
Appaya Dīkshita: history, 514-516; philosophy, 425; and Śrīkaṇṭha, 513; contribution, 685, 630
Apprehend: def., 685
Āraṇyaka: def., 685; *Vedas,* 375
Āratī: def., 685; temple, 305
Arbhuta Tiru Antadi: author and date, 685
Archana: def., 685; worship, 315
Architecture: *Āgama,* 379; in *Purāṇas,* 391; secondary scripture, 389-391; *Sthāpatyaveda,* 826; temple, 301, 627
Ardhanārī Naṭeśvara Stotram: identification, 685
Ardhanārīśvara: Lord Śiva, 685-686; meaning, 57; Śakti, 803
Ārdrā Darśana: def., 686; festival 283, 285
Arduous: def., 686
Arena: def., 686; world, 33
Arguing: family, 247, 667; never with *guru,* 363; and Naraka, 155
Aristotle: importance, 686; dualist, 419
Arjava: def., 686, 862; ethical guideline, 187
Arjuna: profile, 686
Ārogya: āyurveda, diseaselessness, 691
Arrogance: good conduct and, 181; intellect, 141; obstacle, 255
Art: Gaṇeśa, 65; sacred, 39, 261; secondary scriptures, 264, 387
Artha: def., 792-793; goal, 87
Arthaśāstra: manual, art of politics, 618; *Arthaveda,* 686
Arthaveda: scripture, 389; use, 686
Artificial life-extension: dying, 101
Artisans: *dharma,* 171
Arts: boys and girls trained in, 245; *kalā,* 742-743; inner-plane training, 127; sacred, in scripture, 389, 391; *tantras* of life, 255; of *pūjā,* 331; of

worship, 319, 381
Arunagirināthar: life and work, 631, 686
Aruṇeya Upanishad: description, 686
Aryaman: def., 686; prayer, 229
Aryan: invasion, theory of, 608-609; language, William Jones reference, 634; Dravidian racial split, promulgation of theory, 609
Asamprajñāta: samādhi, 805
Āsana: def., 794; description, 686-687; *haṭha yoga,* 728-729; *yoga,* 113
Ascent: def., 687
Ascetic: def., 687; in *Vedas,* 345; description, 361; Pāśupata, 500
Asceticism: def., 687; and renunciation, 345
Ashṭāṅga praṇāma: for men, 305; an aid to faith, 687; def., 787
Ashṭāṅga yoga: rāja yoga, 794; *Yoga,* 814
Ash: def., 687; holy, 315, 321; see also *vibhūti*
Ashes: dispersal after cremation, 277, 695
Ashṭāvaraṇa: shields of Vīra Śaivism, 508
Ashṭādhyāyī: composed, 618
Asian protocol: harmonious, 261
Aśoka: life and work, 619
Āśrama: def., 687, 710-711; home of *guru,* 343; *vānaprastha,* 277; the world as, 145
Āśrama dharma: def., 687, 710-711; description, 173; God's law, 167; and *svadharma,* 175
Assam: location, 687
Assuage: def., 687
Asteya: def., 687, 862; ethical guideline, 187
Āstika: nāstika and, 769
Āstikya: def., 687, 862; ethical guideline, 189; *nāstika* and, 769
Astral body: chart, 867; def., 688; soul, 823; subtle body, 829
Astral plane: creed belief, 471; hell, 155; *loka,* 753-754; prayers and, 331; def., 688; subtle plane, 127, 129; and *vel,* 71
Astrology: *Āgamas,* 381; def., 688; importance, 259; *jyotisha,* 255; marriage, 229, 233; personal, 175; scriptures, 389
Astronomers: method of observation, 612
Astronomy: ancient Hindu dates, 614; Brahmagupta on gravity, 623-624; Indian features, 612; Ptolemy and Indian pupils, 621
Aśuddha tattvas: chart, 867, 869; def., 837
Asuras: attracted, 157; demonic, 63; def., 688; immature, 155; and meat-eaters, 760; not invoked, 63
Aśvaghosha: pantheist, 419; profile, 688
Aśvin: description, 688; prayer, 35
Atala (chakra): chart, 868; description, 688; location, 700
Atattva: chart, 866-867; def., 688; formless, 721; Satchidānanda, 721; *tattva,* 836
Atha: def., 688; use, xxvii
Atharvaśikhā Upanishad: use, 688
Atharva Upaveda: āyurveda, 259
Atharva Veda: contents, 688-689; description, 375; *Vedas,* 851-852
Atheism: Chārvāka, 417; def., 689
Atheistic philosophies: communism, 585-586; existentialism, 587-588; materialism, 584-585; secular humanism, 588-589; summarized, 583-589
Ātman: def., 689; finding, 81, 255; *purusha,* 792; scripture speaks on, 14, 29, 88-89, 440; Śiva, 493; soul, 823; in *Vedas,* 58
Ātma darśana: enlightenment, 716
Ātmārtha pūjā: def., 689, 790; home worship, 335, 319

Ātmasvarūpa: def., 689
Atmosphere: def., 689; "plane of," Bhuvarloka, 694
Atomic bombs: dropped, 642
Atonement: atone, 689; absolution, 676; penance, 783-784; for sin, 153
Attainment: def., 689; God grants, *Bhagavad Gītā,* 25; *nirvikalpa samādhi,* 13; paths of, 35 (see *Path of attainment);* sages, 359
Attendance: temple, 303
Attila the Hun: death, 623
Attire: elegantly modest, 261
Attitude: def., 689; detachment, monastic, 343; belief and, 197; toward sex, 219, 233
Augustine: importance, 689, 419
Aum: meaning, 689-690; mystery, 653; pronunciation, 689; symbol, 3; use, 690; *Veda* on, 116, 382; and *yogīs,* 518
Aura: def., 690, *pāpa,* 779-780; *puṇya,* 790-791; and sin, 818
Aurangzeb: discriminatory policies and practices, 633; Sikh Guru Tegh Bahadur execution, 633
Aurobindo Ghosh: pantheist, 419; profile, 690
Auspicious: def., 690; time in astrology, 259; symbol, 135
Austerity: absolution of sin, 153; born of God, 63; def., 690-691; for goodness, 7; practice of, 189; *tapas,* 835; at temple, 307; *yoga,* 113
Authenticity: def., 691
Authority: def., 691; in *guru's* presence, 363: localized, 357; for *jāpa,* 405; respect for, 247; Siddhānta scriptural, 431; Āgamic, 379; Vedic, 377; woman's, 215
Auvai Kural: written, 626
Auvaiyar: life and work, 626, 691; mystic poetess, 393
Avantīvarman: reign, 691
Avatāra: comparison in Hindu sects, 601; def., 691; doctrine, 601; incarnations of Vishṇu, 25
Avidyā: *āṇava mala,* 682; def., 691; and evil, 717; and sin, 818
Avyakta: *mūrti,* nonmanifest, 765
Awareness: consciousness, 703; def., 691; in *kriyā,* 111; limited, 85, 125; beyond death, 99; *sākshin,* 803; Satchidānanda, 53; in *yoga,* 113
Axioms: def., 692; Chellappan's, 453
Axis: def., 692
Āyurveda: holistic medicine, 691-692; importance, 255, 259; scripture, 389
Āyurveda vaidya: def., 692
Ayyappan: identification, 692; and Śaivism, 491

Bāba, Meher: teachings, 640
Bāba, Neem Karoli: death, 644
Bāba, Satya Sāī: work, 641
Bāba, Śīrdī Sāī: death, 641
Babri Masjid: demolished, 647
Babur: destroys Lord Rāma's birthplace, 631-632; founds Mogul Empire of North India, 631
Backbiting: def., 692; instinctive, 141
Bādarāyaṇa: *Brahma Sūtra,* 697; profile, 692; Vedānta, 852
Bael: *bilva,* 695; symbol, 385
Baha'i: beliefs, 575; founding, 635
Bālasarasvatī: death, 645
Bali: offerings in *bhūta yajña,* 861
Bali: conference, 651; Dutch control, 640; receives Hinduism, 625; Buddhist and Śaiva Hindu princes, 631
Balipīṭha: purpose, 692; temple, 305
Bāṇa: life and work, 624
Bangalore (India): Ṛishi from the Himalayas, 451; Iraivan Temple, 646
Bangladesh: independence, 644;

Islam state religion, 645
Banyan tree: symbol, 17; *vaṭa,* 651
Barbarian period: North India, 618
Bard: def., 692
Basavaṇṇa: life and work, 628, 692, 504-506; philosophy, 425
Batara: other name, 692; Bali, 491
Bathing: affirmation said before, 409; in Ganges River, 722; before worship, 257, 329; *mantras* for, 261; Śivaliṅga, 285
Baudhāyana Dharma Śāstra: use, 692
bce: def., 692
Beads: chanting, 403; *mālā,* 756; *rudrāksha,* 799
Belief: and attitude, 199; Hindu, 19; creeds, 463; in God, 33
Being: def., 692
Beliefs: Buddhism, 536; Christian, 568; Confucianism, 552; Hinduism, 532; Islam, 572; Jainism, 540; Judaism, 564; Shintoism, 556; Sikhism, 544; Taoism, 548; Zoroastrianism, 559
Bell: *ghaṇṭā,* 723; loudly rung, 321; *pūjā,* 790; symbol, 281
Benediction: def., 692
Benevolence: def., 692
Bengal: British rule, 634
Benign: def., 692
Benz, Karl: combustion engine, 639
Berlin wall: fall of, 645
Bernier, François: on Mogul rule, 633
Beseech: def., 692
Bestow: def., 692
Betoken: def., 692
Betrothal: def., 692-693; and marriage, 229; marriage covenant, 758; *niśchitārtha,* 772; rite, 273
Bewilder: def., 693
Bhaga: def., 693; prayer to, 229
Bhagavad Gītā: bhakti, 393; description, 693; Emerson, 635; *Mahābhārata,* 391; Smārtism, 27
Bhāgavata: description, 693; Vaishṇavism, 25, 848-849
Bhāgavata Purāṇa: description, 693
Bhairava: def., 693; Śiva, 57
Bhajana: def., 693; in home shrine, 335; *Āgama* philosophy, 493
Bhakta: def., 693
Bhakti: def., 693; for *guru,* 703-704; heart softening, 653; literature, 393; in Sikhism, 542; scripture on, 336-337; Vaishṇavism, 25, 530-531; Vīra Śaivism, 508
Bhakti yoga: description, 693; focus, 694; *kriyā pāda,* 111; practice of, 257, 694
Bhārata: Vedas, 377; battle, 615; birth, 613; def., 694; holy land, 656
Bhārata Saṁhitā: date written, 615
Bhāshya: commentaries, 694; *Hindu Catechism,* xxvi-xxviii
Bhāskara: contribution, 694; a monistic theist, 425
Bhavabhūti: life and work, 625
Bhāvaliṅga: def., 694
Bhedābheda: def., 694; Vedānta, 853
Bhogar Ṛishi: life and work, 620, 694; Śaiva Siddhānta, 497; *siddha,* 496
Bhṛityāchāra: def., 694, 778
Bhūloka: def., 694, 753; description, 125; creation 123; and subtle plane, 127; see also *Physical plane*
Bhūmikā: def., 694; introduction, xvii
Bhūta yajña: def., 861
Bhūrja pattra: birch bark, xxvii; *olai,* 775
Bhuvarloka: astral plane, 836; def., 694; three worlds and, 839
Bible: Christian scripture, 566; and *Vedas,* 377
Bijjala: profile, 695; and Vīra Śaivism, 505-506
Bilva: symbol, 385; use, 695
Bindu: def., 695; Śakti *tattva,* 837; significance, 695; *tilaka,* 840; *tripuṇḍra,* 31
Birth: and caste, 171; control, 217;

freedom from, 7, 33, 85, 87; marriage, 211, 217, 239; obstacle, 255; preparation 127; purpose, 7; reincarnation, 97; rite, 269, 275; unpleasant, 155; of the world, 41
Birth chart: def., 695; function, 259
Birthstar: def., 695; credentials, 315; Kārttikeya's, 289; *nakshatra,* 767
Bi-sexual: def., 695
Blavatsky, Madame: Theosophy Society, 574, 636
Blessing: def., 695; *guru's,* 363; temple, 303
Bodhaka: def., 695
Bodhidharma: life and work, 622
Bodhi tantra: def., 695
Bodily humors: in *āyurveda,* 259; def., 695
Body: astral, 687; causal plane, 129; def., 695; *kośa,* 749-750; merger in God, 133; soul, 823; subtle, 829; we are not, 5, 97; Vīra Śaivism, 505
Bond: def., 695
Bondage: def., 695; and freedom, 151; *mala,* 756; *pāśa,* 781
Bone-gathering: def., 695-696; part of *antyeshṭi,* 277
Boon: def., 696; grace, 724-725
Bountiful: def., 696
Boys: monastic tendencies, 245; trained in technical skills, 245; rites for, 273
Brahmā: distinction, 696; Śiva, 49; *śuddhavidyā tattva,* 837
Brahmachārī: assistant priests, 319; description, 361; spiritual aspirant, 696; student stage, 696
Brahmachāriṇī: def., 696; description, 361
Brahmacharya: def., 862; description, 687; restraint, 187; *yama,* 862
Brahmacharya: āśrama, 173; guideline, 187; Pāśupata, 499; see also *Āśrama dharma*
Brahmagupta: life of, 623-624
Brāhma muhūrta: def., 696; morning worship during, 257
Brahman: Ādi Śaṅkara on, 27; description, 696; nature, 327; Satchidānanda, 812
Brāhmaṇa: def., 697; dating, 613; *Vedas,* 375, 852
Brahmāṇḍa: cosmology, 866-867; def., 697
Brahma yajña: def., 860
Brahmarandhra: def., 697; door of *Brahman,* 714; *jñāna,* 739; *kuṇḍalinī,* 751; *videhamukti;* 855
Brahma Sūtra: def., 697; and Smārtism, 27; and Vedānta, 852
Brahma Sūtra Bhāshya: Śrīkaṇṭha's, 515; Śaṅkara's, 697
Brāhmin: class, 697; def., 850; *dharma,* 171; Pāśupata, 499; Śaiva, 319
Brāhminical tradition: def., 697; Smārtism and, 27; 821
Brahmotsava: festival, 283; def., 697
Breath control: in *yoga,* 113, *rāja yoga, prāṇāyāma,* 794
Bride: arranged marriage, 229; qualities of, 227
Bṛihadāraṇyaka Upanishad: description, 697
Bṛihaspati: identification, 697; Gaṇeśa, 722
Bṛihatkuṭumba: def., 697; and extended family, 719
Britain: bargains areas of influence with Rañjīt Singh, 635; Bengal rule, 634; captures Delhi, 635; conquers Sind region, 637; defeats Spanish Armada, 632; emigration of Indian indentured laborers, 636; opens trading post in India, 633; Warren Hastings impeached, 634
British Committee for Abolition of Slave Trade: formed, 634
British East India Company: sale of opium in Bengal, 634
British Guyana: Indian laborers, 636

British rule: timeline, 636-639
Brother(s): care of, 247; monks, 343
Buddha: Ajantā cave fresco depiction, 622; birth, 616; dates prior to, 610; founder of Buddhism, 534; life and work, 697-698
Buddhi: antaḥkaraṇa, 684; def., 698; intellect, 11; mind (individual), 762
Buddhi chitta: chart, 686; def., 698; mind (three phases), 762
Buddhism: acceptance in Japan, 623; adherents, 534; beliefs, 536; comparative summary, 534-536; def., 698; founder, 534; founding, 534; goals, 535; path of attainment, scriptures, 534; sects, 534; *siddhas,* 496, 516; synopsis, 534; threat to Śaivism, 495; rejection of *Vedas,* 417; and Vīra Śaivism, 505
Buddhist council: sects split, 621
Buddhist University of Nalanda: destruction, 628
Buddhi tattva: chart, 869; def., 837
Burning prayers: to God, 331; *lekhaprārtha havana,* 752
Business: Gaṇeśa, 287; Śaivite, 39
Business associates: extended family, 231; Pañcha Gaṇapati Utsava, 778
Businessmen: *dharma,* 171; *varṇa dharma,* 850
Butcher: and consumer's desire, 201

ca: See *Circa*
Caldwell, Bishop: coined term *Dravidian,* 637
Calendar: Hindu, 612
Cambodia: Hindu kingdom, 621
Camphor: def., 698; use in worship, 305, 315, 321
Canon: def., 698; of Hindu secondary scripture, 387
Cape Comorin: Muslims conquer, 629
Carbon-14 dating: in support of research dating, 608
Caste: def., 698; discussion, 171, 850-851; *jāti,* 739; Pāśupatas, 501; rejected by Vīra Śaivites, 504; *varṇa dharma,* 850, in *Vedas,* 177
Catalyst: *bodhaka,* 695; def., 698; *karma,* 95
Catechism: how to study, xxix-xxx; creed capsulizes, 463-487; *praśnottaram,* 788; source of, 395
Categories of existence: chart, 867, 869; *padārtha,* 777; *tattvas,* 123, 836-838
Catholic Council of Lyons: reincarnation condemned, 621
Catholics: and Sri Lanka, 453
Caucasoid: Indians as, 531
Causal body: *ānandamaya kośa,* 749-750; chart, 867; def., 698, *śarīra,* 811; soul, 823
Causal plane: belief in, 477; creation of, 123; def., 698; description, 129
Cause: def., 699; three kinds, 419; and God, 5; see also *Karma*
Caves of Jalani: Subramuniyaswami, 455
ce: def., 699
Celestial: def., 699
Celibacy: def., 699; guideline, 187
Cenobite: monk, 343, 764
Centillion: def., 699; *devas,* 333; light particles, 129
Central India: Śaiva Siddhānta, 496
Ceremony: def., 699
Cf: def., 699
Chaitanya, Śrī: life and philosophy, 699; dualist, 419; Vaishṇavism, 25
Chaitanya: def., 699; *antaḥkaraṇa,* 684; consciousness, 703; Śiva consciousness, 819
Chaka: early medical manual, 621
Chakra: chart, 866, 868; description, list, 699-700; and lotus, 121; seven lowest, 155; *yoga pāda,* 113; symbol

lowest, 155; *yoga pāda,* 113; symbol of time, 605
Chakshu tattva: chart, 869; def., 838
Chālukya: contribution, 700; Dynasty, 623-624, 626-627
Chandana: description, 700; sandalwood, 808
Çhandas Vedāṅga: def., 700; *Vedāṅga,* 852
Chaṇḍidās, Baru: writings, 630
Çhāndogya Upanishad: contents, 700
Chandra: def., 700; symbol, 415
Chandragupta, King: abdication, 619; defeats Greeks, 618
Chandragupta II: birth and reign, 622
Chandraśekarendra, Swāmī: life, 639-640
Charity: virtue, 263; cultivation, 183
Charms: *Atharva Veda,* 375
Chārvāka: life and philosophy, 700, *nāstika,* rejected *Vedas,* 417, 769
Charyā: Āgamas, 379, 492; belief, 481; description, 109; path, 107; Śaivism, 526; *Tirumantiram* on, 495; worship in, 327; *yamas,* 187
Charyā pāda: def., 776; stage of service, 700
Chastity: children, 219, 241; of God, 63; *sannyāsa,* 351; vow of, 273
Chaturdharma: description *(dharma),* 710; list, 700
Chela: def., 700
Chellachiamman: death, 642
Chellappaswāmī: axioms, 453; dates, 449, 637; biography, 700; at Nallur, 453; and Yogaswāmī, 455
Chennabasavaṇṇa: contribution, 507, 700
Chidambaram temple: Hall of Thousand Pillars, 632; location, 701
Chidānand Saraswatī, Swāmī: Hindu of Year award, 646
Child-bearing: rites, 275, 806
Children: art and sacred symbols in teaching, xxxi; conceiving, 239; debt to parents, 243; discipline, 247; need for mother, 213, 215; never beaten, 243; older care for younger, 247; mixed marriages, 227; marriage, 211; raising, 225, 239-247; *saṁskāras,* 271; scripture on, 248-249; strictness, 243
Chinese inventions: use in India, 627
Chinmayānanda, Swāmī: founds Chinmāya Mission, 641; Hindu of Year award, 647
Chinmoy, Śrī: birth, 642
Chinna Bomman: Appaya Dīkshita, 514; reign, 701
Chit: def., 701
Chitsabhā: consciousness, hall of, xix; def., 701; and *Naṭarāja*
Chitta: consciousness, 11, 703; def. 701
Chola Empire: founding, 620; prominence, timeline, 625-628
Christian Council of Florence: position on reincarnation, 622
Christianity: adherents, 566; beliefs, 568; comparative summary, 566-568; comparison with Judaism and Islam, 598-599; founder, 566; founding, 566; genesis, 599; goals, 567; man's obligation to God, 599; original sin, 599; path of attainment, 567; proof of God's power, 599; salvation, means to, 599; scriptures, 566; sects, 566; synopsis, 566; true religion, 598
Christian missionaries: Indians vulnerable to conversion by, 609
Chronological Framework of Indian Protohistory (Roy): Use in HIndu timeline dating, 608
Chūḍākaraṇa: def., 701; description, 807; rite, 271, 670; scripture enjoins, 279
Chulavaṁśa: Sri Lankan historical chronicle, 623
Cinnamon: export, Middle East, 615

Circumambulate: def., 701; scripture speaks on, 309; in temple, 305
Citadel: def., 701
Citizens: children as good, 215, holy *vel* and, 71; Śaivites, 35
Civil institution: marriage, 211
Civil law: obeying, 241
Civil War (U.S.): begins, 638
Clairaudience: def., 701; scriptural revelation, 373; *siddhi,* 817
Clairvoyance: def., 701; scriptural revelation, 373; *siddhi,* 817
Class: caste, 698, and *dharma,* 171; *varṇa dharma,* 850
Clive, Robert: seizes Arcot, 634
Clothing: for child, 241; for worship, 329; in home, 667
Coarse: def., 701
Coconut: offering, 315; symbol, 311
Codes: *Dharma Śāstra,* 712; *guru* protocol, 363; Hippocratic oath, 618; legal and social, in Hindu Malla dynasty, 626
Coexistent: def., 701
Cognition: def., 701; guideline, 189
Cognitive body: def., 701; Kārttikeya, God of, 69
Cohesive: def., 701
Coined: def., 701
Collection of 10,000 Leaves: Shinto scripture, 554
Columbus, Christopher: lands in San Salvador, 631
Coming of age: rites, 273, 807
Commemorative: death ceremony, 277; def., 701; *śrāddha,* 825
Commencement: def., 701; of formal study, rite, 271
Commission: def., 701
Commitment: betrothal, 273; to religious conversion, 704; def., 702; to the spiritual path, 7
Communism: beliefs, 586-587; summary, 585
Commune: def., 702
Communion: worship, 313
Community: and *dharma,* 173, 171
Companions: supervision by parents, 243
Compass: Chinese invent, 627
Compassion: and evil, 143; God, 55, 157; guideline, 187; and meat-eating, 201; source, 141
Compatibility: def., 702; in marriage, 229
Compensate: def., 702
Competitiveness: source of violence, 199
Component: def., 702
Comprehend: def., 702
Comprehensive: def., 702
Comprise: def., 702
Concealing (or obscuring) grace: grace, 724-725; Naṭarāja, 769-770; Pañchākshara Mantra, 401; *tirodhāna śakti,* 840
Conceit: binds soul, 139
Conceive: def., 702
Concentration: def., 702; *rāja yoga, dhāraṇā,* 794; *yoga,* 113
Concentration camps: discovery, 642
Concept: def., 702
Conception: def., 702; apex of, 129, 702; preparation, 239; rite, 269, 275
Concomitant: def., 702
Concord: def., 702; Pañcha Gaṇapati Utsava, 287; prayers for, 35, 219, 227, 247, 361
Condone: def., 702
Confer: def., 702
Confession: absolution, 676; def., 702; in worship, 313
Confidentiality: def., 702; vow, 351
Confine: def., 702
Conflagration: def., 702
Conflict(s): belief, 227; so-called righteous, 199; peace on earth, 203
Conform: def., 702
Conformity: def., 702; *dharma,* 167
Confucianism: adherents, 550;

beliefs, 552; comparative summary, 550-552; founder, 550; founding, 550; goals, 551; path of attainment, 551; scriptures, 550; sects, 550; synopsis, 550
Confucius: founder of Confucianism, 550; life, 617
Confusion: *chakra,* 868; conquered, 71; of good and evil, 421; Naraka, 155 selfish acts yeild, 95; state before *charyā,* 107
Congregational worship: def., 702; in Hinduism, 307
Conquest: def., 702; of *karma,* 93; light over darkness, 289
Conscience: def., 702; soul's voice, 157; *sannyāsin's* obedience to, 351; good conduct, 185; Western and Eastern beliefs compared, 703
Conscious mind: def., 703; mind (five states), 761
Consciousness: def., 703; gradations, 703; hellish states, 155; limited, 125; of nature, 169; symbolized in Naṭarāja, 41; understanding, 11
Consecrate: def., 703
Consecrated temple: def., 703
Consent: def., 703; marriage by, 229
Console: def., 703
Consolidate: def., 703
Consort: def., 703
Contemplation: def., 704
Contend: def., 704
Contentment: guideline, 189
Continence: def., 703; vow, 351
Contract: marriage as, 211
Conversely: def., 704
Conversion: Hindu view on, xviii; to Hinduism, 704-705, 603; and marriage, 227; naming rite in Hinduism, 704; peoples of India vulnerable to, 609; requirements, to Hinduism, 704-705
Coomaraswāmy, Ānanda: life, 638
Cope: def., 705
Copernicus: Earth orbits sun, 632
Corn: first cultivation, 613
Cornwallis: Tipu Sahib defeat, 635
Cosmic: def., 705
Cosmic cycle: def., 705; description, 131, 439, 705-706; periods of, 705
Cosmic Dance: Śiva's, 9, 41; see also *Naṭarāja*
Cosmic dissolution: two views of, 439; see also *Mahāpralaya*
Cosmic order: and *dharma,* 167, 169; see also *Dharma*
Cosmic Soul: other terms for, 706
Cosmology: *Āgamas,* 381; chart, 866-867; def., 706
Cosmos: creation, 433; dance of, 41; def., 706; *jyotisha,* 259; man as part, 259; perfection, 437; Naṭarāja, 41
Cosmotheandrism: explained under *monotheism,* 764
Covenant: def., 706; marriage, 225, 233
Covet: *asteya* (nonstealing), 187; def., 706; and *sannyāsin,* 351
Cow: reverence for, 193; symbol, 193
Cranial *chakras:* def., 706; clear white light, 129
Creation: apex of, 702, 129; cause, 419; def., 706; *dharma,* 167; Eastern-Western views, 593; emanation, 433; Kashmīr Śaivism, 511; Naṭarāja, 41; pluralism on, 433; Śaiva Siddhānta, 433; source, 9; three worlds and, 123
Creative arts: *tantra,* 255; see *Arts*
Creator: def., 706
Creed: def., 463, 706; need for, 463; Śaivite Hindu, 463-487; *śraddhādhāraṇā,* 825
Cremation: def., 706; funeral, 277; and soul, xxvi; method, 706; purpose, 706
Cringe: def., 707; fear of transgression, 55
Criticism: family, 247; *guru,* not of,

363; marriage, 233; not dancing with Śiva, 9
Crown chakra: def., 707; exiting the body through at death, 101; see also *Sahasrāra chakra*
Crucial: def., 707; junctures in life, 269
Crude: def., 707
Cruelty: meat-eating, 201; overcoming, 187
Crux: def., 707
Culminate: def., 707
Cultural changes: adaptation to, 37
Culture: *charyā pāda,* 109; common to all Hindu sects, 19; def., 707; fine arts; 654; Gaṇeśa festival, 287; importance, 261; result of good conduct, 157; Śaivism, 39; training for girls, 245; training on subtle plane, 127
Curson, Lord: resignation, 640
Customs: in matters of sex, 217; nonconflicting, in marriage, 227; Asian, 261
Cycles: of birth and death, 87; of the universe, 131

D

da Gama, Vasco: rounds Cape of Good Hope, 631
Daily practices: in *Āgamas,* 381; of Hindus, 257
Dakshiṇa mārga: tantrism, right-hand path, 835
Dakshiṇāmūrti: description, 707; Śiva, 57
Dalai Lama: refuge, North India, 643
Dampatī: def., 707
Dāna: def., 707, 862; giving, Hindu view, 263; guide, 189
Dance: gesture, 253; scripture of, 387; scripture speaks on, 15; spiritual experience, 261; of Śiva, xiv, 9, 15, 41; temple activity, 307; meaning, 9; see also *Tāṇḍava; Naṭarāja*
Dancing with Śiva: explanation, 9, xviii; learning to, 11
Dancing with Śiva: new presentation of ancient knowledge, xxxii; permission to use, xxx; study methods, xxix-xxx; teaching of, xxxi-xxxii; translating, xxix
Daṇḍa: purpose, 707
Darius I: invades Indus Valley, 617
Darśana: children taught to seek, 666; def., 819; explained, 707; philosophy, 417; scripture, 387, 393; *shaḍ darśana,* 814-815; Śiva consciousness, 819
Darwin's theory: evolution of the soul and, 718; explained, 707-708; and nonhuman birth, 773-774
Daśama bhāga vrata: def., 708; tithing vow, 263
Daśamāṁśa: def., 708; giving, 263
Dāsa mārga: def., 708; *charyā pāda,* 109, 776
Daśanāmī: def., 708; monastic orders, 27, 708; Śaṅkarāchārya *pīṭha,* 808-809
Daśaratha: reign, 614
Daughters: joint family, 231, 740; raised to be mothers, 245
Daurmanasya: def., 708
David, King: empire formed, 616
Dayā: def., 708, 862; guideline, 187
Death: rites of, 277; def., 708; life after, 97; an obstacle, 255; preparation, 99, 101; scripture on, 14; subtle plane, 127; suicide, 829; in Śiva Advaita, 513; transition, 843
Debt: guideline, 187, *purushārtha (artha),* freedom from, 792
Deceit: def., 708
Decentralized: def., 708; Hinduism, 357
Deception: def., 708
Decked: def., 708

Defiled: def., 708
def.: abbreviation for *definition*
Deformity: def., 708
de Goubineau, Joseph: writes *The Inequality of Human Races,* 637
Deha: def., 709
Deism: def., 709; *Dharma Śāstra,* 712
Deities: common to sects, 19; def., 709
Delhi: Lodi sultans, timeline, 629-630; Mogul sultans, timeline, 630-635; slave-sultans, timeline, 627; Tughlak sultans, timeline, 628-629
Delineate: def., 709
Delude: def., 709
Delusion: def., 709; obstacle, 255
Demons: attracting, 155
Denial: def., 709
de Nobili, Robert: arrives in Madurai, 633
Denomination: def., 709; Hindu; see *Hindu sects*
Denote: def., 709
Deplore: violence, 203; def., 709
Deploy: def., 709
Deportment: def., 709
Depraved: def., 709
Depresssion: and Naraka, 155
Deśikar, Vedānta: life and work, 629
Desire: control of, 181; deeds, 93, 139; freedom from, 157; in *guru's* presence, 365; for meat, 201; and physical plane, 125; rebirth, 97; scripture on, 352
Desirous: def., 709
Despair: def., 709; obstacle, 255
Despise: def., 709
Destiny: *adṛishṭa,* 678; free will, 93; def., 709; *dharma* is, 167; Gaṇeśa guides, 65; fate, 720; liberation, 87; merger with God, 81; *niyati,* 837; Paraśiva, 13; *ṛita,* 169; shaped in the world, 145
Destroyer: def., 709
Destruction: in Naṭarāja, 41
Deterministic materialism: See *Materialism*
Detachment: *yoga,* 113
Devaloka: chart, 866; def., 709; Maharloka, 755; three worlds, 839
Devamandira: def., 709
Devanāgarī: alphabet key, xxxv; def., 709
Devas: benevolent, 63; centillion, 333; children are, 195; def., 709; devotionals, xxi; God, 597; guardian, 239; home shrine, 335; invoking, 313; nonintervention by, 331; response to prayers, 331; and worship, xix, 63, 333
Deva yajña: def., 860-861
Devī: def., 709; Divine Mother, 23; Śakti, 803-804
Devī Bhāgavata Purāṇa: def., 709
Devī Gītā: role in worship, 710
Devīkālottara Āgama: contents, 710
Devī Upanishad: contents, 710
Devoid: def., 710
Devonic: army, 69; def., 710
Devotee: conduct, 181; def., 710; and the temple, 299; *mantra* initiation, 405; Nandi symbolizes, 77; and *satguru,* 365; temples, 301
Devotion: cultivation, 183; to *guru,* 363; of holy men and women, 357; and worship, 329; see also *Bhakti*
Devotional hymns: Hindu, 393
Dhammapada: Buddhist scripture, 534, 710; *Vedas,* 377
Dhanurveda: contents, 710; scripture, 389; *Upaveda,* 847
Dhāraṇā: def., 710; in *yoga,* 113, *rāja yoga,* 794-795
Dharma: and belief, 199; children's, 243; def., 710; fourfold, 167-175; in marriage, 211; Gaṇeśa is guardian of, 65, 91; a goal of life, 87; good conduct and, 181, 185; lights the path, 143; of husband, 213; need to perform, 87; positive approach,

145; in the *Purāṇas,* 391; *purushārtha,* 792; scripture speaks on, 176-7; sin and, 153; and temples, 301; of wife, 215; *Vedas,* 375, 377; see also *Universal, Human, Social and Personal dharma*
Dharmabuddhi: conscience, 702
Dharmapuram Aadheenam: founding, 633
Dharmasabhā: def., 712
Dharma Śāstra: description, 712; *Kalpa Vedāṅga,* 744; *Manu Dharma Śāstra,* 758; *pāpa,* gives penance for, 780; Hindu scripture, 389; *Vedāṅga,* 852
Dhotī: description, 712; in temple, 329; home apparel, 667
Dhṛitarāshṭra: reign, 615
Dhṛiti: def., 712, 862; guideline, 187
Dhvaja: purpose, 712
Dhvajastambha: prostrating before, 305; purpose, 712
Dhyāna: def., 713, 795; *mudrā, 765;* in *yoga,* 113, *rāja yoga,* 794-795
Dialectical materialism: See *Materialism*
Dichotomy: def., 713
Diet: vegetarian, 201, 259, 351; *mitāhāra,* 763
Dieu Siva est amour omniprésent et Réalité transcendante: affirmation of faith in French, 713
Differentiation: def., 713
Digambara: Jain sect, 620
Dīkshā: def., 713; Pañchākshara Mantra, 405; from *satguru,* 365; and *paramparā,* 456; *sannyāsa,* 277, 349, 455; on Vaikāsi Viśākham, 289
Dīpastambha: kuttuvilaku, lamp, 751
Dīpāvalī: description, 713; festival, 291
Dipolar: def., 713; monistic theism, 763-764
Dīptachakra: aura, 690
Directions: of *guru,* 363
Discipline: *ahiṁsā,* 195; of children, 241-243; by father, 247; on Mahāśivarātri, 285; peerless path, 7; *sādhana,* 800; spiritual, 11
Discordant: def., 713
Discourses: at temple, 307
Discrimination: def., 713; and *vel,* 71
Discussion: needed in marriage, 233
Disease: and *āyurveda,* 259
Disheveled: def., 713
Dismay: def., 713
Dispassionate: def., 713
Dispatch: def., 713
Dispel: def., 714
Disputes: family settlement, 247
Dissolution: def., 714
Distort: def., 714
Distress: and affirmation of faith, 407; call on Kārttikeya, 69
Divergent: def., 714
Divine incarnation: def., 733
Divine judgment: Eastern-Western views, 594
Divine law: of *karma,* 95; and sin, 153; see also *Dharma*
Divine Mother: def., 714
Divine presence: after worship, 333; *sānnidhya,* 809
Divodāsa: reign, 614
Divorce: Hindu view, 219, 217
Divyadṛishṭi: clairvoyance, 701; far-seeing (divine sight), 719
Divyaśravana: clairaudience, 701
Doctrines: and creeds, 463; *Doctrine of the Mean,* 550; Hindu, in *Āgamas,* 381; nature of, Eastern-Western, 595-596
Don: def., 714
Door of Brahman: def., 714; *jñāna,* 739; *kuṇḍalinī,* 751; *videhamukti;* 855
Dormant: def., 714; *karma,* 746
Doshas: āyurveda, 259, 691; def., 714; *upasarga,* 847
Drama: spiritual experience, 261

Drama: spiritual experience, 261
Dravidian: and Aryans, 609
Dravya: yajña, sacrificial substances essential for, 860
Dream: to found temples, 301; violence committed in; *Śiva Sūtra,* 510
Dṛidhavāchana: affirmation, 679
Dross: def., 714
Drug culture: beliefs, 576-577; philosophy, 576
Drugs: avoided at pending death, 101
Drum: of creation, 41; Naṭarāja, 770
Dual: def., 714
Dualism: in *Āgamas,* 492; difference from monism, 419; *dvaita-advaita,* 714-715; flaws, 421, 423; antagonism, 199; Hindu view, xxv; Mādhva's, 25, 754; monistic theism, 421; philosophy, 417, 512; scripture, 426; on God, 419; see also *Dvaita*
Dualists: notable, 419
Duality: nature of world, 151
Duly: def., 714
Dūradarśana: far-seeing, 719
Durban: indentured servants, 638
Durgā: def., 714; Śakti, 803, 23
Durrani, Ahmed Shah: Afghan army annihilates Hindu Marāṭhas, 634
Durvāsas: profile, 714; revived Śaivism, 509
Duties: *pañcha nitya karmas,* 185, minimal for teaching *dharma,* 651
Duty: *charyā,* 109; *dharma,* 167, 173; Gaṇeśa's, 67; husband's, 213, 233, 239; neglect of, 181; priest's, 319, 321; wife's, 215, 239; *Vedas* guide, 377; see also *Dharma*
Dvaita: philosophy, 417; in Śaivism, 33; in Siddha Siddhānta, 518; Vedānta, 852-853
Dvaita-advaita: def., 714-715
Dvaita school of Vedānta: founding, 628-629
Dvaitic Siddhānta: def., 715
Dvija: upanayana, twice-born, 848
Ear-piercing: rite, 269, 271, 807
Earrings: purpose, 715
Earth: cow represents, 193; sacred, 654
Earth Summit (UNCED): environmental gathering, 647
Eastern religions: comparisons with Western views, 592-603, xxiv; similarities with Western religions, 597
East India Company: formed by English Royal Charter, 632; sale of opium in Bengal, 634
Ecclesiastical: def., 715; hierarchy, in Hinduism, 357
Eckhart, Meister: birth, 629
Ecology: def., 715; philosophy, 578-580
Ecstasy: def., 715; and enstasy, 716
Ecumenical: def., 715; gatherings, 35
Ecumenical Council, Fifth: on reincarnation, 623
Ecumenism: def., 715
Edison, Thomas: light bulb, 638
Education: boys and girls taught *kalās,* 245, 742-743; *brahmacharya āśrama,* 173; marriage compatibility, 229; parental duty, 241, 243; rite of, 271; Śaivism, 37; about sex, 243
Efficacious: def., 715
Efficient cause: def., 699, 715; in monism and dualism, 419; in Śaiva Siddhānta, 431-433
Effulgent: def., 715
Egalitarian: def., 715
Eggs: nonconsumption of, 187, 201
Ego: at cosmic dissolution, 439; *antaḥkaraṇa,* 684; in *charyā,* 109; def., 715; and Naṭarāja, 41; purpose, 85; self-perpetuating, 365; and *satguru,* 365; *sannyāsin* renounces, 351

Ekanātha, saint: contribution, 632
Elamite Dynasty: dates, 616
Elders: advise on personal *dharma,* 175; advise on sexual matters, 217; consulting, 185; *dharma* of, 173; are honored, 277; in joint and extended family, 231, 247; have the last word, 247; marriage arranging, 229; marriage problems, 233; respect for, 241
Eliezer: death, 634
Eligible: def., 716
Eliminate: def., 716
Elixir: *amṛita,* 682; def., 716
Elliptical: def., 716
Elusive: def., 716
Emanation: belief, 471; def., 716; God creates through, 123, 433; soul as, of God, 435
Emancipation Proclamation: Lincoln frees slaves, 638
Emancipator: def., 716
Emerson, Ralph Waldo: popularizes *Bhagavad Gītā* and *Upanishads,* 635
Emigration: indentured servant system abolished, 641; see also *Indian laborers*
Eminent: def., 716
Emotion(s): antagonistic, 155; astral plane, 127; intellect bound in, 153; maturing of, 173; moon, 415; "We are not...," 5, 79
Empower(s): def., 716; *japa,* 405; sacraments, 269; *vel,* 71
Emulate: def., 716; *satguru's* awakening, 363
Encompass: def., 716
Encyclopedia of Hinduism: project begun, 646
Endow: def., 716
Energy: of physical plane, 125
English: *Vedas,* 377
Enhance: def., 716
Enlightened: def., 716
Enlightenment: def., 716; Eastern-Western views, 596; God Realization, 724; path of, 107, 189; terms for, 716; Tirumular, 451; *Vedas* are guide to, 377
Enshrine: def., 716
Enstasy: def., 716; *samādhi,* 805
Enthrall: def., 716
Entourage: def., 716
Entreat: def., 716
Environment: attitudes of *ahiṁsā,* 195; and subtle plane, 127
Epics: Hindu, 391
Epic history: def., 716; *Itihāsa,* 391, 737
Equanimity: def., 717; fruit of understanding, 9
Equilibrium: def., 717; of *iḍā* and *piṅgalā,* 347
Equinoxes: precession in dating scriptural references, 607
Equivalent: def., 717
Erotic: def., 717; *Sūtras,* 389
Erroneous: belief, 199; def., 717
Eschew: def., 717
Esoteric: def., 717
Essence: def., 717; soul, 717; Śiva, 83
Esteem: def., 717
Estranged: def., 717
Eternity: def., 717
Ether: def., 717
Ethical conduct: *charyā,* 109
Ethics, Hindu: def., 717; scripture on, 387; summarized, 187-195
Etymology: def., 717; scripture, 389
Evil: apparent, 137, 139; def., 717; discussion, 139-143; Eastern-Western views, 595; and God, 143; and good conduct, 185; Hindu view of, xxv; intrinsic, 453; monistic theism, 421; Siddhānta views, 431, 437; and *pāpa,* 779-780; Śaivite creed belief, 483
Evoke: def., 718
Evolution of soul: completion of, 131; def., 718; *devas* guide, 63; dif-

131; def., 718; *devas* guide, 63; difficult experiences, 139; God Realization, 81; in inner worlds, 97; limiting of consciousness, 85; Nātha path, 447; nonhuman birth, 773-774; world is arena, 33; process, 137; individuality during, 435
Exalt: def., 718
Excel: def., 718
Excitement: obstacle, 255
Exclusive: def., 718
Exemplar: def., 718
Exhaustive: def., 718
Existence: def., 718
Existentialism: beliefs, 587-588; summary, 587
Experience: *anubhava,* 684; base of Hindus, xiv; def., 718; needed, 7
Expound: def., 719
Extended family: def., 719, joint family, 740-741; description, 231; children, 239
Extol: def., 719
Exultant: def., 719

Fable: def., 719
Faith: def., 719; *Bhagavad Gītā* on, 391; guide, 189; and worship, 329
Faiths: list, 574-575; sample beliefs, 575-576; shamanism, 574; spiritualism, 574; summarized, 573-581; theosophy, 574; universalism, 574
Falsehood: not before *guru,* 363
Family: astrologer, 259; *āyurveda vaidya,* 259; and children, 239; cornerstone of culture, 655; *dharma* of, 173, 171; extended, 231, 719; *gṛihastha dharma,* 725; harmony, 247; husband's role, 213; joint, 231; *jyotisha śāstrī,* 259; *karma,* 747; larger, stable, 239; limit on size, 239; living within means, 247; marriage problems, 233; monk does not desire, 343; Śaivite values toward, 37; *sannyāsin* separated from, 347; sharing at rites of passage, 269
Farming: earliest, 611
Far-seeing: def., 719
Fast: def., 719-720
Fasting: to death, 101; and festivals, 283; *kriyā,* 111; *prāyopaveśa,* 788; scripture, 102; suicide, 829
Fate: *adṛishṭa,* 678; def., 720; and *karma,* 93
Father: daughter's marriage, 229; disciplines, 247; duties toward children, 239-245; head of family, 231
Fear: bondage of, 107; *chakra* of, 868; and children, 243; of death, 97, 99; of God, never, 159; of unrighteousness, 141; hellish, 155; ingested by the meat-eater, 201; lower nature, 199, 201; maturing out of, 7; not fearing the world, 145; obstacle, 255; overcoming, 187, 351; release from, 71, 423
Feedings: first, 269; at temple, 307
Feet of *guru: pādukā,* 777, symbol, 355, *ucçhishṭa,* 845
Fellowship: def., 720; devotees in Śaiva Siddhānta, 431
Female: Goddess, 63; energies balanced, 347; soul is not, 79
Ferdinand of Austria, Archduke: assassinated, 641
Festival: def., 720; aphorism, 660
Festivals: culture, 261; narratives at, 391; def., 720; of lights, 291; scripture on, 292; chapter on, 283-291; temple, 303, 307
Fetch: def., 720
Fiji: Indian indentured laborers, 638
Financial year: and Dīpāvalī, 291
Finesse: def., 720
Fire: altar, 267; analogy of creation,

331; in *shaṭkoṇa,* 223; in *trikoṇa,* 371; Vedic rites, 373; weddings, 273; *yajña,* 860
Firewalking: def., 720; in Śāktism, 23
Firsts: beard shaving, 273; *guru,* Kārttikeya, 69; first learning rite, 269
Fives: categories of Pāśupatas, 502; elements and Pañchākshara, 401; obligatory duties of good conduct, 185; powers of Śiva, 49, 492; sacred syllables, 487
Five acts of Śiva: list, 720; Sadāśiva, 799-780
Flag: *dhvaja,* 305, 712
Flux: def., 720
Folk narrative: def., 720; *Purāṇas,* 391
Folk-shamanic: def., 720-721
Food: first solid, 271; giving to *swāmīs,* 263; *satguru's* leavings, 363; *mitāhāra,* 763; offering of, 111, 321; parents provide, 241; vegetarian, 187, 201
Forbearance: cultivating humility through, 183; def., 721
Ford, Henry: assembly line production, 639
Forests: harmed by meat-eating, 201
Form: formless, 721; *māyā,* 759; mind (universal), 762; Śiva creates, sustains and absorbs, 123; cosmic cycles of, 131, 439
Formerly: def., 721
Formless: *atattva,* 688; Brahman, 696; mind (universal), 762; pantheism, 779; philosophic meaning, 721; Satchidānanda, 812; Self God, 49; ultimate goal, 13; unmanifest, 845-846; *Vedas* speak of, 51
Fortress: def., 721
Foster: def., 721
Fountainhead: def., 721
Fowl: not consumed, 187, 201
Francis Xavier, Saint: life of, 631
Frawley, David: on precessional changes, 608
Free will: and *karma,* 93
Freedom: and bondage, 151; and children, 243; and evil, 143; from rebirth, 7; world, not found in, 151
French: affirmation of faith, 407; *Vedas,* 377
French Revolution; storming of Basstille, 635
Friday: holy day in the South, 283
Friends: in extended family, 231; and Pañcha Gaṇapati Utsava, 778; at rites of passage, 269
Fruition: def., 721
Full moon: July-August, *guru* festival, 291; May-June, Vaikāsi Viśākham, 289
Fundamentalism: beliefs, 581; denominations, 580
Funeral: *antyeshṭi,* 807; bone-gathering, 695-696; cremation, 706; rites, 269, 277; *sannyāsa* initiation, 349

Gaja: significance, 721
Gajahasta: *anugraha,* *mudrā* of, 770
Galactic: def., 721
Galileo: invents telescope, 632
Gaṇāchāra: def., 508, 721, 778
Gaṇapati: def., 721; festivals, 287; and Pañcha Gaṇapati Utsava, 778; in Smārtism, 27
Gaṇapati Upanishad: def., 721
Gaṇas: def., 721; and Gaṇeśa, 65
Gāndharvaveda: def., 722; scripture, 389; *Upaveda,* 847
Gandha tattva: chart, 869; def., 838
Gāndhi, Indirā: assassination, 645; becomes Prime Minister, 644
Gāndhi, Mahātma (Mohandās K.): agitates for better working conditions, 640; assassinated, 643; dates, 638; protests indentured servant

system, 639; program of noncooperation and nonviolence, 641
Gāndhi, Rajīv: assassinated, 646
Gaṇeśa: and *aṅkuśa,* 165; and *Aum,* 3; coconut, 311; description, 65-67, 91, 722; festivals, 287; *mankolam,* 209; monthly holy days, 283, 287; and mouse, 237; and personal *dharma,* 175; Śaivite creed belief, 471; *śaktis,* five, 287; and Lord Śiva, 63; *Veda* prayer to, 67; worship of, 305, 321
Gaṇeśa Chaturthī: 287, 722
Gaṇeśa Visarjana: 287, 722
Ganges: description, 722
Ganges bath: *Padma Purāṇa* on, 279; Śaivas clash with Sikh ascetics, 635; *Vārāṇasī,* 849
Gangetic Plain: description, 722
Garbagṛiha: temple, 305
Garbha: def., 722
Garbhādhāna: def., 722, 806; prenatal rite, 275
Gārgya: def., 722
Gautama (Ṛishi): profile, 722; Nyāya Darśana, 814; philosophy, 393
Gautama, Siddhārtha: birth, 616; contribution, 722; Buddhism, 534
Gay: def., 722
Gāyatrī: def., 722-723
Gāyatrī Mantra: description, 723; alternate translation, 336; chanted at *pūjā,* 335; Tryambaka, 844
Generosity: scripture on, 264-265
Genghis Khan: death of, 628
Gentleness: and *ahiṁsā,* 195
Geography: Hindu sects, 602-603; population map, xxii, xxiii
German: *Veda* translations, 377
Germinate: def., 723
Gettysburg Address: delivered, 638
Ghaṇṭā: def. 723; symbol, 281
Ghee: affirmation of faith, 407; def., 723; offering in fire, 201; *yajña,* 860
Gheraṇḍa Saṁhitā: description, 723; Siddha Siddhānta, 518; written, 633; *yoga* text, 393
Ghosh, Śri Aurobindo: philosophy, 638, notable pantheist, 419
Ghrāṇa tattva: chart, 869; def., 838
Ghṛita: ghee, 723
Girls: household arts and culture, training, 245; rite of passage, 273; *kalās*-64 taught to, 742-743
Giving: guideline, 189; as a *tantra,* 255; Hindu view, 263
Global Forum of Spiritual and Parliamentary Leaders for Human Survival: First, 645; Fourth, 647; Second, 646; Third, 646-647
Gloom: def., 723
Go: symbol, 193; 723
Goad: *aṅkuśa,* 660; Gaṇeśa's, 67; symbol, 165
Goals: Buddhist, 535; Christian, 567; Confucian, 551; Hindu sects, 529-530; Islam, 571; Jains, 539; Judaic, 563; life, 13; Shinto, 555; Sikhist, 543; Taoist, 547; Zoroastrian, 559
God: absolutely real, 131; affirmation of faith, 409; *Āgamas,* 379; *ahiṁsā* belief, 197; creation, 159; creator, preserver, destroyer, 469; and *devas,* 597; divine judgment, 594; Eastern-Western views, 593-594; and evil, 139, 143; existence, 593; festivals, during, 283; form, 59; friend-to-friend, 113; gender, xxviii-xxix, 59; Hindu sects, 529; Kashmīr Śaivism, 511; knowers, 366; law, 167; life, 5; love, 157, 336-337; Mahādeva, 754-755; manifest nature, 467; monism, 417; motion, 9; nature, 42, 72, 419, 423, 467; oneness, 435; opposites, 151; Pāśupata system, 502; path, xxiv, 7, 594; perception, 116; personal experience, 594; personal Lord and creator, 469; powers in Naṭarāja, 41; presence, 137, 317, 333; punish-

ment, 159; qualities, 159; reality, 423; Śaivite values, 37; scripture, 58; separation, 5; servant-to-master, 109; Siddhānta, pluralistic, 433; son-to-parent, 111; soul in Śaiva Siddhānta, 83, 431; soul's origin, 5; temple image, 317; temples, 301; true and absolute, 593; union, 113; unmanifest reality, 465; *Vedas,* 377; Vīra Śaivism, 397; worship, 327; see also *Absolute Being; All-pervasive God; Pati; Śiva; Supreme Being*

Goddess: def., 723; not male or female, 63

Godhead: def., 723

God Realization: in Advaita Siddhānta, 678-679; attainment, xxvi; def., 724; goal of *sannyāsin,* 345; initiation, 347; *nāga* symbolizes, *nirvāṇī* and *upadeśī,* 772, 489; and *jñāna,* 107

Gods: bells invoke, 281; causal plane, 129; creation, 132; description, 63-71; distinguished from God, 724; invoked, 333; invoked in *Vedas,* 373; Mahādeva, 755-756; not male or female, 63; worship of through fire, 267; and rites of passage, 269

God Śiva is Immanent Love and Transcendent Reality: See *Affirmation of faith*

Good: monistic theism, 421; source, 141

Good company: need for, 181; negative *karma,* 95

Good conduct: main discussion, 181-185; four keys, 183; parental guideline, 667; scripture on, 190-191; views on, 597; *yamas* and *niyamas,* 189

Good deeds: and sin, 153

Goodness: scripture on, 146; of soul and world, 137, 483

Gopura: description, 724; entering temple, 305; symbol, 297

Gorakh: def., 519

Gorakshanātha: and Ādinātha, 447; contribution, 724; life and work, 626; monistic theist, 425; *samādhi,* 518; *siddha,* 496

Gorakshanātha Śaivism: discussion, 516-519; alternative names, 519; def., 724; philosophy, 518; school of, 21; and *siddha yoga,* 517; see also *Siddha Siddhānta*

Gorakshapantha: def., 724

Gorakshaśataka: contents, 724

Goraksha Upanishad: written, 630

Gotra: archana credentials, 315; def., 724

Grace: *advaita,* 515; all is, 437; def. 724-725; exoneration, 153; of holy one's, 357; home supplication, 335; *mahāpralaya,* 131; and penance, 153; Realization and *satguru,* 113; revealing, 798; Sāktism, 23; Śiva Advaita, 513; Śiva's, 41, 49, 147, 285, 347, 451; temple, 299; *Va,* 401; Vaishṇavism, 25, 530-531

Graha: Rāhu, 794

Grāmadevatā: Amman, 682

Grandeur: def., 725

Grantha: def., 725

Granthavidyā: def., 725

Great Learning: scripture, 550

Great Wall of China: date, 619

Greed: instinctive nature, 141; obstacle, 255; scripture on, 264-265

Greeks: influences in India, 618

Gṛihastha: def., 725; description, 687

Gṛihastha dharma: āśrama, 173, 725; children are fulfillment of, 239; def., 725-726; description, 711, 726; duties, 726; see also *Children; Family; Marriage*

Gṛiheśvara: def., 726; family head, 213

Gṛihinī: wife, 215; def., 726

Gṛihya Śāstras: scripture, 389

Gṛihya Sūtras: contents, 726; *Kalpa Vedāṅga,* 744; *Vedāṅga,* 852

Vedāṅga, 744; *Vedāṅga,* 852
Groom: evaluating, 229
Gross plane: chart, 866; def., 726, *loka,* 753-754
Guardian *devas:* at birth, 239
Guénon, René: adopts Vedānta, 639
Guests: treated as God, 263
Guha: See *Kārttikeya*
Guhā: def., 726
Guhāvāsī Siddha: contribution, 727
Guheśvara: def., 727
Gujarat: location, 727
Guṇa: def., 727; *dosha,* 714; *prakṛiti tattva,* 837; and *triśūla,* 445
Gunpowder: Chinese use, 627
Gupta dynasty: founding, overthrown, 623
Gurkha: description, 727
guru: def., 727; description, 361; extended family, 231; festivals, 283; grace of, 89; guidance, 175, 655; *Guru Gītā,* 363; Kārttikeya as supreme, 69; Kashmīr Śaivism, 511; lineages, 449; and *mantra* initiation, 405; personal *dharma,* 175; prefixes, 727; protocol, 363; *pūjā* days 291; Pūrṇimā, 291; *sādhanas* from, 11; Śaiva Siddhānta, 431; Śaivism, 21, 37; scripture on, 352, 367, 456-457; Smārtism, 531; teachings, 11; Vīra Śaivism, 507-508; water from foot-washing, 293
Guru bhakti: def., 727; *tapas,* 835
Gurudeva: def., 727
Guru-disciple: Hinduism, 19; Vīra Śaivism, 507
Guru Gītā: contents, 727; *guru* protocol, 363
Guru Jayantī: festival, 727
Gurukal: scripture on, 323
Gurukula: def., 727
Guru paramparā: def., 728; See *Paramparā*
Guru Pūrṇimā: festival, 291; occurrence, 728
Guru-śishya system: def., 728; and Nātha Sampradāya, 447; relationships within, 728
Gush: def., 728
Gutenberg: printing press, 630
Gypsies: ancestors to, 627

H

Hair-parting: rite, 269, 275
Hallowed: def., 728
Hammurabi: birth, 614
Haṁsa: symbolic meaning, 728
Hand gestures: symbol of, 253
Happiness: and good conduct, 157; and the world, 151
Harappa: beginnings, 612; destroyed in Battle of Ten Kings, 614
Hardwar: sacked by Tamerlane, 630
Hari-Hara: description, 728; worshipful icon, 57
Harijan: jāti, "child of God," 850
Harmony: with *guru,* 363; and worship, 331
Harsha: reign, 624
Harvest: Tai Pongal, 291
Hastings, Warren: impeachment, 634
Haṭha yoga: daily, 257; def. and purpose, 728, 655; Gorakshanātha, 516
Haṭha Yoga Pradīpikā: contents, 729; importance, 520; yoga text, 393, 518; written, 629
Hatred: instinctive nature, 141
Havana: def., 729; *yajña,* 860
Hazrat Inayat Khan: brings Islamic mysticism to West, 639
Head-shaving: rite, 269, 271, 670, 807
Healing powers: mind, 259
Health: *āyurveda,* 259, 691; child's, 241; scriptures, 389
Heart *chakra:* chart, 868, def., 729
Heaven: causal plane, 129; def., 729; Gaṇeśa oversees, 65; and hell, 199;

327, 333, 361
Hedgewar, K.V.: founds Rāshṭrīya Swayamsevak Sangh (RSS), 641
Hedonistic materialism: See *Materialism*
Heed: def., 729
Hell: chart, 866; def., 729; Eastern-Western views, 594-595; heaven and, 199; Hindu view, xxv; Mādhva's view, 754; Naraka, 155, 768-769; subtle plane, 127
Hephtalites: defeat by Persians, 623; overthrow Gupta Empire, 623
Hereditary: Āgamic knowledge, 381; class and caste, 171; def., 729; priests, 319; *sthapati,* 301
Heresy: def., 729
Heterodox: def., 729
Heterosexual: def., 729
Heretics: Hindu view, xvii
Hierarchy: def., 729
Higher-nature: def., 729
High soul: bringing through to physical birth, 275
Himālayas: def., 730
Hiṁsā: def., 730; scripture on, 205
Hindu: attire, 261; basis, xvii; and civil law, 171; daily practices, 257; greeting, 179; heritage for children, 241; New Year, 291; perfection of art or craft, 261; population, 19; rites of passage, 269; sacredness, 195; sects, 19-27, 529-531; solidarity, 291; and *Vedas,* 377
Hinduism: adherents, 528; ancient inventions, 607; banyan symbolizes, 17; beliefs, xx, xxv, 532; catechism, xviii-xix; comparative summary, 528-532; conversion requirements, 704-705; cosmology, see *Loka;* denominations, see *Hindu sects;* dates, 528; *dharma,* 167, 730-731; def., 19; Eastern religion, xxiv; follower, 730; formal entry, 271; founder, 528; founding, 528; Gods, 63; liberal, 752; monistic theism, 425; paths of attainment, 530-531; perpetuation, 263; practices, xxv-xxvi; principles, 730; revival, 625; Śaivism, 33; scriptures, xxvii, 528, 617; sects, 19-27; 528-530; spiritual leaders, 357; synopsis, 528; temples in U.S., 645; three worlds of existence, xxv; three pillars, xxv; *Vedas,* 377; view of life, xxiv-xxvi
Hinduism Today: founding of, 644
Hindu Malla dynasty: codes introduced, 626
Hindu sects: *avatāra* doctrine, 601; common beliefs, 600-603; comparisons, 600-603; goals, 529-530; major scriptures, 602; nature of Śakti, 601; personal God, 600-601, 601; regions of influence, 602-603; soul and God, 602; spiritual practice, 602
Hindu of the Year: award, 646-647
Hindu solidarity: def., 731; Dīpāvalī, day of, 713
Hippocrates: medical ethics codified, 618
His/her: linguistic dilemma in referring to God, xxviii-xxix
Hiuen Tsang: importance, 731; Pāśupatas, 502; travels, 547
Hoard: def., 731
Holy day: weekly, 283; and good conduct, 185; see also *Festival*
Holy men and women: conclaves on Vaikāsi Viśākham, 289; esteem for, 357; scripture speaks on, 367; respectful terms for, 361
Holy feet: def., 731-732; *pādapūjā,* 777; *pādukā* worship, 291, 777; symbol, 355
Holy orders: def., 732; vows of *sannyāsa,* 351; *sannyāsa dīkshā,* 810
Homa: def., 732; symbol, 267; *yajña* and, 860
Homakuṇḍa: yajña, fire pit, 860;

symbol, 267
Home: as a sanctuary, 195, 215, 247, 39; dying at, 101; festivals, 283; industry and wife, 215; purification after death, 277; wife's domain, 213; worship, 335
Home shrine: 261, 313, 333, 335; children taught, 665; *dharma svagṛiha,* 667
Homosexuals: def., 732; Hinduism, 217; loyalty and community pressure, 245; and marriage, 245
Honesty: good conduct, 181, 187
Honey: and new-born child, 275
Household arts: for girls, 245
Household chores: husband, 213
Householder: *dharma* of, 173; *grihastha dharma,* 725; path of, 245, 343; saints, 359
Hrī: def., 732, 862; guideline, 189
Hued: def., 732
Human *dharma:* def., 732, *āśrama dharma,* 710-711; description, 173; God's law, 167
Humanitarianism: belief, 575
Humility: cultivation, 183; and good conduct, 181; temple, approaching, 303; *sannyāsa* vow, 351
Humors (bodily): *dosha,* 714
Hunger: obstacle, 255
Huns: invasion of Europe, 622; invasions of North India, 622
Hurt: and *ahiṁsā,* 195
Husband: conversion before marriage, 227; *dharma* of, 173; duties of, 211, 213; duty to children, 239; elder rite of passage, 277; leadership of, 233; masculinity, 233; needs from wife, 211; qualities, 213; rites, 275; scripture on, 220-221; sexual union, 217; wife, treatment of, 233
Hymns: in scripture, 387; singing at temple, 305
I am God: in *Vedas,* 425
Icçhā śakti: Āgamas, 492; def., 732; aspect of Śakti, 803; *prakṛiti tattva,* 837; *triśūla,* 844
Iconography: *Āgamas,* 379
Icon: def., 732; *mūrti,* 765
Iconoclastic: def., 732; Śaivism, 493
Iḍā nāḍī: def., 732; and moon, 415; odic, 775; *nāḍī,* 766-767; and *triśūla,* 445
Ignorance: conquest of, 9, 71; evil, as source of, 141, 153; revealed by Pañchākshara Mantra, 401
Ilangovadikal: writes on music and dance, 620
Illusion: cosmic dissolution, 439; def., 732; *māyā,* 759; world, 131
Illustrious: def., 732
Immanent: def., 732; immanence of God, 425; love at core of soul, 83
Immature: def., 733; soul; See *Soul*
Immemorial: def., 733
Immigration: Indian workers to Reunion and Mauritius, 636; U.S. cancels racial qualifications, 644
Immutable: def., 733
Impasse: def., 733
Impede: def., 733
Impediment: def., 733
Imperishable: def., 733
Impermanence: def., 733
Impersonal: def., 733
Impersonal being: def., 733
Impersonal God: def., 733
Impetus: def., 733
Implore: def., 733
Impoverished: def., 733
Impressions, past: See *Saṁskāra*
Inanimate: See *Animate-inanimate*
Inauspicious: def., 733
Incandescent: def., 733

Incantation: def., 733
Incarnation: def., 733; divine, 733
Incarnation: balance *karma,* 197; def., 733; divine, 733; God, Hindu sects on, 528; of Vishṇu, 25; see also *Reincarnation*
Incense: def., 733-734; in temple rites, 315, 321
Incisive: def., 734
Incognito: def., 734
Increment: def., 734
Indentured servants: See *Indian laborers*
Independence, Indian: timeline, 639-643
India: colonial conquest, 631; declared secular republic, 643; holy land, 656; independence from Britain, 642; independence timeline, 639-643; map, 610; sea route to, 631
Indian constitution: on discrimination and untouchability, 643
Indian government: reorganized, 643
Indian immigration: South Africa's prohibition of, 641; U.S.'s exclusion, 641
Indian laborers: to British Guyana, 636; immigration to Reunion and Mauritius, 636; indentured to Britain, 636; indentured to Fiji, 638; indentured to Durban, South Africa, 638; indentured to Mauritius, 636; indentured servant system abolished, 641; to Trinidad, 637
Indian National Congress: founding, 639
Indian nationalism: Śivaji festival, 640
Indian naturalization: U.S. exclusion, 641
Indian trade: earliest known, 611; products at Sumerian sites, 612
Indian workers: See *Indian laborers*
Individuality: def., 734; and return to Śiva, 131; soul, 734
Indomitable: def., 734
Indra: created by Śiva, 63; def., 734; seers on, 28; Vedic Deity date, 615
Indriya: def., 734; *jñānendriyas* and *karmendriyas,* 838
Induce: def., 734
Indus Valley: cities, 608, 614; civilization, 611-614; description, 734; Hindu civilization, 641; location, 612; Muslim conquest, 626; and Śaivism, 492; timeline, 611-614
Indwell: def., 734
Inequality of Human Races, The (de Goubineau): Aryan class doctrine, 637
I-ness: *ahaṁkāra,* 680; def., 734; see also *Āṇava; Ego*
Inexhaustible: def., 734
Initiation: in *Āgamas,* 492; in Pañchākshara Mantra, 405; and *paramparā,* 456; and state of neutrality, 89; in Vīra Śaivism, 508
Inexplicable: def., 734
Inextricable: def., 734
Infatuation: def., 734
Infinitesimal: def., 734
Inflict: def., 734
Infuse: def., 734
Ingest: def., 735
Inherent: def., 735
Inherit: def., 735
Initiation: def., 735; from *satguru,* 365; see *Dīkshā*
Injunction: def., 735
Injure: no intent to, 195
Inmost: def., 735
Inner: def., 735; advancement, 735; bodies, 735; discovery, 735; form, 735; law, 735; life, 735; light, 255, 257, 735, 819; mind, 735; plane, 735; sanctum, 319; self, 735; sky, 735; truth, 735; unfoldment, 735; universes, 735; worlds, 331
Innumerable: def., 735

Inscrutable: def., 735
Insignia: def., 735
Insight: source in soul, 141
Instinctive: def., 735-736, 762
Instinctive-intellectual mind and nature: evil, source, 143; *kriyā pāda,* overcome, 111; purpose, 143
Instinctive mind/nature: *charyā pāda,* 109; def., 736; good and evil, 139, 141; *manas,* 756-757, *manomaya kośa,* 757-758; mind, 762; Namaḥ Śivāya quells, 401, 403; and the causal plane, 129; restraining, 187; *sādhana,* 11; *sannyāsa,* 351; sexuality, 217; seeking understanding of, 11; violence, 199; young soul, 115
Instruction: at temple, 307
Instrumental cause: def., 699, 736; God as, in monism and dualism, 419; in Śaiva Siddhānta, 431, 433
Integration: of belief with daily life, xxxiii
Intellect: *buddhi,* 698; def., 736; and emotion, 153; and good and evil, 141; and instinctive nature, 141; and intuition, 255; and Namaḥ Śivāya, 401; *sādhana,* 11; shattered by *yoga,* 115; softened in *kriyā pāda,* 111; and the sun, 415; seeking understanding of, 11
Intellectual mind: def., 736, 762; of soul, 115; causal plane, 129
Internalize: def., 736
Internalized worship: def., 736; *yoga* as 113
International Green Cross: founding, 647
International Society for Kṛishṇa Consciousness: founding, 640
Interplay: def., 736
Intervene: def., 736
Interweave: def., 736
Intimacy: def., 736; with God, 55; physical, 217, 219
Intrigue: def., 736
Intrinsic: def., 736; evil; see *Evil*
Intuition: def., 736; guide intellect, 255; importance, xvii; *jñāna,* 115
Intuitive: knowledge, in Namaḥ Śivāya, 401; woman's nature, 215
Invigorate: def., 736
Invocation: *charyā,* 107; conceiving child, 275; def., 736; of peace, 203; *pūjā,* 789
Iraivan: def., 736; *Tirumantiram* quotation on, 379
Iraivan Temple: project, 646; *San Mārga Sanctuary,* 809
Iron: early use, 616
Irrigation: development, 620
Īśa: def., 736
Īśānya guru: and Basavaṇṇa, 504; identification, 736-737
Īśa Upanishad: def., 737
Ishṭa Devatā: def. and forms, 737; in Smārtism, 27
Ishṭaliṅga: def., 737; Vīra Śaivism, 505
ISKCON: founded, 640
Islam: adherents, 570; beliefs, 571; comparative summary, 570-572; comparison with Christianity and Judaism, 598-599; def., 737; founder, 570; founding, 570; genesis, 599; goals, 571; man's obligation to God, 599; original sin, 599; path of attainment, 571; proof of God's power, 599; salvation, means to, 599; scripture, 570; sects, 570; synopsis, 570; true religion, 598
Islamic invasions: impact on Śaiva Siddhānta, 497
Issue forth: def., 737
Īśvara: def., 737
Īśvarapūjana: def., 737, 862; guideline, 189
Īśvara tattva: chart, 869; def., 836
Itihāsa: def., 737; epic history, 387, 391
Itinerant: def., 737

Jābāla Upanishad: contents, 738
Jaffna: Catholic control, 632; Kailāsa Paramparā, 453
Jagadāchārya: def., listing, 738
Jāgrat: consciousness, wakeful, 703
Jāgrat chitta: Nivṛittikalā, 866; conscious mind, 761
Jahan, Shah: completes Red Fort, 633; completes Tāj Mahal, 633; Peacock Throne, 632
Jaimini: darśana, 393, identification, 738; Mīmāṁsā, 814-815
Jaiminīya Brāhmaṇa Upanishad: contents, 738
Jainism: adherents, 538; *Āgamas,* 538; beliefs, 540; comparative summary, 538-540; founder, 538; founding, 538; goals, 539; key features, 738; path of attainment, 539; Śaivism, threat to, 495; scriptures, 538; sects, 538, 620; synopsis, 538; *Vedas,* rejects, 417; and Vīra Śaivism, 505
Janābāī: life and work, 629
Janaloka: chart, 866; def., 738; *loka,* 753-754
Jaṅgama: def., 738; Vīra Śaivism, 507, 509
Japa: daily practice, 257; def., 738; empowers mind, 656; guideline, 189; holy days, 283; home shrine, 335; kinds, 738-739; *kriyā pāda,* 111; performance, 403; preparation for death, 101; purpose, 738, 862; necessity, 405; Pañchākshara Mantra, 401; rage, prohibited to those prone to, 403; scripture on, 410-411
Jātakarma: def., 739; description, 806-807; rite of passage, 275
Jāti: caste, 173, 698; def., 739, 850
Jāti dharma: varṇa dharma, 850
Jātihīta: jāti, outcaste, 850
Java: Buddhist and Śaiva princes expelled, 631; and Śaivism, 491
Jayantī: def., 739; festival, 291; see also *Guru Jayantī*
Jealousy: chakra chart, 867; instinctive nature, 141; and marriage, 233
Jewelry: gift from husband, 275
Jesus of Nazareth: birth, 620; founder of Christianity, 566
Jinnah, Mohammed Ali: call for separate Muslim state, 642
Jīva: def., 739; *jīva* is Śiva, 13; *jīva* becomes Śiva, 439, 495
Jīvayajña: def., 739, 860-861; marriage, 211
Jīvanmukta: def., 739; description, 361; and *jñāna pāda,* 115; *satguru* is, 812; in Smārtism, 530
Jīvanmuktī: def., 739
Jñāna: creed belief on, 481; def., 739-740; *japa* leads to, 403; misunderstanding of, 739; *pāda,* 107, 115; in Śaivism, 530; in *Tirumantram,* 495; *Vedas* are guide, 377
Jñānadeva: life and work, 629
Jñānakāṇda: Veda, knowledge section, 852
Jñānāmṛita: def., 740; text of Siddha Siddhānta, 518
Jñāna pāda: def., 740, 776; description, 115; worship in, 327; *Āgama* section, 379, 492
Jñāna śakti: Āgamas, 492; def., 740; aspect of Śakti, 803; *prakṛiti tattva,* 837; *triśūla,* 844; and *vel,* 289
Jñāna yoga: def., 740; Smārtism, 527
Jñānendriya: aśuddha māyā, 867; def. 838; *indriya,* 734
Jñāneśvarī: def., 740; *yoga* text, 393
Jñānī: def., 740; Self Realization, 115
Joan of Arc: victory over English, 630
Joint family: def., 740; description, 231, 247; extended family, 719

Jones, William: postulates Nostratic root language, 634
Joy: good conduct, 181; nature of the soul, 137; and pain, 95, and sorrow, 3, 123, 151; 215, 437
Joyously: life to be lived, 145
Judaism: beliefs, 564; summary, 562-564; comparison with Christianity and Islam, 598-599; founding, 564; genesis, 599; goals, 563; man's obligation to God, 599; original sin, 599; path of attainment, 563; proof of God's power, 599; salvation, means to, 599; scriptures, 564; synopsis, 564; true religion, 598
Juncture: def., 741
Jyoti: def., 819
Jyotisha: def., 741; importance, 259; *śāstrī,* 741; *tantra,* 255; *Vedāṅga,* 259, 616, 741; scripture, 389

Kabīr: life and work, 630
Kadaitswāmī, Siddha: life, 635, 741; and Kailāsa Paramparā, 449, 453
Kadavul: def., 741
Kailāsa: def., 741
Kailāsa Paramparā: def., 449-455; basis of this catechism, 395; lineage, 419, 741-742
Kailāsa temple: carved at Ellora, 625
Kaivalya: def., 742; state of liberation, 115
Kaivalya Upanishad: contents, 742
Kalā (cosmology): chart, 867, 869; def., 742
Kalā-64 (chatuḥ shashṭi kalā): listed, 742-743; def., 742; skills taught to boys and girls, 245, 261
Kāla: def., 742
Kālāmukha: description, 743-744; sect, 503; and Vīra Śaivas, 504
Kalaśa: def., 744; symbol, 311
Kalā tattva: chart, 867, 869; def., 837
Kalayāna: history, 506; location, 744
Kālī: description, 744; Śakti, 803; Śāktism, 23
Kālidāsa: lifetime, 622
Kali Yuga: beginning, 612; in cosmic cycle, 705; def., 744, four *yugas,* 864
Kallaṭa: identification, 744, 510
Kalpa: def., 744; cosmic cycle, 705; *nirvikalpa samādhi,* 772
Kalpa Vedāṅga: contents, 744; scripture, 389; *Vedāṅga,* 852
Kāma: def., 744, 793; goal of life, 87; *purushārtha,* 793
Kamaṇḍalu: def., 744; symbol, 341
Kāma Sūtra(s): contents, 744-745; scripture, 389, *Vedāṅga,* 852
Kāmika Āgama: contents, 745
Kaṇāda: Vaiśeshika Darśana, 393; indentified, 745; Vaiśeshika, 814
Kandar Anubhuti: contents, 745
Kannada: spoken by, 745; Vīra Śaiva texts, 506
Kānphaṭi: practice, 745; Muslims joined, 517; *yogī* sect, 517
Kant: notable dualist, 419
Kāpālika: description, 745; sect, 502
Kapha: def., 745; *dosha,* 714
Kapila: Sāṅkhya Darśana, 393, 814; contribution, 617, 745; dualist, 419
Karaikkal Ammaiyar: life and work, 626; writings, 685
Kāraṇa Āgama: purpose, 745
Kāraṇa chitta: def., 745; mind of *ānandamaya kośa,* 750; superconscious mind, 761
Karaṇa Hasuge: author, 745; Vīra Śaiva scripture, 507
Kāraṇaloka: Śivaloka, 866
Kāraṇa Śarīra: ānandamaya kośa, 750; chart, 867; def., 745; *śarīra,* 811; soul, 823
Karavaṇa Māhātmya: Pāśupata Śaivism, 782

karma: *Āgamas,* 492; and *ahiṁsā,* 197; aspects, 746-747; Hindu belief, 19; bond of soul, 85; Jain view, 539; law, xx; children, 243, 664; comparisons, 746; conquering, 93; at cosmic dissolution, 439; creation of negative, 157; def., 745-746; dimensions, 747; discussion, 93-95; elimination, 113; and evil, 137, 139, 153; evolution of soul, 79; frying seeds, 13; fulfillment of laws, 159; and Gaṇeśa, 65, 91; harsh, 95, 159; kinds, 93; *jñāna pāda,* 115; neutral principle, 95; *niyati tattva,* 837; and personal *dharma,* 175; physical plane, 125; pluralist view, 433, 437, 439; positive approach, 145; resolution, 87, 101, 185, 747; results, 746; Śaivite creed, 479; self-determined, 656; Siddhānta, 439; Śiva Advaita, 514; stars, influence of, 259; suicide, 101; timing, 67; and *tripuṇḍra,* 31; waning, 343; wife working, 215; *yoga pāda,* 113

Karmakāṇḍa: *Veda,* ritual section, 852

Karmaphala: *karma's* fruit, 745; *pāpa,* 779; *puṇya,* 790

Karmasamāya: def., 747; *karma,* 746

Karmāśaya: def., 747; *Ānandamaya kośa,* 750

Karma yoga: def., 747; *charyā pāda,* 109; practice, 257; and path, 107

Karnataka: and Kālāmukhas, 503; location, 747; Vīra Śaivism in, 509

Karṇaveda: def., 747; description, 807; rite, 271, 670

Karmendriya: *aśuddha māyā,* 867; def., 838; *indriya,* 734

Kārttikeya: description, 69, 71; festivals, 289; and peacock, 61; profile, 747; Śaivite creed, 473; and Śiva, 63, 289; *Stotram,* 747; worship of, 283, 289

Karuṇā: def., 747; Pāśupatas, 499

Kāruṇa Āgama: def., 747

Kāruṇya: def., 747

Kāshāya: def., 747; *kavi,* 748-749

Kashmir: and Śaiva Siddhānta, 494; separation from Sikhs, 637; location, 747-748

Kashmīr Śaivism: description, 748; founding, 509, 625-626; goals, Śaivism, 21; *siddha yoga,* 510

Kashmir Valley: Hindus persecuted, 645

Kāśī: Varanasi, 849

Kathā: def., 748; Hindu stories, 391

Kaṭha Upanishad: contents, 748

Kathirgāma Purāṇa: contents, 748

Kauai Aadheenam: established, 644

Kauṇḍinya: identification, 748; and Pāśupatas, 501

Kaurusha: identification, 748, 501

Kauṭilya: writings, 618

Kavadi: public penance, 784; description, 748; Tai Pusam, 289

Kavi: def., 748-749; robes of *sannyāsin,* 349

Kāyāvarohaṇa: location, 749; Lakulīśa, 501

Kāya siddhi: Siddha Siddhānta, 518; process, 749

Kedāreśvara Temple: inscriptions, 749

Kekhrāj, Dādā: founds Brahma Kumārīs, 640

Kena Upanishad: discourse, 749

Kerala: location, 749

Keśānta: def., 749; description, 807; rite, 273; scripture enjoins, 279

Khalsa: Sikh sect, 542

Killing: for sake of, 199; *ahiṁsā,* 195; vegetarianism, 201; meat-eater, 760

Kindred: vigil at death, 101

Kīrtana: Chaitanya taught, 669; def., 749; Vaishṇavism, 25

Klesha: *upasarga,* obstacle, 847

Klostermaier, Klaus K.: on Müller chronology, 608

Knower: def., 749

Knowledge: soul's limited, 85

Know thy Self by thyself: saying of Yogaswāmī, v
Kokiji: Shinto scripture, 554
Konrai: def., 749; symbol of Śiva's grace, 253; *Tirumurai* on, 383
Koran: Islamic scripture, 570; source, 749; and *Vedas,* 377
Kośa: astral body, 687-688; chart, 866; def., 749-750; enumerated, 749-750; *śarīra,* 811; soul, 823; subtle body, 829
Koyil: temple, 838
Kṛipā: grace, compassion, 725
Kṛishṇa: Bhagavad Gītā, 391, 693, importance, 750; incarnation of Vishṇu, 25; Ishṭa Devatā, 737; *pañchāyatana pūjā,* 779; in Vaishṇavism, 849
Kṛishṇadevarāya: ascends throne of Vijayanagara Empire, 631
Kṛishṇamūrti, J.: death, 645
Kṛittikā Dīpa: description, 750; festival, 283, 285; *nakshatra,* 289
Kriyā: in *Āgamas,* 492; def., 750; and *niyamas,* 189; *pāda,* 111, 327, 379, 481; path of, 107; in Śaivism, 530; *Tirumantram* on, 495
Kriyākramadyotikā: contents and use, 750, 498
Kriyamāna karma: def., 93, 746
Kriyā pāda: def., 750-751, 776
Kriyā śakti: def., 751; aspect of Śakti, 803; *prakṛiti tattva,* 837; *triśūla* symbolizes, 844
Kshamā: def., 751, 862; guideline, 187
Kshatriya: Arthaveda, 686; caste, 698; def., 751, 850; *dharma,* 171
Ku: Aum, 689
Kuḍalasaṅgama: and Basavaṇṇa, 505; def., 751
Kudṛishṭi: bindu protects from 695
Kula: def., 751; joint family, 740
Kula guru: def., 751
Kulārṇava Tantra: contents, 751; *guru* protocol, 363
Kumāra: def., 751; Smārtism, 27
Kumaraguruparar: life and work, 632
Kumbha: def., 751
Kumbha Mela: festival, 291
Kuṇḍalinī: adhyātma vikāsa, 677; *Āgamas* on, 379; caution, 347; desires, unharnessed, 257; def., 751; *dīkshā,* 713; door of Brahman, 714; fire of consciousness, 113; *jñāna,* 739; *karma,* frying seeds of, 747; Kārttikeya controls, 69; Kashmīr Śaivism, 510; monistic insight, 421; *kriyā,* 750; *mayūra,* 759; *nāḍī (sushumnā),* 767; Naṭarāja, symbolized in, 41; *nāga,* 489, 767; Nātha Sampradāya, 447; Pāśupatas, 500; Pāśupata Śaivism, 782; *satguru* safely guides, 365; Śaivism, 21; Śakti, 804; Śaktipāta, 804; Śāktism, 23; *sannyāsin,* path, 347; Self Realization, 816; Siddha Siddhānta, 518; Śivasāyujya, 821; spiritual unfoldment, 824-825; *tantrism,* 834; *tapas,* 835; truth, to know, 421; and *vel,* 71; *videhamukti,* 855; *yajña,* 861; in *yoga pāda,* 107; *yoga tapas,* 863
Kuṇḍalinī yoga: Gorakshaśataka, 724; Kanphaṭi, 745; Kashmīr Śaivism, 748; Siddha Siddhānta, 816
K'ung-fu-tsu: Confucius, 550
Kuṅkuma: bindu, 695; def., 751
Kūrma Purāṇa: content, 751
Kurukshetra: battle of, 391; location, 751
Kushan Empire: beginnings, 620; timeline, 620-621
Kuśika: identification, 751
Kuttuvilaku: description and use, 751; symbol, 325
Kuṭumba: def., 751; joint family, 740; see also *Family*

Laborers: *dharma,* 171; see also *Indian Laborers*
Lakshmī: def., 752; Śākti, 803
Lakulīśa: Pāśupata *satguru,* 501; profile, 752; reform, 621; temples, 501
Lallā of Kashmir: develops Kashmīri language, 629; profile, 752
Lance: def., 752; symbol, 429; *vel,* 854
Language: ancestry, 609; Purāṇic literature, 391; scriptures, 309
Lao-tzu: dates, 617; Taoism, 546
Larder: def., 752
Latter life: rites of, 277
Laud: def., 752
Lavish: def., 752
Law: *Arthaveda,* 686; *Vedas* on, 63; *dharma* as, 167; *Dharma Śāstra,* 712
Law-enforcers: *dharma* of, 171, 850
Law-makers: *dharma* of, 171, 850
Laxman Joo, Swāmī: and Kashmīr Śaivism, 512
Laziness: obstacle, 255
Leadership: holy men and women, 357; *sannyāsin,* 345, 351
Left-hand: def., 752; Śākta Tantrism, 835; Śāktism, 23; *vāma,* 849
Legend: def., 752; scripture, 387
Legislate: def., 752
Legitimate: def., 752
Lekhaprārtha havana: def., 752
Lest: def., 752
Liberal Hinduism: def., 752; neo-Indian religion, 771; and *Smārtism,* 821-822
Liberation (from rebirth): in *Āgamas,* 379; and *ahiṁsā,* 195; attainment, 87; creed belief, 479; def., 752-753; Eastern-Western views, 596; desire, 102; and *dharma,* 167; God grants, 87, 159, 285; *moksha,* 763; Śaivism, 33; Self Realization, 13; scripture on, 116; and Śiva's dance, 41; in Vaishṇavism, 530-531
Licchavi dynasty: Hindu rule, 622
Licentious: def., 753
Life: four goals, 87; harmony of, 143; living joyously, 145; obstacles in, 255; pilgrimage, 195, 269; sacredness, in *Vedas,* 377
Life energy: all-pervasive, 819; God in all things, 5
Light: *āratī,* 305, 335; clear white, 101, 753; from darkness to, xix, 145; def., 753; festivals of, 289, 291; inner, 255, 753, 819; *jīvanmukta,* 115; life of, 107; moon-like inner, 257, 753; quantum particles, 793; Śiva's 49, 53, 347; soul body, 81, 79
Light of Truth Universal Shrine (LOTUS): dedication, 645
Lineage: marrying within same, 227; scripture recognized by, 387
Liṅga: and *bilva* leaves, 105; def., 753; Śaiva Siddhānta, 431; scripture, 308; Śivaliṅga, 819-820; symbol, 461; and Vīra Śaivas, 431, 504
Liṅgāchāra: code, 753, 508; among the *pañchāchāra,* 778
Liṅga Dikshā: ceremony, 753; Vīra Śaivism, 508, 856
Liṅga Purāṇa: contents, 753
Liṅgāshṭakam: def., 753
Liṅgavanta: def., 753; Vīra Śaivism, 856
Liṅgayat: def., 753; Vīra Śaivism, 504, 856; scriptures, 507
Liturgy: *Āgamas,* 381; def., 753; *pujārīs* learn, 319; *Vedas,* 377,
Livelihood: def., 753
Living with Śiva: Asian protocol, 261
Loka: chart, 866, def., 753-754; three worlds, 839; world, 859
Lord of Obstacles: See *Gaṇeśa*
LOTUS: Light of Truth Universal Shrine, 645
Lotus: *āsana,* def., 754; of the heart,

657; symbol, 121
Love: of God, 336-337; God is, 407, 409; in *kriyā pāda,* 111; mature in marriage, 225; offering in worship, 329; and purity, 183; radiated by soul, 137; sexual expression, 217; Śiva's immanent, 53, 381
Lower nature: def., 729-730; description, 107; and evil, 141; source of violence, 199, 203
Loyalty: importance in marriage, 219
Lust: *atala chakra,* 700; before *charyā,* 107; control, 187; obstacle, 255; *sannyāsin* protects mind from, 351
Lute: def., 754
Luther, Martin: Protestant, 631

Macaulay: Neo-Indian religion, and, 771
Macrocosm: def., 754, 761; *loka,* 754; *piṇḍa,* 784
Madhumateya Order: founded, 754; Śaiva Siddhānta, 496
Mādhva: Appaya Dīkshita on, 515; life and work, 628; philosophy, 417, 419, 512; profile, 754; Vaishṇavism, 25; Vedānta, 852-853
Madurai Tamil Saṅgam: held at Thiruparankundram, 614
Magic: *Atharva Veda,* 688-699; black, 503; elixir, 716; folk-shamanic, 720-721; incantation, 733; *kalā,* 743; in Purāṇic literature, 391; in Śāktism, 23; *siddhi,* 817; *tantra,* 834; in the *Vedas,* 375
Magna Carta: signed, 628
Mahā: def., 754
Mahā Bodhi Society: founded, 639
Mahābhārata: Hindu epic, 391; interpolations, 615; profile, 754; and Śaivism, 492; written, 615
Mahādeva: belief, 469; causal plane, 129; def., 754-755; Gods, 65, 724
Mahādeva Mountain: Vasugupta, 851
Mahādevī: life and work, 628
Mahākāla: def., 755; and Naṭarāja, 41; symbol, 149; description and worship of, 308
Mahākuṭumba: def., 755; extended family, 719
Mahāmagham: festival, 644
Mahāmaṇḍapa: approaching, 305; def., 755
Mahānārāyaṇa Upanishad: identification, 755
Mahānirvāṇa Tantra: contents, 755
Mahāpralaya: def., 755; discussion, 439; process, 755; Śiva, 131; *tattva,* 836; see also *Pralaya*
Mahāprasthāna: def., 755; positive view of death, 99
Mahārāja: def., 755
Maharashtra: location, 755
Maharishi: def., 755
Maharloka: chart, 866, def., 755, *loka,* 753
Mahāsākāra-piṇḍa: def., 755; Siddha Siddhānta, 517
Mahāsamādhi: day, 756; def., 755-756; observance, 291
Mahāśivarātri: def., 756; festival of, 283, 285, 303
Mahātala (chakra): chart, 868; def., 756; location, 700
Mahātma: great soul, 756; description, 361
Mahāvairochana Sūtra: Chinese translation, 625
Mahāvākya: great saying, 756; creedal sayings, 463
Mahāvaṁsa: written, 623
Mahāvihāra: founding, 621-622
Mahāvīra: founder of Jainism, 538; life and contributions, 617
Mahendra: work, 619
Maheśa: def., 756, 856; selfless service, 508

Maheśvara: def., 756; Śiva, 49
Maitreya: identification, 756
Maitrī Upanishad: description, 756
Major religions: summary of beliefs section, xxviii
Mala(s): darkness of, 347; def., 756; liberation, 752-753; three bonds, 85; world, 859; see also *Pāsa*
Mālā: chanting, 399, 403; def., 756
Malaparipāka: and *anugraha śakti,* 684; maturing of *mala,* 756; *karma,* equivalence brings, 746
Mālatī-Mādhava: contents, 756; written, 625
Malaysia: Hindu kingdom established, 621
Male: and female energies, 347; soul is not, 79
Malice: def., 756; *pātāla chakra* is seat of, 868, 872
Man: evolution in Śaivism, 21; and God, 528; mixed religious marriage, 227; plight, views compared, 594; and woman, natures, 215
Manana: reflection, 756; Smārta path of attainment, 531
Manas: antaḥkaraṇa, 684; def., 756-757, 762; instinctive mind, 11
Manas chitta: chart, 686; def., 757
Manas tattva: chart, 867, 869; def., 837-838
Maṇḍala: chapter, contents, xxx; def., 757; in *Ṛig Veda,* 798
Maṇḍapa: def., 757; *yajña,* place of, 860; *mahāmaṇḍapa,* 305
Mandira: temple, 757
Māṇḍūkya Upanishad: def., 757
Maṅgala kriyā: auspicious practice, 757
Maṅgala sūtra: wedding pendant, 859
Mangalavede: location, 757
Manifest: def., 757
Manifest Sacred Form: aspect of Śiva consciousness, 819
Manifold: def., 757
Manikkavasagar: life and work, 626, 757; *bhakti* movement, 495
Maṇipūra chakra: chart, 868; def., 757, 700; seat of Kārttikeya, 69
Mankolam: def., 757; symbol, 209
Manomaya kośa: chart, 867; def., 749-750, 757-758; dropped off, 87; instinctive-intellectual sheath, 79; *śarīra,* 811; soul, 823
Mānsāhārī: def., 758; meat-eater, 760
Mantra: in *Āgamas,* 379, 381, 492; Aum, 689; *āyurveda,* 259; conception, 275; daily acts, 261; def., 758; Gāyatrī, 723; incantation, 733; *japa,* 738; Namaḥ Śivāya, 405; priest, 319; root, 3; Śāktism, 23, 530; Śaivite Creed, 487; scripture, 410; Śiva's Absolute Being, 51; Vīra Śaivism, 508; worship, 321
Mantra Gopya: identification, 758; Vīra Śaiva scripture, 507
Manu Dharma Śāstra: contents, 758; *Dharma Śāstra,* 712; Kalpa Vedāṅga, 744; Vedāṅga, 852; written, 622
Manushya yajña: def., 861
Mārga: def., 758; *pāda,* 776; *sādhana,* 800; Sān, 809; *tantra,* 835
Mariyamman: Amman, 682; def., 758
Mārjāra: grace, cat analogy, 725
Markaṭa: grace, monkey analogy, 725
Marriage: age, 225; appropriateness, 245; arranged, 225, 229; children, 239; covenant, 225, 758; criticism, 233; def., 758; faithfulness, 187; family union, 229; *gṛihastha dharma,* 725-726; problem resolution, 225, 233; purpose, 211; religion, 227; renewal, 277; rite of passage, 269, 273; scripture on, 220-221, 234-235; sex, 219; success, 225; *Vedas,* 211
Masturbation: view of, 217
Mātaṅga Parameśvara Āgama: contents, 758
Mataramas dynasty: reversion to

Śaivism, 626
Material cause: def., 699, 758; monism and dualism, 419, 431, 433
Materialism: beliefs, 584-585; def., 759; summary, 584
Maṭha: home of *guru,* 343
Mathura: sacked by Mahmud of Ghazni, 627
Mati: def., 759, 862; guideline, 189
Matrimonial: def., 759
Matsyendranātha: Gorakshanātha, 516; life and work, 626; profile, 759
Mattamayūra Order: description, 759; Śaiva Siddhānta, 496
Matter: def., 759
Mature: def., 759
Mauna: silence, 657, 765
Mauritius: indentured laborers from India, 636
Maurya: timeline, 618-619
Maya: def., 759
Māyā: Āgamas, 492; bond, 85; def., 759; and God, 57; material cause, 758; monistic view, 433; origins, 759; physical plane, 131; pluralist view, 433, 437; *pralaya,* 439; scripture on, 147, 440; Sikh view, 544; source of evil and suffering, 137; and *tripuṇḍra,* 31; world, 859
Māyā tattva: chart, 867, 869; def., 837
Mayūra: symbol, 61, 759
Mean: def., 760
Meat: consumption of, 187, 201, 760; harmfulness, 201; scripture on, 205
Meat-eater: *ahiṁsā,* 201; def., 760
Mediatrix: def., 760
Medicine: See *Āyurveda*
Meditation: in *Āgamas*, 379; conception, prior to, 239; daily practice of, 257; def., 760; on God, 14, 159; *haṭha yoga,* 728; holy men and women, 357; home shrine, 335; on path, 7; for peace, 203; for perspective, 143; *rāja yoga,* 794-795; in Śiva Advaita, 513; at temple, 307; in *yoga pāda,* 113, 361
Meditator: experience of Śiva, 85
Mediumship: def., 760
Meenakshi temple: date, 619
Megasthenes: describes irrigation in India, 618
Meghadūta: authorship, 622
Mehrgarh civilization: timeline, 611
Memory: Gaṇeśa God of, 67
Men: law of being, 167; monastic life, 343; *purusha dharma,* 711; settle family disputes, 247; temple priests, 319
Menander: reign, 620
Mencius: second sage of Confucianism, 550
Mencius: Confucian scripture, 550
Mendicant: cenobite, 343; def., 760; *sādhu,* 361; sages, 359
Meng-tzu: Mencius, 550
Menses: def., 760; rite of passage, 273; temple and, 303
Mental body (sheath): chart, 867; def., 760; *vijñānamaya kośa,* 79, 750, 855
Mental plane: def., 760
Merchants: *dharma* of, 171
Merge: def., 760
Merger of the soul: def., 760; *viśvagrāsa,* 87, 857
Meritorious: def., 760
Mesmerizing: def., 760
Metamorphosis: def., 760; soul's evolution, 107
Metaphysics: def., 760; ontology, 776; in secondary scriptures, 387
Method: See *Tantra*
Mexico: Aztec civilization established, 630; Toltec Empire crumbles, 628
Meykandar: dualist, 419; life and work, 628; Nātha school, 431; profile, 761; and Śaiva Siddhānta, 498
Meykandar Śāstras: authors and contents, 761; pluralism, 431

Microcosm-macrocosm: def., 761; *loka,* 754; *piṇḍa,* 784
Migrations: prehistory, 611
Mīrābāī: life and work, 631
Milestone: def., 761
Milieu: def., 761
Millenium: def., 761
Mīmāṁsā: def., 761, 815; *darśana,* 417, *Sūtras,* 620; Vedānta, 853
Mind: bondage and release, 141; cleared by *vel,* 71; cunning, 365; nature of, 5; peace of, 203; pure and impure, 157; purifying, 257; after Self Realization, 13; subliminal traits, 255; transcending, 365
Mind, five states: chart, 867; conscious, 761; subconscious, 761; subsubconscious, 761; subsuperconscious, 762; superconscious, 761-762
Mind, individual: *antaḥkaraṇa,* 684; explanation, 762
Mind, three phases: chart, 867; instinctive, 762; intellectual, 762; superconscious, 762
Mind, universal: explanation, 762; *māyā,* 759; world, 859
Mingdi, King: conversion of, 620
Minister: def., 762-763
Minutiae: def., 763; God's care, 55
Mīrābāī: poetess, 739; profile, 763
Mirific: def., 763; *māyā,* 131, 759
Misconception: def., 763
Missionaries: Appaya Dīkshita, 515; Christian, 609
Mitāhāra: def., 763, 862; *niyama,* 187
Modaka: def., 763
Modesty: of attire, 261; good conduct, 181, 183, 189; soul quality, 141; vanity to, 71; woman's, 215
Mohammed: founder of Islam, 570; life and work, 623
Mohammed of Ghur: conquers Punjab and Lahore, 628
Mohenjo-daro: beginnings, 612
Moksha: belief, 479; children taught, 664; def., 763, 793; liberation, 752-753; in *guru's* palm, 455; Jain view, 539; reaching, xxv; reincarnation, 797; Śaivism, 21, 525; Śāktism, 529; Sikh view, 543; Smārtism, 530-531; and spiritual knowledge, xix
Monastic: blessing for family, 245; def., 763; monk, 764; path of, 245, 343-351; *sannyāsa dharma,* 809-810; scripture, 352; water pot, 341
Monastic initiation: guidelines for, 349; rites of, 349; *sannyāsa dīkshā,* 810; vows of, 351
Monastic orders: created by Gorakshanātha, 516; *daśanāmi,* 708; in Śaivism, 21; in Smārtism, 27; spread Śaiva Siddhānta, 496-497
Monastic tradition: description, 343-351; scripture on, 352-353; *sannyāsa dharma,* 809-810; in Vaishṇavism, 25
Monday: holy day, 283, 303
Mongol dynasty: translation of Sanskṛit into Chinese, 629
Monism: in *Āgamas,* 492; def., 763; difference from dualism, 419; flaws, 423; *dvaita-advaita,* 714-715; Hindu acceptance, xxv; limitation, 421; and monistic theism, 421; Nandinātha, 495; philosophy, 417; Śaivism, 33; Vallabha, 25; in *Vedas, Āgamas* and hymns of saints, 425
Monistic Śaiva Siddhānta: Advaita Siddhānta, 679; basis of this catechism, 395; compared with pluralism, 431-439; Śuddha Śaiva Siddhānta, 829
Monistic theism: Advaita Īsvaravāda, 678; scriptures, 431; cosmic dissolution, 439; creation, 433; def., 714, 763-764; *dvaita-advaita,* 714-715; on evil, 437; on God, 435; monism and dualism, 421, 423; Nātha Sampradāya, 447; panentheism, 779;

pluralist comparison, 431; Śaiva theology, 33; Tirumular, 495; Vedānta, 852-853; *Vedas,* 425
Monists: notable, 419
Monk: def., 764; see *Monastic*
Monotheism: def., 764; Biblical religions, 598; Islam, 570; Judaism, 562, 564; Zoroastrianism, 558
Montessori, Maria: in India, 642
Moon: symbol, 415
Moral law: and *dharma,* 171
Morning worship: *brāhma muhūrta,* 696; *sandhyā upāsanā,* 257, 808
Mortal: def., 764
Mortal sin: def., 764, 818; Hindu view, 153
Moses: founder of Judaism, 564
Mother: duties of, 215, 231; children, 243; rite during pregnancy, 275
Mountain: analogy, 421
Mouse: and Gaṇeśa, 237
Moveable type: Chinese invent, 627
Movement: primal act, xix; Śiva's dance, 9
Mṛigendra Āgama: contents, 764; meaning of *sūtra,* xxvi-xxvii
Mṛityu: death, 708
Mudrā: def. and list, 764-765; Naṭarāja, 769-770; in worship, 321
Muhūrta: def., 765; importance, 259; lucky, 279; systems, 765
Mukhamaṇḍapa: maṇḍapa, 757
Mukhya: def., 765; head of joint family, 740
Muktābāi: life and work, 629
Muktānanda, Swāmī: founds Siddha Yoga Dhām, 640
Mukti: def., 765
Mukti Upanishad: description, 765
Mūla: def., 765
Mūlādhāra chakra: chart, 868; def., 765; Gaṇeśa sits on, 67; location, 699; *nāḍī,* 767; Naraka below, 155
Mūla mantra: def., 765; see *Aum*
Müller, Max: Aryan language, 639; chronology method, 608-609; *Sacred Books of the East,* 638; theory of Aryan race, 637
Muṇḍaka Upanishad: description, 765
Muni: def., 765; description, 359, 361
Mūrti: def., 765; temple image, 317
Murugan: creed belief, 473; def., 765; scripture on, 73; *vel,* 429
Muse: def., 766
Mūshika: def., 766; symbol, 237
Music: Śaivite, as sacred, 39; scriptures, 387, 389; spiritual, 261
Muslim: def., 766; impact on Śaivism, 516; Indus Valley conquest, 626; see also *Islam*
Muslim League: political party formed, 640
Mutual: def., 766
Mystery: of image worship, 317; ultimate reality, 51; soul's two perfections, 83; theology expresses, 417
Mysticism: belief, 575; def., 766
Myth: def., 766; in Hinduism, 391
Mythology: def., 766; scripture, 387

Nabhānedishṭha: birth, 612
Nāda: in cosmology, 866, 869; def., 766; sacred sound, 819; Śiva *tattva,* 836; sound, 823; *tattvas,* 41
Nādānusandhāna: sound, *yoga,* 824
Nādanāḍī śakti: def., 766; *nāda,* 766
Nāḍī: def., 766-767; husband-wife, 219; *kuṇḍalinī,* 751; odic, 775; *tantrism,* 834-835; *triśūla,* 445
Nāga: def., 767; symbol, 489
Nāgasvara: woodwind, 859
Naivedya: def., 767; *pūjā,* 790
Nakshatra: credentials for *archana,* 315; def., 767
Nallur temple: Chellappan, 453; Yogaswāmī, 455

Nalvar: def., 767; named, 767
Nāmadeva: life and work, 629
Nāmadīkshā: def., 767
Namaḥ Śivāya: chakras and, 868; def., 767; description, 401, 767; five sacred syllables, 487; proper chanting, 403; scripture on, 411; Śiva's form, 403; *Vedas,* 410; Vīra Śaivism, 508; see also *Pañchākshara Mantra*
Nāmakaraṇa: converts, 704; def., 768; description, 271, 669, 807; Hindu acceptance rite, 730
Namaskāra: def., 768
Namaste: def., 768
Name-giving: baby, 271; rite, 269; rules, 279; see *Nāmakaraṇa*
Names: guidelines for women's names, 279
Nammalvar: life and work, 625
Namo Nārāyaṇāya: def., 768
Nānak, Guru: life and work, 630; Sikh *guru,* 544
Nandī: def., 768; symbol, 77; *Tirumantiram* on, 309
Nandikeśvara: identification, 768
Nandikeśvara Kāśikā: contents, 768; early Śaiva Siddhānta, 494
Nandinātha: disciples, 619; def., 768; life, 619; and Kailāsa Paramparā, 449; monism, 495; and Śaiva Siddhānta, 494; scripture, 457; stream of Nātha Sampradāya, 447
Nandinātha Sampradāya: ; discussion, 447-455; Kailāsa Paramparā, 449; Nātha Sampradāya, 771; of Tirumular, 495; see also *Nātha Sampradāya*
Napoleon: retreat from Moscow, 635
Nārada Parivrājaka: contents, 768
Nārada Sūtras: bhakti text, 393; contents, 768
Naraka: abode of *asuras,* 63; astral plane, 688; def., 768; description, 155; Gaṇeśa and, 65; meat-eater and, 760; regions, 768-769; subtle plane, 127
Narasiṅha Pūrvatāpanīya: description, 769
Narasiṅhavarman, King: builds China Pagoda, 624
Nārāyaṇa: def., 769
Nārāyaṇakaṇṭha: identification, 769
Nārāyaṇ, Shah Pṛithivī: establishes Hindu state of Nepal, 634
Nastika: def., 769; and *Vedas,* 417
Nataputta Vardhamana: founder of Jainism, 538
Naṭarāja: Ārdhrā Darśana; Cosmic Dance, 41; description, 769; icon of Primal Soul, 57; symbol, 47
Natchintanai: and this catechism, 395; contents, 770; Yogaswāmī, 455
Nātha: def., 770; and Gorakshanātha, 495, 516; and Meykandar school, 431; practice, 770; scripture, 457
Nātha Maṭha: def., 770-771
Nātha Sampradāya: def., 771; Kailāsa Paramparā, 741; lineages, 771
Nation: and *dharma,* 171; peace in, 203; *varṇa dharma,* 710
National: celebrations, 291; *karma,* 93, 747
Naturalistic materialism: See *Materialism*
Nature: Cosmic order, *ṛita,* 167, 169, 710; *prakṛiti,* 125; responsibilities to, 169; sacredness, 195; *Vedas,* 375
Navalar, Arumuga: life and work, 635
Nayanar: Appar, 685; def., 771; hymns, 393; Nalvar, 767; Sambandar, 805; Sundarar, 830
Nebuchadnezzar: dates, 616
Necklace: betrothal, 229
Nehru, Jawaharlal: plan for free India, 642
Neo-Indian religion: description, 771; liberal Hinduism, 752
Nepal: Gorakshanātha, 516; location,

771; and Matsyendranātha, 516; Pāśupatas, 502; Śaivism, 491, 517
Neti neti: def., 771; inner quest for the Self, 51
Neuter: def., 771
Neutron star: def., 771-772; Self God more solid than, 13
New age: beliefs, 577-578; def., 772; enlightenment teachings, 577
Newborn child: rites, 275; *saṁskāras* of birth, 806
New Testament: Christian *Bible,* 566
New Year: def., 772; Dīpāvalī and others, 291
Nikongi: Shinto scripture, 554
Nimbārka: life and work, 628; profile, 772; Vaishṇavism, 25, 417
Nimitta kāraṇa: efficient cause, 699, 715
Nirguṇa Brahman: Brahman, 696; Appaya Dīkshita on, 515; def., 772
Nirukta Vedāṅga: texts on etymology, 772; *Vedāṅga,* 852
Nirvāhaṇa: def., 772
Nirvāṇa: Buddhism, 534, 535
Nirvāṇī and *upadeśī:* def., 772
Nirvāṇīs: sages, 359
Nirvikalpa samādhi: def., 772; *jñāna pāda,* 115; *sannyāsin,* 347; Śaivism, 13, 81; Śiva's Absolute Being, 51; see also *Self Realization*
Niśchitārtha: betrothal, 273; def., 772; description, 807
Nityānanda, Swāmī: monistic theist, 425; profile, 832
Nivedana: def., 773
Nivṛittikalā: chart, 866; *kalā,* 742
Nivṛitti mārga: āśrama dharma, 687
Niyamas: def., 773, 794; discussion, 189; list, 862; and Pāśupatas, 500; scripture on, 191
Niyati: def., 773; *tattva,* 837
Nondual: *dvaita-advaita,* 714-715
Nondualism: Rāmānuja, qualified, 25, 512; in scripture, 427; see *Monism; Monistic theism*
Non-Hindus: and Śaivism, 520
Nonhuman birth: clarification, 773-774
Noninjurious: def., 774
Noninjury: *ahiṁsā,* 680; guideline, 187; inner source of, 197; scripture on, 204-205; summary, 195; vegetarianism, 201
Nonperseverance: def., 774; overcoming, 189
Non-stealing: ethical guideline, 187
Nonviolence: and *ahiṁsā,* 195
Noose: Gaṇeśa's, 67
Northern Śaivism: def., 509
Nostradamus: life and work, 631
Nostratic: parent language, 609
Notable: def., 774
Novelty: def., 774
Novitiate: def., 774; description, 361
Nucleus of soul: discussion, 83; references—*ātman,* 689; impersonal being, 733; soul, 79, 435, 823
Nunk: def., 774
Nurturance: def., 774
Nyāya: def., 774; description, 814; of six systems of philosophy, 417

Obedience: *sannyāsa* vow, 351
Objective: def., 774; of monastic life, 345
Oblation: def., 774; *havana,* 729; *homa,* 732; *yajña,* 860
Obscuring grace: symbolized in Naṭarāja, 41; *tirobhāva,* 770; *tirodhāna śakti,* 840; see also *Grace*
Observances: *niyamas,* 189, 862; in *kriyā pāda,* 111
Obstacles: and Gaṇeśa, 65, 91; purpose of, 67; to spiritual progress, 255; see also *Upasarga*
Obstinate: def., 774

Ocean: Bhedābheda, 694; depositing ashes, 696; Gaṇeśa Visarjana, 722; metaphor, 433, 435, 494, 508
Occult: def., 775
Occultism: belief, 575
Occupation: Śaivism, 37; caste, 171
Odic energy: actinodic, 677; *aśuddha tattvas,* 837; chart, 869; def., 775; *kośa,* 749-750; *manomaya kośa,* 757
Offering: temple, 305, 312, 315, 329
Offset: def., 775
Offspring: def., 775
Oil lamp: Dīpāvalī, 291; *kuttuvilaku,* 751; symbol, 325
Olai: def., 775; palm leaves, xxv
Old soul: def., 775; quest for Self, 87
Old Testament: Christian scripture, 566; Judaic scripture, 562
Olympic Games: first, 616
Om: def., 775; Aum, 689
Ominous: def., 775
Omnipotent: def., 775
Omnipresent: def., 775
Omniscience: def., 775; God, xviii; soul lacks, 85
Oneness: def., 775
Ontology: def., 776
Opposites: and evil, 437; truth beyond, 151
Oral teachings: *Āgamas,* 493; scripture, 373
Orbit: def., 776
Ordain: def., 776
Organization: Hinduism, 357
Oriental religions: major, xxii
Original sin: Hindu view, 153, 818
Origin of Species (Darwin): theory of evolution, 637-638; 707-708
Orissa: timeline, 626-629
Orthodox: def., 776; *nāstika* (opposite to), 769
Outgrow: def., 776
Outstretch: def., 776
Overshadow: def., 776
Overwhelm: def., 776
Pada: def., 776
Pāda: Āgamas, 492; def., 776; fulfillment, 776-777; path of soul, 107-115; stages, 776; see also *Charyā; Jñāna; Kriyā; Yoga*
Pādapūjā: ceremony, 777
Padārtha: def., 777; differences among philosophical schools, 777
Paddhati: def., 777; and *Āgamas,* 493; Aghoraśiva's, 498; manuals for temple priests, 389
Pāda tattva: chart, 869; def., 838
Padma: def., 777; symbol of 121
Padma Purāṇa: def., 777
Padmāsana: āsana, 686
Pādukā: def., 777; symbol, 355
Pagan: def., 777; dualist attitude, 199
Pageantry: def., 777; sacred literature and, 387
Pain: ingested with meat, 201; not inflicting, 195; selfishness brings, 95
Paiṅgala Upanishad: topics, 777
Paisley: symbol, 209
Pakistan independence: from Britain, 642; timeline, 639-643
Palani Hills temple: date, 620
Pallava dynasty: established, 621; timeline, 620-625
Pañchabhūta: def., 777; five elements, 123
Pañchāchāra: codes of Vīra Śaivism, 508; def., 777-778
Pañcha Gaṇapati Utsava: description, 778; festival, 287
Pañcha kañchuka: niyati, 773; *purusha tattva,* 837
Pañchakrityā: (five powers of Śiva), absorption, 676
Pañcha kriyā: duties, 665-666
Pañcha kuṭumba sādhana: five parenting guidelines, 667
Pañchākshara Mantra: def.; 778; ini-

tiation, 405, 409; proper chanting, 403; Śaivite creed, 487; scripture on, 411; *ślokas,* 401-405
Pañcha mahāyajña: def., 861
Pañchamukha Gaṇapati: def., 778
Pañchāṅga praṇāma: def., 787; in temple, 305
Pañcha nitya karmas: children taught, 665-666; and good conduct, 185; listed duties, 778
Pañcharātra sect: def., 778; date, 618; Vaishṇavism, 25, 542
Pañchārtha Bhāshya: Kauṇḍinya, 500
Pañcha śraddhā: def., 778; five precepts, 663
Pañchatantra: animal stories, 391; background and influences, 778
Pañchāyatana pūjā: description, 779
Paṇḍita: description, 361; *pundit,* 790
Panentheism: def., 779; philosophy, 423; theology of Śaivism, 33; see also *Monistic theism*
Pāṇini: composes Sanskṛit grammar, 615, 618
Pāṇi tattva: chart, 869; def., 838
Pantheism: def., 779
Pantheists: list, 419
Pāpa: consequences of acts, 779-780; creation, 157; evil, 717; penance, 780; sin, 817-818; unkindness, 95
Pāpadṛishṭi: and *bindu,* 695
Pāpa-duḥkha: def., 780
Paper: invented in China, 621
Pāpman: def., 780; evil, 717
Para: def., 780
Parabindu: bindu, 695; Śakti *tattva,* 836
Parable: def., 780
Parabrahman: def., 780; Brahman, 696
Paradox: def., 780; oneness and twoness, 83
Parākhya Āgama: def., 780
Parama: def., 780
Paramaguru: def., 780
Paramahaṁsa: def., 780
Paramātman: ātman, 689; def., 781; in Jainism, 539
Parameśvara: ; creed belief, 469; def., 781; invoked on Ārdrā Darśana, 285; Primal Soul, 55; Sadāśiva, 799-800; Śakti *tattva,* 836; Śiva, 818; three perfections, 785; worship of, 57; see also *Primal Soul*
Parameśvara of Malaysia: conversion to Islam, 630
Paramparā: def., 781; *gurus,* 449; scripture on, 456-457
Parārtha pūjā: def., 781, 790; qualifications, 319
Parāśakti: core of soul, 83; creed belief, 467; def., 781; description, 53; Kṛittikā Dīpa, 285; other names, 781; and *pīṭha,* 47; Śiva, 818; Śiva *tattva,* 836; three perfections, 785; worship, 57, 333
Parāsamvid: def., 781; Śiva, 517
Paraśiva: belief, 465; def., 781; description, 51; and *jñāna pāda,* 115; knowing through persistence, 87, 345; Mahāśivarātri, 285; monistic theism, 423; Śiva, 818; Śivaliṅga, 47; soul, 79, 83, 435; superconsciousness, 53; three perfections, 785; *yoga pāda,* 113; you are, 569
Parents: advise on sexuality, 217; debt to children, 243; duty of, 241; five guidelines, 667; five practices, 665-666; five precepts to teach children, 663-664
Parīkshit: birth, 615
Pārvatī: def., 781; Śāktism, 23
Pāśa: Āgamas on, 492; creation of, 433; def., 781; liberation, 752-753; and *māyā,* 759; monotheism, 764; *Pati-paśu-pāśa,* 783; Śaiva Siddhānta, 492; *tattvatrayī,* 838; world, 859; see also *Mala*
Passion: obstacle, 255
Past lives: and *karma,* 93; reincarna-

tion, 796
Paśu: *Āgamas,* 492; def., 782; monotheism, 764; *padārtha,* 777; *Pati-paśu-pāśa,* 783; Śaiva Siddhānta, 492; *tattvatrayī,* 838; world, 859
Paśupālaka: def., 782
Pāśupata Śaivism: appearance, 499; description, 782; originally dualist, 417, 502; path of, 21, 499; relation to Vedic society, 499; scripture, 502
Pāśupata Sūtra(s): contents, 782
Paśupati: def., 782; Indus Valley, earliest date, 613
Pāśupatinātha temple: identification, 782; Nepal, 501
Pātāla (chakra): chart, 868; def., 782; location, 700; Naraka, 769; in subtle plane, 127
Patañjali: and *ahiṁsā,* 195; Kailāsa Paramparā, 449; life and work, 615, 619; 782-783; and Nandinātha, 494; *rāja yoga,* 794; scripture, 457; *yoga,* 393, 814, 863
Path: def., 7, 783; elements of progress, 11; enlightenment, 783; four stages, 107-115; our right, 783; peerless/highest, 783; Truth is one, paths are many, 783; two, 783
Pāṭhaka: def., 783
Paths of attainment: Buddhism, 535; Christianity, 567; Confucianism, 551; Hinduism, 530-531; Islam, 571; Jainism, 539; Judaism, 563; Shintoism, 555; Sikhism, 543; Taoism, 547; Zoroastrianism, 559
Pati: *Āgamas*, 492; def., 783; monotheism, 764; *padārtha,* 777; *Pati-paśu-pāśa,* 783; Śiva, 49
Patience: and humility, 183
Pati-paśu-pāśa: def., 783; elements described, 783; monotheism, cosmotheandrism, 764; *padārtha,* 777; Śaiva Siddhānta, 492, symbolized in temple, 309; *tattvatrayī,* 838
Paushkara Āgama: contents, 783
Pāyu tattva: chart, 869; def., 838
Peace: and *ahiṁsā,* 195; out of conflict into, 7; on earth, 203; following *dharma* brings, 175; all peoples find in the One Supreme Being, 35; prayer for, 315; saints reflect, 359
Peacock: Kārttikeya, 61
Penance: def., 783-784; 65; *kavadi,* 748; *kriyā pāda,* 111; performance, 189; *pāpa,* 780; purity-impurity, 791-792; release for unvirtuous, 157; sin, 153, 718; Tai Pusam festival, 289; *tapas,* 835; worship, 313
Pendant: def., 784; see *Wedding pendant*
Pentateuch: revealed Judaic scripture, 598
Perfections (Śiva's three): def., 784; description, 49-55; exist alone at *mahāpralaya,* 131; realization of, 115; soul's oneness with, 81, 83; Śiva, 818; traditional icons, 57
Periyapurāṇam: identification, 784; Nayanar, 771; written, 628
Persia: Vedic peoples in, 614
Persian wheel: innovation, 632
Personal *dharma:* def., 784, 711; description, 175; God's law, 167
Personal God: Hindu sects, 523, 601-602; references for, 784
Perspective: def., 784; mountaintop, reconciles duality, 143; 421
Peru: Sun temple built, 622
Petition: of God, 67, 307
Petting: Hindu view, 217; sexuality, 814
Philosophy, Hindu: in *Āgamas*, 379, 381; overview, 417-425; in Purāṇas, 391; reading and *jñāna,* 115; in scripture, 387; *shaḍ darśana,* 814-815; six Śaiva schools, 491-520; Vedānta, 852-853; *Vedas* focus, 377
Physical body: chart, 867; *annamaya kośa,* 749; reincarnation, 796-797; Self Realization and, 13;

and soul, 79, 823
Physical plane: Bhūloka, 753; chart, 866; creed belief, 477; description, 125; enhanced from subtle plane, 127; Śiva's creation, 123; and three worlds, 839
Pilgrim: mendicant, 343
Pilgrimage: children taught, 666; def., 784; good conduct, 185; Hindu culture, 261; *kriyā pāda,* 111; life is, 195; negative *karma,* 95
Pillars of Śaivism (three): temples, scriptures and *satgurus,* 39, 101, 299
Piṇḍa: def., 784; in *pitṛi yajña,* 861; symbolic meaning, 784
Piṅgalā: def., 784; *nāḍī,* 767; odic, 775; and sun, 415; and *triśūla,* 445
Pir: def., 784, Muslim holy man, 517
Pīṭha: def., 784; Liṅga base, 461
Pitṛi: ancestors, homage to, 861
Pitṛiloka: astral plane, 688; of Bhuvarloka, 694; chart, 866, def., 784; three worlds, 839
Pitṛi yajña: def., 861
Pitta: def., 784-785; *dosha,* 714
Plague: def., 785; of tormenting moods, 155
Plane: def., 785; see *Loka*
Planes of existence: gross, subtle and causal, 477; see *Loka*
Planets: birth chart, 695; *chakras,* 868; influence of, 259; *jyotisha,* 741; Rāhu, 794
Planets (other): birth on (entry: *nonhuman birth),* 773; Lord Kārttikeya, 69
Planet (Earth): Hindus as guests, 169; man's purpose on, *Vedas,* 373
Plato: birth, 618
Pleasure: a goal of life, 87; see *Kāma*
Pleiades: importance, 785; and Kārttikeya, 69
Pliant: def., 785
Plotinus: pantheist, 419; philosophy, 785; practices and teachings, 621
Pluralism: def., 715, 785; views of, Siddhānta, 431-439
Pluralistic realism: def., 785; Meykandar, 431, 498; synopsis, 498; see also *Pluralistic theism*
Pluralistic theism: Aghoraśiva, 497; on cosmic dissolution, 439; on creation, 433; on evil, 437; on God, 435; monistic theism comparison, 431; scriptures, 431
Point of conception: def., 702
Politics: *Arthaveda,* 686; 389
Polo, Marco: visits India, 629
Polygamy: def., 785; Hinduism, 217
Polynesians: arrival in New Zealand, 627; Hawaii and Easter Island reached, 622
Polytheism: def., 785; monotheism, comparison, 764
Pomp: def., 785; Gaṇeśa, 65
Pontifical: def., 785, Śaṅkarāchārya *pītha,* 808; Smārta centers, 27
Poor: giving charity, 263; *manushya yajña,* 861
Positive affirmation: and affirmation of faith, 407; see *affirmation,* 679
Possessiveness: source of violence, 199
Potent: def., 785
Potentialities: def., 785; pluralistic Siddhānta, 439
Potter analogy: cause, 699; views on creation, 419, 433
Pottu: bindu, in Tamil, 695
Poverty: *sannyāsa* vow, 351
Prabhāmaṇḍala: aura, 690; Naṭarāja, ring of fire, 770
Prabhupāda, Bhaktivedānta Swāmī: International Society for Kṛishṇa Consciousness (ISKCON), 640
Pradakshiṇa: def., 785
Pradhāna: prakṛiti tattva, 837
Pradosha: def., 785-786; Śiva worship, 285
Pragmatic: def., 786
Prajāpati: Vedas on, 72, 88

Prajña: cognition and *samādhi,* 805
Prakara: temple, 305
Prakṛiti: def., 786; depiction, 786; primal nature, 125; *purusha* and, 792; Sāṅkhya, 814; *shaṭkoṇa,* 223
Prakṛiti tattva: chart, 867, 869; def., 837
Prākṛits: language development, 616
Pralaya: def., 786; scripture, 440-441; Siddhanta view, 439; types, 786
Pramukh Swāmī: birth, 641
Prāṇa: def., 786, 819
Prāṇāgnihotra Upanishad: contents, 786
Prāṇaliṅga: def., 786
Praṇāma: def., 786-787; worshipful prostration, 305
Praṇāmāñjali: añjali mudrā, 683
Prāṇamaya kośa: chart, 867; def., 749, 786; *prāṇic* sheath, 79; *śarīra,* 811; soul, 823
Prāṇatyāga: def., abandoning life, 787; suicide, 829
Praṇava: Aum, 689-690; def., 787; symbol, 3
Prāṇāyāma: def., 787, 794; *haṭha yoga,* 728; Śiva's Absolute Being, 51; *yoga pāda,* 113
Prāṇic body (sheath): chart, 867; def., 787; soul, 79
Praṇipāta: term for *praṇāma,* 787
Prapatti: bhakti, 693; *bhakti yoga,* 694; def., 787; grace, 725; *siddhis,* 817; *tapas,* 835; Vishṇu, 25, 531
Prārabdha karma: def., 93, 787, 746
Prasāda: archana, 315; def., 787; *pādapūjā,* 777; temple, 305; *ucçhishṭa,* 845; Vīra Śaivism, 508
Praśna Upanishad: description, 787
Praśnottaram: ; contemporary catechism, xxix; def., 788; Kailāsa Paramparā, 395
Pratimā: mūrti, reflected image, 765
Pratishṭhākalā: chart, 866; *kalā,* 742
Pratyabhijñā: def., 788
Pratyabhijñā Darśana: identification, 788; Kashmīr Śaivism, 510-511
Pratyabhijñā Śāstra: Kashmīr Śaivism, 510
Pratyabhijñā Sūtra: identification, 788
Pratyāhāra: def., 788, 794; *yoga,* 113
Pravṛitti mārga: āśrama dharma, 687
Prāyaśchitta: def., 788; *Dharma Śāstra,* 712; *pāpa,* 780; penance, 783; purity-impurity, 791-792; sin, 153; 818
Prayer: conception of child, 239, 275; conveyed during worship, 331; daily acts, 261; in *Vedas,* 375; holy days, 283
Prayojaka: def., 788
Prāyopaveśa: death, 708; def., 788, fasting to death, 101; suicide, 829
Precede: def., 788
Precinct: def., 788
Precursor: def., 788
Preferred Deity: Smārtism, 27; see *Ishṭa Devatā*
Pregnancy: rites, 275; *saṁskāras* of birth, 806
Premaiva Śivamaya: Satyam eva Paraśivaḥ: def., 788
Prenatal: def., 788
Preservation: chart of *tattvas,* 867, 869; def., 788; in Naṭarāja's Cosmic Dance, 41, 770; Sadāśiva, 799
Preside: def., 788
Pretaloka: chart, 867; of Bhuvarloka, 694; def., 788; three worlds, 839
Prevail: def., 788
Pride: removal through *kavadi,* 289; *sannyāsin* protects mind from, 351
Priest: description, 319-321, 361; *dharma* of, 171; invokes God, 313, 321; manuals, 389; performing *archana,* 315
Priest manuals: and *Āgamas,* 493; see also *Paddhati*
Primal Soul: belief, 469; causal plane,

129; def., 788-789; description, 55; perfection of Śiva, 49; scriptures speak on, 58-59; soul's difference from, 81; worship, 57
Primal Sound: def., 789; Śiva, 55; symbol of, 3; see also *Aum,* 689
Primal Substance: belief, 467; def., 789; description, 53; Śiva, 49; see also *Pure Consciousness*
Principle: def., 789
Pristine: def., 789
Pṛithivī tattva: chart, 867, 869; def., 838
Procreation: def., 789; in marriage, 213, 217
Procurer: def., 789
Profession: and personal *dharma,* 175; sons follow father's, 245
Professionals: *dharma,* 171
Progeny: def., 789; future monks, 245; *Vedas* give prayers for, 375
Prohibit: def., 789
Prohibitions: *guru,* 363; sexual, 217
Prominent: def., 789
Promiscuity: def., 789; impact on marriage, 219
Prone: def., 789
Pronged: def., 789
Propel: def., 789
Property: *artha,* 792; and monk, 343
Prophecy: def., 789; Śāktism, 23
Propound: def., 789
Prostration: to *guru,* 363; in temple, 305; see *Praṇāma*
Protocol: culture, 261; def., 789; *guru,* 363; temple, 329
Protrude: def., 789
Province: def., 789
Prow: def., 789
Prudent: def., 789
Psalm: def., 789
Psychic: currents, husband and wife, 219; def., 789
Ptolemy: and Indian pupils, 621
Puberty: rite of passage, 269, 273; studentship, 173
Pūjā: Āgamas, 493; and bell, 281; daily practice, 257; def., 789; description, 313, 321, 323, 789-790; gestures, 253; God invoked, 321; *kalaśa,* 311; *kriyā pāda,* 111; manual by Appaya Dīkshita, 514; Pāśupata, 499; purpose, 788; Śāktism, 23; scriptures speak on, 322-323; temple activity, 307; times of day, 307
Pujārī: def., 790; duties, 313, 321, 361; training, 319
Pulsate: def., 790
Punarjanma: def., 790; reincarnation, 97, 796; *saṁsāra* and, 806
Pundit: def., 790
Punjab: and Gorakshanātha, 516; location, 790
Punsavana: def., 790; description, 806; rite, 275
Puṇya: consequences of acts, 790-791; def., 790; result of kindness, 95
Puṇya śāstra: scripture, 387
Purāṇas: Āgamas reflected in, 493; astrological observations, 611; contents, 387, 391; def., 791; edited, 615; Goddesses, earliest references, 611; Śāktism, 23; subjects, 791; written, 623, 630
Purāṇic kings: timeline, 612-617
Pure Consciousness: creed belief, 467; perfection of Śiva, 49, 53
Pure Trika System: Kashmīr Śaivism, 510
Purgatory: def., 791; hell, 155; see also *Naraka,* 768
Puritans: def., 791; ignorance, 141
Purity: cultivation, 183; guideline, 187; importance, 357; saint, sage and *satguru,* 359
Purity-impurity: understanding in Hindu culture, 791-792
Pūrṇimā: def., 792
Purohita: def., 792

Pursue: def., 792
Purusha: def., 792; description, 792; and Prakṛiti, 786; Sāṅkhya, 814; *shaṭkoṇa,* 223; soul, 823
Purusha dharma: def., 792; description, 213, 711
Purushārtha: def., 792-793; and life's stages, 171
Purusha tattva: chart, 867, 869; def., 837
Pushya nakshatra: Tai Pusam, 289
Pythagoras: teachings, 617

Qualified nondualism: Vedānta, 853; Viśishṭādvaita, 793
Quantum: def., 793; healing powers, 259; levels of mind, 793; light particles, 129, 793; soul, 823
Quell: def., 793

Race: description, 793; and Hindu populations, 793; riots, U.S. West Coast, 641
Rādhākṛishṇan, Dr. Sarvepalli: genesis of word *Hindu,* 731; life, 639, 794; philosophy, 425; on religious faith, xvii
Rāga tattva: chart, 867, 869; def., 837
Rage: before *charyā,* 107; chart, 868; def., 794; *japa* forbidden, 403
Rāhu: def., 794; effects, 794; Vedic prayer regarding, 259
Railroad track: Indian figures, 637
Rainfall: measurement by early Indian scientists, 618
Rājanya: def. 794, *kshatriya,* 850, *Ṛig Veda* on 177
Rājarāja I: reign, 627
Rajas: def., 727, 794; Śiva as Brahmā, 49; and *triśūla,* 445
Rājasiṅha: reign, 624
Rāja yoga: in *Āgamas,* 379; def., 794; Patañjali, 782; Śaivism stresses, 21; stages, 794; *yoga,* 863
Rajneeshism: belief, 575
Rājput paintings: reproductions, xxv
Rāma: birth, 614; importance, 795; story of, 391; *Rāmāyaṇa,* 795; Vaishṇavism, 25
Rāmacharitamānasa: Tulasīdāsa, 844
Rāmakaṇṭha I: identification, 795
Rāmakaṇṭha II: identification, 795
Rāmakṛishṇa, Śrī: beliefs, 636, ; monistic theist, 425; profile, 795; and Śāktism, 23
Rāmaliṅga, Swāmī: profile, 635
Rāmana Maharshi: life, 639
Rāmānuja: philosophy, 627; profile, 795, Vaishṇavism, 25, 417, 512; Vedānta, 852-853
Rāmarāja: identification, 795
Rāmāyaṇa: contents, 795; Hindi version, 391, 631; interpolations, 615; and Śaivism, 492
Rāmdās, Swāmī "Pāpā:" life, 639
Rāmprasād: identification, 795, 393
Rasātala (chakra): chart, 868; def., 795; location, 700; Naraka, 768-769
Rasa tattva: chart, 869; def., 838
Rashṭrakuṭa: timeline, 624-625
Rationalize: def., 795; righteous wars, 199
Raurava Āgama: contents, 796; Sadyojyoti, 497; Śivajñānabodham, 819
Rāvaṇa: identification, 796
Razor: boy's first, 273
Reabsorption: def., 796
Reaction: def., 796; *karma,* law of, 85, 93, 745-746; vis-a-vis understanding, 183
Reaffirmation: def., 796; of marriage covenant, 233
Realism: pluralistic, 785

Reality: Absolute, 676; def., 796; ; of God Śiva, 49; nature of, 597; relative reality, 797; Paraśiva, 781; Śaṅkara's view, 27
Realization: see *Enlightenment; Self Realization*
Realized soul: near at death, 99
Realm: def., 796; see *Loka*
Reap: def., 796; see *Karma*
Rebellious: *charyā,* 109; def., 796
Rebirth: events preceding, 97; scriptures speak on, 249; see also *Reincarnation*
Rebound: def., 796
Recitation: religious practice, 189, 862; *japa,* 738
Recluse: def., 796
Recognition school: Kashmīr Śaivism, 509, 511
Reconcile: def., 796
Redeem: def., 796
Reembody: def., 796
Reincarnation: avoiding, 87, 97; belief common to Hindu sects, 19; description, 97; evolution of soul, xviii-xix; nonhuman birth, 773; process, 796-797; rejected by Christians, 546; scriptures speak on, 102; soul, 79
Relative: def., 797; reality, 797
Relatively real: universe, 131
Religion: creed of each, 463; differences, 35; East and West compared, xxiv; comparison of Eastern-Western views, 592-603; comparisons of Judaism, Christianity and Islam, 598-599; def., 797; derivation, 797; education of children, 243; inner intent, 35; law and *dharma,* 171; marrying outside one's, 227; neo-Indian, 771; one God, 159; oneness God, 7; origin of, Eastern-Western views, 595; preservation of, 37
Religious leaders: ecumenical gatherings, 35; extended family, 231; listing of, 357; role in peace, 203; *sannyāsins* are, 351
Religious pictures: adornment, 261
Religious solitaire: *āśrama dharma,* 687; *dharma,* 173; forth stage of life, 277
Relinquish: def., 797
Remarriage: in Hinduism, 217
Remorse: def., 797; guideline *(hrī),* 189, 862
Remote: def., 797
Renaissance: def., 797
Render: def., 797
Renowned: def., 797
Reṇukāchārya: identification, 797
Renunciation: def., 797; description, 361; goal, 345; initiation, 343; Kārttikeya, 69; and Paraśiva, 13; path, 343; sages and *satgurus,* 359; time for, 278
Replenish: def., 797
Repose: def., 797; in one's realization, 797
Repudiation: def., 797; of worldly *dharma* by *sannyāsin,* 351
Rescind: def., 797
Resemble: def., 797
Resent: def., 797
Residue: def., 797
Respect: in family, 247
Resplendence: def., 797
Restive: def., 797
Restraints: *charyā pāda,* 247; description, 187; *yama-niyama,* 797
Retirement: *dharma* of, 173
Revealed scripture: *Āgamas,* 379, 381, 679; description, 373-381; scripture speaks on, 382-384; *śruti,* 826; *Vedas,* 375, 377, 851-852
Revealing grace: grace, 724; and Pañchākshara Mantra, 401; symbolized in Naṭarāja, 41
Reverence: approaching temple, 303
Rigorous: def., 798
Righteousness: goal of life, 87

Ṛig Veda: contents and history, 798; date of early hymns, 611; dating of sixth *maṇḍala,* 614; description, 375; earliest eclipse noted in, 612, end of *Saṁhitā* narration, 615; *Veda,* 751
Rinzi Zen sect: founded by Eisai, 628
Ṛishi: def., 798; described, 361
Ṛishi from the Himalayas: Kailāsa Paramparā, 449, 451; life, 634
Ṛita: def., 710, 798; description, 169; God's law, 167; scripture on, 176
Rites: childhood, 271; def., 798; of passage, 269, 798; sacrament, 799; scripture, 279; temple, 313-336; see also *Pūjā*
Ritual: pollution-purity and Vīra Śaivites, 504; in Purāṇic literature, 391; in *Vedas,* 375
Ṛitukāla: def., 798, 807; description, 273
Rivers: Ganges, 722; Indus Valley, 734; Kṛishṇa and Malaprabhā, 808; and Liṅga stones, 818, 832; sacred, 195; Sarasvatī, 811; Sindu, 731; Ujjain, 845
Robes: discolored, 345; saffron, 343; *sannyāsin,* 351
Roy, Rām Mohan: beliefs, 636; Chronological Framework of Indian Protohistory, 608; chronology method, 607-608
Rudra: def., 799; Śiva, 49; *śuddha-vidyā tattva,* 837; *Veda* prayers to, 42, 58, 72
Rudrāksha: def., 799; *mālā* for chanting sacred *mantras,* 403; symbol of, 399; Vīra Śaivism, 508
Rudrasambhu: identification, 799
Rudrāyamala Tantra: identification, 799
Rukminī Devī Śrīmatī: life, 642
Rulers: empowered by Kārttikeya, 71
Rūpa tattva: chart, 869; def., 838
Śabda kośa: def., 799
Śabda tattva: chart, 869; def., 838
Sacrament(s): common to all Hindu sects, 19; def., 799; marriage, 211; children, 241; good conduct, 185; scripture on, 278; temple, 305; see *Saṁskāras*
Sacred and profane: Western perspective, xxii
Sacred Books of the East (Müller): published, 638
Sacred literature: Hinduism, 387
Sacredness: of all things, 197
Sacred Sound: Śivachaitanya, 819
Sacred texts: types, 393
Sacred thread: def., 799; bestowed during *upanayana,* 671, 846
Sacred vows: guideline, *vrata,* 189
Sacrifice: animal, 23; def., 799; knowledge, 391; marriage, 211, 225, 80; monastic, 345; part of *tapas,* 189; *Vedas* on, 301, 313, 321, 331, 377; and Vegetarianism, 201; *yajña,* 860-861
Sadāchāra: chapter on, 181-185; def., 778, 799; five duties, 185
Sādāraṇa dharma: description, 711
Sadāśiva: def., 799-800; five faces, 800; Parameśvara, 781; Śiva, 49
Sadāśiva tattva: chart, 867, 869; def., 837
Sādhaka: def., 800; description, 361
Sādhana: absolving sin, 153; affirmation of faith, 409; as death approaches, 99; def., 800; festivals, 283; home shrine, 335; importance, 11; Kārttikeya's realm, 69; Kashmīr Śaivism, 511-512; *kriyā pāda,* 111; life in world, 145; monastic, 341; Nātha Sampradāya, 447; negative *karma,* 95; path of enlightenment,

107; performance of, 11, 189; *Purāṇic* literature, 391; *satguru* guides, 365; secondary scriptures, 387; Tai Pusam festival, 289; *tantra,* 255; Vaishṇavism, 25; of worship, 327; Yogaswāmī, 455
Sādhana mārga: def., 800; *sannyāsin* is on, 345
Sādhanas: range of beliefs on, xxv; see *Path of attainment*
Sādhu: def., 800; description, 361, 343; Gorakshanātha, 518
Sādhvī: def., 800; description, 361
Sadyojyoti: spreading of Śaiva Siddhānta, 496-497
Safety: child's, 241
Sage: description, 359, 361; spiritual leaders, 357
Saguṇa Brahmaṇ: Appaya Dīkshita on, 515; def., 800, 696-697
Sahajānandaswami: work, 634
Sahakāri kāraṇa: cause, instrumental, 699, 736
Sahasra lekhana sādhana: def., 800; writing *mantras,* 409
Sahasrāra chakra: causal plane, 129; def., 800; door of Brahman, 714; and *kuṇḍalinī,* 23, 751; location, 700; lotus symbol, 121; trance, 843
Sahib, Tipu: killed, 635
Sainthood: path to, Eastern-Western views, 596
Saints: Hindu, 359; *sant,* 811; spiritual leaders, 357
Saism: belief, 575
Śaiva: def., 800
Śaiva Āgamas: basis, 395; contents, divisions and names, 800-801; earliest recording, 613—or 614; Kashmīr Śaivism, 510; Śaiva Siddhānta, 492, 494; and Tirumular, 451
Śaiva Śraddhādhāraṇā: creedal summation of *Śaivism,* 463-487
Śaiva Siddhānta: Advaita Siddhānta, 678-679; beliefs described, 801; founding of a school, 619; history, 801; India, 496, 497; Kailāsa Paramparā, 449; overview, 494-498; Śaivism, 21; *siddha yoga,* 495; Tamil Nadu, 491; Tirumular, 451; today, 498; two schools, 431-439,
Śaiva Siddhānta Church: founded, 643
Śaiva Upāgamas: Āgama texts, 389
Śaiva Viśishṭādvaita: def., 802; Śiva Advaita philosophy, 512-513
Śaivism: adaptability, 37; affirmation of faith, 407; *Āgamas,* 379; all-India, 491; *avatāra* doctrine, 601; beliefs, 463-487; common devotees, 494; description, 21, 33-41; festivals, 283; history, 802; in Java, 491; life, 494; monistic theism, 425; Muslim impact, 517; Nātha Sampradāya, 447; Nepal, 491; origin of, 21; other Hindu sects, 529-530; Pañchākshara Mantra, 401; path of attainment, 530; personal God, 600-601; principal doctrines, 802; regions of influence, 602; sacredness of life, 39; on the nature of Śakti, 601; schools, 491-492, 802; scriptures, 602; sect, 19; *siddha yoga,* 21; 16th century revival, 695; soul and God, 602; spiritual practice, 602; ultimate goals, 529
Śaivite creed: articles of faith, 463-487; creation of soul and identity with God, 475; God's manifest nature of all-pervading love, 467; God's unmanifest reality, 465; God as personal lord and creator of all, 469; goodness of all, 483; *karma,* 479; liberation from rebirth, 479; Mahādeva Kārttikeya, 473; Mahādeva Gaṇeśa, 471; *moksha,* 479; Pañchākshara Mantra, 487; planes of existence, 477; *saṁsāra,* 479; stages of inner progress, 481; temple worship, purpose of, 485

Śaivite (six) schools: background, 491-492, description, 802; summaries, 491-522; relation to one other, 520
Śakāhāra: ahiṁsā, 201; def., 803; vegetarian, 854
Śaka Hindu calendar: beginning, 620
Sakhā mārga: def., 803; *pāda, yoga,* 776; relationship to God, 113
Sākshin: def., 803
Śākta(s): def., 803; devotional songs, 633-634; Gorakshanātha, 518
Sākta Āgamas: in Śāktism, 23, 679
Śākta Tantrism: def., 834-835
Śakti: aspects, 803-804; comparison in Hindu sects, 601; def., 803, 819; Divine Mother, 23; instrumental cause in Śaiva Siddhānta, 419, 431; Kashmīr Śaivism, 511; representation, 803; Smārtism, 27; scriptures speak on, 29; *shaṭkoṇa,* 223; Siddha Siddhānta, 517; Śiva Advaita, 513; temple vibration, 299, 303, 307; *vel* power, 71; worship of, 803-804; in *yoga* mysticism, 804
Śaktipāta: def., 804; *dīkshā,* 713; grace, 725; from *satguru,* 365
Śāktism: Āgamas, 379; *avatāra,* 524, 601; compared with Śaivism, 804; def., 804; description, 23; earliest worship, 611; expressions, 804-805; goals, 529, major scriptures, 602; nature of God, 601; nature of Śakti, 601; path of attainment, 530; personal God, 600; regions of influence, 602; sect of Hinduism, 19; soul and God, 602; spiritual practice, 602
Śakti tattva: chart, 867, 869; def., 836
Śakti Viśishṭādvaita: def., 804; Vīra Śaivism, 507-508
Śāktopāya: def., 804, 847; Kashmīr Śaivism, 511
Śakuntalā: authorship, 622
Śākya: identification, 804
Śālagrāma: Ishṭa Devatā, 736
Sālokya: charyā's attainment, 689, 777
Salt in water: analogy, 435
Salvation: Eastern and Western views, 595; and God's will, 597; Hindu belief, xix; see also *Moksha*
Samādhi: Buddhist view, 535; def., 805; enstasy, 716; Gorakshanātha on, 517-518; *nirvikalpa,* 13, 51, 27, 113, 115, 118; *rāja yoga's* culminations, 795; Ṛishi from the Himalayas, 451; *savikalpa,* 113, 529, 812; trance, 843
Samādhi shrine: cremation tomb, 706; Ṛishi Tirumular's, 962
Sāmānya dharma: description, 711
Samarasa: def., 805; realization, 518
Samāvartana: def., 805; description, 807; Vedic study, 271
Sāma Veda: description, 375; contents, 805; *Veda,* 852
Sambandar: bhakti movement, 495; profile, 805; Nalvar, 767; Nayanar, 771; *Tirumurai,* 841-842
Śāmbhavopāya: def., 847-848; Kashmīr Śaivism, 511
Saṁhāra: absorption, 676; def., 805, Naṭarāja, 770; *pralaya,* 786
Saṁhitā: def., 805; *Vedas,* 375
Sāmīpya: kriyā's attainment, 689; 777
Saṁjñāna: conscience, 702
Sampradāya: def., 806; and *mantra* initiation, 357, 405, 447
Samprajñāta: samādhi, 805
Saṁsāra: belief, 479; def., 806; Jain view, 539, 540; Smārta view, 530; Śaivite creed, 479; soul and, 97; Vaishṇava view, 530
Saṁsārī: Āgamas guide, 381; def., 806; San Mārga, 809
Saṁskāra (rite): adulthood, 807; birth, 806; chapter on, 269-277; childhood, 271, 806-807; children learn, 666; def., 806; good conduct, 185; later life, 807; scripture, 279;

synopsis/art, 669-671
Saṁskāra (impression): def., 806; remolding the subconscious, 673; subliminal traits, 255, *vāsanā,* 851
Saṁskāra chitta: Nivṛittikalā, 866; subconscious mind, 761
Sāmvat calendar: beginning of, 620
Samyama: meditation, 805
Samyutta-Nikaya: Buddhist scripture, 534
Sanātana Dharma: eternal religion, xx; def., 807; guide of righteous life, xxv; Hinduism as, 19, 167; perpetuated through giving, 263; role of holy men and women in proclaiming, xxvi
Sanatkumāra: def., 807; in Kailāsa Paramparā, 449; prayer to, 69; *shaṭkoṇa,* 223
Sañchita karma: def., 93, 746, 808; and *satguru,* 365; *tapas* burns, 835
Sanctify: def., 808
Sanctum: temple, 305
Sanctum sanctorum: def., 808
Sandals: of *guru,* 355; see *Holy feet*
Sandalwood: *bindu,* 695; def., 808; *mālā,* 756; *pūjā,* paste offered in, 790; *tilaka,* 840
Śaṇḍilya: life and work, 621
Śaṇḍilya Upanishad: contents, 808
Saṅdhyā upāsanā: daily vigil, 257; def., 808
Saṅga: fellowship of devotees, 431
Saṅgama: def., 808
Saṅkalpa: def., 808; preparation for worship, 333
Śaṅkar, Uday: popularizes Hindu dance, 640
Śaṅkara: Appaya Dīkshita, 514; *daśanāmi,* 708; life and work, 625; philosophy, 417, 513; profile, 808; Smārtism, 27, 821-822, 27
Śaṅkarāchārya pīṭha: locations of centers, 808-809
Sāṅkhya: def., 809; description, 814; of six systems, 417
San Mārga: def., 809; scripture on, 116; spiritual path, 7, 107, 447
San Mārga Sanctuary: def., 809
Sannidhāna: def., 809
Sānnidhya: def., 809; worship, 333
Sannyāsa: def., 809; description, 687; motivations, 809
Sannyāsa āśrama: def., 809; entering, 277; stage of life, 173
Sannyāsa dharma: chapter on, 343-351; def., 809-810; description, 711; qualifications, 810
Sannyāsa dīkshā: def., 810; elder advisor stage, 277; guidelines for, 349; initiation rites, 343; requirements, 810; taken at early age, 87; vows, 351; and women, 349
Sannyāsa Upanishad: contents, 810
Sannyāsin: def., 810; description, 361; disciplines, 810; lives in *sushumṇā* current, 347; religious leaders, 351; scripture on, 353; vows, 351
Sanskṛit: affirmation of faith, 407; breakdown as spoken language, 616; def., 811; *Devanāgarī,* 709; grammar, 615; priestly revival, 616; pronunciation chart, xxxv; scriptural language, 373; terms in *Dancing with Śiva,* xxvii; *Vedas,* 377; works translated into Chinese, 624
Sant: def., 811; saints, 359
Śāntikalā: chart, 866; *kalā,* 742
Santosha: def., 811, 862; ethical guideline, 189
Śāntyatītakalā: chart, 866; *kalā,* 742
Śāradā Devī, Śrī: dates, 637
Śaraṇā: def., 811
Sarasvatī: def., 811; Śakti, 803
Sarasvatī, Dayānanda: life and work, 635-636
Sarasvatī River: research dating, 608
Śaravaṇa: def., 811; and Lord Kārttikeya, 69

Sārī: description, 811; girl's first, 273; proper temple garb, 329; traditional home garb, 667
Śarīra: chart, 866; def., 811; *kośa,* 750; list, 811; soul, 823; subtle body, 829
Sārūpya: attainment of *yoga pāda,* likeness to God, 689; 777
Sarvabhadra: def., 811
Sarvajñānottara Āgama: content, 811
Sarvāṅgāsana: *āsana,* 686
Śashṭāṅga praṇāma: alternate term for *ashṭāṅga praṇāma,* 787
Śāstra: def., 811
Śāstrī: def., 811; description, 361
Sat: def., 812
Śātakarnī: destroys Śaka kingdom, 621
Satan: def., 812; nonexistence, 155
Śatapatha Brāhmaṇa: contents, 812
Satchidānanda: def., 812; icons representing, 57; and *jñāna pāda,* 115; monistic theism, 423; Parāśakti, 53; realization of, 51, 113; Śaiva Siddānta and Smārta views, 812; soul's oneness with, 83, 137, 435
Satchidānanda, Swāmī: founds Integral Yoga Institute and Light of Truth Universal Shrine, 641
Satguru: *Āgamas,* 492; children taught to follow, 664; creed belief, 481; def., 812; description, 359; *dharma saṅga,* 667; guides *sannyāsins,* 345; guides in *yoga pāda,* 113; initiation from, 349; need for, 151, 185, 365; role, 812; spiritual leader, 357; spiritually awakened master, xxi; unique function, 365
Satgurunātha: def., 812
Satputra mārga: *charyā pāda,* 776, 111
Sattva: def., 727; Śiva as Vishṇu, 49; and *triśūla,* 445
Sattva guṇa: def., 812; *guṇa,* 727
Satya: def., 812, 862; guideline, 187
Satyaloka: chart, 866; def., 812; *loka,* 754
Śaucha: def., 812, 862; guideline, 187; purity-impurity, 791
Saumanasya: def., 812
Savikalpa Samādhi: def., 812; Parāśakti, experience of, 781; in Śaivism, 113, 529
Sāyujya: def., 813; Pāśupata, 502; Śivasāyujya, 820-821, 365
Scarlet: def., 813
Scepter: def., 813; of rulers, Kārttikeya empowers, 71
School: on subtle plane, 127
Science(s): Gaṇeśa, patron of, 65; *kalā-64,* 742-743; in scripture, 387
Scientology: belief, 575
Scriptural references: dating by precession of equinoxes, 607
Scriptures: *Āgamas,* 528; Buddhist, 534; Christian, 566; Confucian, 550; daily study, 257; death, reading before, 101; def., 813; of Hindu sects, 524, 602; Hindu, 373; Islamic, 570; Jain, 538; Judaic, 564; Kashmīr Śaiva, 510; key to marriage problems, 233; learning in *kriyā pāda,* 111; listening to, 189, 283; secondary, 387-393; sectarian, 373; Shinto, 554; Sikh, 542; Taoist, 546; Vaishṇava, 25; *Vedas,* 375, 377, 528; Zoroastrian, 558
Sculpture: Indian medieval style, 623
Secluded: def., 813
Secrets: *guru* protocol, 363
Sects: Buddhist, 534; Christian, 566; Confucian, 550; Hindu, see *Sects, Hindu,* below; Islamic, 570; Jain, 538; Judaic, 562; Sikh, 542; Taoist, 546; Zoroastrian, 558
Sects, Hindu: *Āgamas* unify, 381; compared, 528-531; Hindu solidarity, 731; marrying within same, 227
Sectarian(ism): identity marks, 261; Smārtism discourages, 822; *tilaka,* 840; universalist, 845

Secular humanism: beliefs, 588-589; summary, 588
Secular movements: comparative summaries, 573-581
Seed *karma:* def., 813, 746
Seer(s): def., 813; lineage of, 395; *ṛishi,* 361, 798
Sekkilar: life and work, 628; *Periyapurāṇam,* 784
Self (God): attainability, 11; def., 813; nature of, 13, 51, 83; *satguru* leads one to, 365; scripture on, 14; Śiva Advaita, 513; Śiva is, 49; sought at death, 101; sought after worship, 307; *Yajur Veda,* 88
Self-assertive: def., 813; society's antagonists, 199
Self-control: and good conduct, 181; needed for peace on earth, 203
Selfishness: removing through *kavadi,* 289; results of, 95
Selflessness: in marriage, 225; monastic goal, 343; results of, 95
Selfless service: and path of enlightenment, 107; see also *Charyā*
Self-luminous: def., 813
Self Realization: *abhaya* is fruit of, 675; all strive for at death, 87; *annamaya kośa* needed, 749; *anupāya,* 684; beyond the mind (universal); def., 813; door of Brahman, 714; enlightenment, 716; evolution after, 81; evolution of the soul, 718; God Realization (terms compared), 724; and grace, 725; *jñāna* is the fruit of, 107; Kashmīr Śaivism, 748; life's purpose, 7, 13; Paraśiva, 762; *purushārtha,* 792; San Mārga leads to, 808; *sannyāsa dīkshā,* 810; *satguru* guides, 363, 812; scripture speaks on, 14, 88-89; and *siddhis,* 817; Śivasāyujya, 820-821
Self-reflection: def., 813; leads to oneness with God, 11
Sembiyan Mā, Devī: reign and contributions, 626
Sen, Keshab Chandra: founds Brāhmo Samāj, 636-637
Senses (five): chart, 868, 869; faith and, 719; *indriya,* 734; *manomaya kośa* is seat of, 749-750; physical plane, 125; *tattva,* 838
Sense withdrawal: *pratyāhāra,* 794; *yoga,* description, 113
Sepoy Mutiny: first Indian Revolution, 637
Servitude: def., 813
Sevā: in *charyā pāda,* 109; def., 812-813
Seval: description, 813; symbol, 385
Seven steps: of marriage rite, 273
Sex: education for children, 241; Hindu view, 217, 219; *Kāma,* a goal of life, 793; in marriage, 219, 233; purity, 187
Sexuality: def., 814; nunk transmutes, 774; purity-impurity, 792
Shaḍ darśana: descriptions, 814
Shamanism: def., 815
Shame: *niyama (hrī),* 189, 862; obstacle, 255
Shaṅkar, Ravi: founds National Orchestra of India, 641
Shaṇmata sthāpanāchārya: def., 815
Shaṇmukha: def., 815
Shaṇmukha Gāyatrī: description, 815
Shashṭyābda pūrti: def., 815; marriage renewal at age sixty, 277
Shaṭkoṇa: def., 815; symbol, 223
Shaṭsthala: def., 815; six-fold Vīra Śaiva path, 508
Shatter: def., 815
Shaṭuraṅga: forerunner of chess, 622
Shaven head: ascetic, 345; *chūḍākaraṇa,* 670, 701 807; *sannyāsa* initiation, 349
Shaving beard: *keśānta,* 749, 807
Sheath: cosmology, 866-867; def., 815; *kośa,* 79, 749
Shelter: for child, 241

Shintoism: adherents, 554; beliefs, 556; comparative summary, 554-556; founder, 554; founding, 554; goals, 555; path of attainment, 555; scriptures, 554; synopsis, 554
Shoḍaśa upāchāras: sixteen acts of worship, 493
Shum: description, 815
Shuttle: def., 815
Siddha: def., 816; description, 361; Gorakshanātha, 517; Kadaitswāmī, 453; Kailāsa Paramparā, 449, 742; Kashmīr Śaivism, 510; Nātha, 770; Sadyojyoti, 496; Tirumular, 494
Siddha Mārga: def., 816
Siddhānta: def., 816; extolled, 395; Jain scripture, 538; growth of Indian spirituality, xx; see *Śaiva Siddhānta*
Siddhānta Śravaṇa: religious practice, 189; def., 817, 862
Siddha Siddhānta: history, philosophy, 516-520; def., 816; school, 21
Siddha Siddhānta Paddhati: contents, 816; and Gorakshanātha, 516; *yoga* text, 393; written, 627
Siddha yoga: def., 816; Gorakshanātha, 516-519, 724; Kailāsa Paramparā, 449; Kashmīr Śaivism, 510, 748; Nātha, 770; Śaiva sects, 21; Śaiva Siddhānta, 495; *Tirumantiram,* treatise of, 395, 841
Siddha yogī: def., 816-817; Gorakshanātha, 517; Nātha, 770
Siddha Yogī Sampradāya: def., 817
Siddhi: def., 817; Kadaitswāmī, 453; Nātha, 770; Tirumular, 451
Śikhara: def., 817
Sikhism: adherents, 542; beliefs, 544; comparative summary, 542-544; def., 817; founder, 542; founding, 542, 818; goals, 543; path of attainment, 543; scripture, 542; sects, 542; synopsis, 542; *Vedas,* 417
Sikh kingdoms: timeline, 629-634
Sikshā Vedāṅga: description, 817; *Vedāṅga,* 852
Silappathikaram: written, 620
Śilpani: works of art, 264
Śilpa Śāstra: contents, 817
Śilpi: scriptures on, 264, 308
Sīmantonnayana: def., 817; description, 806; prenatal rite, 275
Sin: def., 817-818; evil and, 717; Hindu view, 151-159; inherent, 735; mortal, 764; release from, 71; scripture, 146, 160-161
Sind region: Muslim conquest, 625
Singh, Govind: assassination, 634
Singh, Dr. Karan: life, 642
Singh, Rañjīt: defeated, 636
Singing: temple, 307
Śishya: def., 818; description, 361; and *satguru,* 365
Sisters: safety and care of, 247
Śiva: abides in all, 21, 123, 129; Absolute Being, 51; *Āgamas* on, 43; *ātman,* 493; cause in Śaiva Siddhānta, 431; cosmic body, 513, 517; cosmic dissolution, 439; and His creation, 63, 79, 123, 145, 433, 513; def., 818; description, 49-57; destroyer, 493; divine dance, xviii, 59; and evil, 437; feet of, 59; festivals, 285; grace, 515; Indus Valley, 611; invoking, 313; Ishṭa Devatā (25 forms), 737; Kashmīr Śaivism, 511-512; life energy, 5; love, 33, 409; merger in, 13; mind, 53; Namaḥ Śivāya, 403, 405; Nātha Sampradāya, 447; Pañchākshara Mantra, 401; Parameśvara, 781; Parāśakti, 781; Pāśupatas, 500, 502; perfections, 49; Rudra, 799; *Sadāśiva,* 799-800; *satguru,* 365; scripture speaks on, 15, 42; *shaṭkona,* 223; Siddha Siddhānta, 517, 518; silent sage, 17; soul, 23, 81, 83, 425; Tryambaka, 844; Vīra Śaivism, 508; visions, 55; worship, 27, 35, 57, 63,

283; and wrongdoers, 159
Śivāchāra: def., 818; among *pañchāchāra*, 777-778
Śiva Advaita: explanation, 818-819; history and philosophy, 512-516; school of Śaivism, 21
Śivachaitanya: def., 818, Śiva consciousness, 819
Śivāchārya: def., 818-819; training and duties, 319
Śiva consciousness: def., 819
Śivadayāl: life, 635
Śiva Dṛishṭi: authorship, 819
Śivaji: restores Muslim territory to Hindu control, 632
Śivajñānabodham: contents, 819; Meykandar, 498
Śivakarṇāmṛita: contents, 819
Śivālaya: def., 819
Śivaliṅga: def., 819-820; scriptures speak on, 322-323, 336-337; significance, 57; see also *Liṅga*
Śivaloka: chart, 866; def., 753-754, 820; description, 129; Śiva's creation, 123; soul's evolution, 87; three worlds, highest of, 839-840
Śivamaya: def., 820
Śivamayakośa: def., 820; *kośa,* 750
Sivanadiyar: def., 820
Śivānanda: Śāntyatītakalā, superconsciousness, 866
Śivānanda, Swāmī: Divine Life Society founder, born, 639; profile, 832
Śivaness: def., 820
Śivānubhava Maṇḍapa: def., 820, Vīra Śaivism, 505
Śiva Purāṇa: def., 820; on Śiva, 493
Śiva Rakshāmaṇi Dīpikā: def., 820
Śivarātrī: def., 820; see *Mahāśivarātri*
Śiva-Śakti: creed belief, 469; def., 820; Parameśvara, 781; Primal Soul, 55; *Tirumantiram* on, 57
Śiva Saṁhitā: contents, 820; Siddha Siddhānta, 518; written, 633
Śivaśaraṇā: def., 820; Vīra Śaiva saints, 504
Śivasāyujya: def., 820-821; *kuṇḍalinī,* 751; path to, 365
Śiva Sūtra(s): contents, 821; date, 626; finding, 510; *yoga* text, 393
Śiva tattva: chart, 867, 869; def., 836
Śiva temple: 299-307; see *Temple*
Sivathondan: def., 821
Sivathondu: def., 821
Śivāya Namaḥ: def., 403, 821
Skanda: flag, 27; creed belief, 473 def., 821
Skanda Shashṭhī: description, 821; festival, 283, 289
Skills: *kalā,* traditional list, 742-743; taught to boys and girls, 245
Skin color: caste and, 171
Skull: Kāpālikas, 502-503; penance, emblem of, for murder, 780
Slavery: abolished in British Commonwealth, 636; ban on importation in U.S., 635; Emancipation Proclamation, 638
Sleep: gaining knowledge, 409; people in, 127; subtle plane, 127
Śloka: def., 821; Hindu catechism, xxvi-xxvii; study method, xxx
Smārta: def., 821
Smārta Sampradāya: def., 821
Smārtism: on *avatāra* doctrine, 601; description, 821-822; emergence, 616; goals, 530; major scriptures, 602; path of attainment, 531; personal God, 600, 601; regions of influence, 603; on Śakti, 601; on soul and God, 602; spiritual practice, 602
Smṛiti: contents, 822; date of composition, 617; devotional hymns, 393; epics and myths, 391; philosophy, 393; recognition of, 387; and sacred literature, 387; Smārta, 27; synopsis, 822; touchstone of culture, 387; *Vedas* and *Āgamas* amplified in, 389; *yoga,* 393

Snare: def., 822; bird analogy, 139
Social changes: adaptation, 37
Social *dharma:* description, 171; God's law, 167; see also *Dharma*
Society: and absolution 153; Bhārata, 377; class and caste, 171, and marriage, 211; needs religious people, 35; defines *varṇa dharma,* 850; withdrawal from, 277
Socrates: dates, 618
Solace: def., 822
Soldier: Kārttikeya, 69
Solemn: def., 822
Soliloquy: def., 822
Solitaire: def., 822
Solomon, King: fleet in India, 616
Soma: amṛita, 682; elixir, 716
Somānanda: life and work, 822-823
Somanātha: location, 823; Pāśupata temple, 501
Son: duties of eldest, 231; follows father's profession, 245
Song: and *Āgama* philosophy, 493; Gāyatrī, 723; *Sāma Veda,* 805; in secondary scriptures, 387
Sorrow: bound to joy, 151; obstacle, 255; see *Joy*
Soul: *Āgamas,* 379; *ātman,* 689; body, 79, 423, 425, 823; bringing into birth, 239; creation, 435, 471, 475; creed belief, 471; death transition, 277; def., 79, 823; description, 79-85; destiny, 13, 81, 87, 597, 425; East-West views of, xxiv; essence, 823; eternality, 99; evolution, 107, 717-718; five sheaths, 79; God, identity with, 83, 431, 435; God Śiva's child, 137; good and evil, 141; goodness of, 137; Hindu sects' views, 528, 602; individual, 734; intellect, 141; *jīva,* 739; *jñāna pāda,* 115; *kriyā pāda,* 111; limitlessness, 159; merger, 760, 81, 439; monism, 417; Pāśupata view, 502; Primal, 789; purity, 181; reincarnation, 79, 97, 796; scripture on, 88; Siddhānta views, 433, 435, 437; Śiva Advaita, 513; Śiva likeness, 55, 81, 123; suffering, 151; in Vīra Śaivism, 508; world, attitude toward, 145
Sound: def., 823-824; *nāda,* 766
Soundless Sound: level of *nāda,* 766; Śiva *tattva* (Paranāda), 837
Sovereign: def., 824
Sow: def., 824
Space: cosmic dissolution, 131, 439
Space age: inner and outer, xvii
Span: def., 824
Spanda: Kashmīr Śaivism, 511
Spanda Kārikā: contents, 824
Spanda Śāstra: Kashmīr Śaivism, 510
Spanish influenza: epidemic toll, 641
Spanish Inquisition: beginning, 630
Spark: analogy, 419, 716; def., 824
Sparśa tattva: chart, 869; def., 838
Spectrum: def., 824
Speculate: def., 824
Sphaṭika: def., 824
Sphaṭika Śivaliṅga: def., 824
Sphere: def., 824
Spinoza, Baruch: contribution, 824; pantheist, 419
Spiritual evolution: *adhyātma prasāra,* 677; def., 824
Spiritualism: trance, 843
Spirituality: cognition and Kārttikeya, 69; consciousness and peace, 203; development and temple worship, 327; discipline, 11, 195; growth and suffering, 151; is honored, 357; knowledge and *vel,* 71; lineage of *gurus,* 449; mysticism, 766; practice, Hindu, 602; qualities, 39; preceptor relationship, 363; path of striving, 7; rites of passage, 269
Spiritual unfoldment: *adhyātma vikāsa,* 677; catalyst, 698; def., 824-825; *jñāna,* 739; *jñāna pāda,* 740; *karma* catalyzes, 95; in marriage,

227; *padma* symbolizes, 121, 777; *sādhana,* 800, *śaktipāta,* 804; *seval* symbolizes, 385
Splendor: def., 825
Spokes of a wheel: analogy, 275, 377
Spouse: def., 825; and joint family, 231, 740; loyalty, 219; selecting, 229
Sraddhā: def., 825; faith, 719; Hindu beliefs, xx; Śaivite creed, 463-487
Srāddha: death commemoration, 277; def., 825; timing, 825
Śraddhādhāraṇā: def., 825; Śaivite creed, 463-487
Śrauta: def., 825
Śrauta Śāstra: contents, 825; *Kalpa Vedāṅga,* 744; scripture, 389; *Vedāṅga,* 852; *yajña rites* in, 860
Śrī: def., 825; Śakti, 804
Śrī Chakra: description, 863; in Śāktism, 23; *yantra,* 862-863
Śrīkaṇṭha: and Appaya Dīkshita, 514; life and work, 512; profile, 825; and Śiva Advaita, 512
Śrīkṛishṇakīrtan: written, 630
Śrīkula: Śakti, Goddess family, 804
Śrīkumāra: life and work, 825; and Śaiva Siddhānta, 497
Sri Lanka: civil war, 645; dominion status, 642; and Kailāsa Paramparā, 449; location, 825; Yogaswāmī, 455
Srinagara: and Kashmīr Śaivism, 509; location, 825
Śrīnātha: identification, 825; and monistic theism, 509
Śrī pādukā: identification, 825; symbol, 355; see *Holy feet*
Śrī Rudram: chanted at Mahāśivarātri, 285*:* description, 826
Sṛishṭi: def., 770, 826
Śrotra tattva: chart, 869; def., 838
Śruti: amplified in *smṛiti,* 387; *Āgamas,* 379, 381; dating, 375, 379; discussion, 373; orally conveyed, 373; scripture speaks on, 382, 383; synopsis, 826; *Vedas,* 375, 377
Stages: attainment in Kashmīr Śaivism, 511; life and *dharma,* 173; manifestation in 36 *tattvas,* 123; of inner progress, 481
Stars: influence, 259; *jyotisha,* 741; *nakshatra,* 767; *ṛita* guides, 169
Stave off: def., 826
Steadfast: def., 826; guideline, 187
Steam locomotive: built, 635
Stein, Sir Aurel: finds shards, 642
Sterilization: in Hinduism, 217
Sthapati: defin, 826; hereditary temple builders, 301
Sthāpatyaveda: contents, 826; scripture, 389; *Upaveda,* 847
Sthiti: def., 770, 826
Sthūla śarīra: chart, 867; def., 826-827; *śarīra,* 811
Stinginess: def., 827; obstacle, 255
Stoics: def., 827; pantheist, 419
Strangers: hospitality, 263
Strī dharma: def., 827; description, 215, 711
Stubbornness: dancing with Śiva, 9
Student: stage in *āśrama dharma,* 687, 173; *brahmachārī,* 696
Subāla Upanishad: contents, 827
Subatomic: def., 827; *ṛita,* 169
Subconscious: aura reflects, 690; conscience, 702-703; def., 761; dross and *satguru,* 365; impressed by rites of passage, 269; and sin, 818; *saṁskāra chitta,* 866; subliminal traits, 255; *vāsanā,* 851
Śubha muhūrta: def., 827; morning worship and *sādhana,* 259
Subjective: def., 827; world, 125
Sublime: def., 827
Subliminal: def., 827; traits, 255
Subramaṇya: def., 827
Subramuniyaswami, Sivaya: satguru Kailāsa Paramparā, 449, 641-642; ordination, 455; life and work, 827; meaning of term, 827; teaching mission, 643

Subside: def., 828
Substance: def., 828; Primal, 789
Substratum: def., 828
Subsubconscious mind: aura reflects; def., 761; *vāsanā chitta,* 866
Subsuperconscious mind: *anukāraṇa chitta,* 762, 866; def., 761; *kriyā,* 115
Subtle body: def., 829
Subtle plane: astral plane, 688; chart, 866; def., 753-754; description, 127; three worlds, 123, 839
Successor: def., 829
Śuchi of Magadha: birth, 616
Sūchi: def., 829
Sudāsa I, King: birth, 614
Śuddha māyā: actinic, 677; def., 836
Śuddha Śaiva Siddhānta: Advaita Siddhānta, 678-679; def., 829; philosophy, 395; *Tirumantiram* on, 33, 495, 381
Śuddhāśuddha tattvas: chart, 867, 869; def., 837
Śuddha tattvas: chart, 867, 869; def., 836-837
Śuddhavidyā tattva: chart, 867, 869; def., 829, 837
Śūdra: caste, 698; def., 829, 850; *dharma,* 171
Suffering: attitude of wise, 151; creation of, 157; *karma,* 139; scripture, 160-161; and sin, 153; source, 137
Suicide: consequences, 101; def., 829
Śukla Yajur Veda: See *Yajur Veda*
Sūkshma śarīra: chart, 868; def., 830; *śarīra,* 811
Sūkta: Ṛig Veda, hymns of, 798
Śulba Śāstras: def., 830; *Kalpa Vedāṅga,* 744, 389; *Vedāṅga,* 852
Sully: def., 830
Sultan of Delhi: Muhammedan, 628
Sun: Sūrya, 831; symbol, 415
Sundaranāthar: identification, 830; see *Tirumular*
Sundararar: bhakti movement, 495; life, 624, Nalvar, 767; Nayanar, 771; profile, 830; *Tirumurai,* 841-842
Suṅga: timeline, 619-620
Sunnis: Islam sect, 570
Śūnya: Buddhism, 536; in Vīra Śaivism, 507; *sahasrāra chakra,* 868
Śūnya Sampādane: contents, 830; Vīra Śaiva scripture, 508
Superconscious (mind): causal plane, 129; chart, 866; conscience, 702-703; def., 761, 762; good conduct, 157; good and evil, 141; Satchidānanda, 812; soul, 79; *yoga,* 115
Supernatural: def., 830
Supplicate: def., 830
Suprabheda Āgama: contents, 830
Supreme: def., 830
Supreme Being: form, xxv; see *Absolute Being; All-pervasive God; God*
Supreme God: def., 830
Sūrdās: life and work, 393, 830-831
Surgery: father of, 616-617
Surinam: prejudice, 644
Surpass: def., 831
Surrender: def., 831; *prapatti,* 787
Sūrya: importance, 831; Smārtism, 27; symbol, 415; Tai Pongal, 291
Sushumṇā (nāḍī): Ardhanārīśvara, 665; def., 831; central *nāḍī,* 767; *daṇḍa,* 707; door of Brahman, 714; *kuṇḍalinī,* 751; monastic, 347; *namaskāra,* 768; Śakti, 804; spiritual unfoldment, 824; *tantra,* 834; *tantrism,* 834; *triśūla,* 445; *videhamukti,* 855
Sushupti: consciousness, 703
Suśruta, Vaidya: father of surgery, 616-617
Sustainable: def., 831
Sustenance: def., 831
Sutala (chakra): chart, 868; def., 831; location, 700, Naraka, 768
Sūta Saṁhitā: contents, 831
Sūtra: def., xxvi-xxvii; structure, 831
Sutta-Nipatta: scripture, 534
Sūryavarman I, King: builds Angkor

Wat, 628
Svadharma: def., 831; description, 175, 711; one's own way, 167
Svādhishṭhāna chakra: chart, 868; def., 831; location, 700
Svādhyāya: def., 831; parental guideline, 667; *niyama,* 862
Svānubhuti: evolution of the soul, 718
Svapna: consciousness, astral, 703
Svarga: def., 831; and Svarloka, 832
Svarloka: astral plane, 688; chart, 866; def., 832; three worlds, 838
Svātmarāma: writing, 629, 729
Svayambhū Liṅga: def., 832
Svāyambhuva Āgama: def., 832
Svāyambhuva Sūtra(s): def., 832
Śvetāmbara: Jain sect, 620
Śvetāśvatara Upanishad: contents, 832
Swāmī: def., 832; consulting, 185; description, 343, 361; honored, 263
Swāminī: def., 832
Swastika: def., 832; symbol, 135
Swirl: def., 832
Symbolism: def., 832
Syncretism: def., 832; Hindu, 417; universalist, 845
Synonymous: def., 833
Synthesis: def., 833

Tagore, Rabīndranāth: life and work, 833; Nobel Prize, 638; poet, 393
Tai Pongal: description, 833; harvest festival, 291
Tai Pusam: description, 833; Kārttikeya festival, 283, 289
Taittirīya Āraṇyaka: def., 833
Taittirīya Saṁhitā: Yajur Veda, 861
Taittirīya Upanishad: contents, 833
Tala: chart, 868; def., 833; Naraka, 768
Talātala (chakra): chart, 868; def., 700, 833, Naraka, 768-769
Tali: wedding pendant, 859
Tamas: guṇa, 727; Śiva as Rudra, 49; and *triśūla,* 445
Tamasic: def., 833
Tamerlane: invades India, 630
Tamil: affirmation of faith, 407; def., 834; and Tirumular, 495
Tamil karttanam: written, 633
Tamil Nadu: location, 834; and Śaivism, 491
Tamil Saṅgam: timeline, 617-618
Tāṇḍava: def., 834, Naṭarāja, 769
Tanmatra: def., 838
Tantra: āyurveda, 259; def., 834; Śiva's Absolute Being, 51; Śāktism, 23; Vedic methods, 255
Tantrāloka: Abhinavagupta, 510; author, 834
Tantrika: def., 834
Tantrism: def., 834-835
Tantric rites: Śāktism, 23, 527
Tao: def., 835; *ṛita,* 169
Taoism: adherents, 546; beliefs, 548; comparative summary, 546-548; founding, 546; goals, 547; path of attainment, 547; scripture, 546; sects, 546; synopsis, 546-548
Tao-te-Ching: scripture, 546; 377
Tapas: Advaita Siddhānta, 679; austerity, 690-691; *daṇḍa,* 707; def., 835, 862; *jīvanmukta,* 739; Kadaitswāmī, 741; *karma,* 747; liberation, 151; monastic, 341; and Nātha Sampradāya, 447; *pāpa,* 780; Pāśupata, 499; penance, 783; performance of, 189; *puṇya,* 791; purity-impurity, 791; *sannyāsin,* 810; and *satguru,* 365; *siddhi,* 817; sin, 818; *vel,* 71; *yoga tapas,* 115
Tapasvin: def., 361, 835; *haṭha yoga,* 728; monastic, 763
Tapoloka: chart, 866; def., 835; *loka,* 754; three worlds, 839
Tarnished: def., 835
Tat: def., 835

Tātparyadīpikā: contents, 835; Śrikumāra, 497
Tat Sat: def., 836
Tattva: chart, 867, 869; creation, 123; def., 836-838; groups, 836; scripture on, 427
Tattva Prakāśa: def., 838; and Śaiva Siddhānta, 497
Tayumanavar: life and work, 634, 838
Teachers: *swāmīs* as, 345
Tears: Rudra, 799; Śiva, 399; see also *Rudkrāksha,* 799
Technical skills: training boys, 245
Technology: and religion, 37; training on subtle plane, 127
Tejas tattva: chart, 867, 869; def., 838
Temper: def., 838
Temple: activities, 307; *Āgamas,* 373, 379, 493; attendance, 303; behavior, 305; building, 301; center of Śaivism, 39; def., 838; description, 299-307; entry, 305; festivals, 283; flag, 461; gateways, 297; and Kālāmukhas, 503; North Indian, 105; priests, 319; scripture, 308-309
Temple worship: common to Hindu sects, 19, 485; culture and, 707; Nātha Sampradāya, 447; purpose, 485; Śaiva Siddhānta, 21, 431; relation to the fine arts, 261; scripture, 322-323; *Vedas* used daily, 377
Temporal: def., 838
Temporary body: image of God, 317
Tend: def., 838
Ten-day festival: annual, Brahmotsava, 697; Śiva temples, 307
Teotihuacan: growth of, 621
Teradi: abode of Chellappan, 453; def., 838-839
Terminable: def., 839
Terminal: def., 839
Terminal illness: def., 839; self-willed death, 101; suicide, 829-830
Terror: ingested, 201
That: def., 839
Theater: secondary scriptures, 387
Theism: belief, 419; def., 839; monistic theism, 763-763; monotheism, 764; panentheism, 779; pantheism, 779; presence in *Vedas, Āgamas* and hymns of saints, 425; reality of God, 423; Śaivism, 33
Theodosius, Emperor: pagan temples destroyed, 622
Theologians: *swāmīs* as, 345
Theological tradition: Hindu, 447
Theology: def., 839
Thirst: obstacle, 255
Three-hundred-thirty million Gods: created by Śiva, 63; Mahādevas, 775
Thither: def., 839
Thomas, Saint: death, 60
Thou/thy: def., 839
Three bonds: in *Āgamas*, 492; see *Pāśa; Mala*
Three perfections: existence after *mahāpralaya,* 131; of Śiva, 49; see also *Perfections (Śiva's three)*
Three pillars: of Śaivism, 39, 101, 299
Three worlds: belief in, 477; chart, 866-867, commune at temple, 299, 301, 331; def., 839; dissolved at *mahāpralaya,* 131; scripture on, 132; Śiva is source, 49, 123; sustained by Śiva, 53
Thugees: suppressed by British, 636
Thwart: def., 840
Thy: See *Thou/thy*
Tilaka: applied, 257; def., 840; Hindu identity, 261; importance, 840; sacred symbol of, xxvi
Time: cosmic dissolution, 439; created by Śiva, 123; cyclic dissolution by Śiva, 131; Gaṇeśa, God of, 67; in Naṭarāja, 41; symbol of, 605
Timeless: def., 840
Timeline: chronology of events, xxviii; dating dispute, 607; Hindu, 607-647; how to read, 610
Timepiece: first worn, 625

Timing events: *Jyotisha Vedāṅga,* 389
Tirobhāva: def., 770, 840
Tirodhāna Śakti: def., 840
Tīrtha, Mādhya Ānanda: life and work, 628
Tīrtha: holy sites, 840
Tīrtha, Rāma: spreads Vedānta, 638
Tīrthayātrā: children taught, 666; def., 840; good conduct, 185
Tiru: def., 840
Tirukural: basis, 395; charity, 263; contents, 840-841; Tiruvalluvar, 842; written, 620
Tirumantiram: Āgama authority, 431; basis of this catechism, 395; *charyā pāda,* 109; *kriyā pāda,* 111; synopsis, 841; teaching, 494-495; and Tirumular, 451; treatise of *siddha yoga,* 395; *yoga* text, 393
Tirumular: Śaiva Siddhānta, 495; and Kailāsa Paramparā, 449; life and work, 619; Meykandar comparison, 431; monistic theist, 425; profile, 841; saying of praise, xix; *siddha,* 496; on Śiva's dance, v, xix; story of, 451
Tirumurai: anthologized, 627; authors, 841-842; basis, 395; contents, 842; Nayanar, authors, 771; Śaiva saints, 495
Tiruvalluvar: life and work, 620, 842; *Tirukural,* 840-841
Tiruvasagam: contents, 842; Maṇikkavasagar, 393, 495; written, 626
Tiruvavaduthurai: Tirumular, 451
Tithe: def., 842; Hindus, 263; religious practice, 189
Tithis: days of worship, 285; def., 842-843; names listed, 843
TM: Transcendental Meditation, prominence, 644
Tolerance: acknowledgement of many paths, xviii; *ahiṁsā,* 197; children learn, 663; openmindedness, 658; peace, 203
Torah: Judaic scripture, 562, 377
Torment: and Naraka, 155
Touchstone: def., 843; sacred literature, 387
Trade: British trading post in India, 633; Indus Valley cities with Mesopotamia, 614; Silk Roads, 621
Tradition: Śaivite, 39; *sannyāsin* follows, 351; *smṛiti* as, 387
Traits: def., 843; source in *saṁskāras,* 255; see also *Vāsanā*
Trance: def., 843; mediumship in Śāktism, 23
Tranquil: def., 843
Transcend: def., 843
Transcendence: God, 425
Transcendent: def., 843
Transcendental Meditation (TM), practice of, 644
Transfix: def., 843
Transgress: def., 843
Transient: def., 843
Transition: def., 843
Traverse: def., 843
Treacherous: def., 843
Tread: def., 843
Treatise: def., 843
Trepidation: def., 843
Tribal: def., 843, Hinduism, 417; shamanism, 815
Tribalism: belief, 576
Trickery: def., 844
Trident: def., 844; Pāśupatas, 499; symbol, 445, *triśūla,* 844
Trikaśāsana: def., 844; Kashmīr Śaivism, 510, philosophy, 844
Trikoṇa: def., 844; symbol, 371
Triloka: def., 844
Trimūrti: def., 844; see Brahmā, 696
Trinidad: Indian laborers to, 637
Tripitaka: Buddhist scripture, 534
Triple bondage: belief, 471; soul, 85; see also *Mala; Pāśa*
Tripuṇḍra: def., 844; symbol, 31; *tilaka,* 840

Triśūla: symbol, 445, 844; worshipful icon, 57
Truth: def., 844; one, 35; search, 151
Truthfulness: guideline, 187
Tryambaka: def., 844; emblems, 844; Gāyatrī Mantra, 723; Śaivism, 509
Tukārām: life and work, 632, 844
Tulasīdāsa: life and work, 631,844
Tumult: def., 844
Turbulent: def., 844
Turks: defeat Hindu confederacy, 627; Mahmud plunders Somanāth Śiva temple, 627
Turīya: consciousness, 703; reincarnation, 797; superconscious, 761
Turmeric: def., 844
Tvak tattva: chart, 869; def., 838
Twain, Mark: visits India, 640
Tyaf: def., 844; *lekhaprārtha havana,* 752
Tyāga: def., 845; in *yajña,* 860

Ucçhāraṇa vyākhyā: def., 845
Ucçhishṭa: def., 845; *guru's* sandals, 363
Udgāta: Sāma Veda, priests of, 805
Uganda: Indians expelled, 644
Ujjain: location, 845
Ultimate: def., 845
Umā: def., 845; in Śāktism, 23
UNCED: See *Earth Summit*
Unconnectedness: def., 845
Uncreated: def., 845
Undecaying: def., 845
Undifferentiated: def., 845
Unerring: def., 845
Unevolutionary perfection: def., 845; Primal Soul, 81
Unfold: def., 845
Unharness: def., 845
Unhindered: def., 845
United Nations: founding, 642
Universal *dharma:* def., 845; God's law, 167, 169; see also *Ṛita*
Universal dissolution: def., 845; see *Mahāpralaya*
Universalism: belief, 575
Universalist: def., 845
Universe: cosmology chart, 866; description, 131; and Parāśakti, 53; revealed in Namaḥ Śivāya, 405; scripture on, 133; Śiva's dance, 9; three worlds, 839; world, 859-860
Unleash: def., 845
Unmanifest Reality: description, 51; def., 845-846; see *Absolute Being*
Unoriginated: def., 846
Unpretentiousness: def., 846
Unrepressed: def., 846
Unshrouded: def., 846
Unwind: def., 846
Upa: def., 846
Upādāna kāraṇa: cause, 699; material cause, 758
Upadeśa: def., 846
Upadeśī: def., 846; *satgurus* as, 359; see also *Nirvāṇī* and *upadeśī*
Upāgama: contents, 846; secondary scripture, 389
Upagrantha: def., 846
Upanayana: description, 807; initiation, 846, 671, 271
Upanishad: advaita, 678; contents, 846; dates, 847; and Emerson, 635; parts, xxix; *Ṛig Veda,* 798; Śaiva Siddhānta, 498; and Smārtism, 27; translation, 377; Vedānta, 852; Vedas, 375
Upāsanā: children taught, 665; def., 847; religious practice, 185; *sannyāsin's,* 810; *Vedas* guide, 377
Upasarga: def. and lists, 847; twenty obstacles, 255
Upastha tattva: chart, 869; def., 838
Upaveda: contents, 847; secondary scripture, 389

Upāya: def., 847-848; Kashmīr Śaivism, 511
Upbringing: def., 848
Utpaladeva: life and work, 848
USSR: Communist leadership collapses, 646
Utmost: def., 848
Utopian materialism: See *Materialism*
Utsava: aphorism on, 660; children taught, 665; def., 848; religious practice, 185
Utsavaka: def., 848
Uttaraphala: karma, after-effect, 745
Uttarāphalgunī nakshatra: Naṭarāja worship, 285

Vachanas: def., 848, of Vīra Śaivism, 393, 506-507
Vāgbhaṭa: writings, 624
Vāgdāna: betrothal, 273; def., 848
Vāhana: def., 848; of Śiva, 77
Vaidya: def., 848
Vaikāsi Viśākham: description, 848; festival, 283, 289
Vaikuṇṭha: def., 848
Vairāgi: def., 848; Mahāśivarātri, 285
Vaiśeshika: def., 848; description, 814; philosophy, 417
Vaishṇava: Alvar saints, 624; def., 848; renaissance, 621
Vaishṇava vairāgīs: battle for control of Kumbha Mela area, 634
Vaishṇavism: Āgamas, 379; *avatāra* doctrine, 601; description, 25, 848-849; goals, 529-530; on God, 600-601; influence, 602; major scriptures, 602; path of attainment, 530-531; Śakti, 601; sect of Hinduism, 19; soul and God, 602; spiritual practice, 602; Vedānta, 417
Vaishṇavite: def., 849
Vaiśya: caste, 698; def., 849, 850; *dharma,* 171
Vaivasvata: birth, 612
Vakarī school: founding, 629
Vāk tattva: chart, 869; def., 838
Valipadu: def., 849; Śaiva Siddhānta, 431
Vallabhāchārya: life and work, 25, 630, 849; monistic theist, 425
Vāma: def., 849; left-handed, 752; *tantrism,* 835
Vānaprastha āśrama: ceremony, 807; def., 849; description *(āśrama dharma),* 687; retirement, 173
Vanity: release from, 71; removal through *kavadi,* 289
Vanquish: def., 849
Vārāṇasī: earliest records, 617; location, 849; Pāśupatas, 501
Varṇa: caste, 698; def., 850; descriptions, 850-851; *dharma,* 167, 171, 710
Varṇāśrama dharma: def., 851
Vartamāna: kriyamāna, 746
Vāsanā: def., 851; *saṁskāras,* 255; *Yajur Veda* on, 265
Vāsanā chitta: mind (five states), subsubconscious, 761
Vasishṭha: life and work, 851; and Nandinātha, 494
Vasugupta: life and work, 510, 625, 851; philosophy, 425; *Śiva Sūtras* discovered, 626
Vāswanī, Sādhu T.L.: missions and educational institutions, 638-639
Vaṭa: def., 851; symbol, 17
Vāta: def., 851; *dosha,* 714
Vatican: Congregation for Doctrine of Faith condemns *yoga,* 646; papal doctrine of infallibility, 638
Vātsyāyana: writes *Kāma Sūtra,* 622
Vault: def., 851
Vāyu tattva: chart, 867, 869; def., 838
Vedāṇga: Çhandas, 700; synopsis,

852; Jyotisha, 741; Kalpa, 744; Nirukta, 772; among scripture, 389; Śiksha, 817; Vyākaraṇa, 858
Vedānta: advaita, 678; Advaita Siddhānta, 679-680; Advaita Vedānta, 679; on *antaḥkaraṇa,* 684; *bhedābheda,* 694; *Brahma Sūtra,* 697; central scriptures, 512; def., 852-854; Indian spirituality, growth, xx; interpretation, 512; on *māyā,* 759; and monistic theism, 425; *padārtha,* 777; on Satchidānanda, 812; Smārtism, 821; school summaries, 853; among six systems, 417; synopsis, 815; *Upanishad,* 846; Vedic-Āgamic, 854; Viśishṭadvaita, 857
Vedas: Aryans as authors, 609; authority, xxvi, 19; basis, 395; contents, 375, 396; description, 851-852; divinity, xx; Hindu use, 377; monistic theism, 425; Namaḥ Śivāya, 401; number of verses, 660; realizing truth, xxv; rejection, 417; Śāktism, 23; scorned in Vīra Śaivism, 507; scripture on, 373, 382-383, 528; significance, 377; *śruti:* 826; study purpose, 11
Vedic-Āgamic: comparison with Vedānta, 854
Vedic Age: beginning, 613; end, 616
Vedic Saṁhitās: dates, 611, 613
Vegetarianism: *āyurveda,* 259; def., 854; importance, 201; *sannyāsa,* 351, scriptures speak on, 205
Veil: def., 854
Veiling grace: def., 854; Naṭarāja, 770
Vel: def., 854; description, 71; belief, 473; Kārttikeya, 289; symbol, 429
Vellore: See *Chinna Bomman*
Venerate: def., 854
Vengeful: def., 854
Venture: def., 854
Veracity: def., 854
Vermillion: def., 854; dot, 333
Veshṭi: def., 854; temple garb, 329
Vestments: def., 854; *sannyāsin's,* 349
Vibhūti: def., 854-855; temple, 321, 329; Vīra Śaivism, 508
Vice: def., 855
Victoria, Queen: proclaimed ruler of India, 637
Victors and vanquished: attitude of violence, 199; def., 855
Vid: def., 855; *Vedas,* 373
Videhamukti: jīvanmukti and, 739; def., 855; sought at death, 101
Vidyā: def., 855
Vidyākalā: chart, 866; *kalā,* 742
Vidyārambha: childhood rite, 271; def., 855; description, 670, 807
Vidyā tattva: chart, 867, 869; def., 837
Vighneśvara: def., 855; Lord of Obstacles, 67
Vigil: performed daily, 257
Vijaya, Prince: founds Sri Lanka kingdom, 618
Vijayālaya: reestablishes Chola dynasty, 626
Vijayanagara: and Appaya Dīkshita, 514; location, 855
Vijayanagara Empire: destroyed, 632; founded, 629; timeline, 628-630
Vijñānamaya kośa: and astral body, 687-688; def., 750, 855; *māyā tattva,* 837; mental sheath, 79; *śarīra,* 811; soul, 823
Vikings: land in Nova Scotia, 627
Vināyaka: def., 855-856; scripture, 73
Vināyaka Ahaval: identification, 856
Vināyaka Vratam: description, 856; festival, 283, 287
Violence: and *ahiṁsā,* 195; meat eating, 201; returns to originator, 197; source of, 199
Vīra, King: enlarges Śiva temple, 626-627
Vīra Śaivism: aspects, 856; synopsis, 856-857; and Hinduism, 507; Kālāmukhas, 504; history and philoso-

phy, 504-509; school of Śaivism, 21, 802; scriptures, 856
Virginal: def., 856-857
Virginity: and marriage stability, 219; good conduct, 183
Virtue: Eastern and Western views, 595; good conduct, 181, 185; lack of, 157; spiritual path, 107
Visarjana: def., 857; festival, 287
Vishṇu: def., 857; incarnations, 25; Śiva, 49; *śuddhavidyā tattva,* 837; worship in Smārtism, 27
Visions: of Śiva, 55; and temples, 301
Visionary: def., 857
Viśishṭādvaita: description, 857; Vedānta, 853; monistic theism, difference, 423
Visualize: def., 857
Viśuddha chakra: chart, 867; def., 857, 700, subtle plane, 127
Viśvagrāsa: *ānandamaya kośa,* 750; chart, 867; def., 857; destiny beyond *moksha,* 87; evolution of the soul, 718
Viśva Hindu Parishad (VHP): founded, 644
Viśvāsa, faith, 719
Vitala (chakra): chart, 868; def., 857s; location, 700
Vital Breath: def., 819
Vivāha: def., 857; description, 807; marriage rite, 273, 671
Viveka: discrimination, 713
Viveka Chūḍāmaṇi: commentary written, 625; contents, 858
Viveka Mārtaṇḍa: of Gorakshanātha, 517; identification, 858
Vivekānanda, Swāmī: life and work, 638, 858; Parliament of Religions in Chicago, 639
Vivify: def., 858
Void: def., 858
Votary: def., 858
Vrata: def., 858; *niyama,* 189, 862
Vrātyastoma: conversion rite, 705
Vṛitti: def., 858; Satchidānanda and, 812; *vāsanā, 851*
Vyāghrapāda: Kailāsa Paramparā, 449; life and work, 858; in the line of Nandinātha, 494
Vyākaraṇa Vedāṅga: contents, 858; *Vedāṅga,* 852

Wane: def., 859
War: and belief, 199; scriptures on, 389
Warp and woof: def., 859; God is, 147
Warsaw Pact: dissolution, 645
Washington, George: defeats British at Yorktown, 634
Waver: def., 859
Wealth: def., 859; distribution, 263; ear piercing, 271; a goal of life, 87, 263, 792
Weaving: basketry, 613; *kalā,* 743
Weddings: pendant, 273, 859; temple, 307; Vaikāsi Viśākham, 289
Western calendar: timeline, 620-643
Western religions: comparisons with Eastern views, 592-603; major, xxiv; similarities with Eastern religions, 597
Wheel: Vedic analogy, 275, 377
Whence: def., 859
Whirling: def., 859
Whitney, Eli: invents cotton gin, 635
Who am I?: answer, 5
Wickedness: right response to, 141
Widowers: as assistant priests, 319
Wield: def., 859
Wife: adopts religion and lifestyle of husband, 227; aggressiveness, 233; ceremonies during pregnancy, 275; *dharma* of, 173, 211, 215; duty to have children, 239; elder rite of passage, 277; femininity, 233; needs from husband, 211; scripture on,

220-221; sexual union, 217; treatment of husband, 233; working in the world, 215
Will: of God, 55; indomitable, in *yoga,* 51; Kārttikeya, God of, 69
Wisdom: def., 859; *jñāna pāda,* 115; path of enlightenment, 107; rigid rule, 217
Wise: consulting, 357
Withholding: def., 859
Women: and mixed religious marriage, 227; qualities, 215; and *sannyāsa,* 349; scripture, 235; temple during menses, 303
Women saints: Andal, 626, 683; Auvaiyar, 626, 691; Chellachiamman, 642; Janābāī, 629; Karaikkal Ammaiyar, 626; Lallā, 752; Mahādevī, 628; Mīrābāī, 631, 763
Wondrous: def., 859
Woodwind: def., 859
Woof: See *Warp and woof*
Word of God: scripture, 373
Words of Our Master: contents, 859
Work: husband, 213; wife, 215
Workers: See *Indian laborers*
World: in *Āgamas*, 379; best attitude toward, 145; cosmology, 866; def., 859-860; goodness of, 137; monistic view, 417; origin, 132; and Pañchākshara Mantra, 401; renunciation, 343; sacredness, 9; Siddhānta views, 433, 437, 439; threefold, 137, 145, 151; and time, 149
Worldliness: affirmation of faith, 407, 860; *sannyāsin* repudiates, 351
Worldly: def., 860; worldly wise, 860
World religions: Buddhism, 534-536; Christianity, 566-568; comparative summaries, 525-572; Confucianism, 550-552; Hinduism, 528-532; Islam, 570-572; Jainism, 538-540; Judaism, 562-564; populations of, xxi; Shintoism, 554-556; Sikhism, 542-544; Taoism, 546-548; Zoroastrianism, 558-560
World Religious Parliament: titles of "world teacher" bestowed, 645
World War I: ends, 641
World War II: begins, 642
Worship: absolves sin, 153; *Āgamas*, 373, 379, 493; aftermath, 333; belief, 485; ceased, 309; children with parents, 241, 663; before death, 101; description, 313; effect, 331; evening, 333; Gaṇeśa first, 65; God's presence during, 317; good conduct, 185; guide, 189; home shrine, 335; how to, 307; and human *dharma,* 173; importance, 313; individual, 315; inner, 307; internalized, 736; *kriyā pāda,* 111; nature of, Eastern-Western, 596; never outgrown, 327; outer, 307; outside temples, 333; and the path, 107; preparation, 329; priests, 319; reaches causal plane, 129; steps, 321; in the current age, 37; temple, 307; and the *Vedas,* 375, 377
Wrath: def., 860
Written prayers: to God, 331; *lekhaprārtha havana,* 752
Wrongdoing: and God, 157
Wrought: def., 860
Wu, Emperor: reign, 620

Yāgaśālā: yajña, place of, 860
Yajña: def., 860; practices, 860-861; in *Vedas,* 373
Yājñavalkya Smṛiti: contents, 861
Yājñavalkya Upanishad: form, 861
Yajñopavīta: def., 861; *upanayana,* 846
Yajur Veda: contents, 861; among four *Vedas,* 375
Yama (Lord of death): def., 861; *videhamukti,* 855

Yama (restraints): def., 794, 862; description, 187
Yama-niyama: yama, listed, 862; Pāśupata vow, 499
Yantra: Āgamas, 379; def., 862-863; Śāktism, 23
Yea: def., 863
Yengishiki: Shinto scripture, 554
Yield: def., 863
Yoga: Āgamas, 379, 492; and *āyurveda,* 259; *bhakti yoga,* 693-694; causal plane, 129; daily life, 257; when nearing death, 101; def., 863; description, 814-815; Gorakshanātha def., 517; *guru* directs, 257; *haṭha yoga,* 728-729; history, 863; and human *dharma,* 173; in Jainism, 539; Kārttikeya's realm, 69; Kashmīr Śaivism, 511; and Nātha Sampradāya, 447; Patañjali, 782; path to God, 7; postures, 113; *rāja yoga,* 794; Śaivism, 21; Śāktism, 23; *sannyāsa,* 347; scripture, 353; as *tantra,* 255; *Tirumantram,* 495; treatises, 393
Yogānanda, Paramahaṁsa: Self Realization Fellowship, 639
Yoga pāda: Āgamas section, 379; belief in, 481; description, 113; 776; stage, 863; temple worship, 327
Yoga Sampradāya: def., 863
Yoga schools: roots in Siddha Siddhānta, 519; today, 519
Yoga Sūtras: def., 782 (Patañjali); text, 393; written, 619
Yogaswāmī, Sage: initiation, 455, 640; and Kailāsa Paramparā, 449; life, 638; monistic theist, 425: profile, 863; sayings of, v; successor, 643
Yoga tapas: def., 863; *jñāna pāda* fruition, 115
Yogas: of *āyurveda,* 259
Yogatattva Upanishad: contents, 863
Yoga Vasishṭha: contents, 863; written, 625; *yoga* text, 393
Yoga Yājñavalkya: written, 628
Yogī: def., 863; description, 361; search for Reality, 51; worship, 333
Yoginī: def., 864; description, 361
Yon: def., 864
Yoni: def., 864
Young soul: *charyā pāda,* 109; def., 864; sin, 153
Yore: def., 864
Yudhisṭhira: reign, 615
Yuga: def., 864; list and colors, 864

Zarathustra: *Zend Avesta:* Zoroastrian scripture, 558
Zenith: def., 864
Zhang Qian: Opens trade routes to India and the West, 621
Zoroaster: contributions, 616
Zoroastrian: def., 864
Zoroastrianism: adherents, 558; beliefs, 560; comparative summary, 558-560; founder, 558; founding, 558; goals, 559; path of attainment, 559; scripture, 558; sects, 558; synopsis, 558

Index of Scriptural Verses

Śāstra Uddharaṇasūchī

शास्त्र उद्धरणसूची

On virtually every text-page of *Dancing with Śiva,* verses from Hindu scripture appear. This index lists the reference for each quote. The number at the left is the page on which the verse appears, followed by the scriptural reference, sourcebook and page number. Scriptures and sources are abbreviated. At the end of the index, a key to abbreviations and a bibliography are provided.

Mandala 1: Self Realization

PAGE SCRIPTURE SOURCE, PAGE

v *TMan* 2789, 2749, 2757. *TM*
xix *TMan* 3021, 3043, 3045. *TM*
BrihadU 1.3.28. *HH*, 202
xxvi *VishnPur.*, 3.5.1. *SA*, 233
MrigAG 1.49KH–50K. SA, 233
xxxiii *TV* 74, 214. *GT*, 182, 249
5 *SYV, BrihadU* 4.4.18. *UpP*, 179
7 *KYV, MaitrU* 4.3. *UpR*, 810
9 *AV, MundU* 2.1.10. BO *UpR*, 682
11 *AV, MundU* 3.2.4. BO *UpM*, 81
13 *SYV, PaingU* 4.10. *UpR*, 921
14 *SYV, BrihadU* 1.3.28. *HH*, 202
AV, KaivU 16. *UpH*, 930
SYV, SataBR 10.6.3.2. *VE*, 705
KYV, SvetU 3.20. *VE*, 735
KYV, SvetU 1.10. *VE*, 762
Devik. AG, JAV 50–51. *RM*, 114
Sarva, AG, Atma S. 29. *RM*, 108
15 *AV, MandU* 7. *VE*, 723
Siva Sutras 2.5. *YS*, 99
TMant 2786. *TM*
Karunakarak Kadavul 6.3. *PT*, 33
SarvAG, AtmaS. 50–51, *RM*, 109
Nat, "I am He." *NT*, 8

Mandala 2: Hinduism

19 *AV, KaivU* 8. BO *UpR*, 928
21 *KYV, SvetU* 4.16. BO *UpR*, 736
23 *Devi Gita*, 5.52. *DG*, 88
25 *BGita* 9.22. *VE*, 160
27 *Crest JD. CJ*, 89
28 *RV S.* 1.164.46. *VE*, 660
KYV, SvetU 5.13. *UpH*, 407
RV S. 10.121.3. *VE*, 71
RV S. 1.89.10. *HP*, 114
RV S. 1.154.5. *VE*, 152
RV S. 10.125.3. *VE*, 97
SYV, IsU 1. *EH*, 45
29 *Devik. AG, JAV* 14. *RM*, 112
Crest JD. CJ, 146
Tayumanavar 1.2. *PT*, 14
Tayumanavar 6.5. *PT*, 34
Nat, "The Wisdom..." *NT*, 202
TMant 1557. *TM*

Mandala 3: Saivite Hinduism

33 *TMant* 1432. *TM*
35 *AV S.* 7.52.1
37 *RV, Aitareya U* Inv. *UpP*, 95
39 *RV S.* 1.89.8. *RvP*, 287
41 *MrigAGj* 2.A3. *MA*, 58
42 *RV S.* 1.114.1. *RvG*, vol. 1, 161
RV S. 10.25.1. *VE*, 302
KYV, SvetU 6.16. *UpM*, 96
KYV, SvetU 3.11. *UpM*, 90
KYV, SvetU 3.15–16. *UpM*, 90

KYV, SvetU 4.14. *UpM*, 92
43 *Ajita AG* 2.2618.1. *SA*, 56
Svayambhuva AG 4.3. *SA*, 56
TMant 1563. *TM*
TMant 1438. *TM*
TMurai 4.81.4 (Appar). *PS*, 31
Nat, "Hara! Siva..." *NT*, 209
TMurai, Saint Appar. *LG*, 152

Mandala 4: Our Supreme God
49 *KYV, MaitU* 5.2. BO *UpH*, 423
51 *AV, MundU* 2.1.2
53 *KYV, SvetU* 6.11. *UpM*, 95
55 *Raurava AGk* 63.2–6. *AK*, 51
57 *TMant* 2722. *TM*
58 *SV, KenaU* 1.3. *UpM*, 51
SYV, BrihadU 2.5.15. *VE*, 716
AV, MundU 2.1.4. *EH*, 159-160
SYV, BrihadU 4.5.15. *VE*, 421
RV S. 43.4–5. *RvG*, 64
SV, ChandU 1.6.6–7. *UpH*, 183
59 *MrigAGj* 3.A.8a–9a. *MA*, 119–20
TMant 2639. *TM*
TMant 1809. *TM*
TMurai 4.8.10. *PS*, 105
Tayumanavar 15.4–5. *HT*, 177
Nat, "Love the Feet..." *NT*, 164

Mandala 5: Lords of Dharma
63 *AV, MundU* 2.1.7. *UpR*, 681
65 *TMant*, Inv. to Vinayaka. *TM*
67 *MrigAGj* 13.A.5. *MA*, 289
69 *SV, ChandU* 7.26.2. *UpH*, 262
71 *TMurai* 11. *KD*, 224
72 *RV S.* 10.151.3. *VE*, 180
KYV, SvetU 3.4. *VE*, 156
Atharva Veda 10.7.25. *VE*, 65
AV S. 10.7.13. *VE*, 64
KYV, MaitU 4.5–6. *UpB*, 343
KYV, SvetU 6.8. *VE*, 156
RV S. 8.1.5–6. *VE*, 202
73 *TMurai* 11 (Nakkirar). *KD*, 224
Kathirgama Pur. KD, 220
KYV, TaitAR 10.6.2–3. *LW*, 112
Saint Auvaiyar. *AG*, 127
GanapatiU 11–12. *HP*, 295
Kandar Anubhuti 15. *KA*, 116
Nat, "Adoration..." *NT*, 222

Mandala 6: The Nature of the Soul
79 *KYV, SvetU* 5.11–12. *UpM*, 94
81 *KYV, SvetU* 1.15. *UpR*, 718
83 *KYV, KathaU* 2.2.12. *UpR*, 640
85 *TMant* 2331. *TM*
87 *KYV, KathaU* 2.3.4
88 *KYV, SvetU* 1.16. *VE*, 711
KYV, KathaU 2.18. *VE*, 566
SV, ChandU 7.25.2. *VE*, 740
KYV, MaitU 2.7. *UpH*, 417
KYV, SvetU 2.15. *VE*, 762
KYV, MaitU 2.4–5. *UpM*, 99
89 *SYV, BrihadU* 3.7.14. *VE*, 708
MrigAGj 2.A.5. *MA*, 60
SupraAG 2.1. *SA*, 102
TMant 2314. *TM*
TMant 1527. *TM*
TMant 2369. *TM*
Nat, "Seek the Profit..." *NT*, 11
Nat, Letter 1. *NT*, 15

Mandala 7: Karma and Rebirth
93 *SYV, BrihadU* 4.4.5. BO *UpH*, 140
95 *SYV, BrihadU* 4.4.5. *UpH*, 140
97 *SYV, BrihadU* 4.4.6
99 *SYV, BrihadU* 4.4.3. BO *UpH*, 140
101 *SYV, BrihadU* 4.3.36. BO *UpH*, 139
102 *AV S.* 10.8.44. *VE*, 538
KYV, KathaU 3.7–8. *UpH*, 352
SYV, IsaU 17. *VE*, 831
SV, ChandU 8.12.1. *UpH*, 272
SYV, PaingU 2.11. *UpR*, 913
SYV, BrihadU 6.2.14. *UpH*, 162
103 *MrigAGj* 8.A.5-6. *MA*, 193–4
MB, Anu. Parva 25.63–64. *HE*, 100
TMant 2132. *TM*
Nat, "Cure for Birth." *NT*, 191
TMurai 11, K. Ammaiyar. *PR*, 132
Tirukural 320. *TW*

Mandala 8: The Way to Liberation
107 *TMant* 1444. *TM*
109 *TMant* 1502. *TM*

111 *TMant* 1496. *TM*
113 *KYV, SvetU* 2.9. *UpP*, 192
115 *AV, MundU* 3.2.5. BO *UpH*, 376
116 *RV S.* 7.1.2. *RvP*, 2341
YV, PaingU 4.19. *UpR*, 923
SYV, PaingU 3.2. *UpR*, 916
SYV, PaingU 4.9. *VE*, 441
KYV, MaitU 6.25. *VE*, 776
KYV, MaitU 6.30. *UpH*, 443
117 *SuprabhedaAG* 3.54–55. BO *SA*, 314
Devik. AG, JAV 7–8. *RM*, 112
Paushkara AG
TMant 1479. *TM*
Tirukural 121. *TW*
Siva S. 1.87, *SS*, 13
Nat, "Path to Liberation." *NT*, 33

Mandala 9: The Three Worlds

123 *AV, MundU* 1.1.7. BO *UpR*, 673
125 *KYV, SvetU* 6.2. *UpR*, 743
127 *SYV, BrihadU* 1.5.16. *UpH*, 89
129 *RV S.*, 9.113.9. *VE*, 634
131 *KYV, SvetU* 3.2. *VE*, 621
132 *SYV, BrihadU* 2.1.20. *UpP*, 141
KYV, KathaU 1.12. *UpP*, 21
KYV, KathaU 6.1. *UpP*, 36
SYV, BrihadU 4.3.9. *UpM*, 134
KYV, SvetU 4.1. *UpM*, 91
KYV, SvetU 1.11. *UpM*, 86
133 *KYV, SvetU* 4.4, *EH*, 5
MrigAGj 13.A.2. *MA*, 286
Sarva. AG 2.9–11
TMant 2130. *TM*
Nat, "Who Can Know?" *NT*, 86
TMurai 8. *TT*, 159
Tirukural 3. *TW*
Tirukural 331. *TW*

Mandala 10: The Goodness of All

137 *KYV, KathaU* 5.11. BO *UpH*, 357
139 *KYV, MaitU* 3.2. *UpH*, 418
141 *KYV, MaitU* 6.34. *UpM*, 104
143 *KYV, MaitU* 3.2. *UpH*, 418
145 *SYV, IsaU* 1. *UpM*, 49
146 *SV, ChandU* 8.3.2. *UpP*, 121
AV S. 10.8.37. *VE*, 828
AV S. 6.45.1. *VE*, 489
SYV, IsaU 18. *VE*, 831
KYV, KathaU 4.14–15. *VE*, 861
KYV, KathaU 4.5. *UpM*, 62
147 *Sarva. AG, AtmaSak.* 62. *RM*, 110
Devik. AG, JAV 31. *RM*, 113
TMant 2599. *TM*, 424
Nat, "Joy and Sorrow…" *NT*, 46
Nat, "Sivadhyana." *NT*, 13
TMurai 5. *HY*, 13
TMurai 8. *HY*, 40

Mandala 11: Sin and Suffering

151 *Ajita AG* 2.10–2.13. *MA*, 94
153 *RV S.* 2.28.5. *VE*, 514
155 *SYV, IsaU* 3. BO *UpR*, 570
157 *KYV, MaitU* 6.34. *UpH*, 447
159 *MrigAGj* 5.A1. *MA*, 138
160 *SYV, IsaU* 7. *VE*, 815
RV S. 10.122.1. *RvP*, 4617
KYV, SvetU 6.19. *UpM*, 96
AV, MundU 3.1.3. *UpR*, 686
KYV, MaitU 6.34. *VE*, 422
KYV, MaitU 6.34. *UpM*, 103
161 *MrigAGj* 7.A.18. *MA*, 184
Devik. AGj 77–78. *RM*, 116
BGita 4.36–37. *BgM*, 64
TMant 532. *TM*
Nat, "Seek the Profit…" *NT*, 11–12
TMurai 4. *HY*, 11
Tirukural 267. *TW*

Mandala 12: Four Dharmas

167 *SYV, BrihadU* 1.4.14. BO *UpH*, 84
169 *RV S.* 10.85.1. *RvP*, 4347
171 *SYV, SataBR* 1.7.2.1. *VE*, 393
173 *KYV, MaitU* 4.3. BO *UpR*, 810
175 *AV S.* 3.22.3. *VE*, 344
176 *RV S.* 9.112. *VE*, 279–280
RV S. 1.124.3. *VE*, 808
RV S. 10.117.8. *VE*, 851
RV S. 10.31.2. *RvG*, 459
AV, SannyasaU 2.1–4. *UpB*, 735–36
AV, NarasinhaU 5.10. *UpB*, 832
177 *RV S.* 10.90.11–12. *UpB*, 894
BGita 18.41–45. *BgM*, 118–19

BGita 18.45–47. *BgM*, 119
TMant 1696. *TM*, 336
Tirukural 214. *TW*
Nat, Letter 7. *NT*, 20

Mandala 13: Good Conduct
181 *KYV, TaitU* 1.11.1. BO *UpR*, 537
183 *KYV, MaitU* 6.18. BO *UpH*, 436
185 *KYV, TaitU* 1.11.4. BO *UpR*, 539
187 *AV, PrasnaU* 1.16. *UpH*, 380
189 *AV, PrasnaU* 1.15. *UpH*, 380
190 *KYV, TaitU* 1.1.1. *VE*, 757
KYV, KathaU 2.24. *VE*, 710
SYV, TrishikhiBR U 32–33. *YM*, 19
KYV, TaitU 2.1. Inv. *UpR*, 541
AV, MundU 3.1.9. *UpR*, 688
SYV, BrihadU 1.4.14. *UpH*, 84–85
Devik AG, JAV 41. *RM*, 114
191 *Devik AG, JAV* 5. *RM*, 111
Devik AG, JAV 12. *RM*, 112
TMant 543. *TM*, 227
TMant 557. *TM*, 230
Nat, "The True Path." *NT*, 4
Tirukural 34. *TW*
Tirukural 31, 33. *TW*
Tirukural 455. *TW*

Mandala 14: Noninjury
195 *AV, SandilyaU* 1.3. *UpA*, 173
197 *SYV, BrihadU* 3.7.15. *UpH*, 116
199 *KYV, MaitU* 3.2. *UpH*, 418
201 *Tirukural* 26.1; 26.9. *TW*
203 *AV S.* 19.9.14. *VE*, 306
204 *KYV, PranaU* 46–8. *VE*, 413–14
AV S. 6.120.1. *VE*, 636
YV S. 12.32. *FS*, 90
SYV S. 36.17. *VE*, 306
RV S. 10.37.11. *VE*, 319
SYV S. 36.18. *VE*, 342
Devik AG, JAV 69–70. *RM*, 116
Patanjali Yoga Sutras 2.35. *YP*, 205
205 *Suta S., SkandaPur.*, 4-5. *FF*, 113
BGita 13.27–28. *BgM*, 101
Mahabharata, Anu. 115.40. *FS*, 90
BGita 16.2–3. *BgM*, 109
Manu DS 5.48. *LM*, 176
Tirukural 155, 206. *TW*

Mandala 15: Husband and Wife
211 *AV S.* 14.2.71. *VE*, 260
213 *AV S.* 6.78.1–2. BO *AvW*, 339
215 *RV S.* 10.85.27. *VE*, 255
217 *RV S.* 10.85.47. *VE*, 257
219 *AV S.* 7.36. *VE*, 259
220 *RV S.* 8.31.5–6. *RvP*, 3015
RV S. 10.85.43. *VE*, 257
RV S. 10.85.26. *VE*, 255
SYJ S. 5.17. *TY*, 44
AV S. 14.1.42. *VE*, 258
RV S. 10.85.44. *VE*, 257
221 *RV S.* 7.2.9. *RvP*, 2355
AV S. 14.2.64. *VE*, 259
AV S. 6.79.1–3. *VE*, 274
Manu DS 9.101–2. *SD*, 161
Paraskara GS 1.8.19. *VE*, 264
Tirukural 60. *TW*
Tirukural 1021. *TW*
Nat, "The True Path." *NT*, 4

Mandala 16: Marriage
225 *RV S.* 8.31.9. *VE*, 265
227 *RV S.* 10.191.4. *VE*, 863
229 *RV S.* 10.85.23. *VE*, 254
231 *RV S.* 10.85.42. *VE*, 256
233 *AV S.* 3.30.5. *VE*, 857
234 *AV S.* 3.30.7. *VE*, 857
AV S. 3.30.6. *VE*, 857
AV S. 3.15.8. *VE*, 295
RV S. 7.63.6. *VE*, 822
AV S. 6.78.1. *AvG*, 236
RV S. 10.85.46. *VE*, 257
AV S. 6.79.1–2. *AvG*, 236
RV S. 8.31.7. *VE*, 265
RV S. 1.1.3 & 9. *VE*,, 329
Tirukural 45. *TW*
235 *RV S.* 10.191.3. *RvP*, 4739
AV S. 6.79.1–2. *AvG* vol 1, 236
Manu DS 3.27. *LM*, 80
Manu DS 3.40. *LM*, 82
Manu DS 3.55–56. *LM*, 85
Paraskara GS 1.8.8. *VE*, 263
Tirukural 43. *TW*

Mandala 17: Children
239 *RV S.* 8.31.8. *RvP,* 3015
241 *AV S.* 3.30.1–2. *VE,* 857
243 *SYV S.* 3.37. BO *VE,* 343
245 *RV S.* 9.43.6. *RvP,* 3675
247 *AV S.* 3.30.4. *VE,* 857
248 *SYV S.* 3.39. *VE,* 343
RV S. 7.2.7. *RvP,* 2355
RV S. 6.9.2. *VE,* 331–332
RV S. 10.37.7. *VE,* 319
AV S. 3.30.3. *VE,* 857
AV S. 3.15.7. *VE,* 295
KYV, TaitU 1.11.1–2. *UpR,* 537–8
249 *SV, JaimU BR* 3.28.3–4. *VO,* 115
Manu DS 2.232–3. *LM,* 72
Tirukural 47. *TW*
Tirukural 66. *TW*
Tirukural 67, 70. *TW*
Tirukural 61, 68. *TW*
Nat, Letter 10. *NT,* 22
Nat, "There Is Not…" *NT,* 34

Mandala 18: Ways of Wisdom
255 *YogatattvaU.* BO *UpA,* 193
KYV, SvetU 2.14. BO *UpH,* 399
257 *KYV, MaitU* 6.34. *VE,* 422
259 *AV S.* 19.9.10. *GK,* 161
261 *RV S.* 8.69.9. BO *GK,* 330
263 *Tirukural* 213, 212. *TW*
RV S. 10.117.5. *VE,* 850–851
264 *RV S.* 7.2.8. *RvP,* 2355
RV S. 10.117. 6–7. *VE,* 851
RV, Aitareya BR 6.5.27. *EI,* 60
SYV, SataBR 11.5.6.1. *VE,* 394
KYV, SvetU 2.10. *UpM,* 88
KYV, SvetU 2.13. *UpR,* 723
265 *SYV, MuktiU* 2. *UpA,* 7
BGita 18.5–6. *BgM,* 115
TMant 252. *TM,* 201
TMurai 2.221.1. *PS,* 109
TMurai (Appar). *SW,* 191
Nat, "Our Duty." *NT,* 178

Mandala 19: Sacraments
269 *AV, MundU* 2.1.6. BO *UpH,* 371
271 *RV S.* 10.101.9. *VE,* 279
273 *Hiranyakesi GS* 1.6.21.2. *VE,* 263
275 *SYV S.* 34.5. *VE,* 799–800
277 *RV S.* 10.18.6. *VE,* 609
278 *RV S.* 10.17.4. *VE,* 608
RV S. 10.18.5. *VE,* 609
RV S. 10.85.36. *RvG,* vol. 2, p. 544; & *Sankh. GS* 1.14.1. *SB,* vol. 29, p. 37
SYV, JabalaU 4. *VE,* 440
AV, KaivU 5. *VE,* 442
Manu DS 2.147–8. *SD,* 156
279 *Manu DS* 2.26. *LM,* 33
Manu DS 2.30. *LM,* 35
Manu DS 2.33. *LM,* 35
Manu DS 6.36. *LM,* 205
TMant 181. *TM*
ParasGS 2.1.1–4. *GS,* vol. 29, 301
PadmaPur., srishti, 60.65. *HE,* 105

Mandala 20: Festivals
283 *RV S.* 10.130.2. *VE,* 356–357
285 *KYV, SvetU* 3.11. *UpP,* 195
287 *RV S.* 2.23.1. *HP,* 291
289 *RV S.* 10.68.1. *VE,* 812
291 *SYV S.* 3.38. *VE,* 362
292 *RV S.* 10.121.6. *RvP,* 4615
RV S. 10.81.7. *VE,* 808
TMurai 11. (Kapiladeva). *AG,* 159
TMurai 5.129.1. *PS,* 180
TMurai 1.71.5. *PS,* 183
TMurai 2.183.7. *PS,* 188
293 *TMurai* 2.192.5. *PS,* 183
TMurai 4.21.2. *PS,* 184
TMurai 4.21.5. *PS,* 185
TMurai 8. *TT,* 151
Guru Gita 29. *GG,* 10
TMant 50. *TM,* 185
Nat, "Give Praise…" *NT,* 199

Mandala 21: Siva Temple
299 *KYV, SvetU* 5.4. *VE,* 335
301 *AV S.* 19.42.1. *VE,* 360
303 *RV S.* 5.13.3. *VE,* 854
305 *KYV, Tait. S.,* 1.6.8.1. *VE,* 401
307 *AV, MundU* 1.2.6. *VE,* 414
308 *RV S.* 7.15.7–8. *VE,* 846
KYV, SvetU 6.7. *VE,* 156

KYV, SvetU 4.21. *UpM,* 93
Karana AG 10. *MT,* 66
SupraAG 21.28–29. *SA,* 180
Karana AG 323–325. *MT,* 200
309 *Karana AG* 446. BO *MT,* 226
Lingashtakam. SW, 8
TMant 2411. *TM,* 406
TMant 518. *TM,* 225
TMurai 4.9.8. *PS,* 44
TMurai 6.309.5. *PS,* 149
PeriyaP, 5.21. verse 252. *PS,* 49

Mandala 22: Temple Rites
313 *RV S.* 10.130.1. *VE,* 356
315 *RV S.* 1.189.2. *VE,* 810
317 *KYV, SvetU* 3.5. *UpM,* 89
319 *Karana AG* 18. BO *MT,* 75
321 *SYV, SataBR* 9.4.4.15. *VE,* 396
322 *RV S.* 7.2.5. *RvP,* 2353
SV, ChandU 5.24.4. *VE,* 412
AV S. 5.24.15. *VE,* 860
Karana AG 11. *MT,* 67
Kamika AG 4.374. *SA,* 248
Karana AG 23. *MT,* 76
Karana AG 202. *MT,* 164
323 *Karana AG* 64. *MT,* 111
Karana AG 190–191. *MT,* 160
Karana AG 274. *MT,* 188
Karana AG 423–426. *MT,* 222
Arputat Tiruvantati 17. *AT,* 18

Mandala 23: Love of God
327 *AV S.* 10.8.1 & 29. *VE,* 824–827
329 *RV S.* 10.151.4–5. *VE,* 180
331 *RV S.* 7.10.3. *VE,* 818
333 *AV S.* 7.21. *VE,* 661
335 *Karana AG* 12. BO *MT,* 67
336 *RV S.* 4.4.7. *VE,* 845
RV S. 3.62.10. *HP,* 345
RV S. 10.4.1. *VE,* 302
RV S. 1.42.10. *VE,* 805
AV, MundU 1.2.1. *VE,* 414
Karana AG 9. *MT,* 66
Karana AG 269–270. *MT,* 186
337 *Karana AG* 46. *MT,* 100
Karana AG 450. *MT,* 227
SP, Rudra S. 23.16. *AI,* vol.1, 380
TMant 1839. *TM,* 349
Nat, "Sivabhakti." NT, 7
PeriyaP. 5.21, verse 253. *PS,* 49
Tirukural 2, 7. *TW*

Mandala 24: Monastic Life
343 *SYV, BrihadU* 4.4.22. *VE,* 717
345 *SYV, JabalaU* 5. *VE,* 440
347 *TMant* 1615. *TM*
349 *AV, MundU* 3.1.5. *EH,* 175
351 *KYV, MaitU* 6.28. *UpR,* 838
352 *RV S.* 10.136.2. *VE,* 436
AV, MundU 1.2.12–13. *EH,* 157
RV S. 10.136.1. *VE,* 436
SYV, BrihadU 4.4.22. *VE,* 717
KYV, MahanU 537–8. *VE,* 439
SV, ChandU 8.5.1. *UpP,* 123
353 *BGita* 6.2–3. *VE,* 445
BGita 6.7–8. *VE,* 445
TMant 1615. *TM*
Nat, "O Sannyasin!" *NT,* 146
Nat, "Body Is a Temple." *NT,* 99
Tirukural 21, 348. *TW*

Mandala 25: Knowers of God
357 *RV S.* 1.164.6. *VE,* 660
359 *RV S.* 7.2.2. BO *AvG,* 3
361 *AV S.* 11.5.1. *AvG,* 55
363 *KulTantra* 9.14. BO *KT,* 84
365 *Svayambhuva-Sutra* 105. *AK,* 98
366 *SYV, PaingU* 3.5. *UpR,* 918
KYV, MaitU 6.28. *VE,* 440
AV, NaradapariU 1. *UpA,* 135
SV, ChandU 8.3.3–4. *UpP,* 122
AV, MundU 1.2.13. *VE,* 415
SYV, JabalaU 6. *VE,* 441
367 *DevikAG, JAV* 83. *RM,* 117
Siva Sutras 2.6. *YS,* 102
BGita 4.34. *BgM,* 64
Guru Gita 97. *GG,* 37
KulTantra 8.1. *KT,* 77
TMant 1868. *TM*
TMant 1624. *TM*
Tirukural 268. *TW*

Mandala 26: Revealed Scripture
373 *TMant* 2404. *TM*
375 *TMant* 51. *TM*
377 *PrasnaU* 2.6. *UpH*, 381
379 *TMant* 2397. *TM*
381 *TMant* 1429. *TM*
382 *SYV, MuktU* 2. *UpA*, 7
SYV, BrihadU 2.4.10. *VE*, 691
KYV, SvetU 4.18. *VE*, 83–84
AV, MundU 2.2.3. *UpH*, 372
KYV, SvetU 6.21. *UpM*, 97
SV, ChandU 1.1.1–2. *VE*, 772
383 *Karana AG* 65. *SA*, 158
TMant 53. *TM*
TMant 85. *TM*
TMurai
Nat, "My Protection." *NT*, 239
TMurai 5.204.6. *PS*, 95
TMurai 7.100.8. *PS*, 322

Mandala 27: Secondary Scripture
387 *AV S.* 10.7.14. *VE*, 64
389 *Jnaneshvari* 1.3–4. *JN*, 25
391 *BGita* 18.70–71. *SH*, 94
393 *BGita* 4.37–38. *VE*, 528
395 *Tayumanavar* 3.2. *PT*, 20
396 *AV S.* 4.1.5–6. *VE*, 105
SV, ChandU 7.2.1. *VE*, 111
BGita 16.23–24. *BgM*, 111
BPur. 11.14.25. *HP*, 378
397 *Panchatantra. PN*, 218
Siva Pur. 1.18.159. *HP*, 227
Lalla. IT, 360
Tukaram. TU, 114–115
Vach.-Basavanna 563. *SO*, 84
TMurai 2.147.1. *PS*, 110
Jnaneshvari 1.5. *JN*, 25

Mandala 28: Affirmations of Faith
401 *Nat*, "Garland..." *NT*, 123
403 *TMant* 941. *TM*
405 *Siva S.* 3.11. *SS*, 25
407 *TMant* 3003. *TM*
409 *TMant* 270. *TM*
410 *YVK, Tait. S* 4.5.8. *YvK*, 359
AV, AtharvasU 2. *UpB*, 782
AV, PrasnaU 5.7. *VE*, 775
KulTantra 11.3. *KT*, 112
KulTantra 11.1. *KT*, 111
411 *KulTantra* 11.4. *KT*, 112
Nat, "Let God Be..." *NT*, 7
Nat, "Adoration..." *NT*, 224
Grace Ambrosia 5. *SY*, 407
TMurai 3.307.3. *PS*, 217
TMurai 3.307.1. *TT*, 61
TMurai 4.48.7. *PS*, 114

Mandala 29: Monism and Dualism
417 *KYV, SvetU* 1.1. BO *UpH*, 394
419 *AV, MundU* 2.1.1. *VE*, 735
421 *KYV, MaitU* 6.35. *VE*, 741
423 *SYV, IsaU* 5–6. *VE*, 811
425 *KYV, SvetU* 6.6. *UpH*, 409
426 *SYV, BrihadU* 4.4.19–20. *UpH*, 143
AV, KaivU 7. *VE*, 764
SYV, BrihadU 4.5.15. *VE*, 420–21
AV, MundU 2.2.8. *EH*, 170
KYV, SvetU 3.9. *UpR*, 727
427 *KYV, MaitU* 6.34.11. *TU*, 103
SarvaAG, AtmaS 14. *RM*, 107
SarvaAG, AtmaS 20–21. *RM*, 107
Siva Sutras 2.3. *YS*, 88
TMant 1441. *TM*
Tayumanavar, 10.3. *PT*, 44
Nat, Letter 2. *NT*, 16

Mandala 30: Views of Reality
431 *TMant* 95. *TM*
433 *SYV*
435 *AV, MundU* 3.2.8. *UpR*, 691
437 *TMant* 1806. *TM*
439 *KYV, SvetU* 3.1. *UpP*, 193
440 *AV, AtharvasU* 2. *UpB*, 782
SYV, BrihadU 4.4.13. *UpR*, 276
KYV, SvetU 4.9–10. *UpM*, 92
KYV, MaitU 7.11.8. *UpH*, 458
KYV, MaitU 7.11.6. *UpH*, 458
KYV, MaitU 6.17. *VE*, 667
441 *Siva Samhita* 1.34. *SS*, 6
TMant 2481. *TM*
TMant 1437. *TM*
Nat, "That." *NT*, 87

Tayumanavar 2.5. *NT,* 8
TMurai 6.308.1. *PS,* 113

Mandala 31: Himalayan Lineage

447 *TMant* 1487. *TM*
449 *TMant* 91. *TM*
451 *TMant* 92. *TM*
453 *Nat,* "My Master." *NT,* 154–5
455 *KulTantra* 8.3. BO *KT,* 79
456 *AV, Yoga–ShikhaU* 5.53. *YT,* 26
AV, MundU 1.2.8. *UpM,* 77
KYV, MahanU 505. *VE,* 439
KYV, SvetU 6.22–23. *UpH,* 411
Guru Gita 43. *GG,* 14
KulTantra 10.1. *KT,* 101
457 *KulTantra* 10.1. *KT,* 101
KulTantra 10.1. *KT,* 101
Guru Gita 115. *GG,* 47
Nat, "Chellappan danced." *NT,* 88
TMant 67. *TM*
TMant 1778. *TM*

Six Schools, Timeline, Lexicon

493 *Kailasasam., SP* 9.23–26. *AI,* 1707
500 *Panchartha B., Kaun.* 3.1. *YT,* 203
503 *Malati–Madhava* 4.27. *KK,* 58
503 *Inscription on Kedaresvara Temple and Maṭha,* 1162 ce. *KK,* 103
506 *Allam. VachCandriki* 959. *SO,* 167
507 *VachGanachara. RL,* 105
VachBasavanna 901. *VB*
SunyaSamp, vol 1, p. 57. *RL,* 99
508 *Renukacharya. SV,* 57
513 *Br. Sutra B., Srikantha. HN,* 391
514 *Br. Sutra B., Srikantha. HN,* 394
515 *Sivakarnamrita. AD,* 105
Sivarakshamani Dipika. AD, 93
517-18 *VM, Gorakshanatha. PG,* 245
608 Letter by M. Müller, *TY,* xxv
731 *RN,* 731

SCRIPTURAL ABBREVIATIONS

AG: Agama
AGj: Agama, Jnana Pada
AGk: Agama, Kriya Pada
Arthavas: Arthavasikha
AV: Atharva Veda
B: Bhashya
BGita: Bhagavad Gita
BPur: Bhagavata Purana
BO: Based on translation from
BR: Brahmana
Brihad: Brihadaranyaka
Chand: Chandogya
CJD: Crest Jewel of Discrimination
Devik: Devikalottara
DS: Dharma Sastras
Inv.: Invocation
Jaim: Jaiminiya
JP: Jnana Pada
JAV: Jnana-archara-vichara
Kaun: Kaundinya
KulTantra: Kularnava Tantra
KYV: Krishna Yajur Veda
Maha: Mahanarayana
MaitU: Maitreya
Mrig: Mrigendra
MundU: Mundaka
Naradapari: Naradaparivrajaka
NaraPur: Narasinhapurvatapaniya
Nat: Natchintanai
PeriyaP: Periyapurana
Prana: Pranagnihotra
Pur: Purana
RV: Rig Veda
S.: Samhita
Sak: Sakshatkara
SarvaAG: Sarvajnanottara Agama
SathaBR: Satapatha Brahmana
SGS: Sankhyananda Grihya Sutras
SP: Siva Purana
Supra: Suprabheda
SU: Svetasvatara Upanishad
SV: Sama Veda
SYV: Sukla Yajur Veda
Tait: Taittiriya
TMan: Tirumantiram
TMurai: Tirumurai
U: Upanishad
Vach: Vachana
VishnPur: Vishnudharmottara Purana
VM: Viveka Martanda

Scriptural Bibliography

Śāstra Vidyānusevana

शास्त्र विद्यानुसेवन

Here are listed the sourcebooks from which were drawn the scriptural and other quotations used in *Dancing with Śiva,* as notated in the preceding "Index of Scriptural Verses."

ABBREVIATION EDITOR-TRANSLATOR SCRIPTURE PUBLISHER

AD: Dr. N. Ramesan, *Sri Appaya Dikshita* (Hyderabad, Srimad Appaya Dikshitendra Granthavali Prakasana Samithi)

AG: Ratna Ma Navaratnam, *Aum Ganesha, The Peace of God* (Jaffna, Vidya Bhavan, 1978)

AI: J.L. Shastri, *Ancient Indian Tradition and Mythology,* vol. 1 & 4 (Delhi, Motilal Banarsidass, 1973)

AK: Prof. S.K. Ramachandra Rao, *Āgama-Kosha (Āgama Encylopaedia),* vol. 2, *Śaiva and Śakta Āgamas* (Bangalore, Kalpatharu Research Academy, 1990)

AT: Karaikkalammaiyar, *The Arputat Tiruvantati* (Pondicherry, Institut Francais d'Indologie, 1956)

AvG: Ralph T.H. Griffith, *Hymns of the Atharva Veda* (New Delhi, Munshiram Manoharlal Publishers Pvt. Ltd., 1985)

AvW: William Dwight Whitney, *Atharva Veda Samhita* (Delhi, Motilal Banarsidass, 1971)

BgM: Juan Mascaro, *The Bhagavad Gita* (Baltimore, Penguin Books, 1966)

CJ: Swami Prabhavananda and Christopher Isherwood, *Shankara's Crest-Jewel of Discrimination* (Hollywood, Vedanta Press, 1947)

DG: Swami Satyananda Saraswati, *Devi Gita* (Napa, California, Devi Mandir Publications, 1991)

EH: Karan Singh, *Essays on Hinduism* (Delhi, Ratna Sagar Ltd., 1990)

EI: Stella Kramrisch, *Exploring India's Sacred Art* (Philadelphia, University of Pennsylvania Press, 1983)

FF: Yogi Raushan Nath, *Flaming Faith* (New Delhi, Rajiv Publications, 1967)

FS: Steven Rosen, *Food for the Spirit, Vegetarianism and the World Religions* (Bala Books, Old Westbury, New York, 1990)

GG: Swami Narayananda, *The Guru Gita* (Bombay, India Book House Pvt. Ltd., 1976)

GK: David Frawley, *Gods, Sages and Kings, Vedic Secrets of Ancient Civiliza-*

tion (Salt Lake City, Utah, Passage Press, 1991)

GS: Herman Oldenberg, *Grihya-Sutras, Sacred Books of the East,* vol. 29 & 30 (Delhi, Motilal Banarsidass, 1973)

GT: G. Vanmikanathan, *God through the Thiruvaachakam, An Original Interpretation & Complete Translation* (Tirupanandal: Sri Kasi Mutt, 1980)

HE: Harold G. Coward, Julius J. Lipner and Katherine K. Young, *Hindu Ethics, Purity, Abortion and Euthanasia* (Albany, State University of New York Press, 1989)

HH: Troy Organ, *Hinduism, Its Historical Development* (Woodbury, New York, Barron's Educational Series, Inc., 1974)

HN: José Pereira, *Hindu Theology* (Delhi, Motilal Banarsidass, 1976)

HP: Alain Danielou, *Hindu Polytheism* (New York, Bollingen Foundation, 1964)

HT: Dr. B. Natarajan, *The Hymns of Saint Tayumanavar* (Kauai Aadheenam, Hawaii. Typescript)

HY: Sri T.B. Siddhalingam, *Hymns and Proverbs* (Tirupanadal, Sri Kasi Mutt, 1964)

IT: W.T. Bary, Stephen Hay, Royal Weiler and Andrew Yarrow, *The Sources of Indian Tradition* (New York, Columbia University Press, 1958)

JN: V.G. Pradhan and H.M. Lambert (ed.), *Jnaneshvari (Bhavarthadipika),* vol. 1 (London, George Allen & Unwin LTD., 1967)

KA: N. V. Karthikeyan, *Kandar Anubhuti* (Uttara Pradesh, India, The Divine Life Society, 1972)

KD: Ratna Navaratnam, *Karttikeya, The Divine Child* (Bombay, Bharatiya Vidya Bhavan, 1973)

KK: David N. Lorenzen, *The Kapalikas and Kalamukhas* (Delhi, Motilal Banarsidass, 1972)

KT: M. P. Pandit, *Kularnava Tantra* (Delhi, Motilal Banarsidass, 1984)

LG: Mariasusai Dhavamony, *Love of God According to Saiva Siddhanta* (London, Oxford University Press, 1971)

LM: Georg Bühler, *The Laws of Manu* (New York, Dover Publications, 1969)

LW: Swami Sivananda, *Lord Shanmukha and His Worship* (Uttara Pradesh, India, The Divine Life Society, 1990)

MA: Michel Hulin, *Mrgendragama, Sections de la Doctrine et du Yoga, Le Florilege de la Doctrine Sivaite, Publications de l'Institut Francais D'Indologie,* vol. 63 (Pondicherry, Institut Francais D'Indologie, 1980)

MT: J. W. V. Curtis, *Motivations of Temple Architecture in Saiva Siddhanta, As Defined by Prescriptions for Daily Worship According to Karanagama* (Madras, Hoe & CO., ca 1970, not dated)

NT: The Sivathondan Society, *Natchintanai, Songs and Sayings of Yogaswami* (Jaffna, The Sivathondan Society, 1974)

PG: Akshaya Kumar Banerjea, *Philosophy of Gorakhnath* (Delhi, Motilal Banarsidass, 1962)
PN: Arthur W. Ryder, *The Panchatantra* (Chicago, U. of Chicago Press, 1972)
PR: E.M. Arumuka Cettiyar, *Periapuranam* (Madras, 1958)
PS: Indira Viswanathan Peterson, *Poems to Siva, The Hymns of the Tamil Saints* (Delhi, Motilal Banarsidass, 1991)
PT: Mutu Coomaraswamy, *The Poems of Tayumanavar* (Petaling Jaya, S. Durai Raja Singam, 1977)
RL: K. Ishwaran, *Religion and Society among the Lingayats of South India* (New Delhi, Vikas Publishing House, 1983)
RM: Arthur Osborne, ed., *The Collected Works of Ramana Maharshi* (London, Rider, 1959)
RN: Janaki Abhisheki, *Religion as Knowledge* (Bombay: Ms. V. Ranade)
RvG: Ralph T.H. Griffith, *Hymns of the Rg Veda* (New Delhi, Munshiram Manoharlal Publishers Pvt. Ltd., 1987)
RvM: Jean Le Mee, *Hymns from the Rig-Veda* (New York, Alfred A. Knopf, Inc., 1975)
RvP: Swami Satya Prakash Sarasvati and Satyakam Vidyalankar, *RgVeda Samhita* (New Delhi, Veda Pratishthana, 1977)
SA: Bruno Dagens, *Saivagamaparibhasmanjari de Vedajnana, Le Florilege de la Doctrine Sivaite, Publications de l'Institut Francais D'Indologie,* vol. 60 (Pondicherry, Institut Francais D'Indologie, 1979)
SD: *Sanatana-Dharma, An Advanced Textbook of Hindu Religion and Ethics* (Madras, Theosophical Publishing House, 1967)
SH: Klaus K. Klostermaier, *A Survey of Hinduism* (Albany, State University of New York Press, 1989)
SO: A.K. Ramanujan (ed.), *Speaking of Siva* (London, Penguin Books, 1973)
SS: Rai Bahadur Srisa Chandra Vasu, *The Siva Samhita* (New Delhi, Oriental Books Reprint Corporation, 1979)
SU: P. Ray, H. Gupta and M. Roy, *Susruta Samhita, A Scientific Synopsis* (New Delhi: Indian National Science Academy, 1980)
SV: R. Chakravarti, *Shakti Vishishtadvaita* (Mysore, Sri Panchacharya Electric Press, 1957)
SW: Swami Sivananda, *Lord Siva and His Worship* (Uttara Pradesh, The Divine Life Society, 1989)
SY: Ratna Chelliah Navaratnam, *Saint Yogaswami and the Testament of Truth* (Columbuturai, Thiru Kasipillai Navaratnam, 1972)
TM: Dr. B. Natarajan et al., *Tirumantiram, Holy Utterances of Saint Tirumular* (Hawaii, Saiva Siddhanta Church, 1982)
TT: K. Chellappa Counder, *Panniru Thirumurai Thirattu* (Durban, Siva Manram, 1975)
TU: J.N. Fraser and K.B. Marathe, *The Poems of Tukaram* (Madras, Christian Literature Society, 1909)

TW: Tiruvalluvar, *Tirukural: The Weaver* (English translation by Himalayan Academy, Concord, California, manuscript)
TY: Devi Chand, *The Yajur Veda* (New Delhi, Munshiram Manoharlal Publishers Pvt. Ltd., fourth edition, 1988)
UpA: K. Narayanasvami Aiyar, *Thirty Minor Upanishads, Including the Yoga Upanishads* (Oklahoma, Santarasa Publications, 1980)
UpB: V.M. Bedekar and G.B. Palsule, *Sixty Upanishads of the Veda* (Delhi, Motilal Banarsidass, 1990)
UpH: Robert E. Hume, *Thirteen Principal Upanishads* (Madras, Oxford University Press, second edition, 1958)
UpM: Juan Mascaro, *The Upanishads* (Baltimore, Penguin Books Inc., 1965)
UpP: Swami Prabhavananda and Frederick Manchester, *The Upanishads, Breath of the Eternal* (Hollywood, Vedanta Press, 1971)
UpR: S. Radhakrishnan, *The Principal Upanishads* (New York: Harper and Brothers, 1953)
VB: R.C. Hiremath, *Vacanas of Basavanna* (Dharwar, Karnatak University, 1968)
VE: Raimundo Panikkar, *The Vedic Experience* (Delhi, Motilal Banarsidass, 1989). Used extensively by permission.
VO: Herman W. Tull, *The Vedic Origins of Karma, Cosmos as Man In Ancient Indian Myth and Ritual* (Albany, State University of New York Press, 1989)
YM: Alain Danielou, *Yoga: The Method of Re-Integration* (New York, University Books, 1955)
YP: Rammurti S. Mishra, *The Textbook of Yoga Psychology* (New York, The Julian Press, Inc., 1963)
YS: Jaideva Singh, *Siva Sutras, The Yoga of Supreme Identity* (Delhi, Motilal Banarsidass, 1979)
YT: Georg Feuerstein, *Yoga, The Technology of Ecstasy* (Los Angeles, Jeremy P. Tarcher, Inc., 1989)
YvG: Ralph T.H. Griffith, *The Texts of the White Yajurveda, Translated with a Popular Commentary,* Chowkhamba Sanskrit Studies vol. 95. (Varanasi, fourth edition, 1976)
YvK: Arthur Berriedale Keith, *The Veda of the Black Yajus School, Taittiriya Sanhita* (Delhi, Motilal Banarsidass, 1967)

Supplementary Reading

Granthavidyā

ग्रन्थविद्या

Books are available directly from the publishers or from distributors, such as: 1) South Asia Books, P.O. Box 502, Columbia, MO 65205 (phone 314/474-0166); 2) Nataraj Books, P.O. Box 5076, Springfield, VA 22150 (phone 703/455-4996); 3) The 21st Century Bookstore, P.O. Box 702, Fairfield, IA 52556. Titles especially recommended are marked with an asterisk.

HINDU SCRIPTURE AND SACRED LITERATURE

Bhatt, N. R. ed., *Mrgendragama* (French translation, two volumes). Pondicherry: Institute Français D'Indologie, 1962.

Bühler, Georg, *The Laws of Manu.* New York: Dover Publications, Inc., 1969.

Cettiyar, E.M. Arumuka, *Periapuranam.* Madras: 1958.

Coomaraswamy, Mutu, *The Poems of Tayumanavar* (anthology). Petaling Jaya, Malaysia: S. Durai Raja Singam, 1977.

Deussen, Paul, **Sixty Upanishads of the Veda.* Delhi: Motilal Banarsidass, 1990.

Easwaran, Eknath, **The Upanishads.* Tomales, California: Blue Mountain Center of Meditation, 1987.

Embree, Ainslie T.(editor), *The Hindu Tradition.* New York: The Modern Library/Random House, 1966.

Fraser, J.N. and K.B. Marathe, *The Poems of Tukaram.* Madras: Christian Literature Society, 1909.

Feuerstein, Georg, *The Yoga Sutra of Patanjali, A New Translation and Commentary.* Rochester, Vermont: Inner Traditions International, 1989.

Ganguli, Kisari Mohan, *The Mahabharata of Krishna-Dwaipayana Vyasa*, 12 volumes. New Delhi: Munshiram Manoharlal Publishers Pvt. Ltd., 1972.

Gounder, K. Chellappa, *Panniru Thirumurai Thirattu.* Durban: Siva Manram, 1975.

Griffith, Ralph T.H., *Hymns of the Atharva Veda*, 2 volumes. New Delhi: Munshiram Manoharlal Publishers Pvt. Ltd., 1985. First published 1895-96.

Griffith, Ralph T.H., *Hymns of the Rg Veda*, 2 volumes. New Delhi: Munshiram Manoharlal Publishers Pvt. Ltd., 1987. First published in 1889.

Hume, Robert Ernest, **The Thirteen Principal Upanishads.* Oxford: Oxford University Press, 1958.

Jyotirmayananda, Swami, *Srimad Bhagavad Gita.* Miami: Yoga Research Foundation, 1986.

Karaikkalammaiyar, *The Arputat Tiruvantati* (translation into French). Pondicherry: Institut Francais d'Indologie, 1956.

Karthikeyan, N. V., *Kandar Anubhuti.* Uttara Pradesh: The Divine Life Society, 1972.

Keith, Arthur Berriedale, *The Veda of the Black Yajus School, Taittiriya Samhita.* Delhi: Motilal Banarsidass, 1967.

Kingsbury, F., and Phillips, G. E., **Hymns of the Tamil Saivite Saints.* Calcutta: Association Press, 1921.

Kirtananda, Swami Bhaktipada, *The Illustrated Ramayana.* Moundsville, West Virginia: Palace Publishing, 1989.

Le Mee, Jean, *Hymns From the Rig-Veda.* New York: Alfred A. Knopf, Inc., 1975.

Madhavananda, Swami, **Minor Upanishads* (8 *Upanishads* with Devanagari, English and notes). Calcutta: Advaita Ashrama, 1988.

Mascaró, Juan, **The Bhagavad Gita.* Baltimore: Penguin Books Inc., 1966.

Mascaró, Juan, **The Upanishads* (selections). Narmondsworth: Penguin Books Ltd., 1965.

Narayananda, Swami, **The Guru Gita.* Bombay: India Book House, 1976.

Narayanasvami, Aiyar K., **Thirty Minor Upanishads.* El Reno: Santarasa Publications, 1980.

Natarajan, Dr. B. (translator), **Tirumantiram, A Tamil Scriptural Classic by Tirumular,* Sri Ramakrishna Math, Mylapore, Madras, 1991.

Navaratnam, Ratna Chelliah, *Saint Yogaswami and the Testament of Truth.* Columbuturai: Thiru Kasipillai Navaratnam, 1972.

O'Flaherty, Wendy Doniger, *The Rig Veda, An Anthology* (108 hymns). London: Penguin Books, 1981.

Oldenberg, Herman, *Grihya-Sutras,* Sacred Books of the East, vol. 29 & 30. Delhi: Motilal Banarsidass, 1973.

Osborne, Arthur (ed.), **The Collected Works of Ramana Maharshi.* London: Rider, 1959.

Pandit, M. P., *Kularnava Tantra.* Delhi: Motilal Banarsidass, 1984.

Panikkar, Raimundo, **The Vedic Experience.* Delhi: Motilal Banarsidass, 1989.

Peterson, Indira Viswanathan, **Poems to Siva, The Hymns of the Tamil Saints.* Delhi: Motilal Banarsidass, 1991.

Pope, G.U., **Tirukkural.* Madras: The South India Saiva Siddhanta Works Publishing Society, 1981.

Pope, G.U., *Tiruvacagam: Sacred Utterances.* Madras: University of Madras, 1970.

Prabhavananda Swami, and Manchester, Frederick, *The Upanishads, Breath of the Eternal.* Hollywood: Vedanta Press, 1971.

Prabhavananda Swami, and Isherwood, Christopher, Shankara's *Crest-Jewel of Discrimination, Viveka-Chudamani.* Hollywood: Vedanta Press, 1947.

Pradhan, V.G., and Lambert, H.M., (ed.), *Jnaneshvari Bhavarthadipika,* vol. 1. London: George Allen and Unwin LTD., 1967.

Prasad, R.C., *Tulasidasa's Shri Ramacharitamanasa.* Delhi: Motilal Banarsidass, 1988.
Radhakrishnan, Dr. S., **The Principal Upanishads.* New York: Harper Brothers, 1953.
Rao, S.K. Ramachandra, *Āgama-Kosha* (Āgamic Encyclopaedia, 4 small volumes). Bangalore: Kalpatharu Research Academy, 1989.
Ramanujam, A.K., *Speaking of Siva.* Baltimore: Penguin, 1973.
Ryder, Arthur W., *The Panchatantra.* Chicago: University of Chicago Press, 1972.
Satchidananda, Sri Swami, *The Yoga Sutras of Patanjali.* Yogaville, VA: Integral Yoga Pub., 1990.
Satyaprakash and Vidyalankar, *Rgveda Samhita* (12 volumes, with Devanagari and English translation). New Delhi: Veda Pratishthana, 1977.
Siddhalingam, T.B., *Hymns and Proverbs* (of Saivite saints). Tirupanandal: Kasi Mutt, 1964.
Singh, Jaideva, *Siva Sutras, The Yoga of Supreme Identity.* Delhi: Motilal Banarsidass, 1979.
Surdam, Wayne Edward, *South Indian Saiva Rites of Initiation: The Diksavidhi of Aghorasivacharya's Kriyakramadhyotika* (Ph.D 1984). University Microfilms International, 300 N. Zeeb Road, Ann Arbor, Michigan 48106.
Vasu, Rai Bahadur Srisa Chandra, *The Siva Samhita.* New Delhi: Oriental Books Reprint Corporation, 1979.
Venkatesananda, Swami, *The Concise Ramayana of Valmiki.* Albany: State University of New York Press, 1988.
Woods, James Houghton, *The Yoga-System of Patanjali.* Cambridge: The Harvard University Press, 1927.
Yogaswami, *Natchintanai.* Jaffna: The Sivathondan Society, 1974.

DICTIONARIES AND REFERENCE TEXTS

Apte, Vaman Shivram, *The Practical Sanskrit-English Dictionary, Revised and Enlarged Edition* (1,022 pages, requires ability to read Devanagari). Delhi: Motilal Banarsidass, 1988. First published ca 1890.
Apte, Vasudeo Govind, *The Concise English-Sanskrit Dictionary* (360 pages, pocketbook size, requires ability to read Devanagari). Delhi: Sri Satguru Publications, 1988.
Apte, Vasudeo Govind, *The Concise Sanskrit-English Dictionary* (366 pages, pocketbook size, Devanagari). Delhi: Sri Satguru Publications, 1988.
Bhattacharya, N.N., *Glossary of Hindu Religious Terms and Concepts* (226 pages). Columbia: South Asia Publications, 1990.
Feuerstein, Georg, **Encyclopedic Dictionary of Yoga* (430 pages). New York: Paragon House, 1990.
Hart, George L., *A Rapid Sanskrit Method.* Delhi: Motilal Banarsidass 1984, reprinted 1989.
Head, Joseph, and Cranston, S.L., *Reincarnation in World Thought, A Living*

study of Reincarnation in all ages. New York, Julian Press, 1967.
India Library, *Religions of India: Hinduism, Jainism, Buddhism, Sikhism, Zoroastrianism, Christianity, Islam and Judaism.* New Delhi: Clarion Books, 1983.
Liebaert, Gosta, *Iconographic Dictionary of the Indian Religions: Hinduism, Buddhism, Jainism* (377 pages). Delhi: Sri Satguru Publications, 1986.
Macdonell, Arthur Anthony, *A Practical Sanskrit Dictionary* (382 pages). London: Oxford University Press 1976; first printed ca 1924.
Ramachandran, T. R., *Tattvaloka, The Splendour of Truth.* Bombay: Sri Abhinava Vidyatheertha Mahaswamigal Education Trust, a periodical journal published six times annually.
Reese, William L., **Dictionary of Philosophy and Religion: Eastern and Western Thought* (644 pages). New Jersey: Humanities Press, 1980 .
Rice, Edward, **Eastern Definitions, A Short Encyclopedia of Religions of the Orient.* Garden City, New York: Anchor Books, 1980.
Satchidananda, Swami, *Dictionary of Sanskrit Names.* Buckingham, Virginia: Integral Yoga Publications, 1989.
Schuhmacher & Woerner (ed.), *Encyclopedia of Eastern Philosophy and Religion: Buddhism, Taoism, Zen, Hinduism.* Boston: Shambhala, 1989 (468 pages).
Schwartzberg, Joseph E. (ed.), **A Historical Atlas of South Asia.* New York and Oxford: Oxford University Press, 1992. First published in 1978.
Stutley, Margaret and James, *Harper's Dictionary of Hinduism: Its Mythology, Folklore, Philosophy, Literature and History* (372 pages). San Francisco: Harper and Row Publishers, 1984.
Subramuniyaswami, Sivaya, **Hinduism Today, The Hindu Family Newspaper* (monthly in 7 editions). Concord, California: Himalayan Academy.
Webster's New World Dictionary of American English: Third College Edition, New York: Webster's New World, 1988.
Williams, Sir M. Monier, **A Sanskrit-English Dictionary* (with full English transliteration, 1,333 pages). Delhi: Motilal Banarsidass, 1990; first published by Oxford University Press, 1899.
Williams, Sir M. Monier, **English-Sanskrit Dictionary.* New Delhi: Munshiram Manoharlal; first Indian Edition 1976, first published ca 1851.

PHILOSOPHY

Banerjea, Akshaya Kumar, *Philosophy of Gorakhnath, with Goraksha-Vacana-Sangraha.* Delhi: Motilal Banarsidass, 1983.
Chatterjee, Satischandra and Datta, Dhirendramohan, **An Introduction to Indian Philosophy.* Calcutta: University of Calcutta, sixth edition, 1960.
Crawford, Cromwell (ed.), *In Search of Hinduism.* Barrytown, New York: Unification Theological Seminary, 1986.
Dasgupta, Surendrananth, **A History of Indian Philosophy* (6 volumes). Delhi: Motilal Banarsidass, 1988.

Curtis, J.W.V. *Motivations of Temple Architecture in Saiva Siddhanta, As Defined by Prescriptions for Daily Worship According to Karanagama.* Madras: Hoe & Company, ca 1970 (date not given).
Ishwaran, K., *Religion and Society among the Lingayats of South India.* New Delhi: Vikas Publishing House, 1983.
Pandey, K.C., *An Outline of History of Saiva Philosophy.* Delhi: Motilal Banarsidass, 1986.
Pereira, José, *Hindu Theology, Themes, Texts and Structures.* Delhi: Motilal Banarsidass; 1991. First published in USA, 1976.
Radhakrishnan, Dr. S., *Indian Philosophy* (2 volumes). Oxford: Oxford University Press, 1923.
Subramuniyaswami, Sivaya, *Monism and Pluralism in Saiva Siddhanta.* Kapaa, Hawaii, Himalayan Academy Publications, 1984.
Tull, Herman W. *The Vedic Origins of Karma: Cosmos as Man in Ancient Indian Myth and Ritual.* Albany: State University of New York Press, 1989.
Tyagi, I.C., *Shaivism in Ancient India (from the Earliest Times to c.* AD 300). New Delhi: Meenakshi Prakashan, 1982.

SUMMARIES ON HINDUISM

Abhisheki, Janaki, *Religion as Knowledge.* Bombay: Ms. V. Ranade.
Arunachalam, M., *Peeps into the Cultural Heritage of Hinduism.* Tirupanandal: Kasi Mutt, 1987.
Balagangadharanath, Sri Sri Sri Swamiji, *Divine Light from Adi Chunchanagiri, Aseervachanas Delivered in India and Abroad.* Bangalore: Sri Adichunchanagiri Educational Trust, 1989.
Bary, W.T., Stephen Hay, Royal Weiler and Andrew Yarrow, *The Sources of Indian Tradition.* New York: Columbia University Press, 1958.
Basham, A. L., **The Wonder That Was India: A Survey of the History and Culture of the Indian Sub-Continent Before the Coming of the Muslims.* New York: Grove Press, 1954.
Chandrasekharendra, Sarasvati Sri, **The Vedas.* Bombay: Bharatiya Vidya Bhavan, 1988.
Dye, Joseph M., **Ways To Shiva—Life and Ritual in Hindu India.* Philadelphia: Philadelphia Museum of Art, 1980.
Klostermaier, Klaus K., **A Survey of Hinduism.* Albany: State University of New York Press, 1989.
Morgan, Kenneth W., *The Religion of the Hindus.* Delhi: Motilal Banarsidass, 1987 (first published, 1953).
Navaratnam, K., **Studies in Hinduism.* Jaffna: Maheswary Navaratnam, 1963.
Organ, Troy Wilson, *Hinduism—Its Historical Development.* Woodbury: Barron's Educational Series, Inc., 1974.
Radhakrishnan, Dr. S., **The Hindu View of Life.* New York: Macmillan Publishing Co., Inc., 1975.

Rawlinson, H.G., *India: A Short Cultural History.* New York: Frederick A. Praeger, 1952.

Renou, Louis, **Religions of Ancient India.* New York: Schocken Books, 1970.

Singh, Dr. Karan, *Essays on Hinduism.* Delhi: Ratna Sagar Ltd., 1990.

Sivananda, Swami, *All About Hinduism.* Shivanandanagar: The Divine Life Society, 1988.

Theosophical Society, **Sanatana Dharma, An Advanced Textbook of Hindu Religion and Ethics.* Adyar, Madras; Wheaton, Illinois; London, England: The Theosophical Publishing House, 1966 (first published, 1940).

YOGA

Danielou, Alain, *Yoga: The Method of Re-Integration.* New York: University Books, 1955.

Desai, Yogi Amrit, *Kripalu Yoga: Meditation-in-Motion.* Lenox, MA: Kripalu Publications, second edition, 1985.

Feuerstein, Georg, *Yoga, The Technology of Ecstasy.* Los Angeles: Jeremy P. Tharcher, Inc., 1989.

Mishra, Rammurti S., *Fundamentals of Yoga, A Handbook of Theory, Practice, and Application.* New York: Harmony Books., 1987.

Mishra, Rammurti S., *Yoga Sutras, The Textbook of Yoga Psychology.* New York: Anchor Books., 1973.

Jyotirmayananda, Swami, *Yoga Essays for Self-Improvement.* Miami: Yoga Research Foundation, 1981.

Radha, Swami Sivananda, *Hatha Yoga: The Hidden Language.* Boston: Shambala Publications, Inc., 1987.

Vishnudevananda, Swami, *The Complete Illustrated Book of Yoga.* New York: Harmony Books, 1988.

CULTURE AND WORSHIP

Arunachalam, M., *Festivals of Tamil Nadu.* Tiruchitrambalam: Gandhi Vidyalayam, 1980.

Coward, Harold G., Julius J. Lipner and Katherine K. Young, *Hindu Ethics, Purity, Abortion and Euthanasia.* Albany: State Univ. of New York Press, 1989.

Frawley, David, *Gods, Sages and Kings, Vedic Secrets of Ancient Civilization.* Salt Lake City, Utah: Passage Press, 1991.

Krishnaswamy, S.Y., *Life and Work of Sri Sivaratnapuri Swamiji* (Tiruchi Swamigal). Bangalore: Sri Kailasa Ashram, 1985.

Lad, Dr. Vasant, **Ayurveda, The Science of Self-Healing,* Santa Fe, New Mexico, Lotus Press, 1985.

McLeod, W.H and Schomer, Karine (editors), *The Sants: Studies in a Devotional Tradition of India.* Delhi: Motilal Banarsidass, 1987.

Pandey, Raj Bali, *Hindu Samskaras.* Delhi: Motilal Banarsidass, 1969.

Sagar, Dr. Vidya, ed., *Mother India Children Abroad—Focus on "Fiji."* New

Delhi: Antar-Rastriya Sahayog Parishad, 1987.
Subramuniyaswami, Sivaya, **Living with Siva: Hinduism's Nandinatha Sutras, Spiritual Rules for the Lion-Hearted.* Concord, California: Himalayan Academy, 1991.

GODS, TEMPLES AND ART

Daniélou, Alain, *Hindu Polytheism.* New York: Bollingen Foundation/Pantheon Books, 1964.
Eck, Diana L., **Darsan, Seeing the Divine Image in India,* Second edition. Chambersburg, Pennsylvania: Anima Books, 1985.
Keshavadas, Sadguru Sant, *Lord Ganesha.* Oakland, California: Vishwa Dharma Pub., 1988.
Kramrisch, Stella, *Exploring India's Sacred Art.* Philadelphia: University of Pennsylvania Press, 1983.
Kramrisch, Stella, **Manifestations of Shiva.* Philadelphia: Philadelphia Museum of Art, 1981.
Kramrisch, Stella, *The Hindu Temple* (two volumes). Delhi: Motilal Banarsidass, 1976 (reprinted 1991).
Kumar, Acharya Prasanna, *The Manasara Series,* 7 volumes: 1) *Dictionary of Hindu Architecture,* 2) *Indian Architecture according to Manasara Silpasastra,* 3) *Manasara on Architecture and Sculpture,* 4-5) **Architecture of Manasara,* 6) *Hindu Architecture in India and abroad,* and 7) *Encyclopedia of Hindu Architecture (with detailed plans and drawings).* New Delhi: Oriental Books Reprint Corp., 1981. First published, 1934, Oxford University Press.
Lal, Lakshmi, *Ganesha Beyond the Form.* Bombay: IBH Publishers, 1991.
Meister, Michael W., *Encyclopedia of Indian Temple Architecture* (2 volumes: North India and South India). New Delhi: American institute of Indian Studies, 1983. Philadelphia: University of Pennsylvania Press, 1983.
Michell, George, **The Hindu Temple—An Introduction to its Meaning and Forms.* New York: Harper & Roe, Publishers, Inc., 1977.
Navaratnam, Ratna Ma, *Aum Ganesha, The Peace of God.* Jaffna: Vidya Bhavan, 1978.
Navaratnam, Ratna Ma, *Karttikeya, The Divine Child.* Bombay: Bharatiya Vidya Bhavan, 1973.
Shastri, J.L., *Ancient Indian Tradition and Mythology.* Delhi: Motilal Banarsidass, 1973.
Sivananda, Swami, *Lord Shanmukha and His Worship.* Uttara Pradesh: The Divine Life Society, 1990.
Sivananda, Swami, *Lord Siva and His Worship.* Uttara Pradesh: The Divine Life Society, 1989.
Subramuniyaswami, Sivaya, **Lord Ganesha: Benevolent Deity for the Modern Hindu World.* Concord, California, Himalayan Academy, 1989.
Waghorne, Joanne Punzo, et. al., *Gods of Flesh Gods of Stone, The Embodiment of Divinity in India.* Chambersburg, Pennsylvania: Anima, 1985.

Colophon

Antyaśabda

अन्त्यशब्द्

D*ANCING WITH ŚIVA: HINDUISM'S CONTEMPORARY CATECHISM* WAS DESIGNED AND ILLUSTRATED BY THE SWĀMĪS OF THE ŚAIVA Siddhānta Yoga Order at Kauai's Hindu Monastery on the Garden Island in Hawaii. This third book in the Ṛishi Collection was composed and assembled using QuarkXpress on DayStar-Powercache-50-mhz-accelerated Macintosh IIs, a Macintosh Portable and a Powerbook 170 on a network established with the help of software designer Bob Roblin. The text was typeset on an Apple LaserWriter Pro 630 in Adobe's Minion family of fonts to which diacritical marks were added with Fontographer. The main verses are set in 12.5-point Minion medium with 15-point linespacing. The lexicon and index are set in 9-point Minion with 11-point linespacing. Devanāgarī and Tamil are set in fonts created by Ecological Linguistics.

Of the 165 Rajput paintings, some were digitized and output to negatives by Vikram Patel at Marvik Colour in New York City. Others were produced conventionally by Honolulu Graphic Arts. Illustrations, patterned graphics and sacred symbols were produced with Adobe's Streamline and Illustrator software and a Wacom graphics tablet, then output directly to negatives at 2,540 dpi on a Linotron Imagesetter by Krishna Copy in San Francisco.

The cover was color proofed on a Tektronix Phaser III, then ported to a Scitex for output on a high-resolution color plotter. The book was printed in Harrisonburg, Virginia, by Banta Company on a Timson web-offset press using 60#

Finch Opaque Book paper. The cover art is an eighteenth-century painting, Chamba School, of Śiva witnessing a devotee's dance, displayed in the National Museum, New Delhi. The end-sheet painting in the hard-cover edition depicts the bathing ghats of a little town, is an eighteenth century piece kept in the Baroda Museum in Gujarat and used with the kind permission of Roland and Sabrina Michaud from their wonderful book, *Mirror of India.* The hardcover edition is cased with Kivar 9 with U.V. coating. San Francisco artist John Kuzich designed the cover and the Himalayan Academy logo. The photo on the back cover was taken by Rohini Kumar at his RK Studios in Kuala Lumpur, Malaysia.

Sanskṛit proofreading and guidance was kindly and patiently provided by Vyaas Houston, founder of the American Sanskṛit Institute; Dr. P. Jayaraman, Executive Director of Bharatiya Vidya Bhavan, Woodside, New York; Pundit and Jyotisha Shastri Laxmishanker Trivedi and his son Devendra of Fremont, California; Dr. George Hart, Professor of Tamil at the University of California at Berkeley; Professor Jayaraman Sethuraman of the University of Florida; Braj B. Kachru and his wife Yamuna, professors of linguistics at the University of Illinois, Urbana; Veda Pundit Ravichandran of Madras and California; and Pundit A.V. Mylvaganam of Jaffna, Sri Lanka.

The multi-level index for further study and research was created with the help of Jordan and Vita Richman of Writer's Anonymous, Phoenix, Arizona.

Dr. Prem Sahai of Webster City, Iowa, contributed to the presentation of the Hindu family structure. In presenting the major sects of Hinduism, C. Ramachandran, editor of *Tattvaloka,* answered several questions on behalf of the Sankaracharya of Sringeri Matha; and three scholars wrote special tracts on Smārtism, Śāktism and Vaishṇavism, respectively, for *Hinduism Today:* T.K. Venkateswaran, Professor of Religious Studies at University of Detroit, Mercy; June MacDaniel, Assistant Professor of Religious Studies at the College of Charleston, South Carolina; and Graham M. Schweig, Director of the Institute for Vaishṇava Studies.

Dr. Virendra Sodhi, Ayurveda Vaidya, kindly confirmed the accuracy of the sections on the ancient science of *āyurveda.* Bill Shurtleff of Lafayette, California, critiqued the Hindu Timeline. Assistance on astrology was provided by Pundit K.N. Navaratnam of Melbourne, Australia; and Chakrapani D. Ullal of Los Angeles.

The Hindu Businessmen's Association of Northern California established a generous, irrevocable endowment to provide needy individuals and worthy institutions with complimentary copies of this important sourcebook.

For all this noble, talented and selfless assistance, we want to offer our heartfelt thanks. May many blessings come to each one who contributed to this tome.

Over a decade ago, when the first edition was being produced, many individuals contributed their time and knowledge. In researching the tradition of *sannyāsa,* two of my monks traveled through South India and Sri Lanka speaking with heads of Hindu monasteries. Particularly helpful were Swami Tapasyananda of the Ramakrishna Mission, Swami Chinmayananda of Chinmaya Missions, Swami Satchidananda of the Integral Yoga Institute and Pundit M. Jnanaprakasam of Erlalai Aadheenam in Jaffna.

Always available to assist in a wide range of philosophical and historical areas was Pundit M. Arunachalam. Information and assistance on clarifying the two schools of Saiva Siddhanta came from numerous devout scholars, including Justice Maharajan of Madras, the world's foremost adept on *Tirumantiram;* Pundit Kandiah of Jaffna, A.P.C. Veerabhagu of Tuticorin; the Guru Mahasannidhanam of the 1,400-year-old Dharmapuram Aadheenam and his pundits, and the Selangor All Ceylon Saivites Association in Kuala Lumpur.

Finally, appreciations to my Śaiva Siddhānta Yoga Order of eleven *swāmīs,* who patiently met daily, month after month to finalize the essential philosophical presentation contained in these pages, and to my tireless band of Śivanadiyars, *yogīs* and *sādhakas,* who also assisted in many ways.

Providing invaluable assistance, information gathering and coordination as our official liaison officers for two decades were Dr. S. Shanmugasundaram in Sri Lanka, and his associate A. Gunanayagam; and in India, Tiru N. K. Murti, retired Aerodrome Officer.

In defining the practical and esoteric aspects of Hindu temple liturgy, we were blessed with the backing of Sri Sambamurthi Sivacharya of the South India Archaka Sangam, who sent two expert priests, Kumaraswami Gurukal and Shanmuga Gurukal, to Hawaii to train my Śaiva Swāmīs in the sacred *parārtha pūjā* for daily performance in the Kadavul Hindu temple.

In the area of scriptural translations, of course, we owe a debt of gratitude to a host of dedicated scholars, including Dr. B. Natarajan, who rendered the entire *Tirumantiram* into English at our behest; Professor Raimundo Panikkar for his beautiful anthology of Vedic texts, *The Vedic Experience,* which he produced over a period of ten years while residing above a Śiva temple in Varanasi; the late Dr. S. Radhakrishnan, former President of India, Robert Hume and Juan Mascaro for their translations of the major *Upanishads;* the Sivathondan Nilayam of Jaffna, Sri Lanka, for its English translation of Sage Yogaswami's *Natchintanai,* and Ratna Ma Navaratnam for her *Testament of Truth, Aum Ganesa* and *Karttikeya, the Divine Child.*

I would also like to honor the Guru Mahasannidhanam of the 2,000-year-old Tiruvavaduthurai Aadheenam, home of the *mahāsamādhi* site of Rishi Tirumular, for his support through the years. And we cannot fail to offer thanks to the late Prof. R. Ramaseshan of Tanjavur, South India, who translated the first edition of *Dancing with Śiva* into lovely Tamil just before he was murdered by atheists who opposed his spiritual work.

Calling forth the blessings of inner worlds, Dr. A. Anandanataraja Deekshidar and others of the ancient hereditary Deekshidar priesthood at Chidambaram Temple in South India performed monthly *pūjās* blessing this work. At Kauai Aadheenam's Kadavul Hindu Temple, on the island Kauai in the Hawaiian Islands, the world's most remote land mass, during the two years it took to create this fourth edition, my monks held successive three-hour vigils around the clock and performed *pūjā* every three hours, night and day, without fail.

Going back even further in our history, we offer our deepest thanks to Tiru Kandiah Chettiar for his early assistance and introducing me at age 21 to the culture and holy people of Jaffna, and most especially for taking me on that never-to-be-forgotten, full-moon day in May to my beloved *satguru,* Sage Yogaswami.

Other Publications From Himalayan Academy

Living with Śiva

Hinduism's Nandinātha Sutras
By Sivaya Subramuniyaswami

Spiritual rules for the lion-hearted, 365 verses on how Hindus approach God, family life, money, food, culture and more. Anyone can pursue a spiritual path for a weekend, even a year or two. But for a lifetime of enlightened exploration, a strict lifestyle must be developed that sustains effort and minimizes distractions. Satguru Sivaya Subramuniyaswami, an illumined master whose *yoga* order is on Hawaii's tropical island of Kauai, offers a detailed and authentic way for his followers, based on the *tantras*, or traditional methods, that Hindus have observed for thousands of years.

If you were ever uncertain about how rigorous to be with yourself, how to approach holy people or relate to members of the opposite sex, what to do about television, alcohol or your career, *Living with Śiva* is for you. Its terse guidelines provide time-tested practices and disciplines for serious seekers.

Anyone of any culture, creed or belief can benefit from reading these *sūtras*, and will in their heart of hearts recognize the valid wisdom of these laws that have matured through the millennia. Different guidelines are provided for varied situations in life to meet the unique needs of the single, married, widowed, householder, monastic, young, elderly, and near-death. Topics of practical concern to modern seekers such as diet and food, health and exercise, tobacco and drugs are all commented upon.

From the Introduction:
"Most people think of themselves as remote from God, but the highest souls are living with Him every day, no matter what they are doing....

Living with Śiva is Śiva consciousness. The reconciled past releases consciousness into the eternal moment in which we see Śiva as the life and light within everyone's eyes."

First Edition, 1991, 5½" x 5½", 208 pages, beautifully illustrated with classical Rajput paintings. Paperback (ISBN 0-945497-44-x) $8.95.

Hinduism Today

"A Hindu family newspaper affirming the *dharma* and recording the modern history of nearly a billion members of a global religion in renaissance" is the bold motto of this colorful, graphically rich monthly newspaper. *Hinduism Today* is an award winning, computer-produced information resource reaching 150,000 readers in 33 countries through eight editions—North America, UK/Europe, India, ASEAN/Malaysia, Africa, Indian Ocean, International and a Dutch Language Digest. Every issue includes a four-color educational poster, personal commentary, editorials, art, metaphysical wisdom and news on a wide spectrum of events, people, issues and lifestyles. Reading *Hinduism Today* is the best way to keep in touch with Hinduism's worldwide impact.

About the Author

In 1949 Sivaya Subramuniyaswami, as a young man of 22, received holy orders of *sannyāsa* from a renowned *siddha yogī* and worshiper of Śiva, Sage Yogaswāmī of Sri Lanka. Today Subramuniyaswami carries forward this lineage as Satguru of Kauai Aadheenam, a 51-acre Hindu temple-monastery complex located on the Hawaiian island of Kauai. He has established teaching centers in North America in Concord, California, and in the beautiful garden-island country of Mauritius in the Indian Ocean.

Satguru Sivaya Subramuniyaswami is founder and publisher of *Hinduism Today*. His published writings, comprising more than 30 books, are unique and practical insights on metaphysics, mysticism, *yoga* and orthodox Hinduism based on many decades of experience in teaching, counseling and initiating devotees.

In 1986 New Delhi's World Council of Religion named him one of five Jagadāchāryas, world teachers, for his international efforts in promoting a Hindu renaissance for half a century. In recent years the Global Forum of Spiritual and Parliamentary Leaders for Human Survival chose Subramuniyaswami as a Hindu representative at its remarkable conferences. At Oxford in 1988, Moscow in 1990, Rio de Janiero in 1992, and Kyoto, Japan, in 1993, religious and political leaders from all religions and countries met for the first time in history to discuss the future of human life on this planet.

Order Form

All prices are listed in U.S. currency. When ordering, specify name of item, quantity and unit prices. Add 10% for postage and handling in USA and 20% foreign, $1.50 minimum. Foreign orders are shipped sea mail unless otherwise specified and additional postage is included. (Add 50% for foreign airmail postage.)

☐ *Yes, I would like to receive a free literature packet.*

☐ *Yes, I would like to subscribe to* Hinduism Today.

☐ 1-year subscription, $24 ☐ 2-year subscription, $36

I would also like to order the following items:

☐ *Dancing with Siva*, Paperback, $19.95

☐ *Dancing with Siva,* Hardcover, $29.95

☐ *Living with Siva,* Paperback, $8.95

☐ My payment is enclosed. Charge to: ☐ Master Card ☐ Visa

Card number: ______________________________

Expiration date: ______________ Total of purchase: __________

Signature: ______________________________

____
First and Last Name (Please Print)

Address: ______________________________

____

____

______________________________ Telephone: __________

Mail orders to Himalayan Academy Publications,
1819 Second Street, Concord, California 94519 USA

These publications are also available in Malaysia and Mauritius. For prices, write to: Siddhanta Publications, P.O. Box 301, 46730 Petaling Jaya, Selangor, Malaysia; or Himalayan Academy Publications, La Pointe, Riviere du Rempart, Mauritius.

The *Dancing with Śiva* Endowment

Himalayan Academy believes *Dancing with Śiva* is an invaluable resource for those seeking to deepen their knowledge of Hinduism and has therefore established the Dancing with Śiva Endowment to facilitate the book's broad distribution in the world's many countries and languages. All donations to this endowment are permanently invested, and the income produced is directed toward:

- funding translations into other languages,
- subsidizing printing outside the USA, and
- making available copies that can be given free of charge.

If *Dancing with Śiva* has provided you with valuable knowledge about Hinduism, perhaps you are inspired to help others have the same opportunity. Send your contribution, which is tax-deductible in the USA, to:

Himalayan Academy, 1819 Second Street
Concord, California 94519 USA

Founded in 1957, Himalayan Academy is a nonprofit educational institution dedicated to the dissemination of information on the Hindu religion. All investments are professionally managed and screened for social responsibility that accords with Hindu ethical principles.

Endowments for *Dancing with Śiva* have also been established in India and Mauritius with affiliated institutions. Donations are tax deductible and may be sent to:

Sanmarga Trust—India, 48-A, South West Boag Road
Thyagaraya Nagar, Madras 600 017, India
(Regd. No. 207/92-93 under I.T. Act. dt.
Nov. 26, 1992 — Madras)

Saiva Siddhanta Church of Mauritius
La Pointe, Riviere du Rempart, Mauritius
(Established by Parliamentary Act No. 22 of 1988)

There are a few unusual men who have had enough of the world and choose to dance with Śiva as Hindu monks.

They follow the path of the traditional Hindu monastic, vowed to poverty, humility, obedience and purity. They pursue the disciplines of *charyā, kriyā, yoga* and *jñāna* that lead to realization of the Self. Knowing God is their only goal in life. They live with others like themselves in monasteries apart from the world to worship, meditate, serve and realize the truth of the *Vedas* and *Āgamas.*

Guided by Satguru Sivaya Subramuniyaswami and headquartered at Kauai Aadheenam in Hawaii, USA, the Śaiva Siddhānta Yoga Order is among the world's foremost traditional Hindu monastic orders, accepting candidates from every nation on earth. Young men considering life's renunciate path who strongly believe they have found their spiritual master in Śrī Śrī Śrī Sivaya Subramuniyaswami are encouraged to write to him sharing their personal history, spiritual aspirations, thoughts and experiences.

Satguru Sivaya Subramuniyaswami
Guru Mahāsannidhānam, Kauai Aadheenam
107 Kaholalele Road, Kapaa, HI 96746, USA

Hail, O sannyāsin, love's embodiment! Does any power exist apart from love? Diffuse thyself throughout the happy world. Let painful māyā cease and never return. Day and night give praise unto the Lord. Pour forth a stream of songs to melt the very stones. Attain the sight where night is not, nor day. See Śiva everywhere and rest in bliss. Live without interest in worldly gain. Here, as thou hast ever been, remain.

NATCHINTANAI 228